Saffet Emre Tonguç

ISTANBUL

THE ULTIMATE GUIDE

Saffet Emre Tonguç

ISTANBUL

THE ULTIMATE GUIDE

ISTANBUL METROPOLITAN MUNICIPALITY

Istanbul The Ultimate Guide, 2021

Project Director
Cengiz Özkarabekir

Publishing Director
Ahmet Bozkurt

Content and Publishing Advisor
Vahit Uysal

Production
D Sinema Destek Sistemleri Ltd. Şti.,2021
info@d-sinema.com

Administrative Coordination
Gökhan Özçevik

Book's Editor
Duygun Soysal

Editing-Proofreading
Barış Cezar

Visual Arts Cosultant
Utku Lomlu

Photo Editor
Serkan Eldeleklioğlu

Cover Design
Utku Lomlu

Cover Photo
Aydın Sertbaş

Page Design
ademsenel.com

Archive Editing
Evren Ertem

Printing and Binding
BPC Matbaacılık Sanayi ve Ticaret A.Ş.
Cevizlik Mah. Hüsreviye Sk. Erşen İş Hanı No:15 Kat:3-38 Bakırköy/İstanbul
info@bpcmatbaacilik.com.tr Tel: 0212 549 53 83

ISBN: 978-625-7288-53-8

Revised & Updated 77rd Edition: Istanbul, December 2023
77rd printing for this book together with its Turkish version *İstanbul Hakkında Her Şey*.

Publisher Certificate Number: 15321
Printers Certificate Number: 48745

Istanbul Culture and Art Products Trade Co.
Maltepe Mah. Topkapı Kültür Parkı Osmanlı Evleri
34010 Topkapı/Zeytinburnu/ISTANBUL/TURKEY
Phone: 0 (212) 467 07 00 Fax: 0 (212) 467 07 99

Saffet Emre Tonguç

ISTANBUL

THE ULTIMATE GUIDE

ISTANBUL
METROPOLITAN
MUNICIPALITY

PREFACE

Ekrem İmamoğlu
Istanbul Metropolitan Municipality Mayor

Dear Friends,

When, years ago, I first read this book written by historian and author Saffet Emre Tonguç - I must admit I loved it. As I always thought Tonguç, who has worked for Istanbul wholeheartedly and covers Istanbul so thoroughly and eloquently, should be published by an institution which properly represents the people of Istanbul. Finally, that day has arrived.

Last year we began to realize this dream and presented our readers with a peerless guide for the Bosphorus and surrounding regions, *Boğaz Hakkında Her Şey*. In English - *Bosphorus The Ultimate Guide*. We now introduce the updated and expanded versions, *Istanbul The Ultimate Guide* - a rare work encompassing not only the Bosphorus but the entirety of Istanbul - and *İstanbul Hakkında Her Şey* (Turkish version.

This book, deemed worthy of the "Best Tourism Publication" award in 2010, was updated after extensive work with the newest images and information and thus transformed into a brand-new reference source and a manifestation of our love for our city.

We present this quite aptly titled book to all Istanbulites, Istanbul lovers, and visitors both foreign and domestic, since it contains everything worthwhile one may need to know about Istanbul. As you turn the pages, you will travel between Istanbul of yesterday and today, accompanied by marvelous photos.

Saffet Emre Tonguç will begin our tour with the Historic Peninsula, starting with the Topkapı Palace and the Blue Mosque (Sultanahmet). We then follow the Marmara coast from Cankurtaran to Bakırköy and continue to explore the Golden Horn. We cross over to Beyoğlu, travel up to Levent and Maslak as we discover Istanbul's modern face. After a delightful cruise along the Bosphorus with its palaces, forests and mansions, we will gaze upon the majestic trees in the Belgrad Forest and the blue waters of the Black Sea in Kilyos, Şile, and Ağva. Our love for Istanbul will take us as far as Gebze, Hereke, and Eskihisar in the east and Beylikdüzü, Büyükçekmece and beyond in the west.

You will be surprised and excited by the myriad details and descriptions of Istanbul's history, nature, legends, buildings old and new - and beyond all, its human stories. On each page you will find countless new treasures, revealing how fortunate you are to explore this unique and multifaceted city. This book will remind you - despite all its hustle and bustle, chaos, and crowds - that Istanbul remains a magnificently beautiful city and worthy of your fervent admiration.

I entrust this precious work to the hands and hearts of all those who love Istanbul. May you enjoy a pleasant journey as you become lost within its pages.

Sincerely yours...

For Istanbul,
The city that stole
my heart eternally...

Saffet Emre Tonguç

Istanbul, not Constantinople

Istanbul was Constantinople
Now it's Istanbul, not Constantinople
Been a long time gone, Constantinople
Now it's Turkish delight on a moonlit night.

Every gal in Constantinople
Lives in Istanbul, not Constantinople
So if you've a date in Constantinople
She'll be waiting in Istanbul.

So take me back to Constantinople
No, you can't go back to Constantinople
Been a long time gone, Constantinople
Why did Constantinople get the works?
That's nobody's business but the Turks.

Jimmy Kennedy

ISTANBUL
The Sultan of Cities

Of all the world's great cities surely few can be as romantic as Istanbul, the sprawling metropolis that straddles the Bosphorus with one foot in Europe and the other in Asia. Byzantium, Constantinople, Istanbul – its three names echo down the ages, speaking of the glories of three empires, the Roman, the Byzantine and the Ottoman. In 1923 Mustafa Kemal Atatürk moved the capital of the new Turkish Republic to Ankara, hoping to shed the historic baggage along the way. Much of the twentieth century was grim for Istanbul but today it has shot back into its own. Ankara may have the politics, but Istanbul has the art, the architecture, the cutting-edge shops, even the gastronomy. Above all it has the spectacular scenery created by the Black Sea, the Bosphorus, the Sea of the Marmara and the Golden Horn. It's modern Turkey's uncrowned capital in all but name.

The heart of touristic Istanbul is Sultanahmet and what is sometimes called the Historic Peninsula, the Old Istanbul that is a UNESCO-listed world heritage site where things kicked off for the city in the 7th century BC. Not surprisingly, this is where all the most famous attractions –Topkapı Palace, Hagia Sophia, Sultanahmet (Blue) Mosque– are to be found, with others such as the Grand Bazaar close by. These are sights that no visitor would want to miss, but the good news about Istanbul is that this is still a relatively under-visited city, which means that there are still plenty of off-the-beaten-track places for independent travelers to make their own. In this book I have divided the city into areas and grouped their attractions.

I have spread my net far and wide, trawling up gems in the unlikeliest of places. Who would have thought, for example, that you could stumble upon a 7th-century open-air cistern in Bakırköy? Or men engaged in dalyan fishing in Beykoz? And who would have dreamed that Hannibal's putative grave could be found in Gebze along with one of the city's finest mosques?

Like every guidebook to Istanbul, this one pays effusive homage to the wonderful Sinan and his successors who did so much to beautify the city. At the same time it also celebrates the best of what has happened to the built landscape over the course of the last couple of centuries, highlighting the mark left on the city by such 19th-century visionaries as the prolific Balyan family, by Raimondo d'Aronco and by Alexandre Vallaury. Even in the much-maligned 20th century I have tipped my hat to Vedat Tek and Kemaleddin Bey, the main proponents of First National Architecture and to Sedad Hakkı Eldem the man behind its less flamboyant second manifestation.

As I worked my way round the city, so I fell more and more in love with it. If you have half as much fun exploring Istanbul as I had researching this book then my task will have been fulfilled.

Saffet Emre Tonguç

November 2023

Birth of a book...

During the 1990s, as I was guiding people all over the world, I began to realize that foreigners sometimes knew and wrote about my country better even than the Turks did. Every year I would buy the latest version of **Lonely Planet Turkey** and began to register the name of **Pat Yale** who wrote it and who obviously loved Turkey so much. I noticed that she wrote well and provided insider tips and interesting information about my homeland. I also noticed that she lived in **Göreme** in Cappadocia. Eventually I started to write for the travel supplement of Hürriyet, Turkey's biggest selling newspaper and used to visit lots of restaurants and hotels for my pieces. While inspecting a newly opened hotel in Cappadocia. I spotted a blonde, short-haired woman whose face was familiar. "**Are you Pat Yale**?" I asked and that was the first step on the journey towards the book that you now hold in your hands.

I started to think that Turks should also be able to write about the places that they want to visit for themselves. Then my first book "**101 Must-See Places in Turkey**" was published in Turkish and became the "**best selling travel book in Turkey**" in 2007. When I decided to produce an English version of it I asked Pat to do the job.

When we embarked on the project I think we were both imagining something fairly small and simple, but as time passed and we delved deeper into the city, so we discovered more and more hidden corners that barely merited a footnote in existing guidebooks. We became more and more interested in what we were discovering and slowly the year that we had imagined it taking to complete the project spun out into three years of combined effort.

And the happy ending...

In 2010 first "**Istanbul Hakkında Her Şey**" and then "**Istanbul The Ultimate Guide**" were published. We were thrilled to have both books in our hands, but still had many questions in our minds. Should we have used the courtyard photo of the Blue Mosque or the one taken from the minaret? Would some of the places mentioned in the book have closed? Were there any mistakes or inconsistencies in the information, etc etc.

Istanbul, a never-ending story...

Our path with Pat Yale, whose efforts I shall never forget, has become separated over the years, but as she said, "Nothing in life is a coincidence."

Duygun Soysal, whom I met when she was a little girl of seven years old, showed up again years later. Like me, she's in love with Istanbul, every corner gives her excitement. She read my book before the first edition and always made valuable contributions. After eight years, I said "Come on!," she replied "Okay" without hesitation and we rolled up our sleeves again to embark on the journey to update it. The city is so dynamic that not only the food and beverage places, but even the seemingly-permanent places have been forgotten in the dusty pages of history or have assumed a sense of misplacement. Despite all these changes, we focus on every corner of the city that has a story at its core and the secrets they whisper to us. As we re-read every line, we admired and fell in love again with this city and its endless stories... Even if we came up with reasons for sadness and anger, we re-edited the book with the joy of remembering the city without judgement.

Züzuniyet and the last laugh

While writing the book we visited Istanbul's many different cemeteries, inspected **Muslim, Greek, Armenian, Jewish, Catholic, Protestant and Anglican** tombstones and even asked someone to translate the **Karamanlı** (see p. 162) tombstones which were written in Turkish but using Greek letters for us. While wandering around the **Protestant Cemetery** in Feriköy (see p. 355) we spotted **C. Robert Avery**'s tombstone with the mysterious word "züzuniyet" carved on it. While finishing work on the 6th edition of the **Redhouse Dictionary** Avery had sneaked in one final made-up word which he translated as meaning "the last word". Inevitably when he died some wag decided to immortalize the prank by carving **"züzuniyet"** on his tombstone. Probably most Redhouse Dictionary users never got the joke. Now I wonder how many perceptive readers will spot the things that we have written between my lines. If you find them and want to let me know I'd love to hear from you.

Saffet Emre Tonguç

After graduating from high school, Saffet Emre studied tourism and hotel management and political science and international relations at **Boğaziçi (Bosphorus) University**. He followed up with a master's degree in Ottoman social history, writing a thesis on "**The Jews and the Ottoman Social Structure**". Later he did doctoral studies in business at **Wirtschaftsuniversität Wien**.

While studying tourism and hotel management, he started work as a professional tour guide, eventually traveling to more than 141 countries either for work or for pleasure. At the same time, he has also designed houses and gardens that have been featured in magazines such as **Maison Française**, **House Beautiful**, **Home Art, Marie Claire, Instyle** and many more. He has also participated as a speaker in programs about Turkey called "**Earth Matters**" and "**World of Wonders**" on **CNN International** as well as being a guest of "**Good Morning America**" on **ABC** television. He has discussed Istanbul and other places in Turkey on the **Dr. Oz Show**, the USA show hosted by world-famous Mehmet Öz and in the documentary "**Hidden Gems of Turkey**" shot for National Geographic. His photographs have also been exhibited in a cistern in Istanbul.

Saffet Emre writes regularly for the **Hürriyet** travel supplement in Turkey and also has been published in various international magazines such as **Conde Nast Traveler**, **Travel and Leisure**, **National Geographic,** and **Lonely Planet**. In May 2007, his "**101 Must See Places in Turkey**" was published both in English and Turkish. In 2010 "**Istanbul Hakkında Her Şey**" and "**Istanbul the Ultimate Guide**" hit the shelves. He wrote 28 books including this one and won more than 30 awards. In 2018 he published **"Privileged Routes"**. Published in 2019, **"Kanatlarımda İstanbul"** earned great success by making nine editions in a short span of time. **"Istanbul: A Bird's Eye View"** and **"Beflügelndes Istanbul"** hit the shelves in 2020. 54th edition of **"Boğaz Hakkında Her Şey"** (also published in English as **"Bosphorus The Ultimate Guide"**) was published by Kültür A.Ş.

He produced **"Priceless Istanbul"** on NTV for two seasons, which got the highest ratings of the channel. He is now shooting the 6th season of **"Privileged Routes"** that began in 2017, traveling Turkey and the world to show amazing places. Along with his works as a professional lecturer and TV host, the writer continues to be a professional guide organizing tours that combine tourism with the sense of exploration. He developed Piri, the first online audio tour guide application in Turkey.

With the Saffet Emre Tonguç (SET) smartphone application that launched in 2021, he brings together suggestions from Turkey and all over the world. The most important feature of the application, which is considered as the "Wikipedia of tourism" and is constantly updated and expanded with new information, is that it is open to everyone and completely free.

They organize tours abroad and produce content and text for TV programs through the company **Best Men Production**, established in 2017 by the writer **Serda Büyükkoyuncu**. He has guided more than 100 internationally renowned people around Istanbul, including the American talk show host **Oprah Winfrey**, who is one of the most influential women of the century, TV Producer and author **Martha Stewart, famous actors Robert Redford, Michael Douglas, Catherine Zeta-Jones, Candice Bergen, Matthew McConaughey, Billy Crystal, Kevin Spacey, Penn Badgley,** the first female USA Secretary of State **Madeleine Albright,** former USA Chief of Defense and Secretary of State **Colin Powell, Prince Edward of England,** Italian President **Carlo Azeglio Ciampi,** Google CEO **Eric Schmidt,** Ford CEO **Alan Mullaly,** General Electric CEO **John Flannery,** Nike CEO **Mark Parker,** Boeing International President **Michael Arthur,** owner of Guess **Paul Marciano,** fashion designers **Calvin Klein, Jeff Koons, Diana Von Fürstenberg, Michael Kors, Eli Tahari** and **Alberta Ferretti.**

Saffet Emre very much believes that life is there to be lived. Consequently, he has always been happy to follow his heart and rarely operates with a Plan B to fall back on. He doesn't like stereotypes and firmly believes that extraordinary people can make a difference to society.

Awards

He was awarded the **"Professional Outstanding Service Award"** by the Rotary Club in 2005, 2010 and 2014. In 2006, he was awarded

Oprah Winfrey

Madeleine Albright

Matthew McConaughey

Kevin Spacey

Robert Redford

Michael Kors

Penn Badgley

Catherine Zeta-Jones / Michael Douglas

"Travel Author of the Year". He was granted the **"Travel Author"** award in the 2007 White Crystal competition. He was named **"Turkey's Best Professional Guide"** by SKAL Club in 2007, 2012 and 2014. Tonguç, one of the authors of the bestselling book titled **"101 Must See Places in Turkey"**, received the **"TUREB Best Book of the Year"** award in 2008 and published his fourth book entitled **"101 Must See Places in Europe"**. He received the **"Best Tourism Publication"** award with his 2010 book **"Istanbul The Ultimate Guide"** and his 2012 book **"Bosphorus The Ultimate Guide"**. In 2015, his **"Priceless Istanbul"** program was granted the **"Best TV Show"**. In 2017, he received the **"Tourism Incentive Publication"** award for his **"Privileged Routes"**; in the same year he was re-granted the **"Best Professional Guide of the Year"** and the **"Professional High Service Award"**. In 2018, the program **"Privileged Routes"** was also granted the **"Best TV Show"** award. He was re-awarded the **"Best Travel Author"** in 2019 and **"Professional Outstanding Service Award"** in 2020. In 2022 he received "**Value Adding Ambassador to Turkey**", "**Best TV Host, 'Privileged Routes'**", "**Best TV Show, 'Privileged Routes'**", and "**Turkey's Promotion and Contribution to Tourism**" awards. In 2023 he received "**Best Historian/Professional Guide Award**".

Thanks to...

Numerous people have contributed to the preparation of this book. **Duygun Soysal** was seven years old when I met her in 1989. Now she reads my books and feeds her intellectual knowledge between the lines. My books are now entrusted to her. **Sevda and Serda Büyükkoyuncu**, in whose ideas and taste I have great trust and **Zeynep Şahin Tutuk**, who is both my communication consultant and my right hand, have obliged me by kindly reading my book within a short period of time. Their contributions are very valuable to me.

A lot of people worked with us on this project. **Zahide Bilsay** acted as a sort of third writer, sprinkling the pages with her ingenuity. Associate Professor **Harry Tzimitras**, a lecturer at **Bilgi** and **Koç** universities, helped with Ancient and Modern Greek translations. **David Thomas Scarff** did the proof-reading. And my mother **Leman Tonguç** always supported me by saying: "Hang on, son! It's almost finished!" I also want to extend special thanks to my good friends who were always supportive and sympathetic during the book's long gestation period.

And the time passes by...

Istanbul the Ultimate Guide came to light in 2010 after a long period of work. My efforts were not wasted and it was regarded as a cult book since the first edition. In a short time more than 50 editions were printed and more than hundred thousand copies were sold. Now I'm taking this journey again with the same enthusiasm. This time I'm accompanied in this journey by **Istanbul Metropolitan Municipality** and **Kültür A.Ş.** I am hoping to keep working and contributing for Istanbul!

Saffet Emre Tonguç

www.saffetemretonguc.com, tonguc2000@gmail.com

@saffetemretonguc

@saffetemretonguc

@saffetemre

Saffet Emre Tonguç

About the Book...

Following in my footsteps

My starting point was **Suriçi,** the historic peninsula that was called Byzantium and Constantinople in ancient times. Since **Topkapı Palace, Hagia Sophia** and the **Sultanahmet (Blue) Mosque** are all located on the first of the seven hills, they got the first pages. Then I made my way around the hills and completed the first section of the book with the land walls that stretch from **Mermerkule to Ayvansaray**. For me the most surprising discovery was the **Cerrahpaşa** district about which I had known almost nothing but where I found enough magnificent Ottoman monuments and works of art to while away several days.

I placed **Cankurtaran** and the sea walls along the Sea of Marmara at the start of the second section and then described everything to be seen along the road including the fish restaurants to be found in **Kumkapı** and the newly discovered remains of the Byzantine port in **Yenikapı**. At first glance **Samatya** didn't seem very exciting, but as I looked more closely I found history adorning every street corner. The second section of the book wound up in **Florya and Yeşilköy**.

In the third section I explored the whole of the Golden Horn, starting at **Gülhane Park** and **Sarayburnu** and heading out to **Sirkeci** and **Eminönü**. The old quarters of the city such as **Fener, Balat a**nd **Eyüp** offered a fascinating mixture of Byzantine relics and Ottoman grandeur, often side by side. Again and again I stumbled upon works of the great architect Sinan in places where I least expected them. One day I watched a Greek Orthodox ceremony in the Greek Patriarchate in Fener, another I admired the beautiful interior decoration of a synagogue in Balat. Still in the vicinity of the Golden Horn I found postmodern art on display at **SantralIstanbul,** cutdown models of Turkish icons at **Miniatürk** and fascinating reminders of industrial history at the **Rahmi M. Koç Museum. Karaköy**, too, was a real discovery, its back streets full of forgotten wonders.

I strolled along **İstiklal Caddesi** to the heart of the modern city for section four. This is a part of town where two worlds really collide as I found as I ambled along the side streets of **Tarlabaşı** and then tucked into Modern Turkish cuisine in the fancy cafes of **Cihangir**. I enjoyed **Nevizade Sokak** and trendy **Asmalımescit**, finding time, of course, to do justice to the impressive **Pera Museum** and the smaller galleries that play host to temporary exhibitions as well.

For section five, I cruised along the European shore of the wonderful **Bosphorus,** ending up in **Rumeli Kavağı,** doing my best to ignore the ugly concrete constructions slotted in amid the delightful mansions and palaces.

Next I explored the Anatolian shore of the Bosphorus for section six, a journey that took me all the way up to **Anadolu Kavağı** and the superb view of the Black Sea from **Yoros Castle**. Afterwards I diverted into **Üsküdar, Kadıköy, Fenerbahçe** and **Kalamış,** before window- shopping my way along **Bağdat Caddesi**, the most popular shopping street on the Asian side of town.

I saved the last section of the book for the hidden places in the city outskirts. Closest to the center were the **Princes' Islands** and the **Belgrade Forest,** but I also ventured much further afield to the beach resorts of **Kilyos, Riva, Şile and Ağva**, to the **Marmara Islands** and then to **Western Istanbul, Gebze, Hereke** and **Eskihisar**, all of them places that deserve to receive far more visitors than they do at the moment.

BAU

101 Places Listed by Geographical Location

THE HISTORIC PENINSULA (INSIDE THE WALLS)

THE COAST ROAD (FROM CANKURTARAN TO YEŞİLKÖY)

THE GOLDEN HORN

FROM TAKSİM TO MASLAK

THE BOSPHORUS (EUROPEAN SHORE)

THE BOSPHORUS (ASIAN SHORE)

ISTANBUL ESCAPES

101 Places Listed Alphabetically

The problem with names

I had a really tough time sorting out the non-Turkish names mentioned in the book since some of them were **Roman, some Ancient Greek, some Modern Greek and some Armenian.** That was bad enough, but to add to the linguistic muddle some names from Byzantine times had been either **Latinized or translated into Turkish**. Over time the transliteration of the names of some emperors and saints had also been changed: Komnenos to Comnenus, Theodosios to Theodosius, Ayios Yeoryios to Aya Yorgi, Ioannes Prodromos (St. John the Baptist) to Aya Yani. I tried to keep family names as they had been originally, but some given names had also been changed or translated; for example, Ioannes is often translated into John. Wherever possible I tried to stick with **the most commonly used versions of names** to avoid confusion but it was very hard to get complete consistency. Associate Professor Harry Tzimitras came to my help with the names in Ancient and Modern Greek, but even where I have used the original Greek name I have sometimes thought it's best to add the more commonly used **Turkish name in parenthesis.** Where the name of the church is something as familiar to Western readers as Sts Peter and Paul I have kept it like that even though for consistency's sake I should have changed their names to Petros and Pavlus. As you can imagine, I was sometimes completely confused and couldn't decide what to do. For instance, I was assured that in Armenian Surp Asdvadzaddin means Virgin Mary, but the Armenian Church in Bakırköy clearly displays a sign reading Astvazazin, so after a while I began to wonder which version was really correct.

I also had some difficulties with the **names of the yalıs** (waterfront mansions). Their names tended to alter with every change of ownership. To make matters worse, different names often cropped up in different sources. Sometimes mansions secretly passed into different hands and the new owners didn't want to be identified, which meant talking to the headmen (muhtar) to try and get the correct name. I may have made some mistakes and will be very grateful for any help in correcting them.

For the **sultans** I retained the **Ottoman-era spelling** of their names: Mehmed, Ahmed, Abdülhamid, Kemaleddin, Hayreddin etc. When I was writing about Sultan Beyazid II, I spelt his name the Ottoman way, but for the square named after him I used the more familiar modern spelling of Beyazıt that appears on signs. When in doubt I consulted the Ottoman-Turkish dictionary by Ferit Devellioğlu.

Please send any comments to: ***tonguc2000@gmail.com***

Exploring Istanbul

The city has an excellent public transport system incorporating buses, trains, metrobuses, trams, funiculars, ferries, seabuses and even cable cars. I suggest that you invest in an **Istanbulkart**, an electronic purse that can be used on every form of local transport except the private dolmuşes (minibuses). You can buy them at main Metro terminals, ferry terminals and transport interchanges and can refill them at machines dotted about the city. For more information please visit: www.istanbulkart.istanbul

Museum Pass

With Museum Pass Turkey, you can visit more than three hundred museums and archeological sites that belong to Republic of Turkey Ministry of Culture and Tourism and enjoy your trip through time. The pass is valid for fifteen days starting from your first museum and archeological site entrance. For more information you can visit: www.muze.gov.tr/MuseumPass

The photographs

By the time I started the design phase of this book, I had accumulated around 26,000 photos. Thanks to the invaluable contribution of other photographers, I ended up with around 32,000 photos to choose from. Some postcards and other images were also selected from my private collection and that of my friends, **Phyllis and Fred Quenault**. Istanbul always looks exceptionally beautiful through the eyes of **Aydın Sertbaş** (@aydinsert), who took unforgettable pictures for my book **"Istanbul by Night"**. Instagram is one of the most effective social media tools for discovering innovations today. I came across **Halit Bilen** through his Instagram account, @bildrone and admired his photographs immediately. He discovers unique angles and captures such magical moments. We prepared my book, **"Istanbul A Bird's Eye View"** together and you will also see amazing photographs taken by him as you turn these pages. I extend my thanks to **Uğur Soyata** (@Emrkrm), **Tolga Sıtkı** (@Tolgy75) and **Barış Hasan Bedir** (@barishasanbedir) for coloring my book with their photographs. I also used the works of more than 60 other photographers, in particular: **Gülgün Asutay**, **Michael Constantini**, **Servet Dilber**, **Sinan Doğan**, **Rebecca Erol**, **Serhan Güngör**, **Aynur Koç**, **Şebnem Köken**, **Aydın Kudu**, **Ozan Kutsal**, **Alex Massavetas**, **Mehmet Özcan**, **Fatih Pınar**, **Kate Russell**, **Ufuk Sarışen** and **Erman Tezgör**. I am very grateful to all of them. You can find a complete list of credits at the end of the book. I was responsible for editing the photos and hope you enjoy my selections.

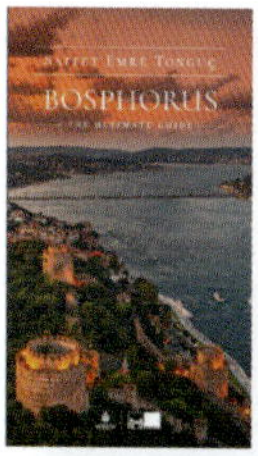

Send us your photos

I tried very hard to come up with the most striking images of the city, but I am still not happy with some of them. If you'd like to share your photos with me, please send them in and I will try and use them in future editions.
tonguc2000@gmail.com

Sister book İstanbul Hakkında Her Şey

The book you are reading now has a sister edition in Turkish. The two books have a lot in common but differ in some details. **İstanbul Hakkında Her Şey** has the point of view of a Turkish man living in İstanbul. It may make a good gift for a Turkish friend who wants to know more about Istanbul. My other books about Istanbul; **Boğaz Hakkında Her Şey**, **Bosphorus The Ultimate Guide**, **İstanbul'un 100 Mücevheri**, **Kanatlarımda İstanbul**, **Istanbul A Bird's Eye View** and **Beflügelndes Istanbul** will also offer you different perspectives about the city.

About Istanbul...

8,500 Years of History

Hagia Sophia is recognized as the most important relic of the Byzantine era.

Pre-Byzantine Period

c. 6000 BC -Neolithic settlement in Yenikapı
c. 680 BC- Megarians settle Chalcedon (see p. 476)
c. 660 – Megarians under Byzas settle Sarayburnu (see p. 202)
512 – Persians seize the city and build a bridge of boats over the Bosphorus (see p. 433)
407 – Byzantium seized by the Athenians
405 –Byzantium falls to the Spartans
340 – Philip of Macedon lays siege to the city
318 – Antigonus takes Byzantium after death of Alexander the Great
64 – Byzantium becomes part of Roman Empire
196 AD – Emperor Septimius Severus demolishes the original city walls (see p. 155)
212 – First major earthquake recorded
258 – Gothic invaders destroy Chalcedon

Byzantine Period

330 – Emperor Constantine the Great makes Byzantium ("Nova Roma") the capital of the Roman Empire as Constantinople
391 - Christianity becomes state religion
395 – Death of Emperor Theodosius heralds final split between Eastern and Western parts of Roman Empire

413-447 – Building of Theodosian City Walls (see p. 155)
527 - Work starts on Church of Sts Sergius & Bacchus (see p. 173)
532 – Nika Riot (see p. 047)
532-537 – Emperor Justinian builds Hagia Sophia (see p. 027)
655-782 – Five Arab raids on Constantinople
730 – Emperor Leo III bans icons in churches

View of Maiden's Tower and Sarayburnu from Üsküdar

842 – Final restoration of icons
1054 – Schism between Catholic and Orthodox churches over religious disagreements
1204 – Fourth Crusade descends on and sacks Constantinople
1261 – Byzantine government restored
1348 - Building of Galata Tower

Galata Tower

1390 – First Ottoman siege under Sultan Bayezid I
1391 – Second Ottoman siege under Sultan Bayezid I
1396 - Sultan Bayezid I builds fort at Anadolu Hisarı (see p. 539)
1412 – Prince Murad besieges Constantinople
1422 – Sultan Murad II besieges Constantinople
1452 – Sultan Mehmed II builds fort at Rumeli Hisarı (see p. 433)

Ottoman Period

1453 – Sultan Mehmed II captures Constantinople for the Ottomans on 29 May
1453 – Work starts on Old Palace (see p. 083)
1455 – Building of Yedikule (see p. 158)
1470 – Building of Fatih Mosque (see p. 115)
1472-1478 – Oldest parts of Topkapı Palace built (see p. 003)
1517 – Istanbul becomes center of Islamic Caliphate under Sultan Selim I
1520 – Sultan Süleyman the Magnificent ascends the throne. Start of Ottoman Golden Age

Rumeli Hisarı

1557 – Completion of Süleymaniye Mosque (see p. 098)
1571 – Ottoman navy defeated at Battle of Lepanto
1609-1616 – Building of Sultanahmet (Blue) Mosque (see p. 063)
1622 – Revolt of Janissaries and murder of the sultan, "Young" Osman

Sultan Ahmed III Library, Topkapı Palace

1660 – Building of Spice Market (see p. 098)
1709-30 – Tulip Age under Sultan Ahmed III (see p. 265)
1730 – Patrona Halil Revolt brings Tulip Era to an end
1807 – Janissary revolt leads to mass destruction
1826 – Sultan Mahmud II disbands the Janissaries ("the Auspicious Event") and creates modern standing army (see p. 382)
1836 – First permanent bridge across Golden Horn (see p. 218)
1839 – Gülhane Decree kicks off Tanzimat period of reform (see p. 202)
1843-56 – Balyan brothers build Dolmabahçe Palace as sultans try to westernize city (see p. 387)
1850 – First ferry service to the Princes' Islands (see p. 591)
1856 – Sultan abandons Topkapı Palace for the Dolmabahçe Palace
1865 – Beylerbeyi Palace built (see p. 417)
1874 – Çırağan Palace built (see p. 407)
1875 – Opening of the Tünel underground railway (see p. 319)

Galata Bridge

1876 – Sultan Abdülhamid II declares, then abolishes constitutional monarchy
1883 – The Orient Express train steams into Sirkeci Station (see p. 206)
1908 – Sultan Abdülhamid II declares second constitutional monarchy
1912 – Bulgarians reach Çatalca during Balkan War
1914-18 – Ottomans enter First World War on side of Germans
1919-23 - Turkish War of Independence under leadership of Mustafa Kemal Atatürk. Istanbul occupied by British and French troops
1922 - Sultanate abolished

Tünel

Republican and Modern Periods

1923 – Treaty of Lausanne ends war. Allied Forces leave 6 October. Capital moved to Ankara 13 October. Republic founded 29 October.
1928 – Turkish alphabet is switched from Arabic to Latin; Istanbul becomes city's official name
1938 – Atatürk dies in Dolmabahçe Palace on 10 November (see p. 391). İsmet İnönü becomes president
1939-45 – Turkey stays neutral during Second World War
1950 - First democratic elections won by Democrat Party under Adnan Menderes
1952 – Turkey joins NATO
1960 – Military coup
1961 – Adnan Menderes hanged on Yassıada (see p. 595). İsmet İnönü becomes prime minister
1965 – Justice Party wins elections. Süleyman Demirel becomes prime minister

Atatürk and the Shah of Iran

1971 – Second military coup leads to a series of figurehead leaders whose policies are dictated by the military.
1973 – First Bosphorus bridge opens (see p. 379)
1974-1980 – Political tension and street fighting ends in third military coup. Kenan Evren becomes president
1983 – Motherland Party wins elections. Prime minister Turgut Özal launches program of economic reforms.
1988 – Opening of second Bosphorus bridge (see p. 370)
1993 – Death of Özal heralds decade of weak coalition governments
1996 – Turkey enters EU Customs Union
1997 – "Post-modern coup" sees off government of Necmettin Erbakan
1999 – Two serious earthquakes devastate north-eastern Turkey and parts of Istanbul

First Bosphorus Bridge

2001 – Economy collapses following banking crisis
2002 – Justice & Development Party (AKP) wins elections. Abdullah Gul becomes prime minister.
2003 – Recep Tayyip Erdoğan, ex-mayor of Istanbul, becomes prime minister on March 14th.
2005 – Talks on Turkey joining EU commence
2006 – Istanbul-born Orhan Pamuk (see p. 347) wins Nobel Prize for Literature
2010 – Istanbul crowned European Capital of Culture. Route of Third Bosphorus Bridge announced (see p. 370). *İstanbul Hakkında Her Şey* published!
2012 – *Bosphorus The Ultimate Guide* (published in Turkish and English) and *Istanbul The Ultimate Guide* were published.
2013 – The protests which began in Gezi Park affected the agenda of the whole country. The Marmaray (see p. 501) line was opened.
2015 – Prof. Dr. Aziz Sancar won the Nobel Prize in chemistry.
2016 – *Istanbul by Night* was published. The 15 July coup attempt occurred. The Third Bosphorus Bridge (see p. 370) and the Eurasian Tunnel (see p. 183) were opened.
2017 – "Yes" won in the referendum on the constitutional amendment.
2018 – Recep Tayyip Erdogan (see p. 265) became the first leader of the presidential system.
2019 – The Gebze-Halkalı suburban line was opened. Istanbul Airport was opened while Atatürk Airport was closed.
2020 – *Istanbul A Bird' s Eye View* published. Covid-19, which left its mark on this year, also adversely affected the lives in Istanbul.

The Byzantines in a nutshell

The great Byzantine Empire started life as a small Greek colony in the 7th century BC but went on to become the capital of the Eastern Roman Empire as sheer size forced the rulers in Rome to share their power. Eventually Rome itself was overrun by invaders, leaving Byzantium – renamed **Constantinople** in his own honor by **Constantine the Great**– as its successor, albeit a far glitzier, more eastern-oriented one. Frequently harried by armies from the newly invigorated Islamic Middle East, Byzantium held its ground until 1071 when defeat by the Selçuk Turks at **Manzikert** in what is now eastern Turkey signaled that the tide had turned against it.

In a particularly disconcerting episode in 1204 the Byzantine emperor was actually forced from the throne by the forces of the **Fourth Crusade** who diverted from their supposed goal of Jerusalem to sack the city, inflicting worse damage on it than the Ottomans when their turn came in 1453. The **Latin Occupation** continued through until 1261 at which time a scion of the imperial family based in **Nicaea** (modern İznik) managed to recapture the city. This achievement was marked by a Byzantine Renaissance in art and architecture, but beneath the glamor the Empire was seriously weakened, its troops no match for **Sultan Mehmed II**'s concerted assault on it in 1453. A breakaway Byzantine "Empire" continued to hold on in Trebizond (modern Trabzon) on the Black Sea, but it too finally fell to the Conqueror in 1461.

The Ottomans in a nutshell

From a base in Bursa the first Ottoman sultans rapidly reached out to snatch most of the territory around Constantinople in the 14th century. Then in the 15th century concerted efforts to conquer the city from their second capital in **Adrianople** (Edirne) in Thrace culminated in the great prize of the Conquest in 1453. Almost immediately the city was renamed Istanbul and became the new capital of the expanding empire.

It's not without reason that **Sultan Süleyman I** is known as "the Magnificent" to Westerners since it was during his long reign that the Ottoman Empire reached its apogee both in terms of territory and in art and culture. By the time Süleyman died, his writ ran through most of the Balkans, the Middle East and parts of North Africa. The Ottomans continued to be a force to reckon with right through until the late 17th century, despite a major setback in 1571 at the **Battle of Lepanto** which put an end to their naval supremacy.

From then on, however, the Empire went into a long period of decline brought on in large part by the failure to establish a clear system of inheritance that would have prevented the massacres and in-fighting that inevitably followed the death of each ruler. By 1923 when the sultanate was finally abolished the great power of the Ottomans had long since crumbled to dust, with the Empire dubbed "the Sick Man of Europe".

The coming of the Turkish Republic

During the 19th century several of the sultans made attempts to modernize the government, some, such as **Sultan Mahmud II** who overthrew the troublesome Janissary army, rather more seriously than others. Under pressure, **Sultan Abdülhamid II** briefly agreed to a parliament that he speedily abolished again. But as the Balkan states rapidly peeled away from the Empire modernization could not be held back and there was a second attempt at establishing a parliament under the **Young Turks** who were instrumental in taking Turkey into the First World War on the side of Germany with disastrous consequences.

Defeat in that war led to the invasion of Turkey by the victorious Allied forces who started to try and carve the country up for themselves. Incensed, the war hero **Mustafa Kemal** gathered together a resistance movement and in the course of the **Turkish War of Independence** drove the invaders out, establishing a new republic within what are its modern borders. Dubbed **Atatürk** ("the Father of the Turks"), Mustafa Kemal moved fast to bring in much-needed reforms that in particular reduced the power of the religious authorities. Almost immediately he moved the capital away from Istanbul with its Ottoman associations to Ankara in the heart of the new **Turkish Republic**.

The expanding city

Today Istanbul is a sprawling metropolis of an estimated 18 million people. However, this is a fairly recent development. It is thought that there were perhaps 100,000 people living here in the 5th century, but it will probably come as quite a shock to learn that at the time of the Conquest in 1453 the number had fallen until there were only about 60,000 residents. The number was brought up to around 300,000 in the early 16th century as settlers were relocated from other parts of the expanding Ottoman Empire, but as recently as 1945 there were still only about one million people living in the city. Most of the rapid expansion has taken place over the last 30 years, as people have poured into Istanbul in search of a better life, especially from the troubled south-east part of the country. In 1990 the population stood at 7.5 million people, by 1997 it was 9.2 million and in 2000 12 million and in 2020 18 million.

30

Istanbul's Rulers

Roman Emperors

Constantine I (324-37) - the Great
Constantius (337-61)
Julianus (361-3) - the Apostate
Jovianus (363-4)
Valens (364-78)
Theodosius I (379-95) - the Great

Byzantine Emperors

Arcadius (395-408)
Theodosius II (408-50)
Marcian (450-57)
Leo I (457-74)
Leo II (474)
Zeno (474-75)
Basilicus (475-76)
Zeno restored (476-91)
Anastasius I (491-518)
Justin I (518-27)
Justinian I (527-65) - the Great
Justin II (565-78)
Tiberius I Constantine (578-82)
Maurice (582-602)
Fokas (602-10)
Heraclius (610-41)
Constantine III & Heraclonas (641)
Constans II (641-68)
Constantine IV (668-85)
Justinian II (685-95)
Leontius (695-98)
Tiberius II (698-705)
Justinian II restored (705-11)
Philippicus Bardanes (711-13)
Anastasius II (713-15)
Theodosius III (715-17)
Leo III (717-41)
Constantine V (741-75)
Leo IV (775-80)
Constantine VI (780-97)
Irene (797-802)
Nicephorus I (802-11)
Stauracius (811)
Michael I Rangabe (811-13)
Leo V (813-20)
Michael II (820-29)
Theophilus (829-42)
Michael III (842-67)
Basil I (867-86)
Leo VI (886-912)
Alexander (912-13)
Constantine VII Porphyrogenitus (913-59)
Romanos I Lecapenus (919-44)
Romanos II (959-63)
Nicephorus II Fokas (963-69)
John I Tzimiskes (969-76)
Basil II (976-1024) – the Bulgar-slayer
Constantine VIII (1025-28)
Romanos III Argyrus (1028-34)
Michael IV (1034-41)
Michael V (1041-42)
Theodora & Zoe (1042-1042)
Constantine IX Monomachos (1042-55)
Theodora restored (1055-56)
Michael VI (1056-57)
Isaac I Comnenos (1057-59)
Constantine X Ducas (1059-67)
Romanos IV Diogenes (1067-81)
Michael VII Ducas (1071-78)
Nicephorus III Botaneiates (1078-81)
Alexios I Comnenos (1081-1118)
John II Comnenos (1118-43)
Manuel I Comnenos (1143-80)
Alexios II Comnenos (1180-83)
Andronicos I Comnenos (1182-85)
Isaac II Angelos (1185-95)
Alexios III Angelos (1195-1203)
Isaac II Angelos restored & Alexios IV Angelos (1203-04)
Alexios V Ducas (1204)

Latin Occupiers

Baudouin I (1204-05)
Henri (1205-16)
Pierre de Cortenoi (1216-19)
Robert (1219-28)
Baudouin II (1228-61)

Byzantine Restoration

Michael VIII Paleologos (1261-82)
Andronicos II Paleologos (1282-1328)
Andronicos III Paleologos (1328-41)
John V Paleologos (1341-91)
John VI Cantacuzenus (1347-54)
Andronicos IV Paleologos (1376-79)
John VII Paleologos (1390)
Manuel II Paleologos (1391-1425)
John VIII Paleologos (1425-48)
Constantine XI Dragases (1449-53)

Ottoman Sultans

Mehmed II (1451-81) – the Conqueror
Bayezid II (1481-1512) – the Thunderbolt
Selim I (1512-20) – the Grim
Süleyman I (1520-66) – the Magnificent
Selim II (1566-74) – the Sot
Murad III (1574-95)
Mehmed III (1595-1603)
Ahmed I (1603-1618)
Mustafa I (1617-18)
Osman II (1618-22) – Young Osman
Mustafa I restored (1622-23)
Murad IV (1623-40)
İbrahim (1640-48)
Mehmed IV (1648-87) – the Hunter
Süleyman II (1687-91)
Ahmed II (1691-95)
Mustafa II (1695-1703)
Ahmed III (1703-30)
Mahmud I (1730-54)
Osman III (1754-57)
Mustafa III (1757-74)
Abdülhamid I (1774-89)
Selim III (1789-1807)
Mustafa IV (1807-08)
Mahmud II (1808-39)
Abdülmecid (1839-61)
Abdülaziz (1861-76)
Murad V (1876)
Abdülhamid II (1876-1909)
Mehmed V (1909-18) – Reşad
Mehmed VI (1918-22) – Vahdeddin
Abdülmecid Efendi (1922-24) – caliph only

The Architects of Istanbul

Many men have left their mark on the stones of Istanbul, most famously Koca Mimar Sinan, the great Ottoman architect who was responsible for a staggering 84 buildings, half of them mosques. Second only to Sinan must come the prolific Balyan family whose baroque 19th-century designs tend to be less popular with contemporary visitors but which are no less ubiquitous. Unlike Sinan's, the Balyans' reach extended across the Bosphorus to the Asian shore, as did that of Kemaleddin Bey who, with Vedat Tek, worked to create a new style of Turkish architecture appropriate to the 20th-century. In the second half of the 20th century Sedad Hakki Eldem fined down Ottoman architecture to its essentials before the city succumbed to the current concrete cancer. These men were not just prolific but versatile as were the foreign architects who visited Istanbul in the 19th-century and moulded the streets of Pera (modern Beyoğlu) in particular in their image, amongst them the Italians Raimondo d'Aronco and Guilio Mongeri and the Levantine Alexandre Vallaury. Oddly enough, some of the city's most famous buildings, including the Beyazıt, Fatih and Sultanahmet Mosques, were designed by men about whom very little is known. Some of the most extraordinary buildings in the city such as the Gümüşsuyu Palas (see p. 285) were designed by men whose names have not even come down to us.

Anthemius of Tralles and Isidore of Miletus

It all began with these two great 6th-century Greek architects who came up with the idea for the vast domes that later became a standard feature of Ottoman architecture.

• Hagia Sophia (see p. 027)

Yakub-Şah ibn Sultan-Şah

Nothing is known about this architect despite the splendor of his creation. He is thought to have been a Turk.

Beyazıt Mosque (see p. 081)

Atik Sinan

Easily confused with the much better known Koca Mimar Sinan, Atik (Old) Sinan (?-1471) was probably a Greek architect who worked for Sultan Mehmed II Virtually nothing definite is known about him.

• Fatih Mosque (see p. 115)

Koca Mimar Sinan

Sinan (c.1490-1588) was born in a village near Kayseri, probably of Greek parents. Taken in as a *devşirme*, he rose through the ranks of the Janissaries to become a commander, before becoming chief imperial architect in around 1540 and staying in post for the rest of his life. His masterpiece is generally said to be the Selimiye Mosque in Edirne but there are several buildings in Istanbul that are almost equally splendid, especially the Süleymaniye Mosque, built for his patron Sultan Süleyman the Magnificent.

• Atik Valide Mosque (see p. 502)
• Azapkapı Mosque (see p. 273)
• Barbarossa's Tomb (see p. 396)
• Büyük Hamam (see p. 265)
• Çemberlitaş Hamam (see p. 068)
• Çinili Hamam (see p. 110)
• Eğrikemer (Crooked Aqueduct, see p. 564)
• Fatih İbrahim Paşa Medrese (see p. 096)
• Gazi Ahmed Paşa Mosque (see p. 146)
• Güzelce Kemer (Charming Aqueduct, see p. 564)
• Hadım İbrahim Paşa Mosque (see p. 160)
• Hagia Sophia - two minarets (see p. 027)
• Haseki Hürrem Hamam (see p. 033)
• Haseki Hürrem Mosque (see p. 095)
• İskele Mosque (see p. 500)
• Mağlova Aqueduct (see p. 564)
• Mesih Mehmed (Ali) Paşa Mosque (see p. 119)
• Mihrimah Sultan Mosque (see p. 384)
• Molla Çelebi Mosque (see p. 382)
• Ortaköy Hamam (see p. 413)
• Paşa Kemer (Paşa's Aqueduct, see p. 564)
• Piyale Paşa Mosque (see p. 264)
• Ramazan Efendi Mosque (see p. 097)
• Rüstem Paşa Han (see p. 273)
• Rüstem Paşa Medrese (see p. 061)
• Rüstem Paşa Mosque (see p. 220)
• Selim II's tomb, Hagia Sophia (see p. 032)
• Semiz Ali Paşa Medrese (see p. 502)
• Sinanpaşa Mosque (see p. 397)
• Sokollu Mehmed Paşa Mosque (see p. 178)
• Sokollu Mehmed Paşa, Siyavuş Paşa and Ayas Mehmed Paşa tombs (see p. 247)
• Sultan Süleyman Bridge (see p. 605)
• Süleymaniye Mosque (see p. 098)
• Şehzade Mosque (see p. 103)
• Şemsi Paşa Mosque (see p. 502)
• Yahya Efendi's shrine (see p. 407)
• Yavuz Sultan Selim Mosque (see p. 122)
• Zal Mahmud Paşa Mosque (see p. 250)

Miniature showing the building of Süleyman the Magnificent's tomb in the grounds of the Süleymaniye Mosque from the Süleymanname by Sinan Çavuş

Davud Ağa

Davud Ağa (?-1599) worked alongside Sinan for many years and succeeded him as chief imperial architect on his death. Stylistically, there is little to distinguish between his buildings and those of Sinan.

- Cerrahpaşa Mosque (see p. 094)
- Hadım Hasan Paşa Medrese (see p. 060)
- Koca Sinan Paşa complex (see p. 068)
- Murad III's tomb, Hagia Sophia (see p. 032)
- Sepetçiler Kasrı (original, see p. 202)
- Yeni (New) Mosque (see p. 213)

New Mosque

Sedefkar Mehmed Ağa

Another architect who had worked and trained under Sinan, Sedefkar Mehmed Ağa (c. 1540-1617) was probably an Albanian who may have come to Istanbul to serve in the Janissary corps. Multi-talented, he trained as a musician as well as a worker in mother-of-pearl (*sedef*). In 1606 he succeeded Dalgıç Ahmed Ağa as chief imperial architect. He may not have left many buildings to the city but his masterpiece is still one of its best known monuments.

- Sultanahmet Mosque (p. 038)

Mehmed Tahir Ağa

Even Mehmed Tahir Ağa's dates of birth and death are a mystery but he was chief imperial architect during the reign of Sultan Mustafa III and was responsible for many of the city's early baroque mosques.

- Ayazma Mosque (see p. 502)
- Beylerbeyi Mosque (see p. 517)
- Fatih Mosque (reconstruction, see p. 115)
- Laleli Mosque (see p. 088)
- Zeynep Sultan Mosque (see p. 202)

Beylerbeyi Mosque

The Balyans

If ever there was a family that stamped their mark on a city it was the Balyans, a family of Ottoman Armenians that produced a string of no less than nine architects in the 18th and 19th centuries: Bali (?-1725), Magar (?-?) Krikor (1764-1831), Senekerim (1768-1833), Garabed Amira (1800-66), Nigoğos (1826-58), Sarkis (1831-99), Hagop (1837-75) and Simon (1848-94). Bali came from a village near Karaman in Central Anatolia and became an architect at the court of Sultan Mehmed IV. Nigoğos, Sarkis, Hagop and Simon were all sons of Garabed who died prematurely of a heart attack. Love them or loathe them, you certainly can't miss their work.

Balyan Family Burial Plot

- Abud Efendi Yalı (see p. 535)
- Adile Sultan Palace (see p. 532)
- Akaretler row-houses (see p. 401)
- Askeri Hastane (Gümüşsuyu Military Hospital) (see p. 285)
- Beyazıt (Serasker) Tower (see p. 083)
- Beylerbeyi Palace (see p. 517)
- Çırağan Palace (original version, see p. 406)
- Dolmabahçe Palace and Mosque (see p. 386)
- Feshane (see p. 251)
- Gümüşsuyu Barracks (see p. 285)
- Ihlamur Kasrı (see p. 399)
- Imperial Tombs, Divan Yolu (see p. 064)
- Kara Todori Yalı (see p. 453)
- Küçük Mecidiye Mosque (see p. 405)
- Küçüksu Kasrı (see p. 537)
- Maçka Kışlası (Maçka Barracks) (see p. 347)
- Mecidiye Pavilion, Topkapı Palace (see p. 018)
- Meclis-i Mebusan Building (see p. 382)
- Mediha Sultan Palace (see p. 437)
- Nusretiye Cami (Victory Mosque, see p. 378)
- Nusretiye Clock Tower (see p. 378)
- Ortaköy Mosque (see p. 413)
- Sadabad Mosque (see p. 256)
- Sarı Köşk, Emirgan Park (see p. 441)
- Selimiye Barracks (see p. 495)
- Surp Asdvadzadzin Church, Beşiktaş (see p. 399)
- Surp Asdvadzadzin Church, Kumkapı (see p. 181)
- Topuzlu Dam (see p. 565)
- Valide Dam (see p. 565)
- Valide Sultan Mosque (see p. 089)
- Yıldız Şale (Yıldız Chalet) and Malta Köşk (see p. 403-04)

Ortaköy Mosque

A mosque designed by Raimondo d'Aronco was lost to road-widening.

Raimondo d'Aronco
Art Nouveau in Istanbul

Raimondo d'Aronco

The Italian architect Raimondo d'Aronco (1857-1932) arrived in Istanbul in 1896 to design the site for a trade fair for Sultan Abdülhamid II. After an earthquake put paid to the exhibition D'Aronco was invited to stay on to repair some of the historic monuments, then to design new government and private buildings. During the 16 years that he lived here he introduced Art Nouveau to Istanbul. He left Istanbul in 1912 when the sultan was deposed. One of Istanbul's big losses is the Küçük (Small) Mosque that used to stand in Karaköy Square over where the underpass is now.

- Casa Botter (Botter Apartments, see p. 314)
- Huber Köşkü (Huber Mansion) (see p. 459)
- Imperial Porcelain Factory (see p. 405)
- Imperial School of Military Medicine (see p. 494)
- Italian Summer Consulate (see p. 460)
- Laleli Çeşme (Tulip Fountain, see p. 329)
- Maçka Fountain (see p. 348)
- Mizzi Köşkü (see p. 591)
- Rectorate, Hippodrome (p. 048)
- Şeyh Zafir complex (see p. 398)
- Şişli Etfal Hospital clock tower (see p. 356)
- Yıldız Palace complex (see p. 402)

Alexandre Vallaury

Born to a pastry chef in Istanbul, Alexandre Vallaury (1850-1921) is assumed to have been of partly French ancestry. He was a lecturer at the Mimar Sinan University of Fine Arts for a quarter of a century and played a big part in plans to reconstruct the damage done by a big earthquake in 1894, sometimes in collaboration with d'Aronco. He was an eclectic architect who mixed and matched elements of Ottoman, Baroque and Art Nouveau in his buildings.

- Abdülmecid Efendi Mansion (Abdülmecid Efendi Köşkü) (see p. 511)
- Ahmet Afif Paşa Yalı (see p. 451)
- Cemil Topuzlu Köşkü (see p. 488)
- Galata Antique Hotel (see p. 339)
- Hezaren Han
- Hidayet Mosque (see p. 209)
- Istanbul Boys' High School (see p. 060)
- Museum of Archeology (see p. 020)
- Ottoman Bank (see p. 274)
- Pera Palas Hotel (see p. 337)
- Rum Yetimhanesi (Greek Orphanage, see p. 591)
- Tophane Müşiri Zeki Paşa Yalı (see p. 437)

A building in Eminönü designed by Kyriakidis

Konstantinos Kyriakidis

A rare Greek architect whose career is on record, Kyriakidis (1881-1942) studied architecture in Istanbul and Paris and went on to build some 60 apartment blocks here.

- 401-3 Istiklal Caddesi (see p. 300)
- Alhambra Cinema building (see p. 339)
- Fatih Belediye (municipality) and İtfaiye (fire station) (see p. 118)
- Frej Apartments (see p. 333)

Hovsep Kerovbet Aznavuryan

Little is known about the Armenian architect Hovsep Kerovbet Aznavuryan (1854-1935) who worked in a mixture of styles.

- Mısır Apartments, İstiklal Caddesi (see p. 310)
- St Stephen of the Bulgars (see p. 233)

G. E. Street

George Edmund Street

George Edmund Street (1824-81) is best known for the Royal Courts of Justice building in The Strand in London but he also injected a dose of high Victorian Gothic into Istanbul with the Crimean Memorial Church.

- Church of all Saints (see p. 483)
- Crimean Church (see p. 315)

Fossati Brothers

Guiseppe Fossati

Gaspare Fossati (1809-83) and Guiseppe Fossati were Swiss brothers whose main gift to Istanbul was the restoration of Hagia Sophia, completed in 1849. Gaspare also left some wonderful drawings of the end result.

- Church of Sts Peter and Paul (see p. 327)
- Dutch Consulate (see p. 311)
- Hagia Sophia (restoration, see p. 030)
- Notre Dame de Sion (see p. 343)
- Press Museum building (see p. 064)
- Russian Consulate (see p. 312)

William James Smith

The British-born architect W. J. Smith lived in Istanbul from 1844 to 1856, but the buildings he designed were in a Neoclassical and European rather than specifically British style.

- British Consulate (see p. 337)
- Selimiye Barracks (see p. 495)
- Naum Theater (see p. 304)
- Taşkışla (Stone Barracks, see p. 283)
- Tophane Pavilion (Tophane Kasrı, see p. 381)

Tophane Pavillion

August Jasmund

Born in 1859, Jasmund arrived in Istanbul in 1887 and in 1894 he became one of the foreign architects invited to help remake the damage done by a major earthquake. Some of his work was carried out in a pointedly orientalist style, although some was Neoclassical.

- Deutsche Bank building (see p. 208)
- Ragip Paşa Mansion (see p. 489)
- Sirkeci Station (see p. 206)

Giulio Mongeri

Giulio Mongeri

The Italian architect Giulio Mongeri worked in Istanbul on and off between 1900 and 1930, mainly leaving his mark on Pera (Beyoğlu).

- Anadolu Teknik Lisesi (Anatolian Technical High School, see p. 347)
- Assicurazioni Generali Han (see p. 274)
- Bulgur Palas (see p. 094)
- Karaköy Palas (see p. 267)
- Maçka Palas (see p. 347)
- St Anthony's Cathedral (see p. 311)
- Taksim Square monument (see p. 281)

Anatolian Technical High School

Mehmed Vedat Tek

Vedat Tek

Istanbul-born Vedat Tek (1873-1942) was one of the main exponents of the style of architecture called First National that drew on motifs from Selçuk and Ottoman buildings to create something that could exemplify the growing mood of Turkish nationalism in stone. Eventually he became chief architect to the sultan. He was the first Turk to teach at the Academy of Fine Arts. In general he favored a more elaborately decorative style than his contemporary and colleague Kemaleddin Bey.

- Air Forces' Martyrs Monument (see p. 118)
- Büyük Postane (Main Post Office, see p. 207)
- Haydarpaşa (see p. 493) and Moda landing stages (see p. 484)
- Hobyar Mescid (see p. 207)
- Land Registry Building (see p. 048)
- Liman Han (see p. 209)
- Maritime Lines Building, Karaköy (see p. 270)
- Milli Emlak Dükkanları (National Estate Agency Shops, see p. 484)
- Nemlizade Tobacco Warehouse (see p. 513)
- Vedat Tek Konağı (see p. 345)
- Veli Efendi Hippodrome (see p. 193)

Ahmed Kemaleddin Bey

Kemaleddin Bey

Istanbul-born Kemaleddin Bey (1870-1927) was the second major exponent of First National Architecture. Having studied under August Jasmund, he went on to work with Vedat Tek and to develop a more pared-down style of architecture that still incorporated Selçuk and Ottoman motifs. At times he also incorporated elements taken from Art Nouveau into his work.

- Bebek Mosque (see p. 427)
- Çamlıca Girls' High School (see p. 505)
- First and Fourth Vakıf Hans (see p. 208)
- Gazi Osman Paşa tomb (see p. 117)
- Reşadiye Primary School, Eyüp (see p. 247)
- Sultan Mehmed Reşad's tomb (see p. 247)
- Tayyare (Harikzedegan) Apartments (see p. 087)
- Yeşilköy (see p. 194) and Bostancı Mosques (see p. 490)

Sedad Hakkı Eldem

Sedad Hakkı Eldem

Istanbul-born Sedad Hakkı Eldem (1908-88) is the best known practioner of what became known as Second National Architecture, a movement that tried to combine some of the features of traditional Ottoman architecture such as overhanging gables and paired windows with the pared-down appearance and use of modern building materials such as concrete espoused by Le Corbusier.

- Atatürk Kitaplığı (Atatürk Library, see p. 283)
- Istanbul Hilton (see p. 343)
- Istanbul University Department of Literature building (see p. 087)
- Rahmi Koç House, Tarabya
- Sosyal Sigortalar Kurumu (Social Security Department, see p. 110)
- Suna-İnan Kıraç Yalı, Tarabya (see p. 524)

HISTORIC PENINSULA

(OLD ISTANBUL INSIDE THE WALLS)

The House of Felicity

Topkapı Palace

001

The most beautiful and best-known of all Istanbul's sights, Topkapı is the palace overlooking the Bosphorus where the sultans made their homes and supervized government during the glory days of the Ottoman Empire; it's here more than anywhere else in the city that you will feel the ghosts of the imperial past brushing up against you. A collection of kiosks and pavilions set in delightful gardens sit alongside the harem, the private quarters of the sultan's family and the source of much western fantasizing. Here too stands Hagia Eirene (Divine Peace), partner to the Emperor Justinian's great church of Hagia Sophia (Divine Wisdom).

Just around the corner from Hagia Sophia, Topkapı Palace has a spectacular location high on the First Hill of the Byzantine city overlooking the confluence of the Golden Horn, the Sea of Marmara and the Bosphorus. This is where the Byzantine emperors had also chosen to site their palace (see p. 043), which reflects the Ottomans, desire to be seen as stepping into the shoes of a line of rulers stretching back to the Romans. Despite its much later date, the high wall that surrounds the palace and stretches from Cankurtaran to Sirkeci looks very similar to the great **Theodosian land walls** that enclosed the Byzantine city (see p. 144); the area inside it corresponds very closely to what would have been the extent of the original Byzantium. Parts of the palace gardens now form **Gülhane Park** (see p. 201), while parts are occupied by **Istanbul Archeology Museum** (see p. 020). Some of the grounds were lost long ago to the railway line from Greece, leaving the pretty little **Sepetçiler Kasrı** (see p. 202) stranded on its own by the waterside.

As you approach the palace you should rid your mind of the idea of a single building usually evoked by the word. Instead the Ottomans, like the Byzantines before them, lived in a collection of relatively small buildings scattered about extensive gardens which were added to as and when the need arose. By the time the sultans abandoned it the Topkapı complex consisted of four courtyards, a set of gardens and terraces and the labyrinthine harem. It continued in use until 1856 when Sultan Abdülmecid chose to move across the Bosphorus and base himself in the brand-new **Dolmabahçe Palace** (see p. 386). His successors also preferred to live in **Dolmabahçe**, **Yıldız Palace** (see p. 406) and a series of more minor palaces dotted around their estates. Just as the **Old Palace** at Beyazıt (see p. 083) had become a retirement home for redundant palace women after the sultans took up residence in Topkapı, so Topkapı itself served a similar function after the sultans relocated across the Bosphorus. It has been a museum since 1926.

@topkapi_sarayi
www.millisaraylar.gov.tr/saraylar/topkapi-sarayi/
Tel: 0212 512 04 80
Closed Tuesdays

Fountain of Sultan Ahmet III

Before you step through the main gate, pause for a moment to admire the magnificent Fountain of Sultan Ahmet III, which was built in 1728 and boasts four **çeşmes** (fountains) as well as four **sebils** (water dispensaries) guarded by elaborate metal grilles at its corners. An inscription written by the sultan himself reads: "Turn on the tap, drink the water and pray for Ahmed Khan."

Topkapı means "Cannon Gate" and refers to an old entrance to the palace near Sarayburnu that was demolished in the 19th century.

Istanbul was designated European Capital of Culture in 2010 and as part of the celebrations restoration of several palace buildings began. Unfortunately the work hasn't always been completed. As a result visitors cannot always see everything they want to.

Old photograph of the Bab-ı Hümayun

Portrait of Sultan Mehmed II by Sibilizade Ahmed, c.1480

Bab-ı Hümayun (Imperial Gate)

Modern visitors enter through the same monumental gateway, the Bab-ı Hümayun (Imperial Gate), as the sultans' visitors did. As you stand beside the **fountain** look up and admire a stunning piece of calligraphy containing a quotation from the Koran that was inserted into the lunette above the gate; it's thought to be the handiwork of Ali Sofi who also worked on the **Murad Paşa Mosque** at Aksaray (see p. 090). Beneath it a rectangular plaque commemorates the building of the palace by Sultan Mehmed II ("the Conqueror") in 1478, describing him as **"the sultan of two continents and the emperor of two seas"**. Finally, the lintel is decorated with the tuğra (monogram) of **Sultan Mahmud II** who had the gate refashioned in the 19th century. Niches on either side of it were used to display the heads of those who had offended the sultan (before they were refaced with marble in the 19th century, of course). A second storey that appears in old images of the gate was demolished by **Sultan Abdülaziz** in 1867.

Sultan Mahmud II

The signature of Sultan Abdülaziz

Darphane (Mint)

First Courtyard (Alay Meydanı)

The first courtyard of the palace feels more like a small park than an integral part of the complex and even in the past this was the part of the palace that was open to everyone provided they had left their weapons at the gate. Here some of the most **important ceremonies** would have taken place, including the funeral of **Sultan Mehmed II** which was attended by 25,000 of the elite foot soldiers called the Janissaries (see p. 495); not surprisingly, it was sometimes known as the **Courtyard of the Janissaries**.

The buildings ringing the walls were mainly used for storage, although a renowned bakery stood against the south wall. Firewood for the palace fetched from the woods of Thrace was stored against the west wall, while there was a mint (darphane) against the north wall which dated back to the 15th century (the surviving buildings are 18th-century replacements). Waterwheels behind what is now the ticket office controled the flow of water to the palace.

A miniature showing the Bab-ı Hümayun from the Şehinşahname of Nakkaş Osman, 1597

You buy a ticket to enter the palace from the booths against the right-hand wall. Once you've done so, be sure to take a look at the **Executioner's Fountain**, also against this wall (it's the fifth along). Supposedly used by the executioner to rinse the blood off his sword, this must be a replacement for the original since its inscription dates it to the reign of **Sultan Abdülhamid II** (r. 1876-1909) when the last such gruesome head-severing had taken place in 1826.

"...a peninsula of pavilions, surrounded by trees and gardens, cascading down to the sea".

Constantinople – City of the World's Desire 1453-1924 **by Philip Mansel, 1995**

Hagia Eirene

Apse of Hagia Eirene

The one unmissable building in the first courtyard is the church of Hagia Eirene (Divine Peace) that was rebuilt by the Emperor Justinian in 537 after an older building was destroyed by the **Nika Riot** of 532. It was patched up again after an earthquake in 740, since when it has been little altered. After the Ottoman conquest it was enclosed inside the walls of Topkapı Palace and used as an arsenal by the Janissaries. Later it became a forerunner of the Military Museum in Harbiye (see p. 341). Today it serves as an occasional **concert hall** but can't be visited at other times, which is a shame as the sight of its great brick dome and its apse adorned with a simple **mosaic cross** is very dramatic. The mosaic itself is of uncertain date, some attributing it to the Justinian period, others to the restoration in 740. The **synthronon** (bench seat ringing the apse) is the only such example known in the city.

The first church on this site appears to have preceded the reign of **Constantine the Great** who probably had it rebuilt. Peaceful as the setting may seem now, it was here in 346 that more than 3,000 people died in a riot over one of those obscure theological squabbles for which early Christianity was renowned (in this case Arianism versus Orthodoxy).

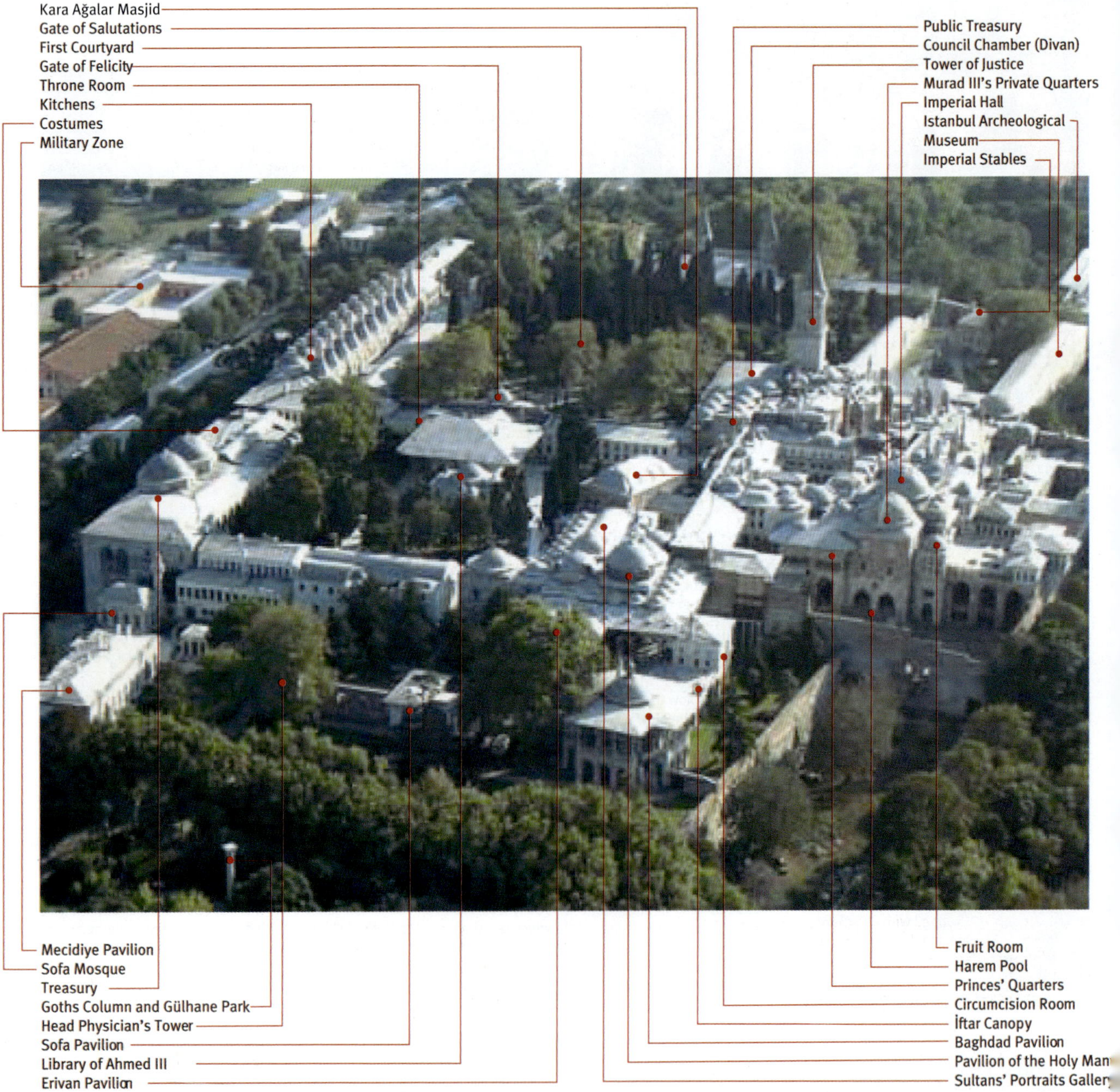

Kara Ağalar Masjid
Gate of Salutations
First Courtyard
Gate of Felicity
Throne Room
Kitchens
Costumes
Military Zone
Public Treasury
Council Chamber (Divan)
Tower of Justice
Murad III's Private Quarters
Imperial Hall
Istanbul Archeological Museum
Imperial Stables
Mecidiye Pavilion
Sofa Mosque
Treasury
Goths Column and Gülhane Park
Head Physician's Tower
Sofa Pavilion
Library of Ahmed III
Erivan Pavilion
Fruit Room
Harem Pool
Princes' Quarters
Circumcision Room
İftar Canopy
Baghdad Pavilion
Pavilion of the Holy Man
Sultans' Portraits Galler

The Kelime-i Tevhid, or Islamic Creed, is inscribed above the Bab-üs Selam

Bab-üs Selam (Gate of Salutations)

After buying your ticket you proceed through the Bab-üs Selam (Gate of Salutations, also known as the Middle Gate) into the second courtyard. Flanked by octagonal towers topped with conical roofs, this is a far grander gate than the Imperial Gate and designed to leave a lasting impression on foreign visitors. Its exact date of construction is unknown although it must have been in existence by 1493 when the towers appear in pictures of the palace. An inscription above the gate records the Islamic creed: **"There is no god but Allah and Mohammed is his prophet."**

In the past visitors would have had to leave their horses here since no one but the sultan could ride through the gate. At this entrance to the inner palace enemies of the sultan were sometimes beheaded and their heads displayed on **"example stones"**.

Second Courtyard (Divan Meydanı)

Little changed from the days of **Sultan Mehmed II**, the second courtyard is ringed with porticoes and adorned with many ancient cypress trees. If you turn left and walk downhill you can peer through a locked gate at the **stable complex** where the sultans' horses were kept. In the rooms behind the portico immediately to the right of the gate some of the **carriages** used by the later sultans and their families are on display; the finest is also the oldest, an 18th-century landau with latticed windows. Continuing to the right you come to the enormous domed **kitchens** whose soaring chimneys are a feature of the Istanbul skyline. This is where the famous Ottoman palace cuisine was prepared and cooked, with up to 300 people working here at any one time. Today the kitchens house an impressive collection of **Chinese porcelain and celadon** mainly built up by sultans Bayezid II, Selim I and Süleyman the Magnificent and ranging in date from the 10th to the 18th centuries. In the **confectioners' kitchen** can be seen some of the huge cauldrons and ladles used to prepare meals for the sultans' extensive household, as well as a collection of porcelain and silverware.

Sultan Bayezid II

Two huge stone **capitals**, one in the grounds of the kitchen complex and one on the lawn just outside, are preserved on the sites where they were dug up; they probably formed part of a late Roman monumental arch. Parts of the brick vaulting of a **Byzantine cistern** can also be seen midway along the path leading from the second to the third courtyard.

Chimneys of the palace kitchens

Tower of Justice

The Tower of Justice and the Divan

A miniature of the Divan in session

The most conspicuous building in the second courtyard is the conical-roofed Tower of Justice that is another prominent feature on the city skyline. The body of the tower dates back to the reign of **Sultan Mehmed II**, although the roof was completely remodelled by **Sultan Mahmud II** in 1820.

In front of it stands the domed Divan, or Council Chamber, where the business of state was conducted and justice administered. Before every meeting of the Divan the **council of viziers (ministers)** would process to the palace along the road now called **Divan Yolu** in their memory (see p. 062). Once in the chamber they would seat themselves on the benches around the wall with the **Grand Vizier**, the Ottoman equivalent of the prime minister, in the middle facing the entrance. Originally the sultans also attended these meetings but over time they prefered to take a back seat, the grille above the Grand Vizier's seat allowing them to eavesdrop on proceedings. The hanging **gold pendant** was a symbol of their continued authority. Fine **İznik tiles** adorn the lower walls of the Divan although much of the decor dates back to an 18th-century restoration by which time state business was being conducted from the Sublime Porte (see p. 203) beyond the palace walls.

Adjoining the Divan is the **Public Records Office**, so that any paperwork needed would be readily to hand. Beyond it the Grand Vizier had a private office that is not currently open to the public.

Entrance to the Divan or Council Chamber

Sultan Süleyman the Magnificent

Next door to the Divan was the **Public Treasury** (Silahlar Seksiyonu) where tax revenues collected from the provinces were stored. Every three months the Janissaries were ceremonially paid from here at which time they were also treated to a specially prepared meal. This building houses the palace **collection of armor and weaponry**, including some of the horsetail standards that would be erected in front of the Gate of Salutations before the sultan set off for war.

Portico in front of the Divan

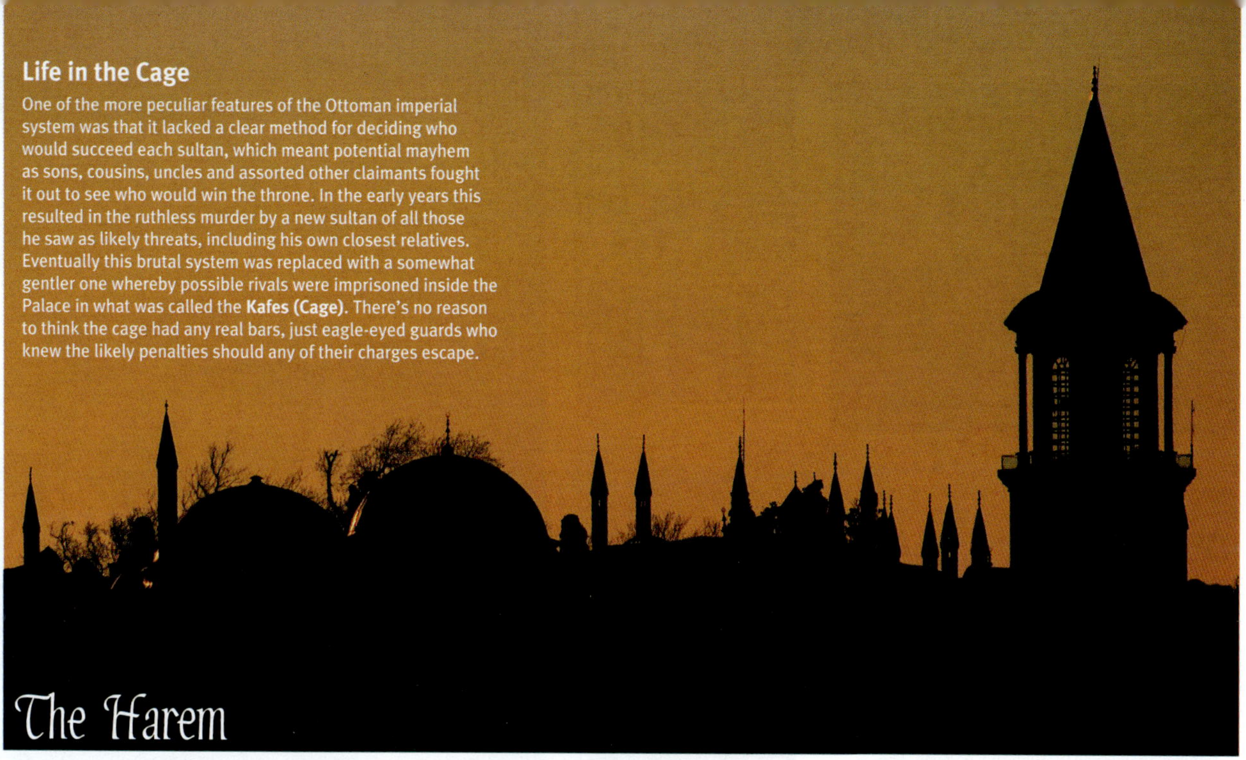

Life in the Cage

One of the more peculiar features of the Ottoman imperial system was that it lacked a clear method for deciding who would succeed each sultan, which meant potential mayhem as sons, cousins, uncles and assorted other claimants fought it out to see who would win the throne. In the early years this resulted in the ruthless murder by a new sultan of all those he saw as likely threats, including his own closest relatives. Eventually this brutal system was replaced with a somewhat gentler one whereby possible rivals were imprisoned inside the Palace in what was called the **Kafes (Cage)**. There's no reason to think the cage had any real bars, just eagle-eyed guards who knew the likely penalties should any of their charges escape.

The Harem

Approached through the **Carriage Gate**, an inconspicuous doorway beyond the Divan, the harem, also known as the House of Felicity, is the part of the palace that has most gripped the imagination of foreigners, probably because the intense privacy with which the sultans' private life was guarded helped fuel their lurid fantasies. In Arabic "harem" means **forbidden** and the harem was the part of the palace that was closed to outsiders, where the sultans (at least from the reign of **Sultan Murad III** onwards) lived with their concubines, their children and the vast entourage required to look after them all. The single most important person here was the **Valide Sultan** (the Queen Mother) who exercised enormous power over the household, often including the sultan. After her, the sultan's women, all of them Christian slaves who had converted to Islam, were ranked in a rigid hierarchy with the **"kadınlar** (the women who most approximated to wives)" at the top and the ordinary **"cariye** (slaves)" at the bottom. The harem was guarded by **eunuchs**, a tradition seemingly adopted from Byzantium. Any woman who stepped out of line risked dire punishment – being stitched up inside a sack and tossed into the Bosphorus.

Courtyard of the Black Eunuchs

The harem buildings are not part of the original palace as Sultan Mehmed II seems to have been happy for his family to live in the **Old Palace** at Beyazıt (see p. 083). The oldest structures that can be dated with certainty were erected under Sultan Murad III (r. 1574-95), but much of the harem had to be reconstructed following a fire in 1665. Although a separate ticket is required to visit the harem, visitors are no longer required to take a guided tour which makes it easier to appreciate the rabbit warren of rooms, many of them much smaller than you might have expected. What is not so easy to imagine amid the constant crush of visitors is the **silence** that reigned here along with the sense of rigid control that was imposed by the **Kızlar Ağası**, the Chief Black Eunch, whose task it was to ensure that everything ran smoothly.

Kızlar Ağası or Chief Black Eunuch

As you pass through the gate to the harem notice on the left the **Dormitory of the Halberdiers with Tresses**, an eccentrically-named slave corps whose long locks meant that they could cover their faces when they brought wood into the harem.

Shopping in the Harem by Rudolf Swoboda (1859-1914)

The Queen Mother's apartment

Sultan Abdülhamid I's apartment

The Sultan's bath

You enter the harem via the **Domed Cupboard**, the harem treasury where deeds of trust and household money were stored. This opens onto the fountainless **Hall of the Fountain** which is decorated with lovely blue and green calligraphic tiles and then to the **Courtyard and Dormitory of the Harem Eunuchs** with cells on the left-hand side where the men charged with ensuing absolute privacy lived; you can see models of two of them warming themselves around a brazier through one of the windows. The current decoration dates back to 1668-9 when the rooms were probably rebuilt after the 1665 fire.

A gateway then leads through to a hallway. The sultan would have proceeded straight ahead along the **Altın Yol (Golden Way)**, while his mother would have stepped into the courtyard beside it. Modern visitors, however, turn left and proceed along a corridor lined with stone benches where food from the kitchens was left for the women. Since this would have had to be passed from hand to hand right the way across the courtyard from the kitchens it's hard to imagine that anyone would ever have eaten a truly hot meal here.

The corridor opens onto the small **Courtyard of the Cariyeler**, where the female slaves slept in dormitories very close to the women in charge of the day-to-day administration of the complex: the head stewardess, the harem treasurer and the harem laundress. 18th-century landscape paintings are preserved on the walls here. A winding corridor then leads through a tiled room equipped with an enormous fireplace into a part of the **Valide Sultan's suite**; the bedroom features a dome decorated with a painted grapevine and frescoed landscapes; a small room off to the side is assumed to have been for prayers. Immediately afterwards you pass through the magnificent **Sultan's Hamam**, which is decked out in marble and goldleaf and superbly illuminated by light streaming in from cutouts in the ceiling. Particularly lovely would have been the **selsebil**, a gold-flecked marble fountain against the far wall down which water would once have cascaded.

The Hünkar Sofası (Imperial Hall). The left side was reserved for women, the gallery for musicians.

Imperial Hall

The Sultan's own suite of rooms was centered on the huge if faded and ecletically decorated **Hünkar Sofası (Imperial Hall),** the largest room in the harem. Tall and light, this room has sometimes been claimed as a work of Sinan but is probably a good hundred years newer than that; the musicians' gallery, where men in blindfolds would have played to the sultan on his throne and the women gathered behind the arcade in front of the windows, was probably added in the 18th century. The walls are partially tiled with blue and white **Delftware** imported from Holland because the great potteries at İznik and Kütahya had passed their prime. This room would have been used for wedding parties and family entertainment, as well as during the main religious holidays.

Much more cohesive and beautiful is the Sinan-designed **Salon of Murad III** dating back to 1578, whose walls are entirely encased in fine examples of İznik ware; when water was still flowing down the selsebil this must have been a truly delightful room, its windows looking out onto the garden. Opening off the far side is a small room known as the **Pavilion of Ahmed I** that is exquisitely encased in tiles whose blue and green hue affects the quality of the light. Even more delightful is the tiny **Fruit Room (Yemiş Odası)** which opens, in turn, off the pavilion and is completely covered with paintings of fruit and flowers prepared for the tulip-loving **Sultan Ahmed III.**

Sultan Murad III's private quarters

On the other side of the Salon of Murad III are a pair of tiled rooms equipped with fireplaces and gorgeous stained glass whose purpose has been the subject of debate but which may have been used by the royal princes. The first of them contains one of the few original inlaid wooden domes to survive in the complex. Shortly afterwards you will arrive in the **Gözdeler Taşlığı (Courtyard of the Favorites)** which overlooks a sunken pool and then the Golden Horn. Despite its name, it doesn't appear to have had anything to do with the "gözdeler", the women who had particularly caught the sultan's eye.

From here visitors walk back along the **Altın Yol (Golden Way)** and emerge through the **Kuşhane Kapısı (Aviary Gate)** into the third courtyard. The story goes that the Golden Way took its name from a custom whereby the sultan handed a gold coin to one of the women waiting in the corridor to indicate that he wished to spend the night with her. However, it's just as likely that it was called this because it was the sultan's main route into the harem, or because he distributed coins to the women here on special occasions. It was near the Aviary Gate, an 18th-century building designed to look like a bird-house, that the powerful **Valide Sultan Kösem** was murdered by the Chief Black Eunuch Süleyman Ağa in 1651.

Royal princes' quarters

Sultan Ahmed III's room

Courtyard of the Favorites

Many books have been written about the Harem, not all of them very sensible. For a historian's take on what went on behind the walls, read **John Freely's "Inside the Seraglio"**; for a novelist's recreation of how life might have been lived there try **Katie Hickman's "The Aviary Gate"** set during the reign of Sultan Mehmed III.

"(The Harem) perfumes the brain. Each breath and breeze is the purest musk and amber of love."

Inscription inside the Harem

The women of Sultan Abdülhamid II's harem and their eunuch guards waiting to go into exile on the proclamation of the Second Constitution in 1908.

The Sultanate of Women

Forget any idea that all the members of the harem were downtrodden females subject to their husband's every whim! For a period of around 130 years in the 16th and 17th centuries a handful of powerful women defied such casual stereotyping and played a major role in the running of the Ottoman Empire. All of them had been born outside the Empire and only converted to Islam once absorbed into the harem.

The first was **Hürrem Sultan** (c.1510-58), the only legal wife of **Sultan Süleyman the Magnificent** and better known to the West as **Roxelana** ("the Russian"). Born in what was then Poland (now Ukraine), she was captured as a slave by the Crimean Tatars and ended up in Istanbul where she succeeded in ousting the Sultan's favorite concubine and giving him five children. She was responsible for the magnificent **Haseki Hürrem Sultan Hamam** in Sultanahmet Square (see p. 033) and is buried in the grounds of the **Süleymaniye** (see p. 101).

Hürrem Sultan

Next in importance was **Nurbanu Sultan** (c.1525-83). Venetian-born and a relative of the Doge, she was captured by Turks and ended up in the harem of **Sultan Selim II** ("the Sot") where she became his favorite wife. As co-regent for Murad III she pursued such a pro-Venetian policy that the powerful Genoese traders in Galata came to hate her. Her death in 1583 looked thoroughly suspicious.

Nurbanu Sultan

Kösem Sultan

Finally, Bosnian-born **Kösem Sultan** (1589-1651) became the wife of **Ahmed I** and then co-regent for her son **Murad IV**, effectively running the empire for him. When he was succeeded by his feeble-minded brother **İbrahim**, Kösem continued as the power behind the throne, then when he was in turn succeeded by her grandson, seven-year-old **Mehmed IV**, she openly became regent again, a situation which persisted until her murder in 1651. She was probably the most powerful Ottoman woman ever to have lived.

Bab-üs Saade (Gate of Felicity)

Although there must have been a gate here at the time of Sultan Mehmed II, the current Gate of Felicity (Bab-üs Saade) with its dome and huge canopy dates back only to the late 16th century; it was completely redecorated in the 18th century when landscape paintings were added to the facade. On feast days and other important occasions the **sultan's throne** would be placed on a carpet in front of the gate so that he could receive homage from his subjects. **Foreign ambassadors** would wait in the area just inside the gate to learn if the sultan would receive them in the Throne Room that blocked their view of the private areas just beyond. A hole in the ground immediately in front of the gate marks where the **holy standard** would be raised before the sultan left for war.

A ceremony in front of the Bab-üs Saade during Sultan Selim II's reign

Janissary band

Gate of Felicity

Third Courtyard

Pause now to consider the unlikely purpose once served by the third courtyard which was primarily a large **school for civil servants** when it was first built. The teenage boys who studied here were Christians who were trained to administer the empire despite having been taken captive, an extraordinary idea that actually worked very well for the first couple of centuries after it was introduced by Sultan Mehmed II. Most of the rooms that ring the square served different functions within this school.

However, the first building that you come to when you pass through the Gate of Felicity is the **Chamber of Petitions (Arz Odası)** or **Throne Room,** a lovely pavilion, largely dating back to the early 16th-century reign of Sultan Selim I but renovated by Sultans Ahmed III and Mahmud II. Here the sultan would listen to the Grand Vizier's reports after the meetings of the Divan and receive foreign ambassadors whose **gifts** would be placed outside the window for him to assess. The gold that once plated the walls was sold to help with the financing of the Dolmabahçe Palace, but the pavilion is now used to display a magnificent throne cover, cushion and curtain embroidered with gold wire, silver thread, pearls, rubies and diamonds.

Throne Room

The sound of silence

Today's visitors to the Topkapı Palace must cope with a multilingual cacophony that makes it almost impossible to believe that the sultans once lived here in a silence so complete that they actually employed mutes to teach their staff sign language (the mutes were, of course, unable to pass on any of the secrets of the palace either).

Library of Ahmed III

Immediately behind the **Throne Room** in the middle of the courtyard is the pretty little **Library of Ahmed III** which dates back to 1719. A domed building with three eyvans, it features mother-of-pearl-inlaid bookcases and stained-glass windows.

Sultan Ahmed III's Library

Imperial Kaftans

Turning right from the gate you will come to the **Seferli Odası,** which is now used to house a splendid collection of kaftans worn by sultans right back to **Sultan Mehmed II,** their patterns clearly the model for many latterday Ottoman fabrics. When a sultan died it was the custom to store away his clothing which is how these garments have managed to survive in such immaculate condition. To look at them is to realise what a deleterious effect too much palace cuisine had on imperial waistlines, while to gaze on the costumes of the later 19th century is to realize how much color drained out of the empire as it slowly westernized.

The Treasury

Continuing round the courtyard you come to one of the oldest remaining parts of the palace, a suite of rooms including a bathhouse used by Sultan Mehmed II where Sultan Selim II later slipped and died. It has now been converted to house the imperial Treasury, surely one of the most eye-poppingly stunning collections of jewels ever assembled in the world. Here are emeralds the size of eggs, rubies the size of cherry tomatoes and diamonds the size of ice cubes sitting alongside gorgeous jewel-encrusted golden thrones.

First Room

• A mid-16th-century **ebony throne** inlaid on the back and sides with ivory and mother-of-pearl, a magnificent example of classic Turkish craftmanship. It was used by Sultan Murad IV during the Baghdad campaign of 1638.

Sultan Mahmud I seated on the Nadir Shah Throne by Constantinos Kapıdağlı

• Sultan Ahmed I's **walnut throne** inlaid with mother-of-pearl and precious stones, designed by Sedefkar Mehmed Ağa, the man responsible for the Sultanahmet (Blue) Mosque.

• The **gold-plated wooden throne** encrusted with turquoise, emeralds, rubies and pearls brought back from India as a trophy by Nadir Shah, one of the 18th-century rulers of Iran and presented to Sultan Mahmud I as a token of friendship. At first glance it resembles a large oval couch. Some historians believe that the throne might originally have belonged to Timurlane.

• The mid-18th-century **gold-plated Bayram Throne** last placed in front of the Gate of Felicity to host Sultan Mehmed V Reşad in 1918. Instructions for how to celebrate the bayrams (holidays) at the palace had been codified in the time of Sultan Mehmed II. On the first day of the bayram the throne was taken from the treasury and set up on a platform covered by a silk carpet in front of the Bab-üs Saade.

Second Room

A richly carved, feminine-looking **ivory mirror** that actually belonged to Sultan Süleyman the Magnificent. For the Ottomans mirrors carried particular religious and moral implications.

Third Room

Two candlesticks, each of them made from 48 kilos of solid gold, that were sent as a gift to the Kaaba. They are encrusted with 6,666 diamonds that represent the number of verses in the Koran. During the British occupation of the city during the First World War they were brought to Istanbul.

Fourth Room

• The absurdly over-the-top 18th-century **Topkapı dagger** intended as a gift from Mahmud I to Nadir Shah of Persia who died before it could be delivered. Its handle is adorned with three priceless emeralds ringed with diamonds. It shot to fame in 1964 on the back of the movie "Topkapı".

• The 86-carat, pear-shaped **Spoonmaker's Diamond.** As romance would have it it was retrieved from a rubbish dump at Eğrikapı and sold for the cost of three spoons. More prosaically a French officer named Pigot may have bought it in India and taken it to France where it was bought at auction by Tepedelenli Ali Paşa and finally ended up in the treasury of Sultan Mahmud II. It's one of the largest diamonds in the world.

• A gold-plated **18th-century cradle** which would have been brought to the palace in a grand ceremony called the Cradle Procession following a new baby's birth. According to Ottoman tradition the Valide Sultan (Queen Mother) was responsible for preparing the cradle and quilt of the sultan's new-born children.

• A **sword of Osman** (possibly Caliph Osman but more probably Osman Gazi) that was used in the ceremonial following the accession of a new sultan.

Entrance to the Pavilion of the Holy Mantle

l in the Third Courtyard

Pavilion of the Holy Mantle

Across the garden, the queues inside the domed **Pavilion of the Holy Mantle** can be equally daunting, but this is still a holy place where many Muslims revere relics of the Prophet Mohammed including teeth, hairs from his beard and the impression of his footsteps. Most important of all are the **holy standard** and a **holy mantle** that he had given to the poet Kaab bin Zuheyr and which passed down from him to the caliphs; the standard is encased in a silver casket and the mantle in a golden one which can only be viewed from afar through a window. These items were all brought from Egypt by **Sultan Selim I** after he conquered the country in 1517. Their presence inside the palace is a reminder that, as caliph, the sultan was also the head of the Islamic congregation worldwide.

Other items on display include the **swords of the first four caliphs**, Abu Bekr, Omar, Osman and Ali; a door from the mosque at Mecca; and beautiful silver-gilt-covered gutters, also from Mecca. Relics of equal interest to Christians include the **rod of Moses**, the **sword of David** and pieces of the **skull of St John the Baptist**. Throughout the day the Koran is recited here, so a respectful attitude is appreciated.

The rooms in which these objects are displayed were once part of the **Privy Chamber**, the sultan's private apartments. Later, Sultan Murad III moved into the harem to be closer to his family.

Piece of the Prophet Mohammed's beard

Portraits of the Sultans

The crush is likely to be less in the **Chamber of the Royal Pages**, a lovely dormitory for the young men studying in the palace that had been created by closing in a portico. It's now used to display portraits of the sultans, although only the later ones were painted during their subject's lifetime. Most are copies of **copies of Veronese originals** made in the late 16th century. Others are part of a series of 28 images created by **Konstantin Kapıdağlı** in 1789 that also list the sultans' achievements. The most famous picture is a portrait of a very hook-nosed Sultan Mehmed II that was painted by Gentile Bellini but later sold by his pious son Sultan Bayezid II who wanted to uphold the Islamic prohibition on images of living things. The original is on display in the **National Gallery** in London, UK.

Portrait of Sultan Mehmed the Conqueror by Gentile Bellini, 1480

The Ottoman family tree painted by Constantinos Kapıdağlı

Mecidiye Pavilion

Baghdad Pavilion

İftar Canopy

Hırka-ı Saadet Fountain

Fourth Courtyard

The gardens

From the back of the third courtyard ramps lead down to a set of gardens and terraces. On the right-hand side stand the **Sofa Mosque,** built by Sultan Mahmud II for his corps of swordbearers and still in use today; and the **Mecidiye Pavilion,** a neoclassical structure built for Sultan Abdülmecid by one of the Balyan in c. 1840 that now houses the Konyalı Restaurant (see below). Beyond it extends one of the best views in the city – straight out over the Golden Horn to the confluence of the Bosphorus and the Sea of Marmara and thence across to Asia.

On the terrace to the left lies what was once the **tulip garden** where Sultan Ahmed III hosted the famous Tulip Era parties (see p. 265); in the center is a 5th-century marble font that was once used as a piggy-bank for gold coins but now has a purely decorative function. The **Head Physician's Tower** at the corner seems to have been one of a series of towers at the edge of the garden from which the sultans could watch games of cirit (mounted javelin) taking place beneath it; at the back is a 6th-century marble bishop's throne reused as a seat for anyone who wanted to watch the game from closer quarters. Past the tower, the **Sofa Pavilion** was probably built so that the sultan could admire his flowers from indoors in poor weather.

At the end of the tulip garden steps lead up to one of the most delightful parts of the whole palace complex with a pair of wonderfully tiled kiosks standing on either side of a pool and with the **Marble Terrace** overlooking the Golden Horn stretching out between them. Centerpiece of this terrace is the charming **İftar Canopy** put here in 1640 during the reign of Sultan İbrahim I; it was where the sultan would break the Ramadan fast at the end of each day while looking out over the stunning view. In general, though, the terrace was mainly used as a place for entertainment.

Of the two kiosks, the one to the right is the domed and porticoed **Baghdad Pavilion,** built by Sultan Murad IV in 1639 to commemorate his capture of that city. Splendidly wallpapered with blue and white tiles, it boasts a magnificent fireplace with a bronze hood and served as a library for many years. Facing it on the opposite side of the terrace is the **Circumcision Room,** built in 1641 and also covered in tiles; some of those on the outside walls are especially notable. This is linked by a portico with yet more tiles to the **Erivan Pavilion,** built by Sultan Murad IV in 1636 to celebrate his capture of the Armenian capital. Ironically, by the time work on the Baghdad and Erivan Pavilions had been completed both cities had been lost to the Ottomans.

Erivan Pavilion

Interior of Erivan Pavilion

The Baghdad Pavilion in Levni's *Surname*, 1720

Miniature depicting circumcision ceremony

Visitors Information

Since Topkapı Palace is a large museum some departments may be occasionally closed to visitors due to restoration work. I therefore recommend you find updated information from www.millisaraylar.gov.tr/saraylar/topkapi-sarayi/ before your visit.

Massed circumcision

In 1595 when **Sultan Mehmed III** became sultan he is thought to have had all 19 of his brothers circumcised in the Circumcision Room before having them killed lest they challenge his right to the throne. Some of them were just infants at the time. They're buried in their father's tomb in the grounds of Hagia Sophia (see p. 032). This was the last such legal fratricide to take place. When **Ahmed I** became sultan in 1603 he merely imprisoned his brothers in the infamous Kafes (Cage).

The Past Uncovered

Istanbul Archeological Museums

002

Housed in a triptych of buildings on the hillside below Topkapı Palace, the Istanbul Archeology Museum contains a treasure trove of finds both from abroad and from the city's own past, including discoveries made during recent excavations to improve the local infrastructure. One building, the Tiled Pavilion (Çinili Köşk), is itself of enormous historic importance as one of the few structures to survive from the reign of Sultan Mehmed the Conqueror.

Alexander Sarcophagus in a photograph of 1890

Tiled Pavilion

Archeological Museum, with Tower of Justice at Topkapı Palace peeping up behind it

On land that once formed part of Topkapı Palace, Istanbul Archeology Museum is actually housed inside three separate buildings, each with its own individual character. The largest and most important is a porticoed building, called the **Museum of Archeology**, which dates back to the time of Osman Hamdi Bey (see p. 335), the artist and archeologist responsible for the foundation of the museum in 1881. The second, just inside the gate on the left-hand side, is the **Museum of the Ancient Orient**, which houses finds from areas that once formed part of the Ottoman Empire. The third, to the rear of the courtyard, is the delightful **Tiled Pavilion** (Çinili Köşk), originally built for Sultan Mehmed the Conqueror in 1472. It houses a fine collection of ceramics but is worth visiting as much for its interior decoration as for its contents.

@istanbularkeolojimuzesi
Closed Mondays.

Hittite lion's head

Alexander Sarcophagus

Sacrophagus of the Mourning Women

On the left Alexander is riding his horse Bucephalus

Museum of Archeology

Although there had been a haphazardly arranged museum of sorts first in the Church of Hagia Eirene and then in the Tiled Pavilion since 1846, it wasn't until the archeologist **Osman Hamdi Bey** became interested in the idea that a more formal museum was created; in 1891 the Levantine architect **Alexandre Vallaury** was commissioned to create the grand building that now houses it, using as his model details taken from the **Sarcophagus of Mourning Women** on display inside.

Reconstructed coloring of Alexander Sarcophagus

As you enter the museum a small exhibition in the hallway details the life of **Osman Hamdi Bey** with photographs of his homes in Kuruçeşme and Eskihisar (see p. 599) and of the important digs he led at Mt **Nemrut, Lagina and Sidon.**

The single most impressive section of the museum is to the left of the hall and houses a collection of sarcophagi excavated from the **Sidon necropolis** in what is now Lebanon by Osman Hamdi Bey in 1887. Some of them resemble massive Egyptian mummy cases even though they were created for Greek occupants, but the most interesting are superb examples of Hellenistic grave art, including the magnificent but erroneously named **Alexander Sarcophagus.** This was probably made to hold the remains of the much less well-known **King Abdalonymos** who was elevated to the throne of Sidon in the wake of Alexander the Great's arrival there in the late 4th century BC. Scenes carved in high relief along the sides of the sarcophagus depict the **Battle of Issos** in 333 BC with naked or half-naked Macedonians battling much better clad but ultimately militarily less successful Persians. Beautiful as these carvings are in their current state, you need to try and imagine what they would have looked like more than two millennia ago when they would have been as vividly colorful as a children's paintbox as shown in illustrations nearby.

Almost as beautiful as the Alexander Sarcophagus is the marginally older **Sarcophagus of the Mourning Women,** which housed the body of **King Straton of Sidon** (? - c.360 BC) and whose sides depict his funerary cortege in loving detail complete with images of the women of his harem grieving for the departed monarch. The **Satrap Sarcophagus** dates back to the 5th century BC and was created for a Persian satrap (local governor) whose name is lost to history but whose way of life complete with panther hunts is reconstructed along its sides. Finally, the glorious, late 5th-century BC **Lycian Sarcophagus** is also a monument to a man whose name escapes us but revels in exuberant scenes of hunting carved in a 3D style that is vaguely reminiscent of Rodin. Despite the name, which is thought to have been given to it because of some supposed resemblance to other Lycian tombs, the design of this sarcophagus links it firmly to the Greek mainland. Don't miss the **griffins** carved on one end of the lid.

Lycian Sarcopha

Statue of a river god

Details from the Classical Sculpture collection.

To the right of the hall when you come in is an extensive collection of Greco-Roman statuery gathered from some of Anatolia's most important archeological sites: **Ephesus, Aphrodisias, Miletus, Tralles (Aydın)** and **Magnesia ad Meandrum,** near Söke. Particularly striking is the statue of **Bes,** a bearded and behorned Egyptian demi-god who stands alone near the entrance holding by its legs what might have been a lion with a hole in its head; some believe the statue was intended as a fountain, although possibly it was adapted to serve this function at a later date. Another memorable statue shows **Marsyas** being flayed alive, a punishment inflicted on him after **King Midas** said he could play the flute better than Apollo. Other important statues include one of **Alexander the Great** and another of a beautiful **hermaphrodite**, both discovered at Pergamum (modern Bergama).

Bust of Alexander the Great

Bust of the poet Sappho from Lesbos (Midilli)

Statue of Hadrian

The first floor houses a fine 2nd-century bronze **statue of Hadrian** found in Adana, while the second floor displays some of Schliemann's dazzling finds from **Troy**, as well as Phrygian finds from **Gordion** and Hittite masonry from **Yazılıkaya**. The third floor has a fine selection of items collected from the Ottoman Middle East, including a large cache of finds from **Cyprus**, some figurative gravestones from **Palmyra** and carved bulls' heads from **Baalbek**.

Easily overlooked to the rear of the ground floor is a small **Children's Museum** complete with a model of the Trojan Horse into whose belly youngsters can climb to imagine what it might have felt like to be a Greek soldier lying in wait for the Trojans to pull their gift into Troy with fatal consequences.

Terracotta oil lamps found during excavations for Marmaray

Finally, those with a particular interest in **Istanbul** will not want to miss the rooms displaying finds from the adjacent provinces of **Thrace and Bithynia** that include a fine sarcophagus from **Bakırköy** (see p. 191) and the finds from a hypogeum (underground tomb) from **Yeşilköy** (see p. 196). It's not immediately obvious from the signs, but this is also where you will find some of the items taken from **the city's Byzantine churches,** including a late medieval fresco that once adorned the church of St Mercurius in Karagümrük (now the Odalar Mosque) and an exquisite icon made from inlaid marble and colored stone that came from the church of Constantine Lips (see p. 090). Here, too, a stone platform and a set of 5th to 4th-century BC sarcophagi are the only remains so far found of **ancient Chalcedon** (now Kadıköy, see p. 476), discovered in 1987.

Medieval weight

Mosaic icon o
Hagia Eudoki
from Church o
Constantine L

Lion relief from Gates of Babylon

Museum of the Ancient Orient

Given that almost the entire Middle East once formed part of the Ottoman Empire it's hardly surprising that the Istanbul Archeology Museum boasts an extensive representative collection of finds from this area, especially from **Mesopotamia**, the strategically vital area that fell between the Tigris and Euphrates rivers. Perhaps the single most important item on display here is a clay tablet inscribed in Akkadian cuneiform. It's a copy of the **Kadesh Treaty**, a document originally inscribed in silver that recorded a peace agreement between the warring Hittites and Egyptians in 1269 BC; it contains many elements that would be familiar to modern peacemakers as regards the treatment of prisoners etc. More visually striking are the colorful **glazed-brick friezes** of lions, bulls and dragons that once ran out from the Ishtar Gate in **Babylon** in what is now Iraq. Turcophiles will also want to look out for the finds from **Samal**, a late Hittite site near Gaziantep that was excavated in the late 19th century and the Assyrian reliefs from **Aslantaş**, near the Syrian border.

The Kadesh Treaty, 1269 BC

Selsebit – beautiful indoor fountain

Tiled Pavilion

One of the gems of Istanbul, this delightful small pavilion was built for **Sultan Mehmed the Conqueror** in 1472 and probably originally served as a pavilion for watching cirit tournaments. Its design, with the exterior walls papered with colorful tiles and the huge entry eyvan, shows the influence of what was then Timurid Persia (now Iran), probably filtered through the medium of Karaman in Central Anatolia. It's the only building of its type to survive to the present day. The marble portico was added in the 18th century after an earlier wooden version burnt down.

The pavilion contains a beautifully displayed collection of tiles and ceramics dating from the Selçuk period through to the 18th and 19th centuries when Kütahya and kitsch Çanakkale wares were fashionable, the highlights being the pieces dating back to the 15th and 16th century from golden age of İznik tiles. (see p. 223) Look out in particular for the star-shaped Selçuk tiles that once adorned the **Kubadâbâd Palace in Konya** and for the glorious 15th-century mihrab taken from the **İbrahim Bey İmaret** (soup kitchen) in Karaman. More local items include wonderful 16th-century İznik panels that used to adorn the outside of the **Haseki Hürrem Sultan Medrese** in Cerrahpaşa (see p. 095) and 18th-century ceramic lamps that used to hang in the **Sokollu Mehmed Paşa Mosque** in Kadırga (see p. 178).

Whatever you do, don't miss the room on the left at the far end of the pavilion whose walls are decorated with navy and turquoise tiles patterned with what is sometimes called **"gold embroidery"**. More importantly it contains an exquisite 16th-century fountain set into the wall. This appears in Osman Hamdi Bey's painting **"The Fountain of Life"**, created in 1904, which is reproduced on the wall facing it.

If you liked this you'll also like:
Museum of Turkish and Islamic Arts (see p. 050)
Rezan Has Museum (see p. 228)
Sadberk Hanım Museum (see p. 465)

Divine Wisdom

Hagia Sophia Mosque and Around

003

The vast 6th-century church of Hagia Sophia (Divine Wisdom) that dominates the Istanbul skyline is one of the best known and most visited sites of the historic peninsula, constantly busy with visitors who come to admire its glittering mosaics and stupendous dome. It sits in Sultanahmet Square, just a stone's throw from Topkapı Palace, the Hippodrome and the Yerebatan Cistern and gazing at the Sultanahmet (Blue) Mosque which mirrors its silhouette across the park.

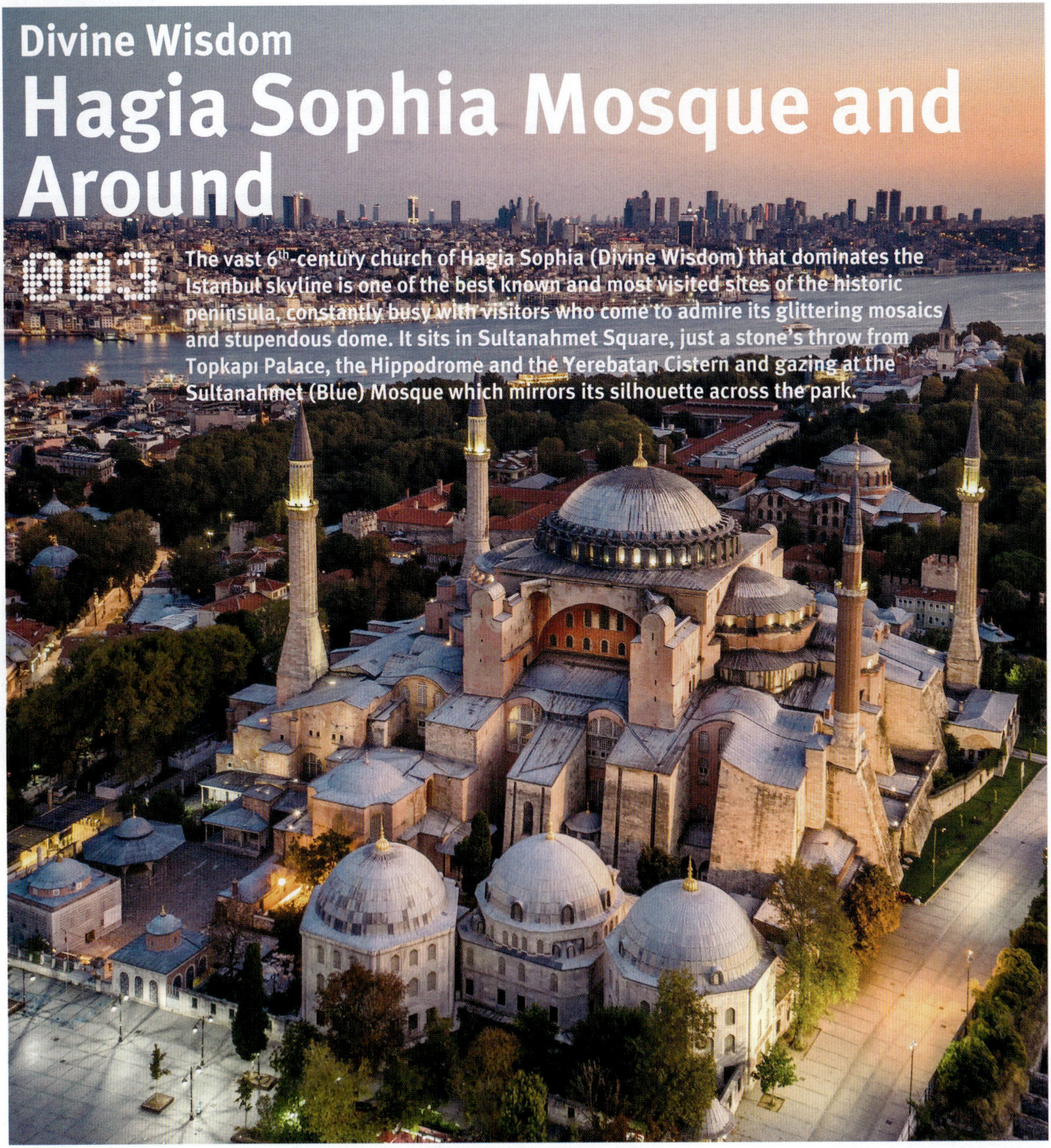

Dedicated to **Divine Wisdom**, the Church of Hagia Sophia is one of the most important architectural structures in the world. It forms a pair with the virtually contemporary Church of **Hagia Eirene** (Divine Peace), behind it in the grounds of Topkapı Palace; together they celebrate two of the most important attributes of Jesus Christ. Completed between 532 and 537 during which time 10,000 workers and 100 masters had a hand in the work, the church was designed by two of the most important architects of the time, the mathematician and physicist **Anthemius of Tralles** and the mechanic **Isidore of Miletus**. For almost a thousand years, it was renowned as the largest church in the world and it served as the center of the Greek Orthodox Patriarchate until the conquest of Istanbul in 1453 when Sultan Mehmed the Conqueror had it converted into the mosque of **Ayasofya** as one of his first acts on entering the vanquished city. In 1935 Atatürk turned it into a **museum**. With the decision announced in 2020, the place is opened for worship once again. The floor is covered with a rug. During the hours of worship, the mosaics are concealed with special methods. Local and foreign tourists can visit Hagia Sophia between the hours of worship.

Justinian's church was not the first to stand on the site. The **Emperor Constantius** had a church erected here in 360, but it was destroyed during a fire in 404. In 415 **Theodosius II** paid for a new church, which was in turn destroyed during the Nika Riot (see p. 047) of 532. Almost immediately Justinian made his mind to replace it with something even more splendid; work began within six weeks of the fire that destroyed the old church and was completed almost six years later on 26 December 537. Part of the architrave from Theodosius' church can still be seen in front of the entrance, while pieces of the grand porticoed entrance lie just past it.

The exterior

To get an idea of what Hagia Sophia originally looked like you must first stand in Sultanahmet Square and mentally strip away many of the later additions to the building starting with the four minarets that were gradually added after it was converted into a mosque (only the brick one dates back to the time of the Conqueror) and going on to the series of imperial tombs that are lined up in front of it. Away, too, will have to go the flying buttresses that were added in 1573 when it looked as if the building might collapse and it was strengthened by Sinan. Once you have done all this you will appreciate that it was the interior of the original church rather than its clumpy exterior that made it so exceptional.

Hagia Sophia in an old postcard

The restoration scaffolding over Hagia Sophia, which has obscured the visual integrity since 1993, was briefly removed for the Istanbul 2010 European Capital of Culture. The beauty of the structure in all its glory was presented to visitors for a short time. In 2020, the scaffolding was completely removed.

Hagia Sophia was built in 5 years, 10 months and 24 days.

"Oh Solomon! I have outdone you."

Emperor Justinian comparing Hagia Sophia to the Temple of Solomon in Jerusalem in 537.

Ablutions fountain

The courtyard

As you enter the grounds, to the right you'll see an attractive domed structure which served as a one-room **primary school**. As you leave the museum you'll see to the right the lovely baroque şadırvan (ablutions fountain) placed in the courtyard in 1740, with the contemporary primary school behind it. Facing it is the pretty domed **muvakkithane** (time-keeper's lodge, see p. 547) added by the Fossati brothers in 1853.

Sarcophagus

Remains of second Hagia Sophia

"It is distinguished by indescribable beauty."

Buildings **by Procopius, c.550**

The interior

The church of Hagia Sophia was entered via a **double narthex**, the outer section being extremely plain while the inner narthex was walled in marble and adorned with glittering **geometric mosaics**. Although these are often overlooked in the rush to view the more striking figurative mosaics, they are actually survivors from Justinian's church, which would have been completely covered in similarly simple golden mosaics. Originally there was an atrium in front of the outer narthex with five gates leading into it. The emperor entered through the central gates, which were known as the **Orea Porta (Beautiful Gate)**.

Nine huge doors apparently dating back to Justinian's time lead from the inner narthex to the nave. The most important were the tall central doors, called the **Imperial Gate**, through which the emperor processed. Above them can be seen a **mosaic** depicting an enthroned Christ with an emperor, assumed to be Leo the Wise (r. 886-912), prostrating himself in front of him. Leo had already gone through three wives without acquiring a male heir and wished to marry for a fourth time, something so frowned on by the Orthodox church that the emperor was for a while banned from entering the building. Consequently the extremity of his prostration may suggest that he was pleading with Christ for forgiveness.

Leo VI prostrates himself before Christ in a mosaic above the Imperial Gate

Reconstruction of second Hagia Sophia

Today's visitors notice the gate once reserved for the emperor, stepping over the deep ruts worn into the marble threshold by centuries of heavy footfall. As soon as you enter the nave you will be struck by the enormous space created by the lofty and dominant **dome**, the two semi-domes and the apse. This sense of space is emphasized by the emptiness of the nave, a consequence of the church's later conversion into a mosque and the removal of all the clutter of Orthodoxy. Eight huge green **marble columns** imported from Thessaly support the dome, which is pierced with windows to admit light. The original dome quickly proved too shallow to stand up to earthquakes and came crashing down in 558, after which the nephew of Isodorus of Miletus, also called Isodorus, recalculated the dimensions and replaced it with a taller dome which now stands 56 meters high above the ground. This dome was originally decorated with a mosaic of Christ the Pantocrator as in the Fethiye Museum (see p. 124), but it was removed when the church became a mosque; the centerpiece is now a verse taken from the Koran. Despite two further partial collapses in 989 and 1346 the dome you see today is substantially the same as it was after Isidorus the Younger completed his alterations.
The apse is decorated with a beautiful **mosaic** showing the enthroned Virgin Mary holding the Christ Child. Dating back to 867, this was the first figurative image to be added to the church after the Iconoclastic period (see p. 583), as recorded in a Greek inscription that is now almost worn away. The arch to the right of the apse features a mosaic of the Archangel Gabriel although the matching image of the Archangel Michael that would have adorned the opposite pillar has been virtually obliterated. Elsewhere in the nave there are three mosaic images of the saints **Ignatius the Younger**, **John Chrysostom** and **Ignatius Theophorus** that are more readily visible from the gallery. Finally, in the pendentives below the dome there are mosaic images of **seraphim or cherubim** (and 19th-century painted replicas of the same) probably dating back to the 14th century. The mosaics were rediscovered in 1933 when layers of whitewash were scrubbed from the walls.

Right "Allah", left "Muhammed"

"...the rustiest old barn in heathendom."

Innocents Abroad **by Mark Twain, 1869**

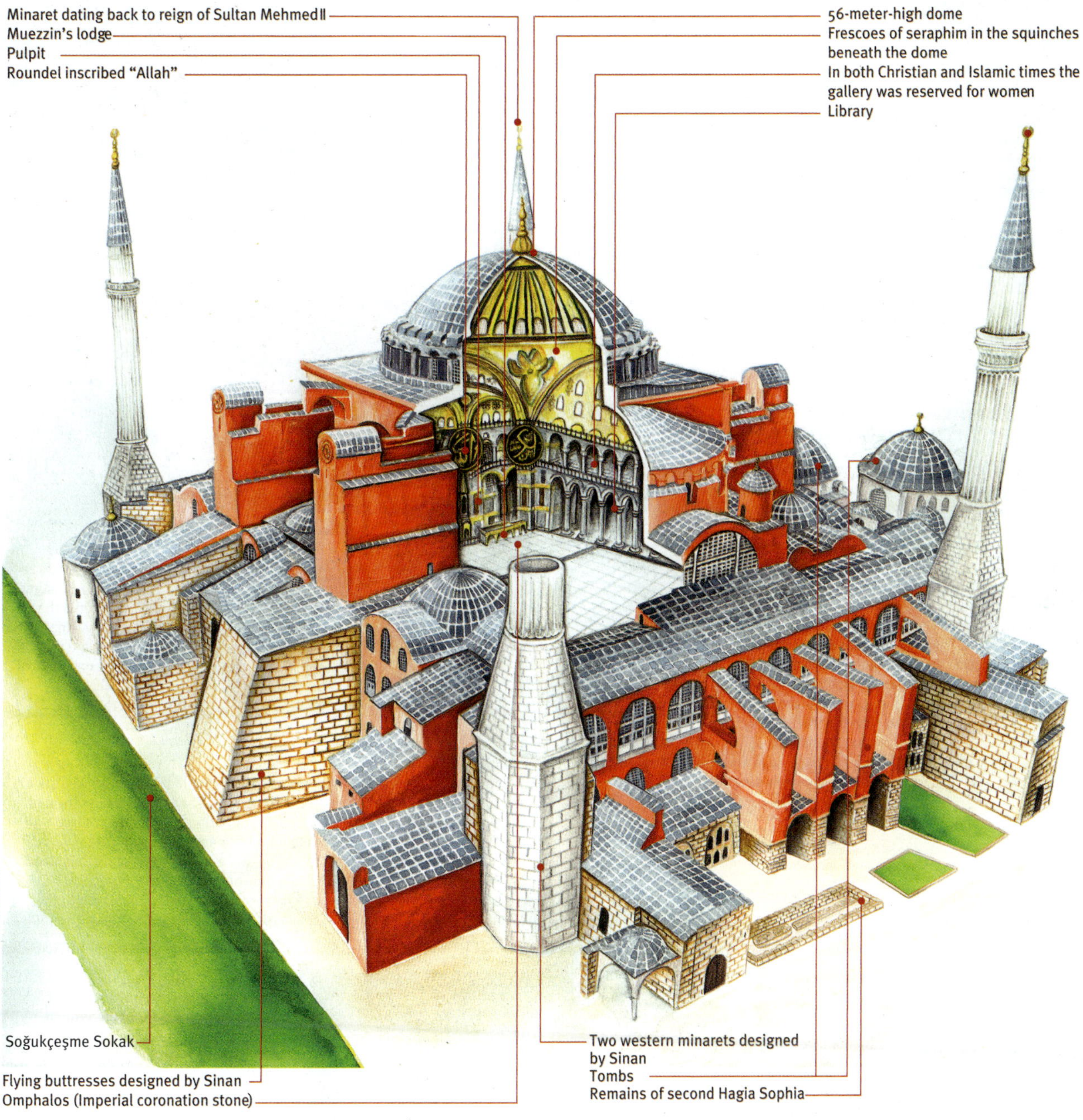

İllüstrasyon: Selda Balcan

A hidden angel
Seraphim

During the restoration in 2009, a painting of a six-winged seraphim that had not been seen for 160 years was revealed. It had been covered up during the previous restoration efforts during the reign of Sultan Abdülmecid and is thought to date from the 14th century.

Hagia Sophia's marble-paneled **walls** are almost as remarkable as the mosaics; the patterns were often created by slicing through a single piece of marble and then opening it out like a book. Especially impressive is the panel high up above the Imperial Gate which depicts curtains drawn back to reveal a cross upon an altar. Look out, too, for a large panel of multi-colored marble called the **Omphalos** set into the floor of the nave; it's believed to mark the site where the Byzantine emperors would have been crowned.

When Hagia Sophia became Ayasofya a **mihrab** was added to the apse and a **minbar** (pulpit) to the nave along with several platforms for the muezzins to lead the chanted responses to the imam at Friday prayers. Two huge Hellenistic **alabaster urns** from Pergamum (Bergama) were also installed to the rear. In 1607 the calligrapher **Mehmed Efendi** added a running tiled inscription to the apse, while in 1739 Sultan Mahmud I had a **library** built against the southern wall. Then between 1847 and 1849 Sultan Abdülmecid commissioned the Swiss **Fossati brothers** to restore the interior at which time a daintily-screened box for the sultan was placed right beside the apse. It was at this time too that the eight **roundels** bearing the names of Allah, Mohammed, Ebubakr, Omar, Osman, Ali, Hasan and Hüseyin in Arabic were hung up. The Fossatis also stenciled imitations of lost mosaic decorations onto the walls.

Panel inscribed Allah

Hagia Sophia in Ottoman times in an old engraving

The weeping column

Don't leave the nave before joining the queue to rotate your finger in a hole set into one of the huge columns to the rear. Called the "weeping column" or the column of St Gregory the Miracle-Worker, it offers a supposed cure for eye infections and boost for fertility on which visitors have been depending since at least the 13th century.

The dome

The galleries

The best places from which to appreciate Hagia Sophia's immense size are the galleries that run along three sides of the building and would have provided space for **female worshippers**. These are supported by columns created from white Proconnesian marble quarried on the Island of Marmara (see p. 597); carved into their lovely capitals can be seen the **monograms** of Justinian and his wife Theodora together with the initials of their titles Basileus (Emperor) and Augusta (Empress). However, what really make the galleries worth the walk up the inclined passage to reach them are the **mosaics** that can be found tucked away up here.

Gates of Heaven and Hell

The western gallery was reserved for the empress and her entourage; a circle of green marble set into the ground marks the site of her throne. The most interesting **mosaics** can be found in the southern gallery which you reach via a pair of fake marble doors known as the **Gates of Heaven and Hell**, placed in the gallery at an unknown date and for an unknown purpose.

-century Deesis Mosaic

The mosaics

Immediately past the Gates on the right is what is perhaps the most impressive mosaic panel. It's a 13th-century **Deesis** that shows St John the Baptist and the Virgin praying to Christ on behalf of mankind, a magnificent example of the art produced during the **Byzantine Renaissance** that followed the eviction of the Latins from the city in 1261.

A little further ahead you'll see another **mosaic panel** depicting the Emperor John Comnenos (r. 1118-43) and his wife Eirene, founders of the Monastery of the Pantokrator (see p. 111), praying to the Virgin Mary. In 1122 the image of their teenaged son Alexios was added to the panel after he became co-emperor with his father. Beside it you'll see Christ offering a blessing to the Emperor Constantine IX Monomachos (r. 1042-55) and his wife Zoe. If you look down into the apse from this point you'll get the best view of the mosaic of the Virgin Mary.

The emperor's portrait

Justinian and Theodora don't appear in the mosaics of Hagia Sophia. Instead they can be seen in the mosaics of the Church of San Vitale in Ravenna, Italy, which dates back to 547.

Changing faces

The Empress Zoe was a much-married woman despite having lived as a virgin until the age of 50. The mosaic panel in Hagia Sophia that immortalizes her originally showed her first husband **Romanos Argyros** (r. 1028-34) beside her. When he proved unsatisfactory, Zoe took one **Michael Psellus** as her lover and in due course he murdered Romanus and took his place on the throne (r. 1034-41) whereupon the mosaic was altered to replace Romanus' image with his own. Michael IV was succeeded by Michael V (r. 1041-42) who locked Zoe away and had both imperial portraits removed. When the people rose up against him Zoe was released and married **Constantine IX Monomachos** whereupon the faces on the panels were redesigned for the last time.

In the north gallery can be seen an image of the **Emperor Alexander** (r. 912-13) whose brief reign was notorious for its brutality and came to an abrupt end when he died of a stroke while playing polo.

Emperor John Comnenos and his wife Eirene

Michael Douglas and Catherine Zeta-Jones with Constantine IX Monomachos and his wife Zoe.

Gravestone of Doge Enrico Dandolo

Dandolo and Halvdan

Opposite the Deesis mosaic look out for a **plain tombstone** that marks the burial site of Enrico Dandolo (1107-1205), the Doge of Venice responsible for the horrific assault on Constantinople during the Fourth Crusade in 1204 and perhaps the most despised man in Istanbul's history (his bones were supposedly thrown to the dogs by the disgusted population when they finally recovered the city). If you inspect the balustrade between these two features you will discover the name of a 9th-century Viking, Halvdan, amid the other **graffiti** left by past visitors.

Tomb of Sultan Selim II

The side door from the narthex be sure to look up at the magnificent **10th-century mosaic** of the Virgin Mary with the Christ Child sitting on her lap; the Emperor Constantine is offering her a stylized model of his city while the Emperor Justinian holds out a model of the church. As you enter the mosque you will be walking through the **Vestibule of the Warriors** where the emperor would have left his crown and sword before entering the nave and where his bodyguard would have awaited his return. Above it was the palace of the patriarch. The **Splendid Door** is a bronze piece taken from a temple in Tarsus (2nd century BC) and brought here in the 9th century by the Emperor Theophilus.

Mosaic showing Constantine on the right and Justinian on the left

The imperial tombs

Accessible (free) via a separate entrance off the road leading up to Topkapı Palace are the tombs of those sultans who were buried in the grounds of Hagia Sophia. As you enter you will see immediately to the left the tomb of **Mehmed III** (r. 1595-1603) and his wife Handan. Next to it is the lovely Sinan-designed tomb of **Sultan Selim II** (r. 1566-74), his wife Nurbanu and five of their sons who were murdered on their father's death to ensure that their brother **Murad III** could accede to the throne without competition. Next to this is the tomb of Murad himself (r. 1574-95), which was designed by Davud Ağa. He is buried with his favorite wife Safiye and 23 of his sons, including the 19 who were murdered on his death to ensure that their brother Mehmed III would face no opposition. It was only after his death that this cruel system was finally abandoned and surplus boy children were imprisoned inside the "kafes (cage)" of the palace (see p. 009) instead of being strangled with a bowstring. The last tomb was originally the Baptistry of Hagia Sophia but was later adapted to serve as a last resting place for **Sultan Mustafa I** (r. 1617- 18) and **Sultan İbrahim I** (r. 1640-48).

If you continue around the perimeter fence towards Topkapı Palace you will see a magnificent side gate on the corner facing the palace. Just behind it the imaret (soup kitchen) built for Ayasofya was restored in 2009, as was the Skeuophylakion, or Byzantine treasury.

If you liked this you'll also like:

Chora Church/Kariye Mosque (see p. 132)
Church of Constantine Lips/Fenari İsa Mosque (see p. 090)
Church of the Myrelaion/Bodrum Mosque (see p. 088)
Church of the Pantokrator/Zeyrek Kilise Mosque (see p. 011)
Church of Pantepoptes/Eski İmaret Mosque (see p. 112)
Church of St Theodore/Vefa Kilise Mosque (see p. 113)
Church of St Theodosia/Gül Mosque (see p. 228)
Church of Theotokos Kyriotissa/Kalenderhane Mosque (see p. 104)
Church of Theotokos Pammakaristos/Fethiye Mosque (see p. 124)

Marble urn brought from Bergama

Hagia Sophia from Sultanahmet Square

Sultanahmet Square

The large square which stands between Hagia Sophia and Sultanahmet Mosque with the Archeology Park running along the far side is very much the heart of touristic Istanbul, constantly awash with visitors from all over the world. This was once the site of a huge square named the **Augusteon** by Constantine the Great in memory of his mother Helena Augusta. Opening off it were the main entrance to the Great Palace known as the **Chalke**, or Bronze House and the palace of the patriarch. Later Justinian had an **equestrian statue** of himself placed right in the center of it. We know from the French writer Pierre Gilles that it survived into the 16th century when it was melted down to make cannons; the only surviving piece of it is thought to be a Greek inscription now built into a small gate in the sea walls near Küçük Ayasofya (see p. 175).

Baths of Roxelana

Designed by Mimar Sinan in 1556, this magnificent double hamam on the corner of Sultanahmet Square was built for **Haseki Hürrem**, the wife of Süleyman the Magnificent and better known to Westerners as Roxelana. With its brick-and-stone-striped walls, its graceful portico and its twin domes topped with lanterns, it's one of the finest surviving examples of an Ottoman bath complex. Interestingly, this 16th-century hamam was built only a short way away from the **Baths of Zeuxippus**, which dated back to 196 and the reign of Septimius Severus.

Roxelana

---

www.ayasofyahamami.com
Tel: 0212 517 35 35

Istanbul Library

Restored wooden houses in Soğukçeşme Sokağı

Soğukçeşme Sokak

Until the 1970s, the street of **wooden houses** that ran between the outer wall of Topkapı Palace and Hagia Sophia stood derelict. Then Çelik Gülersoy of the Turkish Touring and Automobile Association supervised its restoration and conversion into a **hotel**, thereby kickstarting the movement to resurrect the city's old housing stock for touristic purposes. Today Soğuk Çeşme Sokak (Cold Fountain Street) is a delightful cobbled and traffic-free row of houses painted in pastel colors surrounding the **Istanbul Library**, a wonderful airy space in which Gülersoy's book collection is preserved in a setting reminiscent of the library of an Oxbridge college. The cistern, used as a restaurant (see p. 036) also forms part of the complex.

Sarnıç Restaurant

Conservationist extraordinaire

Çelik Gülersoy (1930-2003) was a Hakkari-born lawyer with a vision, the man who more than almost anyone else saw the potential in the rotting buildings of the 19th-century Ottoman Empire and set out to restore them. We have him to thank not just for the restoration of Soğukçeşme Sokak and the Yeşil Ev, but also for the resurrection of the Khedive's Villa (see p. 551), the area around the Chora Church (see p. 132) and the buildings on Çamlıca Hill (see p. 404), in Emirgan Woods (see p. 441), in Yıldız Park (see p. 402) and in Fenerbahçe Park (see p. 474).

Istanbul Handicrafts Center

Housed in the buildings of the 18th-century **Kabasakal Medrese** (theological school), which was restored in 1987, this is a great place to come and watch craft workers in action. It's a haven of serenity from the street hustle outside.

Kabasakal Medrese

Four Seasons Hotel

Sultanahmet Prison/Four Seasons Hotel

Nâzım Hikmet

There are not many luxury hotels in the world that can boast that they were once home to the criminal fraternity, but the Four Seasons in Sultanahmet was, until 1982, a prison whose best-known inmate was probably Billy Hayes, the drug-runner behind the infamous **"Midnight Express"** (during filming a substitute structure on Malta stood in for the original). Other famous inmates, many of them political prisoners, included the poet **Nâzım Hikmet, novelist Yaşar Kemal** and the cartoonist **Orhan Coplu.**

Yaşar Kemal

Built in 1919, the prison was one of the finest examples of the architectural style dubbed First National and may have been a work of the architect **Vedat Tek** (see p. xxix). The inscription above the door reads "Istanbul Criminal Detention Center", fortunately in Arabic lettering so most guests can't read it!

One visitor to Sultanahmet in 2009 was television host Oprah Winfrey. She learnt two words of Turkish: Merhaba (hello) and Nasılsın (how are you)?

Archeology Park

The Archeology Park stands in the grounds of the Four Seasons and contains the remains of the old **Byzantine hamam** discovered during work to expand the hotel. In 1846 Sultan Abdülmecid commissioned the Fossati brothers to design a building for the **Darülfünun** (University) that stood on this same site. Completed in 1863, it was used as a hospital by the French during the Crimean War. In 1877 it was used for the **Second Ottoman Parliament**, then went on to serve as a succession of government offices before becoming the **Palace of Justice**, which finally burnt down in 1933.

The story of Hagia Sophia

The Emperor Justinian once dreamt of a saint radiating light. In the dream the saint gave him a silver tablet with a drawing of a church on it. The Emperor was so charmed by this that, upon waking, he decided to have the church built. The church already had a name, which the saint in the dream had whispered in his ear: the Hagia Sophia. The next day he received another surprise. After telling his head architect about the dream, the architect told him he had the same dream and made a sketch of the church upon awakening. When he saw the sketch, the emperor realised they had seen the same church. And thus construction of one of the most magnificent temples in the world began.

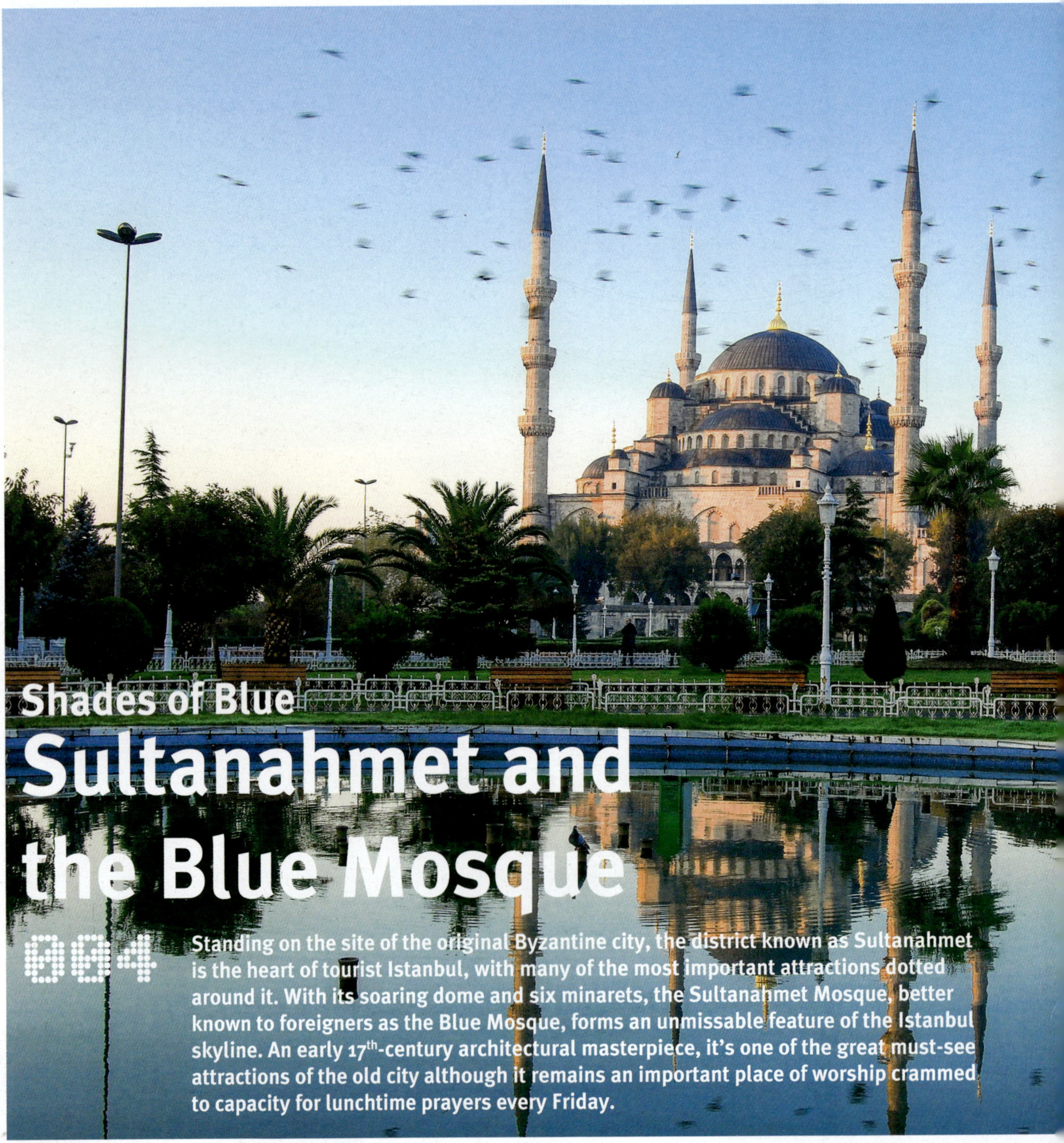

Shades of Blue

Sultanahmet and the Blue Mosque

004

Standing on the site of the original Byzantine city, the district known as Sultanahmet is the heart of tourist Istanbul, with many of the most important attractions dotted around it. With its soaring dome and six minarets, the Sultanahmet Mosque, better known to foreigners as the Blue Mosque, forms an unmissable feature of the Istanbul skyline. An early 17th-century architectural masterpiece, it's one of the great must-see attractions of the old city although it remains an important place of worship crammed to capacity for lunchtime prayers every Friday.

Facing Hagia Sophia across Sultanahmet Square stands the architectural jewel called the **Sultanahmet Mosque**, built more than a thousand years later despite some similarities in their silhouettes. Designed by the architect **Sedefkar Mehmed Ağa** for Sultan Ahmed I between 1609 and 1616, it dramatically changed the city's skyline since it was the first mosque to boast six minarets. Until recently it remained the only mosque thus lavishly endowed, although the **Sabancı Central Mosque** in Adana and **Büyük (Big) Çamlıca Mosque** now also has six minarets. The mosque in **Mecca** has seven minarets, the seventh paid for by Sultan Ahmed I after people complained at his arrogance in trying to outshine the Prophet's own shrine.

"The Mosque of Sultan Achmet, although less spacious than that of St Sophia and less elegant in its details than Suleimanie, is superior to both in exterior effect."

The Beauties of the Bosphorus **by Julia Pardoe, 1840.**

"Nothing resembles this exalted masterpiece, nor ever will do. Let it always be spoken of with praise."

Inscription over the main entrance to Sultanahmet Mosque, 1616

The exterior

Built from a particularly beautiful grey stone, the Sultanahmet Mosque consists of a **mass of semi-domes** that lead the eye remorselessly up to the huge central dome that nestles amid the six minarets. They make a particularly spectacular sight when floodlit at night with the eerie white shapes of seagulls circling over them.

Most visitors enter the grounds via the garden on the side that faces towards Hagia Sophia. The **main entrance** is actually via the second gate down in the wall facing onto the Hippodrome. This leads straight up some steps to the grand colonnaded courtyard centered on a **şadırvan** (ablutions fountain), a much more impressive first view. Over this gateway notice the hanging chains to which a fugitive could cling to claim sanctuary. Notice too the inscription over the main entrance, inscribed by **Derviş Mehmed**, father of the 17th-century Ottoman travel writer **Evliya Çelebi**.

The mosque is the centerpiece of a **külliye**, or complex of other buildings that served a variety of important social functions. The hospital, caravanserai and kitchen have all been lost, but the **primary school** building can be seen right beside the first entrance as you walk down the Hippodrome from Hagia Sophia, while the **medrese** (theological school) still stands disregarded between the entrance facing Hagia Sophia and the tomb of Sultan Ahmed I (see below).

Chain over entrance gate

Ablutions fountain
Sundial
Courtyard
"Elephant's foot' column
43-meter-high dome
Unrestored paintings on arches in this area
Tourist entrance
Sultan's Lodge
Mihrab

The interior

The interior of the Sultanahmet Mosque is virtually square and the massive dome is supported by four enormous columns, often called **"elephants' feet"**, each of them measuring five meters in diameter. At first glance there is nothing remotely blue about it to account for its being dubbed the Blue Mosque (the Rüstem Paşa Mosque is much more obviously blue, for example). However, closer inspection reveals that the lower parts of the walls are covered with more than 20,000 predominantly blue-and-white **İznik tiles** depicting tulips, carnations, roses and lilies. Light

While changing the carpets...

streaming through the 250-plus stained-glass windows also throws different shades of blue onto the carpeted floor at certain times of day.

As is usual with mosques most of the interior consists of empty but comprehensively carpeted space where the congregation can kneel in prayer. However, the **mihrab and minbar** are carved from finest Proconnesian marble quarried on the Island of Marmara (see p. 596) and the exquisite **doors and window shutters** are of wood inlaid with mother-of-pearl and ivory. Most visitors will also be struck by the enormous low-hanging lamp-holders designed to carry **oil lamps** but now fitted with electric light bulbs.

Tomb of Sultan Ahmed I

Sultan Ahmed I (1590-1617), the young man who commissioned the Blue Mosque, was laid to rest in a tomb the size of a small mosque right beside it together with his **wife Kösem** (see p. 014) and the Sultans **Osman II and Murad IV.** The walls are decorated with fine İznik tiles and in an eyvan at the back are displayed items taken from other tombs including that of **Yahya Efendi** (see p. 407).

Sultan Ahmed I

Sultan Murad IV

Kösem Sultan

Milking the goats

Tiger hunt

Great Palace and mosaics

Sultanahmet Mosque stands on the site of part of the **Palatium Magnum**, the Great Palace of the Byzantines, an extensive collection of individual palaces built on terraces stretching down to the Sea of Marmara that went to make up a whole, rather as the collection of individual pavilions and other structures make up what is now Topkapı Palace. Of these palaces, the **Sacred** and **Daphne** stood on the spot now occupied by the Sultanahmet Mosque, while the **Khalke** (Chalke), **Magnaura** and **Mangana** Palaces lay on the hill sloping down to the sea to the south-east of Hagia Sophia. Finally, the **Bucoleon Palace** sat beside the Great Palace's private harbor, near the Ahırkapı (Stable Gate) in the sea walls. At the height of its importance the palace covered an area of some 100,000 square meters.

It was **Constantine the Great** who began work on this complex in 328 in an attempt to provide a counterpart for the Palatine Palace in Rome. Much of the original was destroyed during the **Nika Riot** of 532, but other emperors gradually rebuilt and extended it over the years. Our best source for what it looked like in its heyday is **"The Book of Ceremonies"**, written by Emperor Constantine VII Porphyrogenitus (r. 944-59), which details the various elaborate interiors.

Coin of Constantine

Greatly admired by foreign visitors who wrote gushingly of its beauty, the Great Palace was home to the Byzantine emperors until 1204 when the **Fourth Crusade** hit town and they were driven out in favor of a puppet government installed by the Latins. In 1261 when they recovered the throne they found the palace reduced to such a poor condition that they preferred to start all over again, moving to the **Blachernae Palace** at Ayvansaray (see p. 151) close to the shores of the Golden Horn. Some of the substructures of the individual palaces then became a **prison**. In 1453 the victorious **Sultan Mehmed II** is said to have wandered through the ruins of the original palaces murmuring words taken from the 13th-century Persian traveller and poet Saadi:

"The spider is the curtain-holder in the Palace of the Caesars
The owl hoots its night call on the Towers of Aphrasiab."

You can see a restored portion of the Magnaura Palace in Akbıyık Caddesi

Traces of the **Magnaura Palace** have come to light in the grounds of the Four Seasons Hotel. A poorly restored stretch of wall from the palace also stands in Akbıyık Caddesi (see p. 167). But the most dramatic relic that survives to give some clue to the splendor that has been lost is the huge **mosaic pavement** unearthed beside the Arasta Bazaar in the 1930s and 1950s and now housed in situ in the **Great Palace Mosaics Museum** *(closed Mondays)*.

The huge stretch of mosaic floor on display here dates back at least to the reign of **Justinian the Great** and is made up of an estimated 75-80 million tesserae made from tiny pieces of limestone, marble, colored glass, brick and even semi-precious stones. It shows a wonderful selection of scenes from everyday **Byzantine life** including hunters spearing a tiger, a man milking a goat, a monkey trying to catch birds in a palm tree, children herding ducks and a bear up a tree. One of the most interesting scenes shows children playing with a hoop, a seemingly innocent image except that some commentators believe that the color of their clothing was intended to evoke the **Greens and Blues**, the fiercely competitive chariot teams that vied with one another in the nearby Hippodrome (see p. 047).

1204 – the Fourth Crusade besieges Constantinople

Shops in Arasta Bazaar

The Arasta

Traditionally the money to pay for the upkeep of a mosque came from receipts from its hamam or rents from adjacent shops. In the case of the Sultanahmet Mosque, those rents came from a street of shops at the outer edge of the complex, commonly known as the Arasta Bazaar. Today it's an inviting alley of upscale carpet, tile and antique emporia whose owners, often seated on an inverted Byzantine capital, are always ready with a cup of tea and a chat.

Underground secrets

Just as in London, Paris and other consistently occupied city sites, it is rarely possible to dig far down in central Istanbul without coming to remains first of the medieval and then of the Byzantine and Roman cities. As a result, many buildings are built on historical ruins, as mentioned below.

A carpet shop was built on top of a magnificent 5th-century cistern with great columns. The cistern is also used as an art gallery. A restaurant at 33 Kutlugün Street is the upper floor neighbour of an unusual Byzantine complex, part of the Great Palace. Its caverns lead to another restaurant in Cankurtaran. There is another carpet shop on top of a vaulted Byzantine chapel with a holy water spring. The chapel probably dates back to the 9th Century, the floor mosaics are probably from the 5th or 6th centuries.

Part of the Magnaura Palace lies under a carpet shop

A 6th-century cistern

Istanbul's First Sports Stadium
The Hippodrome

085

In Byzantine times the Hippodrome, which sits next to the Blue Mosque, was a huge open-air sports stadium with banks of seats forming an elongated oval shape around a central arena. In Ottoman times its name was changed to At Meydanı (The Square of the Horses), the official name it still bears today.

The Hippodrome in Byzantine times

The original Hippodrome dates back to 203 and the reign of the Emperor **Septimius Severus**, although it was enlarged by **Constantine the Great** under whom it grew to be an enormous space 480 meters long by 118 meters wide. The best way to appreciate it is to stand near Kaiser Wilhelm's fountain at the northern end where the charioteers and their audience would have entered and gaze down the long stretch of grass in front of you. Originally this would have been the **"spina"** which ran down the center of the arena and was adorned with a variety of statues and monuments. Just a handful of these still remain; most of the others were lost to the rampaging **Fourth Crusaders** who carted off everything they regarded as valuable in 1204. Their booty included the statue of a **quadriga** or four-horse chariot, which stood over the entrance gate to the Hippodrome and which served as the prototype for the many similar statues that came later. A copy now stands on top of **St Mark's Basilica** in Venice while the original is housed in a museum inside it. Another copy stands in front of the **Sakıp Sabancı Museum** (see p. 444).

The Emperor Septimius Severus in the Capitoline Museum, in Rome

The modern road that loops round the green follows the route the charioteers would have taken in Byzantine times. Beyond that you need to forget all the existing buildings and imagine in their place tiered seating able to accommodate more than **30,000 spectators;** close your eyes and imagine the roar of all those people cheering on their favorite teams as they careered round the Hippodrome. An outer wall originally enclosed the Hippodrome and this was topped with decorative arcading which survived until the mid-16th century when the columns were removed for use in other buildings.

"(Kaiser Wilhelm's Fountain) was as ludicrous and out of place as the mechanical canary set amongst the ancient crowns and jewels of the Emperors of the Roman Empire at the Treasury."

Romance of the Bosphorus **by Dorina Lady Neave, 1949.**

Kaiser Wilhelm's Fountain

At the northern end of the Hippodrome, near Hagia Sophia stands a green-domed fountain designed by Max Spitta, the funds for which were given to Sultan Abdülhamid II by Kaiser Wilhelm II in memory of his visit in 1898; the emblems of both rulers appear on the golden mosaic inside the dome. The fountain stands on the site of the Janissary Tree, a plane tree from which many rebellious Janissaries were hanged in 1826. In Turkish it was sometimes called the Vakvak Ağacı (Vakvak Tree) after a tree in hell whose fruits were in the form of human skulls.

The Blues and Greens

In early Byzantine times the supporters of the chariot teams were just as fanatical in their devotions as fans of Galatasaray and Fenerbahçe today. The two most important factions were the Blues (generally the conservative middle and upper classes) and the Greens (the more radical lower classes) whose rivalries were always threatening to get out of hand. In 532 one faction "elected" Justinian's nephew Hypatius to take his place and the ensuing **Nika Riot** spurred his wife Theodora into vengeful action.

Empress Theodora

Count Belisarius (c.500-565) was sent to the Hippodrome to supervise the dispatch of some 30,000 rebels, events described in Robert Graves' novel "Count Belisarius". Amid the chaos the churches of **Hagia Sophia, Hagia Eirene and Hagios Stephanos** were burnt down. Justinian started work on replacements for the first two churches just after the riot was suppressed. The chariot factions never recovered their former power to create mayhem.

Obelisk

The Emperor would have watched the goings-on from the **Kathisma**, a private box facing the referee with a tunnel beneath it so he could make a speedy escape if necessary. This was a wise precaution since the huge crowds who gathered to watch the games could easily be whipped up into a frenzy; the worst such incident, the Nika Riot, occurred in 532 and ended in a bloodbath.

The Hippodrome remained the scene of disturbances right through until Ottoman times. It was also the location for many public executions, including that of Basil, the leader of the heretical Bogomil sect, who was burnt here in 1116, an event vividly described by the Byzantine royal historian **Anna Comnena** in her book, **"The Alexiad"**.

Chariot races stopped in the 13th century and by the 15th century the Hippodrome seems to have been in ruins. Its end finally came in 1609 when what remained of it was cleared away so work could begin on **Sultanahmet Mosque** (the Blue Mosque). Today you can still inspect the support walls for the southern end of the Hippodrome, the **Sphendone** (see p. 178). Some of the structures from the spina that still stand in the modern park also date back to the Hippodrome's heyday – presumably a granite obelisk was just too heavy for the Crusaders to cart away! The vacated space was later used for games of **cirit**, an equestrian sport rather like polo but in which riders try to hit each other with sticks.
The Hippodrome is surrounded by some of Istanbul's most important monuments including the Sultanahmet ("Blue") Mosque (see p. 039) and the 16th-century palace which houses the Museum of Turkish and Islamic Arts (see p. 051). Other less important but still impressive buildings include the imposing **Title Deeds and Land Registry Office**, designed by **Vedat Tek** in 1909 and the **Rectorate Building**, at the far end of the Hippodrome, which was designed by **Raimondo d'Aronco** in the 1890s and served as a school of fine arts and government offices before metamorphosing into the administrative headquarters of Marmara University. This is joined to a small building that once contained a museum dedicated to the Janissaries. The Rectorate houses a fine but little visited **collection of prints** as well as a small private hamam. **The Title Deeds ABD Land Registry Office** building hosts **Hagia Sophia History Museum**. Prepared with a new generation approach, museum invites its visitors to witness the history of one of the most important buildings in the world.

@demmuseums
www.demmuseums.com
Tel: 0850 346 33 36

The Serpentine Column in Levni's *Surname*, 1720

Serpentine Column (Yılanlı Sütun)

In the middle of the spina stood a spiral column topped off with three serpents' heads that acted as the central strut for a golden cauldron supported by a tripod. This was originally created to celebrate the victory of a coalition of Greek city-states over the Persians at Plataea in 478 BC and stood in front of the **Temple of Apollo at Delphi;** the names of the 31 victorious cities were inscribed on the serpents' lower coils and the column was supposedly made out of the shields of the defeated Persians. In c. 330 the Emperor **Constantine the Great** had the monument brought here and possibly erected in the grounds of Hagia Sophia, whence it was brought to the Hippodrome at a later date and adapted to serve as a fountain. The **serpents' heads** are thought to have survived right through until c.1700 when a drunken Polish diplomat may have chopped them off (unless, of course, they fell victim to over-enthusiastic cirit players). Today only a small fragment of one head lives on in the Istanbul Archeology Museum (see p. 020). Legend had it that if the **Serpentine Column** was ever destroyed Istanbul would become a Christian city again. Of course it probably depends on the definition of destroyed...

The Serpentine Column plays a leading role in Jason Goodwin's 19th-century detective novel "The Snake Stone".

Knitted Obelisk (Örme Dikilitaş)

A second rough-hewn obelisk stands at the southern end of the Hippodrome. Little is known about it although it was probably placed here by Constantine the Great or Theodosius I. Once it was covered with **bronze plates** supplied by Constantine VII Porphyryogenitus (r. 913-59), but they were ripped off by the Fourth Crusaders in the mistaken belief that they were gold. Why it would be called the knitted column is a complete mystery.

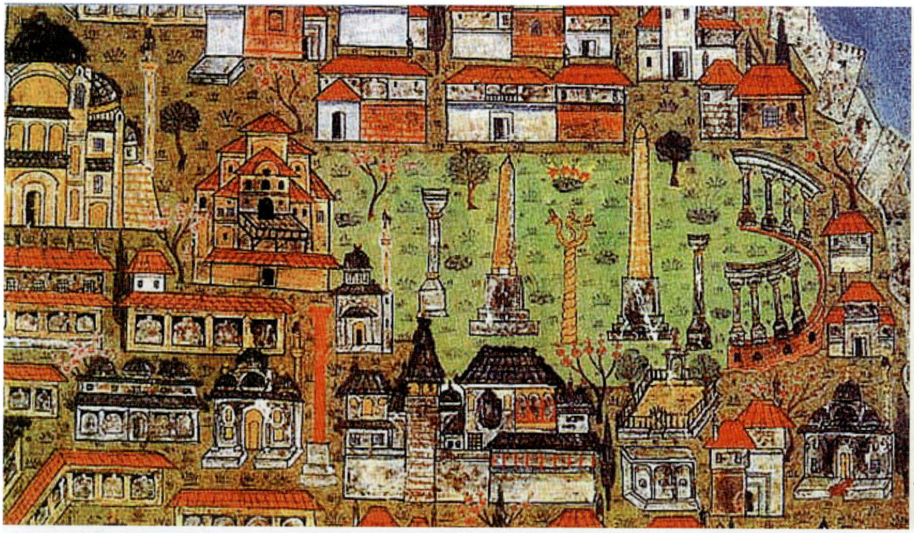

Plinth of the Theodosian Obelisk
The faded carvings on the plinth of the Theodosian Obelisk show the emperor watching a chariot race from the imperial box and awarding a laurel wreath to the victor. They also show him helping with the erection of the column and receiving homage from defeated enemies.

The Hippodrome in the 16th century by Matrakçı Nasuh

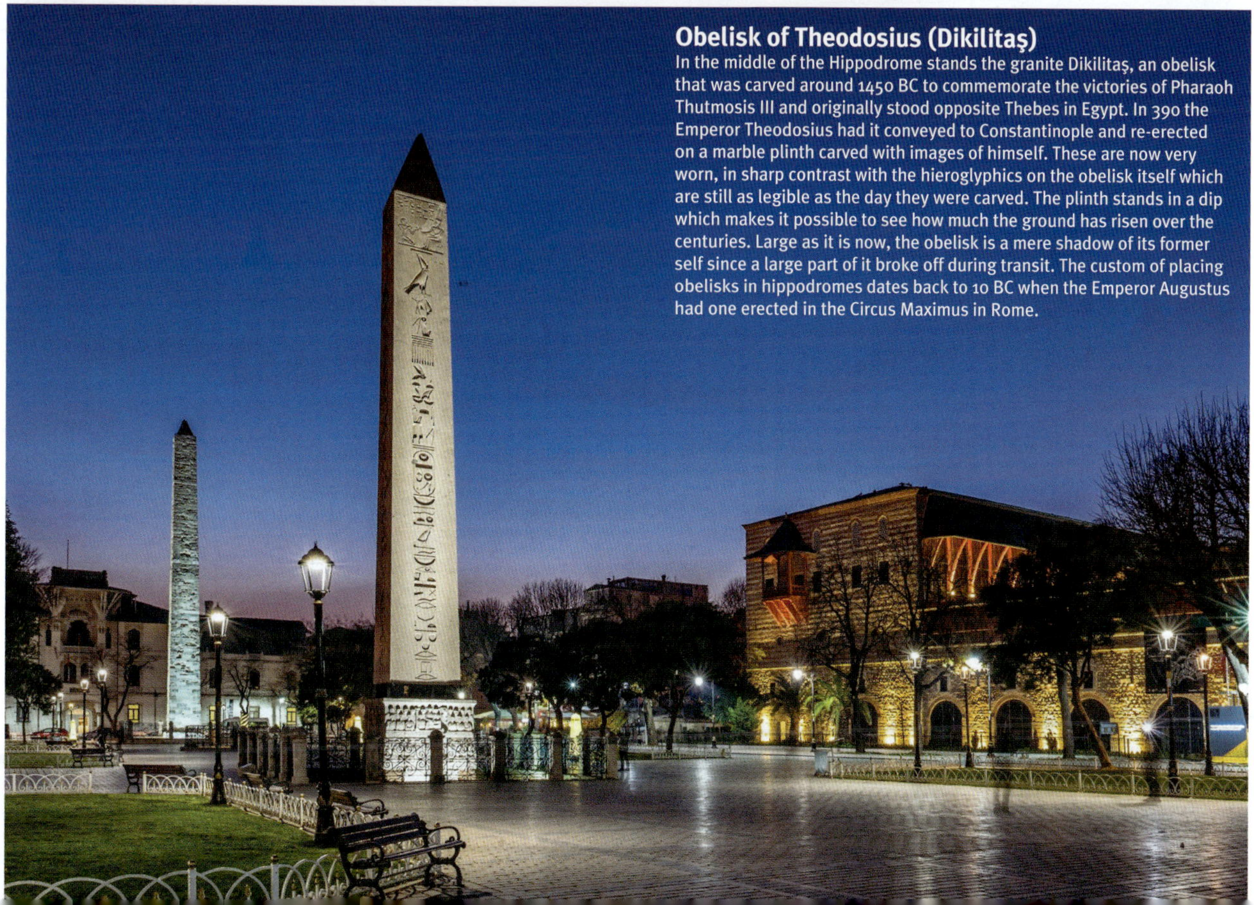

Obelisk of Theodosius (Dikilitaş)

In the middle of the Hippodrome stands the granite Dikilitaş, an obelisk that was carved around 1450 BC to commemorate the victories of Pharaoh Thutmosis III and originally stood opposite Thebes in Egypt. In 390 the Emperor Theodosius had it conveyed to Constantinople and re-erected on a marble plinth carved with images of himself. These are now very worn, in sharp contrast with the hieroglyphics on the obelisk itself which are still as legible as the day they were carved. The plinth stands in a dip which makes it possible to see how much the ground has risen over the centuries. Large as it is now, the obelisk is a mere shadow of its former self since a large part of it broke off during transit. The custom of placing obelisks in hippodromes dates back to 10 BC when the Emperor Augustus had one erected in the Circus Maximus in Rome.

İbrahim's Treasure House

Museum of Turkish and Islamic Arts

086

Right beside the Hippodrome, the Museum of Turkish and Islamic Arts is a treasure trove of exquisite arts and crafts items from around the Middle East housed inside what was once a private palace. Highlights of the collection are some truly magnificent carpets.

The historical archive, which was preserved in the treasure section in the Damascus Umayyad Mosque which was damaged by fire, was brought to Istanbul in 1917 for preservation. The showcase in the Damascus Documents section shows the oldest and most important works of this collection.

Although it's the contents that make the **Museum of Turkish and Islamic Arts** such a must-see attraction, the building in which they are housed is also of enormous importance as the city's only surviving example of an **Ottoman private palace** dating back to the 16th century. Completed in 1524, the palace was home to **Pargalı İbrahim Paşa** (1493-1536), brother-in-law, Grand Vizier and favorite of **Sultan Süleyman the Magnificent** and was built of stone so that it stood out amid its wooden neighbors. Grand as the surviving building is, it was originally even finer and, with its four separate courtyards, was larger even than nearby Topkapı Palace. A graceful wooden loggia enabled the occupants to look directly into the Hippodrome.

In its heyday the palace served as the venue for many important wedding and circumcision parties. However, it's rarely wise for a subject to live in a home that outshines that of their sovereign. Just as Hampton Court Palace, the home of Cardinal Wolsey, chancellor to King Henry VIII of England, attracted the monarch's envy, so İbrahim found the sultan (or at least his powerful wife **Roxelana**) looking on his self-aggrandizement with a jaundiced eye. The result was predictably the same – both Wolsey and İbrahim ended up prematurely dead, their palaces forfeited to the government.

In the aftermath, of course, İbrahim's palace had as checkered a history as most other Istanbul buildings, serving at different times as a barracks, a residence for foreign ambassadors, a land registry office, a clothes factory and a prison. After restoration, some parts of the original building, including a ceremonial hall that features in many Ottoman manuscripts, were opened to the public. Today the palace provides a graceful home for the Museum of Turkish and Islamic Arts, a collection of arts and crafts from around the Islamic world that is just the right size to appreciate without growing weary. Its **carpet collection** alone is rated as one of the best in the world.

Tel: 0212 518 18 05
Closed Mondays

"(The İbrahim Paşa Palace) was erected by a vizier who thought himself to be all-powerful, before he was strangled with the silken bowstring."

***The Janissary Tree* by Jason Goodwin, 2006**

If you liked this you'll also like:
Pera Museum **(see p. 334)**
Sadberk Hanım Museum **(see p. 465)**

Holbein and Lotto carpets

In the 16th century the European artists Hans Holbein the Younger and Lorenzo Lotto often included images of oriental carpets in their paintings with the somewhat perverse result that carpets of their preferred types are now sometimes described as Holbein or Lotto carpets. Perhaps the most famous example is Holbein's **"The Ambassadors"** which hangs in **London's National Gallery;** a carpet is prominently draped over a cupboard in the center. Several "Holbein carpets" are on display in the Museum of Turkish and Islamic Arts.

The room housing the Holbein and Lotto carpets

Doorhandle, Ulu Cami, Cizre

Islamic arts and crafts

The main collection housed in the upper part of the palace is arranged in roughly chronological order with many of the well-labeled exhibits grouped in side rooms off the main corridors. Highlights include finds from the palaces of the Abbasid caliphs at **Baghdad and Samarra,** amongst them colorful mosaics and a beautiful fresco of two dancers; and a superb wooden door rescued from the Great Mosque (Ulu Cami) in **Cizre** in south-eastern Turkey that dates back to 1155. The ceramic artefacts unearthed during the 1905 excavations in the Raqqa section, one of the most important settlements of the Early Islamic Period, are exhibited with the original chests in which they were brought at the time. The layout and design of the exhibition reflects the look of an archeological excavation site.

A large collection of Selçuk pieces includes some unglazed 13th-century ceramics and a number of magnificent bronze boxes and ewers. There's also a fine display of blue and white so-called **Miletus ware** that was in fact manufactured in İznik. Quirkier are the **portraits** of the Qajar shahs of Persia (Iran) that show them wearing bushy beards that look like Santa Claus stick-ons.

Items brought here from elsewhere in Istanbul include 16th and 17th-century inlaid wooden Koran boxes removed from the **tombs** of Rüstem Paşa, Sultan Selim II and Sultan Ahmed I and from the Hagia Sophia Library; a late 19th-century golden **jug and ewer** removed from the Pertevniyal Valide Sultan Mosque (see p. 089); and examples of porcelain-like 19th-century **Beykoz glass** (see p. 554). Do not leave without seeing the Holy Relics Section, which is exhibited in the last three rooms and along the large corridor of the display hall. In the third room of the section, the whiskers belonging to our Prophet, known as Lihye-i Saadet or Sakal-ı Şerif (The Noble Beard of the Holy Prophet), are exhibited in their original containers and boxes.

Sultan's kaftan

Seljuk ceramic panel

Wooden Seljuk sarcophagus

Most large carpets are displayed in the Divanhane.

Turkish carpets

Almost all the carpets on display in the museum would originally have decorated the floors of mosques, in particular mosques in the central Anatolian towns of **Konya** and **Sivrihisar**. The oldest carpets are an important group of seven from the 14th century, some of them mere fragments, that were brought here from the Selçuk-era **Alaeddin Mosque** in Konya, but for most people the most memorable pieces will be the floor-to-ceiling-sized **Uşak carpets** dating back to the 16th century that are on display in the Ceremonial Hall; some used to adorn the **Piyale Paşa Mosque** in Kasımpaşa (see p. 264) and the **Galata Mevlevihanesi** in Tünel (see p. 320). The same room also contains examples of what are called "garden carpets" woven in Persia in the 18th and 19th century and brought here from a mosque in **Erzurum** in north-eastern Turkey. The term "divanhane" refers to the place where the divan (council of state) gathers in palaces. The large halls used as guest reception rooms in large residential buildings like pavilions, mansions and sea-mansions were also named divan. Don't forget to imagine those glorious days while visiting this hall where Ibrahim Paşa, one of the most powerful viziers of the Ottoman Empire, hosted the sultans.

Their removal to a museum was perhaps inevitable both on conservation and security grounds, but today when almost all Turkish mosques are carpeted with machine-made versions, they serve as a poignant reminder of what has been lost.

Şahniş

Şahniş is the name given to the open parts of the residential buildings in traditional Turkish architecture which extend to the street or the courtyard, with windows on three sides or in the form of a balcony. Since the şahniş of Ibrahim Paşa Palace is at a favourable elevation to enjoy the best view of Sultanahmet Square and its surroundings, the sultans used to watch weddings and festivities held in the square from here.

The 200-year-old glorious plane tree attracts the attention of visitors. The tree, which is also depicted in the 16th-century miniatures of the palace, is thought to have been planted in the place of another plane tree which had been felled as part of an Ottoman tradition.

The unearthing of the **"Hall of Hippodrome Ruins"** is another story. This section was being used as a boiler room for many years. The fate of the area changed when excavations and cleaning work during the extensive restoration work in 2014 unearthed strata of the hippodrome and tunnel-shaped galleries beneath the strata.

Underground Medusa

Basilica Cistern

007

Amid Istanbul's many surprises, few places can be more unexpectedly romantic than the wonderful Yerebatan Cistern, which lurks underground just across the tram lines from Hagia Sophia. This magical and mysterious place affects everyone so much that it sometimes appears in a Hollywood movie or an immersive novel.

Another masterpiece of the famed Byzantine emperor **Justinian I** who had it built in 532 to supply water for the **Great Palace**, the Basilica Cistern actually resembles an underground palace itself and is therefore called the Yerebatan Sarayı (Submerged Palace) in Turkish. The name "Basilica Cistern" refers to its presumed location underneath the Roman Ilius Basilica which stood in the second of two great squares in the area.

Yerebatan Cistern in an 19th-century engraving

This 1500-year-old structure consists of 336 columns lined up in 28 rows of 12 and spread over a space measuring 140m / 460ft by 170m / 558ft; most of the columns are 9m / 30ft high and topped with Corinthian and Doric capitals. At the far end of the accessible part of the cistern, two bas-reliefs in the shape of **Gorgons' heads** can be seen serving as column bases; that they were regarded as just so much building rubble is suggested by the fact that one of them is upside down, the other on its side. Water was brought here by means of a series of aqueducts and tunnels that ran from the **Belgrade Forest** (see p. 562), 25 kilometers / 16 miles away. When full it would have held some 80 million liters of water. For a long time the cistern's very existence was forgotten, but then in 1545 the French traveller Pierre Gilles noticed locals lowering buckets to haul water up from underground (as is still possible in some places today). In his **"Antiquities of Constantinople"** Gilles describes how he became the first European in modern times to explore the cistern. He also describes watching it fill up via a huge drainpipe during the winter rains, a rather more dramatic experience than listening to the drips which greet modern-day visitors.

Edmondo De Amicis

Peacock-feather decoration on column

"The torch threw a fiery gleam upon the arches near the door and revealed dropping walls and endless rows of columns wherever one looked, like tree trunks in a dense flooded forest."

Constantinople **by Edmondo de Amicis, 1877**

Esat Efendi Library

The building which was once the Esat Efendi Library dating back to the 19th century stands on Yerebatan Caddesi. Its contents have been moved into the Süleymaniye Library, and the building now houses a souvenir shop.

A fishy story

Before restoration, many visitors were amazed to spot carp and goldfish happily swimming around in the water around the base of the columns, but this is nothing new since Pierre Gilles records going fishing in a boat with the man who showed him how to get into the cistern. Centuries earlier, a Byzantine man living above the forgotten cistern had dug a hole into it and managed to catch a few fish. As the fish grew ever fatter, so did the man as he feasted on his catch!

The cistern was used as a venue for the 2003 Istanbul Biennale

Even after it was rediscovered the Ottomans continued to prefer drinking spring water rather than the still water collected in underground reservoirs, so this particular cistern was used to irrigate the **palace gardens**.

A surviving engraving from the 19th century shows a visitor being rowed round the columns with a little lamp in the prow of the boat guiding the way and **Julia Pardoe** left a harrowing description of a Frenchman who sailed off into the dark in the 1830s and was never seen again, but gradually people started to use the cistern as a rubbish dump. Between 1985 and 1987 it was cleared of all the accumulated junk, restored and fitted out with walkways for visitors. Today with suitably atmospheric lighting and music (usually the haunting sound of the **ney**, a Turkish flute), it makes a great and thoroughly unexpected place to visit, especially if you need a cool place to escape the summer heat.

The entrance to the cistern is on Yerebatan Caddesi, although you will re-emerge into the daylight on Alemdar Caddesi beside the tram lines.

@yerebatansarnic
www.yerebatan.com
Tel: 0212 512 15 70

If you liked this you'll also like...

Binbirdirek Cistern (see p. 064)
Şerefiye Cistern (see p. 064)
Nakkaş Cistern (see p. 044)
Sarnıç Restaurant (see p. 034)
Sultan Sarnıç Restaurant (see p. 123)
Theodosius Cistern (see p. 064)
For information about Istanbul's open-air cisterns, see p. 123.

The freezing smile

According to Greek mythology the Gorgons were a trio of snake-headed women whose smile turned those who looked on it to stone. Of the three, only **Medusa** had any developed personality, hence the assumption that any snake-headed, vaguely female-looking image must represent her. In the most famous story about the Gorgons the hero **Perseus** was dispatched to bring the head of Medusa to King Polydectes. This he succeeded in doing by looking at her reflection in a bronze shield given to him by Athene, the goddess of wisdom, while he cut it off.

Medusa

James Bond in town

In 1964 the Basilica Cistern featured in the James Bond movie **"From Russia with Love"**. Istanbul's cisterns and the network of water tunnels serving them also play a leading role in Jason Goodwin's crime novel "The Snake Stone".

Nightingale's Bathhouse
Cağaloğlu

088

Of all Istanbul's historic hamams (Turkish baths), perhaps the best known is the one in Cağaloğlu, just up the road from the Basilica Cistern, that played host in the past to many famous bathers including Florence Nightingale. Nearby are the Iranian Consulate and the fine building that houses the offices of the Governor of Istanbul.

Yusuf Sinan Paşa

"(The bath attendants) wear no other garments, while on duty, than a small fez, a pair of naelin (clogs) and a peshtamel... which latter...serves as a petticoat or apron."

Three Years in Constantinople
by Charles White, 1846

Cağaloğlu's name is said to be derived from that of **Cigalazade Yusuf Sinan Paşa** (c.1545-1605), a descendant of the Genoese Cicala family who became an Ottoman admiral and politician. It is thought that his name was Turkified to Cigalaoğlu which gradually corrupted to Cağaloğlu. In the early 20th century this part of town was the heart of the **printing industry**. Still today you will find many book and print shops in the back streets.

Cağaloğlu Hamam

Arguably the most beautiful Turkish bath in Istanbul, Cağaloğlu (*Yerebatan Caddesi*, is not actually that old, having been built in 1741 for **Sultan Mahmud I** who wanted to use its revenue to finance a library for Ayasofya; indeed, it was originally called the Yeni, or New, Hamam. Not long after it was built a law was passed forbidding the creation of any more hamams because their proliferation was leading to a shortage of firewood and water; in that sense, then, Cağaloğlu has been described as the last great Ottoman hamam.

Surprisingly little is known about the men who designed the bath, although it is thought that the chief architect **Süleyman Ağa** drew up the plans which were then executed by one **Abdullah Ağa**. When it first opened its doors it quickly attracted an upscale clientele drawn from the palace and its offices.

Cağaloğlu is a double hamam, with separate entrances and facilities for men and women. Access to the men's part is via a tunnel-like corridor lined with mementoes of the glory days of public bathing. Immediately over the entrance is a graceful calligraphic inscription recording the foundation of the baths. The **hararet** (hot room) of the men's section is unusual in that it is square-shaped even though the **göbektaşı** is octagonal. As usual the men get the finer bath, but the women's section is also very beautiful. In both cases the decoration offers baroque flourishes that make it stand out from its more austere rivals. Surprisingly, the heat is provided by burning crushed olive pips brought from Ayvalık on the Aegean.

Hamam entrance

Its great beauty combined with its proximity to the great monuments of Ottoman Istanbul has ensured it a succession of famous visitors, amongst them **Kaiser Wilhelm II** of Germany, **King Edward VIII** of Britain, the Hungarian composer **Franz Liszt**, the British nurse **Florence Nightingale**, the Russian dancer **Rudolf Nureyev** and the Egyptian actor **Omar Sharif**.

Perhaps predictably, the makers of soap ads have shown great interest in Cağaloğlu which also starred in the video made to support Sertab Erener's Eurovision Song Contest-winning effort in 2003. Cağaloğlu popped up again in The Young Indiana Jones Chronicles, the television spin-off from the smash-hit film.

@cagalogluhamami
www.cagalogluhamami.com.tr
Tel: 0212 522 24 24

Iranian Consulate

Midhat Paşa

Iranian Consulate

Walking uphill from the hamam you will pass a fine government building originally designed for the TC Ziraat Bankası. In front of it stands a bust of the reforming politician **Midhat Paşa** (see p. 404). Across the road are the remains of the **Hadım Hasan Paşa Medrese,** built by the architect **Davut Ağa** between 1595 and 1597 for a vizier to Sultan Mehmed III and currently under restoration.

The **Iranian Consulate** is housed in a magnificent mansion dating back to 1866 and designed by the Italian architect **Domenico Stampa.** It was the first consulate building to be built within the old walled city.

Istanbul Boys High School

Turning down Türkocağı Caddesi beside the embassy you will come on the right to a huge building designed in bombastic First National architectural style in 1897 by **Alexandre Vallaury** to house the **Düyun-u Umumiye** (Public Debt Administration). This department had been established in 1882 when it became apparent that the Ottoman Empire was effectively bankrupt and it was administered by foreigners. In 1923 the Turkish Republic canceled the outstanding debt and the building became redundant. Many companies hoped to move into it but **Atatürk** wanted it to become a school so that young Turks would grow up understanding its history. Despite its name the school has been **co-educational** since 1964.

Istanbul Boys High School

Lobby of Istanbul Boys High School

In this photo taken from Karaköy the Nuruosmaniye Mosque is in the center with the Istanbul Boys High School to the left.

Rüstempaşa Medrese

Continuing downhill along Hoca Hanı Sokak, you will come to the Rüstempaşa Medrese (Seminary) designed by Mimar Sinan in 1550. Externally only its fine gateway attracts attention. Internally, however, the medrese is octagonal, the spaces on each side being filled out with bathrooms and toilets to enable the external walls to be straightened into a square. It is restored to serve as a **cultural center.**

Red Mansion

Nearby is the barely visible shell of a wooden building that played a notable part in modern Turkish history. It was in the Red Mansion in Hoca Hanı Sokak that important decisions were made in the period leading up to the start of the Second Constitutional Monarchy (1909-22) and here that the Committee of Union and Progress ("the Young Turks") agreed that Turkey should enter the First World War on the side of the Germans. Unless restoration begins soon the remnants will not be around for much longer.

Red Mansion

Governor's Mansion

A short walk downhill from the Iranian Consulate along Ankara Caddesi, high on a hill overlooking the Golden Horn and the Sea of Marmara, the beautiful building that now houses the Vali (Governor) of Istanbul was originally built for the grand viziers who served the sultans in the nearby Topkapı Palace. When the capital moved to Ankara in 1923 it was converted into a home for the governor who can take advantage of what must be one of the best views in the city. It has its own mosque, the Vilayet Cami (Nallı Mescid), next door.

The Imperial Road

Divan Yolu

009

Since Roman times Divan Yolu has been one of the most important roads in the city; today it is thronged with tourists who walk along it or take the tram to get from Sultanahmet Square to Çemberlitaş and the Grand Bazaar. Historic mosques, old schools and libraries, monuments to the famous, they're all here, alongside many small restaurants and places to stay. The Sultanahmet Hamam offers the services of a newly restored Turkish bath.

Originally what is now Divan Yolu was part of the **Via Egnatia** (see p. 191) that ran for more than 1,000 kilometers from the Augustaion (now Sultanahmet Square) to the port of Dyrrachium (now Durres in Albania). After the city walls were built in the 4th century the name of the stretch inside them was officially changed to the **Via Regia** (the Royal Road), although it was more commonly called the **Mese** (Main Road). In later Byzantine times the road fell into disuse, only to be revived by the Ottomans as Divan Yolu, the road along which the council of ministers processed to the frequent meetings of the Divan inside Topkapı Palace (see p. 008). Today it merges seamlessly into Yeniçeriler Caddesi (Janissary Street) and then Ordu Caddesi (Army Street).

Firuz Ağa Mosque

Near Sultanahmet tram stop stands the elegant little Firuz Ağa Mosque, one of the city's oldest mosques dating back to 1491. It was built for Firuz Ağa, Chief Treasurer to **Bayezid II** and is a pre-classical mosque with a single minaret and triple-arched portico of a type developed in Bursa.

In Ottoman architecture, the single-minaret mosques had their minarets on the right side of the kiblah. However, the Firuz Ağa Mosque contradicts this. There are different opinions about this positioning. One proposition is that the design of the mosque was based on the features of the first mosque built in Mecca. Another opinion holds that the reason was to avoid disturbing the Greek citizens, who were in a majority in the neighborhoods to the right of the mosque, with the sound of the Ezan (Islamic call for prayer).

Just past the mosque and set back from the road in a small park scattered ruins have been identified as the remains of the palaces of two Byzantine noblemen, **Antiochus and Lausus.** Later the site was used as a burial place for **St Euphemia of Chalcedon,** a Christian martyred for her faith in c. 300 (see p. 480). Also here is a monument to **Mehmed Akif Ersoy** (1873-1936), author of the Turkish national anthem, the İstiklal Marşı (Independence March).

"Never fear! For the crimson flag that proudly waves in these dawns shall never fade/before the last fiery hearth that is ablaze within my nation burns out."

"Independence March" by Mehmed Akif Ersoy, 1921

The Milion Stone

One of Divan Yolu's most important monuments is also one of its least obvious and that is the small chunk of marble that stands at the start of the road just as it leaves Sultanahmet Square. It's all that survives of the **Roman Miliarium Aureum** (Golden Milestone) or Milion, usually said to be the milestone from which all distances in the Byzantine Empire were calculated, although recent research suggests that they may have been calculated from the Forum of Constantine, modern Çemberlitaş (see p. 066). To the right of it stand the slight remains of an Ottoman **water tower,** while to the left is the **Beşir Ağa fountain,** built in 1744 for Hacı Beşir Ağa, then the Chief Black Eunuch at the Topkapı Palace.

Cevri Kalfa Primary School

A little further along on the right the Cevri Kalfa Primary School was built by **Sultan Mahmud II** in 1819 to show his gratitude after Cevri Kalfa, a slave girl in the Harem, saved his life during an uprising of the Janissaries when he was a prince. At the time it was Istanbul's largest primary school. The building has had a checkered history. In 1858 it became a girls' school, in 1930 a printing school and in 1945 a primary school once again. In 1985 it was given to the **Türk Edebiyat Vakfı** (Turkish Literature Foundation), after which it languished unloved until the restorers finally moved in in 2009. The pretty fountain set into the outside wall forms an integral part of the main building.

Şerefiye (Theodosius) Cistern

Senator Philoxenos

Cisterns

Turn left along İmran Öktem Caddesi to find the entrance to the **Binbirdirek Cistern** (Cistern of 1001 Columns), the city's second largest cistern after the Basilica Cistern (see p. 054), which can seat 1,500 people in its modern reincarnation as a restaurant. It's possible that a Roman senator called **Philoxenus** started work on it during the reign of Constantine the Great although most of it appears to date from the 5th or 6th centuries. Far from glorying in 1001 columns, it has only 224 of them and column headings in the form of pyramids without any decorations. Unlike the Basilica Cistern, the columns and headings were made for the cistern specially and not brought from other structures. Each column has foundations that go down 5 meters below ground. If you pay special attention to their bodies, you will see Greek inscriptions and letters. It is believed that these signs were left by workers working on the construction of the cistern.

The cistern is associated with a gruesome folk story that tells how a 17th-century woman called **Cevahirli Hanım Sultan** used a beautiful young servant called Tayyarzade to lure men into her gambling den where she would murder them and toss their bodies into the cistern. In his travelogue "Innocents Abroad" the American writer **Mark Twain** reported seeing silk-spinners at work in the cistern in the 1860s. Later, however, it became a garbage dump, the holes in the domes enlarged to make it easy for people to drop their rubbish in. Before it could be restored, 7,000 truckloads of garbage had to be removed.

The least known of the three major cisterns of Istanbul, the Şerefiye Cistern, has a deep-rooted history. After the completion of the eight-year restoration work carried out by **Istanbul Metropolitan Municipality** in 2018, it reclaimed its place among the historical treasures of Istanbul in all its glory. Located on Piyer Loti Street, the cistern was erected on 32 columns by **Emperor Theodosius II** between 428 and 443. Water sources in the Belgrade Forest and its surroundings were distributed through the canal of the **Aqueduct of Valens** (see p.108) to "Nymphaeum", "Zeuxippus Baths" and the "Grand Palace". The Şerefiye Cistern was also added to the system to store the water transported through the aqueduct. The cistern was one of the three cisterns built in the 4th century that supplied Istanbul's water needs. Because we live in a city built on history, **Arif Paşa Mansion** was built on the parcel of Şerefiye in 1910. After the 1950s, **Eminönü City Hall** was based here. Thanks to the completion of long-running restoration works its texture of 1600 years has been preserved and it welcomes visitors with a chilling and extraordinary atmosphere, particularly when viewed from a height. Exhibitions are also occasionally held at the place. The cistern hosted the 'Hiç Hali' exhibition by the Iranian artist Ahmet Nejat to celebrate its opening.

@1001direk
www.binbirdirek.com
Tel: 0212 518 10 01

@serefiyesarnici
Tel: 0212 568 60 80

You can visit the Sultanahmet Hamam located on Dr. Emin Paşa Street. The bath, which was built as a source of income for the Fenari Isa Mosque, (p. 090) has been restored and opened for service (Tel: 0212 513 72 04). You can find the best examples of English books about Turkey and the Middle East in the branches of the Book Shop located on both sides of Sultanahmet tram station.

@bookshopistanbul
www.bookshopistanbul.com
Tel: 0212 512 04 56

Fuad Paşa Mosque

Most people barely give it a second glance, but the octagonal tomb in the grounds of the Fuad Paşa Mosque, very close to the Binbirdirek Cistern in Peykhane Caddesi, is actually a gem of late Ottoman architecture, its exterior densely covered with carvings. It contains the tomb of the reformist Grand Vizier Keçecizade Fuad Paşa (1815-69) who commissioned the unexceptional mosque beside it.

Şerefiye (Theodosios) Cistern in 2018, after restoration.

Sultan Abdülhamid II's tomb

Press Museum

Housed in a fine stone mansion built for a university department in the 19th century by the Grand Vizier **Saffed Paşa** and designed by the **Fossati brothers**, the Press Museum is a reminder of the fact that this part of the city was once the center of the printing industry. Come here to see a giant lithograph machine dating back to 1870, a German offset printing machine of similar vintage and cameras that used to belong to famous journalists. A map in the hall shows all the local sites that have played a part in printing history. The ground floor houses a café and gift shop.

Imperial tombs

A little further west along Divan Yolu stand the tombs of Sultans **Mahmud II** (r. 1808-1838), **Abdülaziz** (r. 1861-1876) and **Abdülhamid II** (r. 1876-1909); the building that houses them was designed by the great Armenian architect **Garabed Amira Balyan** in 1840. The grounds house an impressive sea of late Ottoman marble tombstones, including that of the sociologist and Turkish nationalist writer **Ziya Gökalp** (1876-1924). Şehzade Ertuğrul Osman (1912-2009), known as **"the Last Ottoman"**, was also buried here after dying in New York.

Across the road is the Köprülü Kütüphanesi (Köprülü Library), built in 1661 as the first independent library of the Ottoman period and paid for by **Mehmed Paşa** (1578-1661) and his son **Fazıl Ahmed Paşa** (1635-76), both of them powerful grand viziers in their turn.

Constantine's Last Memorial

Çemberlitaş

010

One tram stop west of Sultanahmet is the district called Çemberlitaş (Hooped Column) after a stone column erected in the reign of Constantine the Great which sits in a pigeon-infested square opposite the Çemberlitaş Hamam, one of the city's finest Turkish baths. There are a few minor mosque complexes nearby and the huge Nuruosmaniye Mosque and Grand Bazaar are just a short walk away.

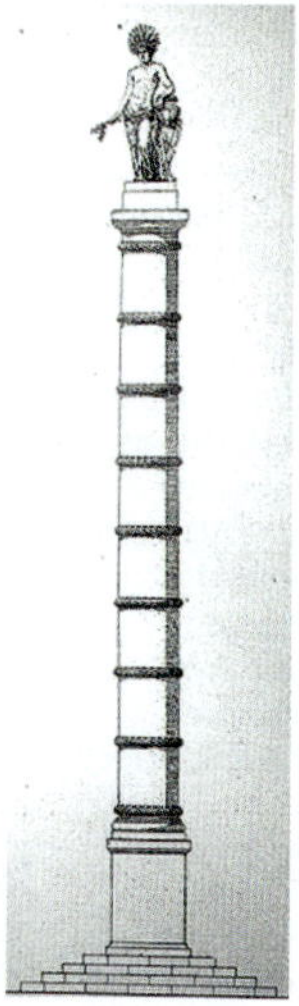

19th-century Çemberlitaş was a popular residential district favored by doctors and lawyers. However, as the 20th century developed, so it fell from fashion as the old residents moved away from the town center leaving it to be colonized by immigrants from eastern Turkey, especially leather workers, who took advantage of the declining rents. This had implications for the hamam in particular which could no longer rely on a stream of wealthy customers to maintain it. After many years in the doldrums, salvation finally arrived in the 1990s with the coming of mass tourism, the revenues from which made up for the shortfall in income from the locals.

Today Çemberlitaş is a rather grim square facing the hamam and dominated by the eponymous "Hooped Column", but in origin it was the glamorous **Forum of Constantine**, an oval-shaped space ringed with porticoes, decorated with statues of the Roman emperors, the pagan gods and the Christian saints and with grand temples and mansions all around it.

The Çemberlitaş

In 330 the Emperor Constantine decided to make Byzantium the capital of the Eastern Roman Empire, renaming it Constantinople and erecting a 35-meter-high porphyry column right in the center of the Forum to commemorate the event. For the top of the column he commissioned a statue that depicted him in the guise of **Apollo**, the sun god, which might suggest that his much-vaunted Christianity was not quite as deep as it appeared (in fact he only formally converted to Christianity on his deathbed in 337).

The Çemberlitaş is not just the world's largest porphyry column but also a stalwart survivor. In 416 it was damaged by an earthquake and iron bands had to be secured around the joints between the seven huge blocks of stone to ensure that it wouldn't fall down. In 1106 a storm brought the statue of Constantine crashing down and **Emperor Manuel I Comnenos** snatched the chance to replace it with a giant cross. After the Turks seized Constantinople in 1453, the cross came down in its turn. Then in 1779 fire swept through the neighborhood and left only the soot-blackened column. **Sultan Abdülhamid** paid for its restoration, during the course of which the lowest layer of porphyry was enclosed inside a stone plinth. In the 1970s the iron hoops were replaced in case they damaged the marble, which is how things remain today.

Hidden treasure

Constantine was supposed to have buried several relics, including pieces of the **True Cross**, the axe Noah used to build the **Ark** and the remains of the **seven loaves** from the miracle of the loaves and fishes, around the base of the column. So far they remain undisturbed.

Fourth Crusade of 1204 by F.V. Delacroix, 1840

If you like this you'll also like:
Column of Arcadius (see p. 093)
Goths Column (see p. 201)
Kıztaşı (see p. 117)

Çemberlitaş Hamam

Immediately across the road from the column and entered through a surprisingly inconspicuous doorway, **Çemberlitaş Hamam** is one of the city's finest Turkish baths, almost certainly a work of Mimar Sinan dating back to 1584. It was built for **Nurbanu Sultan**, the wife of Sultan Selim II and one of the more powerful queen mothers who effectively ruled the Ottoman Empire from 1574 to 1583 as co-regent for her young son Murad III – the story has it that she actually concealed her husband's dead body in ice so that no one would know that he had died until her son could ride in from Manisa and stake his claim to the throne. The hamam was intended to provide financial support for the **Atik Valide Sultan Mosque,** far away in Üsküdar (see p. 503). It was restored by Köprülü Mehmed Paşa in the 17th century, as recorded above the main entrance.

The magnificent bath-house has separate sections for men and women. **Marble screens,** or "halvets", further subdivide the hot rooms to provide more private bathing areas; these screens are adorned with calligraphic verse in Ottoman Turkish. The baths have undergone several refits over the years and in 2008 when better changing facilities for women were installed The original camekan (changing room) was knocked down during road-widening in the 19th century.

@cemberlitashamami
www.cemberlitashamam.com
Tel: 0212 522 79 74

Mosques and complexes

Near the Çemberlitaş a couple of mosque complexes repay a quick look. Almost immediately across the road is the octagonal **Köprülü Mosque,** built in 1659-60 for Köprülü Mehmed Paşa ("Mehmed the Cruel"), the first grand vizier to come from this powerful family (at the age of 80) and his son Fazıl Ahmed Paşa.

Atik Ali Paşa Mosque

Mehmed Paşa's tomb has a metal grille over the top leaving it open to the elements; wags suggested that he had been responsible for the execution of so many people that his tomb had to be left open to the skies so that the rain could cool him down as he burned in hell. The mosque itself started life as a lecture theatre for the complex's medrese. Also part of this complex is the 17th century **Vizier Han,** a little way down the road from the Çemberlitaş Hamam. Once able to accommodate visiting traders and their animals in its double courtyard, it's now somewhat run-down and neglected. At one time a passage connected it directly to the Çemberlitaş Hamam.

Also nearby is the **Atik Ali Paşa Mosque,** built in 1496 for a eunuch who became Grand Vizier to Bayezid II. Enclosed behind a wall of arches, the **Koca Sinan Paşa Complex** was designed by the architect Davud Ağa for the grand vizier who captured Yemen for the Ottomans in 1569. It incorporates a 16-sided tomb and medrese and now houses a cultural center for the Balkan Turkish community. The sebil (water dispensary) on the corner looks across a small side street to the **Çorlulu Ali Paşa Complex,** built in 1708 for a man who served as grand vizier to Sultan Ahmed III until they fell out and he was executed. It's now a popular nargile cafe (see below). Finally, on the opposite side of the road stands the **Kara Mustafa Paşa Complex,** built between 1669 and 1690 for a grand vizier who besieged Vienna in 1683. It includes an overgrown octagonal mosque and a medrese with a half-hearted "museum and institute" to poet Yahya Kemal Beyaltı (1884-1958).

Koca Sinan Paşa Social Complex

Pierre Loti's house

Heading away from Cemberlitaş towards the Grand Bazaar you will pass on the left-hand side of the road the only surviving building in Istanbul in which the French author Pierre Loti (see p. 253) actually lived. He stayed there for nine weeks in 1910. A plaque commemorates his stay.

The severed head

While enjoying your nargile at the Çorlulu Ali Pasa Medrese you might want to spare a thought for the eponymous Ali who fell foul of Sultan Ahmed III and was beheaded on Mytilene (Lesbos) in Greece in 1711. His severed head was returned to Istanbul and buried beneath the mosque complex for which he had paid just three years earlier.

"Oh, to be this one who keeps an eye
on each tobacco bowl,
who adds to the dying embers
a fresh coal, cerise with heat."

Paulann Petersin in "Blood Silk", 2003

Gedikpaşa Hamam

Visit the **Çemberlitaş Hamam** for an excellent scrub in beautiful surroundings. – it's a particularly good place to come if you've never visited a Turkish bath before and are unsure of the etiquette. Less well-known than Çemberlitaş, the **Gedikpaşa Hamam** was built beside the Gedikpaşa Mosque in 1474 for Gedik Ahmed Paşa, one of Sultan Mehmed II's grand viziers and is probably the oldest bathhouse in the city. Restored in 2009, it offers separate sections for men and women.

---

www.gedikpasahamami.com
Tel: 0212 517 89 56

Çorlulu Ali Paşa Medrese

One of the most atmospheric places to smoke a nargile in all Istanbul is the courtyard of the **Çorlulu Ali Paşa Medrese** (seminary) where students from Istanbul University gather to while away an hour or so alongside their flat-capped elders. Despite the tourist shops arraigned along one side it retains a very authentic atmosphere.

The First Shopping Mall

The Grand Bazaar and the Hans

011

Dating back to 1461, Istanbul's Grand Bazaar is one of the liveliest and most colorful parts of the old city where you can find souvenirs to take home in all shapes and sizes. Tourism dominates the main thoroughfares, but off the back streets lie a network of ancient hans where you can still see craftsmen hard at work.

Old sebil turned carpet shop

Set on Istanbul's Second Hill right beside Beyazıt Square, the **Grand Bazaar** (*Covered Bazaar, or Kapalı Çarşı in Turkish*) is one of the oldest and largest markets in the world with nearly 60 frantically busy streets stuffed with around **4,000 shops**. Originally there would have been a series of different markets here all side by side and each specializing in one particular product. Many would have been hans or bedestens, with rooms, often on two levels, opening off a central courtyard, so traders could store their goods and even stay the night. Although some of the originals still survive, over time most were roofed over and the different markets linked together to create the vast complex you'll visit today. The alleys were also lined with wooden stalls, called "**dolaps** (cupboards)" in Turkish, which were very popular with visiting 19th-century artists.

The part of the bazaar closest to the main entrances can feel very touristy, but there are still parts of it that are quieter and more evocative such as the attractive 18th-century **İç Cebeci Han**. Most of these areas are on the far side of the bazaar, near the **Mercan** and **Mahmutpaşa Gates**.

Although some people enter the bazaar through the Market Gate (Çarşıkapı) entrance near the chaotic Beyazıt/Kapalı Çarşı tram stop, a much more attractive approach route brings you from Çemberlitaş through the grounds of the Nuruosmaniye Mosque (see below) to the imposing **Nuruosmaniye Gate** which has a colorful coat of arms above it and a small **sebil** (water dispensary) housing a carpet shop immediately opposite it.

"It is full of life and stir and business, dirt, beggars, asses, yelling peddlers, porters, dervishes, high-born Turkish female shoppers, Greeks and weird-looking, weirdly-dressed Mohammedans..."

Innocents Abroad **by Mark Twain, 1867**

Kalpakçılar Caddesi is full of jewellery shops

Kalpakçılar Street (Kalpakçılar Caddesi)

Running from the Nuruosmaniye Gate to the Beyazıt Gate roughly parallel with Yeniçeriler Caddesi outside, Kalpakçılar Caddesi, the wide, vaulted main street, houses countless jewelry shops and still does quite a lot of business selling gold to locals who give it as a gift at wedding and circumcision parties. A myriad leather, carpet, textile, pottery, copper, antiques and souvenir shops meander back from it. Don't worry about getting lost – it's all part of the fun. And no matter where you shop, expect to be plied with plentiful freshly brewed tea, the essence of Turkish hospitality.

Bargaining

In most parts of Istanbul bargaining ("pazarlık" in Turkish) is fast becoming a thing of the past. However, it lives on in the bazaar where it would almost always be a mistake to pay the first price suggested. There are no hard and fast rules about where to start negotiating. For example, the price of gold and silver jewelry largely depends on its weight and since the price changes daily you can only really bargain over the part of the cost dependent on workmanship. Otherwise there's no substitute for shopping around to get the feel for prices and then deciding what you are happy to pay. In general, if the vendor follows you out of the shop it means that there's still scope for bargaining; if they don't it's probably safe to assume that you've pushed the price as low as it can go.

Café in Old Bedesten

Inner Market

Right at the heart of the complex, the İç Bedesten (also called the Old or Cevahir Bedesten) was the original bazaar dating back to 1461 and the reign of **Sultan Mehmed the Conqueror**. At one time it was where male slaves were sold. Today it's crammed with glittering antique and jewelry shops and is still sealed off at night behind heavy metal-bound wooden doors. It's one of the most atmospheric parts of the bazaar even if you can only afford to window-shop.

What's in a name?

The bazaar mainly sells items that are likely to be of interest to visitor and to judge by the accounts of past travelers this has probably always been the case. However what visitors want to buy has certainly changed over the years and the names of the different streets provide a vivid record of the favored purchases of the past. For example, **Kalpakçılar Caddesi** may now be lined with jeweler's shops but it was once the place to come t buy hats. **Terziler Caddesi** is where the tailors hung out, **Yağlıkçılar Caddesi** is where the sellers of oil lamps congregated, while **Fesciler Sokak** was home to the fez sellers and the **Kürkcüler Çarşısı** to the furriers.

Sandal Bedesten

The second "square" inside the bazaar is the Sandal Bedesten, close to the Nuruosmaniye Gate, which probably dates back to the early 16th century and used to house sellers of luxury fabrics and precious stones; the word **"sandal"** refers to a heavy, expensive cloth that was once produced in Bursa. Today it's much less cramped than the İç Bedesten, which makes it easier to appreciate its ancient architecture and the pleasing brickwork of its **20 domes**. These days it sells lots of pashminas and knock-off textile products and "brand-name" leather bags.

Gates

The bazaar has eleven doors which each open to neighbouring districts: Beyazıt, Çarşıkapı, Çuhacıhan, Kuyumcular, Mahmutpaşa, Nuruosmaniye, Örücüler, Sepetçihan, Takkeciler, Tavukpazarı and Zenneciler.

Bazaar landmarks

For those worried about getting lost there are a couple of specific landmarks in the bazaar. One is a pretty two-storey kiosk that was originally built as the **Çukur Muhallebicisi** (pudding shop) in c. 1850 but now houses the predictable jewelry shop. Another is the delicate wooden "minaret" of the **Cafer Ağa Mosque** which juts out into the alleyways.

Old printing stone showing Virgin Mary and Christ Child

Sahaflar (Secondhand Book) Market

For bibliophiles, the so-called Secondhand Book Market, set round a pretty courtyard between the main shops and the **Beyazıt Mosque** (leave the bazaar via the Beyazıt Gate to find it), is especially interesting. These days almost all the books on sale are brand-new textbooks aimed at students from neighboring Istanbul University although there are also some books of touristic interest and a handful of secondhand novels. At the back of the market look out for some heavy engraved stone plates preserved behind glass. They were used by 19th-century printers from nearby **Bab-ı Ali** where most of the city's printers had their shops.

Tomb of Mahmud Paşa

Mahmud Paşa Mosque

Mahmud Paşa Mosque

Just outside the bazaar stands one of Istanbul's oldest mosques built in 1462 for Sultan Mehmed the Conqueror's Grand Vizier **Mahmud Paşa**, widely regarded as one of the wisest men ever to have held that office (which didn't stop him dying eventually as a prisoner in Yedikule, see p. 158). The building still follows in the tradition established by the Ottomans in Bursa and consists of a colonnaded portico that gives onto a courtyard and then to a rectangular hall divided into two sections, each with their own dome. Rooms on each side appear to have provided accommodation for itinerant dervishes.

But perhaps the most interesting thing to see here is actually the octagonal **tomb of Mahmud Paşa** that lies behind the mosque, unfortunately inaccessible to visitors who must peer through the fence. It's completely covered with blue and turquoise **İznik tiles** so that it looks as if it has accidentally strayed here from Iran or Central Asia.

Nuruosmaniye Mosque with Hagia Sophia Mosque, Topkapı Palace and Çamlıca Hill rising behind it.

Nuruosmaniye Mosque

Visitors to the Grand Bazaar usually pay no attention to the “Light of Osman” as they pass through its courtyard. It overlooks the city from the seven-hilled Istanbul’s second hill in all its glory. This colossal mosque complex, which meets you on the left when you come out of the gate of the Grand Bazaar named after the mosque, was built by Sultan Mahmud I and Sultan Osman III. It is also the first mosque built in Istanbul in the European baroque style. This group of buildings, designed by the architect Mustafa Ağa, initiated a new era in Ottoman architecture. Their authenticity is also proved by some original Ottoman touches. The Social complex includes a mosque, madrasah, a shrine, a library and a fountain. The influence of the baroque style can mostly be seen in the library, shrine and fountains. The entrance with a few steps and the long ramp reaching out to the gathering place of the sultans are remarkable at first sight. The porphry sarcophagus and the library in the courtyard are interesting. Some of the columns you see in the courtyard were brought from an old church in Pergamon. The mosque, which is listed on the temporary list of the UNESCO World Heritage Site, was restored in 2009. During the restoration work, which was restarted in 2010, a cistern and a well for storing the water coming from the mosque and the Grand Bazaar was unearthed 8.5 meters below ground. It was discovered that bored piles were used in these buildings, which are still in use for stabilizing the ground in accordance with the requirements of the earthquake regulations. This feature, as befits the reputation of Nuruosmaniye, was a first in its time. The Nuruosmaniye Cellar was opened for visitors for the first time with an exhibition in 2018.

Büyük Yeni Han

Küçük Yeni Han

Crumbling bird-house on Küçük Yeni Han

Tower of Eirene from Büyük Valide Han

Exploring the hans

In the winding back streets behind the Grand Bazaar it's still possible to explore a series of old hans where in the past merchants would have been able to put up for the night with their animals and also sell their merchandise. Most are two storeys high and set round courtyards, with most of the modern action going on downstairs where the animals might have been stabled. In general they tend to be neglected and soot-blackened, although some have been at least partially restored.

If you leave the Grand Bazaar via the **Mahmutpaşa Gate** you will be able to walk down to the Spice Market along a route that takes you past many of the city's oldest hans. Walk along Mahmutpaşa Yokuşu and then turn left along Tarakçılar Caddesi. At the end of it you will see the huge **Büyük Valide Han,** built by Murad IV's powerful mother **Kösem Valide Sultan** (see p. 014) in 1651; in its prime it could accommodate up to 3,000 traveling traders. There's a Shiite mosque in the center and in the 16th century one of Istanbul's first printing presses was housed here. The han's three courtyards have become very dilapidated, especially since the use of the old weaving machines was banned in 2007, but if you can get up there, the view from the rooftop is absolutely extraordinary, taking in the Bosphorus, the Golden Horn and much of the Old City. From here you will also be able to examine the adjoining Byzantine **Tower of Eirene,** which was badly damaged and cut down in size by an earthquake in 1926. The building currently serves as an art gallery. The third courtyard of the han used to be called the **Sair (Foreigners) Han** because it was inhabited by Persians. Its name has now been corrupted to **Sağır (Deaf) Han**. Deep inside it the remains of what appears to be a **Byzantine chapel** go completely disregarded.

A little further down if you turn right back onto Mahmutpaşa Yokuşu you'll come across the **Küçük Yeni Han**, built in the 18th century with birdhouses on the walls and a mosque on the top. Keep walking down and turn right onto Çarkçılar Sokak. On the right-hand side of the road is the **Büyük Yeni Han (Big New Han)**, built out of brick and stone in 1764 in a style that had probably changed very little since Byzantine times. Facing it across the street is the **Kürkçü (Furriers) Han,** thought to date back to the 15th century when it was built for Sultan Mehmed II's Grand Vizier Mahmud Paşa.

If you turn left onto Mahmutpaşa Hamamı Sokak, then left again on to Vasıf Çınar Caddesi and right onto Sabuncu Han Sokak you should eventually arrive at the back of the Spice Market (see p. 214) where there are plenty more opportunities to shop.

Mahmutpaşa Lane

Around the Old Seraglio

Beyazıt Mosque and Around

012 Often overlooked by shoppers in a rush to get to the Grand Bazaar, the early 16th-century Beyazıt Mosque is one of the city's finest classical mosques, with an exquisite courtyard that makes a pleasant oasis amid the commercialism. Nearby stand the imposing entrance to Istanbul University and the Serasker Tower from which men would keep watch for fires.

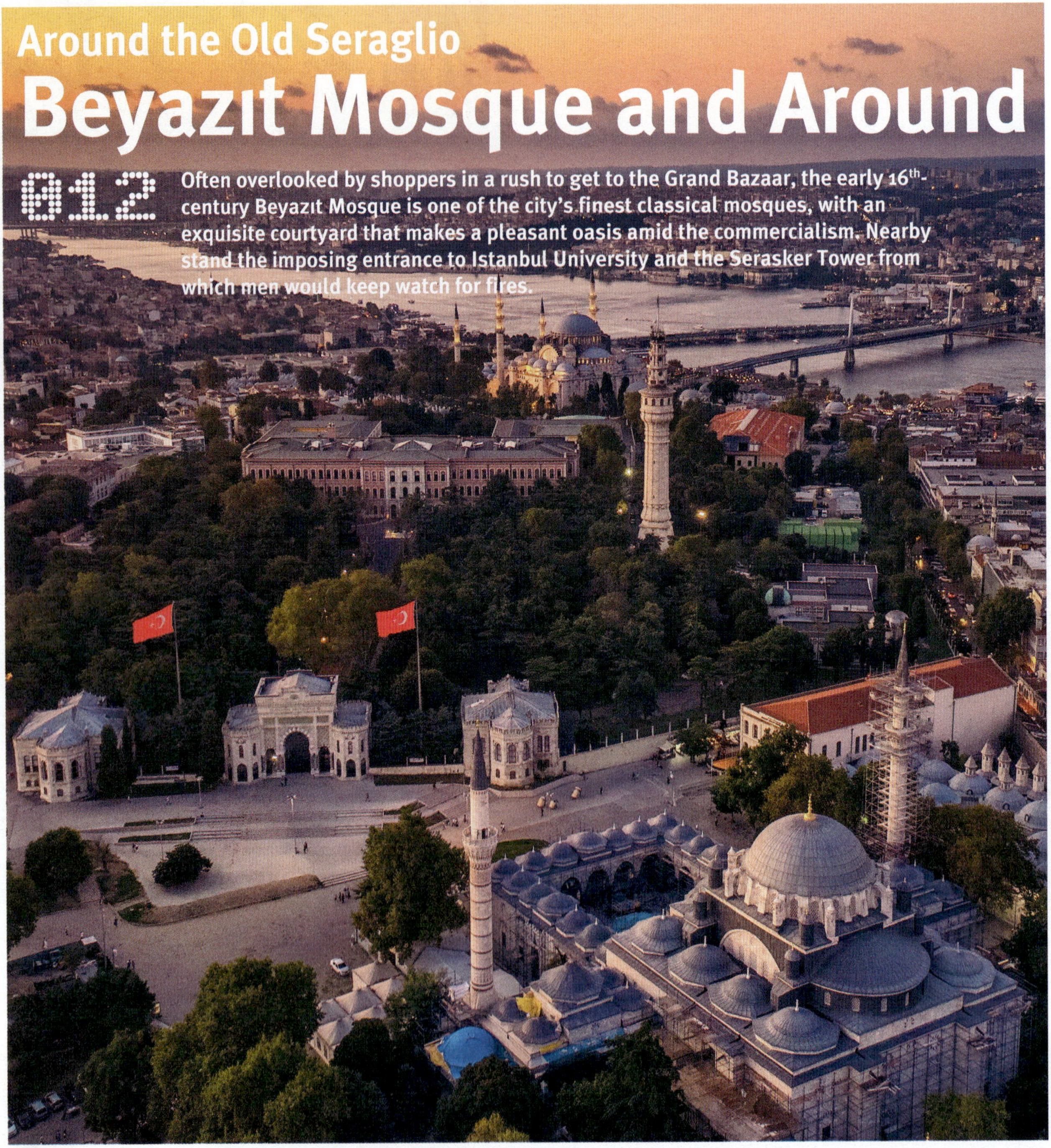

In the 4th century the largest square in Constantinople was the **Forum Tauri**, which was named after the statue of a bull that was its centerpiece. In 393 it was redesigned by the Emperor Theodosius and renamed the **Forum Theodosius** in his honor. Prominent features of the new square, which was surrounded by grand porticoed buildings, were a column rather like Trajan's Column in Rome and one of the huge triumphal arches so beloved of Roman emperors, in this case almost certainly surmounted by statues of Theodosius and his sons Honorius and Arcadius. The forum covered much the same area as the modern **Beyazıt Square**, a sprawling, somewhat featureless space that is always busy with people coming and going between the **Beyazıt Mosque** and **Istanbul University**.

Emperor Theodosius

Remains of triumphal arch from Forum Tauri

Sultan Bayezid II

Bayezid Mosque

The Bayezid Mosque was built between 1501 and 1506 for Beyazid II, the son of Mehmed the Conqueror and was the work of **Yakub-Şah İbn Sultan-Şah**, a little known but probably Turkish architect who appears to have taken Hagia Sophia (Ayasofya) as his model, while adding to the plan all the usual accoutrements of a mosque complex: hamam, madrasah, mektep (school) and imaret (soup kitchen). Although it postdates the **Fatih Mosque**, that mosque was almost completely destroyed by an earthquake in 1766, leaving the Beyazıt as the oldest of Istanbul's big classical mosques to survive intact. So although when people consider the city's greatest mosques they usually think of Sinan, it was actually a far less well-known architect who laid the groundwork for him.

For most visitors the enclosed courtyard, reminiscent of others attached to the Şehzade Mosque (see p. 103) and Yeni Valide Mosque (see p. 500), makes a peaceful contrast with the hustle of the nearby Grand Bazaar. Twenty huge columns of porphyry, verd antique and granite support arches striped in red and cream to create domed porticoes surrounding a fine ablutions fountain. Unusually, an east-west extension of the mosque with a minaret at each end creates something of the impression of the narthexes in Byzantine churches, while aisles run along each side of the main hall of the mosque in imitation of Hagia Sophia. The two minarets are also inlaid with geometric patterns in terracotta.

Outside the mosque peddlers hawk prayer beads, perfumes and other Islamic paraphernalia beneath venerable plane trees while pigeons gather in search of tidbits. In the graveyard behind the mosque lies the beautifully decorated **tomb of Bayezid II** and the far humbler one of his daughter Selçuk Hatun. Here too are buried the Tanzimat-era Grand Vizier **Koca Mustafa Reşid Paşa** (1800-58), whose corner tomb can be identified by the fine green grilles over its windows and the architect **Kemaleddin Bey** (1870-1927). Between the graveyard and the main body of the mosque is the mosque's domed **primary school** building that now houses a Koran school.

"(The Bayezid Mosque) a work of the very first importance, both in its excellence as a building and in its historic importance in the development of Turkish architecture."

Strolling Through Istanbul **by Hilary Sumner-Boyd & John Freely, 1972**

Museum of Calligraphy

Restored in 2009, what was originally the madrasah of the Beyazıt Mosque on the western side of the square now houses the Museum of Calligraphy. Provided it's open, it showcases examples of the different types of calligraphy used in Ottoman times and contains a model of a teacher instructing pupils in the art. The exhibits are housed in what were once the *hücres* or cells of the madrasah ringing a peaceful courtyard.

Tel: 0212 527 58 51, closed Sundays and Mondays

Turkey's first portrait painter

Feyhaman Duran (1886-1970) is usually credited as Turkey's first portait painter even though his work also encompassed landscapes, still lifes and even images of animals. Trained in Paris, Duran went on to teach at the Fine Arts Academy which is where he met his wife and muse, Güzin Hanım, with whom he worked for the rest of his life. You can visit the small wooden house that Güzin inherited from her calligrapher father just a short walk away. The house, which could be subdivided Ottoman-style into public and private areas, contains yet more of Duran's work, including a stunning portrait of Güzin just before they married which hangs in the bedroom. Across a small garden their atelier is still set up as if they might walk in and pick up their brushes at any moment.

Istanbul University

The largest of the city's universities, Istanbul University is also the longest lived as an institution since it can be traced back as an idea to the reign of **Sultan Mehmed the Conqueror** when it was housed in the eight madrasah attached to the **Fatih Mosque** (see p. 114). The madrasah attached to the Beyazıt, Selim I and Süleymaniye Mosques also formed precursors for the university's different faculties. Like most of the institutions of the Ottoman Empire, the "university", at first called **Istanbul Darülfünun**, was in great need of reform by the 19th century. However, the necessary steps could not be taken until after the declaration of the Turkish Republic in 1923 when it was rehoused in what had been the **Seraskerat**, or Ministry of War, at the back of Beyazıt Square. Renamed Istanbul University in 1933, it is now accommodated in buildings designed in 1866 by the French architect Marie-Auguste Antoine **Bourgeois** which are accessed via a magnificent Neo-Renaissance arch. The university has two Nobel laureates among its alumni: Prof. Dr. Aziz Sancar and Orhan Pamuk. Famous alumni include the novelist Ahmet Hamdi Tanpınar, the poet Orhan Veli, the musician Mercan Dede, the İstanbul Metropolitan Municipality Mayor Ekrem İmamoğlu, the doctor Türkan Saylan and the politicians Abdullah Gül, Yıldırım Akbulut and David Ben-Gurion.

Auguste Bourgeois

There is nothing to stop you taking a stroll round the university's leafy grounds. Walk right to the back to inspect the **Beyazıt (Serasker) Tower** (see below) and for a fine view of the **Süleymaniye Mosque**. Here too you'll find a bust commemorating **Turan Emeksiz**, a 20-year-old student who died in Beyazıt Square during the unrest that led up to the coup of 1960. The area in front of the university is sometimes the scene of demonstrations.

Beyazıt State Library

Beyazıt State Library

Immediately opposite the mosque stands what was once its soup kitchen cum caravanserai, but which was converted to house a library by **Sultan Abdülhamid II** in 1832. Since 1884 it has been home to the Beyazıt State Library, which means that casual visitors can no longer see inside it. In 2009 it was completely restored.

Professors' House
Istanbul University

Moving palace

Istanbul University Rectorate

The Byzantine emperors chose to make their home in the area that is now **Sultanahmet** (see p. 043), moving to the **Blachernae Palace** at the Ayvansaray end of the land walls (see p. 151) after the Fourth Crusaders wreaked havoc on the city in 1204. During the fighting of 1453 Blachernae Palace too was virtually destroyed and so the victorious **Sultan Mehmed II** struck camp behind the old Forum of Theodosius where his first Istanbul home, the **Old Palace (Eski Saray)**, was constructed. The sultan commuted between here and another **Old Palace in Edirne** while Topkapı Palace was being built. Then he gradually moved out, leaving the palace buildings to become a sort of retirement home for the wives and concubines of deceased sultans; not surprisingly, it became known as **"the Palace of Tears"**. The Old Palace stood in the grounds of what is now Istanbul University and beneath what is now the Süleymaniye Mosque. The buildings were finally demolished in 1866 to make space for the Ministry of War.

Beyazıt (Serasker) Tower

In the grounds of the university stands this curvaceous 85-meter-high tower that dominates the skyline for miles around. Fire was a perennial problem in old Istanbul (see p. 227) and the city was equipped with four towers from which men would watch out for flames and then raise the alarm. Three wooden towers had already burnt down before the current stone version was built by the architect Senekerim Balyan in 1828 during the reign of the reformist sultan Mahmud II. When the firewatchers saw flames they lowered baskets during the day or lit lamps at night – the number of baskets or lamps indicated the location of the fire. The fire towers play a leading role in Jason Goodwin's crime novel, "The Janissary Tree".

Beyazıt Hamam

Kuyucu Murad Paşa Medrese

Beyazıt Hamam

Half-heartedly restored in 2008, this double hamam on the main road formed part of the Beyazıt Mosque complex and played an important role in history as the place where rebels organized by the Albanian boiler-stoker **Patrona Halil** plotted to overthrow Sultan Ahmed III and his powerful Grand Vizier Damat İbrahim Paşa in 1730 (see p. 265). It houses Turkish Bath Culture Museum.

Up a few steps behind the hamam is the delightful **Hasan Paşa Medrese (Seminary)**, built by the architect Mustafa Çelebi in 1745 for Grand Vizier Tokatlı Hasan Paşa. On its façade can be seen one of the city's finest carved **birdhouses** shaped like a mosque with minarets. There's also a particularly delightful **sebil** (water dispensary, see p. 083) on one corner with a calligraphic inscription by Hocazade Ahmed Efendi. It now houses Istanbul University's Institute of Turkish Studies.

If you continue past Hasan Paşa Medrese and then turn left along Vezneciler Sokak towards the Şehzade Mosque you will pass on the left the **Kuyucu Murad Paşa Medrese**, built in 1606 and most conspicuous for the pollution-besmirched sebil (water dispensary) visible through the gates of Istanbul University's Literature Faculty building. Small shops and street stalls largely obscure the wall of the madrasah to which it is attached. **Murad Paşa** acquired his delightful nickname, "the pit-digger", as a result of the large number of graves that had to be dug to bury all the Anatolian rebels he had killed.

Tel: 0212 440 00 00 - 16120, closed Mondays

Hasan Paşa Medrese

Turkish Bath Culture Museum

Simkeşhane

Back on the main road the **Orhan Kemal Provincial Library** is now housed inside the restored Simkeşhane, a building that started life as a mint during the reign of Sultan Mehmed II but became a base for silver workers when the business of pressing coins was moved to the **Darphane** in Topkapı Palace. As so often, the original structure fell victim to fire and was rebuilt in 1707 by Rabia Gülnüş Ümmetullah, the wife of Sultan Mehmed IV. That building was in turn partially destroyed during road widening in the 1950s.

On the pavement immediately in front of the Simkeşhane stand huge chunks of marble, the last surviving reminders of the **Forum Tauri**. Some of them, including pieces carved with peacock-eye patterns, have been re-erected to suggest the lost triumphal arch that stood nearby.

Hasan Paşa Han

A little way further along Ordu Caddesi (the continuation of Divan Yolu) stand the shattered remains of the **Hasan Paşa Han**, built in 1745 as the Süpürgeciler (Broom Sellers) Han but nowadays named after the grand vizier who commissioned it. Much of its façade was also lost to road widening in the 1950s. The shops inside it mainly sell leather goods.

Hidden Jewels

Laleli and Aksaray

013

Interspersed with the cheap shopping opportunities down the back streets there are a few reminders of the grander past, including the Laleli and Valide Sultan mosque complexes and a couple of ramshackle old hans that have been given new life as mini shopping malls. The Bodrum Mosque was also created out of a cute little Byzantine church.

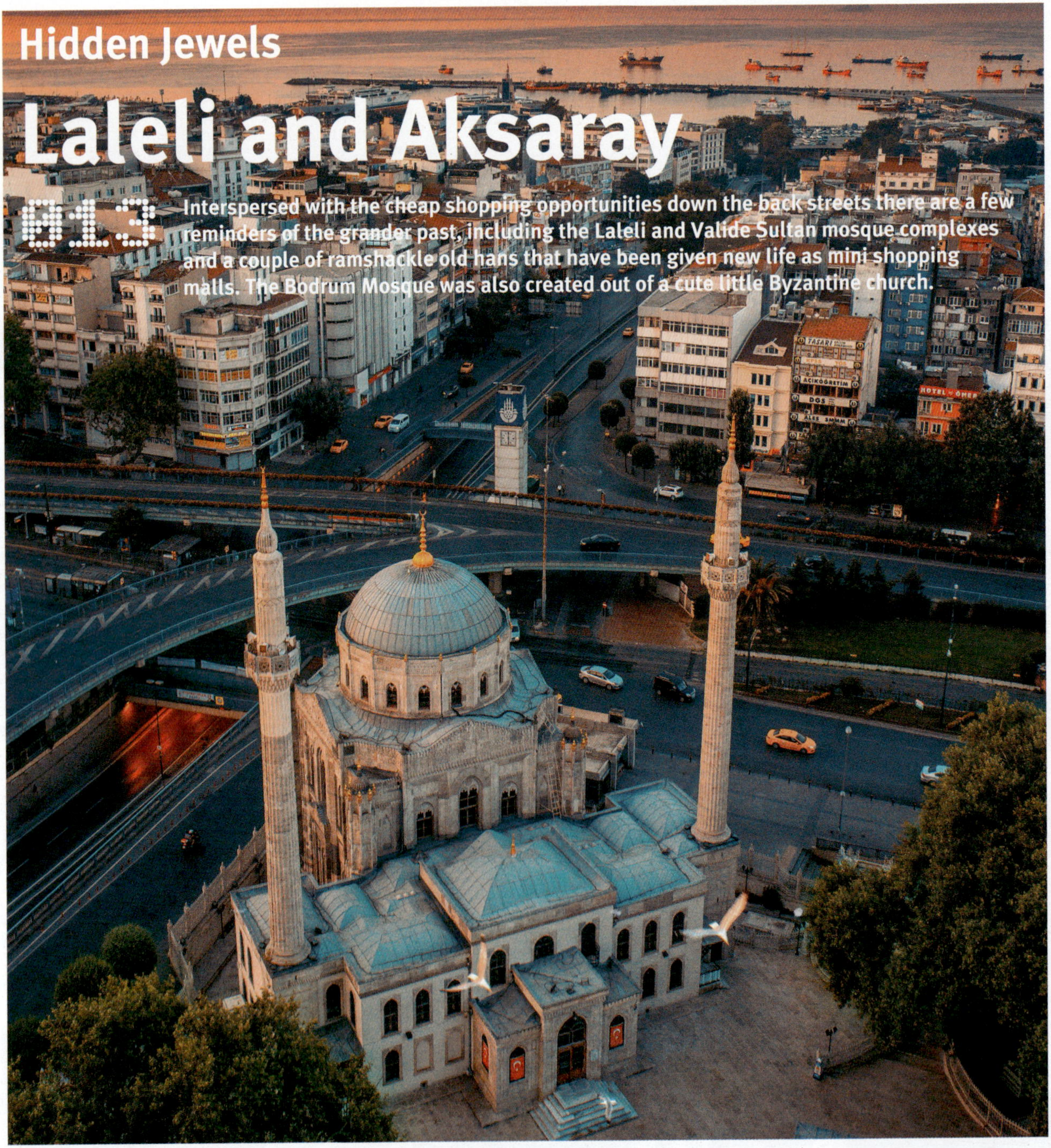

Once upon a time this would have been a lovely part of town adorned with graceful mansions, busy hans and elaborate mosque complexes. Today sadly all that remains of that beauty is Laleli's pretty name which means "with tulips". The name completely belies the area's built-up modern appearance but is said to have been taken from that of a pretty fountain in the courtyard of the local mosque. That in turn seems to have been named after **Laleli Baba**, a teacher to **Sultan Mustafa III**. Today it is known for its cheap textile shops, often staffed by Russians and for its Iranian community.

Building bearing Star of David

Mustafa III

After a terrible fire in Fatih in 1918, survivors were rehoused in the **Tayyare (Harikzedegan) Apartments**, a complex of flats and shops designed by Kemaleddin Bey that was the first building in Istanbul to use reinforced concrete. Walking back towards Beyazıt you pass the austere building that now houses the **Literature and Science Faculty** of Istanbul University and which was designed by **Sedad Hakkı Eldem** and **Emin Onat** between 1942 and 1944. Eldem was also responsible for the award-winning Social Security office buildings in Zeyrek (see p. 110).

Heading west from Laleli, Aksaray was once the site of the **Bovis Forum**, one of the most important squares in Byzantium, but took its modern name after **İshak Paşa**, Grand Vizier to Sultan Mehmed II, resettled a large number of people from Aksaray in central Anatolia here in the 15th century. It's now mainly known as a chaotic transport interchange, but with a lot of restaurants serving south-eastern Turkish food nearby.

Tayyare Apartments 1

Istanbul University Literature and Science Faculty

Laleli Mosque

"The visitor (to the Laleli Mosque)... is immediately charmed by its elegance and the harmony of its interior."

Les Peintres du Bosphore
by A. Boppe, 1911

Büyük Taş Han

Laleli Mosque 2

Restored in 2009, the elegant brick-and-stone-striped Laleli Mosque complex was built between 1759 and 1763 in baroque style by architect **Mehmed Tahir Ağa** for **Sultan Mustafa III** (r. 1757-74). It was the last such complex to have been built in the city (later mosques lack the associated buildings that used to accompany any new mosque); of the complex, the sebil (water dispensary) and imaret (soup kitchen) still survive, along with a türbe (tomb) housing the remains of Mustafa III and his son Selim III. The restored **Büyük Taş Han** (Big Stone Han), originally called the Çukur Çeşme Hanı (Sunken Fountain Han) is also thought to have been attached to the mosque. It's round the corner in Fethi Bey Caddesi and houses a pleasant teahouse as well as a restaurant in underground stables that started life as a cistern.

Laleli Mosque stands on sloping ground with a large basement full of clothes shops forming a platform for it. On the exterior walls of the tomb look out for several small bird-houses. It supposedly stands on the site of the brothel where the Empress Theodora started her working life. The mosque looks especially wonderful when floodlit at night.

Bird house

Myrelaion Church (Bodrum Mosque) 3

Between 920 and 922 the cute little **Church of the Holy Anointing Oil** was built beside the palace of the **Emperor Romanos Lecapenus I** (r. 920-44) whose wife, Theophano, probably turned it into a monastery to which she retreated at the end of her life. It was converted into a mosque in the 15th century by **Mesih Ali Paşa**, a descendant of the Paleologues who had led the Ottomans in an unsuccessful attack on Rhodes in 1479. It was called the Bodrum (Basement) Mosque because of the cellar beneath the church that had made it possible to raise its height to that of the adjacent palace. This may have been circular in design, hence the concrete circle marked out in the empty space beside the mosque. In fact, this place is a **rotunda** which was later turned into a cistern. It is one of the earliest buildings of Byzantine Istanbul which has survived to this day. We don't know the exact reason why it was built but the building, whose construction dates back to the 5th century, is quite similar to the **Pantheon** in Rome in size and form. While Romanos Lekapenos was building a palace and the **Myrelaion Monastery** here in the 10th century, this circular structure, the dome of which had probably already been demolished, was converted into a cistern to enable the new structures to be built on top of the cistern. This hidden treasure, which is now empty and which I hope will be valued as a unique example of its kind, has more recently been used as a bazaar.

Cistern

Valide Sultan Mosque on old postcard

Valide Sultan Mosque 4

Hemmed in by the busy Ordu Caddesi and Atatürk Bulvarı, the Valide Sultan Mosque, designed by the Italian architect **Montani** (or possibly by Sarkis and Agop Balyan) for **Pertevniyal Valide Sultan**, the mother of **Sultan Abdülaziz**, in 1871, deserves to have a much more attractive setting. It is not generally thought to be a particularly fine example of architecture. However, the long wall, standing in a dip, into which is set a grand gateway and four **fountains** is very striking and would be even more so were the fountains ever to run with water again. The mosque was restored in 2009. Round the corner on Atatürk Bulvarı the **Pertevniyal High School** is housed in a building dating back to 1872.

Fountains beside entrance to Valide Sultan Mosque

Koca Ragıp Paşa Library

Mehmed Tahir Ağa was also responsible for the complex built in 1762 across the road from the Laleli Mosque for **Koca Ragıp Paşa**, the erudite Grand Vizier to **Mustafa III**. Ragıp Paşa was a poet who wrote many of the verses that adorn the city's fountains. Thought to have been one of the greatest men to hold the office of grand vizier, he is buried in the courtyard of the library, which is currently inaccessible but can be recognized by the glorious swirling calligraphy above its entrance, now well below street level.

Pertevniyal High School

Murad Paşa Mosque ⑤

Too often overlooked by commuters in their rush to get between the Yusufpaşa and Aksaray stations, this distinctively striped mosque was built in 1473, just 20 years after the conquest of Istanbul. Internally it turns out to be much longer than would be anticipated from the exterior. The fine inscription over the entrance is thought to be the handiwork of **Ali Sofi**, the calligrapher who also created the wonderful inscription over the gateway leading into **Topkapı Palace.**

Interior of Fenari İsa Mosque

Church of Constantine Lips (Fenari İsa Mosque) ⑥

Now here's a building with a really peculiar name! A man called **Constantine Lips** really did exist and worked at the courts of Emperors **Leo the Wise** (886-912) and **Constantine Porphyrogenitus** (913-59). The five-apsed church that he chose to build on this site right beside what is now hectic Vatan Caddesi has been standing since 907 and was dedicated to Theotokos Panachrantos, the Immaculate Mother of God. Originally it was part of a monastic complex. Unusually, it has four chapels on the roof clustered around the dome. Attached to it is a later **Church of St John the Baptist** founded by Theodora, the wife of Michael VIII Palaeologus (1259-82). This church had three apses, one of which it had appropriated from the older church. In all, then, the double church boasted an extraordinary array of **seven apses** of which only six remain today. The church was converted into a dervish lodge by **Fenari Ali Efendi** in the 15th century and was later used by the eminent preacher, Sheikh İsa, hence the compound name "Fenari İsa Mosque".

Motif in masonry

A little further west along Vatan Caddesi is a little noticed work of Sinan dating back to 1549, the **Yavuz Sultan Selim Medrese**, with a row of jaunty chimneys, that is currently used as a clinic. Nearby, don't miss a small stone schoolhouse obscuring the **tomb of Şah Huban Kadın**, one of Selim I's daughters who died in 1572. It's another work of Sinan. Were you to cut south through the back streets at this point you should come out close to the **Çapa Anatolian High School** whose extravagant turquoise-tiled façade is a fine example of First National Architecture, albeit by an unknown architect.

The Story Of Laleli Mosque

Sultan Mustafa III had not given his name to any of the mosques he had had built, but he later decided to give his name to the newest mosque and social complex. But he was unfortunate. The Sultan happened to pay a visit to Laleli Baba, who was living in the neighbourhood during the construction. After an argument broke out between them, Laleli Baba became sick and the doctors couldn't cure the disease. The Sultan took action to make up to Laleli Baba, giving his name, rather than his own name as he had intended, to the social complex. From that day on, not only the complex he built, but the whole neighbourhood, were named after Laleli Baba.

Sofular Hamam

Go for a deep cleansing experience at the **bath** which form part of the 16th-century Sofular Mosque complex near the Aksaray tram stop. Twin buildings serve men and women separately as they have done since the 17th century when travel writer Evliya Çelebi identified these baths as especially popular with local notables.

---

www.sofularhamami.com
Tel: 0212 521 37 59

The Secret of the Lost Foot

The most exciting finding unearthed during excavations in the Myrelaion Rotunda was a piece of sculpture made of porphyry stone. Placed in a corner in the exterior of the Church of San Marco in Venice, the portrait of the **Four Tetrarchs** (Four Emperors) was missing an emperor's foot which had been completed using different material. This little piece of statue challenged the argument that this statue had been brought from Rome. Like many other examples, it was ascertained that the Tetrarchs had been brought to Venice from Constantinople during the **Latin Siege** in the aftermath of the Crusades. This piece is now on display at the Archeological Museum (see p. 020).

Where Slaves Were Sold

Cerrahpaşa and Around

014

Fancy exploring a part of the city with lots of grand mosques and hardly any visitors? Then head straight for the area around Cerrahpaşa Hospital to discover a cluster of forgotten masterpieces including the Haseki and Hekimoğlu Ali Paşa Mosques. Here too are the imposing early 20th-century Bulgur Palas and the remains of the Arcadius Column dating back to Roman times. During the Ottoman era this was where slaves were bought and sold.

Original appearance of Column of Arcadius

Despite its position inside the walled part of the city, the area around Cerrahpaşa Hospital is rarely visited by tourists which is a shame because it's almost as richly endowed with beautiful old mosque complexes as Üsküdar (see p. 498) and can be accessed by taking a quick detour west from busy Aksaray (see p. 086). Cerrahpaşa takes its name from **Cerrah (Surgeon) Mehmed Paşa**, a barber who had the honor to perform the circumcision for the future **Sultan Mehmed III** and was rewarded with the title of surgeon. Although there's no longer anything to show for it the area around the Column of Arcadius was once home to the **Avrat Pazarı (Women's Market)** where slaves were sold throughout much of the Ottoman era. To find the area get out of the tram at Aksaray and then head south-west along Cerrahpaşa Caddesi – to find this look for the small 18th-century **Ebu Bekir Paşa school** building on the corner of Namık Kemal Caddesi.

The Sale of Circassian Captives to a Turkish Paşa by Sir William Allan, 1816

The white slave trade

Unlikely as it may sound, many of the people who rose to positions of authority in the Ottoman Empire, even the grand viziers, started out as slaves, either captured by pirates or collected almost like tax from the different provinces of the empire during what was called the ***devşirme*** (gathering). Most slaves had been brought up as Christians but converted to Islam on arrival in Istanbul. Even the women of the harem were effectively slaves (called "cariyes"); the **Valide Sultan (Queen Mother)** was given her freedom on the death of her husband. Many of them would have been sold at the Avrat Pazarı, the Women's Slave Market that took place in what is now Cerrahpaşa. Amongst the famous women of the harem who seem to have passed through that market were **Roxelana** and **Kösem Sultan** and **Mihrişah Sultan**, the mother of Sultan Selim III. The Market was closed in 1847, although slaves continued to be sold elsewhere in the city until 1922.

"Slaves varied in price according to their age, qualities, or defects. Scanty hair, bad teeth, a dwarfish figure considerably reduced their value. Flat feet were believed to bring bad luck..."

Three Centuries: Family Chronicles of Turkey and Egypt
Emine Foat Tugay, 1963

Base of Column of Arcadius squeezed between two buildings

Column of Arcadius 1

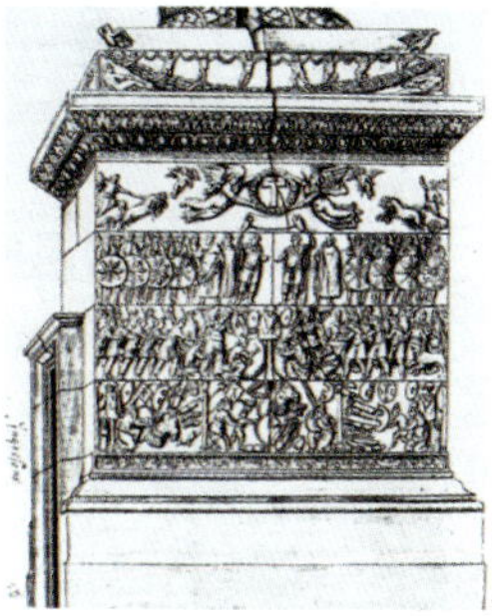

If you turn right along Haseki Kadın Sokağı from Cerrahpaşa Caddesi you will stumble upon a curious relic of the Byzantine city. What is now a densely built-up area near the Haseki Hürrem Mosque was once the **Forum of Arcadius** where the Emperor Arcadius erected a column similar to Trajan's Column in Rome to trumpet his victories in 402 on the summit of the Seventh Hill. In 421 his son Theodosius II had an equestrian statue of his father placed on top of it, but this fell down and was destroyed by an earthquake in 704. In 1715 the column itself was demolished for fear that it would collapse on neighboring properties leaving only the tall base which is now sandwiched in between a house and a car park and largely concealed by a tree. Later, the surrounding area became the site of the **Avrat Pazarı** (the Women's Slave Market).

"This column is covered with reliefs from top to bottom representing some expedition of Arcadius..."

***Turkish Letters*, Ghislain Ogier de Busbecq, 1555**

Bulgur Palas 2

If you turn left off Cerrahpaşa Caddesi along Haseki Kadın Sokağı you will come to a magnificent example of First National Architecture dating back to 1912 and partly the handiwork of the Italian architect **Giulio Mongeri**. It was built for the Bolu MP **Mehmed Habib Bey** who had made his money in cracked wheat, hence its name, the Bulgur Palas (Cracked-Wheat Palace). The tower offers a magnificent view of the Sea of Marmara, a view that passed into the ownership of the **Ottoman Bank** in the 1920s. For many years the building was used to store the bank archives, but these have now been moved into the Ottoman Bank Museum (see p. 274). This impressive building, which was under the ownership of Garanti Bank for a while, was purchased by Istanbul Metropolitan Municipality in 2021 to be organized as a cultural center.

Cerrahpaşa Mosque 3 4

Standing in a pleasant small garden and dating back to 1593 is this graceful, porticoed work of Davud Ağa who succeeded Sinan as chief architect, with, right beside it, the hexagonal tomb of the surgeon-barber himself. Across the street stands the **Gevher Sultan Misafirhanesi (Guesthouse)** built in 1568 for the wife of Admiral Piyale Paşa. It's an attractive small building set round a courtyard and marred only by the brash silver-plating of its domes.

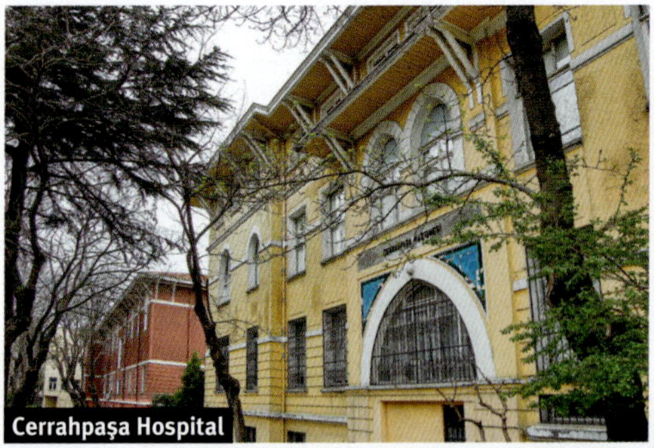
Cerrahpaşa Hospital

Bayrampaşa Complex 5

Walk along Haseki Kadın Sokağı and you will come to the Bayrampaşa complex which is split in two by the road. A son-in-law of Sultan Ahmed I and the man who gave his name to Istanbul's western district of Bayrampaşa, **Bayram Paşa** was Grand Vizier to **Sultan Murad IV** and died during the successful campaign to recapture Baghdad in 1638. In 1634 this delightful cluster of buildings was erected to be his memorial with his enormous tomb as its centerpiece. On the right-hand side of the road stands the **madrasah** (seminary) with shops running along its ground floor and chimneys jutting up from the roofs. On the left-hand side of the road a beautiful **sebil** (water dispensary) sits in front of the **tomb** whose lovely wooden porch is on the verge of collapse. A domed mescit and porticoed tekke (dervish lodge) used as a women's clinic stand in an attractive small garden.

Haseki Hürrem Complex 6 7

Heading west along Haseki Caddesi you'll come to the impressive Haseki Hürrem complex, which is also sliced in two by the road. Better known as **Roxelana**, the much-loved wife of **Sultan Süleyman the Magnificent**, Haseki Hürrem was an extremely powerful woman (see p. 014), so it's hardly surprising that the mosque complex that she endowed in 1539 is the third largest in the city after the Fatih and Süleymaniye complexes. Unfortunately the **mosque** is stranded in the corner of a rather cramped and uninviting courtyard. Immediately across the road, though, the **madrasah** (seminary) is much more impressive even though the fine panels of İznik tiles that once sat in the lunettes above the windows have been moved into the **Istanbul Archeological Museums** (see p. 020) for safekeeping. Beside it stands the small two-storey schoolhouse while behind it are a many-chimneyed **imaret** (soup kitchen) which was one of the last in the city to provide free food to the poor and an impressive octagonal **hospital** which now stands abandoned, over-ambitious plans to convert the complex into a hotel having fallen by the wayside. Perhaps surprisingly, Roxelana was not buried here but beside her husband in the grounds of the **Süleymaniye Mosque**. The complex is long overdue for restoration. The complex was restored in 2012.

Medrese

Davud Paşa Mosque 8 9

If you stroll along Hekimoğlu Ali Paşa Caddesi and turn left along Davut Paşa Medresesi Sokağı you will come to an older mosque built for **Davud Paşa**, grand vizier to **Sultan Bayezid II**, in 1485. With a fine five-arched portico, a conspicuously shallow dome and side chambers where wandering dervishes could pass the night, it's a particularly attractive building with Davud Paşa's tomb in the graveyard behind it. Across the road the **madrasah (seminary)** stands in ruins despite being one of the oldest in the city; there are Byzantine columns that grace its overgrown courtyard.

Column capital in medrese

Fatih İbrahim Paşa Medrese

If you continue south along Davut Paşa Medresesi Sokağı and then turn right along Kocamustafapaşa Caddesi past the Davut Paşa High School which is housed in a 20th-century building on the site of the school attached to the mosque complex you will pass Cerrahpaşa Hospital and come, on the left, to the Fatih İbrahim Paşa Medrese, a work of Sinan which was crudely restored/rebuilt in 2009. It stands on the site of a 14th-century church that was turned into a mosque c.1560 by a eunuch called İbrahim Paşa who had the medrese added to it. The buildings were badly damaged by an earthquake in 1894 and then abandoned. Some locals used to call it the **İsa Kapısı Mescid** (chapel of the Gate of Jesus), a name that might hark back to a gate in the original Constantinian city walls.

Hekimoğlu Ali Paşa Mosque 10 11 12

If you head north along Ese Kapısı Sokağı you will come to the Hekimoğlu Ali Paşa Mosque which, in an area almost over-endowed with great mosques, still stands out for its gracefulness and decorative detail. Created in 1734-5 by **Ömer Ağa** for **Ali Paşa**, the son of a court surgeon (hekimoğlu) and Grand Vizier to **Sultan Mahmud I**, it was described by John Freely as "either the last of the great classical buildings or the first of the new baroque style" for its seamless blending of features of both styles – the main entrance is a case in point, pairing traditional stalactite carvings with more rococo decoration in the spandrels.
The mosque stands in a pleasant garden concealed behind a wall into which is built a **sebil** (water dispensary) with a particularly beautiful metal grille. Even more impressive is the huge arched entrance gate with, above it, a small **library** which has been returned to use despite some impracticalities; the books are contained inside a raised wooden cupboard which must be accessed by a ladder. The adjacent room offers a wonderful view towards the mosque, which is raised on a **stone platform** and has a ground plan very similar to that of the much older Cerrahpaşa Mosque. The tiles on its walls, which include an image of the Kaaba in Mecca, were made at Tekfur Palace (see p. 149).

Altı Mermer Greek Orthodox Church

Surp Agop Armenian Church

Across busy Hekimoğlu Ali Paşa Caddesi stands the 19th-century Greek Orthodox **Church of Dormition of the Virgin Mary (Altı Mermer Panagia)**. If you then head north along Sırrı Paşa Sokağı you will glimpse to the left the large 19th-century Armenian **Church of Surp Agop** and then come to a huge space on the left, now called a "çukurbostan (sunken garden)" although it started life as the 5th-century **Cistern of St Mocius**, the largest of the four Byzantine reservoirs in the city (see p. 023) and named after a church that once stood nearby. Its 25,000 square meters now contain a park and children's sports facilities.

Sultan's box

Library

Fountain

Cistern of St Mocius

Tomb of Ramazan Efendi

Ramazan Efendi Mosque 13

If you a walk west along Kocamustafapaşa Caddesi you will come to a square containing the self-effacing Ramazan Efendi Mosque, commissioned by an official named Hoca Hüsrev in 1586 and richly decorated with beautiful **İznik tiles** despite its apparent simplicity (you may only be able to view them through the windows). Almost unbelievably **Mimar Sinan** designed this, his last mosque, at the age of 96; it was once part of a larger complex that was destroyed by fire in 1782. Ramazan Efendi (1542-1616) is buried in a tomb beside the mosque that contains a lovely calligraphic panel dating back to 1868.

The chained cypress tree

Beside the tomb of the two princesses in the grounds of the Kocamustafapaşa Mosque you will see a cypress tree with a chain attached to it. Legend has it that after the **İmam Hüseyin**'s daughters were buried here the **İmam Cabir** had a tree planted beside their grave. To ensure that it would never lose its branches he wrapped a **chain** around it. According to local lore if a **debtor** sat down under the tree the chain would reach out and touch them, so instead of going to a judge people would head for the tree and await its ruling. Should the chain ever break, the end of the world would apparently be nigh.

Haseki Bostan Hamam

You can visit this double bathhouse, which presumably dates back to the Byzantine era. Stories about the healing properties and reputation of the bath on Hekimoğlu Ali Paşa Street near the Haseki Hürrem Social Complex are still very much alive.

Kocamustafapaşa Primary School

Kocamustafapaşa Mosque/Sümbül Efendi Tomb

Right at the end of Kocamustafapasa Caddesi beside the fine 19th-century mansion that houses the Kocamustafapaşa Primary School is an intriguing building that forms the centerpiece of an important religious complex. As soon as you enter the mosque you should turn sharp right, walk to the end of the building and then turn left. You will find yourself standing in what was probably the outer narthex of the late 13th-century **Church of St Andrew of Crete** whose pillars incorporate capitals taken from a 6th-century church that may also have stood on the same site. Recent repainting has removed all traces of the original building but its shape is unmistakable – if you look straight inwards through the outer narthex you will see first the inner narthex, then the domed nave and then the apse. When the church was converted into a mosque it was rotated through ninety degrees so that the mihrab and minbar are now in what was the south aisle.

The church was converted into a mosque in 1486 by Grand Vizier **Koca Mustafa Paşa** who gave his name to the surrounding area. Mustafa Paşa then had a falling out with **Sultan Selim I** who would have had the building torn down had it not been for the intervention of **Sümbül Sinan** (1451-1529), leader of a branch of the Halveti dervish sect whose lodge (tekke) was linked to the mosque. When Sümbül Efendi died his tomb became a center for pilgrimage, especially by women in search of a husband. The hyacinths painted on the ceiling are a play on his name – "sümbül" is Turkish for hyacinth. It sits inside a much later building, in the entrance to which a baroque rotunda surrounds the tomb of **Serasker Rıza Paşa** (1848-1917), topped off with a carved fez.

In the grounds another tomb might or might not contain the remains of **Safiye Sultan** (c.1550- c. 1619), the mother of Sultan Mehmed III, while an open-sided tomb houses the bodies of the Çifte Sultanlar. In front of the mosque is the humble burial place of the **Byzantine princess** Katherine who converted to Islam as Sıdıka Hatun. The complex also includes a library that now contains a teahouse, a madrasah housing a Koran course and, outside the walls, a hamam.

Kocamustafapaşa Mosque

Sinan's Masterpiece

Süleymaniye Mosque and Around

015

Standing unmissably proud on the Istanbul skyline, the 16th-century Süleymaniye Mosque is one of the city's largest and most beautiful mosque complexes, the burial place of Sultan Süleyman the Magnificent and his wife Roxelana. Nearby the Şehzade Mosque is less visited but almost equally lovely. Many of the old wooden buildings in this area are also being given a much-needed face-lift.

Minbar (pulpit)

Designed by the greatest of all Ottoman architects, **Mimar Sinan** (c. 1490-1588) and regarded by many as the city's most beautiful mosque, the Süleymaniye Mosque is one of its great must-see attractions, especially since its renovation in 2010. It crowns the third hill of Istanbul and can be seen from miles around.

The Süleymaniye was commissioned by **Sultan Süleyman the Magnificent** (r. 1520-66) to celebrate the thirtieth anniversary of his accession to the throne. Work on the mosque began in 1550 and continued for seven years, al though the surrounding complex was not finished until a year later. The end result was what is generally regarded as Sinan's masterpiece in Istanbul, second only in splendor to the **Selimiye**, his great mosque in **Edirne** in Thrace. So impressed was the sultan that on the grand opening day he is said to have allowed the architect the honor of unlocking its doors.

Sultan Süleyman the Magnificent

Burial Area

Süleymaniye Mosque is floodlit at night.

The exterior

The mass of domes and semi-domes of Sinan's masterpiece surely inspired the Sultanahmet (Blue) Mosque with which most visitors will be familiar. Its **minarets** are said to symbolize Süleyman's status: that there are four of them indicates that he was the fourth Ottoman sultan to be based in Istanbul, while the 10 "şerefes (minaret balconies)" reveal that he was the 10th sultan since the establishment of the empire.

Sometimes it's surprising what could be found near a mosque. At one time the street that now dispenses beans to hungry visitors used to be **Tiryaki Çarşısı, the Market of the Addicts**, where opium was on sale alongside the tea and coffee. **Wrestling matches** also used to be held in front of the mosque every week.

Mihrab

The interior

The vast domed interior of the Süleymaniye has a certain austerity about it, even though the walls are decorated with fine **İznik tiles** while the windows are shuttered with wood inlaid with mother-of-pearl, as is the kürsü (preacher's seat). The mihrab and minbar are made from **Proconnesian marble** quarried on Marmara Island (see p. 597). The contemporary stained glass was designed by a glazier glorying in the name of **Sarhoş İbrahim (İbrahim the Drunkard)**, while the calligraphy is by **Ahmed Karahisari** (1468-1556), whose work can also be seen in the Piyale Paşa Mosque (see p. 264) and Hasan Çelebi, his pupil, who is said to have completed the work after his teacher went blind.

The four columns supporting the dome, one said to have come from the Temple of Artemis at Ephesus, another from Egypt and two from ancient sites around Istanbul, are thought to represent the first four caliphs.

The two different techniques that were used inside the mosque evoke admiration even today. First, he put earthenware jars and bricks in different places and left gaps between them, creating beautiful acoustics inside the building. With another method, he created an air stream to collect the smut from the oil lamps in a single place. This prevented the smut from making the mosque dirty. Following a smart path, he created a project that would be called "upcycling" today and used the collected smut as ink.

The Süleymaniye Mosque and tomb from the Serasker Tower by Franz von Alt

The mosque complex and tombs

Much of the pleasure of a visit to the Süleymaniye comes from the fact that so much of the surrounding complex still survives. It consists of a number of structures ranging from a **caravanserai** to a series of **madrasahs** (seminaries) and from a **hamam** (bathhouse) to a **hospital**. The **tombs** of Sultan Süleyman and his Ukrainian-born wife Haseki Hürrem (Roxelana – "the Russian") can be seen in the garden.

Süleyman is buried alongside Sultans Süleyman II and Ahmed II in a building more densely covered in **İznik tiles** than the mosque itself, while Roxelana lies apart from him in a second tomb, also decked out in İznik finery. The domed structure nearby that looks like a third tomb was actually the **Dar-ül Kurra**, a school in which students learnt to read and recite the Koran.

Süleyman the Magnificent's tomb

Medreses

The assorted **madrasahs** (seminaries) on three sides of the mosque formed the foundation for **Istanbul University** (see p. 082) and it was largely their presence which explains why this was such an upscale neighborhood until the 17th century. Architecturally the most interesting of the buildings are the least obvious: the **Dar-ül Hadis**, which was designed as a straight line of cells with a dershane (lecture theater) above them instead of the more familiar square; and the **Mülazim** (preparatory school) which was created on five levels tripping down the hillside in the space beneath the Salis (Third) and Rabi (Fourth) madrasahs and was restored in 2009. The **Salis** and **Rabi** medreses are mirror images of the **Evvel** (First) and **Sani** (Second) madrasahs on the far side of the mosque – each of them taught one of the orthodox schools of Islamic law. The Evvel and Sani medreses now house the closely guarded **Süleymaniye Library.**

Roxelana's Tomb

"(The sultan's tomb) looks like a temple dedicated to cheerfulness, rather than a shrine for the ashes of the dead."

The Beauties of the Bosphorus **by Julia Pardoe, 1840**

Spectacular view from Botanical Garden

Mimar Sinan's humble tomb

Botanical Garden

Across the road from Sinan's tomb is a grand gateway that leads to the offices of the Istanbul Müftülüğü and to the botanical garden. Provided you don't come here expecting Kew Gardens, you'll probably find it a pleasant oasis in which to while away half an hour. From the terrace there's a fine view of the confluence of the **Sea of Marmara**, the **Bosphorus** and the **Golden Horn**. To find it, ignore what looks like the gate on the right and instead go inside the building straight ahead, turn left and go downstairs to find the entrance.

Twisted Mosque (Burmalı Cami)

If you walk up Atatürk Bulvarı and under the Aqueduct of Valens to get to the Şehzade Mosque, you will pass on the left the small but very cute Twisted Mosque, so named because of the raised pattern that spirals up the outside of its single minaret, something that is unique in Istanbul despite its similarity to the much-photographed **Yivli Mosque** (Grooved Mosque) in **Antalya**. It was built in 1540 for the Egyptian judge Emin Nureddin Osman and features an attractive triple-arched porch that reuses old **Byzantine capitals**.

İmaret (Soup Kitchen)

The former imaret, which once produced food for several thousand people daily, now houses the rather more exclusive **Darüzziyafe restaurant** (see below) whose porticoes shelter an old mill and a marble ice-box weighing 7,000 kilograms; a plane tree shading the courtyard is said to date back to the 15th century. Right next door was the **caravanserai** where travelers and their pack animals could be accommodated overnight. It's not currently accessible. Nor is the huge **Dar-üs Şifa (hospital)** building, which was also restored in 2010. As for the great architect **Sinan**, he lived on the outskirts of the site for many years and is buried there in a pretty open-sided **tomb** which he designed for himself inside a walled garden with an attractive sebil (water dispensary).

The soup kitchen houses the Darüzziyafe restaurant.

Şehzade Mosque

Şehzade Mosque and Damat İbrahim Paşa Sebil in an old painting

Such is the fame of the Süleymaniye that the almost equally beautiful but slightly smaller Şehzade Mosque (the Mosque of the Crown Prince) tends to get overlooked. Built in memory of Sultan Süleyman the Magnificent's much-loved son **Mehmed** who died of smallpox in 1543, it was the first of the large imperial mosques designed by **Mimar Sinan** and is approached via a wonderful porticoed courtyard where the lovely red, white and blue lunettes over the paired windows make a dramatic contrast with the whiteness of the surrounding stone. Unusually, the two minarets are decorated with relief carvings. Internally, the mosque is a vast empty square beneath a soaring dome – it's the exterior that will strike most visitors as the most memorable part of it.

The mosque stands in a large garden with, near the gate, a cluster of tombs, the most important being that of the Crown Prince (Şehzade) Mehmed, an octagonal building with a double dome in which is also buried his brother **Prince Cihangir**, said to have died of grief after the murder of his half-brother Prince Mustafa in 1553 (see p. 297). Beside this tomb stand the last resting places of **Rüstem Paşa** (see p. 222), as designed by Sinan and of the Grand Vizier **İbrahim Paşa** as designed in 1603 by Dalgıç Mehmed Ağa. All three tombs contain magnificent examples of **İznik tiles** so it's a shame that they are not open to the public.

Also in the garden are the **tombs** of Sultan Mehmed III's son Mahmud, Sultan Murad III's daughter Hatice Sultan and Şehzade Mehmed's granddaughter Fatma Sultan. One more unusual rectangular tomb is set apart from the others near the entrance from Şehzadebaşı Caddesi; it contains the remains of Destari Mustafa, a statesman in the reign of Sultan Ahmed I and his wife Ayşe Hatun and also contains some fine tiles.

Some of the buildings of the **mosque complex (külliye)** still run along the outside wall of the garden. The madrasah with a dershane (lecture theater) on the east side. Beyond it is a **kervansaray** (caravanserai) which must be entered from the street outside. Across Dedeefendi Caddesi stand the abandoned remains of the small **primary school and soup kitchen**.

Kaptan Paşa Fountain

Damat İbrahim Paşa Medrese

A little way along Şehzadebaşı Caddesi at the junction with Dedeefendi Caddesi a fine street corner sebil (water dispensary) is attached to the madrasah (seminary) built by Sultan Ahmed III's Grand Vizier **Nevşehirli Damat İbrahim Paşa** in 1720. The grounds contained a library and a dershane (lecture theater) that has since been converted into a mosque. The grand vizier's own modest gravestone hardly suggests the big part he played in court life until he was strangled in 1730 during the Patrona Halil revolt (see p. 265).

Nevşehirli Damat İbrahim Paşa Mosque

Kalenderhane Mosque

Right up against a stretch of the old aqueduct in a particularly picturesque corner of the Süleymaniye neighborhood stands what was once the large and impressive 12th-century Byzantine **Church of Theotokas Kyriotissa**, now a mosque named after the Kalender dervishes who used it as a lodge (tekke) in the years after the Ottoman conquest. The church's greatest treasure was a series of **frescoes of St Francis of Assisi** that are believed to have been painted c. 1250 during the Latin occupation of the city, making them the oldest paintings of the saint to have been discovered; they are now in the Istanbul Archeology Museum although not on display. Also found in the church was a mosaic showing the presentation of Christ in the Temple believed to date back to the 7th century and the only **pre-Iconoclastic mosaic** to have been discovered in the city.

Excavations beside the church uncovered the remains of a 4th-5th-century **bathhouse** and two previous churches.

Kalenderhane Mosque

Istanbul Metropolitan Municipality Building (Istanbul Büyükşehir Belediyesi)

Immediately across Şehzadebaşı Caddesi from the mosque stands the L-shaped building that houses the metropolitan authority, with a line-up of busts of eminent Turks in front of it. It was designed in 1953 by Nevzat Erol. The structure has a lean style and differs from the historical architecture of its region, but is still very much in harmony with the surrounding texture. Numerous Roman and Byzantine mosaics were unearthed during the construction of the building. These historical pieces are on display at the Istanbul Museum of Archeology (see p. 020).

Local houses

Until recently many of the houses near the Süleymaniye were in a very poor state of repair and it was hard to credit that this was once such an upscale neighborhood that people were prepared to pay for the privilege of being allowed to live here. Slowly but surely some of them are now being restored under the auspices of **KUDEB**, a government department dedicated to finding new uses for old buildings and itself housed in the splendid **Kayserili Ahmed Paşa Konağı** in Kayserili Ahmed Paşa Sokağı. This is one of the best examples of the sort of mansion 19th-century statesmen expected to inhabit. Ahmed Paşa (1806-78) was a **Minister for the Ottoman Navy** but was also one of the men involved in the plot to remove Sultan Abdülaziz from the throne in 1876. Despite its wonderful painted walls and ceilings, his grand Empire Style house narrowly escaped demolition in the 1970s.

Ramadan between the arches

These days during Ramadan people flock into the Hippodrome (see p. 046) as soon as iftar (the break of fast meal) is over. In the past, however, the place to celebrate used to be the area known as **Direklerarası** around the Şehzade Mosque where an arcade of shops ("direklerarası" means "between the arches" in Turkish) provided funds for its maintenance. At first magicians, acrobats and Karagöz puppeteers would amuse the crowds. Later, theaters and movie houses also put down roots here. In the 1950s the nightlife center relocated to the northern side of the Golden Horn and then to Taksim. Today there's nothing but a giant shoeshop housed in a redundant cinema to remind visitors of a little piece of entertainment history.

Sinan and the *devşirme* system

A uniquely Ottoman institution, the ***devşirme* (gathering)** was an annual rounding up of young Christian boys to serve the sultan, a sort of tax in the form of human beings. Born in Ağırnas near Kayseri in 1490, Mimar Sinan was one of the boys gathered in this way and given a schooling in Istanbul where he converted to Islam. Like many others, he was sent to serve with the **Janissaries**, an elite corps of soldiers, but unlike the others he went on to become a revered architect credited with more than 320 works. Of these 84 are still standing in Istanbul, including 42 mosques. The last known devşirme took place in 1703.

Süleymaniye Hamam

One of the favourite baths of the Architect Sinan, was not built as a double bath, since it was planned to be used mainly by employees of the social complex. It is still used today and attracts great attention from tourists.

www.suleymaniyehamami.com.tr, Tel: 0212 519 55 69

The Very Center of the City

You will see a green column in the corner of the wall of the Şehzade Mosque complex towards Istanbul University. This column was erected there to mark the exact centre of 16th-century Istanbul. **Evliya Çelebi** also writes in his "Seyahatname (Book of Travels)" that this point was chosen following meticulous work carried out by all the engineers.

The Water Carrier

Aqueduct of Valens, Zeyrek and Vefa

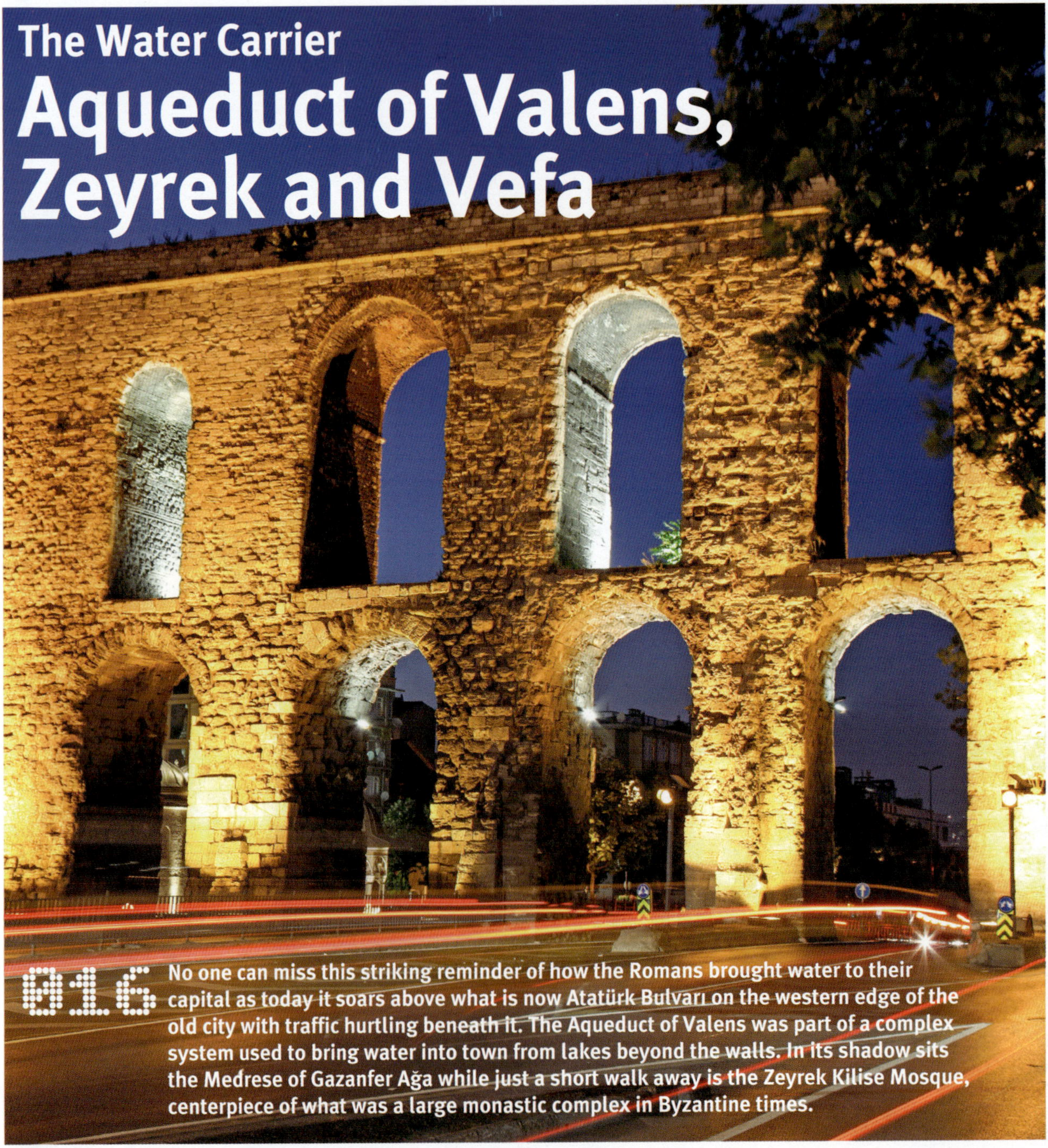

016

No one can miss this striking reminder of how the Romans brought water to their capital as today it soars above what is now Atatürk Bulvarı on the western edge of the old city with traffic hurtling beneath it. The Aqueduct of Valens was part of a complex system used to bring water into town from lakes beyond the walls. In its shadow sits the Medrese of Gazanfer Ağa while just a short walk away is the Zeyrek Kilise Mosque, centerpiece of what was a large monastic complex in Byzantine times.

"Of all the antiquities of Constantinople, none form so prominent a feature in the landscape (as the Aqueduct)."

***The Beauties of the Bosphorus* by Julia Pardoe, 1840**

The Aqueduct ①

Known as Bozdoğan Kemeri (Bozdoğan Aqueduct) in Turkish, this kilometer-long aqueduct of which about 800 meters still survive was built by the Roman Emperor **Valens** in 375, almost certainly on the site of an older version. It was created out of stones taken from the walls of **Chalcedon** that had been demolished after the locals rose up in support of Procopius, the cousin of the Emperor Julian, against the Emperor Valens in 365. For much of its length it features a double tier of arches 18.5 meters high.

Emperor Valens

Impressive as the aqueduct is, it is just one of the more dramatic reminders of a hugely complex system that used to bring water from lakes outside the walls into the town center. The water is believed to have been brought to **Edirnekapı** (see p. 127) in an underground pipe and then channeled along the ridges of the **Sixth**, **Fifth and Fourth Hills** before being carried across the valley between the **Third and Fourth Hills** by the aqueduct. It ended up in the **Nymphaeum Maximum (the Great Fountain)**, a cistern close to Beyazıt Square, the precise site of which is no longer known. During the last days of Byzantium it fell into disrepair as a shrinking population reduced the quantity of water the city required. The Ottomans, however, repaired and maintained it and it continued in use right through to the 19th century, hence its current surprisingly good condition.

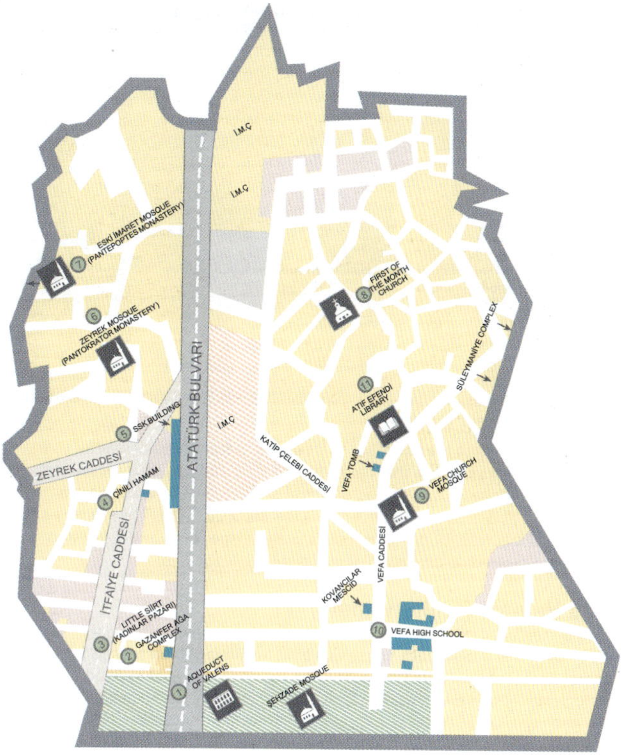

Bringing water to the city

A survey carried out by the Leverhulme Trust between 2000 and 2005 has brought to light the full complexity of the system developed to bring water into the city, as symbolized by the aqueduct. In its heyday the network is thought to have brought water to the city from over 400 kilometers away, with one particular part from **Vize** in **Thrace** stretching for 250 kilometers. Over **100 covered cisterns** connected to the system have been identified, as well as **four open reservoirs.** There were three separate systems: the **Kırkçeşme system** that brought water from the Belgrade Forest to Egrikapi, the **Taksim system** that brought it from the Forest to Taksim Square and the **Halkali system** that brought water from Thrace to Beyazıt Square. The Aqueduct of Valens is a relic of the latter system, the only one no longer in use.

This water distribution system has been described as "one of the greatest achievements of hydraulic engineering known from antiquity". Today stretches of aqueduct still await excavation in the dense woodlands of northern Thrace.

Print by William Henry Bartlett, 1838

Gazanfer Ağa Külliye ②

Immediately next to the aqueduct on its northern side is the delightful **Medrese of Gazanfer Ağa** that dates back to 1599 and was built for the last Chief of the White Eunuchs to keep control of what went on in the harem before that power passed to the Chief of the Black Eunuchs. The complex still includes a medrese, türbe (tomb), sebil (water dispensary) and rose-filled courtyard centred on a fountain. It was restored in 2009-10.

Tiled Hamam (Çinili Hamam) ④

Not to be confused with the Turkish bath of the same name in Üsküdar (see p. 506), this double bath-house was built by **Mimar Sinan** in 1546 for **Admiral Barbaros Hayrettin Paşa** who intended its revenues to support a theological school in Beşiktaş. The **İznik tiles** which gave it its name are long gone although it does retain an impressive marble fountain said to have been donated by a 19th-century Iranian ruler. The frilly arches and the domes over the lavatories mark this hamam out from its more mundane competitors. Although the well that supplied the water and the stables for the horses that used to draw it are no more you can still see the remains of the **boiler room** where a "külhanbey (stoker)" and his team would have fed the flames that kept the baths hot. Unfortunately, the magnificent blue and white tiles of this building were also destroyed in the same period as it suffered its share from the earthquakes. In 1874, a Parisian antique dealer bought thousands of tiles from here and took them abroad. You have to go to Victoria&Albert, the Louvre or the British Museum to see the beautiful tiles of the bath today. Fortunately, the building, which is one of the rare non-touristic baths in Istanbul, did not collapse. After 13 years of restoration with the devoted efforts of the Gürsel Family, it was brought back into the cultural life of the city. This was the hamam used for **Ferzan Özpetek**'s award-winning film 1997 **"Hamam"**.

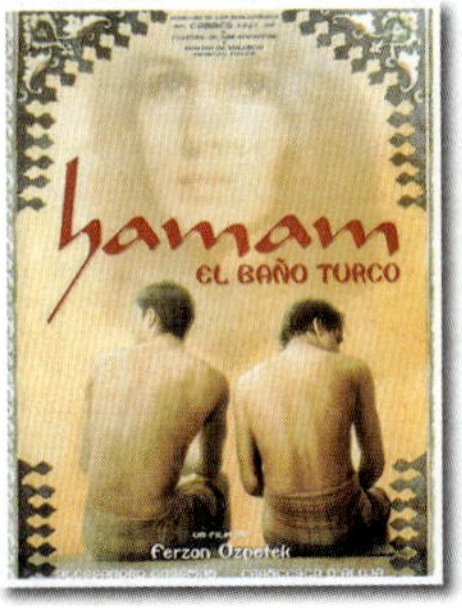

Kadınlar Pazarı ③ ("Little Siirt")

Right next to the medrese is a district popularly known as Little Siirt because many of its workers come from this town in South-eastern Turkey. Centered on the architecturally non-descript but very busy **Hüsambey Tezgahçılar Mosque**, it's full of butcher shops, groceries selling south-eastern Turkish cheeses and *tandır ekmek* (pit-baked bread that requires rehydrating) and small restaurants specializing in *büryan kebap* which is also baked in a pit before being finished off in an oven. Hard now to believe that this was until recently a thoroughly neglected and run-down part of town where people came to buy cheap and dubious cuts of meat.

Atatürk Bulvarı ⑤

SSK Building

Part of a piece of much-panned town planning by the French architect **Henri Prost** (1874-1959) that destroyed many old buildings in its path, Atatürk Bulvarı is one of those roads that makes the heart sink. So heavy is the traffic along it that you can only cross safely by using the underpasses. However, amid the concrete jungle there are still a few things to look out for. Walking downhill from the aqueduct on the left-hand side of the road you will pass but may not notice the buildings that house the **Sosyal Sigortalar Kurumu** (SSK, Social Security Department). These were designed in 1963 by **Sedad Hakkı Eldem** who attempted to imitate some of the traditional buildings of the surrounding neighborhood using modern materials (i.e. concrete). For his efforts he was awarded an **Aga Khan Award for Architecture** in 1986. Nearby is a stretch of curvy wall which conceals the **Zeynek Cistern**, the only such structure in the city that was built overground rather than underground.

Sedad Hakkı Eldem

Monastery of the Pantokrator (Zeyrek Kilise Mosque) 6

Walking downhill along Atatürk Bulvarı you will eventually come on the left to **Zeyrek**, a small, run-down neighborhood with many crumbling wooden houses that are slowly being restored by KUDEB, an organization dedicated to finding new uses for old buildings.

It also harbors what was once the huge monastic complex of the Pantokrator which consisted of two churches, a chapel and other monastic buildings, including a mental hospital, a general hospital and a hospice for elderly men. Of the two churches, the southerly one, the **Church of Pantokrator (St Savior)**, was built for the **Empress Eirene** and the northern one, the **Church of the Virgin Elousa**, for the **Emperor John II Comnenos (John the Good)** between

John Comnenos and his sons

1120 and 1136. In between the two a mortuary chapel, called a Heroon, was built for the Comneni family. Such was the importance of this monastery that it owed allegiance directly to the emperor rather than to the patriarch.

In 1204 the church's treasury was raided and the contents carried off to Venice; part of the **Pala d'Oro** (Golden Cloth) that now serves as the altarpiece of **St Mark's Basilica** is said to have come from the Pantokrator. However, in 1261 when the Byzantine emperor was reinstated a hugely important **icon of the Virgin Mary Hodegetria** was installed here; in 1453 it was moved to the Chora Church (Kariye Mosque).

After the conquest the chapel was converted into a mosque, named **Molla Zeyrek Mehmed Efendi** after its imam and the monastic buildings were turned into an Islamic theological school that continued in use until the medreses attached to the Fatih Mosque (see p. 115) were completed. During

renovations in the 1950s a wonderful opus sectile floor was found beneath the floorboards. The extensive restoration that began in 2009 ended after ten years. As a result of the work, many pieces were brought to light including glass antiques dating back to different periods. The mosque was ranked in UNESCO's Cultural Heritage List in 1985 along with other historic areas of Istanbul.

Interior of Zeyrek Mosque

Pala d'Oro in Venice

Old Zeyrek houses

Pantepoptes Convent

Convent of Pantepoptes ⑦ (Eski İmaret Mosque)

This beautiful and little-visited mosque started life as the church for a convent built in c. 1185 by the **Empress Anna Dalassene** who governed Byzantium for 20 years with her young son Emperor Alexius I Comnenos (1081-1118) before spending the last five years of her life here in retreat. The church's Byzantine name meant **"Christ the All-Seeing"**, but the mosque took its name, which means **"Old Soup Kitchen"** in Turkish, from the fact that it was converted into a soup kitchen for travelers immediately after the conquest of 1453; it maintained this function until the vast Fatih Mosque (see p. 115) nearby was up and running. The church's most striking features are its attractive brickwork and 12-sided dome, although it also features some fine red marble around the doorways and in some of the columns. To find it walk along Haydar Caddesi, then climb the steps up Haydar Yokuşu and turn left at the top.

On Haydar Caddesi stand the ruins of the **Haydar Hamam**, named after the same 16th-century vizier who gave his name to Haydarpaşa station (see p. 492). It's sometimes listed as a work of Mimar Sinan although without much evidence.

Şebsafa Kadın Mosque

Across Atatürk Bulvarı in the area known as Küçükpazarı you will see the attractive **Şebsafa Kadın Mosque**. The school attached to it was built in 1787 by Fatma Şebsafa Kadın, a member of Abdülhamid I's harem, in memory of her son, Şehzade Mehmed. It's also known as **Zeyrek Mosque** which is likely to lead to some confusion with the much older Zeyrek Kilise Mosque or Monastery of the Pantokrator (see p. 111).

The tomb of Istanbul's first mayor Hızır Bey is near the church.

First of the Month Church

First of the Month Church (Ayın Biri Kilisesi) ⑧

This church, with a sacred spring underneath it, is tucked away behind the Third Block of the İMÇ off the east side of Atatürk Bulvarı. On the first day of each month Christian, Jewish and Muslim women come here to pray to **St Mary** for help in conceiving a baby. Salesmen outside the gates sell charms for all sorts of other desirable things such as a new car or success at work, while inside small silver and gold **"wishing keys"** are on sale; people rub these on the various icons dotted about the church while they say their prayers.

Vefa Kilise (Church) Mosque

Vefa (9) (10) (11)

Once one of inner-city Istanbul's more upscale neighborhoods, Vefa, which lies to the east of Atatürk Bulvarı, is now home to many poor migrants from Eastern Turkey as well as to the pretty stone and brick **Vefa Kilise Mosque (Church Mosque)** in Molla Şemsettin Camii Sokak, also known as the Church of St Theodore, which probably dates back to between the 10th and 12th centuries, despite incorporating pieces of marble from a much earlier Byzantine structure. The outer narthex was probably built in the 14th century and contains some frescoes in its domes that resemble those in the Chora Church (see p. 132).

Vefa Kilise Mosque in 19th century

Vefa High School

In Dedeefendi Caddesi, on the way to the Şehzade Mosque (see p. 103), stands the **Vefa High School,** dating back to 1872 and now housed in a fine example of First National Architecture from the 1920s designed by the architect **Kemaleddin Bey**. Its grounds conceal the multi-domed **Şehid Ali Paşa Library** that was founded in 1715; its contents have long since been moved into the Süleymaniye Library.

Vefa Mosque in Vefa Caddesi is a modern building on the site of a 15th-century model and is of interest primarily because its grounds house the tomb of **Şeyh Muslihiddin Vefa,** a late 15th-century holy man with a strong and enduring following. Of passing interest is the **çilehane**, a cell in which a holy man would have fasted in solitude. A little further along the road on the left is the fortress-like **Atıf Efendi Library**, the second such building to be founded in Istanbul in 1741-2 after the Köprülü Library (see p. 065). It once contained a collection of more than 25,000 manuscripts housed inside a very appealing complex that included accommodation for its workers.

Atıf Efendi Library

Vefa Boza

Stop for a drink at the cute little shop which has been serving *boza*, a drink of fermented barley, to an appreciative clientele since 1876. It still preserves the mug from which Atatürk tried a sample in a glass case in the wall. In summer the *boza* is supplemented with *şıra*, a refreshing drink made from raisins.

İMÇ (Istanbul Manifaturacılar Çarşısı)

The Istanbul Drapers' Market (IMÇ) is an important example of modern Turkish Architecture. It also hosts nine works of eight contemporary Turkish artists. The place is almost a modern outdoor museum. But unfortunately, the pieces of art share the fate of the bazaar, which has been neglected. While explanatory plates were mounted during restoration work, which was carried out under the leadership of the Cultural Awareness Foundation, these have not alleviated the situation. Since the works of art are placed on the exteriors of the blocks, you have to walk through all the blocks to see them. The most well-known of these works is the mosaic panel made by the poet-artist Bedri Rahmi Eyüboğlu in 1965. In this abstract panel, Eyüboğlu depicts Istanbul as a vibrant meandering river with fish, birds, minarets, towers and domes. Other works are:

1. The mosaic panel named "Horses" and made by Nedim Günsur in 1967 in the 6th block of the bazaar. Nedim Günsur was among the founders of the group of "10'lar".
2. The ceramic panel in the 5th block belongs to Sadi Diren.
3. The wall-relief made of natural stone by Ali Teoman Germaner; this piece is in the worst condition.
4. In the 2nd block bazaar, the "White Marble Fountain" by Yavuz Görey, who was one of the first sculptors of the Republican era and who introduced modernism to Turkish Sculpture Art.
5. The mosaic panel reflecting Anatolian life and folkloric elements made in 1965 by Eren Eyüboğlu in the 1st block
6. The mosaic panel, Bedri Rahmi Eyüboğlu's second work in the bazaar which was made in 1965.
7. The ceramic panel by Füreya Koral, which was inspired by the mood created by the Süleymaniye Complex (see p. 098)
8. The statue of "Birds" which was dismantled in 2013 for repair and returned to its original place after it was exhibited at the Sakıp Sabancı Museum (see p. 444) in 2013. The work belongs to Kuzgun Acar and his 1965 piece is one of the most important works of Turkish sculptural art.

The mosaic panel by Bedri Rahmi Eyüboğlu

The Conqueror's Mosque

Fatih

017

Fatih is thought of as one of Istanbul's most conservative districts. Its focal point is the fortress-like Fatih Mosque, which was built in celebration of the sultan, but there are other things to look out for too including the Byzantine Kıztaşı (Maiden's Stone), a tall column that has given its name to the surrounding district and the Hırka-i Şerif Mosque which houses a cloak once owned by the Prophet Mohammed.

Fatih was named after Sultan Mehmed II, the great Ottoman leader who, aged only 21, wrested control of Constantinople from the Byzantines and was accordingly nicknamed "Fatih" (the Conqueror). At first glance it may strike casual visitors as more obsessed with weddings than religion since its main street, Fevzi Paşa Caddesi, is lined with shops selling alarmingly over-the-top wedding dresses. To see real religious conservatism in action you need to exit the Fatih Mosque on the north side and explore the district of Çarşamba (see p. 120).

Fatih Monument

Fatih Mosque 1

Istanbul's first large mosque complex, the Fatih Külliyesi, was constructed immediately after the conquest of the city in 1453 over the ruins of what had been the enormous **Church of the Holy Apostles** where many of the Byzantine emperors and their families had been buried. It was designed by an architect called **Atik Sinan** who should not be confused with the 16th-century genius generally known as Koca Mimar (Architect) Sinan and the sturdy walls of the surrounding medreses make it look almost as fortified as a castle. An earthquake in 1766 badly damaged the original mosque, which was reconstructed in baroque style by **Mehmed Tahir Ağa** between 1767 and 1771; of the original building little remains bar the courtyard, the entrance gateway, the mihrab and the lower parts of the minarets. Since then some parts of the complex have also been torn down although the **eight medreses** still survive, along with the 18th-century **Carullah Efendi Library**. At one time the complex may have been able to accommodate almost 1,000 students.

One of the more unusual features of the mosque complex is the restored **tabhane**, or dervish inn, whose 20 domes are supported on columns that may have been taken from the Church of the Holy Apostles. Opposite it and in striking contrast, is the baroque **tomb of Nakşidil Valide Sultan**, the wife of Abdülhamid I and possibly a cousin of the Emperor Napoleon's wife Josephine, who had been captured by Algerian pirates and who is often credited with inspiring the pro-French policies of the Ottoman Empire in the early 19th century. The mosque was completely restored in 2009.

Fatih Mosque in old photograph

"(Fatih Mosque) imposes a feeling of physical, as well as religious, humility on the faithful."

***Constantinople - City of the World's Desire* by Philip Mansel, 1995**

Nakşidil Sultan 2

One of the more fantastic stories told about the Ottoman harem is that of Nakşidil Sultan, the wife of Sultan Abdülhamid I and mother of Sultan Mahmud II. In the late 18th century **Aimee du Buc de Rivery**, the 11-year-old daughter of a Martinique plantation owner and the cousin of the Empress Josephine, vanished at sea on her way back home from school in France. Somehow the story developed that she had been seized by pirates and sold into the harem where she later saved her son Mahmud from the murderous Janissaries by hiding him in a furnace. Sadly, there is no historic data to support any of this and to have been Mahmud's mother she would have to have given birth aged nine, which hasn't stopped at least 174 novelists jumping on the bandwagon alongside several film-makers.

Portrait of Aimee du Buc de Rivery (Nakşidil Sultan?) aged just 12

Fatih Mehmed's Tomb

Fatih Mehmed himself is buried in a superb tomb to the rear of the mosque where the reverent can always be found reciting passages from the Koran. It was the custom for newly crowned sultans to come here immediately after visiting the mosque at Eyüp in the hope that they would soak up some of the Conqueror's greatness for themselves. Fatih Mehmed's wife **Gülbahar Sultan** is buried more modestly nearby.

Ahmed Mithad Efendi

The tombs

The collection of Ottoman tombstones assembled in the cemetery attached to the Fatih Mosque rivals that at Eyüp in splendor and several famous individuals are buried here. They include **Gazi Osman Paşa** (1832-1900), a great Ottoman general who survived the five-month Russian siege of Plevne in Bulgaria in 1877 and was treated as a hero by both sides. He died in Istanbul and his tomb was designed by **Kemaleddin Bey**, the architect responsible for the fine building that now houses the Legacy Ottoman Hotel in Sirkeci. Other names to look out for include those of historian and statesman **Ahmed Cevded Paşa** (1865-1935) and journalist and writer **Ahmed Mithad Efendi** (1844-1912). As for the architect **Atik Sinan**, he is buried in the small **Kumrulu Mescidi** in Edirnekapı. The graveyard is especially pretty in summer when the roses planted in each burial plot come into bloom.

Gazi Osman Paşa

Gazi Osman Paşa's Tomb

Millet Library 3

Across Fevzi Paşa Caddesi from the mosque is the Millet (People's) Library, which was established by Diyarbakır-born traveler and bibliophile **Ali Emiri Efendi** (1857-1924). It is housed in the old **Feyzullah Efendi Medrese** which dates back to c. 1700 and was completely restored in 2008. A pretty courtyard garden adorned with a well, fountain and palm trees faces steps that lead up to the medrese where two domed lecture rooms now house a collection of almost 7,000 manuscripts and 20,000 books, many of them first editions or rare books in Arabic. In pride of place is the **Dîvânu Lugâti't-Türk**, the earliest known Turkish dictionary which was hand-written in Baghdad in the 11th century. Kashgar Mahmud's book also served to shine a light on early Turkish history. Admission is free although you will need to leave your bag at the door.

11th-century map in the Dîvânu Lugâti't-Türk

Dîvânu Lugâti't-Türk

Maiden's Stone (Kıztaşı) 4

A short walk away from Fatih Mosque along Kıztaşı Caddesi, a Byzantine column made out of granite with a statue of Nike, the winged Greek goddess of victory, at its base stands in a small square named after it. Built for the Emperor Marcian (450-57), it is formally known as Marcian's Column and an inscription lists it as the work of the Prefect Tatianus Decius. Originally it would have had a statue of the emperor on the top of it, but this was probably stolen by the Venetians in 1204 and may now be in Bari.

Because of its name the Kıztaşı has sometimes been confused with the lost Column of Venus which was supposed to sway slightly to acknowledge truly virgin passers-by from those who were only pretending to be. In fact it took its name from the image of Nike. The Kıztaşı is one of four such Byzantine columns to survive in Istanbul, the others being Çemberlitaş (see p. 067), the Goths Column in Gülhane Park (see p. 201) and the Column of Arcadius in Cerrahpaşa (see p. 093).

Dülgerzade Mosque

Amcazade Hüseyin Paşa Mosque 5 6 7

If you walk west along Fevzi Çakmak Caddesi you will pass the old but not especially interesting **Dülgerzade Mosque** before arriving at the junction with Eski Saraçhane Sokak where another grimy but picturesque mosque, the **Amcazade Hüseyin Paşa,** still forms a complex with a medrese, mescit, library, fountain and sebil. The mosque seems to have served primarily as a lecture theater for the medrese and was built for **Hüseyin Paşa,** Grand Vizier to **Mustafa II** from 1697 to 1702 and a relative of the Köprülüs, one of the city's most wealthy and distinguished families who owned what is now the oldest surviving yalı on the Bosphorus (see p. 544). It supposedly houses a small **Museum of Turkish Construction,** but I never found it open.

Church of Hagios Polyeuktos

Across Horhor Caddesi there's a small park with, at the back, the excavated remains of the huge **Church of Hagios Polieuktos,** built for Anikla Juliana, the daughter of the last Western Roman Emperor Anikius Olybrius (r. 430-72). Old capitals and pieces of column dotted about the park presumably come from this building and the old mansions known to have stood nearby. As you walk through Haşim İşcan Underpass towards Aksaray, don't be misled by the broken appearance of the wall stones to the right. This is part of the altar of the church. Unfortunately it's not possible to read the brass plate on it, but we can surmise that the road along which traffic flows today was probably the cemetery of the church in the past.

Nearby are two striking and restored examples of First National Architecture built for the **Fatih Belediye** (municipality) and **İtfaiye** (fire brigade). Both date back to 1914 and were designed by **Kostantinos Kiriakidis.** In front of them is the **Air Forces' Martyrs Monument** designed by architect **Vedat Tek** in 1916.

Amcazade Hüseyin Paşa Complex

Former Fatih Municipiality building

Air Force Martyrs Memorial

Sacred Cloak (Hırka-ı Şerif) Mosque 8 9

This elegant mosque, built in a style that reflected contemporary western tastes, was constructed in 1851 by **Sultan Abdülmecid** to house a cloak that had belonged to the Prophet Mohammed but had been given to a contemporary ascetic called Veysel Karani who had been living in Yemen. In 1611 **Sultan Ahmed I** had the cloak brought to Istanbul where it was originally housed in a single room. Today several other sacred relics are on display in a small building facing the mosque. The cloak itself is housed in a room attached to it and is put **on display to visitors** from the first Friday of Ramazan until the end of the fasting period; a descendant of the original owner still opens the door to visitors on the first day. This cloak should not be confused with the **Holy Mantle** (Hırka-ı Saadet) on display in Topkapı Palace (see p. 017).

Hırka-i Şerif door knocker

As you walk here from Fevzi Paşa Caddesi you can pass through the pretty courtyard of the **Mesih Mehmed Paşa Mosque**, which may have been built by **Sinan** in 1585-6. The tomb of the founder, who became a grand vizier at the grand old age of 90, stands where you might have expected to find the ablutions fountains which are, instead, housed inside the surrounding portico.

Hırka-i Şerif Mosque

Mesih Mehmed (Ali) Paşa tomb

Piece of Prophet Mohammed's beard

Horhor Flea Market

It could hardly be housed in a less inspiring building, nor could its name be more misleading, but this market is a treasure-trove of antiques spread out over seven floors off Horhor Caddesi close to the Kıztaşı.

Mesih Mehmed (Ali) Paşa Mosque

Mosque Interior

Le Corbusier's Favorite Mosque

Çarşamba and Sultan Selim Mosque

018

Çarşamba, the even more pious district that abuts Fatih, is home to the huge Sultan Selim Mosque as well as to the remains of a curious Byzantine cistern which stood open to the elements. Here too is the restored Sultan Cistern that houses a restaurant. The back streets offer superb views over Fener and the Golden Horn.

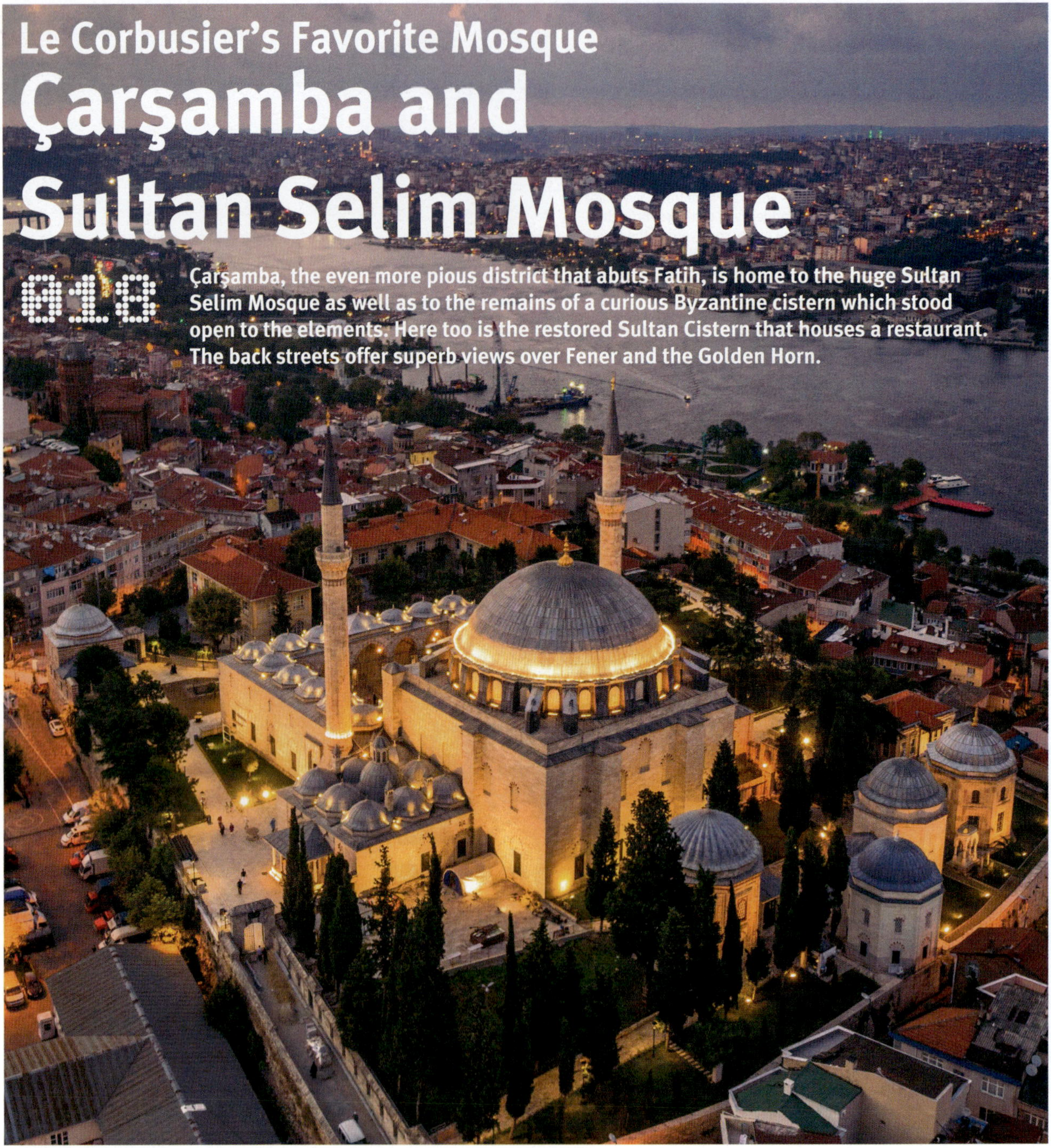

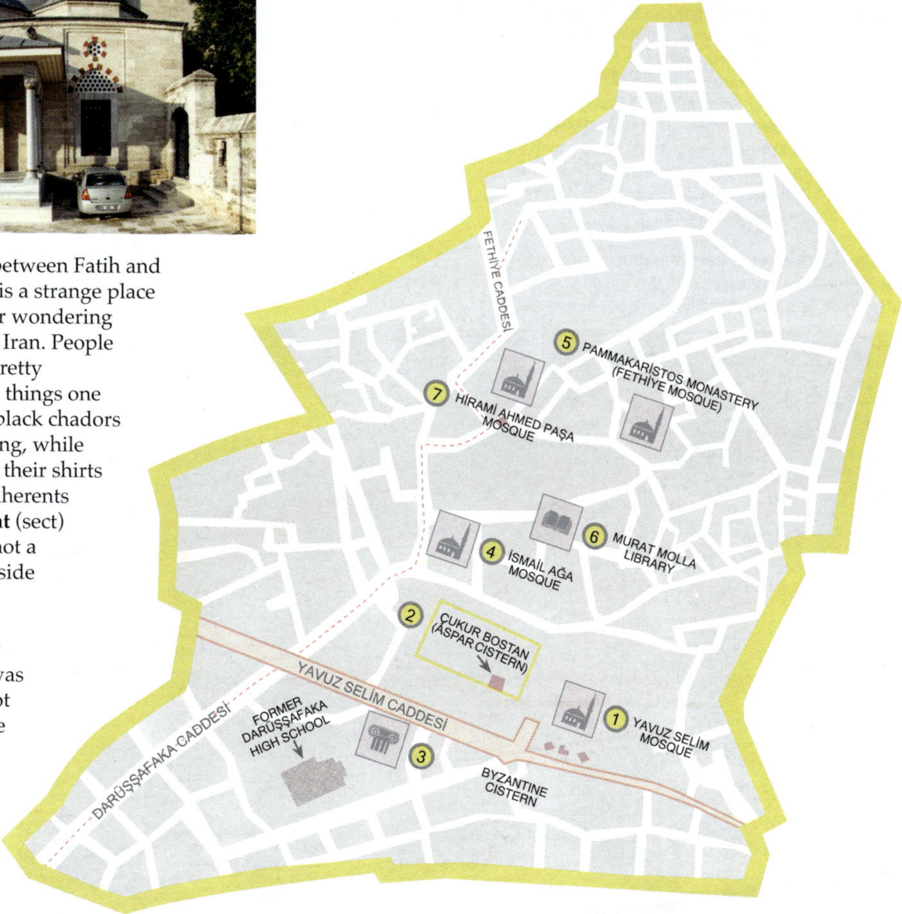

Çarşamba, the area squeezed in between Fatih and the shores of the Golden Horn, is a strange place where you could be forgiven for wondering if you had side-stepped suddenly into Iran. People usually think of Fatih in general as a pretty conservative area, but Çarşamba takes things one step further. Many women here wear black chadors with only a triangle of pale face showing, while their men sport thick beards and wear their shirts loose over baggy trousers. They are adherents of a branch of the **Nakshibendi Tarikat** (sect) centered on the **İsmail Ağa Mosque**, not a place that expects to receive many outside visitors.

There are two conflicting stories about how **Çarşamba** (Wednesday), which was called Deuteron in Byzantine times, got its modern name. The first would have it that after the Ottoman conquest in 1453 **Sultan Mehmed II** brought people from the Black Sea district of Çarşamba to settle here. Others claim that it took its name from the **market** that takes place here every Wednesday.

Sultan Selim Mosque crowning the Fifth Hill as seen from the Golden Horn

"...the twin minarets of Sultan Selim stood out like two black chimneys against the scudding clouds."

Sweet Waters **by Harold Nicholson, 1921**

Sultan Selim Mosque (1)

This fine if rather austere mosque was built by **Sultan Süleyman the Magnificent** for his father **Yavuz Selim (Selim the Grim)**, although it's probable that the father had actually initiated work on the site before his death. A fine building decorated with İznik tiles, it's often attributed to Mimar Sinan although there is no record of it in the **"Tezkere"**, which is the officially recognized list of Sinan's works. In the grounds can be seen the tomb of Sultan Selim (1512-20), during whose brief reign the Ottoman Empire doubled in size; this was definitely designed by **Sinan**.

The Swiss-French architect **Le Corbusier** (1887-1965) was especially impressed with this mosque, which he described as having "the suave melody of very gentle forms", an opinion with which you are likely to concur if your tastes run to architectural simplicity. The mosque was restored inside and out in 2009.

Selim was the first Ottoman to have himself declared **Caliph** (head of the Islamic congregation worldwide), a title claimed by his successors right down to Abdülmecid Efendi, the prince deposed during the Turkish War of Independence. Nearby is the tomb of **Sultan Abdülmecid** (1839-61), which was designed by **Garabed Balyan**, a member of the talented family of architects who designed the Dolmabahçe Palace. The **views** of the Golden Horn from the mosque's terrace are spectacular.

Sultan Selim the Grim's tomb

Mosque interior

Why was Sultan Selim called "the Grim"?

Like his near contemporary the Tudor King Henry VIII of England, Sultan Selim I had a reputation for ruthlessly disposing of those who annoyed him. In his eight-year reign he got through eight grand viziers, all of whom were executed. There's even a suspicion that he had his own father, Bayezid II, assassinated to ease his path to the throne. Certainly he had his brothers and nephews executed to make sure they could not challenge him for supremacy. Interestingly, his Turkish nickname "Yavuz" has much more positive connotations, celebrating his fearlessness rather than his brutality.

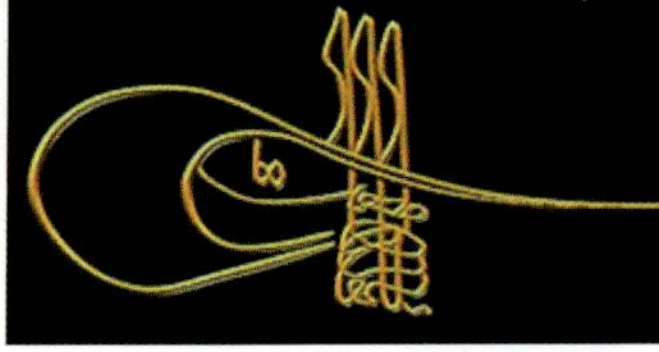

İsmail Ağa Mosque (4)

Built in 1724, this spatially cramped but ideologically important mosque was supposedly designed to evoke the Kaaba in Mecca although that is not especially apparent on a brief visit. The complex still retains a **sibyan mektebi** (school) and a **medrese** (seminary) converted for use as a Koran school. It is named after local boy **İsmail Efendi** (1645-1725) who rose to become Şeyhülislam or minister for Islamic Affairs. In 1998 and 2006 fatal shootings took place in mysterious circumstances inside this mosque.

Cistern of Aspar (Çukur Bostan) (2)

The covered cisterns of Istanbul, especially the **Basilica Cistern** (see p. 054), have attracted a lot of attention but less interest has been focused on the few remaining open cisterns whose precise purpose is unclear; some people have suggested that they were left open to the skies so that the air could purify the water, although it seems more likely that they were simply large reservoirs from which water could be drawn to irrigate the fields. They seem to have fallen into disuse once a series of dams were built in the **Belgrade Forest** (see p. 562). The **Cistern of Aspar** takes its name from an Alan Arian general from southern Russia who was executed by Emperor Leo I in 471. It stands just across the street from the Sultan Selim Mosque and as recently as the 1970s housed an entire village, now cleared away to make space for a small park and sports facilities. It forms the picturesque backdrop for much of the action in American crime writer Jenny White's book "The Abyssinian Proof". Its Turkish name means "sunken market garden".

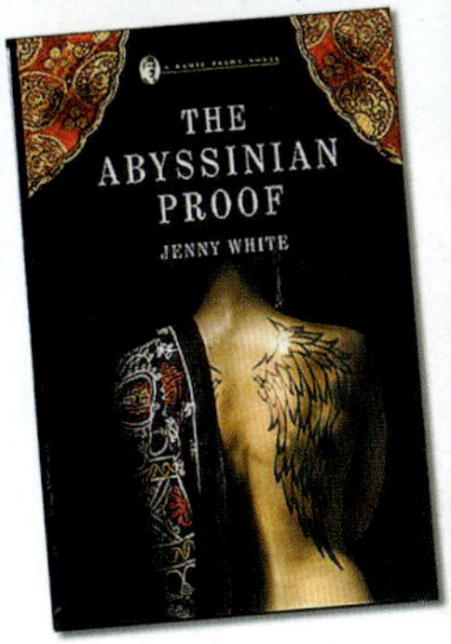

If you like this you'll also like: Aetios Cistern (see p. 129) Fildamı (see p. 192) St Mocius Cistern (see p. 096)

Corinthian capitals top columns in cistern

Sultan Cistern (Sultan Sarnıcı) (3)

Across the street from the open Cistern of Aspar is a more conventional covered cistern that houses a restaurant. Probably dating back to the reign of the **Emperor Theodosius I** (379-95), the cistern was later reused as a workplace by carpenters and cotton ginners, before being abandoned altogether. It then became a rubbish dump and was only reopened after seven years of restorative work.

Theodosius

www.sultansarnic.com
Tel: 0212 521 07 20

Mosaic showing Christ offering a blessing

Twelve Apostles mosaic

Minbar detail

Monastery of Theotokos Pammakaristos (Fethiye Mosque and Museum) ⑤

Built by **Emperor John Comnenos** and his wife Anna Doukaina, the **Church of the Joyous Mother of God** is a fine example of 12th-century Byzantine brick-and-stone architecture. Unlike most of the city's old Byzantine churches it stands on a piece of open ground that makes it possible to appreciate the external brickwork and multiple apses. The chapel on the south side was added by a nobleman called Michael Glabas Ducas Tarchaniotes in the 13th century and has a **collection of mosaics** second only in interest to the one in Chora Church (see p. 132). From 1456 to 1568 the church served as the seat of the patriarchate. In 1573 it was converted into a mosque and given the name **Fethiye Camii (Mosque of Conquest)** to commemorate Sultan Murad III's victories in Georgia and Azerbaijan. Today it has been divided into two parts, with one side continuing to serve as a mosque while the adjacent chapel has become a **museum.**

A library and church (6) (7)

West of the Sultan Selim Mosque along Fethiye Caddesi you can divert briefly to inspect the cute little **Library of Murat Molla,** built for a scholar-judge in 1775 in a style that looks to have come straight down from Byzantium. It was originally attached to a dervish lodge (tekke) that has long been lost although restoration is completed in 2018. Also nearby is the tiny Byzantine **Church of Hagios Ioannis in Trullo,** now called the Hirami Ahmed Paşa Mosque after the man who converted it into a mosque but thought to date back to the 12th century. From 1456 to 1586 it served as a convent for nuns who had been evicted from the nearby **Church of Theotokos Pammakaristos** when Patriarch Gennadius decided to make it his base. Otherwise, very little is known about it.

Hirami Ahmed Paşa Mosque

Çarşamba Market

Every Wednesday a big **street market** takes place in the streets north of the Fatih Mosque, which explains why this district is called Çarşamba (Wednesday). It's a great place to come to shop for fruit and vegetables and for household goods amid a sea of black-clad women and heavily-bearded men.

Murat Molla Library

Sultan Selim Mosque

The Sixth Hill

Edirnekapı and Karagümrük

019

Easily overlooked in the rush to visit the Chora Museum and the nearby land walls, Edirnekapı is the neighborhood just inside the walls whose most prominent monument is the Mihrimah Mosque, a work of Sinan. Nearby is an open-air cistern dating back to the 5th century and a lodge (tekke) where whirling dervishes are taught their art.

Fatih Sultan Mehmed at the Gates of Istanbul, by Fausto Zonaro (Zonaro painted himself as a Janissary to the sultan's left)

The **Edirnekapı** neighborhood takes its name from its proximity to the gate in the Theodosian land walls through which ran the road to **Edirne in Thrace**, a city that retained its importance well into the Ottoman era. Immediately to the east is the district called **Karagümrük** (Land Customs) which may have acquired this name after Sultan Mehmed II bestowed the right to collect customs dues on a local boiler-stoker named Kara Davud. Alternatively, it may simply refer to the fact that this was where taxes were levied on goods arriving in the city by land (kara).

Seven hills

Like Rome, ancient Byzantium was built on seven hills ("yedi tepe" in Turkish), most of them topped with forums. After the Conquest in 1453 the original Turkish city covered much the same area, but grand imperial structures were erected on six of the hills. Topkapı Palace stands on the First Hill, Nuruosmaniye Mosque on the Second, Istanbul University and Süleymaniye Mosque on the Third, Fatih Mosque on the Fourth, Yavuz Selim Mosque on the Fifth and the Mihrimah Sultan Mosque on the Sixth. The Seventh Hill in Cerrahpaşa is crowned with Haseki Hürrem Complex.

Mihrimah Sultan Mosque

Perched right on top of the Sixth Hill just inside Edirnekapı, the impressive Mihrimah Mosque was built by **Sinan** between 1562 and 1565 for Mihrimah Sultan, the favorite daughter of **Sultan Süleyman the Magnificent** and dominates the landscape for miles around despite having only a measly single minaret. The mosque complex, which included a seminary, primary school and hamam, was badly damaged by earthquakes in 1766 and 1894 but was being completely restored in 2009. Its double hamam is still open to visitors. Mihrimah Sultan was also responsible for the **Harbor (İskele) Mosque** in Üsküdar (see p. 500).

Mihrimah Sultan

Mihrimah Sultan Mosque

Stars of David beneath bay windows.

Only the gate of the Kastoria synagogue remains

Memories of more cosmopolitan times

Ten minutes' walk away from the Mihrimah Sultan Mosque in Sultan Çeşme Caddesi stands a unique building, Istanbul's only wooden synagogue, the İştipol, a virtually windowless structure hidden behind high walls. Facing it across the street are three lovely wooden houses. If you look up at their jutting cumbas (bay windows) you will notice that two of them have stars of David carved into them, a sign that the residents were Jewish (three brothers apparently). Nearby only the gateway of the old **Kastoria Synagogue** survives.

Just streets away from these reminders of a time when there was a flourishing local Jewish population stands the Greek Orthodox **Church of Panagia (St Mary),** locked up and with nothing on the outside to identify it. When I talked to people nearby, I found some who remembered living happily side by side with their Jewish neighbors, while others looked astonished when I asked about the church. Today, of course, there are plenty of non-Muslims wandering around the area, but they are tourists rather than residents. The buildings are silent witnesses to a time when this was a far more culturally diverse part of town.

Fortunately, another piece of good news came from Edirnekapı **Aya Yorgi Church.** After a comprehensive restoration, the church opened its doors for worship again in 2017; there are plans for the school building, which is part of the complex, to serve as a music institute. The existence of the church has been known to exist with certainty since the 9th century.

Greek Orthodox Church of Virgin Mary

Wooden İştipol Synagogue

Cistern of Aetios

How many people taking their seats to watch a match in the Vefa Stadium ever look round and consider the antiquity of their setting? For the football stadium has been created inside the walls of what was once the smallest of Istanbul's four open-air cisterns (see p. 123), where water was collected and stored. It was probably commissioned by the prefect **Aetios** in 421.

Turkish take on New York's Flatiron building.

Atik Ali Paşa Mosque

Madrasah, mosque and tomb

Immediately east of the cistern on Fevzi Paşa Caddesi is the **madrasah (seminary)** built some time before 1564 by **Sinan** for **Semiz Ali (Fat Ali) Paşa**, a Grand Vizier to **Sultan Süleyman the Magnificent** who reveled in a reputation as the life and soul of the party. Badly damaged by fire and earthquakes, it's now restored and used as a children's clinic.

Just down the road is the **Atik Ali Paşa Mosque,** also known as the Zincirli Kuyu (Chained Well) Mosque, built in 1512 in a style that recalls the multi-domed Great Mosque in Bursa for one of the grand viziers of **Sultan Bayezid II**. Facing it is the **tomb** of **Hattat Rakım Efendi**, a calligrapher responsible for the ornamentation of the tomb of Sultan Abdülhamid I's wife **Nakşidil Valide Sultan**, even further down the road behind the Fatih Mosque (see p. 115).

Tomb of calligrapher Rakım Efendi

Nureddin Lodge (Nureddin Tekkesi)

If you keep walking south-east along Fevzi Paşa Caddesi and then turn left along Nurettin Tekkesi Sokağı you will come to a dervish lodge (tekke) that is still in use today and where on Monday evenings you can watch young men learning the skills of a **whirling dervish.** Many long-gone dervishes are interred here in a spacious room whose floors are still covered with individual rugs, making it especially beautiful. The dervishes belong to the **Cerrahi Tarikat** that was founded in the 17th century by a man with a tongue-twister of a name, Nureddin Mohammed İbni Abdullah er-Rumi el-Istanbuli el-Cerrahi. **Sultans Mustafa II, Ahmed III** and **Abdülmecid** were all apparent adherents.

Nişancı Mehmed Paşa Mosque

In this neighborhood it tends to be the Mihrimah Sultan Mosque that scoops all the attention. However, if you head a little further north to Fatih Nişanca Caddesi in Karagümrük you will come to the magnificent **Nişancı Mehmed Paşa Mosque,** a building that looks as if it should be by Mimar Sinan but in fact appears to be the work of an unknown 16th-century architect who designed it for Mehmed Paşa, the then Keeper of the Seal which is what "nişancı" means in Turkish. It was extensively restored in 1766, probably after an earthquake. The mosque stands in an attractive courtyard where, following the Balkan Wars of the early 20th century, large numbers of refugees were fed.

A little way to the east you might want to glance into the graveyard of the appallingly restored **Kumrulu Mosque** to see the grave of **Atik Sinan,** the architect responsible for the Fatih Mosque who was apparently executed by the Conqueror in 1471 which might offer credence to the 17th-century writer Evliya Çelebi's claim that Fatih Mehmed ordered the architect's hands cut off because the dome of his mosque did not outstrip that of Hagia Sophia in height. The building takes its name, Dove Mosque, from a piece of decorative Byzantine marble embedded in the wall.

Heading back along Kurtağa Çeşmesi Caddesi to Edirnekapı you will pass on the right on Sarayağası Caddesi the unexceptional 16th-century **Üç Baş (Three-headed) Mosque** with, opposite it, a crumbling **madrasah** dating back to 1575. They form a pleasing group with a fountain adorning the road junction.

Üç Baş (Three Heads) Mosque

Mihrimah Sultan Hamam

Bathe in the **Mihrimah Sultan Hamam,** a historic bath with separate sections for men and women. The sauna and plunge pool are recent additions. Prices are still very reasonable.

www.mihrimahsultanhamami.com, Tel:0212 523 04 87

Here the great architect shows his genius again, once a year it meets with the namesake mosque on the other side in a spectacular way. This meeting was such an engineering marvel that it led to rumours that Sinan was platonically in love with Mihrimah Sultan. "Mihr" means sun while "mah" means moon. And Sinan virtually wrote this name in the sky on both sides of Istanbul. Every year on March 21, when the lengths of day and night are equal, the sun setting over the minaret of the mosque in Edirnekapı meets the moon rising over the minaret in Üsküdar (see p. 500). Some say March 21 is the birthday of Mihrimah Sultan.

The Church in the Country

Kariye Mosque (Chora Church)

020

Easily overlooked in the back streets near the city walls at Edirnekapı, the Byzantine Church of St Savior in Chora is one of Old Istanbul's most amazing sights, full of stunning frescoes and mosaics. Nearby some old wooden houses have also been given an attractive makeover.

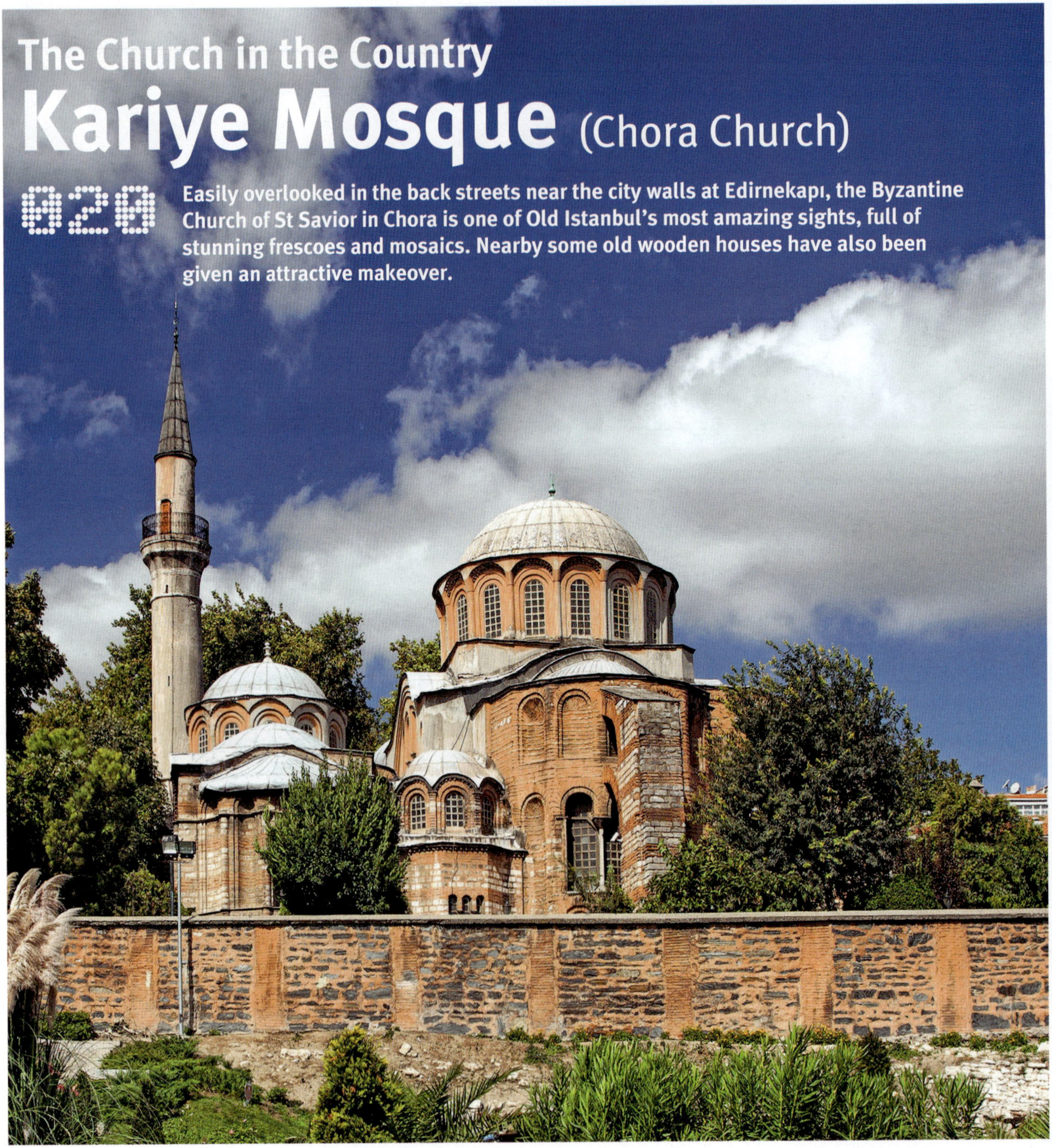

What is now the **Chora Museum** started life as the Church of St Savior in Chora, taking its name from the Greek word "chora" meaning "country". Today there's precious little sign of any country-side here, but when the original church was built it lay outside the Constantinian city walls and somehow the name stuck even after the arrival of the Theodosian walls (see p. 144) rendered it redundant. Instead the name appears to have acquired a more metaplysical meaning, with mosaics referring to Christ as the "country (chora)" of the living and to the Virgin Mary as the "dwelling place (chora)" of the uncontainable, meaning Jesus Christ.

Why Kariye?
In old Turkish "kariye", like chora, meant a village or the countryside.

Chora Church in old photograph

After **Saint Babylas** and his 84 disciples were martyred in **Nicomedia** in 298, **Emperor Constantine** liberated the Christian faith with the **Decree of Milano** in 313. Legend has it that the relics were transported here and the region became a sacred necropolis. **Saint Theodore**, who was related to **Emperor Justinian**'s wife **Theodora**, founded the first monastery here. The monastery and its church were destroyed with earthquakes repeatedly. The present version was built between 1077 and 1081 for **Maria Doukaina**, the mother-in-law of Emperor Alexius I Comnenus, although it was much remodeled and strengthened by her grandson **Isaac Comnenos**. Then between 1315 and 1321 the church was expanded with the addition of a northern corridor, outer narthex and parecclesion or side chapel after the damage done by the Crusaders during their occupation from 1204 to 1261. That is more or less the church that has survived until today.

Externally Chora is a pretty domed Byzantine building but with nothing much to distinguish it from several others that can be seen around town. Inside, however, it's another matter and

Tomb near the entrance to the museum

Theodore Metochites presenting a model of the church to Christ

the mosaics and frescoes on the walls far exceed in quantity those to be seen in the much larger Hagia Sophia (see p. 026). I owe the splendor of the décor to the Byzantine statesman and poet **Theodore Metochites** (1270-1332), a wealthy and powerful advisor to **Emperor Andronikos II Paleologos**, who not only paid for it but also added an image of himself dressed in a preposterous hat to a mosaic of Jesus. Like so many court favorites, Metochites lost his position when **Andronikos III Paleologos** usurped his grandfather's position as emperor. Exiled to Didymoteichon near Evros in what is now Greece, he was only able to return to the city in 1330 whereupon he became a priest, renamed **Theoleptos**, in his own church.

In 1511 the church was converted into a mosque with the addition of a minaret and mihrab by **Atik Ali Paşa**, Grand Vizier to **Sultan Bayezid II**. At this time the mosaics and frescoes were largely covered over with whitewash and plaster. Between 1948 and 1958 all this was slowly peeled away by the Byzantine Institute of America and the mosaics were comprehensively documented by **Paul A. Underwood** in a four-volume work "The Kariye Djami". The church finally became a museum in 1947. With the decision announced in 2020, it is decided that the place is going to be opened for worship once again. The mosaics will be concealed during worship with the same method carried out in Hagia Sophia, at other times the mosque will be open for touristic visits.

Emperor Andronikos II Paleologos

Restored houses near Chora Church

Thomas Whitemore

Thomas Whitemore worked on the restoration of the church with Paul A. Underwood

Outer narthex

Many of the images depicted in the narthex will be familiar to Western visitors from their own churches. You can, for example, see mosaics of the **Three Magi** arriving to visit the Baby Jesus and Mary and Joseph on the **Flight into Egypt** after they learnt of Herod's intended **Massacre of the Innocents**, which is also vividly depicted.

Outer narthex

One of the more intriguing groups of images is high on the vaults where the **Temptation of Christ** in the desert is rendered in four scenes: Satan tries to persuade him to turn rocks into bread, or jump off a tower in Jerusalem to prove his divinity, before offering him endless riches if he will only bow down and worship him.

Familiar to Christian visitors, too, will be the scenes of Christ's miracles: the **loaves and fishes**, the **wine at Cana**, the **healing of the blind and the lame** (Lazarus is a conspicuous omission from the line-up). There are, however, many twists that are peculiar to Orthodox representations of Bible stories: for example, **the Nativity** includes an image of women bathing the new-born Jesus which never appears in Western versions of the story (the diminutive ox and ass peering into the manger will be more familiar). The details of Byzantine clothing and furniture are also particularly interesting; it was not only Metochites, for instance, who favored outlandish headgear since the tax-gathering Syrian Governor Cyrenius is also shown wearing something that wouldn't look out of place on the most flamboyant of catwalks.

The Entry into Bethlehem: On the left in a dream Joseph is told of Mary's pregnancy by an angel. Mary and Joseph ride to Bethlehem to take part in the census.

The Governor Cyrenius carries out a census before levying tax

Birth of Jesus

Mosaics

All but three of the mosaics can be found in the two narthexes where they can be read like a storybook by anyone who knows their Bible (there are also helpful inscriptions in Greek for those who're feeling rusty). The mosaics depict the main events in the **life of Christ**, starting with the story of how the Virgin Mary was born to the elderly Anne and Joachim. Interestingly you need to go into the inner narthex to "read" the story of Mary before returning to the outer narthex to read that of her son. Then you must return to the inner narthex and inspect, over the entrance to the nave, a huge image of Christ. On either side are images showing him healing the deaf, the blind and the lame. Mosaics in the dome show Christ's family tree traced back to Adam and Jacob.

Miracle at Cana

The Three Wise Men (Herod and the Fortune-Tellers)

Massacre of the Innocents

Inner narthex

The mosaics here tell the story of Mary's elderly parents **Anne and Joachim** and of the birth of their daughter. The family of Mother Mary, the birth and the events she went through her childhood and marriage were depicted according to the story written in Protovangelium, one of the Apocryphia Bibles instead of the Holy Scripture. Orthodox Christians respect Apocryphia Bibles as well as the Canonic Bibles (the four Bibles that are approved). Unusually in the story of Christ himself there are no depictions of the events surrounding his death or of the Crucifixion or Resurrection, although the latter is depicted in the frescoes of the parecclesion. The domes of the inner narthex depict **Christ's lineage** traced back to **Adam and Jacob** and that of the Virgin Mary's running back through a line of 15 kings to **David**.

The inner narthex is like a corridor.

Family tree of Jesus

Family tree of Mary

In the narthex a few of the scenes from the **life of the Virgin Mary** are rather unusual. For example, one shows an angel feeding her bread while she was living in the temple, while another shows her being handed purple wool with which to knit a veil for it. In another scene we see a row of sticks laid out on an altar by widowers who fancied their chance at winning her hand in marriage; when these were returned to the widowers it was the stick belonging to Joseph that had started to sprout leaves, hence her betrothal to him.

St Peter holds the keys to heaven.

St Paul, once Saul of Tarsus holds a holy book.

Before you go into the nave look to the right in the narthex at a wonderful representation of **Christ** which is believed to be a copy of an icon that could be seen above the entrance to the **Khalke (Chalke)**, part of the Byzantine Great Palace in Sultanahmet (see p. 043). To his right is an image of his mother Mary, with, at her feet, another of **Isaac Comnenos**, the prince responsible for the rebuilding of the church. This would once have been matched by an image of "Melane the nun", possibly but not certainly the half-sister of Andronikos II who was responsible for the church of St Mary of the Mongols (see p. 234).

The upper part of the mosaic shows the childhood of Mary, the lower part her birth

The top mosaic shows the Consecration of Mary. The lower mosaic shows Mary entrusted to Joseph. On the right Joseph brings Mary to his home.

Nave

The nave of the church is more conspicuous for the beauty of the **marble panels** decorating its walls, some of them created by slicing a single sheet of marble down the middle and then placing the two pieces side by side, a technique also used in Hagia Sophia (see p. 026). However, the three mosaic panels to be seen here are as important as those in the narthex.

Dormition of Virgin Mary

Immediately above the entrance a large panel depicts the **Dormition of the Virgin.** Beside her, enclosed in a mandorla, stands Christ holding a baby that represents her soul. Above him hovers a seraphim with six wings that looks very like a flower.

Jesus inscribes the names of believers on the open pages of a book.

The other two panels depict a splendid blue-robed **Virgin Hodegetria** (She who Shows the Way) to the right of the apse, where she is described as "the dwelling-place (*chora*) of the uncontainable"; Christ to the left is described as "the dwelling-place (*chora*) of the living."

The Virgin Mary and the Christ Child.

Pareccleslon and the frescoes

The wonderful parecclesion served as a funerary chapel and feels almost like a separate building. Not all the eight people buried here have been identified but among them were **Michael Tornikos,** a friend of Metochites and his wife; **Irene Raoulaina Palaeologina**, a princess with ties by marriage to Metochites; and the despot **Demetrius Doukas Angelus Paleologos**. Most importantly the tomb in the north wall is believed to have been the last resting place of **Metochites** himself.

The mosaics of the nave and narthex may be impressive but it's the **frescoes** of the parecclesion that will probably leave the strongest impression on many visitors, mainly because the contrast between the pastel colors and bold black and white designs is so visually stunning.

Parecclesion

The Last Judgment

The second most extraordinary scene in the parecclesion is the image of the **Last Judgment** spread across the ceiling vault. Always a favorite with iconographers because of the potential it offered for mischief-making, this depicts **Christ** sitting in judgment between the souls of the saved on his right and the condemned on his left. Below him to his left a spreading red blot symbolizes **Hell** and the river of fire awaiting the guilty. Immediately beneath him **Adam and Eve** kneel in front of a throne that will remain empty until the Second Coming of Christ. Above him **Heaven** is represented as what looks like a giant white snail borne aloft by an angel.

As soon as you enter the parecclesion you will notice the dramatic image of the **Anastasis** (Resurrection, Harrowing of Hell) covering the ceiling of the apse. In the center Christ surrounded by a double mandorla decorated with stars reaches out his hands to raise **Adam and Eve** from their tombs. Beneath his feet the **Gates of Hell** lie broken in pieces while **Satan** appears as a prisoner in handcuffs. Behind the white-bearded **Adam** stand **St John the Baptist** and the righteous kings, **David** and **Solomon.** Behind Eve, **Abel** stands in an open sarcophagus holding a staff, while behind him are assembled more of the righteous.

The Harrowing of Hell (Anastasis)

"The fresco of the Anastasis in the apse of the side chapel...is perhaps the supreme masterpiece of all Christian art."

Byzantium: The Decline and Fall **by John Julius Norwich, 1995**

Lined up under the Anastasis and clad in glorious black and white robes are the **Fathers of the Church**: St Athanasius, St John Chrysostom, St Basil, St Nicholas of Myra (alias Father Christmas), St Gregory the Theologian and St Cyril of Alexandria.

Fethiye Museum

The mosaics of Chora are so splendid that it's easy to overlook the fact that other churches were almost as richly decorated. A short walk east along Draman and then Fethiye Caddesis will bring you to the Fethiye Museum where more glittering mosaics can be seen (see p. 124).

Palace and Pottery

The Land Walls I

(From Topkapı to Ayvansaray)

021

The stretch of the great land walls from Topkapı to Ayvansaray on the Golden Horn tends to attract less attention than the southern stretch through which pass the road from the airport and the suburban railway. However, it was to this part of the city that the Byzantine emperors retired in the 13th century, building a new palace at Blachernae to replace their old one. It was here too that an 18th-century pottery was established which went on to produce what are called Tekfur Palace tiles and ceramics.

The most northerly stretch of the land walls beyond the **Tekfur Palace** (Tekfur Sarayı) was rebuilt between the 7th and 12th centuries and it's no longer clear what precise route the earlier Theodosian Walls followed. The stretch of wall immediately beyond the palace was rebuilt during the reign of **Manuel Comnenos** (r. 1143-80) and incorporates nine towers and a gate. There then followed a stretch of wall that appears to have been pieced together during the reigns of **Isaac II Angelos** (r. 1185-95) a**ndronicos II Paleologos** (r. 1282-1328) and **John VIII Paleologos** (r. 1445-48). Finally, the stretch of walls running from the Blachernae Palace down to the Golden Horn appears to have been rebuilt in two stages: the inner wall by the **Emperor Heraclius** in 627 as a defense against the Avars and Persians and the outer wall by the **Emperor Leo V** in 813 as protection against the Bulgars.

Tekfur Palace (1)

Gate of Romanos

Cannon Gate (Topkapı/Gate of Romanus)

The "Cannon Gate" has nothing at all to do with distant Topkapı Palace, but did play a leading role in the siege of 1453 when some of the heaviest fighting took place around what was the weakest stretch of the walls. It was here that the Hungarian engineer **Urban** placed a huge cannon that finally blasted the walls apart; some of the cannonballs are still preserved here. Poignantly, it was also here that the last Byzantine emperor **Constantine XI Dragases** is believed to have died in the futile battle to hold onto the city.

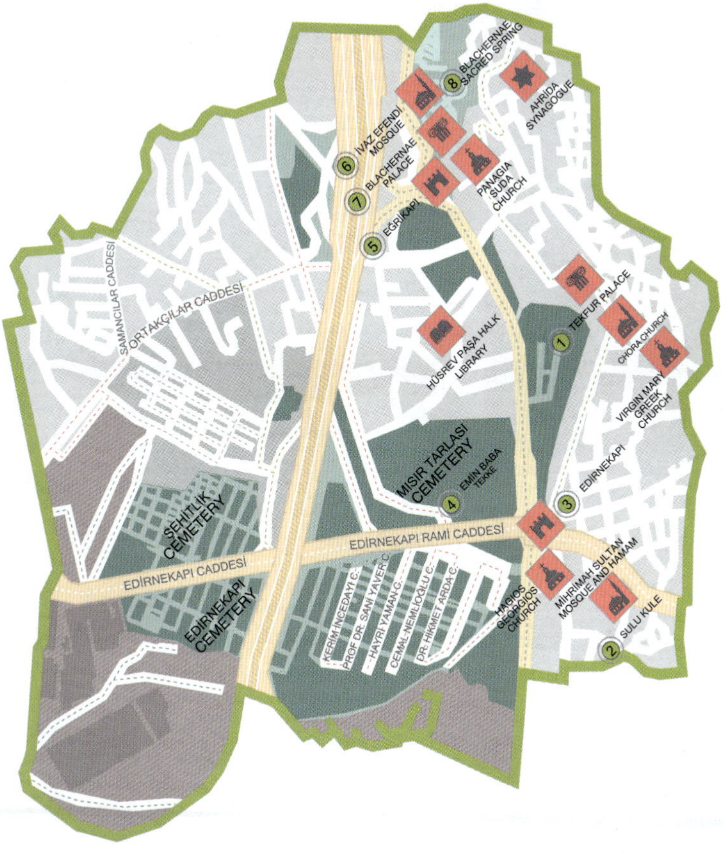

Panorama 1453 History Museum

Fatih Mehmed riding a white horse

Gazi Ahmed Paşa Mosque

Panorama 1453 History Museum

Near this hugely significant site, the **Panorama 1453 History Museum** uses 3,000 square meters of paintings and the sound effects of a Mehter band playing and cannons exploding to recreate what the surrounding area would have looked like on 29 May 1453, the day that Constantinople finally fell to the Ottomans. Plenty of information is also provided about the events leading up to the conquest.

@panorama1453
www.panoramikmuze.com
Tel: 0212 415 14 53

Adnan Menderes memorial

Just inside the walls at this point is the **Gazi (Kara) Ahmed Paşa Mosque,** a magnificent work of Sinan dating back to 1554 and built for one of Sultan Süleyman the Magnificent's grand viziers. It contains some fine late-period İznik tiles and the porticoed courtyard provides a **peaceful oasis** in a somewhat hectic part of town. The grand vizier's tomb stands just outside the mosque on Millet Caddesi. A short walk further east along Millet Caddesi brings you to the small 16th-century **Kürkçübaşı Mosque,** interesting because its porch incorporates capitals from **old Roman columns,** while its minaret bears a faded scratch sundial.

Outside the walls beside busy Vatan Caddesi stand **monumental modern tombs** in memory of **Adnan Menderes** (1899-1961), Turkey's first democratically elected prime minister who was hanged after the military coup of 1960 and **Turgut Özal** (1927-93), the modernizing prime minister responsible for starting to reopen Turkey to the outside world (his is the one with the metal ball on the top).

Turgut Özal memorial

Takkeci İbrahim Ağa Mosque

A short walk west of Topkapı across a newly landscaped park will bring you to Istanbul's only **wooden mosque** that survives more or less in its original form, perhaps because it was far enough out of the city center to avoid the many fires. It dates back to 1591 and was commissioned by a man who made "takkes (skullcaps)". Unexpectedly, it boasts a fine selection of **İznik tiles,** although its finest feature is the restored wooden ceiling with its **internal dome.**

Believe it or not, busy Vatan Caddesi was once the course of the Lycus river.

Sulukule (Water Tower) 2

Sulukule takes its name from the Lycus river that used to flow nearby. In 2008 it became something of a cause célèbre when it was announced that the entire area between Topkapı and Edirnekapı was to be demolished for redevelopment and its Romany population moved elsewhere. Opponents of the scheme pointed out that the area was home to the world's oldest settled population of **Romany**, one that traced its origins back to the days of **Sultan Mehmed II** (and one that had also featured in the James Bond film **"From Russia with Love"**). Its supporters retorted that it had become an inner-city slum after losing its raison d'etre in 1992 when the old music and belly-dancing venues that used to exist here were closed down. Whatever the truth of the matter, most of the buildings have long since been torn down and their inhabitants moved elsewhere.

Historic gateway into Sulukule

Surp Nigoğos Armenian Church

Sulukule is tucked inside the walls. Just ahead is the Mihrimah Sultan Mosque.

Churches

Tucked inside the walls are two 19th-century churches. The Armenian one is dedicated to **Surp Nigoğos** and dates back to the 1620s although the present version was built in 1831. The Greek Orthodox church is dedicated to **Hagios Nikolaos**. It dates back to the 16th century but was also completely rebuilt in 1831.

Hagios Nikolaos Greek Orthodox Church

Edirne Gate (Edirnekapı) 3

Right on the summit of the Sixth Hill, the Edirne Gate (Edirnekapı) was, at 77m, the highest point in the entire city and it was through this gate that **Sultan Mehmed II** eventually rode into Constantinople in 1453. Sometimes known as the **Gate of Charisius**, it was also called the **Porta Polyandrium** (Gate of the Cemetery) because of the vast necropolises that stretched out to the west of it and still do today.

Emin Baba Dervish Lodge

Emin Baba Tekke 4

Across the road from Edirnekapı the **Emin Baba Tekke** was virtually rebuilt in 1997. Built for the Bektaşi sect, it had already been extensively repaired by Sultan Abdülaziz's mother, **Pertevniyal Valide Sultan**. The overgrown graveyard behind it contains many unusual grey pillar memorial columns.

Gate of the Wooden Circus/Porta Xylokerkou

North of Edirnekapı the small gateway known as the Gate of the Wooden Circus after a nearby **hippodrome** was where the first of Mehmed the Conqueror's Janissaries managed to enter the city. Nearby was the tower mounted by the soldier **Ulubatlı Hasan** to raise the Ottoman standard – the Topkapı Metro station commemorates his name today. The gate is sometimes called the **Kerkoporta** (Little Gate).

Ulubatlı Hasan - a true Turkish hero

Hasan of Ulubat (1428-53) was the hero who climbed onto the walls near Topkapı in 1453 to raise the standard of the Ottomans, providing inspiration to the other soldiers until he was mown down in a hail of arrows. You can see him standing astride the battlements at the **Panorama 1453 History Museum**.

Panagia Suda Greek Orthodox Church

Crooked Gate (Eğrikapı) ⑤

The Crooked Gate cuts through the walls built by Emperor Manuel Comnenos at a point where it is believed horseshoes used to be made in Byzantine times, hence its original name, the **Gate of the Kaligaria,** derived from "caligae (horseshoe)". It acquired its Turkish name from the presence on the site of the tomb of **Hazreti Hafız,** the nephew of Eyüp Sultan, round which the road was forced to divert. Hazreti Hafız was probably killed nearby during the first Arab invasion of the city in the seventh century. In 1453 many of the occupying Turks entered the city through this gate.

Until 1939 there was a small **cemetery** beside this gate that had served the Jewish community since Byzantine times. The gravestones found here have now been relocated to **Hasköy cemetery** (see p. 261). If you pass through the walls and bear left down the hill you will glimpse the 19th-century Greek Orthdox **Church of Panagia Suda** behind a high wall. There's an **ayazma** (sacred spring) here that is meant to help those suffering from nervous diseases although you're unlikely to be able to visit it.

Outside the gate on the left you'll see the Sinan-designed **Kırkçeşme Maksem,** one of two final collection points for water brought from the Belgrade Forest (see p. 562). The other such collection point is in Taksim Square (see p. 283).

Hazreti Hafız's tomb beside the Crooked Gate

A Star of David in the glass of a house near the Tekfur Palaces shows that it once had a Jewish owner.

Hidden cemetery of the Prophet's Companions

The palace and pottery at Tekfur Palace

Built in the 13th or 14th century, the **Palace of the Porphyrogenitus** ("Born in the Purple", a synonym for the Byzantine emperor) was a substantial building that may have formed part of the nearby Blachernae Palace complex (see below) in the same way that a series of separate buildings made up the complexes of the Byzantine Great Palace (see p. 043) and the Ottoman Topkapı Palace. Much of the external structure still survives complete with attractive decoration in brick and marble.

The restoration of the building, which lasted for almost ten years, was completed in 2014.

The palace came to be known in Turkish as **Tekfur Sarayı** (Palace of the Emperor). After the Conquest it had a chequered history, serving for a while as a menagerie for exotic animals (where in 1597 a guest of the English ambassador Edward Barton recorded how he had had to duck to avoid the "familiar kisses" of a giraffe), then as a brothel. Then in 1719 it acquired new life as a pottery producing Tekfur Palace **tiles and ceramics.** While regarded as inferior to the products of the İznik kilns at their best, these ceramics are still highly prized. However, by the late 18th century production had ceased and the building was turned into a poorhouse. Later **Cyrus Hamlin,** the missionary who founded **Robert College** (present-day Bosphorus University, see p. 429) in the 1860s, actually considered incorporating the remains of the palace into the campus.

In 2019, the palace was opened for visitors as a museum exhibiting the tiles and ceramics produced here.

@tekfursarayi
www.tekfursarayi.istanbul
Tel. 0212 525 61 30

İvaz Efendi Mosque

İvaz Efendi Mosque 6

This imposing mosque with a single minaret at its south-east corner dates back to the 1580s and stands on a terrace immediately above the remains of the Blachernae Palace and against the towers that formed part of it. The mihrab is faced with fine **İznik tiles** and the internal porticoes are made from **wood**, a unique and somewhat disconcerting feature. Stones with hollows in them on the terrace probably once supported flagpoles. It's not known who was the architect behind the design.

Emir Buhari Dervish Lodge

A short way downhill on the right the **Emir Buhari Tekke (dervish lodge)**, dating back to 1513 but rebuilt in the 19th century, was completely restored in 2009.

Greek Orthodox churches

There are 96 Greek Orthdox churches in Istanbul. Ten of them are attached to monasteries, 12 are in cemeteries, one is privately owned and seven are representatives of other churches that are recognized by statute. Fifty-three of the churches were built before the Tanzimat Edict (see p. 202) and another 42 immediately after it. Just one church, St Mary of the Mongols (see p. 234), survives unchanged since Byzantine times.

Hançerli Panagia Greek Orthodox Church

Blachernae Palace (7)

Close to the point where the land walls met the sea walls on the shores of the Golden Horn, the Blachernae Palace complex was built by the **Emperor Anastasios** in c. 500. It took its name from a hugely revered nearby **ayazma** (sacred spring, see below) and was used by the imperial family when they were visiting it. It was extensively rebuilt in the 11th or 12th centuries after which it started to supplant the **Great Palace** as the preferred imperial residence. After the brief period of Latin government from 1204 to 1261 left the Great Palace in ruins, the emperors made it their permanent home. Of the splendor once hymned by Western commentators, there is little left to show today: just the substructures required to fit it into the hillside and the **Dungeon of Anemas** and **Tower of Isaac II Angelos** which may have served as a private apartment.

Ayvansaray (Eyvan Palace), the surrounding neighborhood, appears to have taken its name from the palace, the "ayvan" part being a corruption of the Persian word **"eyvan"** which meant the sort of large arched recesses that probably graced the building.

"To this Palace (Blachernae) are brought the annual tributes, both in gold and in garments of purple and scarlet, with which the towers are filled to bursting."

Benjamin of Tudela quoted in *Byzantine Empress* by Charles Diehl, 1904

İvaz Efendi Mosque rising above the walls at Ayvansaray

Dungeon of Anemas

This prison, a part of the Blachernae Palace complex, housed many unhappy captives, including several emperors, two of whom, **Isaac II Angelos** and **Alexius IV Angelos**, were murdered here. Originally it appears to have had 42 rooms spread out over three floors, but because the floors no longer exist modern visitors receive a rather misleading impression of space. The complex was restored in 2014.

Michael Anemas was a descendant of an Arab Emir of Crete who was brought as a prisoner to Constantinople in the 12th century but whose courageous demeanor won him the respect of the Byzantine emperor. However, Anemas became involved in a plot against **Alexios II Comnenos** for which he was punished by being paraded through the streets dressed in rags and with his beard plucked out. Fortunately for him, the Empress took pity on him and pleaded with her husband not to blind him. Instead Anemas was thrown into the dungeon that went on to bear his name.

Emperor Isaac II Angelos

"Our disgruntled old guide... showed us the chute down which the corpses of prisoners were flung out to sea... There was a blood-curdling atmosphere in the (Anemas) dungeon... everything was suggestive of death and destruction."

***Romance of the Bosphorus*, Dorina Lady Neave, 1949**

Secret cemetery

At the point where the land walls finally meet the sea walls at Ayvansaray there is now a walled garden surrounding the small **Hacı Hüsrev Mescid** which probably dates back to the 17th century but was virtually rebuilt in 2009. From here there is a spectacular view of the last three **polygonal towers** of the land walls. Here too, tucked out of sight in the space between the walls, is a very pretty small cemetery containing a shrine to **Ebu Şeybet-ül Hudri**. Buried in the cemetery are **Ebu Ahmed El Ansari** and **Hamidullah El Ansari**, believed to have been companions of the Prophet Mohammed and **Toklu İbrahim Dede**, who is thought to have taken part in the battle for the city in 1453.

According to a survey carried out in 1990 there are approximately **200 ayazmas** (sacred springs) in Istanbul. There's even a spring dating back to Byzantine times in the grounds of the **Zarif Mustafa Paşa Yalı** (see p. 542). Unfortunately many of these springs are inaccessible including the one dedicated to the 7th-century saint Hagios Therapon close to Gülhane tram stop that used to be popular with Muslims and Christians. I think this is a great shame since all such sites form part of Istanbul's incredible heritage.

Entrance to the Blachernae sacred spring

Blachernae Ayazma (8)

A **spring** believed to have curative powers in what is now Ayvansaray Kuyu Sokağı was already attracting pilgrims in pre-Christian times, but in 451 **Pulcheria**, the wife of the Emperor Marcian, had a church built on the site, thereby hugely increasing its profile. Later two pilgrims returning from the Holy Land donated **clothing** believed to have been worn by the Virgin Mary which they had stolen in Jerusalem, thereby setting the stage for this to become the most sacred shrine in the city, hence the frequent visits made by the emperors and their need for a palace nearby (see Blachernae Palace above). To add to the hysteria, in 627 the **Virgin Blacherniotissa** was believed to have appeared on the city walls to spur on the soldiers fighting to drive out the Avars – every year there are still celebrations here on the anniversary of their defeat on 7th August.

Fire destroyed the original church in 1434, although it was rebuilt in the 19th century with an attractive little dome. The spring is now enclosed inside the church.

From the Bloody Tower

The Land Walls II

(From Yedikule to Topkapı)

022

One of Istanbul's most impressive sights, the land walls built from the Sea of Marmara to the Golden Horn during the reign of the Emperor Theodosius still stand to a considerable height despite the battering they have received across the centuries. Some stretches have been restored with mixed results. A walk along them –ideally in company– is one of the unexpected treats of a trip to the city. Start from Yedikule, a collection of towers that was turned into a fortress and head north.

The original Byzantium, the small town that stood on the site of what is now the Topkapı Palace, was a walled enclave whose fortifications stood up to several onslaughts before finally being destroyed by the **Emperor Septimius Severus** in an act of revenge following his capture of the city in 196. When the emperor was persuaded by his son **Caracalla** to rebuild them, he moved the western wall some 500 meters westwards, thereby more than doubling the size of the city. Unfortunately no trace of the original walls or their Severan successors survives today.

Septimius Severus

In 324 the **Emperor Constantine the Great** started to reinforce Nova Roma, his new capital, with land walls, the work being completed during the reign of his son and successor **Constantius**. Once again the land walls migrated westwards and the area enclosed within this third set of walls was perhaps four or five times as large as it had been in the Severan era.

Constantius II

Septimius Severus, his wife Julia Domna and their sons Caracalla and Geta. Geta's image was erased after Caracalla murdered him.

Area enclosed by the city walls in old engraving

The moat in front of the walls is now full of vegetable gardens.

When a single-layer wall proved inadequate to meet the needs of the expanding city, work began on the construction of the present-day walls 1.5 kilometers further west in 413; they had to be speedily rebuilt again in 447 after an earthquake struck just as **Attila the Hun** was approaching and it was at this point that the outer wall and ditch were added. Following another earthquake in 740, they were completely repaired by the **Emperor Leo III**. When the emperors moved house to the **Blachernae Palace** in the 11th century 13 more bastions were added to the section of wall around it. The walls were extensively repaired again after yet another earthquake in 1509. Long sections of the inner walls still stand intact and make one of Istanbul's most impressive sights.

The land defenses consisted of inner and outer walls with a road between them and a ditch in front of them. **Towers** were built roughly every 55 meters, while a series of **gates** provided access for the military and civilians. These were mainly named after the destinations of the roads that passed through them or after important buildings in the vicinity, although there is some debate over the names of some of them as they have changed frequently over the centuries. Since it was next to impossible to seize the city from the sea and as there was already a heavy chain closing off access to the Golden Horn, the sea walls didn't need to be as elaborate as the land fortifications; today you can inspect a few wretched remains in **Cibali**, **Fener** and **Balat** and more impressive stretches along the **Sea of Marmara**.

The walls were only ever **breached twice**: once in **1204** when the Crusaders came bursting through the sea defences and again in **1453** when Sultan Mehmed II and his army finally breached the land walls and captured Constantinople.

Parts of the sea walls have been lost to road widening or railway lines. Restoration of the land walls and of the Propontine walls along the Sea of Marmara began in 1953 as part of the celebrations for the 500th anniversary of the Ottoman conquest. During the 1980s the section of wall between Yedikule and the Belgradkapı was virtually rebuilt with little regard for the ancient stonework. Recently work on the project has speeded up with yet more heavy-handed rebuilding taking the place of meticulous restoration. The end results have come in for criticism from **UNESCO**, which recommended in 2006 that all work on the walls should stop pending further consultation.

Part of the chain that blocked the entrance to the Golden Horn

Parts of the wall are decorated will old religious motifs.

Whose walls?

Although the walls are often called Theodosian, Theodosius II was just a child of seven when work started on them. They are really the handiwork of his regent **Anthemius**.

Gold coin of Theodosius

Inscription on the wall reading: "Restored by the Roman Emperor Manuel".

Sadly some stretches of the wall are so "restored" that they look new.

Like Rome...

Once the land walls had been completed they enclosed a "New Rome" that stood on seven hills just like the original Rome in Italy.

The walls in numbers

- Total length of land and sea walls: 20.5km
- Length of land walls from the Mermerkule to Blachernae: 6.5km
- Height of inner wall: 12m
- Width of inner wall: 5m
- Height of outer wall: 8.5m
- Number of gates: 81
- Number of towers: 96 (outer wall) + 96 (inner wall)
- Distance between outer and inner walls: 15-20m
- Width of moat: 20m
- Depth of moat: 10m

Marble Tower (Mermerkule)

At the point where the land and sea walls met stood the **Marble Tower**, with the sea lapping at its base; it may once have formed part of a **separate palace** or castle. Today the coastal road built on reclaimed land separates it from the sea. When you are coming into Istanbul from the airport this is one of the first parts of the old city that you will see.

"The picturesque ruins were overgrown with creepers and scrub and ivy clung to the stonework which in many places was cracked from top to bottom."

Romance of the Bosphorus **by Dorina Lady Neave, 1949**

Yedikule ①

Today Yedkule is a museum.

Originally a cluster of four towers close to where the land and sea walls joined, **Yedikule** acquired another three towers after Sultan Mehmed II's conquest of Istanbul when it was converted into a fortress. During the Ottoman period it was used first as the treasury, then as a prison. As a prison it became something like the Turkish equivalent of the Tower of London in the UK, a place where those who had fallen from imperial favor were tortured and executed; heads were apparently tossed into the *kanlı kuyu* (bloody well) just inside the gate whence they eventually ended up in the Sea of Marmara. Famous prisoners who were put to death here included **Mahmud Paşa**, widely regarded as the best of the early Ottoman grand viziers, who was strangled in 1474 and the 17-year-old sultan **Genç (Young) Osman** who was executed by having his testicles compressed, a punishment intended to prevent the spilling of imperial blood, after he threatened the power of the Janissaries in 1622.

Osman II (the Young)

Graffiti etched on the walls of the **Ambassadors' Tower** (also known as the Yazılı Kule or "tower with inscriptions") recall long-dead prisoners from foreign countries that had offended the sultan. As recently as the Napoleonic Wars (1803-15), French prisoners-of-war languished in Yedikule; amongst them was **Francois Pouqueville** (1770-1838) who went on to write a book about his experiences.

François Pouqueville

Yedikule Gas Works, which was built by the French company in 1873 in Yedikule to provide gas and electricity to the Old City neighborhoods of Istanbul, was established as both a factory and a social purpose building. **Yedikule Gazhanesi**, which was brought into the cultural life of Istanbul as a result of the restoration works initiated by Istanbul Metropolitan Municipality, is a new meeting point for Istanbulites on the European side after the Gazhane Museum (p.482).

The towers were used as a prison.

If you like this you'll also like:
Anadolu Hisarı (see p. 538)
Galata Tower (see p. 324)
Rumeli Hisarı (see p. 432)

The Golden Gate (Porta Aurea) 1

Built into the walls of Yedikule you can still make out the partial outline of the gate the Byzantines called the **Porta Aurea** (Golden Gate; Altınkapı), which gave access to the **Via Egnatia** (see p. 191). This started life as a typical tripartite monumental arch built to celebrate the victory of **Emperor Theodosius I** over Magnus Maximus in 388; in 408 Theodosius II had it incorporated into the surrounding walls. Covered with statues and inscriptions, it would once have been far more impressive than it is today; the original gates, for example, were gold-plated, hence the Latin name. The gates were kept closed except after a victory when the emperor and his generals would parade through them to the roar of applause from the gathered crowds.

The Porta Aurea continued in use until 1261 when the **Emperor Michael VIII Palaeologos** rode through it to celebrate his return to power after ridding the city of the Fourth Crusaders. After that, however, the arch was sealed up for good.

The Golden Gate from outside Yedikule

Goose Fountain (Kazlıçeşme) 2

A pretty story recounts how thirsty soldiers besieging Constantinople in 1453 were advised to find water by following a flock of passing geese. In 1537 a fountain was erected on the site where the geese supposedly led them to water on land outside Yedikule. Later this area was designated for leather-working, an industry which continued here right through until 1993; the 17th-century travel writer **Evliya Çelebi** memorably described the dreadful stench while also suggesting that the locals became so accustomed to it that they were more bothered by the smell of perfume on a dandy!

Rome in Zeytinburnu

At the basement of the old Municipality building that is not being used as a museum and showroom at the coast of Kazlıçeşme, Roman mosaics from 2nd Century BC were unearthed. With the help of Istanbul Archeology Museums Department, this area was arranged as a **"Mosaic Room"** and opened to visit in a short time. With its vivid colors and very little damage, this artefact sets light to the unique style of the era. The mosaics are compared to the **Hadrian Villa Mosaics** in Tivoli, which are part of the National Museum of Rome and the **Dionysos Villa Mosaics** in Knossos.

Belgrade Gate (Belgradkapı) 3

This gate acquired its name after **Sultan Süleyman the Magnificent** resettled prisoners-of-war from **Belgrade** (Serbia) nearby in 1512. Just inside the wall is a **shrine** dedicated to **Uykulu (Sleepy) Muhiddin Efendi** who is supposed to be able to help those suffering from insomnia. At this point the walls have been particularly crudely restored.

"He who built this Gate of Gold brings back the Golden Age".

Lost inscription from the Porta Aurea.

Silivrikapı

Hadım İbrahim Paşa Mosque

Silivri Gate 4 (Silivrikapı/Gate of Selebria)

Once called the **Mukaddes Kaynak Gate** after a nearby sacred spring, this gate was later renamed after the road to Silivri, which passed through it. It was through it that an army from the Byzantine statelet of Nicaea (now İznik) marched to drive out the Latins in 1261.

Just inside the walls in Silivrikapı Caddesi is the elegant **Hadım (the Eunuch) İbrahim Paşa Mosque**, a work of **Sinan** that dates back to 1551. The founder is buried in the grounds.

Round the corner in unexpectedly rustic Tekke Maslağı Sokak is the **Bala Külliyesi (social complex)**, a mosque complex originally built by **Topçubaşı (Chief Cannon Master) Bala Süleyman Ağa** who had taken part in the siege of Constantinople. It was completely rebuilt in 1863 by Sazkar Kalfa as a Nakshibendi lodge, while **Piriüstü Valide Sultan**, the last official queen mother, added a school and fountain (currently lived in). In 1894 an earthquake badly damaged the complex which was repaired by Adile Sultan (see p. 532).

Living inside the walls

Fountain donated by Piristü Valide Sultan

The Bala complex

Narthex of church

Sacred spring

Balıklı Rum Church 5

At the back of a large cemetery across the busy road outside the gate is the **Balıklı Rum Church (Greek Orthodox Church with Fish)** built beside a sacred spring. While suffering from kidney problems, the **Emperor Justinian** is said to have drunk water from it and been cured, after which he had some of the stones intended for **Hagia Sophia** diverted here to build another church. As the story goes, during the siege of Constantinople in 1453 a monk was frying himself some fish beside the pool while muttering "the Turks are about as likely to occupy the city as these fish are to come back to life", when the fish jumped out of the pan and into the pool and shortly afterwards the city fell to the Ottomans. Fish still live in the pool, which is now housed beneath a beautiful chapel and very busy with visitors.

Tombs of the patriarchs with that of Patriarch Demetrios I in the foreground

Church courtyard

Nuns preparing for Easter

Hrant Dink's tomb in the Armenian cemetery

The current church on the site dates back only to 1833 and its courtyard contains many old **gravestones** moved from the cemeteries that used to exist here. Some are written in **Karamanlı** (Turkish written in Greek characters) and bear emblems to suggest the occupations of the deceased. During the anti-Greek rioting in 1955 the church was badly damaged and the tombs of some of the patriarchs buried behind it were ransacked.

Armenian cemetery next to the Balıklı Rum Church

A Karamanlı gravestone in which Turkish is written using the Greek alphabet. It reads: In this grave lies Vithleem (Bethlehem), wife of the tavern-keeper Sava from the village of Iloson in Niğde. May God bless her soul. 2 July 1897

Mevlevi Gate (Mevlevikapı) 6

This gate took its name from a nearby dervish tekke (lodge). The **Yenikapı Mevlevihanesi** was established in 1598 by the Janissary leader **Malkoç Mehmed Efendi**; it was the second oldest Mevlevi lodge in Istanbul after the Galata Mevlevihanesi (see p. 320) and by far the largest. In 1911 the lodge was repaired after a suspicious fire in 1906. After Atatürk banned the dervish orders in 1925, the buildings were turned into a student hostel much of which was destroyed by another fire in 1961. Yet another fire in 1997 wrote off more of the complex. However, in 2009 the entire complex was rebuilt as part of a **"Cultural Valley"** project to improve this whole area. The new **semahane** (ritual hall), with a wooden floor beneath a shallow dome, is absolutely stunning, as is the restoration of the surrounding complex.

To find it, cross over the busy main road and walk through peaceful Merkez Efendi cemetery in the direction of the Merkez Efendi Mosque; the complex is behind the row of restaurants.

Other Mevlevi lodges in Istanbul:

- Galata Mevlevi Lodge (p. 320)
- Kasımpaşa Mevlevi Lodge
- Beşiktaş (Bahariye) Mevlevi Lodge
- Üsküdar Mevlevi Lodge

Among the Mevlevi Lodges in Turkey, only The Galata Lodge, which serves as a museum and belongs to the Ministry of Culture and Tourism in Turkey, hosts sufi music concerts and whirling performances.

Merkez Efendi and the magical "*Mesir Macunu*"

Born in a village near Denizli, Merkez Efendi was living and teaching in Manisa when Sultan Süleyman the Magnificent's mother, **Hafsa Valide Sultan**, fell ill.

The sheikh mixed together **41 different ingredients** to create a remedy that he called "*mesir macunu*". The queen mother made such a rapid recovery that the mixture was soon in great demand and every 22 March Merkez Efendi would go to the Sultan Mosque, built by the grateful queen and toss samples to the assembled crowd from the minarets. The tradition continues to this day and the recipe also features prominently in the annual **Traditional Medicine Festival** held near his tomb in Istanbul.

Merkez Efendi Mosque 7 8

The **Merkez Efendi Mosque** dates back to 1580 and was built with the assistance of Sultan Selim II's daughter **Şah Sultan**; originally it formed part of a large complex, but most of the other buildings are now lost. The mosque was completely made over in 1837 and the stone exterior conceals a pretty little wooden interior with a curtained mihrab painted on the back wall. Attached to it is the **tomb of Merkez Efendi** (1463-1552), which still attracts many pilgrims. Just outside the gate the attractive **Abdülbaki Paşa Library (Neyhane)** was originally a primary school but had long served as a storage unit until it was restored in 2007; it now houses a small tearoom, library and cultural center, named Nağmeda, with some pretty painted panels reworked on its domed ceiling. Nearby the large wooden **Merkezefendi Konağı** (mansion) was restored in 2009. The hamam linked to the mosque is also slated for restoration.

---

www.nagmedar.com, Tel: 0212 415 58 58

Medieval ships full of produce-carrying amphorae emerging from the mud at Yenikapı during excavations for the Marmaray. The site of the old Theodosius Harbor later became the Langa fruit and vegetable gardens.

THE COAST ROAD
(FROM CANKURTARAN TO YEŞİLKÖY)

Beyond the Stable Gate

Cankurtaran and the Sea Walls

023

The back streets of Cankurtaran, tucked in between the Topkapı Palace walls and Kumkapı, stand on the site of the remains of the old Byzantine Great Palace whose remains crop up unexpectedly here and there. It is also home to the frequently overlooked Dede Efendi House Museum.

Hidrellez festivities in days gone by

"Life-saver" might seem rather a strange name for a neighborhood, but Cankurtaran is thought to have acquired it because it was at one time home to a **lifeboat station**. Alternatively, it may have been given the name in memory of a soldier called Ni'me'l-Ceyş'ten Seyyid Hasan Ağa who was nicknamed "**the Life-Saver**" because of his valor in battle against the Byzantines.

Resident of Cankurtaran

In the 16th century the Ottoman admiral known to the west as **Barbarossa** (see p. 396) had barracks built here to house his sailors when they returned from a voyage. The original buildings were lost to an 18th-century fire; a hotel now stands on the site. Today this is a district that is rapidly surrendering to tourism. Although hotels are increasingly encroaching on the area, it still has the feel of a traditional Istanbul ***mahalle*** (neighborhood) and retains many old **wooden houses** – often in a sorry state of disrepair – and small shops catering for the locals. Still pockets of glaring poverty continue to rub awkwardly against such speedy gentrification.

Magnaura Palace

Akbıyık St (Akbıyık Caddesi)

The heart of Cankurtaran, **"White Moustache Street"** is a funny place, part Turkish take on Bangkok's famous Khao San Road backpacker enclave, part fast-gentrifying hotel-land. Bars, restaurants, cafes, souvenir shops, grocery shops, book exchanges, they're all here and in summer life on the street can be raucous They soon re-open and life returns to normal. Near the junction with Mimar Mehmet Ağa Caddesi a stretch of the Byzantine **Magnaura Palace**, which formed part of the Great Palace (see p. 043), has been rather crudely restored. The palace is known to be the largest of the four large palaces built in the region by the Byzantine Emperor Constantine I, founder of Eastern Rome, when he settled in Istanbul. The building, which served as the senate and a university in different eras, was acquired by Istanbul Metropolitan Municipality in 2017.

Akbıyık Street

İshak Paşa Mosque

Often overlooked despite its position at one end of Akbıyık Caddesi this small mosque dating back to 1482 is one of the oldest in the city as it was built for **İshak Paşa**, Grand Vizier to **Mehmed II** and **Bayezid II**. Across the road the remains of its large **hamam** crumble away unloved; some parts are incorporated into the garden of a hotel.

İshak Paşa Hamam

Dede Efendi House Museum

This lovely old wooden mansion was once home to **Dede Efendi** (1778-1846) who was one of Turkey's finest composers of classical music. After his death it was used for a while as the local police station before falling into disrepair. Restored in the 1980s, it now houses a small **museum of musical instruments,** but is mostly worth visiting to get a sense of what some of the other houses crumbling away nearby might have looked like in their heyday. Watch for signs advertising occasional **concerts.** Right beside the museum stands an elaborate **fountain** dating back to 1734 and paid for by the mother of the Grand Vizier **Hekimoğlu Ali Paşa.**

@dedeefendievi
www.turkev.org.tr
Tel: 0212 516 43 14

Who was Dede Efendi?

Born in Istanbul and resident for a while in Eyüp, Dede Efendi studied the **ney** (reed flute) and wrote hundreds of songs and pieces of music for the **Mevlevi dervishes.** His works were popular with Sultan **Selim III** for whom he often performed. In 1846, while on pilgrimage to Saudi Arabia, he died of cholera. He is buried in Mecca. Some of his songs remain popular even today.

Restored wooden houses of Cankurtaran

Traces of Church of Savior Philanthropos

The Propontine Sea Walls

If you stroll down from Küçük Ayasofya to Kennedy Caddesi and the seashore you will be able to inspect the remains of the Byzantine sea walls that ran all the way from the **Marble Tower** (Mermer Kule) in the west (see p. 157) to **Ayvansaray** in the north (see p. 151). Despite the heavy traffic on Kennedy Caddesi, the coast road, it's a pleasant half-hour **walk** from Ahırkapı or Çatladıkapı to Sarayburnu. As you walk along you will be able to inspect the mish-mash of masonry and look out for two particular landmarks. The first is the support wall that is all that remains of the marble **İncili Köşk (Pearl Pavilion),** built into the perimeter of Topkapı Palace in 1578. According to the story, at the very end of his life **Sultan Murad III** (r. 1574-95) was listening to music while gazing out to sea from this pavilion when the passing navy fired their guns in his honor, causing such vibrations that part of the ceiling fell down on him. The Pearl Pavilion was also the last known resting place of a famous **organ** sent as a gift to Sultan Mehmed III by **Queen Elizabeth I of England**.

Just past the pavilion patterns in the brickwork of the wall and the shapes of arches and windows are all that remain of the 12th-century **Church of Savior Philanthropos (Jesus the Charitable)** which was popular with medieval Russian pilgrims who reported a miracle-working statue there. Greek pilgrims visited an **ayazma** (sacred spring) here until well into the 19th century.

Pearl Pavilion

Ahırkapı

Cankurtaran lurks behind the remains of the old **Byzantine sea walls,** which, here, have a railway line running immediately behind them. Occasionally there are breaks in the wall where the railway line is forced to run across the old gateways. Ahırkapı (Stable Gate) was one such gateway that offered access to the **imperial mews** in Ottoman times.

Statue of Admiral Turgut Reis in front of the sea walls

Hagia Sophia's Older Sister

Küçük Ayasofya

024

A short walk away from the Blue Mosque, Küçük Ayasofya (Little Hagia Sophia), a wonderful small church dating back to the 6th century, is now a mosque with an inviting courtyard ringed with craft workshops. Nearby stand ruinous stretches of the Byzantine sea walls and the last remnants of the Great Palace.

In the early 6th century, **Justinian**, who was to become one of the greatest builders of the Byzantine Empire, was accused of plotting against his uncle, the then emperor **Anastasius** and was facing probable execution. Fortunately for him his uncle had a dream in which **Sts Sergius** and **Bacchus** appeared to him and pleaded for his nephew's life. Not surprisingly, when Justinian succeeded to the throne the very first church for which he was responsible was dedicated to the soldier saints.

Church of San Vitale in Ravenna

Little Hagia Sophia (Küçük Ayasofya)

Justinian paid for the church to be built in 527, five years before work began on his version of the more famous Hagia Sophia (see p. 026). The design is said to have been inspired by that of the **Church of San Vitale in Ravenna**, Italy, which contains a mosaic image of Justinian. Despite its beauty, the church was the setting for an undignified squabble in 547 when Justinian invited **Pope Vigilius** to visit him and settle an obscure theological dispute. During the course of events the Pope clung to the altar, which was pulled down before he could be separated from it. Perhaps inevitably it was Justinian who emerged the victor in the quarrel.

The Church of Sts Sergius and Bacchus is more dazzling even than the sun."
Buildings **by Procopius, c. 550**

Writing in Greek and Arabic scripts side by side.

Inside the church-mosque

While the exterior of Little Ayasofya with its shallow dome is striking it's really the interior that wins it the plaudits. Once you cross the porch that formed part of Hüseyin Ağa's additions you pass through the cluttered narthex into an interior that feels circular but is in fact roughly octagonal. It's ringed with a two-storey-high **colonnade** that has no counterpart in Istanbul and is its most striking feature. The columns themselves are made of green, red and black marble and are topped with exquisite Byzantine basketwork capitals. There's also a fine and deeply carved **entablature** bearing an inscription commemorating Justinian and his wife Theodora's dedication of the church to St Sergius although not, rather oddly, to St Bacchus. You can ascend to the gallery to inspect the upper columns using stairs at the back of the building; the bird's-eye view down into what was once the nave is stunning.

During the 16th century conversion a mihrab and minbar were added to the church. So far, so conventional. More unusual are the stone pump and hamam basin that stand on what looks like a large millstone to the rear of the nave. They were apparently used for baptisms in the later Christian period, with the water being pumped up from a well below the building.

View of Little Ayasofya's stunning dome

Hüseyin Ağa's tomb

Byzantine capitals in Küçük Ayasofya

Hüseyin Ağa Medrese

After you've finished inspecting the church-mosque it's worth taking a turn around the cells of the **madrasah** (seminary) where you will find craftsmen and women hard at work, producing ebru pictures, painted tiles, inlaid boxes and Ottoman-style miniatures. An office sells copies of the Yesevi magazine that perpetuates the teachings of **Ahmed Yesevi** (1093-1166), a Turkic **poet and sufi** from what is now Kazakhstan who founded the **Yeseviye Tarikat** (religious order).

The church-mosque overlooking the Sea of Marmara

Not so great after all?

Emperor Justinian

The **Emperor Justinian** (483-565) is usually nicknamed "the Great" and is revered as a saint in the Eastern Church. However, in **"The Secret History"** the contemporary historian **Procopius** presents a very different picture of a man he calls a "demon in human form". In this extended piece of character assassination, he depicts Justinian as indecisive, vicious, greedy and in thrall to his wife **Theodora** who, he says, had started out as the lowest of prostitutes.

The Bucoleon Palace and the Cracked Gate (Çatladıkapı)

On the waterfront, near the Stable Gate (Ahırkapı, see p. 169) stood the **Bucoleon Palace**; you will notice its walls and marble window frames set into the sea walls as you head west towards the Cracked Gate (Çatladıkapı). Dating back to the 5th century, the palace faced onto the **harbor** that served the Great Palace (see p. 043), so the window frames are some of its very last vestiges.

Apparently taking its name from the Greek words for "bull" and "lion" after statues of these animals with which it was adorned, the Bucoleon Palace was restored during the reign of **Justinian** and expanded by **Emperor Theophilus** in the 9th century when a sea-facing balcony may have been added. During the **Fourth Crusade** of 1204 the palace was seized by **Boniface of Montferrat** who went on to marry Princess Margaret of Hungary, a refugee there. After the restoration of the Byzantine monarchy in 1261, it was gradually **abandoned** in favor of the Blachernae Palace at Ayvansaray (see p. 151). By the time the Ottomans arrived in 1453 the building seems to have been in ruins. It was effectively **dismantled** to make way for the railway in 1873.

As for the **Cracked Gate**, which probably led from the Bucoleon Harbor to the Great Palace, it seems to have suffered the damage from which it acquired its name during an **earthquake** in 1532.

---

www.byzantium1200.com/boucoleon.html

Remains of the Bucoleon Palace in 2010 before restoration

Beyond the Hippodrome

Sokollu Mehmed Paşa Mosque and Kadırga

025

Just a short walk south-west of the Hippodrome, the beautiful 16th-century Sokollu Mehmed Paşa was designed by Mimar Sinan but attracts much less attention than some of his other works despite containing an impressive array of İznik tiles. On the way to inspect it you will pass the Byzantine Sphendone which used to support the southern end of the Hippodrome. Here, too, is the restored 19th-century Uzbek Lodge, which has a long tradition of training students in the art of "ebru" (paper marbling).

The massive façade of the Sokollu Mehmed Paşa Mosque faces straight onto Kadırga, a residential neighborhood largely ignored by tourists where crumbling **wooden houses** and unexpected pieces of ancient masonry stand as reminders of a grander past. Once upon a time there was a huge **harbor** here, originally created in 362 by **Emperor Julian the Apostate** and revived in 570 by **Emperor Julian II.** It continued in use through to Ottoman times and its name is thought to be a corruption of the Greek "katerga" which meant "**forced labor**", a reference to the men who

Julian II

would have rowed the galleys. Visiting in the 16th century the French writer and traveler **Pierre Gilles** thought the name commemorated the sunken galleys that were sometimes uncovered here; interestingly it was at Yenikapı, just a little way further along the shore (see p. 185), that a series of galleys were dredged intact from the mud during excavation work for the Marmaray project (see p. 500).

Somewhat run-down and overcrowded, modern **Kadırga** is an area where the shops exist to serve the locals rather than the tourists and where the small lokantas serve pide and lentil soup to an appreciative regular clientele. It has something of the feel of the East End of London, England, where waves of immigrants have passed through and then moved on again. The latest incomers are **Ethiopians** and **East Europeans** who are served by an extraordinary number of cheap phone shops.

Old Kadırga houses

Recently some of the old **wooden houses** in the streets leading off Kadırga Limanı Square have been pleasingly restored. Most are small family houses although there are also some imposing *konaks* (mansions). Here and there you will also see fine stone fountains from which local residents would have fetched their water before the days of in-house plumbing. The **Kadırga Hamam** is still open to visitors. Commissioned by Governor General Yahya Paşa in 1506 to provide funding for a soup kitchen in **Skopje**, this bath-house, facing the park, used to be a first port of call for sailors returning from voyages. Rebuilt in 1734, it still serves both men and women in separate sections and is pleasingly authentic. but the early 16th-century **Çardaklı Hamam** stands in ruins.

www.kadirgahamami.com
Tel: 0212 518 19 48

Sokollu Mehmed Paşa Mosque and Kadırga

Built by **Mimar Sinan** for **Esmahan Sultan**, the wife of the Grand Vizier Sokullu Mehmed Paşa, in 1571 on the supposed site of the **church of St Anastasia**, this superb mosque is best known for the lovely **İznik tiles** that adorn its walls, although the stained glass in its windows is also very impressive. It is also interesting because of the architectural difficulties presented by the need to build on such a steeply sloping site. Unusually, you approach it via steps that pass under an arch above which sits the dershane (lecture theatre) of the **madrasah** (seminary) whose cells wrap around the courtyard.

Externally the mosque gives the impression of great size. Inside, however, it feels very compact and cut off from the outside world. Small pieces removed from the Kaaba in Mecca have been incorporated into the mihrab and minbar. The columns on either side of the mihrab are able to revolve which is meant to ensure earthquake-proofing.

Sokollu Mehmed Paşa

Born a Bosnian Serb in the town of Sokol, Sokollu Mehmed Paşa (1506-79) was brought to Istanbul through the **devşirme** system (see p. 106) to serve as a janissary and rose through the ranks to become grand vizier to three sultans, **Süleyman the Magnificent**, **Selim II** and **Murad III**. Educated inside Topkapı Palace, he became a soldier who fought at **Mohacs** in 1526 and at **Vienna** in 1529, going on to succeed Barbaros Hayreddin as **admiral of the Ottoman navy**. For the last 15 years before he was assassinated by a dervish, he was effectively the ruler of the Ottoman Empire. Aside from the mosque in Kadırga that bears his name, Mehmed Paşa was also responsible for the fine Sinan-designed **Azapkapı Mosque** (see p. 273). His tomb, also designed by Sinan, is at **Eyüp** (see p. 247).

Ruins of Helvacıbaşı İskenderağa Mosque (front) with Sokollu Mehmed Paşa Mosque (back)

"Color is the glory of this mosque."
Sinan **by Arthur Stratton, 1972**

Uzbek Lodge (Özbekler Tekkesi)

If you leave the mosque from the right-hand side of the courtyard you will come out facing the Uzbek Lodge. Originally built in 1692 but completely rebuilt in 1887, this rose-colored tekke (Sufi lodge), with its minaret right above the entrance, was probably erected to serve as a guesthouse for visiting dervishes and clergy from **Central Asia**. It is associated with the Uzbek religious leader **Sheikh Sadık Efendi** (? – 1846) who is thought to have studied paper marbling (*ebru*) in his home town of Bukhara and then passed his knowledge down to his sons. Restored in 2008, it now houses Istanbul Design Center, as an arts and crafts school.

@istanbultasarimmerkezi, www.istanbultasarimmerkezi.org

Building directly on top of the Sphendone.

Sphendone

As you walk down from the Hippodrome (see p. 046) to the Sokollu Mehmed Paşa Mosque you will pass the remains of the huge semi-circular wall that used to support the southern end of the **stadium.** Today they are mostly of interest for their great age rather than their beauty but behind them you should try to imagine a long corridor with branches off it leading to the different sections of seating just as you might find in a modern football stadium. Later the corridor was converted into a cistern to provide water for the surrounding neighborhood.

Kadırga Park

Heart of Kadırga is Kadırga Limanı (Kadırga Harbor) Square which contains a small park popular with locals. Easily overlooked behind a fence stands what looks like a simple free-standing fountain but is actually the **Esma Sultan Namazgah**, one of Istanbul's few remaining outdoor places for prayer. Built in 1781 for **Esma Sultan** (1726-88), the daughter of **Sultan Ahmed III**, it was accessible via stairs that led up to the top.

What is ebru?

The art of paper marbling, *ebru* is known to have existed in Turkey since at least the 16th century. The marbling effect is created by carefully transferring layers of paint from the surface of a viscous solution to paper, using a horsehair brush and small combs to create patterns in the color. After a period in the doldrums, *ebru* has been rediscovered recently and you should be able to see people carrying it out in the Caferağa Medrese (see p. 203) or Kabasakal Medrese (see p. 034).

Esma Sultan Namazgah is in Kadırga Park

Behind the Sand Gate

Kumkapı

026

Best known for the many fish restaurants that spill out into the main square in summer, Kumkapı is an old Armenian and Greek neighborhood just inside the sea walls between Kadırga and Yenikapı. In Byzantine times there was a busy port here as well as a fleet of fishing boats, which was how the tradition of eating fish here originally started. The area grew in importance in the 17th century when the Armenian Patriarchate moved here from nearby Samatya.

Old photograph of Kumkapı

Kumkapı Fish Market

In Byzantine times what is now Kumkapı (Sand Gate) was the site of the **Kontoskalion Harbor** which was originally built by the **Emperor Julian** (r. 361-63) and repaired and upgraded over the centuries until **Michael VIII Paleologos** made it the city's main naval base after the Latins were driven out in 1261. As so often, the harbor gradually silted up and had to be abandoned, but recently a new harbor was built to serve the modern fishing fleet that ploughs back and further from the Sea of Marmara to the Black Sea. A lively fish market has grown up alongside the harbor, selling some of the freshest fish in town; some of the action on the fish-eating front has also migrated to this side of the main road too. Some of the fine **wooden houses** of Kumkapı have been given a much-needed facelift, although this is still a very run-down and neglected area, especially once you cross over the main square and start walking towards Nişanca and Yenikapı.

Mikhail Palaeologos

Armenian Patriarchate

Surp Asdvadzadzin (Virgin Mary) Church

Armenian Patriarchate

As late as the 1850s, the majority of the local population was Armenian and they lived a life not unlike that of their Turkish neighbors, with separate male and female quarters in their homes and their women similarly covered up. Since then, most of them have moved away, their place taken by Armenians from the Anatolian heartlands and, perhaps surprisingly, from Armenia itself.

Today the Armenian Patriarchate is housed inside the **Church of Surp Asdvadzadzin** (the Holy Mother of God), which stands on the site of a Byzantine church. It moved here from Samatya in 1641 but the buildings that housed it have been destroyed twice in huge conflagrations, first in 1762 and then again in 1826. The current complex only dates back to 1828 and incorporates a school as well as three churches; the plans were drawn up by members of the famous **Balyan** family. It stands over a sacred **spring** (ayazma) dedicated to St Theodore which is accessed via steps down from the Surp Harutyun church. The striking **bell tower** with crosses cut out of its facades was added in 1870. As well as by the local Armenians, the church is used today by Istanbul's small Ethiopian population. With the artworks exhibited in all rooms and the hallways, the Patriarchate resembles a museum. During the restoration between 2001-2004, the basement floor that was not in use, was turned into an exhibition area. The collection of Patriarch Hovhannes Golod, which includes more than 300 objects dating from the 18th century to present day, was opened for visits in 2006. To see the collection, you need to contact Diyakos Vagarsak Seropyan beforehand to get an appointment

www.turkiyeermenileripatrikligi.org

Tel: 0212 517 09 70, closed weekends

Panagia Elpida Church

Greek Churches

Although the old Greek population has completely vanished, Kumkapı still retains two enormous Greek Orthodox churches, both of them rebuilt in the 19th century. The glistening white **Church of Panagia Elpida** probably dates back to the 15th century and stands over a sacred spring dedicated to St George. Completely rebuilt in 1895 in a style that mixes neoclassicism with rococo, it is being painstakingly restored. The **Church of Hagia Kyriake** probably dates back to the 16th century but was completely rebuilt in neo-Byzantine style between 1895 and 1901 by the architect **Pericles Fotiades.** It boasts one of the largest domes in town and stands over a sacred spring dedicated to St Basil. The size of these churches suggests the great wealth and confidence of the community who used to live here.

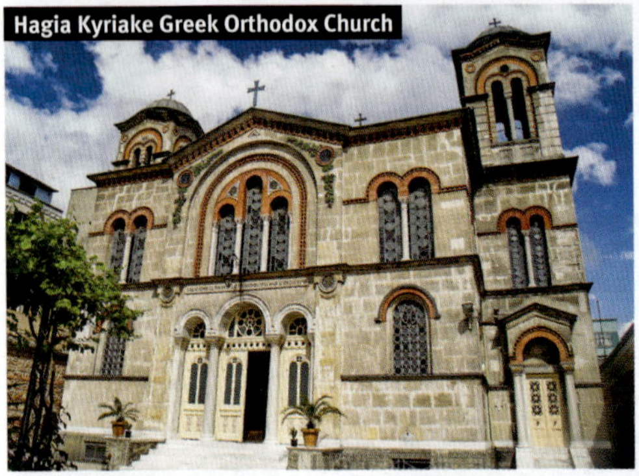

Hagia Kyriake Greek Orthodox Church

Interior of Panagia Elpida

Tavaşi Süleyman Ağa Mosque

The **Tavaşi Süleyman Ağa Mosque** dates back to the 17th century although the current building is a 19th-century remake, distinguished only by the interest of its **wooden minaret.** More intriguing is the story attached to its name. A "tavaşi" was a **black slave** who had been castrated and sold into service at the palace, but from such seemingly unpromising beginnings **Süleyman Ağa** rose to become Chief Black Eunuch (Kızlar Ağası) at Topkapı Palace, an enormously important position which gave him effective control over the harem and of a network of spies.

Tavaşı Süleyman Ağa Mosque

Nişancı Mehmed Paşa Mosque

The **Nişancı Mehmed Paşa Mosque** was originally built in 1475 for Mehmed II's last grand vizier, the Nişancı or Keeper of the Seal **Karamanlı Mehmed Paşa**, but it has been rebuilt many times since then. The current manifestation is a wooden Ottoman construction, which still retains its original double **hamam** (Turkish bath), one of the oldest in Istanbul and still in business today. Mehmed Paşa is buried in the grounds of the second mosque to bear his name in **Karagümrük** (see p. 130).

Some of Kumkapı's Ethiopian community

Eurasia Tunnel

Designed to ease the traffic density of Istanbul, the tunnel was opened in 2016. The 5.4 km section of the project, whose entrances are located in Koşuyolu and Kumkapı, consists of a two-storey tunnel built underneath the seafloor with special technology and connection tunnels built with other methods. The fee is a little high, but it can be life-saving in emergencies.

Night in Kumkapı

The colorful atmosphere of Kumkapı Square on summer evenings when tables spill out of the restaurants and fill the area around the fountain is hard to beat. However, this is an area that has long been notorious for price-gouging and other rip-offs.

There's always fresh fish in Kumkapı.

Let the musicians serenade you over dinner in Kumkapı.

New Life for the New Gate

Yenikapı and Samatya

027

Home to an enormous harbor since Byzantine times, Yenikapı is now the site of the docks used by the huge sea buses to the Marmara Islands, Bursa, Yalova and Bandırma. A treasure trove of medieval ships has just been discovered here. Once the base for the Armenian patriarchate, Samatya is a little visited suburb with one particularly significant monument, the ruined Church of St John the Baptist of Studios, heart of one of the most important of all Byzantine monasteries.

Yenikapı

At first sight Yenikapı (New Gate) is a pretty unprepossessing place, hemmed in by busy Kennedy Street (Caddesi) and a large car showroom. However, it has a venerable history as the site of the huge, stone-walled **Theodosius (Eleutherius) Harbor** built during the reign of the Emperor Theodosius (379-95). As so often this harbor slowly silted up; by 1500 it had fallen into disuse and the neighborhood went on to grow fat on the proceeds of market gardening. Since then, however, it has recovered its original purpose as the dock for the huge sea buses that crisscross the Sea of Marmara.

During the course of preparatory work for a new station of Marmaray Project (see p. 501) here the sites of the **Theodosian and Ottoman harbors** were uncovered and excavated. The most exciting discoveries were the remains of **37 medieval shipwrecks** dating from the 5th to the 11th centuries, perfectly preserved in the mud with their contents intact and a permanent museum to house the finds is expected to form part of the new Yenikapı station. The **Institute of Nautical Archeology** has said of the finds: "The work at Yenikapı will rewrite the book on Byzantine shipbuilding as well as the role of maritime trade in the history of Constantinople and the late Roman Empire."

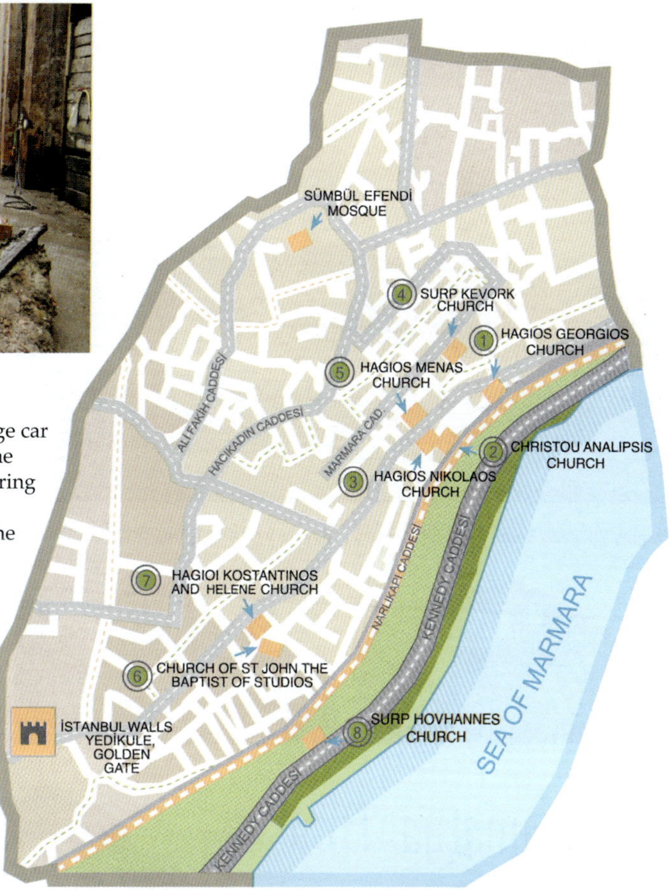

Greeks, Armenians and Turks

Yenikapı was originally a Greek neighborhood, but after 1453 Sultan Mehmed II resettled many Armenians here. Gradually Turkish Muslims also started to move in, adding mosques to the mix of religious buildings. In the 21st century Yenikapı is well known for its bars and rather seedy nightclubs.

Samatya shoreline

Samatya ① ② ③

Like nearby Kumkapı, Samatya has a name that commemorates the extensive sands that once existed where now there is only the busy main road; it's a corruption of the Greek word "**psamathion**" meaning **sandy**. Officially the area is now called **Kocamustafapaşa** but most people stick with Samatya, a rare instance of a name that has survived virtually intact since Byzantine times (others are Tarabya, Pendik and Langa).

Assyrian Church

The square at the center of Samatya is still very picturesque and the surrounding area was used during the filming of **Nuri Bilge Ceylan**'s award-winning film on the topic of family honor, "**Üç Maymun (Three Monkeys)**". In the streets immediately behind the square stand the Greek Orthodox churches of **Christou Analipsis** and **Hagios Nikolaos**, both of them generally kept locked. Next to the Gençosman primary school there's also a modern Italian church with a curious metal tower that looks as if it came from a prisoner-of-war camp. It's used by the local **Assyrian community**.

Hagios Nikolaos Greek Orthodox Church

Hagios Georgios Greek Orthodox Church on the main road

Old Samatya Houses

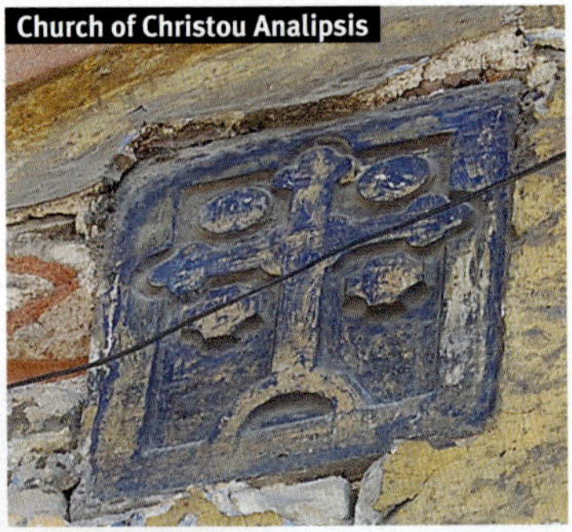
Church of Christou Analipsis

Inscription on the monastery

Old monastery building

Surp Kevork Kilisesi ④ ⑤

The **Samatya Gate** in the sea walls gave access to what started life in 1031 as the Church of Panaghia Peribleptos (St Mary the All-Seeing) on Samatya Caddesi but is now the imposing **Church of Surp Kevork,** also known as the **Sulu Monastery (Water Monastery)** because of the sacred spring in the grounds. After the church was sacked during the **Fourth Crusade** of 1204, **Michael VIII Paleaologos** had it restored and reopened. Following the conquest of Istanbul, **Sultan Mehmed II** brought some Armenians here from Bursa and gave them the church to serve as a patriarchate. Over the decades there were so many arguments between the Greek and Armenian communities over possession of the building that it came to be nicknamed "**the Bloody Church**". In 1641 the patriarchate moved to Kumkapı but the church remained in the hands of the local Armenians. Repeatedly burnt down and then restored, it was used by soldiers for target practice during the First World War. It was restored yet again in 1993.

Surp Kevork Armenian Church

Main entrance to church grounds

The church of Surp Kevork is in the grounds of the Sahakyan Nunyan School

Today Samatya has the city's biggest Armenian population along with Kurtuluş and Şişli. There's a large school in the church grounds but when I visited during break time all the children were speaking Turkish. I chatted with Halis Hanım whose family originally came from Anatolia and whose family name was Alis - the "H" was added during the program of Turkification.

Nearby on the main road the much smaller **Church of Hagios Menas** was built in 1833 and destroyed during the riots of 1955, only to be rebuilt again immediately. Beneath it is the brick-domed **Mausoleum of Sts Karpos and Papylos,** obscure saints who were martyred during the 3rd-century Decian persecutions. Although this was be the **oldest such mausoleum in the city**, today it's hidden behind a teahouse. The owner showed us a short stretch of the circular wall with the aid of a gas lamp.

Ayios Minas Church

Looking for Sts Karpos and Papylos Mausoleum

Abandoned shell of Studion Monastery

“A monk (at the Studion) was not allowed to kiss his mother... under penalty of excommunication for fifty days.”

Byzantine Churches in Constantinople **by Alexander van Millingen, 1912**

Abbot Theodore the Studite

Church of St John the Baptist of Studios ⑥ ⑦

Samatya’s most important monument is the ruined Church of St John the Baptist of Studios (also known as the Church of Ioannes Prodromos) in İmrahor İlyas Bey Caddesi which was built between 454 and 463 and is thought to be Istanbul’s **oldest surviving Byzantine church**. It was once part of an important monastic complex, the **Studion**, housing about 1,000 monks and taking its name from that of the Roman consul Studios. The monks here were keen **iconodules** (see p. 583) and their rules formed the basis for those followed on **Mt Athos** in Greece.

After being exiled to Prinkipo (Büyükada, see p. 588), its most famous abbot, **Theodore the Studite** (759-826), was eventually canonized and is buried in the grounds. Under his leadership the monastery became the center of a brief **Byzantine revival** during which the monks were responsible for producing many wonderful **illuminated manuscripts**, some of which found their way to Europe during the Renaissance.

Relief from Church of Hagioi Konstantinos and Helene

The Studion was sacked by the Crusaders in **1204**, but became the focal point for celebrations when **Michael VIII Paleologos** was restored to the throne in 1261.

Sundial

Rebuilt in 1293 with fortress-like walls, it remained a center of intellectual brilliance right through until 1453.

St John’s was converted into the **İmrahor (Master of the Horse) İlyas Bey Mosque** after the Turkish conquest of the city but was virtually destroyed by an earthquake in 1894. It retains some of its original floor mosaics. Unfortunately you will not be able to see them since, even though the church has had restoration work carried out on it, it is now locked and abandoned to the taggers, a particular shame given its illustrious history (the most beautiful are in any case on display at the **Benaki Museum in Athens**).

It’s also worth taking a look at the nearby **Church of Hagioi Konstantinos and Helene**, on Hacı Manav Sokak. It’s known as the church of the Karamanlıs because it was used by Greeks from the Karaman province of central Anatolia who spoke Turkish but wrote it in the Greek alphabet, a mongrel linguistic form called **Karamanlı**. The church dates back to 1805 but has been extensively repaired, most recently in 1963.

Church of Hagioi Konstantinos and Helene

Inscription in Arabic script above the Narlıkapı

Pomegranate Gate 8

The **Pomegranate Gate (Narlıkapı)** through the city wall used to provide access for the emperors when they came to visit the monastery every 29 August, the feast day commemorating the execution of St John the Baptist. Today it still survives but is obscured from view behind the Armenian **Church of Surp Hovhannes** which is open Sunday mornings; it's worth taking a look as it's still attached to a long stretch of **unrestored wall.** The emperors also came to pray at the Studite monastery whenever they entered the city via the Pomegranate Gate.

Surp Hovhannes Church

Church Interior

At the Seventh Mile

Bakırköy and Ataköy

028

For most visitors Bakırköy and Ataköy are just part of the sprawling new Istanbul that they were whisked through on the way to and from the airport. However, both suburbs contain one or two historical surprises, including the most westerly of the city's four open-air reservoirs dating back to Byzantine times. The area around Ataköy Marina on the Sea of Marmara is also quite charming if you can ignore the busy coast road rushing past behind you.

Shoreline at Bakırköy

In Turkish **Bakırköy** means "**Copper Village**". However, its original name seems to have been **Makriköy**, a corruption of the Greek Makrohori that meant "a far place"; it was changed to Bakırköy as part of a general policy of Turkifying place names in 1925. Why "a far place"? Well, originally this was a separate settlement, called **Hebdomon**, which was outside the city walls at a point that was exactly seven miles (11 kilometers) from the **Milion** marker in Sultanahmet (see p. 063). The **Emperor Valens** built himself a seaside palace here and until 474 this was where new emperors were crowned before they processed ceremonially into the city along the **Via Egnatia** (from 474 onwards they were crowned in Hagia Sophia). A large military training ground was also established here and named the **Campus Martius** (Field of Mars) after its counterpart in Rome. Much of the **limestone** used in building the land walls is thought to have been quarried in Makrohori (the same quarries later supplied many of the stones used to build the Süleymaniye Mosque).

The coming of the railway in the 19th century turned Bakırköy into a popular middle-class residential area. Since then it has grown more and more built-up and congested. Today it takes a considerable leap of the imagination to conjure up what it might have looked like in its glory days when its street would have been lined with grand monuments instead of branches of chain stores.

One of Turkey's first planned suburbs, **Ataköy** was named after Turkey's founding father, **Mustafa Kemal Atatürk**; unfortunately it's full of the sort of high-rise apartment blocks that most people who don't have live in them find rather depressing.

Opened in 1988, the **Galleria** was the first of the city's now seemingly endless shopping malls and was built at the urging of **Prime Minister Turgut Özal** who had been very impressed by the **Houston Galleria**.

Baruthane Public Garden

Emperor Valens

The road to Albania

The **Via Egnatia** was one of the great highways of the Roman world, stretching for 1,120 kilometers from **Dyrrachium** (Durres) on the Adriatic coast of what is now Albania all the way to Byzantium; from Dyrrachium travelers would have been able to take ship across the Adriatic and then continue their journey along the **Via Appia** to Rome, thus linking what were to become the twin capitals of the Roman Empire.

It seems to have taken its name from **Gnaeus Egnatius,** a proconsul of Macedonia who, inscriptions suggest, initiated what is thought to have been the upgrading of an earlier road some time in the 2nd century BC. By the 5th century AD the road had fallen into neglect, although that tireless builder, the **Emperor Justinian**, had it repaired and the eastern section of it continued to be a major trade route during Byzantine times. The **Crusaders** also made use of the road on their way to the Middle East, but by the time of the Ottoman conquest it had lost most of its importance.

Stretch of Via Egnatia in Greece

Dadyan Armenian Church

Bakırköy back streets

At first glance it looks as if there's nothing left of a Bakırköy that preceded the 1990s. However, if you wander around the network of streets immediately to the south of the suburban train station you'll find some surprisingly impressive wooden and stone houses interspersed amid the concrete. There's a concentration of them in **Istanbul Caddesi, Heyvet Sokak, Yurt Sahibi Sokak** and **Hazırlık Sokak** where you'll find the huge **Taş Okul**, a stone-built 19th-century primary school. The building and adjacent stone bridge on the train line were constructed with tiles and bricks brought from Marseille by **Count Alleon**, an expert on urban development who was invited from Paris in 1864. The building, which changed hands in various periods and was also used as a school for a semester, was restored in 2014. Today it serves as a continuous education center. The stone building at Hallaç Hüseyin Street was built as a police station by the French in 1884. The building, which later hosted different schools, was bought by **Tarık Akan**, one of the famous actors of the Yeşilçam cinema period (p.304) and has served as the Taş Private Elementary School since 1991. On Ebuzziya Caddesi which runs down to the harbor you'll see the 19th-century Armenian **Church of Surp Asdvadzadzin,** with a large schoolhouse dating back to 1844, just across the road from the old Greek Orthodox church (the old Greek primary school building survives on Istanbul Caddesi), both of them reminders of a time when this was a much more ethnically diverse neighborhood. On Reyhan Sokak a small **art gallery** is housed in what started life in 1908 as a French school.

Taş Okul (Stone School)

Fildamı (Elephants' Stables)

This curiously named structure in Bakırköy near Veli Efendi race course is one of four 5th-century **open-air cisterns** or reservoirs that have been identified in Istanbul and by far the **most impressive** as a piece of architecture. The others are all inside the area enclosed by the Theodosian Land Walls, so presumably this one played a role in the expansion of the city towards the west. Unlike the others it had a **control tower** in one corner. The reservoir probably supplied water for **Valens' palace**, although it may also have been connected via lost aqueducts to other parts of Constantinople's water supply system (see p. 109). Given that it measures 127 meters by 76 meters, it's hardly surprising that it came to be called the Elephants' Stables. Today it's home to a somewhat dejected football pitch.

Private Greek Orthodox School

Surp Asdvadzadzin Armenian Church

One of the old houses

Ataköy Marina

Set in the Sea of Marmara, Turkey's first five-star marina opened in 1998.

www.atakoymarina.com.tr

Church of Christou Analipsis

In the grounds of the Greek Orthodox cemetery, this triple-aisled basilica was built in the 19th century by the architect Akilepsos Aleksios.

Tomb of Zuhurat Baba

Fair-faced and white-bearded, Zuhurat Baba is believed to have assisted the Ottoman forces during the siege of Istanbul in 1453. His tomb is crowded with visitors every Friday.

Veliefendi Hippodrome

Watch the races at the Turkey's largest and oldest horse racing stadium, which was designed by Vedat Tek in 1922 and paid for by Sir Loftus Banks, the owner of a stadium in Scotland. It has two tracks, the larger of which is 2400 meters/7875 feet long. The stadium can seat 7,600 spectators and has a small museum and picnic area. The most important race, the **Gazi Derby**, is held every year on 28 June.

Siyavuşpaşa Köşkü (Mansion)

Havuzlu Köşk (Pool Mansion) also called Çavuşbaşı, which is located within Milli Egemenlik Park, was named after Siyavuş Paşa, who was the Grand Vizier to Sultan Mehmed III for two terms. The mansion, which currently functions as a children's library, reflects the civil architecture of the 16th century.

Atatürk's Summer Retreat

Florya and Yeşilköy

029

Florya is an upscale suburb facing the Sea of Marmara that has a wonderful monument to Mustafa Kemal Atatürk in the shape of the unique Art Deco Sea Pavilion. The sea-facing restaurants are popular places to come for slap-up breakfasts or meaty evening meals. Nearby Yeşilköy is equally upscale, with leafy residential streets boasting a fine array of pastel-colored wooden houses.

Reflexology Garden

Delightful **Florya** has a long stretch of **sandy beach** lining the Sea of Marmara and plenty of restaurants set in **parkland** looking out to sea. It acquired its name either from the Greek word "florion", or from Florina in Albania, the original home of İskender Çelebi, the treasurer of Sultan Süleyman the Magnificent, who had a mansion here.

Yeşilköy (Green Village) is rather like a cross between Bebek and Kuzguncuk, a fine place to live.

Istanbul Aquarium

Opened in 2011, Istanbul Aquarium attracts the attention of both adults and children ever since. Following a geographical route from the Black Sea to the Pacific, you can see a 2.5 meters tall anaconda, sharks, rays, piranhas and many other sea and land creatures through 17 themes and a rainforest. You also have the chance to dive with sharks and rays in the main tank with a capacity of 4 thousand cubic meters that hosts 5 thousand creatures.

Sea Pavilion (Deniz Köşkü)

This delightful structure, which resembles the piers to be found in British seaside resorts, was designed in 1935 by the architect **Seyfi Arkan** and shows the influence of the European **Bauhaus movement** in the smooth surfaces of the walls and the wide windows. It consists of a long walkway with a suite of rooms at the end in which **Atatürk** passed 42 intermittent summer days before his death in 1938. The rooms are still furnished as they would have been in his day and there are plenty of photographs of Atatürk enjoying himself on the sandy beach and taking a dip in the sea.

Guests who stayed at the Sea Pavilion included **King Edward VIII** of England and his partner, later wife, **Mrs Simpson**. After Atatürk's death it was used by other important dignitaries of the early Turkish Republic, including presidents **İsmet İnönü, Celal Bayar, Cemal Gürsel, Cevdet Sunay, Fahri Korutürk** and **Kenan Evren.**

Tel: 0212 426 51 51
closed Mondays

Florya Sosyal Tesisleri

Behind this unimaginative name, which just means Florya Social Facilities, lies a delightful sea-facing park filled with cafes, restaurants, children's play areas and flower gardens. It even boasts what must be Turkey's first **reflexology garden** where visitors are invited to remove their shoes and walk over semi-precious stones embedded in the ground.

The Taking of Constantinople, by Palma Le Jeune (1544-1628)

Site of signing of Treaty of San Stefano

St Stephen's Roman Catholic Church

From San Stefano to Yeşilköy

Modern Yeşilköy stands on the site of the village of **San Stefano**, the Byzantine Hagios Stephanos, which had acquired its name after a ship carrying the bones of the first Christian martyr **St Stephen** from Constantinople to Rome was forced to pause here during a storm. In 1203 this was also where the **Crusaders** landed to begin their assault on Constantinople.

St Stephen

During the 19th century the whole village belonged to one Armenian family, the **Dadyans**. During the Crimean War **French soldiers** stationed here built one of three historic lighthouses, which still stands today. In 1876 **Russian soldiers** marched into town, offering support to the Bulgarians who had declared independence from the Ottoman Empire. Their arrival forced **Sultan Abdülhamid II** to sue for peace and the **Treaty of San Stefano**, signed in the beautiful wooden mansion belonging to the Simeonoğlu family, acknowledged a new Bulgaria that stretched all the way from the Danube to the Aegean. The **Treaty of Berlin**, also signed in 1878, redrew the borders of Bulgaria to create a much smaller entity and in 1909 the Committee for Union and Progress (CUP, "Young Turks") made the decision to send Abdülhamid into exile in Salonica from San Stefano.

Turkey's first movie

In 1895 the Russians erected an elaborate **war memorial** in Yeşilköy to mark the furthest point that they reached during the **Ottoman-Russian War** of 1877-78. The monument stood as a powerful symbol of Ottoman defeat, so in 1914 the CUP had it dynamited, an event that featured in Turkey's first motion picture **"The Destruction of the Russian Monument in San Stefano"** which was produced by **Fuat Uzkınay** in 1914.

Fight Near Ivanova Farm on 2 October, 1877, by Pavel Kovalevsky (1843-1903)

Today's Yeşilköy

Unlikely as it sounds, the center of Yeşilköy has something of the feel of a British market town or even a small Massachusetts settlement about it. Many beautiful 19th-century **wooden houses** have been repaired and repainted and now house shops, restaurants and bars. It's a delightful place to spend an evening.

In Cümbüş Sokağı stands the huge **Catholic Church of St Stephen**, with a painting above the altar that depicts St Stephen being stoned to death in 34 or 35. Just round the corner a pretty small **harbor** offers fine views out to the Princes' Islands. In İnci Çiçeği Sokağı can be found the **Armenian Church of Surp Istepanos** (St Stephen), while in Mirasyedi Sokak is the **Greek Orthodox Church of Hagios Stephanos** (St Stephen once again).

Yeşilköy Station

While seving in the army in 1909 Atatürk used this station which dates back to 1871. The oldest surviving part of it is the water storage tank.

The Semprini houses

Three houses designed by the Italian architect **Guglielmo Semprini** can be found side by side in Yeşilköy. Semprini was also the architect of the **Büyük Londra Oteli** (see p. 336) in Tepebaşı as well as of the **current** version of the **Church of Santa Maria Draperis** (see p. 312) on İstiklal Caddesi. He also worked as a contractor on the German School and Hospital.

Self Portrait, by Amadeo Preziosi

A bullet too far

Born in Malta in 1816, the artist **Amadeo Preziosi** arrived in Istanbul in 1842, married a Greek woman and set up home in Beyoğlu. Unfortunately, in 1882 he accidentally shot himself while out hunting in Yeşilköy's extensive forests and died of his injuries the next day. He is buried in the cemetery in Yeşil Zeytin Sokağı. Some of his drawings of Istanbul street life can be seen in the **Pera Museum** (see p. 334).

Istanbul Coffee-house, by Amadeo Preziosi

Yeşilköy Lighthouse

THE GOLDEN HORN

Park and Porte

Gülhane Park and Sarayburnu

038

One of the gems of Old Istanbul is Gülhane Park (House of Roses Park), once the lower part of the Topkapı Palace gardens and now, after considerable renovation, a popular place for local families to pass their spare time beneath a canopy of tall trees amid well-kept flowerbeds. There are several minor monuments within the park, including the ancient Goths Column, as well as a few simple teahouses. The park is at its best in April during the tulip festival and in high summer.

Gülhane Park

At 100,000 square meters, Gülhane Park is roughly half the size of St James's Park in London. Dotted about its fringes are several minor historic monuments, including the slight remains of what looks like a church but may have been the 6th-century **orphanage of St Paul** which ended up housing the University of Constantinople in the 13th century. There are also several important monuments and buildings attached to the surrounding walls and lining the tram tracks as they head downhill to Eminönü.

Gülhane Cistern

The Byzantine cistern with 12 columns dates back to the first half of the 5th century. It is estimated that Gülhane Cistern was an affiliated structure of a monastery or a bath in the past. It was used as an aquarium for a while; There is also a baroque fountain at the entrance. The cistern, one of the oldest historical buildings of the city, was revived thanks to Istanbul Metropolitan Municipality.

Closed on Mondays.

"I am a walnut tree in Gülhane Park/an old walnut tree with knots and scars."

The Walnut Tree **by Nâzım Hikmet, 1957**

The Goths Column

Inside the park on top of the hillside overlooking Seraglio Point (Sarayburnu) stands a 15-meter-tall granite column with a Corinthian capital perched on top which the Byzantine historian Nicephorus Gregoras tells us once carried a **statue of Byzas**, the founder of Byzantium.

A barely discernible **Latin inscription** on its base reads, "To Fortune, who returns by reason of the victory over the Goths", which leaves it unclear whether it was erected during the reign of **Claudius II Gothicus** (r. 268-70) or that of **Constantine the Great** (r. 324-337), both of whom won battles against the Goths.

Museum of the History of Islamic Science and Technology

Housed in the rebuilt stables that ring the inside of the park walls, this museum may be of rather specialist interest but is nonetheless very atmospheric, with sections devoted to time, navigation and medicine as well as zoology and architecture. Many of the exhibits are either copies of items held in foreign museums or models based on written accounts, but there are also some fine original musical instruments on display. It's almost worth paying the entrance fee just to see the lovely drawings on the ceiling by the Istanbul artist **Nusret Çolpan** whose delightful miniatures also adorn the tram stops.

Near the museum can be seen a fine **rose garden** as well as a small garden displaying the flora of the Turkish Republic of Northern Cyprus.

The birds of Gülhane

In spring the park is full of birdsong. Look out for hooded crows, turtle and collared doves and bright green and red parakeets. In winter and spring a large **heronry** is audible and visible amid the naked branches of the trees.

First statue of Atatürk

Basketmakers' Pavilion

Sultan İbrahim I

Seraglio Point (Sarayburnu)

If you walk right across the park from the Soğukçeşme (Cold Fountain) Gate on the tramway side you will exit facing Seraglio Point (Sarayburnu) which offers great views across the Sea of Marmara. Here stands what was the first **statue of Atatürk** (or any other Turk, for that matter) to be erected in the country in 1926. Designed by the Austrian sculptor Heinrinck Krippel, it shows Atatürk gazing across to Kadıköy and Haydarpaşa. It was from this spot that Atatürk set sail for Samsun in 1919 at the start of the **Turkish War of Independence.**

A short walk along the road towards Sirkeci takes you past the dainty **Basketmakers' Pavilion (Sepetçiler Kasrı),** a boathouse with rooms above it whence the sultans would embark on cruises across the Bosphorus or up the Golden Horn. The existing version was built in 1643 for **Sultan İbrahim I,** although there seems to have been a building on the site since the 5th century. Derelict for much of the 20th century, it was restored in 1980 and again in 1990 and is best appreciated from the water as you sail towards Kadıköy.

Zeynep Sultan Mosque

Most people enter Gülhane Park either downhill from the Archeological Museum or via the Soğukçeşme Gate entrance at the bottom of Soğukçeşme Sokak (see p. 034). Across the tramlines from this entrance stands the baroque-style Zeynep Sultan Mosque, built in 1769 for Sultan Ahmed III's daughter Zeynep by **Mehmed Tahir Ağa,** who was also responsible for the **Laleli Mosque** (see p. 088). The mosque could easily be mistaken for a Byzantine church, not just because of its dome, which undulates around the arches of the windows beneath it, but also because of its alternating layers of brick and stone, a style of masonry that seems to have continued straight through from Byzantine times into the 18th century. Behind the mosque a small building of similar construction was once an Ottoman **primary school** and is now the office of the Ottoman Researches Foundation.

Immediately in front of the mosque is a prominent **sebil,** now serving as a kiosk, which turns out not to belong to the mosque at all but was moved here from Sirkeci when the roads were widened. It dates back to 1778 and used to be attached to the tomb of **Sultan Abdülhamid I** (see p. 205).

The Gülhane Decree

Gülhane Park provided the location for an important event in later Ottoman history. In 1839, during the **Tanzimat (Reform)** era, it was here that **Sultan Abdülmecid** proclaimed the Gülhane Decree (Hattı Şerif), which kickstarted only partially successful efforts to strengthen the empire by modernizing its institutions.

By the 19th century the once vibrant Ottoman Empire was stagnating, nicknamed **"the Sick Man of Europe"** by the Western powers. Starting with the Gülhane Edict (also called the Tanzimat Fermanı) in 1839, the reforming sultans **Mahmud II** and **Abdülmecid** and the grand viziers **Ali Paşa, Fuad Paşa, Ahmed Cevdet Paşa** and **Midhat Paşa,** attempted to drag the empire into the modern era by abolishing the old "millet" system whereby its different nationalities more or less governed themselves. Instead they tried to forge a true **Ottoman identity,** with a new flag and national anthem and universal conscription for males of all religions. They were only partially successful in their modernizing endeavors and the Tanzimat era effectively came to an end in 1876.

The Sublime Porte

Across the road from the Parade Pavilion stands the **Bab-i Ali**, a dramatic canopied gateway dating back to around 1840. Today it gives onto mundane government offices but this was once the **Sublime Porte** through which guests were admitted to the inner sanctum of the grand viziers, men who held an office somewhat akin to that of a prime minister today. The first grand vizier to build himself a palace here was **Sokollu Mehmed Paşa** (see p. 178) who moved in in 1564. As time passed and more and more Ottoman business was conducted here the Sublime Porte came to symbolize the government, especially as many visitors were not allowed to venture beyond it. So ambassadors would be said to be accredited to the Sublime Porte rather than to the Ottoman Empire just as they are said to be accredited to the Court of St James rather than to the British government today. In 1839 the grand viziers moved up the road to what is now the Governor's Office (see p. 061) but the old name lingered on to refer to the empire.

Church of St Mary Chalcoprateia

Walking uphill towards Hagia Sophia you pass on the right the site of the **Church of St Mary Chalcoprateia (St Mary of the Copper Market),** which was built in about 450 over the site of an old synagogue and used to contain a particularly potent relic, **the girdle of St Mary**, the mother of Jesus. When Hagia Sophia was destroyed during the **Nika Riot** in 532 (see p. 047), St Mary's briefly took its place in importance, only to be destroyed in its turn.

Charioteers in the Hippodrome

Caferağa Medrese

Immediately across the road is a work of **Mimar Sinan** that goes virtually unnoticed amid the souvenir shops. The Caferağa Medrese was built in the 1550s for **Cafer** and **Gazanfer Ağa**, brothers who held the post of Chief Black Eunuch at Topkapı Palace during the reign of Sultan Süleyman the Magnificent. A gate leads into a lovely **secluded courtyard** ringed with student cells turned into craft workshops and with a bust of Sinan by the gate. As you turn right, on the main street you'll pass a grand **three-faced fountain** dating back to 1911.

Parade Pavilion (Alay Köşkü)

Heading downhill following the tramlines and Gülhane Park's outer wall, you will pass an imposing mansion which now houses Istanbul Univercity, Faculty of Social Sciences but which was originally built in 1875 to serve as a **military college.** Across the road and jutting out from the walls as they make a sharp turn to the right is the graceful Parade Pavilion, a gazebo from which the sultans would watch ceremonial processions, including the **Processions of the Gilds**, a colorful feature of life until the 18th century vividly described by the 17th-century travel writer Evliya Çelebi who makes them sound a bit like an Ottoman version of the Notting Hill carnival in London, UK. No doubt it was more than mere coincidence that the location of the gazebo also enabled the sultan to keep an eye on what was going on across the road at the Sublime Porte, the home of their grand viziers. The original gazebo was probably built for **Sultan Mehmed II** although the current version only dates back to 1819 and the reign of **Mahmud II**. A long stone ramp just inside the park gate enabled people to ride their horses right up to its door.

Basketmakers' Pavillion with Gülhane Park and Topkapı Palace rising up behind it.

Oriental Business District

Sirkeci and Eminönü

031

Sirkeci railway station is renowned as the terminus for the old Orient Express trains and, after the completion of the Marmaray project, it remain the starting point for train services to Europe. A short walk away is the main post office, a building so beautiful that it's worth visiting to take a look around. The Main Post Office dates back to the start of the 20th century and was built in a style that came to be associated with the young Turkish Republic which can also be seen in the First Vakıf Han and in the Fourth Vakıf Han in surrounding Eminönü.

Sirkeci Harbor in the past

Nimet Abla (1899-1978) was Istanbul's most famous lottery ticket agent

The narrow streets of **Eminönü** between the New Mosque and Sirkeci were substantially rebuilt in the 19th century and since then more and more businesses have been shoehorned into the limited space. This is a good place to come in search of cheap electronic goods, as well as low-budget meals in the many small kebaberies.

In Turkish Eminönü means "in front of justice", a name it may have taken from the **courts** or customs houses associated with the docks. **Sirkeci** means "vinegar-seller" in Turkish although there don't seem to be any records of vinegar being sold here! In fact the name is probably a corruption of the Greek "Strategion", meaning "**the place of the commander**".

Tomb of Abdülhamid I

Opposite the Fourth Vakıf Han in Hamidiye Caddesi stands the lovely **tomb** of **Abdülhamid I** (1774-89), buried in a small precinct along with his son, **Mustafa IV** (1807-08), whose short reign became particularly bloodthirsty as he struggled to contain a Janissary revolt. Beautifully restored, it features some especially wonderful 18th-century **tiled calligraphy**. A set of Mohammed's footprints are also preserved in a niche in the wall.

Sirkeci Station (Istanbul Gar)

Sirkeci Station was designed in Oriental-Gothic style in 1887-89 by the German architect **August Jasmund**, who was also responsible for the Deutsche Bank building (see below). It was specifically intended to serve the needs of passengers arriving from Europe on the **Orient Express**, but unfortunately present-day access to the railway concourse is via a mundane modern entrance while the fine original façade, with its circular stained-glass windows, is almost hidden.

Marmaray at the first stage is now serving in the Gebze-Halkalı commuter train line. The restaurant inside the terminal offers pleasant flavors in its nostalgic atmosphere. Inside the original part of the building a small **museum** contains pictures of what the station originally looked like, as well as souvenirs of the Orient Express in its heyday. Scenes shot for the film of Agatha Christie's famous thriller **"Murder on the Orient Express"** bring to life the colorful hustle and bustle that once took place on the platforms.

Tel: 0212 527 12 01
closed Sundays and Mondays.

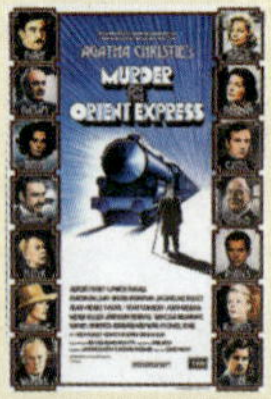

The incomparable Orient Express

Surely one of the world's most famous and glamorous train services, the Orient Express first steamed out of London heading for Istanbul via Paris in 1888. At that time the journey took nearly three days to complete but the train was equipped with every modern comfort to suit its upscale clientele. The journey was immortalized by **Agatha Christie** in her crime novel "Murder on the Orient Express", starring the Belgian detective **Hercule Poirot** and filmed in 1974, 2001 and 2017.

Murder on the Orient Express **author Agatha Christie's room in the Pera Palace Hotel**

Main Post Office

Main Post Office (Büyük Postane)

This imposing building, given added gravitas by the stone steps leading up to it, was designed between 1905 and 1909 by **Vedat Tek**, one of the stars of the First National Architecture movement. The small domed rooms at each end were an attempt to meld a newly emerging **Turkish national style** with more familiar Western elements, while the **Kütahya tiles** used to decorate the façade were chosen in an attempt to breathe new life into a faltering industry.

Philatelists love the small **museum** inside the post office that contains some of the original wooden furnishings and a collection of old postboxes and stamps. It was mainly interesting, though, as a chance to see the lovely staircase, ceilings and other interior design details. But a five-year restoration and organization plan at the museum was initiated in 2018.

Hobyar Mosque

Frequently overlooked to the rear of the post office is the small hexagonal **Hobyar Mosque,** also by Vedat Tek and also adorned with Kütahya tiles although the roof of the minaret looks to have stepped straight from Syria. This was the only mosque designed by the architect.

The Hobyar Mosque is called a mescid in some sources.

Vlora Han

Vlora Han

If you stand on the steps of the post office and look to your right you will see the fine Art Nouveau **Vlora Han,** its façade adorned with stone roses like those on the better-known **Casa Botter** (see p. 314) on İstiklal Caddesi.

A short walk down Yeni Postane Caddesi brings you to a fine restored building in First National Architectural style that was created for the **Yapı ve Kredi Bank**. Immediately facing it is a far more austere Teutonic building designed to house the **Deutsche Bank** by **August Jasmund** in 1890.

Detail from the Vlora Han

Old Deutsche Bank building

Fourth Vakıf Han

Old postcard showing sebil in front of Türkiye İş Bankası Museum on right and part of Fourth Vakıf Han on left.

First and Fourth Vakıf Hans

In the 1910s architect **Kemaleddin Bey,** the second of the main movers behind the First National Architecture movement, built four large hans that were really Istanbul's first modern office blocks in the streets between Sirkeci and Eminönü. **The Fourth Vakıf Han** is the more obvious of the two surviving buildings as it stands opposite the famous **Ali Muhiddin Hacı Bekir** shop where Turkish delight (lokum) was first created. After the First World War it served as the headquarters of the French army, before going into a long decline during which it became the haunt of glue-sniffers until finally being rescued and turned into a hotel in 2005. Like the Post Office building, it has domed rooms at each corner. There's also an original hamam in the basement.

Detail from Liman Han (Harbor Building)

First National Architecture

This was the name given to a style of architecture characteristic of the first half of the 20th century that pulled together elements of the Selçuk and Ottoman to create something entirely new. Features include overhanging roofs, thick lancet windows, panels of tiling on the façade and obtruding semi-spherical ornaments. Its two leading lights were **Vedat Tek** (1873-1942) and **Kemaleddin Bey** (1870-1927) whose moustachioed face now peers out of the 20TL note. Aside from the **Main Post Office**, other fine examples include the **Land Registry** and **Rectorate buildings** in the Hippodrome (see p. 048), the **Four Seasons Hotel** in Sultanahmet (see p. 035) and the **Sütlüce Convention Center** (see p. 255).

Türkiye İş Bankası Museum

Between the Main Post Office and the New Mosque several fine 19th and early 20th-century buildings house branches of major banks. The Türkiye İş Bankası building dates back to 1898 and was originally used first as the post office and then as a parcel sorting office. In 1928 it passed into the care of Türkiye İş Bankası and now boasts a small state-of-the-art **museum**. The paperwork on display may be of interest only to true banking devotees, but children will enjoy being able to go inside the **basement vaults** with their enormous doors and peeking inside **safe-boxes** to see what sort of things people valued enough to store in them.

You might also want to spare a glance at the elegant **Garanti Bankası** building across the road, another fine example of the First National style of architecture.

www.muze.isbank.com.tr
Tel: 0212 511 13 31, closed Mondays

Garanti Bankası building

Harbor Building (Liman Han)

If you cut up Yalı Köşkü Caddesi from the waterfront you will see on the right the huge Liman Han designed by **Vedat Tek** in 1907, with its beautiful tiled façade. At the end of the road is the **Hidayet Mosque,** designed by **Alexandre Vallaury**. Dating back to 1887, it stands on the site of an older wooden mosque.

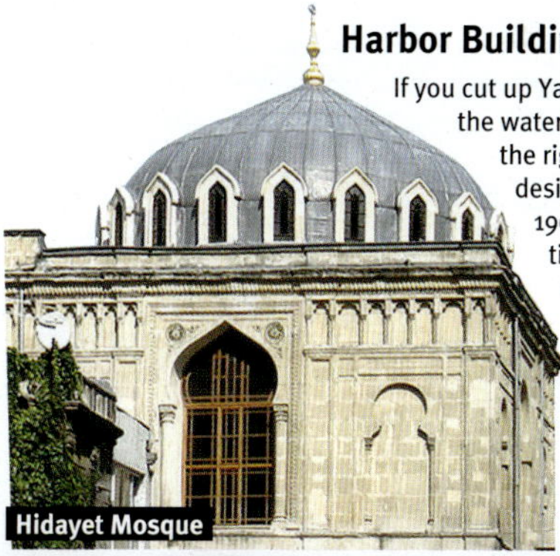

Hidayet Mosque

Liman Han

"(At Haci Bekir's) the cook ladled a great coil of the stiffened syrup and with a dextrous twist of the wrist threw the sticky substance like a coil of rope into the air and it was caught on a huge hook on the wall."

***Romance of the Bosphorus* by Dorina Lady Neave, 1949**

Ali Muhiddin Hacı Bekir

Hamidiye Caddesi was the first place to stock **Turkish delight** in Istanbul and its windows are still full of the gummy sweet in an astonishing variety of different flavors.

Religion and Commerce

New Mosque and the Spice Market

032

Officially known as the Mısır Çarşısı (Egyptian Bazaar), the Spice Bazaar is a particularly popular stop on most tours of Istanbul. Housed in a building dating back to 1660, the Spice Market today sells a wide variety of goods, many of them aimed at tourists. The surrounding streets, however, still stock a wide choice of staple foodstuffs. The bazaar was originally part of the complex attached to the huge and impressive New Mosque although today they are completely separate.

"(The New Mosque) seems to share the life of the city in a way that no other imperial mosque quite does and at no loss to her dignity."

***Stamboul Sketches* by John Freely, 1974**

Courtyard

Today the Eminönü waterfront is a ferociously busy transport interchange. Until the late 19th century though this was where the fish market stood and before that it was where the Venetians and the Amalfians had their trading colonies.

New Mosque (Yeni Cami)

The large mosque that dominates the waterfront has the apparently perverse name New Mosque (Yeni Cami), even though it dates back to 1591, which makes it very old by most people's standards. Foreigners have a hard time understanding why this mosque is called "new" but in Turkey those which are older than a thousand years are "historical", while the ones that are younger are "new".

Work on the mosque was started by **Safiye Sultan** (1550-1605), at a time when this was a predominantly Jewish neighborhood occupied by tall wooden apartment blocks called Jeweries. The Jews were relocated to **Hasköy** (see p. 261) on the far side of the Golden Horn, but progress on the mosque was slow because Safiye Sultan lost her power on the death of her son **Sultan Mehmed III** in 1603. Like so many modern buildings in Turkey, the mosque was left incomplete and eventually caught fire. It was only completed in 1633 by which time **Hatice Turhan Sultan**, the mother of **Sultan Mehmed IV**, had taken charge of things. Her architect, **Mustafa Ağa**, completed the work in 1663 using the plans drawn up by the original architect, a pupil of Sinan's called **Davud Ağa**.

The mosque, one of the last such large buildings to be completed in the classical Ottoman style, boasts two minarets, a flurry of 66 domes and a secluded courtyard centered on an attractive şadırvan (ablutions fountain). Tiles and calligraphic inscriptions decorate the courtyard walls. Unusually, the mosque has open galleries on each side of the exterior, while the minarets each boast triple balconies which meant that in the days before loudspeakers half a dozen müezzins could give the call to prayer at the same time. When it was first completed the mosque would have stood right on the shore with the water lapping at its steps.

Starlings circle above the New Mosque.

Internally the mosque is very elegant, its walls covered with tiles that, while not of the finest quality, are nevertheless very pretty, its windows filled with richly colored stained glass. The **minbar** (pulpit) and **müezzin mahfili** (muezzin's pew) are of marble and the **kürsü** (imam's prayer seat) is of wood inlaid with mother-of-pearl. Above the windows verses from the Koran were beautifully inscribed by **Mustafa Çelebi**.

Attached to the shore side of the mosque is a brick-and-stone structure accessible via a ramp to the rear. This is the newly restored **hünkar kasrı (sultan's lodge)** which housed private quarters for the sultan offering direct access to the mosque's interior. The restoration won a Europa Nostra award in 2010. Across the road on the inland side is a small precinct that contains the **tombs** of **Hatice Turhan Sultan**, her son **Sultan Mehmed IV** and those of sultans **Mustafa II**, **Ahmed III**, **Mahmud I**, **Osman III** and **Murad V**. Facing it across the street a now derelict **time-keeper's lodge** is built into the walls of the mosque.

A little further along the road on the same side as the tombs the elaborate **sebil** (water dispensary) that formed part of the mosque complex was badly damaged by a fire that destroyed the surrounding buildings in the late 19th century. Its restoration was originally supervised by **Osman Hamdi Bey**, the archeologist who founded the Istanbul Archeological Museums. It has recently been restored again, although sadly today the water is dispensed from a mundane machine plonked down beside it.

Spice Market

When you stand on Galata Bridge and look inland you will see a small but sturdy multi-domed building immediately to the right of the New Mosque. This is the Spice Market or Egyptian Bazaar (*Mısır Çarşısı*), which was built in 1660 and took its name from the fact that goods from the **Far East** and **India** arrived here from Egypt on the so-called **Mısır Kervanı** (**Egyptian Caravan**). L-shaped in layout, the bazaar nurtures almost 100 shops beneath its vaulted ceilings plus two restaurants above the main entrances: the famous Pandeli and less well-known Bab-ı Hayat. The Spice Market, together with a hamam that has since been lost, was originally built so that its shops could provide financial support for the neighboring mosque.

The Spice Market gained its hauntingly romantic nickname because at one time the majority of its shops sold herbs and spices. Today you can still come here to shop for cooking ingredients although you will have to search harder for them amid the more prominent souvenir tea sets and trays of lokum (Turkish delight) aimed at tourists. A few of the shops have given up selling foodstuffs altogether and now sell much the same sort of things as you could find in the **Grand Bazaar** (Kapalı Çarşı, see p. 070).

Outside, however, it's a different story. The surrounding streets still stock a wide choice of staple foodstuffs: cheeses, fruit and vegetables and meat, on one side; pet food, flowers and leeches on the other. On the side of the bazaar closest to the New Mosque an attractive outdoor market primarily sells seeds and plants as well as a rather disheartening selection of animals and birds in overcrowded cages. Here, too, you will find plastic bottles full of leeches that are still used in traditional medicine. On the side facing **Tahtakale** you'll find a mouth-watering array of local cheeses, jars of honey and mountains of fresh fruit and vegetables. To the rear of the bazaar a string of small shops sell kitchenware and other basic household goods. The bazaar was originally part of the complex attached to the New Mosque although today they are completely separate.

Pampered pigeons

In front of the New Mosque stand a row of kiosks from which licensed retailers sell small trays of birdseed for visitors to feed the many appreciative pigeons. This is a common sight outside Turkish mosques since pigeons are revered here rather than treated as pests. The reason lies in a story often told about the Prophet Mohammed who had taken refuge from his enemies in a cave. A spider wove a web across the entrance and a pigeon nested in front of it, thereby putting pursuers off the scent and guaranteeing its descendants a lifetime of pampering.

Kurukahveci
Mehmet Efendi

Pandeli

In business since 1901, Pandeli is housed in a set of exquisite turquoise-tiled rooms over the bazaar's main entrance. It's wonderfully "oriental" and the views of the Golden Horn, if you can land a front-window table, are unforgettable. The food is also pretty good. It's only open from noon until 4 pm and closed altogether on Sundays.

@pandeliistanbul
www.pandeli.com.tr
Tel: 0212 527 39 09

Bridging the Old and New

Galata Bridge

033

Until the 19th century the old Byzantine city of Constantinople was completely separated from Galata and Pera by the Haliç or Golden Horn, the stretch of water that cuts inland at the point where the Sea of Marmara and the Bosphorus meet. Several bridges have been built across it over the centuries. The current Galata Bridge is the fifth on the site.

As long ago as the reign of the **Emperor Justinian** there had been attempts to bridge the Golden Horn and there are known to have been early bridges upstream at Ayvansaray and Kağıthane. However, both were destroyed during the disastrous Fourth Crusade that diverted to Constantinople in 1204. Renaissance polymath **Leonardo da Vinci** came up with a design for a new bridge, but it wasn't until 1836 that a permanent crossing of rafts was strung out between **Unkapanı** on the southern shore of the Horn and **Azapkapı**, to the north. Since then there have been several more Galata Bridges culminating in the current model that links **Eminönü** on the southern shore with **Karaköy** to the north. This latest incarnation is not especially beautiful although it has an iconic status, famous as much for the myriad fishermen who dangle their rods over its sides whatever the weather as for its engineering. The line of fish restaurants nestling beneath it make great places to watch the sun go down over the Horn.

Leonardo's Bridge as constructed at Aas in Norway.

Leonardo's bridge

So obvious was the need for a bridge across the Horn that both Leonardo da Vinci and Michelangelo came up with plans that they submitted to the sultan. Leonardo's drawing, completed in 1502 for Sultan Bayezid II, has received the most publicity and in 2001 a scale model of it was constructed in Aas in Norway as part of the Leonardo Bridge Project. In 2010 work on a new footbridge based on da Vinci's ideas began as part of the Marmaray Project. It crosses between the existing Galata and Unkapanı bridges since 2014.

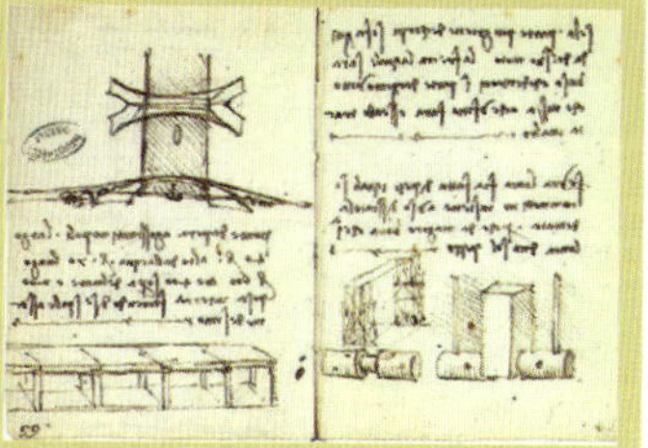

www.leonardobridgeproject.org

"On the bridge you don't make friends/from the bridge you watch and see."

The Bridge **by Sait Faik Abasıyanık**

Waiting for the fish to bite.

Earlier bridges

Inconceivable as the idea seems now, it wasn't until the mid-19th century that there was a proper permanent bridge across the Golden Horn; until then, people made do with boats that served as water taxis. In 1845 **Bezm-i Alem Valide Sultan**, the mother of Sultan Abdülmecid, paid for a permanent bridge to be built across the Golden Horn to facilitate access to Galata. Her bridge had several different names: **Yeni Köprü** (New Bridge), **Cisr-i Cedid** (New Bridge) and **Valide Köprüsü** (Queen Mother's Bridge) in honor of its founder. In 1863 **Ateş Ahmed Paşa** paid for a new bridge, which was, in turn, replaced in iron in 1875 and 1912; in 1878 restaurants and teahouses were added to its underside. Many writers, including **Edmondo de Amicis**, have left vivid descriptions of the colorful throng that was forever passing over what became known as **"the most wonderful pathway of Europe."** In 1910 a new wood-and-iron model, the most famous of all the Galata bridges, was built. This was designed in such a way that it could be opened to allow larger ships to pass from the Bosphorus into the Golden Horn. The latest concrete version opened in 1994.

Most famous Galata Bridge

When people murmur nostalgically about the old Galata Bridge they are usually referring to the elegant 1912 version which served the city faithfully for 80 years and whose underside was festooned with picturesque fish restaurants. Just before it was due to be decommissioned in 1992, this bridge caught fire. However, as soon as its replacement was in position, it was speedily repaired. It served as a footbridge linking Eyüp and Sütlüce and was completely removed in 2016.

"The bridge where Turkey and Europe had met until old age and fire had done for it."

***A Fez of the Heart* by Jeremy Seal, 1995**

Why the Golden Horn?

Many reasons have been given for how the Golden Horn acquired its picturesque name. Some focus on the horn shape created by the two streams –the Alibey and Kağıthane rivers– that flow into it from the west, others on the way that the setting sun is reflected on the water. Yet others suggest that it acquired its name because of the quantity of gold tossed into the waters by the Byzantines as they confronted defeat at the hands of the Turks in 1453. In fact the name is a translation of the Greek word **"chrysokeras"** whose precise derivation is unclear.

The Turkish name for this stretch of water, **Haliç**, is not a translation of "Golden Horn" but an abbreviation for the less romantic **Haliç-i Dersaadet**, meaning "Bay of Istanbul" in Ottoman Turkish, the language of the Ottoman Empire.

The bridge behind bridge

The Galata Bridge must be the only bridge in the world to have bestowed its name on a card game. According to a 1901 guide to this quintessentially British game, it was originally dreamt up by a group of British soldiers who were based in Galata during the Crimean War. Every evening they would walk across the Galata Bridge to coffeehouses in the Old City where they could play the game, so when pressed to come up with a name for it they called it simply "bridge".

Geert Mak's best-selling book "The Bridge" lifts the lid on the underside of life in Istanbul through interviews with the men and women who eke out a living on and around the Galata Bridge.

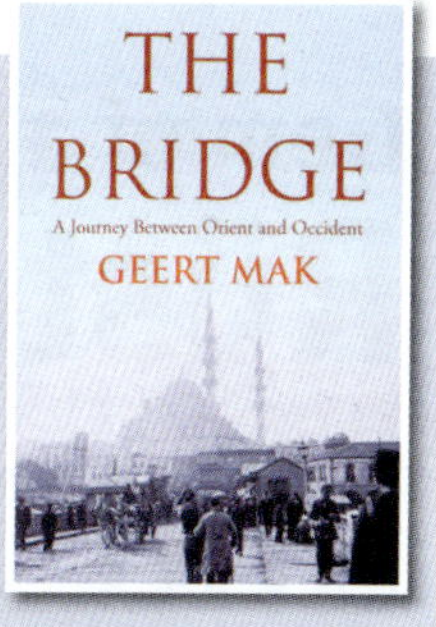

Haliç Metro Bridge

The metro bridge project was first begun in 2004. In 2009 Unesco issued a report detailing its harmful effect on the silhouette of the Süleymaniye Mosque and recommended another project for a flat bridge to replace it. The ongoing work was discontinued briefly and the project was revised. The towers, which were first planned at 82m, were reduced to 65m. The bridge was opened for service in 2014 as the connection line for Hacıosman-Yenikapı metro line.

Cruising the Golden Horn

It costs almost nothing, but one of the most enjoyable things to do on a trip to Istanbul is cruise up or down the Golden Horn. A ferry (www.istanbulsehirhatlari.com) leaves from Karaköy (see p. 266) and criss-crosses the Horn, calling in at Kasımpaşa (see p. 262), Fener (see p. 230), Balat (see p. 240), Hasköy (see p. 258), Ayvansaray (see p. 151), Sütlüce (see p. 255) and Eyüp (see p. 244). Amongst the buildings most easily seen from the boat are the Naval Command Office (Bahriye Nezareti) and Istanbul Naval Hospital at Kasımpaşa and the Greek High School for Boys at Fener.

Gem of a Small Mosque

Rüstem Paşa Mosque and Tahtakale

034

Built in 1561 for Rüstem Paşa, son-in-law and Grand Vizier to Süleyman the Magnificent, the Rüstem Paşa Mosque is one of Mimar Sinan's most widely admired small mosques and is adorned with a wonderful collection of İznik tiles. It stands right in the heart of Tahtakale, the tight-knit network of market streets that sprawls to the south-west of the Spice Market. This is a great place to while away a few hours, shopping for the sort of items desired by locals rather than tourists.

e mosque exterior is decorated with İznik tiles.

Tahtakale

Exploring the maze-like streets of Tahtakale (Wooden Castle) will give you a flavor of the old Istanbul, a place where people were more interested in buying wooden spoons than souvenir T-shirts and which is still one of the best places to come in search of all kinds of packing materials, children's games and assorted hardware items. There are whole shops here dedicated to the sale of knives or scales or colorful quilts and in the weeks leading up to 1 January the bazaar is stuffed full of what Westerners perceive as Christmas decorations but which are bought here to celebrate **Yılbaşı (New Year**).

Close to the steps leading up to the Rüstem Paşa Mosque is the old Tahtakale Hamam, which dates back to the 15th century and was built with separate sections for men and women. Today it houses a pleasant café and shops selling baskets from all over the country.

Tahtakale Hamam Cafe

The mosque as it was

"Rüstem Pasha bequeathed Sinan a miser's collection of hundreds and thousands of Iznik tiles."

***Sinan* by Arthur Stratton, 1972**

Rüstem Paşa Mosque

It's easier to spot the Rüstem Paşa Mosque from the water than when you're closer to it because it's almost completely buried amid the chaos of surrounding Tahtakale. Unlike most of his mosques, **Sinan** decided to build this one on a raised platform, which means that you actually approach it from underneath, making its exquisite perfection all the more of a surprise when you finally pop up in front of it. Although the **İznik tiles** that line the walls inside are especially beautiful, even the exterior is encased in tiles.

The mosque was probably paid for by Rüstem Paşa's widow **Mihrimah**, the daughter of the famous **Roxelana** (see p. 014), in memory of her recently-deceased husband. Although it has only one minaret and so might seem relatively insignificant in a city where at least two minarets are de rigueur, this mosque is renowned for its wonderful galleried interior with tiles covering everything from the walls to the mihrab and minbar. Particularly beautiful are the designs of tulips and carnations which make delightful use of the slightly raised coral-red glaze for which İznik tiles were famed (see opposite). A **Newsweek** journalist was once sufficiently smitten with the mosque to list it as one of the world's fifty real gems.

Tile depicting the Kaaba in Mecca

The 15th-century Saman Emin-i Evvel Mosque near the the Rüstem Paşa Mosque has a distinctive minaret.

Who was Rüstem Paşa?

Damat Rüstem Paşa (1500-61) served for two separate periods as Grand Vizier to **Sultan Süleyman the Magnificent.** Through marriage to **Mihrimah Sultan**, he was also the sultan's son-in-law, hence the epithet "damat (son-in-law)" which precedes his name. He also gloried in the less pleasant nickname, **"the louse of fortune"**, acquired after he was allowed to go ahead and marry the sultan's favorite daughter despite being infested with lice. Rüstem is also believed to have plotted with the sultan's wife Roxelana to have Süleyman's favorite son Mustafa strangled so that her son could succeed him instead. At one time he was believed to be the richest man in the empire after the sultan; some of this wealth was poured into the creation of the **Rüstem Paşa Medrese** in **Cağaloğlu** (see p. 061) and the **Rüstem Paşa Han** in Karaköy (see p. 273). He is buried in the grounds of the **Şehzade Mosque** beside Şehzade Mehmed, the crown prince for whom the complex was built.

İznik tiles

Turkey has a long history of tile-making dating back to c.7000 BC, but the most valued of all its tiles were those produced in the small town of İznik in the 16th century after the conquest of Tabriz in 1514 resulted in the resettlement there of many highly skilled Persian tile makers. It was in İznik that ceramicists first worked out how to make the rare and valuable coral-red glaze called **Armenian bole** that was so useful for depicting tulips and carnations, but by the 17th century the torch was already passing to Kütahya.

Beneath the mosque second-hand goods are on sale.

Küçük Çukur Han

Hans

Part of the original mosque complex are two hans, one called the **Büyük Çukur (Big Sunken) Han**, the other the **Küçük Çukur (Small Sunken) Han**. To reach them you follow a winding, sweet-scented and utterly medieval street behind the mosque where hamals (porters) still wait for business. Both are used for storing spices.

The oldest of all the hans is probably the **Balkapanı Han** whose round arches suggest that it may date back to the 5th century. Its name also suggests that it was used for storing honey (bal). Nearby is the only slightly newer **Hurmalı (Date) Han** which retains some fine Byzantine brick vaulting. Both these hans are near the Rüstem Paşa Mosque.

Dome of the Büyük Çukur Han

If you liked this you'll also like:

Blue Mosque (see p. 038)
Eyüp Sultan Mosque (see p. 245)
Piyale Paşa Mosque (see p. 264)
Ramazan Efendi Mosque (see p. 097)
Sokollu Mehmed Paşa Mosque (see p. 178)
Takkeci İbrahim Ağa Mosque (see p. 146)
Tomb of Sultan Süleyman the Magnificent (see p. 101)

Bismillahirrahmanirrahim
Tarihi Eminönü Balık Ekmek

View from Hamdi Et Lokantası with the New Mosque to the right

Eminönü Square is always crowded. The building draped with a flag is the Zindan Han with the Cafer Baba Tower right beside it.

Zindan Han

Right on the waterfront close to where the Golden Horn ferry docks at Eminönü, the Zindan (Dungeon) Han was the third largest han built in Western architectural style in the 19th century.

Attached to the side of the han is the rectangular **Cafer Baba Tower**, the only tower from the ancient sea walls that lined the Golden Horn to have survived intact from Byzantine times. Inside it is the grave of Cafer Baba who came to Constantinople as the envoy of the Abbasid ruler **Harun al-Rashid** in the 9th century, only to be thrown into prison where he died. His grave on the ground floor became **a place of pilgrimage** especially for ex-prisoners, as recorded by the 17th-century traveller and historian **Evliya Çelebi**. The Ali Baba who is buried alongside him has nothing to do with the 40 thieves but was his jailer who converted to Islam.

Also near here is the small **Ahi Çelebi Mosque**, built in 1523 by a physician who was on his way home from Mecca. According to Evliya Çelebi, he began his own travels and working on the **"Seyahatname (Book of Travels)"** that described them after dreaming that he had fallen asleep inside this mosque and learning that he would become a great traveller with the blessing of the Prophet Mohammed.

Ahi Çelebi Mosque

It may be nothing much now but Uzunçarşı (Long Market) Caddesi was once, as the Makros Embolos (Great Colonnade), a vitally important link between the Forum of Constantine (today's Çemberlitaş) and the Golden Horn.

Ancient Fire Trap

Cibali and the Sea Walls

035

Cibali is an impoverished but colorful neighborhood on the southern shore of the Golden Horn between the Atatürk Bridge and Fener. It has gained new life since the Kadir Has University was established inside the huge old tobacco factory that dominates the area close to the bridge and houses a small archeological museum. Cibali is also home to the enormous Gül Camii which started life as a Byzantine church. Ruins of the old sea walls that protected the city from invasion via the Golden Horn can also be seen here.

Cibali is named after **Cebe Ali**, the Ottoman soldier who is believed to have forced his way through the Cibali Gate in the sea walls during the 1453 invasion of Constantinople. In the distant past this was a wealthy, cosmopolitan area where many **Greeks and Jews** lived and which was famous for its lively meyhanes (taverns). In the mid-18th century Turks moved in and founded several mosques and dervish lodges. Later still it was well known as the place where materials used for waterproofing boats were stored. Since these materials were highly flammable, Cibali became infamous as the starting point for many of the fires that ravaged the city; the worst conflagrations were known as "**Cibali fires**".

The adjoining district is called **Küçükmustafapaşa** which means "Little Mustafa Paşa" in Turkish. It was probably named after **Koca Mustafa Paşa**, a Grand Vizier to Sultan Beyazid II.

Cibali Gate

Cebe Ali is believed to have carved out this gate by hand on the day that Constantinople was captured in 1453. Since then his tomb, decked out with cannonballs, has been preserved here.

Tulumbacıs (original fire-fighters)

Fire! Fire!

Now that wooden buildings are an increasingly rare sight in Istanbul it's hard to imagine what it must have been like in the days when fires were an ever-present hazard, threatening to wipe out entire districts in next to no time. Reading through accounts of old Istanbul one comes across frequent references to buildings been rebuilt over and over again as each new version was written off by fire. To guard against the danger Istanbul had several fire-watch towers including **Galata Tower** (see p. 324) and the **Beyazıt/ Serasker Tower** (see p. 083). Men living in the towers would signal that they had spotted a fire to the **"tulumbacı"**, the teams of unruly fire fighters whose job it was to try and douse the flames. One of the worst fires of all was the one that ripped through **Pera** in 1870, killing around 900 people and leaving thousands of families homeless. In **"Constantinople"**, his lyrical account of a visit to late 19th-century Istanbul, **Edmondo de Amicis** recounts how a concubine was primed to inform the sultan of a fire by entering his presence wearing a red dress, while in **"Portrait of a Turkish Family" Irfan Orga** describes the horrific night when his own family lost their home to a conflagration.

Cibali Police Station

The police station that used to stand beside the Cibali Gate provided the setting for Pierre Weber's successful play "Düğün Gecesi (Wedding Night)", first staged in the 1950s, which went on to be turned into a film.

Atatürk Bridge

Cibali sits on one side of the frantically busy Atatürk Bridge, which was erected in 1940. The point from which it crosses to the northern shore of the Golden Horn is called **Unkapanı**, which may be a corruption of **Odun Kapısı** (Firewood Gate). Alternatively, it could be derived from **"un kapanı"**, meaning **"wheat warehouse"**, a reminder of the produce that used to be offloaded from ships here.

Kadir Has University

Cibali Tütün Fabrikası Cibali Tobacco Factory

Buhari Dervish Lodge

The **Kadir Has University** is housed inside what was once the Cibali Tobacco Factory, the huge building rising up on the bluff to the right shortly after you pass the Atatürk Bridge that was founded in 1884. Here men and women worked side by side and many generations of the same families followed each other into the business. At the height of its prosperity, the factory operated almost like a town within a town, having its own police force, hospital, kindergarten, shops and restaurants. It was nationalized in 1925 and closed down in 1995. Between 1998 and 2002 the old building was transformed into a modern campus for the University, which was founded by the industrialist responsible for bringing Coca-Cola to Turkey.

Inside the building, the **Rezan Has Museum** provides space for high-quality art and history exhibitions. The permanent collection, which consists of artefacts dating from the Neolithic to the Selçuk periods, is atmospherically housed inside the remains of an 11th-century Byzantine cistern known as the Karanlık Çeşme (Dark Fountain) and of a 17th-century Ottoman hamam (Turkish bath). On the way through to the museum, take a quick look at the photographs on the walls which show the factory as it was in its heyday.

Immediately behind the university building stands the elegant and well-maintained **tomb of Emir Ahmed Buhari**, a Nakshibendi sheikh who arrived here from Buhara in the 16th century. It is just along the road from the late 18th-century **Şazeli Mosque** which was home to a dervish order with their roots in North Africa. If it's interesting for anything it's because its founder, **Ali eş-Şazeli**, is revered as the protector of Istanbul's many coffee-house owners. The same dervish order used the **Ertuğrul (Şeyh Zafir) Tekke** in Beşiktaş (see p.398)

www.rhm.org.tr
Tel: 0212 533 65 32

Şazeli Mosque

Church of St Theodosia (Gül Mosque)

This imposing, triple-apsed Byzantine church in Şair Nebi Sokak was built in the 9th or 10th century and was probably converted into a mosque c.1490; the dome and minaret are Turkish additions. A pretty story explains its Turkish name, the "Rose Mosque". The feast day of St Theodosia was 29th May and on that day in 1453 large crowds gathered in the church and festooned it with garlands of roses as they prayed to be protected from the encroaching Turks. When the victorious soldiers eventually entered the church they were amazed to see the roses, hence the name.

A slight complication is that the church has also been claimed as the last resting place of a Muslim holy man called **Gül Baba** who may or may not be entombed in a burial chamber inside one of the columns; others assert that this was the last resting place of **Constantine XI Dragases**, the last Byzantine emperor, who had died trying to defend the walls but whose body was never found. To further complicate matters a mysterious Ottoman inscription above the entrance to the tomb reads: "Tomb of the Apostle, disciple of Jesus. Peace be upon him." To whom it refers, no one knows.

Beneath this 11th-century structure is a crypt that was reserved for the graves of the empire's most distinguished individuals. Opposite the church stands a **library** commissioned by **Adile Sultan**, a 19th-century Ottoman princess, renowned Divan poet and philanthropist, whose palace was converted into the **Kandilli High School for Girls** on the Asian side of the city (see p. 532).

Rezan Has Museum

Gül (Rose) Mosque interior

Gül (Rose) Mosque

Church of Hagios Nikolaos

Right beside the main shore road a church built in 1837 stands in the courtyard of what was once a Byzantine church dedicated to Hagios Nikolaos, the patron saint of mariners. The narthex contains a **model of a ship**, hung there in gratitude by sailors who had returned safely from a voyage, as is also the case in the Church of the Panagia in Karaköy (see p. 276). The church was a dependency of the **Vatopedi Monastery** on **Mt Athos** in Greece. A sacred spring in the grounds is dedicated to the obscure St Charalambos according to an inscription on the outside wall where you can easily see how much the ground has risen over the centuries.

The Sea Walls

Houses built right on top of the old sea walls.

Although it's Istanbul's land walls (see p. 144 & p. 154) that garner most of the attention, long stretches of the old sea walls that protected the southern side of the city also still survive. The most impressive sections run from **Mermerkule** to the west almost as far as **Sarayburnu** and the mouth of the Bosphorus and used to protect the city from invaders arriving via the Sea of Marmara; since this was called Propontis in ancient times, these parts of the wall are sometimes called the **Propontine Walls**. Gates through these walls were specially designed to allow boats to pass through into the inner harbors. Some parts of the walls were lost when the railway was laid in the late 19th century and a road now runs in front of them on reclaimed land, but enough still survives to get a good idea of what they must have looked like in their heyday.

Parts of the walls that defended Istanbul from enemies who had managed to enter the Golden Horn still run alongside the busy main road skirting the shore. They are mostly in a shocking state of disrepair, especially in comparison with the Propontine section (see p. 069); frequently the ruins have been incorporated into other later buildings or knocked down altogether to make space for the road. Studying them is made all the more difficult by the narrowness of the pavements hereabouts.

The development of the sea walls mirrors that of the land walls. The earliest defences were probably erected by **Septimius Severus** in the 2nd century, then rebuilt by **Constantine the Great** in the 4th century and **Theodosius II** in the 5th century. The sea walls were lower than the land walls and proved less robust since the **Fourth Crusaders** were able to force their way through them in 1204.

"(29 May, 1453) In the terrible darkness, the church of St Theodosia, ablaze with lighted tapers, gleamed like a beacon of hope."

Byzantine Churches in Constantinople
by Alexander van Millingen, 1912

The walls in numbers

Length (Propontine): 9km	No. of towers (Propontine): 188
Length (Golden Horn): 5km	No. of towers (Golden Horn): 110
Height (Propontine): 12-15m	No. of gates (Propontine): 13
Height (Golden Horn): 10m	No. of gates (Golden Horn): 20

Küçük Mustafa Paşa Hamam

In the back streets of Cibali, near the Gül Mosque this once big and beautiful Turkish bath is believed to have been built for **Koca Mustafa Paşa**, Grand Vizier to **Bayezid II**, which would make it one of the oldest baths in the city. Thanks to restoration works initiated by a businessperson and completed in 2018, it has now become part of Istanbul's cultural and art life as a "multi-functional events venue."

www.kucukmustafapasahamami.com
Tel:0212 358 01 85

The Vatican of Greek Orthodoxy
Fener

036

On the southern shore of the Golden Horn, Fener is a fascinating district with several small but interesting churches including St Stephen of the Bulgars, a rare example of a church built entirely out of cast iron. It's best known as home to the Greek Patriarchate, still the mother-church for Greek Orthodox Christianity worldwide. Greeks continued to live here until the middle of the 20th century and it was home to several men who went on to hold high office at the Ottoman court. Dominated by the dramatic Fener Greek High School for Boys, Fener is a very hilly area, which has been more or less taken over by poor immigrants from Eastern Turkey.
A UNESCO/EU project to restore some of the buildings here and in adjacent Balat is completed in 2018.

Tucked inside the sea walls of Byzantium, Fener (Lighthouse) was once a wealthy area whose **Greek** population initially fled before the Ottoman conquest of the city but then returned after **Sultan Mehmed II** assured them that they would be safe. Greeks, called **Phanariots**, continued to live here throughout the Ottoman years, growing rich from trade and commerce. Some of them went on to hold high office in the state, especially as interpreters and secretaries. One example was **Rum (Greek) Mehmed Paşa** who was Grand Vizier to Mehmed II from 1466 to 1469 and is buried in Üsküdar (see p. 502). Another was **Dimitri Cantemir**, a historian who became Prince of Moldavia. Yet a third was **Alexander Mavrokordato**, who became Grand Dragoman (official translator) to Sultan Mehmed IV but wielded much greater power at court than his innocent title might suggest.

Alexandros Mavrokordato

Following a nationalist uprising in Greece in 1821, many of the Phanariotes fled Istanbul, fearing persecution. When that didn't happen, many returned, but by then Fener had had its day and most preferred to settle in Pera, on the Princes' Islands, or in the Bosphorus villages.

It is hard now to imagine how rich Fener once was since the grand mansions that used to stand here are mostly long gone and those that survive are usually ruinous. Today, hundreds of children play in streets festooned with washing and you're more likely to overhear the dialects of the Black Sea than Istanbul Turkish.

In Fener's streets there are still some majestic buildings.

"...the silent and melancholy quarter of Fener, where the soul of old Byzantium has taken refuge."

***Constantinople*, Edmondo de Amicis, 1877**

A Fener diva

Arms of an aristocratic Phanariot family

Fantastic Phanariotes

Fener was home to an elite group of Ottoman Greeks whose ancestors settled here immediately after the Turkish conquest of Istanbul when Sultan Mehmed II invited them to make their homes on the Golden Horn as he strove to recreate his new capital as a world city. Most of the rich Phanariote families originally made their fortunes from trade, although over time they also became indispensable as **translators (dragomans)** and then as governors (ospedars) of **Wallachia and Moldova.** At the same time they put a lot of emphasis on education and preserving traditional Greek culture. Closely linked to the Ottoman government, the Phanariotes were hardly in the forefront of revolutionary fervor. However, when the Greek uprising of 1821 broke out inside the areas they governed, many Phanariotes paid the price as vengeful mobs burned their homes and slaughtered their occupants. After the Patriarch was hanged despite his opposition to the revolt, many Phanariotes fled abroad or at least to Pera. Fener never really recovered.

Greek Patriarchate Church of St George

Icon showing Fatih Sultan Mehmed granting Patriarch Gennadios II political and ecclesiastical authority over the Greek Orthodox Church on 1 June 1453

Middle Gate

The Patriarchate

Relief depicting St George

Tucked up inside the remains of the old sea walls is the Church of St George which is home to the Greek Patriarchate, still revered as the mother-church by members of the Greek Orthodox congregation worldwide. The patriarchate moved to this site in 1602, after starting life in **Hagia Eirene** and **Hagia Sophia**, then rotating around assorted other city churches.

Byzantine double-headed eagle

A huge fire wrote off the original basilica on the site and what you see now is an undistinguished building dating back only to 1720. It forms the centerpiece of a complex arranged around a central courtyard which is entered via a tripartite gate. Its central section, the **Orta Kapı (Middle Gate)**, is permanently closed and painted black in memory of **Patriarch Gregory** V who was hanged in front of it in 1821 when Greece started a war to free itself from Ottoman control. A second fire in 1941 destroyed many of the older outbuildings, leaving behind only the attractive old library, hidden away at the end of the garden behind the church. In the 1990s it was restored to its former glory.

Virgin Mary

If there is anywhere in Istanbul where it's still possible to get a feel for what Byzantine churches might have looked like in their heyday, it's here at the Patriarchate where the soaring iconostasis glitters with gold in the otherwise dimly-lit interior. Its most important panel can be found on the far right-hand side where there is a rare 12th-century mosaic **icon of St John the Baptist**. Nearby, overlooking a separate altar, is a second mosaic icon, this time depicting the **Panagia Pammakaristos (the Most Happy Mother of God)**. Set into the wall between these two treasures is a section of what is supposed to be the **stone pillar** against which Jesus was flogged. Nearby the bodies of **saints Omonia, Theophano and Euphemia** (see p. 480) lie in caskets with identifying icons in front of them. The patriarch's throne is thought to date back to the early 5th century and may have been made for **St John Chrysostom**, the then patriarch. The lofty pulpit and two small octagonal tables are inlaid with mother-of-pearl.

During Orthodox holidays such as **Christmas** and **Easter** the church heaves with visitors, many of whom come all the way from Greece especially for the occasion. Don't forget that the Greek Orthodox holidays fall one week later than the Protestant/Catholic versions.

Interior of church

Patriarch Bartholomew I

Patriarch Bartholomew I

The current patriarch was born Dimitris Arhondonis in Zeytinli on Gökçeada in 1940. In 1991 he was chosen to lead the Greek Orthodox Church and took the name Bartholomew I; US Vice-President Al Gore later dubbed him the "Green Patriarch" in recognition of the work he had done to improve the surroundings of the patriarchate. The Turkish state does not recognize his leadership of the Orthodox world, as ecumenic.

Patriarchal offices

Church of St Stephen of the Bulgars

Where else could you expect to stumble across a rusty church? Right by the waterside stands this curious example of Gothic architecture, cast out of iron in **Vienna** in 1871 and then shipped down the **Danube** in pieces to be reconstructed in a small garden on the shore of the Golden Horn (a previous wooden church on the site had already burnt down). Built for the Bulgarian Church which was eager to shake off the authority of the Greeks, it became the seat of a **Bulgarian Exarchate**, in what was a slap in the face to the patriarch just up the road. After being closed for nine years, the church was restored and opened in 2018. It's a dramatic building with stained-glass windows and striking ornaments. It has overtones of both neo-baroque and neo-gothic styles. The exterior is covered with galvanise and cast sheets. All parts are connected with bolts and nuts or welded together. The chorus section upstairs is also used as a gallery where you can see photographs of the building before and after its restoration.

Since there are only a few other such buildings in the world it certainly merits a quick look. The large, building facing it across the road and now partly below street level was once the **school** associated with the church. It has been successfully renovated to resemble its original looks. There are plans to turn it into a museum where works related to the life of Bulgarians in Istanbul and the history of the Bulgarian Church will be on permanent display.

Church from the gallery

Bulgarians and Macedonians

Instead of by a Bulgarian congregation down to around 400 people, St Stephen's is mainly used today by **"Macedonians"** from the Greek province of that name, most of whom come from Kastoria and speak Macedonian. In the past these people used to rear buffaloes, tend gardens and sell milk products. The Sütte, Milka and Çerkezo delicatessens were all founded by Macedonians.

The erstwhile large Bulgarian congregation used to support schools in Beyoğlu, Fener and Kumkapı, all of them now closed. In Şişli the **Church of Sveti Ivan Rilski** is currently used by Moldovans; the Bulgarians celebrate Christmas there but use the church in Fener for Easter and weddings. A third church of **St Demetrios** in Feriköy cemetery is used for funerals, while a fourth Bulgarian church inside the Bulgarian Hospital is now a mescid inside the **Türkiye Hospital** (see p. 355). Unfortunately, the Kaymakçı (clotted-cream shop) Pando, which had been relishing our palates for many years and was the Bulgarian's place in Beşiktaş Çarşı (Bazaar) (p. 400) was also closed. With its departure the city has lost another valuable reminder of the old Istanbul.

Stepped Street

Because Fener was built on such a steep slope several of its streets were equipped with steps to make access easier for the locals. Merdivenli Mektep Sokağı (Stepped School Street) leads up to the Greek High School, bypassing the house of Dimitri Cantemir on the right. At the top a cluster of fine stone houses hint at Fener's lost grandeur. The road then twists round on the left passing the abandoned **Yuvakimyon High School** for Girls before bearing right past a large, ruined **dining hall** to St Mary of the Mongols in Fırketeci Sokak.

Dimitri Cantemir's house

Who was Dimitri Cantemir?

Exiled to Istanbul from his homeland of Moldavia in 1687, Dimitri Cantemir (1673-1723) was a Greek philosopher and historian who wrote a **"History of the Growth and Decay of the Ottoman Empire"**, which remains an important source of information for the years 1688 to 1710, as well as a **Greek translation of the Koran** and a treatise on Ottoman music. Cantemir went on to fight alongside Peter the Great of Russia against the Ottomans. Defeated in 1711, he ended his life in Russia. His house in Fener, near the Merdivenli Mektep Sokağı, has been restored.

Church of St Mary of the Mongols

Church of St Mary of the Mongols (Panagia Muhliotissa)

The only church to have been in Greek hands continuously since before the Ottoman conquest of Istanbul, St Mary of the Mongols is associated with the story of **Princess Maria Paleologina**, an illegitimate daughter of **Emperor Michael VIII Paleologos**, despite evidence that it was actually built by the emperor's uncle Isaac Dukas in 1261. Poor Maria was one of those women who became a pawn in the diplomatic game, being sent far from home to marry **Hulagu**, the Great Khan of the Mongols, in 1265. Hulagu died before she could meet him, so she was married instead to his son **Abagu** and spent 15 years at the Mongol court, before finally rebelling when it was suggested that she marry yet another Mongol after her husband was murdered. Whether she founded the church named after her or merely embellished it, Maria retired to the convent attached to it for the remainder of her life.

St Mary of the Mongols (Panagia Muhliotissa, sometimes known as **Theotokos Panagiotissa**) is the only remaining Byzantine church preserved in its original form. In 1453 the architect, **Atik Sinan (Christodoulos)**, the Greek architect who was responsible for Fatih Mosque, succeeded in persuading Sultan Mehmed II to allow St Mary's to continue as a church rather than being turned into a mosque; a copy of the decree ensuring its survival is still preserved inside the building. Unfortunately crude restoration of the dome detracts from its aesthetic.

St Mary of the Mongols in Chora Church fresco

The clover-shaped church in an old drawing

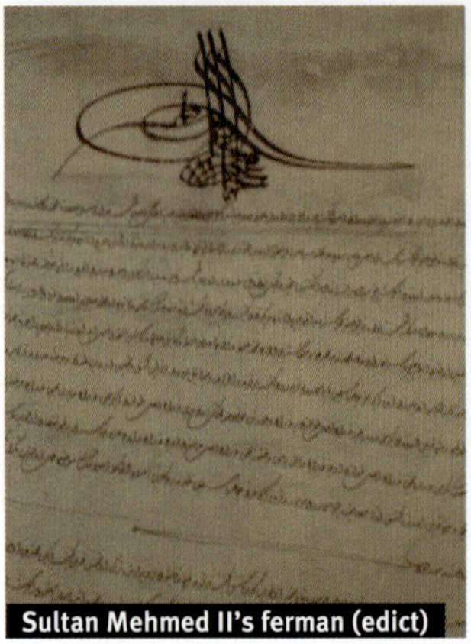

Sultan Mehmed II's ferman (edict)

Iconostasis

Above the door is written "High School of the Greek Orthodox community"

Fener Greek High School

Built in 1881 by the architect **Pericles Dimadis** using materials imported from France, this huge and unmissable red-brick building, sometimes called **"the Red Castle"**, looks especially impressive when viewed from the deck of one of the Golden Horn ferries. Its sheer size is a reminder of how wealthy an area this once was. Of an earlier university on the site dating back as far as 1454, there is no longer any trace, but many important individuals graduated from it, including the historian **Dimitri Cantemir** (1673-1723).

You probably won't be able to see inside the school, but if you do you will find the first-floor chamber of ceremonies decorated with murals depicting Pericles, Alexander the Great, Constantine and the Apostle Paul interspersed with motifs taken from classical Athenian pottery. The views from the windows are predictably gorgeous. Despite its name this is now a co-ed school. And in spite of what many people think this is not the Patriarchate!

Mural of Alexander the Great

The shape of old Fener

Mural of saints

Church hidden behind high wall

Church of Hagios Georgios Metochi

This small and not especially distinguished church seems to have started life in the 12th century as a chapel for a governor of Wallachia. In the mid-17th century it was bought to serve as a **"metochion"**, or daughter-church of the Holy Sepulchre in Jerusalem. The current building post-dates an 18th-century fire.

Archimedes' Palimpsest

An unbelievable treasure

What makes the church so interesting is not its architecture but what was found inside it: namely a 10th-century edition of seven works of the great Greek mathematician **Archimedes**, including three – "The Method", "The Stomachion" and "On Floating Bodies" – for which it is a **unique source.** They survived because the parchment they were written on was reused to create a 13th-century prayerbook. The so-called Archimedes Palimpsest was almost certainly made in Constantinople, but was only rediscovered in 1906 when John Ludwig Heiberg made a study of it. It is now housed in the **Walters Art Museum in Baltimore, USA.**

Archimedes (287-21 BC)

Ayakapı

A busy main road separates Fener from the Golden Horn. For much of its length traces of the old sea walls can still be seen. However, they are in a very poor state of repair after their battering first by the Crusaders in 1204 and then by the Ottomans in 1453. Several gateways through the walls also continue to survive, including the Ayakapı, built by Mimar Sinan in 1582. Right beside this is a wooden mescit (chapel) over the tomb of Sekbanbaşı Abdurrahman Ağa who died during the conquest of Istanbul in 1453. Beside that in turn is a building that used to be a base for the Janissaries and then became a police station after Sultan Mahmud II had them disbanded in 1826. From here it is just possible to make out the dome of the Church of St Nicholas (see p. 229) peeping over the walls.

Fener's past splendor reduced to today's poverty

For this local woman the long history of the Greek High School is irrelevant.

Fener's old houses

Most of Fener's wonderful **mansions** have long since disappeared but near the Church of St Stephen stand two that have been restored: one houses a **women's library**, the other a **glass workshop**. Steps down to their entrances indicate how much the ground has risen over the centuries. Fener was unusual in that the locals continued to build in stone even after wood had become the favored building material elsewhere in the city. Today the back streets are filled with what are called row-houses, small houses of two or three floors joined to each other and with jutting "cumbas (bay windows)" on their first floors. Built to house single families, many of them are now in multiple occupation. A few were restored during the early 2000s with funding from the European Union in an attempt to improve the neighborhood. Istanbul Metropolitan Municipality brought Fener Houses, one of the most original examples of 18th century Istanbul civil architecture, back to the city as contemporary art galleries and living spaces. **Haliç Sanat** hosts art lovers at 3 different addresses in the first phase of the project to create an art route along the Golden Horn coast.

Women's Library

Maraşlı Greek School

Was the Golden Horn so named because the waters reflected the setting sun or because it was such a wealthy harbor?

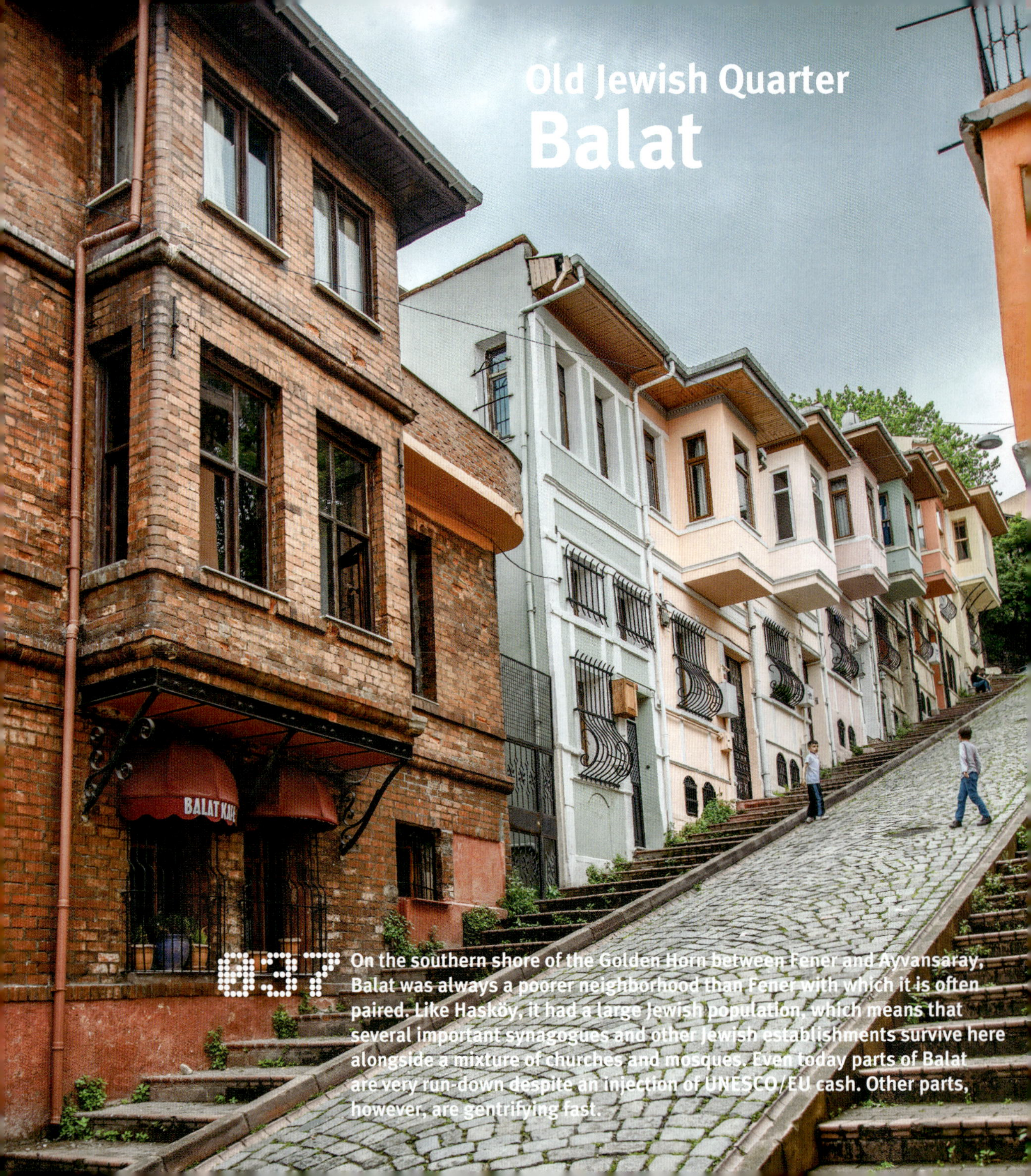

Old Jewish Quarter

Balat

037 On the southern shore of the Golden Horn between Fener and Ayvansaray, Balat was always a poorer neighborhood than Fener with which it is often paired. Like Hasköy, it had a large Jewish population, which means that several important synagogues and other Jewish establishments survive here alongside a mixture of churches and mosques. Even today parts of Balat are very run-down despite an injection of UNESCO/EU cash. Other parts, however, are gentrifying fast.

Balat street scenes

Balat market

If you cut inland and walk along Leblebiciler Caddesi you will come to Balat's attractively old-fashioned shopping area, where small family-owned shops are accommodated in a variety of buildings of different ages. Here you'll see the entrance gate to the **Yanbol synagogue,** which takes its name from Yanbol in Bulgaria, original home to its congregation. The current building, once able to accommodate 300 worshippers, dates back only to 1895 despite the venerable history of Judaism on the site.

Balat's original community was made up of **Jews from Macedonia**. However, in 1492 Sultan Bayezid II invited the **Spanish Jews** who had been expelled by Ferdinand and Isabella to settle here, thus superimposing a population of Judeo-Spanish speakers (and Ladino writers) on to the original Greek speakers. Later more refugees arrived first from Portugal (the Marranos), then from Rhodes and Balat became known as **"Yahudi Balat (Jewish Balat)"**. The newcomers brought with them many new-fangled inventions, including the **printing press**, which appears to have been introduced to Constantinople in 1493. Although there were once 19 synagogues in the area, no more than a handful of Jews still live in Balat; most have long since emigrated to Israel, their place taken by poor immigrants from Eastern Turkey.

Ironically, Balat takes its name from the Greek word **"palation (palace)"**, a reference to its proximity to the **Blachernae Palace** (see p. 151).

Ferruh Kethüda Mosque

For those who believe Sinan only ever built on a grand scale, this relatively small mosque, built in 1562, will come as a surprise. Its most interesting internal feature is the mihrab, which is decorated with tiles from nearby **Tekfur Palace** (see p. 149), but unfortunately its external appearance is marred by an ugly modern porch. **Balat Court**, one of Istanbul's four religious courts, used to meet in the grounds. **Ferruh Ağa** was a steward to Semiz Ali Paşa (Fat Ali) whose medrese can be seen near Edirnekapı (see p. 129).

Vodina Caddesi

Many of the houses and shops along this street have been restored by the European Union and UNESCO. At its easterly end where Balat merges into Fener there's a large walled compound with an old brick building clinging on to one end. Behind the wall, but barely visible, there are actually two churches, one dedicated to **St George**, the other to **Panagia Paramithas (St Mary the Comforter)**. St George was given to the Patriarch of Jerusalem by the Fener nobleman **Michael Cantacuzenus** in the 17th century and his family used it as a private chapel for their mansion which may have stood behind the walls. Panagia Paramithas served as the seat of the patriarchate from 1586 to 1596, but also seems to have been linked to the Cantacuzenuses, who were governors of Wallachia, so that it was known locally as the **Vlach Saray (Vlach Palace)**. The building burnt down in 1976.

Ahrida Synagogue

Founded in the 15th century, this synagogue in Kürkçü Çeşmesi Sokağı, the oldest in Istanbul, takes its name from **Ohrid in Macedonia** which is where its congregation came from. Following a fire, it was rebuilt in 1694 with an internal dome that was invisible from outside since the minority populations were forbidden to build domes. The shape of its **bema** (prayer platform) has been compared to that of the bow of the ship that brought the Jews from Spain to Balat, although others believe it is intended to evoke Noah's Ark. The synagogue was big enough to accommodate 500 worshippers, an indication of the size of the lost Jewish population. It was here that the self-proclaimed Jewish Messiah **Sabbetai Tsvi** from Smyrna (modern İzmir) proclaimed his creed in 1666, creating a schism that has continued to this day (see p. 346). Restored in 1992 for the 500th anniversary of the arrival of the Jews in Turkey, the synagogue is still in use today.

Entrance to Ahrida

La Senyora

The wealthy Marrano banker **Dona Gracia Mendes Nasi** (La Senyora) put up the money to support the naval battle of **Lepanto** in 1571. The Ottomans lost the engagement to a coalition of Spain, Venice and the Papacy, which is usually seen as a turning-point in their history.

Visiting the Synagogues

For security reasons those wanting to visit Istanbul's synagogues must visit the Chief Rabbinate website: www.turkyahudileri.com

Hazreti Cabir Mosque

Although it goes little noticed this pretty little brick building in Çember Sokağı started life as a **9th-century church** with a dome and three apses. It then became the Atik Mustafa Paşa Mosque before being renamed after Hazreti Cabir, a holy man who lived from 604 to 697.

If you continue up the road and turn right you will come to the ayazma of Blachernae (see p. 153).

"Here the metropolis has become a hamlet and rediscovered its identity."

Dervish **by Tim Kelsey, 1996**

Or-Ahayim Jewish Hospital

Beautifully situated on the shores of the Golden Horn in a district once inhabited by Jewish fishermen, this hospital was founded in 1899 and designed by the architect **Gabriel Tedeşci**. Money to endow it came in from all the big names of the Jewish diaspora: **the Goldschmidts, de Hirsches and Rothschilds**. The Kadoorie synagogue inside is named after the Iraqi family who paid for it.

Jewish Hospital

Surp Hreşdagabed

"(Surp Hreşdagabed Church) may be the only place in the world where Christians and Muslims meet to worship seriously."

***Dervish* by Tim Kelsey, 1996**

Surp Hreşdagabed Church

Dating back to the 16th century, this huge Armenian church was rebuilt in the 18th century over a sacred spring. On the feast date of the saint, both Christians and Muslims gather here in eager anticipation of a **miracle**. The adjoining 19th-century **schoolhouse** is now used as a warehouse.

Church of St John the Baptist

Metokion

The Church of Hagios Ioannis Prodromos (St John the Baptist) on Mürsel Paşa Caddesi originally had a link with the church of **St Catherine in Sinai, Egypt**. There was certainly a church here from as early as the 14th century but the current model dates back only to 1830; it is probably the worst restored church in Istanbul. Behind it are the remains of an associated **library** and **guesthouse**, now inhabited by Christians from South-eastern Turkey. Attached to them are the remains of the grand house that was once home to the 17th-century politician Panagotaki Nikosi; over the years the ground has risen so much that the gate is half-buried. This was once a very impressive **mansion** so it's to be hoped that it will also be restored soon.

Church of Hagios Demetrios Kanabu

If you walk along the main road following the sea wall you will come to a plaque commemorating the start of the siege of Constantinople on 23 April 1453. Just past it the roof of the Church of Hagios Demetrios Kanabu can be glimpsed. A church is known to have existed on this site since at least the 14th century; it served very briefly as home to the patriarchate from 1597 to 1601. The present building, however, dates back no further than 1730.

"On Monday 23 April 1453 Sultan Fatih Mehmed set up a bridge to scale the walls here."

Hagios Demetrios Kanabu Church

If you walk through the car park beside the church, turn left and walk along Kırkambar Caddesi to its junction with Mahkeme Altı Caddesi you will come to the 19th-century Church of Panagia Balinu which dates back to at least 1597 although the current build- ing is an 18th and 19th century structure.

Church of Hagios Ioannis Prodromos

The Struma Disaster

The ship, which brought 764 Jews who had escaped from Nazi Germany from Romania during the Second World War, stayed anchored offshore Sarayburnu (p.202) for 71 days in harsh conditions. During this period passengers, except for a lucky few with special permission or those who got sick, were not allowed to land or receive help due to Turkey's neutrality in the war. After the ship was pulled to the shores of Şile (p.568) on 24 February 1942, it was torpedoed by a Russian submarine. The ship sank with all its passengers onboard. The author Zülfü Livaneli has written about this shameful tragedy in his book "Serenad (Serenade)".

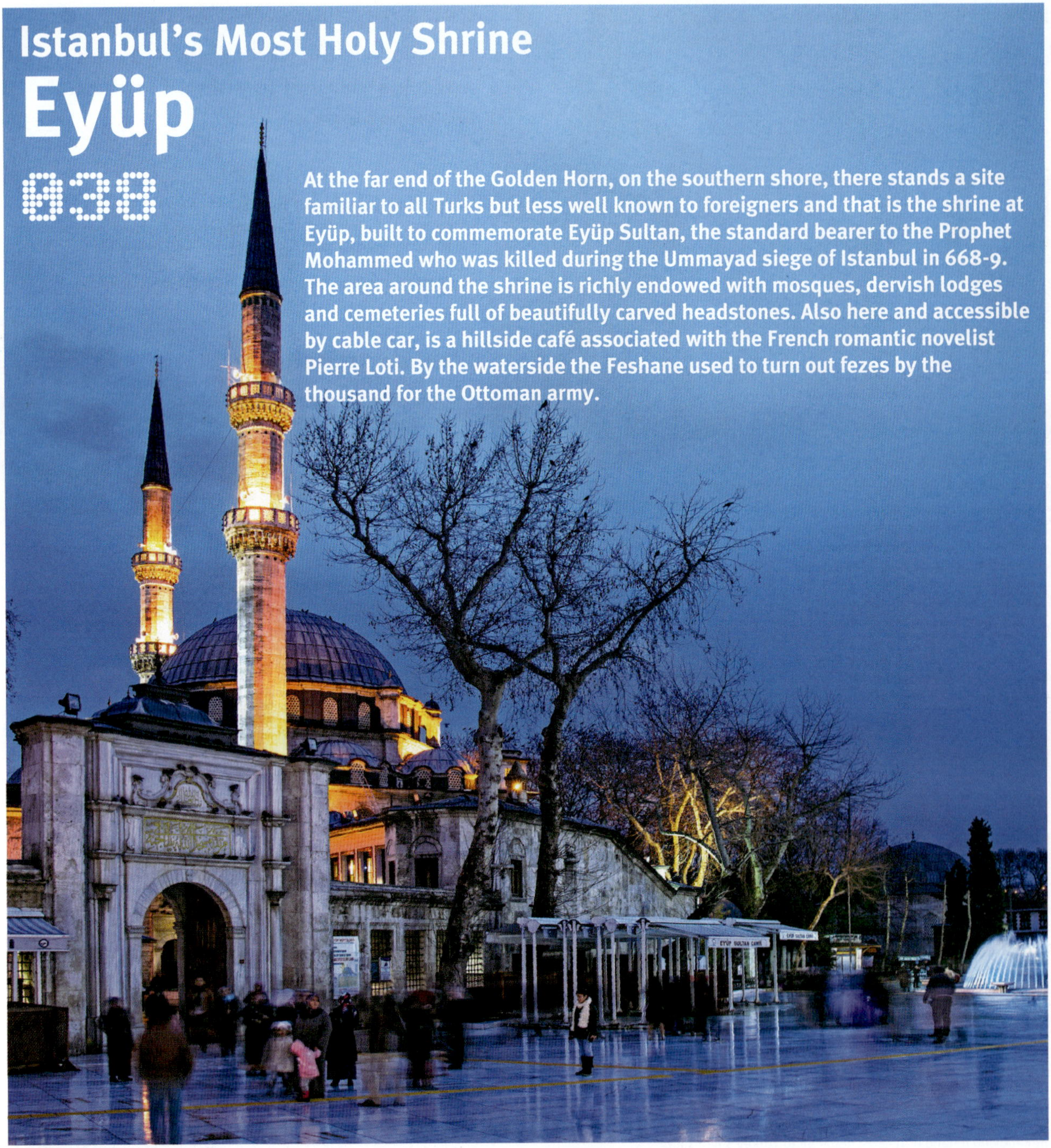

Istanbul's Most Holy Shrine

Eyüp

038

At the far end of the Golden Horn, on the southern shore, there stands a site familiar to all Turks but less well known to foreigners and that is the shrine at Eyüp, built to commemorate Eyüp Sultan, the standard bearer to the Prophet Mohammed who was killed during the Ummayad siege of Istanbul in 668-9. The area around the shrine is richly endowed with mosques, dervish lodges and cemeteries full of beautifully carved headstones. Also here and accessible by cable car, is a hillside café associated with the French romantic novelist Pierre Loti. By the waterside the Feshane used to turn out fezes by the thousand for the Ottoman army.

View of Golden Horn from Pierre Loti Café

Ebu Eyüp el-Ensari was the standard bearer who accompanied the **Prophet Mohammed** on his many military campaigns and went on to become his close friend. So when Sultan Mehmed II's teacher **Akşemseddin** claimed to have found his remains in Istanbul immediately after the conquest in 1453, the Conqueror was only too pleased that the first mosque built after his victory should be dedicated to this important man (in fact there is plenty of written evidence to suggest that the shrine was already very well known, so perhaps the Conqueror merely rebuilt it). Once the mosque had been built, many dignitaries wished to be buried close to someone whom they believed could intercede for them after their death and so built their own mosques here too. Since the wealthy had much the same thought in mind, many of them were buried here and the local **cemeteries** now form outdoor museums of the finest Ottoman calligraphy and stone carving. The site chosen for the mosque had been used for the coronation of the Ottoman sultans who came here to strap on the revered **sword of Osman**, founder of the Ottoman Empire.

Eyüp has lots of stalls selling religious paraphernalia.

Eyüp is a strange place. Like Lourdes in France, it can appear at first sight to be drowning beneath the sea of religious paraphernalia on sale in stalls that ring the main square. However, once you escape into the streets around the Mihrişah Valide Sultan Külliye (complex) you may well have the **tomb-lined streets** to yourself, a real treat.

Eyüp Sultan Mosque (1)

Of the many mosques in Eyüp, far and away the most important is the one that made the area what it is and where the remains of Ebu Eyüp el-Ensari are buried inside a tomb dating back to 1458. The original structure fell victim to an earthquake in 1766, so the building that you see today dates back only to 1800 when it was rebuilt by **Sultan Selim III** (1789-1807). The minarets were added by **Sultan Ahmed III** (1703-30).

The mosque is approached via a double courtyard adorned with venerable plane trees; although there is no longer any sign of the lame storks that used to live in their hollows or of the gray herons which used to nest in them, as reported by John Freely and Hilary Sumner-Boyd in 1972, there are always hundreds of pigeons here, tucking into the easy pickings provided by indulgent pilgrims. The stepped corridor that used to lead to the **sultan's pew** inside the mosque is now reserved for women worshippers.

Inside the mosque itself honey-colored walls set off to perfection a huge chandelier that is suspended over a sea of turquoise carpet. Of the mosque's külliye (complex), only the **hamam** (Turkish bath) survives, the medrese (theological school) and imaret (soup kitchen) having been demolished long ago to create pedestrianized **Eyüp Square**. The hamam was restored in 2010.

Eyüp Square

Interior of mosque

Fountain in the square

Courtyard

Tiles near the entrance to the shrine

Ebu Eyüp el-Ensari's Tomb

The entrance to the shrine is just next to the gate of the mosque's courtyard. Exits are made from the door to the inner courtyard, which was used for both entry and exit.
Inside, the remains of Ebu Eyüp el-Ensari rest behind a solid silver grille donated by Selim III. This is a very holy site and a place of pilgrimage, so no matter when you visit you are likely to find people praying.

The tombs ② ③

Amid the many large tombs to be seen around the Eyüp Sultan Mosque it's worth looking for that of **Sokollu Mehmed Paşa,** which was designed for the powerful Grand Vizier by Sinan in c.1572 and contains some wonderful stained glass; that of **Siyavuş Paşa,** also by Sinan and probably built for the young children of this Grand Vizier before being commandeered for the body of the father; that of **Mirimirman Mehmed Paşa** which has a stone wishing well in the courtyard; and that of **Lala Mustafa Paşa** (c.1500-80), the brutal conqueror of Cyprus. If you're tiring of the classical style, the tomb of **Posta Telgraf Nazırı İzzet Efendi,** who died in 1891, is in the Empire style. Further away but also worth a quick look is the tomb of **Sultan Mehmed V Reşat** (1909-18), the last sultan to die and be buried in Turkey, which stands right beside a school designed by **Kemaladdin Bey,** a star of the First National Architecture movement.

Sultan Mehmed V Reşad

Amongst the gravestones lining peaceful Beybaba Sokağı, behind the Eyüp Sultan Mosque, it's worth looking for the Sinan-designed tomb of **Ayas Mehmed Paşa** (? – 1539), a notorious womanizer who gave his name to the area at the top of Gümüşsuyu Caddesi just off Taksim Square (see p. 284).

Sultan Mehmed V Reşad's tomb

Mirimirman Mehmed Paşa's tomb

Horse-mounting step

View of Golden Horn from Pierre Loti Café showing the Bahariye Islands

The Executioners' Cemetery

Ottoman executioners, always deaf mutes, adapted the method of execution to the status of the condemned person and the nature of their crime. Given the Islamic prohibition on killing, other people rarely wanted to be buried near them, so they were generally buried in the most out of the way places. There were two cemeteries for executioners, one of them in Eyüp. To find it walk past the Pierre Loti Café towards the **Karyağdıbaba Tekke** (dervish lodge) and it's a short way ahead. The executioners' tombstones look different from those around them. This rather grim place features in Selçuk Altun's novel "Songs My Mother Never Taught Me".

Ceremony to recognize new sultan

Cülus Yolu (Accession Road) 4

In the past new sultans would come to Eyüp by caique, disembarking at the Bostan landing stage and processing towards the Eyüp Sultan Mosque along the Cülus Yolu which was lined with the finest tombs and complexes, including the **Hüsrev Paşa complex, the Mihrişah Valide Sultan complex** and the **Adile Sultan tomb.** Unfortunately later realignment of the roads and landing stages means that modern visitors can only recreate their procession in their imaginations.

One of Eyüp's old wooden houses

Hüsrev Paşa Complex 5

Koca Mehmed Hüsrev Paşa (1769-1855) served as Grand Vizier to Sultan Abdülmecid but is best known as the man responsible for bringing a **fez** back to Turkey from his travels in Tunisia and persuading Sultan Mahmud II that it should replace the turban as the headgear of choice for the Ottomans. He was also involved in the overthrow of the Janissaries in 1826 and the creation of the new model army in its aftermath. His complex consists of a tomb, library and dervish lodge straddling both sides of the Cülus Yolu.

Adile Sultan's Tomb

Adile Sultan (1825-98), the daughter of **Sultan Mahmud II** and wife of **Admiral Mehmed Ali Paşa**, is buried in a somewhat austere tomb. A tragic woman, Adile Sultan saw all her children and her husband predecease her. Her brother **Sultan Abdülaziz** may have committed suicide but was also almost certainly murdered. Not surprisingly, she devoted the latter part of her life to charity and religious contemplation. Her palace in **Kandilli** (see p. 532) now houses an upscale restaurant.

Eyüp is full of historic houses.

Mihrişah Valide Sultan Complex ⑥

One of the largest complexes in Eyüp was designed in baroque style for Mihrişah Valide Sultan, the Genoese mother of **Sultan Selim III**, in 1791; it included a tomb, school, superbly decorative sebil and fountains. A peaceful courtyard surrounded on three sides by porticoes was the complex's **imaret** (soup kitchen) where food used to be dispensed to the poor every morning. In front of it a marble block of stone was used by the sultans to mount and dismount their horses.

Mihrişah Valide Sultan's mosque complex

Zal Mahmud Paşa Mosque ⑦

The second most important mosque in Eyüp is significant not so much for religious as for architectural reasons as it is a hugely impressive work of the great Ottoman architect **Sinan** dating back to the 1570s. Much of the split-level complex also survives, including two **medreses** and the **türbe** (tomb) of Zal and his wife who died, remarkably, on the same night in 1580. Zal was the man who personally strangled **Süleyman the Magnificent's son Mustafa** once the order for his death was given. Not withstanding that, he went on to become Grand Vizier.

If you leave the complex by the upper exit you will come out opposite the pretty 16th-century **Silahi Mehmed Bey Mescit (Chapel)**, which has an unusual hexagonal brick and stone minaret with an open-sided lantern at the top.

The Bronze Inkwell ⑨

All Istanbul mosques have crescents topping off their domes but only the 18th-century **Defterdar Mosque** in Eyüp has a bronze inkwell and pen, a reminder that its founder, Defterdar Mahmud Efendi, was a talented **calligrapher**.

Defterdar Mosque

Şah Sultan Complex

Near the Zal Mahmud Paşa Mosque is an impressive 18th-century complex paid for by Sultan Selim III's sister Şah Sultan. It consists of a tomb, sebil and school with birdhouses carved on its facades.

Zal Mahmud Paşa's tomb

Silahi Mehmed Bey Mescid

Cezari Kasım Paşa Mosque ⑧

This small mosque to the west of the Şah Sultan complex dates back to 1515 and used to have one great claim to fame which was a fine panel of **Tekfur Palace tiling** (see p. 149) dating back to 1726 that depicted tents gathered around the **Kaaba** at Mecca. Unfortunately this was stolen and removed from Turkey. Although it has since been returned, it has not been replaced in the mosque where visitors can only look at but not photograph a copy.

"In the shadow of the mosque is the green-roofed (Feshane) that since the time of Mahmud II had pointed towards a western future..."

***A Fez of the Heart* by Jeremy Seal 1995**

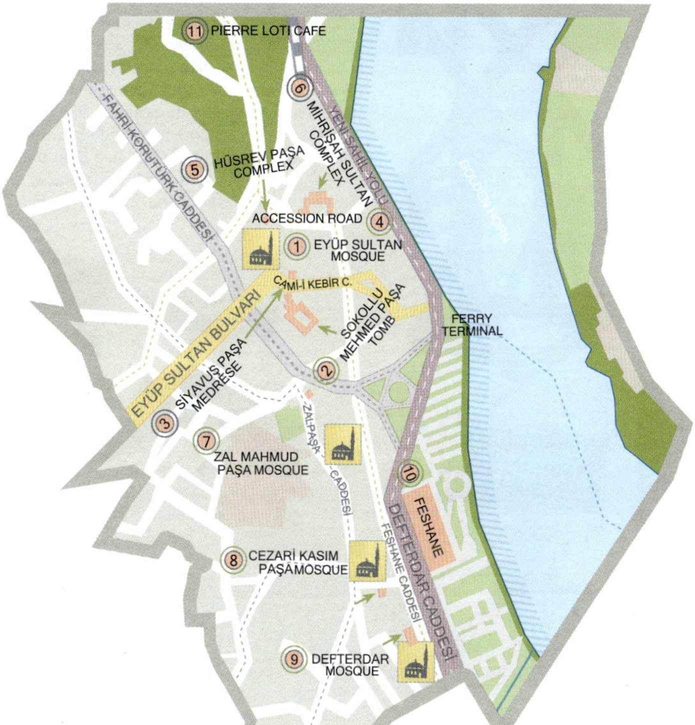

Ottoman coat of arms above entrance to Feshane

Feshane (10)

In 1833 a huge factory for the production of fezes for **Sultan Mahmud II**'s new army, the New Guard, was built right on the waterfront on the southern shore of the Golden Horn. Remodeled in 1843, it was given a complete makeover by the Armenian architect **Krikor Balyan** in 1894. The factory continued in business until 1937, but parts of the building had already been demolished when it finally closed altogether in 1986.
In 2023, **Artİstanbul Feshane** was opened as one of the largest art centers in the city. Located on an area of 8 thousand square meters, Artİstanbul; It is a breathing space for Istanbulites with its exhibition halls, rich library, social venues, congress, workshop and reading areas, as well as cafes, restaurants, shops and green areas.
It provides a memorable opening scene for Jeremy Seal's 1995 Turkey travelogue, **"A Fez of the Heart"**.

@artistanbulfeshane
Closed Mondays.

Fez facts

In 1829 the reforming sultan **Mahmud II** decreed that men should abandon turbans in favor of the more modern fez, a maroon-colored, round head covering with a tassel instead of a brim. One hundred years later **Atatürk** decided that the fez, too, had had its day. In 1925 he introduced the **Hat Law** which insisted that men should wear "Western"-style hats with brims. Today, of course, no one wears a fez except tourists and people working in the tourism industry.

Sultan Mahmud II

Traditional Eyüp Toys

Eyüp Sultan was believed to have had a particular love for children, which is partly why so many parents bring their sons here before their circumcision. Expect to see them parading around in their satin and feather crowns and topcoats, clutching white scepters like Harry Potter wands. Not surprisingly a flourishing trade in wooden toys grew up in the area. Until recently this had died out, although some examples of what was produced can be seen in the City Museum at Yıldız (see p. 404) and the Toy Museum in Göztepe (see p. 488). The **Eyüp Toy Workshop** (Eyüp Oyuncakları Atölyesi) in the grounds of the Zal Mahmud Paşa Mosque is trying to revive the tradition. The "Toy Workshops", organized at the Traditional Eyüp Toy Shop, keeps this almost 500-year-old art alive for the future generations. There is also a museum on the upper floor of the toy shop.

www.eyupoyuncakcisi.com

Pierre Loti's house in Rochefort, France, is now a museum

"There is a splendid view from my roof... the gloomy plain of Eyoub, its sacred mosque rising in marble whiteness from the mysterious depths of immemorial trees...the vast cemeteries that form a veritable city of the dead."

Aziyade **by Pierre Loti, 1877**

Who was Pierre Loti? (11)

Romance clings like a veil to the name of this French novelist who arrived in Istanbul in 1876 and went on to write **Aziyade**, an apparently autobiographical novel detailing his love affair with the Circassian Aziyade, a member of a wealthy merchant's harem. Pierre Loti was actually **Julien Viaud** (1850-1923), a Turcophile naval officer who traveled the world and wrote a string of books. His home in **Rochefort, France,** is now a museum with one room resembling a somewhat fantastical mosque. His story is recounted in **Lesley Blanch**'s book "Pierre Loti: Travels with the Legendary Romantic". Sadly for romantics the café he actually frequented, **Rabia Kadın Kahvesi**, is no more.

Pierre Loti at home in Rochefort

Pierre Loti Café

Come up here to sit at the spot where the French novelist supposedly found inspiration, even though the view that will greet you is far more built-up than the one that so enthralled him. A few outdoor tables are lined up to scoop a panorama that takes in the two rather rustic Bahariye islands at the end of the Golden Horn. Teas, coffees and cold drinks are the order of the day. There's a cozy indoor café for winter. Beside the Café, a small bookshop sells copies of his works as well as pictures and souvenirs of the writer.

New Life for an Industrial Wasteland

Sütlüce, Miniatürk and SantralIstanbul

039

At the far end of the northern shore of the Golden Horn is Sütlüce, a once-beautiful district that was zoned for industrial development in the 1930s. Today's visitors come here mainly to visit Miniatürk, a curious collection of cut-down versions of Turkey's most famous sites intended to appeal to children. Adults may be more interested in the giant slaughterhouse nearby which has been converted into a cultural center. Come here, too, to eyeball the artworks on display at SantralIstanbul.

Arriving in Sütlüce, it's worth pausing for a moment to reflect on what has been lost. Back in the 18th century this was one of Istanbul's many leafy playgrounds, with people flocking by boat or carriage to frolic on the banks of the **Kağıthane** and **Alibey streams** where they merged with the Golden Horn in an area nicknamed **"the Sweet Waters of Europe"**. As far back as Byzantine times, this had been thought of as a particularly beautiful region. Then in the 17th century the wealthy began to build grand homes on the banks of the rivers, giving it the same sort of cachet as Ortaköy has today. The most impressive of all these palaces and mansions was the **Sadabad (Eternal Happiness) Summer Palace**, whose rooms jutted out over the river (you can see a painting of it in the Pera Museum, see p. 334). The excitement reached a peak during the **Tulip Age** at the beginning of the 18th century (see p. 265), when cooling water from the river was channeled down through a series of pools and waterfalls (hence the name of the next neighborhood up, **Çağlayan**, which means "waterfall" in Turkish) and the gardens were awash with tulips during the spring festivals. But by then tensions had been building up inside the Empire and in 1730 during the **Patrona Halil Rebellion** the wonderful buildings of Kağıthane were burnt down.

"Why shouldn't the heart flow like water towards Sa'adabad?"
Nedim (1681-1730)

During the reign of the reformist **Sultan Selim III** in the 18th century the pleasure gardens experienced something of a revival and in the 19th century the Armenian architect **Krikor Balyan** was commissioned to rebuild some of the palaces. All that came to an abrupt end in the 1930s when **industrialization** hit Sütlüce and it's only in the last few years that an attempt has been made to revive the idea of traveling to the far reaches of the Golden Horn for pleasure. **Parks and promenades** now stretch for most of the way from the Sütlüce Cultural Center to SantralIstanbul.

Golden Horn Conference Center (Haliç Kongre Merkezi)

The giant **abbatoir** (mezbaha) at the end of the Golden Horn dates back exactly to the birth of the Turkish Republic in 1923 when it was designed in First National Architectural style by **Osman Fitri** and **Marko Logos** as the largest place for the slaughter and sale of meat in the city. Its most outstanding feature is two tall towers that served as an **icehouse** in the days before refrigeration. In the 1980s the slaughterhouse was decommissioned as part of an attempt to start cleaning up the Golden Horn. Converted into a cultural center, it opened for conference business in 2009.

Küçük Çavuşbaşı Mosque

Sütlüce Hamam

The Turkish bath near the slaughterhouse has been attributed extremely tenuously to Mimar Sinan. Even were that to be the case, there's not much left to show for his efforts today. The bath was renovated in the reign of Sultan Abdülhamid II (1876-1909); once again in 2009.

Behind the hamam the small, newly restored **Çavuşbaşı Mosque** in Talatpaşa Arkası Sokak has also been attributed to Mimar Sinan. Beside it the **Hasîrîzâde Elif Efendi Tekke** was a famous dervish lodge, built in 1784. It is restored in 2012.

Sadabad Mosque (Kağıthane Mosque)

The first mosque built in the reign of **Sultan Ahmed III** was in Kağıthane. It was restored during the reign of Sultans Selim III and Mahmud II, before being completely rebuilt by the **Balyans** in 1862 for Sultan Abdülaziz.

Kağıthane

The area around Santral is called Kağıthane (Paper House), a name it acquired from a paper factory and printing house established here in 1727; both collapsed after the Islamic authorities refused the owner permission to print copies of the Koran. Although much of this part of the Golden Horn is still rather depressing, the last few years have seen efforts made to cheer things up with new parks and a promenade that runs most of the way from Bilgi University to Miniatürk following the banks of the Golden Horn.

Lost Sadabad Pavilion

Miniatürk

Miniatürk is a large gathering of miniature versions of all Turkey's best-known monuments set in landscaped gardens. Inside the grounds the small **Victory Museum** contains photos of Atatürk along with information and a diorama depicting the **Battle of Çanakkale** (Gallipoli) that took place during the First World War. There's a model railway and other **children's playground** apparatus here too, but people who're going to visit the actual monuments may prefer to give it a miss.

@miniaturk1
www.miniaturk.com.tr
Tel:0212 222 28 82

Maiden's Tower

"There (under Sultan Ahmed III) grew up as by magic a continuous line of villas and gardens from the village of Kiat Haneh (Kağıthane) to that of Sütlüjeh (Sütlüce)."

Constantinople, Settings and Traits **by H. G. Dwight, 1927**

Santralİstanbul

Santralİstanbul started life in 1911 as the vast **Silahtarağa Power Plant**, the first power station to be built in Istanbul and in service until 1983. Taking a leaf out of the success of Tate Modern in London, UK, it was converted into a **contemporary art space** under the aegis of Bilgi University and reopened to the public in 2007.

From 1914 to 1952 Santral provided all the electricity Istanbul needed. Built by an Austro-Hungarian company, it covered 118,000 square meters of land what had become Istanbul's first industrial zone. Electricity was supplied first of all to the European side of the town where most of the commerce took place. Then in 1926 an underwater cable made it possible to extend the supply to the Anatolian side of the city too. In 1937 the company was taken over by the state and given to **İETT** (Istanbul Elektrik, Tramvay ve Tünel); today İETT still runs Istanbul's public transport and has retained its initials even though it no longer has anything to do with electricity. In 1970 the plant was given to TEK, the new electricity-generating company but already it was nearing the end of its life. In 2007 it opened to the public as a museum and art gallery hosting short-term but often excellent art exhibitions, all of them cutting edge and conceptual. Don't come here expecting Renoir.

www.santralistanbul.org
Tel: 0212 311 78 09

Museum of Energy

This is Turkey's first industrial archeological museum. Unlike other abandoned industrial sites that have been restored, such as the Feshane on the opposite shore of the Golden Horn, the Santral still retained its original machinery and this has been preserved and used as the basis for a Museum of Energy inside the same building as the art gallery. Visitors can inspect the original turbine generators which were, at the time, state of the art machinery and visit the old Control Room, still with most of its equipment intact. On the ground floor of the museum is an Energy Playground where visitors can conduct experiments on electricity and energy. The museum was awarded the "DASA Award" by the European Museum Academy in 2012.

closed Mondays

Istanbul's Industrial Heritage

Hasköy and the Rahmi M. Koç Museum

048

On the northern shore of the Golden Horn, Turkey's first industrial museum occupies the site of an old shipyard and anchor-making factory. Privately funded by one of Turkey's wealthiest families of industrialists, it's a state of the art museum with lots to interest older children as well as a lovely café to entertain their elders. Hasköy itself was one of the districts to which Turkey's Karaite Jewish population was relocated from Eminönü in 1591 when their land was expropriated to make way for the New Mosque.

Old anchor factory turned museum

Hasköy is not an especially beautiful suburb but it does have two considerable attractions: the old **Jewish cemetery** up on the hillside and Turkey's first **museum of industrial heritage**. The Rahmi M. Koç Museum has two separate sections on either side of Hasköy Caddesi. The first section is housed inside what was once a gracefully domed lengerhane (anchor-making factory) dating back to the reign of **Sultan Ahmed III** (1703-30). In the 1950s this building was used to store industrial alcohol, but it had become redundant by the time **Rahmi M. Koç** bought it in 1991 with a view to opening Turkey's first industrial museum. The second part, across the street, is an open-air museum on the site of an abandoned tersane (shipyard) dating back to 1861 where some of the early ferry boats were built. It was purchased in 1996 and opened as a museum in 2001. A temporary exhibition hall also lurks behind the Café du Levant.

---

rahmi_m_koc_muzesi, www.rmk-museum.org.tr
Tel: 0212 369 66 00, closed Mondays

Who is Rahmi M. Koç?

Born in 1930, Rahmi Mustafa Koç was the only son of Vehbi Koç who founded one of Turkey's most successful industrial empires. In 1984 he took over as chairman of the Koç Holding Company from his father, relinquishing the position to his own eldest son Mustafa in 2003.
He has become one of the country's most conspicuous philanthropists, responsible for the museums that bear his name in Istanbul, Ankara and Ayvalık amongst many other things. The Koç family has two more museums in town: Pera (see p. 334) and Sadberk Hanım (see p. 464). Rahmi Koç lives in Kandilli (see p. 528).

The anchor-making factory (Lengerhane)

That the lengerhane is accessed down steps beside the road is an indication of how much the local ground level has risen over the last three centuries. The interior of the building itself is superb, reminiscent of the inside of a mosque rather than of something as prosaic as a factory. The collections, however, are of rather specialist interest: glass-cases full of old radios, endless models of trains, many pictures of boats etc. Two stand-out sections are the **captain's bridge** complete with sound effects and a tableau of a family sharing a meal in 1453 just before the Turks breached the walls of Constantinople that was used in the 1996 Turkish film **"Love Under Siege"**. This building was named after Mustafa V. Koç, the businessperson who died in 2016.

Sultan Abdülaziz' s state carriage

Sultan Abdülaziz' s tuğra (monogram) on state carriage

Boats, a train and a submarine

At weekends it's possible to take a 40-minute tour along the Golden Horn in the restored Liman II and Rosalie tugs, or to board a restored train and trundle along the foreshore as far as Sütlüce. Groups of up to 12 people at a time can also descend into a submarine which is moored just off shore.

The museum is very popular with students and young people and takes a pride in its educational role. It even has a museum bus that tours some of the exhibits following the mantra that if some students won't come to the museum the museum must go to them. There's also a workshop for kindergarten-aged children.

The world's longest-serving submarine, Uluç Ali Reis was in service from 1944 to 2004

The Shipyard (Tersane)

The main part of the museum houses an enormous **collection of cars**, with everything from an original Turkish Tofaş, through a Trabant and a Mini, to the real glamor cars, the Chevys, Cadillacs, Daimlers and Rolls'. Here, too, are galleries containing a wide array of **boats**, including one of the caiques that used to ferry the nobility around the Bosphorus. Carefully preserved is a **satin-lined carriage** from the train in which **Sultan Abdülaziz** travelled to Paris and London in 1867 (the first and last sultan to travel to Europe for pleasure rather than war), as well as one of the **original trams** that served the Kadıköy to Moda route from 1934 to 1966 and one of the horse-drawn trams that operated between Azapkapı and Ortaköy between 1872 and 1914.

Indoors, a section of the museum is devoted to explaining the workings of everyday **household machinery** such as washing machines and cookers (many of them made by Koç Holding companies). There are also working models of an **olive-oil factory** and a **sawmill**.

The shipyard grounds contained the remains of 14 buildings, some of them now restored and converted into the sort of **shops** to make older people go misty-eyed over remembrance of their childhoods: a cobbler's, an old-fashioned pharmacy full of giant bottles of medicine, a blacksmith's forge, a ship's chandler's, a watchmaker's and a toyshop.

Original horse-drawn tram

Who was Abraham Kamondo?

Abraham Kamondo (1781-1873) who was responsible for the **Kamondo Steps** (see p. 274) and the **Galata Residence** was born in Constantinople to a family of Jewish-Italian descent, Abraham inherited a fortune from his childless brother Isaac and went on to become banker to the Ottoman court before the creation of the **Ottoman Bank** (see p. 274). He was so powerful that he managed to persuade the sultans to overturn a law that prohibited foreign nationals from owning real estate in the city. He died in Paris but was buried in Hasköy Cemetery. You can find out more about the Kamondo family at the **Turkish Jewish Museum** (see p. 328).

The Kamondo tomb

Hasköy's Jewish Cemetery

Hasköy Jewish Cemetery

Overgrown and neglected, Hasköy Cemetery, which dates back to 1582, was once a thriving Jewish burial ground which still contains some **20,000 graves** with inscriptions mainly in Hebrew and Turkish, but also in Ladino and Greek (written in Hebrew script). Buried here are Jews of Sephardic, Karaite and Romaniot persuasion. Perhaps the most famous of them is **Abraham Kamondo** whose tomb can be seen to the right of the D-100 as you drive from Okmeydan to the Golden Horn. Sadly, it has been vandalized and is in dire need of restoration.

Church of Hagia Paraskeve (St Paraskevi)

Slightly inland from the waterfront in Baçtar Sokak, this small church, dating back to Byzantine times, was rebuilt in 1692 by **Constantine Brankovanos,** a Governor of Wallachia and extensively restored in the early 19th century. Its courtyard contains several Byzantine gravestones. Paraskeve's feast day, **26 July**, is still celebrated here. Women also come here to pray for children.

Maalem Synagogue

In the Lion's Footsteps

Aynalıkavak Pavilion and Kasımpaşa

041

During the Tulip Era, Sultan Ahmed III decided to locate a small but exquisite hunting lodge in extensive grounds right on the northern shores of the Golden Horn. Today what remains of the Aynalıkavak Pavilion houses a small museum of Turkish musical instruments. Further east towards the Galata Bridge is the run-down suburb of Kasımpaşa, once an important shipbuilding area and home to a large barracks. A little way inland the Piyale Paşa Mosque has an unusual multi-domed silhouette.

Aynalıkavak Pavilion (Aynalıkavak Kasrı)

The original wooden palace on this site, the Tersane (Shipyard) Palace, was created for **Sultan Ahmed I** (1603-17), a keen archer who would come here to practice at Okmeydanı (Arrow Square) on Hasköy hill. During the reign of **Sultan Ahmed III** (1703-1730), the sultan who presided over the Tulip Age, the palace was expanded and became one of the locations for the sultan's popular tulip parties.

Delicate little Aynalıkavak Kasrı (the Pavilion of the Mirrored Poplars), with its many windows, is the last surviving remnant of Ahmed's palace and contains the only **Tulip Age ceiling** to survive in Istanbul. How it acquired its rather strange name is not entirely clear, although it may commemorate some conspicuously tall **Venetian mirrors** that had been given to the sultan.

Sultan Selim III

In 1784 representatives of Russia and the Ottoman Empire met here to sign what became known as the **Treaty of Aynalıkavak** recognizing the Russian occupation of Crimea. Later the poet and musician **Sultan Selim III** (1789-1807) had the palace restored. He was especially fond of Aynalıkavak and spent much of his time here, organizing concerts at which his own compositions would be performed. In the 19th century Sultan Mahmud II (1808-39) had the building restored again and given the present extensive gardens.

Today the pavilion houses a small **Museum of Musical Instruments**. The most important rooms are the imperial audience chamber (arz odası), the council chamber (divanhane), the Composition Room where Selim III is believed to have worked and a room containing a suite of furniture inlaid with gorgeous mother-of-pearl. The lodge is a beautiful gem set in a sea of surrounding ugliness which makes it all the more disappointing that it has been closed to the public for many years.

www.millisaraylar.gov.tr
Tel : 0212 227 34 41

Levni's Surname

In 1720 the famous Ottoman miniaturist Abdülcelil Levni Çelebi illustrated a copy of a book called the Surname to commemorate the 15-day celebrations for the circumcision of Sultan Ahmed III's sons. Images inside it show the sultan watching waterside entertainments from the Aynalıkavak Pavilion. They are reproduced in tile in the building housing the cable-car to the Pierre Loti café (see p. 253).

Venetian mirror

Music Room

Aynalıkavak Kasrı by J.B. Hillair, 1782

Council Chamber

Kasımpaşa

It was at Kasımpasa that Sultan Mehmed II's boats were launched into the Golden Horn after being dragged overland from near what is now Dolmabahçe Palace in 1453. Later the area was settled by **Genoese traders** and went on to become famous for its shipyards. The beauty of the surrounding hillside soon attracted the imperial eye and a garden, called the **Shipyard Imperial Garden** (Tersane Hasbahçesi) started to take shape, followed in due course by a Shipyard Palace (Tersane Sarayı) – Aynalıkavak Pavilion is the last relic of that palace and stands today amid the squalor of an area that quickly fell from favor when the Golden Horn was turned into an industrial zone.

Its main mosque, the **Cami-i Kebir**, is named after Güzelce (Quite Beautiful) Kasım Paşa (? – 1543), one of Sultan Süleyman the Magnificent's commanders who fought at the **first siege of Vienna** in 1529. In 1530 he succeeded in seizing Buda in return for which the sultan bestowed on him the area that now bears his name. The mosque is a work of **Sinan** dating back to 1533-34, but was almost completely rebuilt after a fire in the 19th century.

Güzelce Kasım Paşa Mosque

Piyale Paşa Mosque

This is the least Sinan-like of all **Sinan**'s Istanbul mosques. He built it in 1573, but in designing it he harked back to an earlier style of design which included multiple equally-sized domes so that it looks more like the Ulu Mosque in Bursa than other Istanbul places of worship. Unusually it also has a **single minaret** arising from the center of the western façade. Internally the mosque boasts some beautiful İznik tiles and a frieze designed by the great calligrapher **Karahisari** who also worked on the Süleymaniye (see p. 098). As for **Piyale Paşa** (1515-78), he was a Croatian shoemaker who went on to become a lord high admiral, capture Chios for the Ottomans and marry one of Sultan Selim II's daughters.

"...upon the shore, you see the immense arsenal of Tersane; a labyrinth of docks, factories, squares, storehouses and the barracks, that extends for a mile..."

***Constantinople* by Edmondo de Amicis, 1877**

Barracks of the Galleymen (Kalyoncu Kışlası)

As soon as you disembark at Kasımpaşa jetty, you will see the Barracks facing you across a small park. This vast complex was built in 1785 by **Grand Admiral Cezayirli (Algerian) Gazi Hasan Paşa** (1713-90) to house the Ottoman marine corps. The park in front of it bears his name and right in the middle of it is a statue showing the grand admiral accompanied by the **pet lion** which he had apparently domesticated in Africa and with which he would walk around the shipyard, much to the consternation, one might imagine, of its workers.

Cezayirli Gazi Hasan Paşa

Tiles in Şişhane Metro station

The Tulip Age

This was the name given to the period at the start of the 18th century when such was the demand for tulips at the Ottoman court that their prices rose to extraordinary levels. It coincided with the reign of **Sultan Ahmed III** and the supremacy of his Grand Vizier and son-in-law **Damat İbrahim Paşa** who was famous for throwing extravagant parties at which guests could admire rare plants. The Tulip Age came to an effective end in 1730 with the **Patrona Halil Revolt** which culminated in the abdication of the sultan.

Harem **by Jean Baptiste Vanmour , 1724**
The Dutch artist Vanmour is known for his paintings of the Tulip Age

Patrona Halil by Jean Baptiste Vanmour, 1730

The Patrona Halil Revolt

In 1730, sickened by the conspicuous consumption associated with the Ottoman court at a time when ordinary people were struggling, Patrona Halil, an Albanian worker in the **Beyazıt Hamam**, led an uprising which resulted in the removal of **Sultan Ahmed III** and his replacement with **Mahmud I**. For a couple of months Halil threw his weight around and dictated official appointments. Then the Janissaries had had enough of him too and he was murdered during a meeting of the Divan during which he had demanded that the sultan declare war on Russia.

Büyük Hamam

The **Büyük Hamam**, inland in Potinciler Sokak, off Bahriye Caddesi, was built in 1533 by Mimar Sinan and is the largest hamam in Istanbul that is still operational, with an amazing 60 basins and separate sections for men and women. Unfortunately it has been clumsily restored and a visit, at least to the women's side, can be a little too authentically rough and ready for comfort. It's right beside the **Güzelce Kasımpaşa Mosque** (Cami-i Kebir).

Tel: 0212 253 42 29

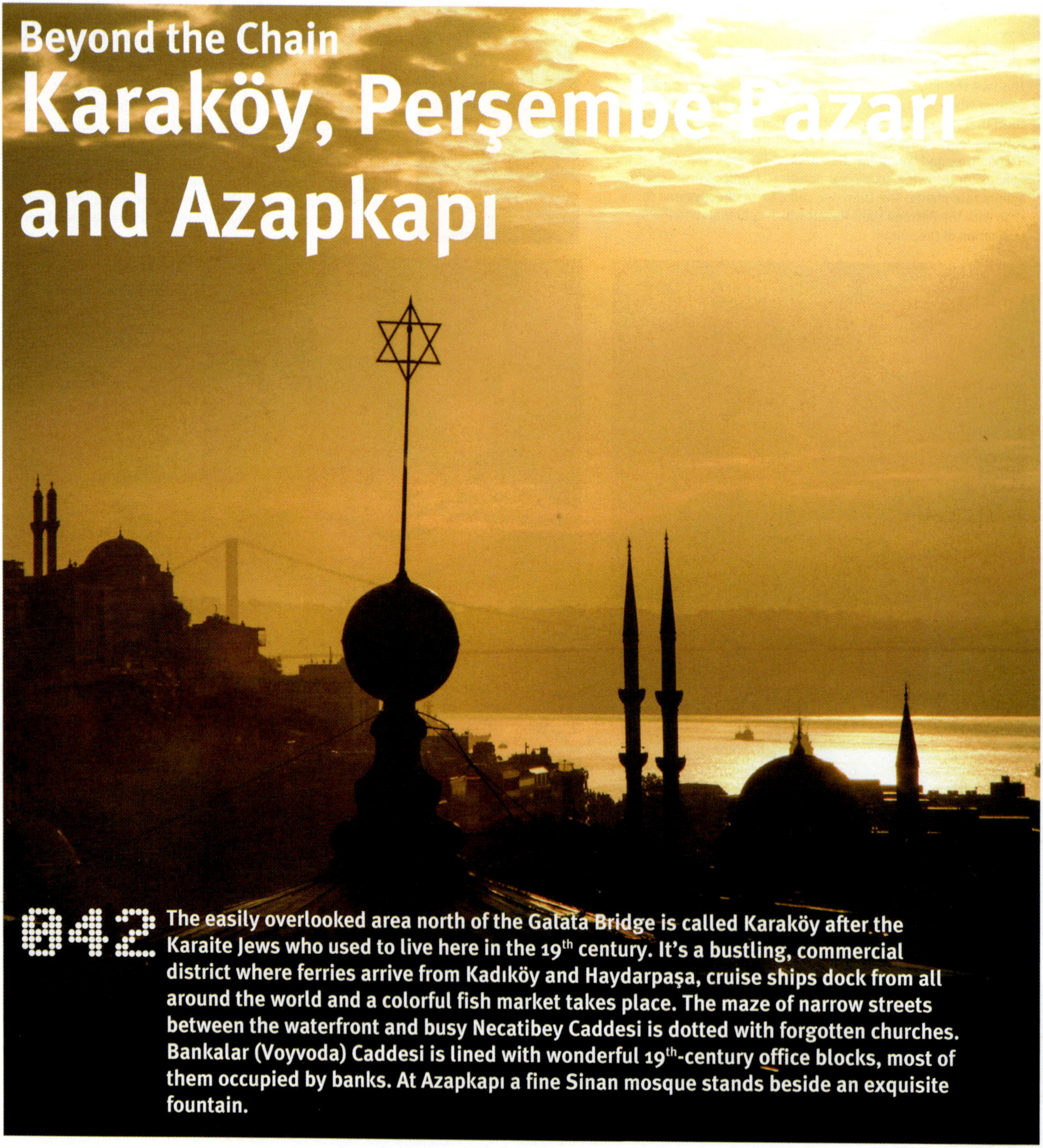

Beyond the Chain

Karaköy, Perşembe Pazarı and Azapkapı

042 The easily overlooked area north of the Galata Bridge is called Karaköy after the Karaite Jews who used to live here in the 19th century. It's a bustling, commercial district where ferries arrive from Kadıköy and Haydarpaşa, cruise ships dock from all around the world and a colorful fish market takes place. The maze of narrow streets between the waterfront and busy Necatibey Caddesi is dotted with forgotten churches. Bankalar (Voyvoda) Caddesi is lined with wonderful 19th-century office blocks, most of them occupied by banks. At Azapkapı a fine Sinan mosque stands beside an exquisite fountain.

öy Harbor

y Palas

Karaköy Square 1

The Karaköy tram stop deposits its passengers in Karaköy Square, the rather messy area immediately north of Galata Bridge that was once the heart of Genoese Galata, a virtually independent, walled trading colony that flourished under the Byzantines. At its height it stretched all the way from Azapkapı where the Atatürk Bridge now stands to Tophane (see p. 376) and uphill as far as the Galata Tower (see p. 325).

Standing on the tram platform it's possible to admire, amid the chaos of traffic, the **Karaköy Palas** building which was designed by the Italian architect **Guilio Mongeri** in 1920 in a style that mixes and matches Byzantine, Selçuk and Ottoman features. It now houses branche of Yapı Kredi. Facing it across the tramlines is the **Nordstern Han,** also apparently designed by an Italian architect.

The harbor area ② ③

Heading down towards the Karaköy ferry you pass, on the corner, the imposing Neoclassical façade of the **TC Ziraat Bankası,** built immediately before the First World War to house the Vienna Bank. Its parapet supports two statues, the female said to represent **commerce,** the male **industry**. Alternatively the figures may be of **Master Hiram** from the Old Testament and his **widowed mother** (characters, incidentally, who crop up in Masonic ritual). In either case they are very early instances of figurative sculpture in the city.

Strolling along the waterfront you will have a fine view across to **Sarayburnu** and **Topkapı Palace** and to the pretty little **Basketmakers' Pavilion** at Eminönü (see p. 202). In 2008 the ferry landing stage sank in heavy winds. The modern floating pier constructed in Tuzla Shipyard was put into service in 2018. Facing it, the **Uğurlu Han** is a fine example of First National Architecture, as is the tiny health center next door. A third example of the style at the end of the harbor was beautifully restored in 2010.

Former landing stage

Turkish Maritime Lines building and former Istanbul Port

Turkish Maritime Lines Building (4)

At the far end of the harbor stands the sturdy **Deniz Yolları Building**, the headquarters of the Turkish Maritime Lines company. It was built between 1912 and 1914 in grand, if eclectic, style. The building that was restored as part of the Galataport Project, will be the first enterprise of the famous Peninsula hotel chain in Turkey.

Decorated (previously Voyvoda) Police Station from reign of Sultan Abdülaziz

Christos Kremastos Monastery

The picture on the left shows this ancient Byzantine structure in 2005, while the one on the right shows it in 2010. By that time parts of it had been demolished to make way for a car park which is a bit like demolishing parts of Hagia Sophia. Let's see how well the rest of it survives the test of time.

Tomb of Arab warrior

Underground Mosque (Yeraltı Camii) 5

One of Karaköy's more unexpected treasures is this small underground mosque hidden amid the workaday shops of Kemankeş Caddesi. It's thought that a **tower** originally stood on this site; to it was attached the **chain** that was strung across the Golden Horn to close it to intruders (stretches of this chain still survive in the Naval [see p. 396] and Military [see p. 341] museums). After the tower was demolished following the Ottoman conquest of Istanbul, the site was used to house a **gunpowder depot**. Later a shrine was built inside the cellar after, in 1640, a şeyh (religious leader) of the Nakshibendi sect claimed to have found the bodies of two men killed during the **Arab siege of Byzantium in the 7th century**. In 1757 Grand Vizier Köse Mustafa Paşa paid to have the shrine upgraded to a mosque. The novelty of its being underground aside, the mosque is of no great architectural significance.

Fountain in front of Kemankeş Mosque

Zülfaris Synagogue 6

Tucked away in Perçemli Sokak, just round the corner from the Tünel entrance, **Zülfaris Synagogue,** is easy to miss, There had been a synagogue on this site since the 17th century, but the current building was paid for by the wealthy **Kamondo family** in 1890. It became redundant in 1985 and reopened as a museum in 2001.

In the courtyard a statue called "The Soaring Flame" welcomes guests. The statue, by Nadia Arditti, commemorates Turkish Jews who have died in different parts of the world. The restoration of the synagogue fully revived its neoclassical grandeur and the main body of the museum housed what was once the prayer hall. However, the fate of the synagogue was repeated and its doors were closed again in 2015. The Turkish Jewish Museum was moved to the Neve Shalom Synagogue (see p. 328) in Galata. Today it serves as a cultural center.

Who were the Karaite Jews?

The Karaites are non-Orthodox Jews who reject the Talmud and the rabbinaical tradition, accepting only the Tanakh (Bible) as a source of authority. Unlike most Jews, they are patrilineal (i.e. if the father is a Jew so is the child). They worship in **underground synagogues** of which there is a single example in Hasköy, the **Bene Mikra**, that was rebuilt in 1800 after a fire. Karaite Jews appear to have arrived in Byzantium some time in the 8th century. Others arrived from Russia and were settled in the Karaköy area by **Sultan Mehmed II**. Their numbers were further augmented in the late 18th century when the Russians seized the Crimea and its Karaite population fled. Nowadays only a few remain in the city.

Arab Mosque (Arap Camii) 7

The entrance to the Tünel leading up to Galata is on Yarbay S. Evren Caddesi which continues as Tersane Caddesi and runs as far as Atatürk Köprüsü, the second bridge across the Golden Horn. Although this is predominantly a business area known for its many **hardware shops** there are several reminders of the distant past mixed in with the modernity. The finest of these reminders can be found by walking along the road as far as Sırmalı Nafe Sokak and then turning right along this road until you reach the enormous Arab Mosque (*Galata Mahkemesi Sokak*) which dates back to 1323-37 and features an unusual square bell tower topped with a **spire**. The church was apparently built by **Dominican friars** on the site of an earlier church of St Paul and appears to have been used by the **Genoese** community since excavations in the nave uncovered many Genoese tombstones. In the early 16th century it was taken over by **Moors** who had been expelled from Spain, hence its current name, the Arap (Arab) Camii. Inside, the elongated space immediately suggests that the building started life as a church.

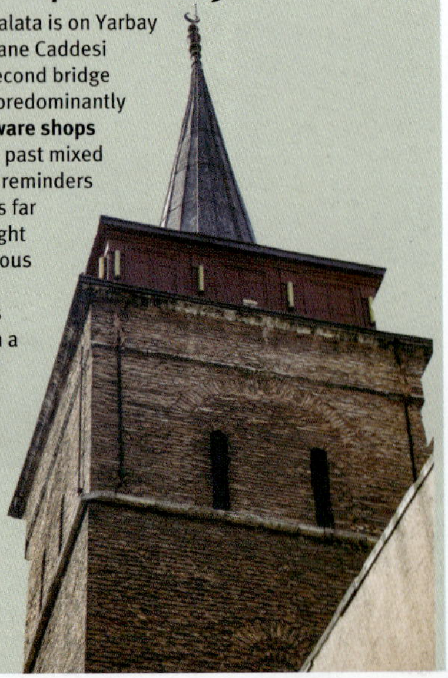

The elongated interior of the Arab Mosque is very striking.

Ancient hans continue in use today.

Rüstem Paşa Han

Karaköy hans 8

On the water side of Yarbay S. Evren Caddesi are two early Ottoman hans. The first is the picturesque, vine-shaded **Rüstem Paşa Han** (also called the Kurşunlu Han) which was built by **Sinan** for the Grand Vizier Rüstem Paşa between 1544 and 1550 on the site of the old Genoese Cathedral of St Michael. Its two courtyards are separated by a double flight of steps leading up to the upper storey whose brick arches are ogival in shape.

A little further along a cluster of nine domes bestrides the roof of the old **Bedesten,** also known as the **Fatih Han,** that almost certainly dates back to the reign of Sultan Mehmed II.

Perşembe Pazarı

For a glimpse of what **18th-century Galata** might have looked like, cut inland off Yab. S Evren Caddesi along the street called Perşembe Pazarı (Thursday Market), where a series of old brick houses with corbelled upper storeys perpetuate an architectural style that probably passed straight from the Byzantines to the Genoese and then to the Turks.

Azapkapı Mosque 9

Right at the end of Tersane Caddesi and overshadowed by the busy Atatürk Bridge stand the Azapkapı Mosque and the regilded **fountain** paid for by **Saliha Valide Hatun,** the mother of **Sultan Mahmud I,** in 1733. The mosque itself is a work of the famous Ottoman architect **Sinan** who designed it for **Sokollu Mehmed Paşa,** Grand Vizier to Sultans Süleyman the Magnificent, Selim II and Murad III, in 1577. It stands on a raised platform which would once have been filled with **shops** whose profits would have supported the mosque. Interestingly, it also has a **detached minaret** which is linked to the rest of the building by an arched corridor over the porch. In the 1930s the mosque was narrowly saved from demolition to make way for the bridge by public protests.

Saliha Valide Hatun Fountain

Azapkapı mosque

Minerva Han

Bankalar (Voyvoda) Caddesi (10)

Often overlooked by visitors who prefer to take the Tünel rather than climb the hill from Karaköy to Pera, Voyvoda Caddesi was one of the most important streets of 19th-century Istanbul and many banks and insurance companies set up their head offices here, hence its nickname "Bankalar Caddesi (the Banks Street)". To find the street look for the colorful **Minerva Han** building which stands at the junction with Yüksek Kaldırım Caddesi, the road that leads directly to the Galata Tower. The Han boasts a blue-tiled façade adorned with cherubs that dates back to 1911-13 when it may have been designed by the architect Basile Couremenos.

At first glance Bankalar Caddesi has something of the look of the City of London about it, an impression created by the serried ranks of imposing buildings that line both sides of the street. In particular look out for the **Assicurazioni Generali Han** that was designed by **Giulio Mongeri** in 1909 and for the **Hezaren Han** designed by **Alexandre Vallaury** (the man responsible for the Pera Palas Hotel) in 1902. Between 1890 and 1892 Vallaury also designed the splendid building that houses the Ottoman and Central Banks in a style that has been described as **"Banker's Renaissance"**. Today the Ottoman Bank has ceased to exist and the building contains the **Ottoman Bank Museum**, which accommodates a museum of banking history as well as SALT, a hall for temporary exhibitions, often with nothing to do with banking at all.

The street fell quiet when most of the banks moved their headquarters to Ankara after the founding of the Turkish Republic in 1923. Today the city's main banking districts are Levent and Maslak (see p. 362).

@salt_online, www.saltonline.org
Tel: 0212 334 22 00, closed Mondays

Minerva Han when it housed the Deutsche Bank

Ottoman Bank Museum

Kamondo Steps

Midway along Bankalar Caddesi are the curvaceously lovely **Kamondo Steps,** which were photographed in 1964 by **Henri Cartier-Bresson** and feature in British crime writer **Barbara Nadel**'s novel "Pretty Dead Things". They are named after the Jewish banking family (see p. 261) that is thought to have paid for their construction by an unknown architect in the 1880s. They provide a short cut for getting up to the Galata Tower (see p. 325).

Kamondo Steps

"The Kamondo Steps represented a strange fusion between utility and art."

Pretty Dead Things **by Barbara Nadel, 2007**

Yüksek Kaldırım 11 12

Just to the north of Bankalar Caddesi a second road climbs up to Pera by a more direct and steeper route. This is Yüksek Kaldırım (High Pavement), originally a street of 118 stone steps which connected with what is now **Galipdede Caddesi** (see p. 321). Not surprisingly once the funicular railway opened, traffic on this street slackened off – one look up it and you'll understand why. This was always a very **cosmopolitan area**, with all sorts of interesting shops. Today the shops mainly sell electrical appliances, the steps have been replaced with asphalt and the colorfulness reported by many 19th-century visitors has completely drained away. To get an idea of what it might have looked like, peer up nearby Hacı Ali Sokağı which still retains its steps.

Just off Yüksek Kaldırım, a Moorish-style **Ashkenazi Synagogue** dating back to 1901 stands on the site of an older wooden building. It mostly served refugees from Russia and Eastern Europe.

St. Benoit High School 13

On Kemeraltı Caddesi a long wall closes off an L-shaped building that houses the St Benoit High School. Its most prominent feature is a **bell tower** dating back to 1427 when **Benedictine monks** founded the church of St Benoit (Benedict) here. In 1583 **Jesuit missionaries** established a school for Greek and Jewish boys on the site; when the Jesuit order was abolished in 1773, it was given to the Lazarist sect instead (see p. 428). In 1839 a school for girls was added to the complex. In 1987 the two parts of the school merged and became co-ed. It's not normally open to the public even though what is now the school chapel contains the **tombs** of several early French ambassadors to the Ottomans.

Greek Orthodox Primary School on Kemeraltı Caddesi

Ashkenazi synagogue, off Yüksek Kaldırım

Ashkenazi synagogue

Surp Krikor Lusavoriç Armenian Church

Karaköy's forgotten churches (14) (15)

The most visible of Karaköy's many churches is the huge **Surp Krikor Lusavoriç (St Gregory the Illuminator) Church** which stands right beside Tophane Caddesi. Greatly in need of a spring-clean, it is still an imposing building with the raised dome and blind arcading typical of Armenian architecture. A church seems to have stood on this site since 1431 when the Armenians bought the land from the Genoese. However, the original building was damaged by a series of fires in the 18th century and was then demolished when the road was widened in 1958. So, despite its appearance of great age, the current church only dates back to 1966 when it was rebuilt by **Bedros Zobyan**, basing the design on that of the church in **Echmiadzin in Armenia**. Access to the church is via a side entrance which passes under the belltower. Inside you will find tiles from the original church decorating the basement chapel.

Surp Hisus Pirgiç Church

Right next door to St Benoit High School is the Armenian Catholic **Church of Surp Hisus Pirgiç (Jesus Christ the Savior),** product of a breakaway group of Armenians led by an early 18th-century monk called Mekhitar from Sivas who thought salvation could be found in union with Rome. The Armenian Catholics took to speaking French and their church, built in 1834, has an unexpected whiff of Italy about its decoration. I never found it open. You may be luckier.

St John the Baptist Church

The Turkish Orthodox Patriarchate

Tucked into the back streets in Ali Paşa Değirmen Sokak you will eventually stumble upon the **Church of Panagia Kafatiani (Church of St Mary)**, the only functioning church belonging to the obscure and controversial Turkish Orthodox Church, which broke away from the Greek Orthodox Patriarchate in 1922. The original church on the site dated back to the 16th century, although this particular version was built in 1840. In 1924 it was occupied by **Papa Eftim I** as the headquarters of his new movement. The present patriarch is **Papa Eftim IV** who succeeded to the position in 2002. Today the church is in the possession of the Erenerol family, its only congregation.

Church doorknocker

Normally only the narthex is open to the public who will find small silver ships hanging from the ceiling, offerings placed there by mariners in thanks to **St Nicholas** for a safe voyage. The pretty courtyard is lined with 19th-century tombstones.

Russian Orthodox churches 16

The most extraordinary of Karaköy's forgotten places of worship are four rooftop **Russian Orthodox churches,** complete with cupolas, which were originally built as chapels above hostels, called "podvoriyes", where **Russian pilgrims** en route to Mt Athos (Greece) or Jerusalem could break their journeys; the clergy would stay on the floor immediately beneath the chapel, everyone else on the lower floors. The first to go up in 1870 was the St Andrei Podvoriye. It was followed in quick succession by the St Panteleimon Podvoriye in 1878, the St Ilya (Elijah) Podvoriye in 1879 and the Triotskoye (Trinity) Podvoriye in 1880. All four were officially linked to Russian monasteries on **Mt Athos**.

The chapels were at their busiest between 1920 and 1924 when **White Russians** fleeing the Bolshevik advance into the Crimea flooded into Istanbul. By then at least two of the churches already boasted bright blue walls and murals in the style of the Russian Symbolist painter **Mikhail Vassiliyevich Nesterov** (1862-1942). Of the four churches, St Pantaleimon in Hoca Tahsin Sokağı is the prayer-house of choice for most modern Russians; a handful of elderly White Russians still attend St Andrei's, the most beautiful of them all, in Galata Mumhanesi Caddesi while the other two chapels are effectively derelict.

The lady in the photograph was one of the last remaining White Russians. She has sadly also passed away.

St Andrei Church

The rooftop Russian churches and their congregations

FROM TAKSİM TO MASLAK

The Heart of Modern Turkey

Taksim Square and Gümüşsuyu

043

Taksim Square, with its monument to the founding of the Turkish Republic, is very much the symbolic heart of modern Istanbul, a busy transport intersection within walking distance of all sorts of hotels, bars, cafes and restaurants.

Atatürk and followers on the Republic Monument

Pietro Canonica

Taksim Square

Taksim Square plays much the same role in Turkish life as Trafalgar Square in London does in British life. Its Nelson's Column is a monument to the **Turkish War of Independence** and the founding of the **Turkish Republic** designed by the Italian sculptor Pietro Canonica and with a plinth by Giulio Mongeri. It was erected in 1928. Almost immediately the square became a focal point for gatherings and demonstrations. Today it's still where people congregate in great numbers to see in the New Year, although protest meetings are rarely permitted. Even though the square lost its former mission since being closed to traffic, it can still be a romantic scene for meetings.

After its rearrangement the square was opened to pedestrians and car traffic was channelled through subways and ring roads. Facing the Republic Monument, behind the long stone wall, rises the Taksim Mosque which you see on the right as you start down İstiklal Caddesi.

Taksim Square in deepest winter

Standing on the site of an old cemetery, **Taksim Gezi Park** up the steps, is a pleasant place to take a break from the hustle during the daytime, although perhaps best avoided after dark.

In 2013, the protests started as a reaction to the cutting down of the trees in the park and turned into a symbol of resistance.

A number of important streets converge on Taksim. These include **Sıraselviler Caddesi**, the main thoroughfare of Cihangir (see p. 297), pedestrianised **İstiklal Caddesi** (see pp.300-17), Cumhuriyet Cad. (see p. 289) and **Gümüşsuyu Caddesi** (see p. 284). Taksim also offers access to Talimhane Tarlabaşı and Elmadağ (see p. 288).

Interior of water distribution building

Atatürk Cultural Center

Atatürk Cultural Center (AKM) was designed by Hayatı Tabanlıoğlu, is a controversial piece of architecture, loved by some, loathed by others and the subject of sporadic demands that it be torn down and replaced with something more conventionally beautiful. It was opened in 1969 but immediately burnt down and had to start life all over again in 1978. The cultural centre was closed in 2008 and left to its fate for a while. After the new project was presented to the public in 2017, Atatürk Cultural Center (AKM) opened its doors on October 29, 2021 with great excitement. The center that was reintroduced to art life has an opera hall with a capacity of 2040, a theater with a capacity of 802, a 410 m2 gallery and a multi-purpose hall. Keeping the connection with the past with its structure similar to its old architecture, AKM will play a major role in the revival of art life in and around Taksim.

Former Atatürk Cultural Center (AKM) building

Water distribution buildings

Facing the Republic Monument is a long, low stone building which was once a water storage unit joined by pipes to the small octagonal structure (**the "taksim"**) dating back to 1723 which you see on the right as you start down İstiklal Caddesi. From here water brought from the **Belgrade Forest** used to be distributed around the adjoining area in Ottoman times. Above the fountain against the exterior wall of the taksim is a quotation from the Koran that reads: "Everything was created from water". The façade is also decorated with miniature buildings designed to serve as **birdhouses**.

Atatürk Library (Atatürk Kitaplığı)

Atatürk Kitaplığı is a beautiful hexagonal library designed by the award-winning Turkish architect **Sedad Hakkı Eldem** in 1976. It's said to have one of the finest views in the world and few would probably dispute that as they open their books to start work in front of the Bosphorus.

---

www.ataturkkitapligi.ibb.gov.tr
Tel: 0212 249 95 65

"(The Park Hotel) was an important junction between Taksim and Ayaspaşa on the map of the pleasure-grounds of Istanbul."

***A Taste of Old Istanbul* by Jak Deleon, 1989**

Taksim Mosque

The mosque that was being planned for many years began to be built in 2017. Located right behind Taksim Maksemi (water reservoir), the mosque spreads over an area of 2,482 square meters. The dome height of the 3-floor building is 9.6 meters. While the mosque was being designed, calculations were made taking the heights of the Aya Triada Greek Orthodox Church and the Surp Asdvadzadzin Armenian Catholic Church, which are located nearby, into account. The mosque that changed the silhouette of Taksim Square was opened for worship in 2021.

Stone Barracks (Taşkışla)

Designed by the British architect **William James Smith**, who also worked on the British Consulate building, in 1846, this vast edifice was built as a **military hospital** and was used to treat the French soldiers during the Crimean War. In the 1860s it became a barracks known as the **Mecidiye Barracks** because it had been built for Sultan Abdülmecid. Restored in the reign of Sultan Abdülaziz, it is now used as the **Taşkışla Campus** of **Istanbul Technical University**. The İTÜ Science Center was opened in 2007 to raise scientific awareness in public by enabling students of all ages to learn about the basics of science and nature through observation and the application of various experiments.

Gümüşsuyu from Üsküdar

Back streets of Ayaspaşa

Gümüşsuyu (İnönü) Caddesi

Gümüşsuyu Caddesi is one of Istanbul's grandest streets with a central boulevard at the Taksim end that briefly gives it the look of the Barcelona Ramblas. Its name appears to mean "**silver water**" in Turkish but is probably a corruption of "gömüşsuyu (reservoir water)", a reference to the water emerging from a fountain in the walls of the Military Hospital (see p. 285). It was renamed in honor of the second president of the Republic, **İsmet İnönü** (1884-1973), but the original name has proved surprisingly tenacious.

The district immediately adjacent to Taksim square at the top end of the road is called **Ayaspaşa** after one of Sultan Süleyman the Magnificent's grand viziers. Hard though it is to imagine it now, this was once a wide open space occupied only by the **Ayaspaşa Muslim Cemetery** which extended from the site of the Atatürk Cultural Center downhill as far as the site of the German Consulate; as a result the street was sometimes called **Le Grand Champs des Morts**; it was much admired by foreign visitors. Today a part of that ground is covered by the brooding shell of a building which has been standing for two decades on a piece of prime real estate within spitting distance of Taksim Square. A mansion here was originally intended to be the home of the Italian Consulate but when the Italians proved unable to pay for it **Sultan Abdülhamid II** gave the land to **Ahmed Tevfik Paşa** (1845-1936), the last of the Ottoman grand viziers. After a fire burnt it down in 1911, a hotel was opened on the site in 1930. As the **Park Hotel** it went on to host the likes of **Atatürk** and the poet **Yahya Kemal Beyaltı** who lived here for 16 years from 1942. It was demolished in 1978. The building, which was used as car parking area for a period and stood as a monument of ugliness in the centre of the city, was reconstructed and opened again as a hotel in 2013.

Atatürk's wife

Born in İzmir in 1898, Latife Uşşaki studied in Paris and London before returning to Turkey immediately after the Turkish War of Independence. In 1923 she married Atatürk although their union survived for less than two years. For many years after their divorce she lived in Ayaspaşa.

Latife Hanım's house (now lost)

German Consulate in old postcard

Gümüşsuyu Palas

Heading down the street you quickly come to the huge and rather austere **German Consulate** on the right which was built between 1874 and 1877 and hosted Kaiser Wilhelm II on his three visits to Turkey (although he stayed at the Yıldız Palace, see p. 403).

A little further down on the same side of the street is the distinctive wooden building that used to house the **Japanese Consulate.** It was originally built in 1904 as a home for the manager of the Osmanlı Bank, but became the Japanese Embassy in the 1920s. When the embassy was relocated to Ankara in 1937 it became a consulate and summer residence. The consulate has now moved to 4. Levent, leaving the building empty.

In striking contrast to the simplicity of the ex-Japanese Consulate is the **Gümüşsuyu Palas**, originally the Azaryan Apartments, right next door which was one of the first – and surely one of the most exuberant – apartment blocks to be built in Istanbul. Surprisingly, the name of the architect responsible for this Art Nouveau-meets-baroque extravaganza is unknown. Across the road the **Gümüşsuyu Military Hospital (Askeri Hastanesi)** is housed in a delicate-looking building designed by **Garabed Balyan** in 1848. Given a garden and swimming pool in 1885, it was expanded again in 1978 and still serves its original purpose.

Beyond the hospital the road swings to the left and passes what was the **Gümüşsuyu Barracks**, designed by **Sarkis Balyan** in 1861-2 to replace an older wooden building. It was here that the soldiers who overthrew Sultan Abdülaziz in 1876 were based. Today it forms the **Gümüşsuyu Campus of Istanbul Technical University (ITU)**.

Beşiktaş Vodafone Park

As you go down the hill, you'll come across a stadium. The stadium standing there today is on the site of the original stadium, which was initially constructed for **Beşiktaş Football Club** in 1947 and had the name **İnönü Stadium.** That stadium was demolished for renovation but its replacement, Turkey's first smart stadium, was reopened in 2016 with the name Vodafone Park. The **Beşiktaş Museum** inside the sports complex, which has a contemporary museology perspective, was also opened.

@besiktasjkmuze, www.bjk.com.tr
Tel: 0212 948 19 03, closed Mondays

BURGER KING

Taksim Square is the gateway to İstiklal Caddesi

Taksim in Rome

Have you visited the Borghese Gardens in Rome? The park, covering a total area of 1700 acres, is now located in the centre, but in the past it used to be outside the city. It's a huge dreamlike garden with statues, fountains, groves, lakes and walking trails. The songs of birds, the dance of butterflies, the dizzying magic of flowers surround you, particularly in springtime. There are 87 places worth seeing in the park. Eight of which are museums – yes, there are eight museums in only one park! There is a striking museum in the park which will surprise you with its statues of a donkey and a man. This is the home and studio of **Pietro Canonica** which was later turned into a museum. Another great surprise welcomes you once you enter the museum: **Republic Monument** is on the right, with Atatürk in the middle. Entering the hall, **İzmir Monument** is on your left. Isn't it nice to see Republic Monument and the İzmir Monument in the middle of Rome? The reliefs of the Monument and the busts of **Atatürk** and **İnönü** wait for you in an exhibition hall in the museum. Seeing such a place in the middle of Rome make me arouse all my feelings of national pride.

Taksim's Forgotten Back Streets

Talimhane, Tarlabaşı and Dolapdere

044

Cumhuriyet Caddesi is the busy main road heading north through the curiously named Elmadağ (Apple Mountain) to Harbiye from Taksim Square. Directly to the east is Talimhane, a network of roads harboring many smaller hotels which has become very fashionable, its streets recobbled, its mansion houses restored and a bevy of shops and cafes opened. Beyond Talimhane is run-down Tarlabaşı, currently occupied mainly by poor immigrants from Eastern Turkey. Bringing up the rear is even more neglected Dolapdere at the bottom of a ravine.

Cumhuriyet Caddesi

Cumhuriyet Caddesi (Republic Street) is so busy with traffic that it's easy to overlook the fine 19th-century mansions that look onto **Gezi Park**, a small, undistinguished patch of greenery that backs onto Taksim Square. Many airlines have their offices here and several of the big chain hotels are grouped together around the junction with Asker Ocağı Caddesi. The Taksim end of the street is disfigured by a collection of fast-food shops, but immediately across the road the shops on the corner of Şehit Muhtar Bey Caddesi announces the way into Talimhane and its increasingly lively streetlife.

Talimhane

Talimhane has changed very rapidly over the last years. Buildings have been restored, signs spruced up, pavements relaid and shops and cafes opened. At the last count 35 hotels were clustered together in a location which is perfect for visitors wanting to take advantage of İstiklal Caddesi's hectic nightlife (see p. 300).

Tarlabaşı

Busy Tarlabaşı Bulvarı heads south towards the Golden Horn, paralleling İstiklal Caddesi for some of the way. To the north lies **Tarlabaşı** which is full of the same sort of fine mansions as İstiklal Caddesi and Cihangir, albeit on a smaller scale. In the 19th century many of the people who worked for Istanbul's wealthier families and for the embassies on İstiklal Caddesi lived in this part of town which was conveniently close to their work. When Atatürk moved the Turkish capital to Ankara in 1923, the embassies moved too and many Tarlabaşı residents lost their livelihood. Other residents were forced to move out in the mid-20th century when a hefty **wealth tax** levied on minorities in 1942 made it virtually impossible for them to remain. In their place came **migrants from Eastern Turkey** who divided what had been single-family homes into apartment blocks.

"Tarlabaşı, the very navel of Istanbul."

***Songs My Mother Never Taught Me* by Selçuk Altun, 2008**

Buildings being torn down to create Tarlabaşı Bulvarı.

In the 1980s Tarlabaşı Bulvarı was widened, with the loss of hundreds of historic houses. Most of those that survive are in a parlous state of disrepair although since 2005 gentrification of the area has been on the cards. As with **SoHo** in New York and **Hoxton** in London, it's the artists and media folk who are already moving in to be at the birth of the "new" Tarlabaşı.But the project is cancelled In the meantime, washing hangs across child-filled streets which fall prey, after dark, to a mixed bag of drug dealers, prostitutes and transvestites. If you want to wander around here, do so in daylight and preferably in company.

In Tarlabaşı's narrow streets you never know what you'll see.

Dolapdere

North of Talimhane and Tarlabaşı lies the poor neighborhood of Dolapdere, most famous recently as the birthplace of the **Dolapdere Big Gang**, a group of cover artistes so good that it's hard to distinguish their take on the likes of Sting from the originals.

Dolapdere Big Gang

The many faces of Tarlabaşı

Assyrian Ancient Virgin Mary Church

Church of Panayia Evangelistria

Hagioi Konstantinos and Helene Church

Nineteenth-century churches

The back streets of Tarlabaşı and Dolapdere harbor several 19th-century churches. Unfortunately you will find them locked except on the rare occasions when there are services. You are most likely to be able to see inside them on Sunday mornings.

In Karakurum Caddesi in Tarlabaşı the **Church of Virgin Mary,** built by the Syrian Orthodox community, was also used by the Armenian congregation in the past. The original church on the site dated back to 1844, but it was replaced in 1863 by a basilica modeled by the architect Master Serope. Restored after a huge fire in 1870, it was completely rebuilt in 1963 from Mardin stone and then restored again in 2006.

At the junction of Kalyoncu Kulluğu Caddesi and Kemerbostanı Caddesi is the gorgeous Greek Orthodox **Church of Hagioi Konstantinos and Helene** that dates back to 1861. Its iconostasis resembles the façade of a Greek temple.

At the junction of Mirimiran and Kasap Ali Sokaks in Dolapdere is the huge and elaborate Greek Orthodox **Church of Panagia Evangelistria** that dates back to 1894. Work on restoration has started and stopped again in spite of which there are still services here on Sunday mornings.

Adam Mickiewicz Museum

A Polish Romantic poet and patriot, **Adam Mickiewicz** (1798-1855) arrived in Istanbul in 1854 at the start of the **Crimean War**, hoping to rally Polish forces to fight against Russia which had occupied part of his country. He died of cholera in Tarlabaşı a year later and there's a symbolic tomb in the basement of the building which now occupies the site of the one in which he lived (the original burnt down in 1870) and which is theoretically open to the public as a small museum. His remains have been returned to **Cracow** in Poland.

Adam Mickiewicz's cenotaph

VKV Contemporary Art Collection in Dolapdere

Arter is an important centre for the art community, hosting continuous activities on İstiklal Avenue since 2010. In September in 2019, in celebration of the 50th anniversary of the Vehbi Koç Foundation, the gallery was moved to its new 18,000-square-meter building in Dolapdere and a new chapter was opened in its activities. The architecture was designed by the British Grimshaw Architects. Within this modern building, Arter also offers art lovers the VKV Contemporary Art Collection and exhibitions outside the collection, as well as performance halls, learning and activity areas, a library, a conservation laboratory, a bookstore specialising in art publications, cafes and restaurants.

@arteristanbul
www.arter.org.tr, Tel: 0212 708 58 00

Panagia Evangelistria Greek Orthodox Church

Antiques Central

Cihangir and Çukurcuma

845

Named after Sultan Süleyman the Magnificent's son, Cihangir is one of the most fashionable places to live in Istanbul, partly because of its proximity to the many and varied attractions of İstiklal Caddesi. Its main thoroughfare is Sıraselviler Caddesi, a narrow, congested street that links Taksim Square with Tophane, passing the Firuz Ağa Mosque on the way. A short diversion from Sıraselviler Caddesi will bring you to Çukurcuma, well known for its many antique and curio shops.

Cihangir

Cihangir is a surprisingly fashionable part of town where much of the expat population has made a home, spawning all sorts of street cafes and restaurants offering ethnic cuisine. It's a part of town where you'll hear many different languages being spoken. It's also a part of town where it's almost de rigueur to adopt some of the myriad street cats.

View of the Historic Peninsula from Cihangir

The main street, **Sıraselviler Caddesi** (Row of Cypresses Street), heads towards the Bosphorus from Taksim Square, passing a shabby building, the former **Taksim Sahnesi**, designed by Giulio Mongeri (1875-1953), that once housed the Maksim Music Hall and the Majik, Istanbul's first cinema. It continues past the **Romanian Consulate** housed in a 19th-century mansion that used to belong to the London envoy to the Ottoman court and the even more imposing **Belgian Consulate,** which was designed by the Greek architect Kampanaki. At one time there would have been many more equally impressive mansions here but most of them have long since fallen victim to modern development.

Two soot-blackened buildings on Meşelik Sokak to the right were built in the late 19th century as **girls' schools:** the Zappion was for Greeks and the Eseyan for Armenians.

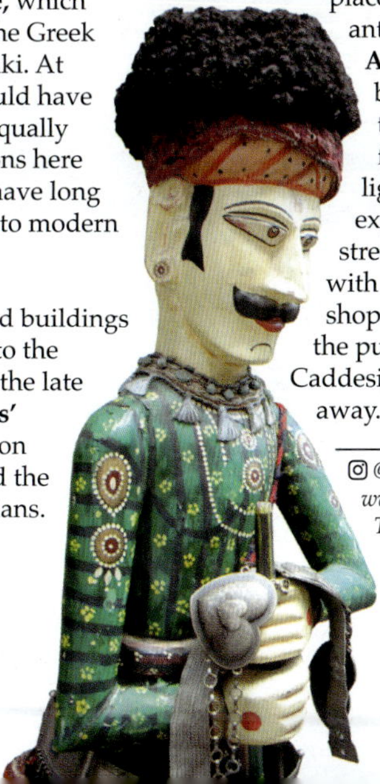

Çukurcuma

A short walk west of Firuz Ağa Mosque is Çukurcuma, a quiet district whose name means "Lower Friday", apparently because Sultan Mehmed II came here to pray on a Friday before the conquest of Istanbul. Despite the obvious poverty of some of its inhabitants, it has earned itself a reputation as the best place in Istanbul to shop for antiques. Here, too, is the **Ağa Hamam**, a Turkish bath dating back to 1562 that was built to provide funds for the Fenerbahçe lighthouse. It's well worth exploring the narrow streets of Çukurcuma, which, with their many small local shops, are a world away from the pushy modernity of İstiklal Caddesi, just a short uphill walk away.

@agahamami
www.agahamami.com
Tel: 0212 249 50 27

Cihangir Mosque

Perched high on the hillside overlooking the Bosphorus, this is the building that gave its name to the area. In the 16th century the famous architect Sinan built a mosque here to commemorate Sultan Süleyman the Magnificent's son **Cihangir** who had died in 1553, supposedly from grief after the **murder** of his half-brother Mustafa on the instructions of their father. The original mosque long ago burnt down and the one currently on the site dates back to 1874 when **Abdülhamid II** ordered its construction. It looks rather like the **Balyan mosques** at Dolmabahçe and Ortaköy although the famous brothers were not apparently the architects. Inside, the mihrab is painted with clouds which makes it look rather like a stage set.

Old Ottoman Parliament building below Cihangir Mosque

Firuz Ağa Mosque

At the point where Sıraselviler Caddesi changes its names to Defterdar Yokuşu the **Firuz Ağa Mosque** is a green-and-white raised structure with the prayer hall up a long flight of stairs and a couple of very popular teahouses sheltering beneath the vines underneath it. It's a popular meeting place with locals. The original 15th-century building burnt down in 1823 and was rebuilt in the same year.

Innocence in Çukurcuma

The Museum of Innocence in Çukurcuma is named after the first Nobel Prize-winning author Orhan Pamuk's (see p. 347) novel dedicated to his daughter. The museum, which was inspired by the novel, opened in 2012. As the first city museum in Istanbul, it is located in a three-story building in Çukurcuma which dates back to 1897.

@themuseumofinnocence, www.masumiyetmuzesi.org
Tel: 0212 252 97 38, closed Mondays

Orhan Kemal Museum

Just as the Liverpool authorities saw fit to knock down the Cavern Club where The Beatles first performed and were then forced to build a replica, so the original **İkbal Kahvesi** where novelist **Orhan Kemal** (1914-70) and his friends used to hang out in **Nuruosmaniye**, near the Grand Bazaar, was torn down and a replica has been built on Akarsu Caddesi. A small museum contains some of the writer's personal effects and letters, first editions of his books and a mock-up of the room where he used to work; the photographs of Kemal with fellow scribes **Nâzım Hikmet**, **Yaşar Kemal**, **Haldun Taner** and **Sait Faik** are especially interesting. Copies of his books translated into English are on sale in the bookshop attached to the İkbal.

Orhan Kemal

www.orhankemal.org
Tel: 0212 292 92 45

Istanbul's Most Crowded Street

İstiklal Caddesi I

(Taksim Square to the Galatasaray High School)

046

A stroll down pedestrianised İstiklal Caddesi (Independence Street) is a must for any visitor to Istanbul. No matter what the time of day or year it is virtually guaranteed to be wall-to-wall bodies as people visit the shops, while away their hours in the cafes and bars, pop into the churches, window-shop and just plain promenade.

İstiklal Caddesi (once known as **Grande Rue de Pera** or **Cadde-i Kebir**) was the most important thoroughfare in 19th-century **Pera**, the place with the most fashionable shops and most of the embassies. It runs all the way from **Taksim Square** at the northern end to **Tünel Square** at the southern end, with a break about halfway along where **Yeni Çarşı Caddesi** bisects it beside the imposing **Galatasaray Lisesi** (High School). The north-easterly end of the street used to be the most fashionable part although these days the action extends all the way down to Tünel Square in the south-west. It's a pedestrianized street along which trundles a cute **19th-century tram** which makes three leisurely stops before reaching the terminus at the Tünel end of the street. From end to end it is lined with shops, restaurants, museums, cinemas and bars which explains why it is the city's number one place for promenading.

The Greek community's single creche can be found in the Zapyon High School

Church of the Holy Trinity (Hagia Trias) 1 2

While standing in Taksim Square you will be able to see the dome and twin bell towers of the huge and newly restored Greek Church of Holy Trinity located to the left of Taksim Mosque. To reach it you need to turn left off İstiklal Caddesi along Meşelik Sokak.

The Holy Trinity was designed by **Vasilaki Ioannidi** in 1880 and was one of the first churches in Istanbul to be given a **dome** after a law forbidding such ostentation on anything other than mosques was repealed. Unless you visit on Sunday morning you may only be able to see the narthex, but if you do manage to get inside the main body of the church you will find a vast but colorful empty space in front of a soaring iconostasis. On Meşelik Sokak don't miss the soot-blackened Zapyon and Esayan Schools (see p. 297)

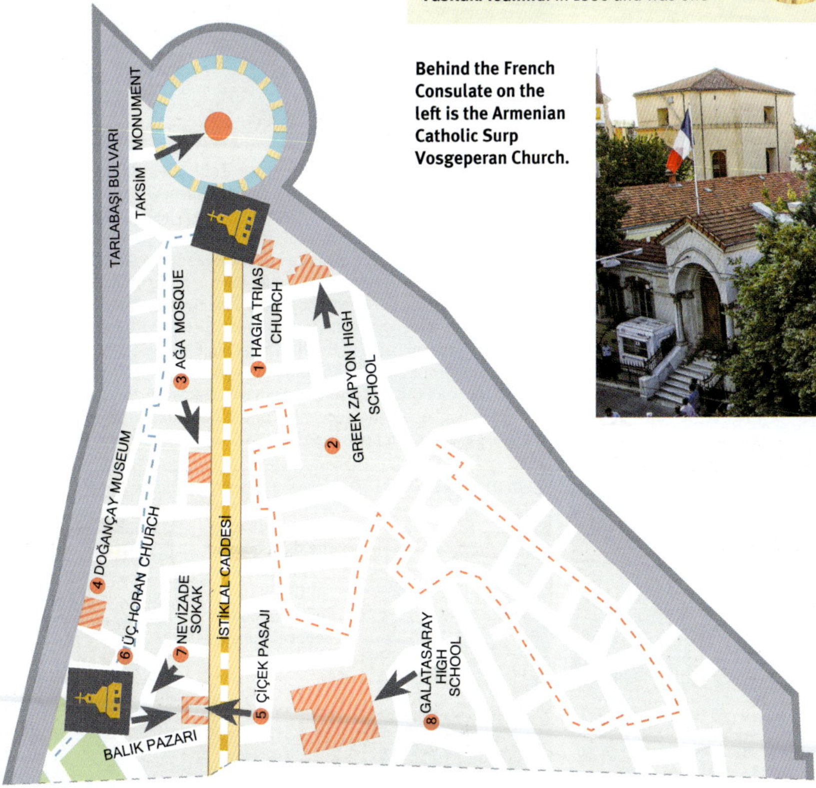

Behind the French Consulate on the left is the Armenian Catholic Surp Vosgeperan Church.

French Consulate

Just a short walk along İstiklal Caddesi on the right is a rather unusual low-slung building dating back to 1898, which houses the French Consulate. It was erected on the site of an 18th-century **plague hospital**.The building also includes language courses, a library, cinema and exhibition halls and a cafe as well as the consulate. The courtyard in the middle makes you feel far away from the crowd of İstiklal Street.

The enormous Armenian **Church of Surp Vosgeperan** lurks behind the French Consulate.

Rumeli Pasajı

Ağa Mosque ③

The only mosque along İstiklal Caddesi before the mosque in Taksim Square was erected, is the Ağa Mosque that was built in 1594 at the same time as the Galatasaray Hamam for **Hüseyin Ağa** who was the local governor. If you wander into the rear courtyard you will find a fine **fountain** that was brought here from a redundant dervish lodge. The mosque was rebuilt after a fire in 1934.

Just before the mosque is an elaborately carved apartment block, called the **Citè de Roumelie/Agora Romelias**, which was built over a shopping "passage", one of the many **arcades** that took over from hans as the shopping complexes of the 19th century. Its inscriptions in French, Greek and Ottoman are a reminder of how cosmopolitan an area this once was. The han was one of three dedicated to three "continents", the other two being Africa and Anatolia. The **Afrika Han** can still be seen in Büyük Parmakkapı Sokak. They were paid for by **Ragip Paşa** (1857-1920), a bureaucrat in the court of Sultan Abdülhamid II who built himself a fine house in Caddebostan (see p. 489).

Cercle d'Orient

Built in 1884 for the Armenian businessman **Abraham Paşa** (see p. 554), **Emek Pasajı** (Arcade) was once home to the Cercle d'Orient, a social club where foreigners and Tuks could get together and that had its counterpart on the Asian side of the city in the **Büyük Külüp** (Big Club, see p. 488). The building was restored and opened as a shopping mall with the name Grand Pera. Although there were objections to the moving of **Emek Cinema**, it was re-opened for service in its new location as part of the redevelopment project. The shopping-mall is also home to **Madam Tussauds Istanbul** where wax sculptures of famous people from Turkey and around the world are exhibited. Just next to it is a shopping mall, discordant with the fabric of the street, built in place of the old **Saray Cinema**. A little further down the road on the right the **Greek Consulate** now occupies a mansion built for the Greek Şişmanoğlu family. Keep going and you will come to the **Halep Pasajı** (Cite d'Alep, Aleppo Arcade) built for a Syrian Christian in 1885 and once used as a circus. Across the road the grand **Atlas Pasajı** was created in the 1870s for an Armenian banker named Köçeoğlu. **Sultan Abdülaziz** is said to have maintained a bachelor pad there where he could meet women.

Halep Pasajı (Cité d'Alep)

@mt_istanbul, www.madamtussauds.com/istanbul/tr, Tel: 444 3 253

The building on the right housed the Cercle d'Orient. It is now slated for redevelopment.

İstiklal Caddesi when it was the Grande Rue de Pera.

Burhan Doğançay Museum (4)

Divert to the end of Balo Sokak to find this museum which houses a small collection of paintings and montages by Burhan Doğançay (1929-2013), one of Turkey's best-known modern artists and sometimes known as the "father of wall art" because of his preoccupation with the multiple uses of city walls.

www.burhandogancay.org
Tel: 0212 244 77 70
closed Mondays

"Blue Symphony" is Burhan Doğançay's most highly priced montage.

An unknown family who lived along the Grand Rue, perhaps Levantines, perhaps White Russians.

The historic tram

While in Istanbul you will surely want to trundle along İstiklal Caddesi in the dinky, two-carriage, red and white tram with wood-trimmed interior. The tram first started running in 1875, but was taken out of service in 1961. In 1990 it was reinstated and now makes its stately passage through the crowds three times an hour, often with young boys hanging off its platforms.

Yeşilçam

At the start of the 21st century Turkish cinema is undergoing a renaissance in the hands of directors such as Nuri Bilge Ceylan, but midway along İstiklal Caddesi the name of one street – Yeşilcam (Green Pine) Sokak – lives on as a reminder of the flourishing film industry, high on melodrama if low on production values, that already existed here in the mid-20th century. Yeşilcam flourished from the 1950s through to the '70s.

Nuri Bilge Ceylan

Flower Arcade (Çiçek Pasajı) 5

Continuing down İstiklal Caddesi you pass on the right the **Tokatlıyan Han** which stands on the site of the Tokatlıyan Hotel, the second biggest hotel after Pera Palas in 19th-century Istanbul. Next to it is the beautifully decorated Flower Arcade with a sign over the entrance reading "Cite de Pera". This is especially famous as a place to tuck into a dinner of **mezes** (appetizers) washed down with **rakı** in a glass-roofed, cobblestoned courtyard where **gypsy musicians** serenade diners at their tables. The building that stands on the site today is a replacement for the **Naum Theater** that burnt down in 1870 and was redeveloped as a complex of shops and apartments. In the 1930s, some of the restaurants started to move their tables outside and at one time **White Russian refugees** fleeing the Bolshevik Revolution used to sell **flowers** here, hence its pretty name. One of the most famous musicians to play here was the accordion-player **Madam Anahit.**

In 1978 the original Flower Arcade collapsed overnight from neglect. It was completely restored in 1988 and again more recently, each time becoming more sanitized and less atmospheric. It's still a popular place to come for a night out, although most of the local action has migrated to **Nevizade Sokak** at the back.

Madam Anahit

Nevizade Sokak 7

Although the Flower Arcade meyhanes still have their fans, these days much of the meze-eating and rakı-drinking action has migrated down through the **Fish Market** to Nevizade Sokak which is one big gathering of places to eat, drink and be merry. It hardly seems worth trying to recommend any specific venues as all too often it's a question of homing in on wherever there's an empty table. Come in a group to get the most out of the choice of mezes and generally feel part of things.

"And, oh, the unbelievably lovely White Russian girls whose beauty outmatched even the rose-buds there!"

The Greek bon viveur Todori remembers the Flower Arcade in *A Taste of Old Istanbul* by Jak Deleon, 1989

Galatasaray Hamam

Galatasaray Hamam

Across from the Flower Arcade a small alley runs down from beside the Konak restaurant, passing the **Zografyon Greek School (Zografyon Rum Lisesi),** built by a wealthy Greek banker and opened in 1893. A little further along it doglegs to the right and there is the Galatasaray Hamam, one of Istanbul's most famous Turkish baths with separate sections for men and women.

A hamam was originally built served as part of a school complex founded by **Sultan Bayezid II** to educate the brightest of Balkan children who would then continue their education at the Topkapı Palace school. In 1715 **Sultan Ahmed III** had a new hamam built here and this was eventually incorporated into the Galatasaray High School. The women's section (not a match on the men's for atmosphere) was added in 1965. In 2008 actor John Travolta added his name to the baths' list of illustrious patrons which has also included singer Johnny Halliday and actor Tony Curtis.

Zografyon Greek High School

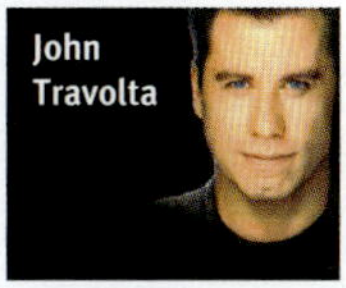
John Travolta

Fish Market 6

Right beside the Flower Arcade is the **Fish Market (Balık Pazarı)** which was renovated recently as part of the **Beyoğlu Beautification Project.** Unfortunately this seems to have stripped it of much of its erstwhile rambunctious character, although it's still worth coming here to snack on *kokoreç* (grilled intestines) and *midye tava* (fried mussels), or to shop at the many greengrocers and delicatessens.

Üç Horon Armenian Church

It's also worth walking along here to visit the Armenian **Üç Horan (Three Altars)** church, otherwise known as "the Church in the Cupboard", which lurks behind a double door and down a flight of steps in compliance with a law that forbade non-Muslim religious buildings to impose themselves on the skyline. The current building dates back to 1838 but stands on a site which had been occupied by a church since 1503.

Also accessible from the Fish Market are the attractive **Avrupa Pasajı (European Arcade),** decorated with classical statues and filled with antique and souvenir shops and the **Aslıhan Pasajı,** where shops sell a wide range of second-hand books.

Galatasaray High School (Galatasaray Lisesi) 8

Opposite the Flower Arcade, the Galatasaray High School stands in extensive grounds behind elaborately decorated wrought-iron gates. The school was founded in 1868, although the current building dates back only to 1907. It is not normally possible to go inside, but if you take the elevator up to one of the small cafes on the top floors of the buildings opposite you will be able to look down into its grounds and then to the Bosphorus beyond. Famous past students include the poet Tevfik Fikret (see p. 435), the journalist Abdi İpekci (see p. 345) and pop star Barış Manço (see p. 484).

Across the road the grand, restored post office dating back to 1875 how houses a small **philately museum** and an upstairs exhibition space.

Tel: 0212 293 49 86, closed Mondays

The Cite de Roumelie building near the Ağa Mosque retains its past splendor.

Fransız Sokağı (French St)

Tucked away in the back streets just off İstiklal Caddesi is a novelty known as Fransız (French) Sokak which came into being in 2004 when the old Cezayir (Algeria) Sokak was tarted up and had its walls painted fuschia pink prior to the introduction of a string of supposedly French restaurants. Best of them all is probably Cezayir, although as time has passed, so even the superficial "Frenchness" has given way to a familiar mix of Turkish and international cuisine.

Hacı Abdullah Restaurant

The jars of pickles and fruit in the window are a well-known feature of this restaurant which has been in business since 1888 and serves an excellent choice of food including many dishes that you won't find on menus elsewhere such as *fukara keşkülü*, a rice-flour custard flavored with almonds (but no alcohol). Of the more than 250 eggplant dishes cooked in the Ottoman palace cuisine, 70 of them can still be tasted here with their old recipes.

Istanbul's Most Crowded Street

İstiklal Caddesi II

(Galatasaray Square to Tünel)

047 Past the Galatasaray High School İstiklal Caddesi slopes gradually upwards and runs past several consulates housed in grand 19th-century buildings. This was the original Grande Rue de Pera and there are several important churches along this stretch of the street, including the conspicuous St Anthony's Cathedral. You'll find art galleries here, but just as many shops, restaurants and cafes. Finally you'll fetch up in Tünel Square, the gateway to vibrant Tepebaşı.

Danışman Geçidi tea garden

Artist and opera singer Semiha Berksoy's room in Gümüşsuyu recreated for a Yapı Kredi Nedim Tör Museum exhibition.

Monument to 50th anniversary of Turkish Republic in the square

Panagia Eisodion Greek Orthodox Church

Around Galatasaray Square

In the small square where Yeni Çarşı Caddesi cuts across İstiklal Caddesi there stands a monument to the 50th anniversary of the Turkish Republic in 1973 designed by the sculptor Şadi Çalık.On the corner of Galatsaray Square facing the war memorial is the Yapı Kredi bookshop with, attached to it, the wonderful Yapı Kredi Vedat Nedim Tör Museum and Kazım Taşkent Art Gallery. This hosts a regular program of classy free exhibitions covering everything from history and archeology to painting and photography. The building was renovated and opened again with all its units. It has now taken its place in the cultural life of İstiklal Street. One of the İlhan Koman's sculptures, named Akdeniz, relocated many times across İstanbul, has finally found an appropriate resting place. Today it salutes passers-by on İstiklal from the glass façade of the building and embraces Galatasaray Square.

Nearby the Danışman Geçidi (once the Hazzopulo Pasajı) leads past a few shops to a cobbled courtyard which houses one of İstiklal Caddesi's few remaining traditional tea gardens. It was here that leading lights of the Young Turk movement including Ahmed Midhat Efendi and Namık Kemal published their controversial newspaper İbret (Warning).

Egypt Apartments (Mısır Apartmanı)

This exuberant apartment block was designed by the Armenian architect **Hovsep Aznavuryan** (1854-1935) in 1910 in a style that pays homage to Art Nouveau while being entirely original and was intended to provide a winter home for the **Egyptian Prince Abbas Halim Paşa**. On his death it was converted into apartments for his relatives, but eventually it evolved into a multi-purpose block that housed galleries, a theater and, for a while, the home of the poet **Mehmed Akif Ersoy** (1873-1936), author of the lyrics for the Turkish national anthem. Another resident was **Virginia Bruce** (1910-82), star of such early Hollywood hits as "The Great Zeigfeld", who moved in after her marriage to then owner Ali Ipar. Another resident was Sami Günzberg, a Jewish dentist who was visited here by **Atatürk**. For a while the many tailors here also attracted a well-heeled crowd of society customers.

Ali İpar and Virginia Bruce

Today the building has been restored and houses a small theater and gallery as well as several cafes.

Egypt Apartments

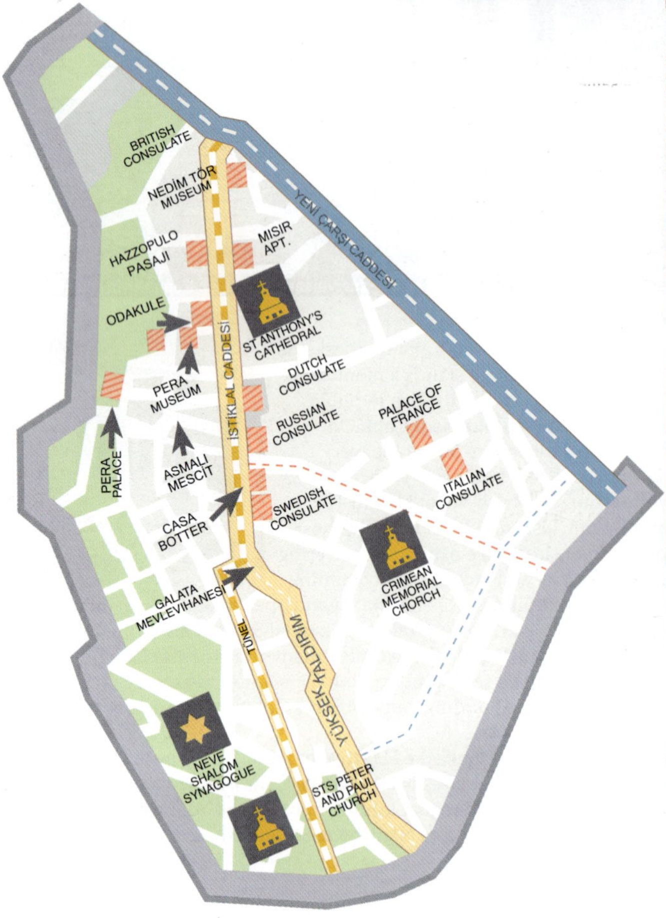

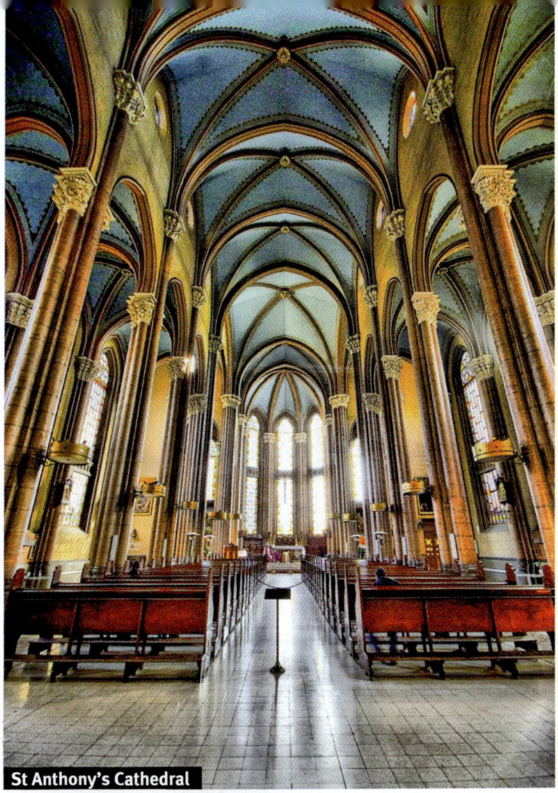

St Anthony's Cathedral

Giulio Mongeri

St Anthony's Cathedral

Built between 1906 and 1911, St Anthony's was designed by the Italian architect **Giulio Mongeri** (1875-1953), who also designed the plinth for the monument in Taksim Square (see p. 281). It replaced an earlier church that dated back to 1763 but had been demolished to make space for the tram. **St Antoine's**, as it is usually called, stands just back from İstiklal Caddesi in a small courtyard on the site of an old theater, but the surrounding buildings and the arch through which visitors approach it are all part of the same design and are all built in red brick which stands out from the mainly stone structures that line the street. Inside, the lofty, spacious church is **neo-gothic** in design and feels as if it could have been imported from France, although the exterior would be more at home in Italy. The balconies on the apartments facing into the courtyard are pure Romeo and Juliet.

---

www.sentantuan.com

Elhamra Cinema once frequented by Atatürk

Dutch and Italian Consulates

Behind iron gates stands the **Dutch Consulate** which was built in 1855 by the Swiss architects **Gaspare and Guiseppe Fossati** who also restored Hagia Sophia (see p. 026). In Tomtom Kaptan Sokak, the steep street that runs down beside it, you'll find the **Dutch Chapel**, the first Protestant place of worship in the city, then, if you keep going, an imposing mansion in extensive grounds, the **Palazzo de Venezia,** that was built in 1782 to house the Venetian embassy in the days when the Italians ruled the roost around here. In 1744 **Casanova** was a visitor to the palace, staying for a relatively chaste three months. In 1797 the Venetian Republic ceased to exist and the palace was taken over first by the Austrians, then by the French, then by the Austrians again. In 1919 it became the **Italian Embassy**, changing into the Consulate when the Embassy moved to Ankara.

Just past the Dutch Embassy was Ravouna Building. Today it houses a cafe. Even if you don't want to buy anything it's worth popping your head round the door to admire its glistening glass-and-wood **Art Nouveau interior**. (At the time of writing the shop had just been sold.)

Dutch Chapel

Italian Consulate

French Court

Dutch Consulate

Palace of France

Odakule

An unexciting high-rise block, Odakule (Chamber Tower) nevertheless contains a small first-floor **art gallery** which hosts changing free exhibitions. Walk through the arched passage beside it and you will emerge close to the Pera Museum (see p. 334). The sea-urchin-like **abstract sculpture** in front of Odakule was designed by Atilla Onaran in 1973.

Suriye Pasajı

Statue of St Mary over entrance

Santa Maria Draperis Church

Santa Maria Draperis Church

A little further up the road on the left an arched gateway with a statue of the Virgin Mary above it is set into an otherwise unexceptional apartment block that opens onto a steep flight of steps down to the delightful barrel-vaulted church of Santa Maria Draperis, designed by the architect **Guglielmo Semprini** in 1904. It replaced previous churches dedicated to St Mary and dating back to 1584, which repeatedly burnt down and took its name from that of the Genoese woman who gave the land for the church, **Clara Bratola Draperis**. The atmospheric interior glitters with stained glass and the flickering light cast by candles.

Just past the church you'll see the closely guarded **Russian Consulate** housed in another building designed in 1837 by the **Fossati brothers** who had worked as official architects to the tsar in Moscow, hence the commission.

Gaspare Fossati

Casa Garibaldi Societa Operaia (Italian Workers Union Building)

Did you know that **Giuseppe Garibaldi**, İtaly's national hero who united the country lived in Beyoğlu between 1828-31? Facing the Deva and Perukar blinds, the "Società Operaia" building that was named after its founding president as Casa Garibaldi is a hidden treasure of Beyoğlu. Although its architect was thought to be Alexandre Vallaury, it was actually designed by the Lombardian architect **Bernardo Bottarlini**. The renewal work in order to meet the need for more space as the number of the people gathering increased was done by architects **Giulio Mongeri** and **Edoardo de Nari**. The institution is the only known example in Turkey of the Italian workers' solidarity unions that were first founded in Italy in 1848 and spread around the country in a short span of time. The building also has an important archive since it also serves as a meeting point for Italians living in Istanbul.

Autumn on the left panel and spring on the right

Markiz Cake Shop

A little further up on the right-hand side of the road is the delightful Markiz cake shop, established in 1940 on the site of an almost equally popular patisserie. **The Lebon** was created by Edouard Lebon, brother-in-law to the architect Alexandre Vallaury, who ordered wonderful Mucha-style tile representations of the four seasons by **J A Arnoux** to decorate the walls; made in France, the panels were shipped to Istanbul but only two spring and autumn survived the journey. In its heyday the Lebon was a popular meeting place, patronized by the likes of the writer **Namık Kemal** (1840-88) and the poet-reformer **Ziya Paşa** (1829-1880). After he took over the Lebon and renamed it the Markiz, Avedis Ohanyan supplied it with striking **Art Deco stained-glass** windows which are very unusual for Istanbul. The Markiz closed in 1977 and stood abandoned throughout the 1990s. It was eventually restored and reopened in 2003, but has struggled to re-establish an identity. For a long time its door was locked and this nostalgic place is left to its fate.

Casa Botter

Casa Botter

Of all the crumbling 19th-century buildings along İstiklal Caddesi, perhaps the most beautiful is the Casa Botter at No. 475-77 which was designed in flamboyant Art Nouveau style by **Raimondo d'Aronco** in 1901 for **Jan Botter**, a Dutch tailor and couturier to **Sultan Abdülhamid II**. While the fashion house on the ground floor competes with its peers abroad, the upper floors are arranged as a living space for the Botter Family. The building's exterior is dressed up with stone roses and huge female heads and decorated with elaborate wrought-iron balconies, while the interior boasts stained glass (now sadly broken) and an elaborate elevator shaft and banister railings, all designed by d'Aronco. Despite this, time has not been kind to the building . In 2021, the luck of the building turned and its restoration started by Istanbul Metropolitan Municipality. Casa Botter, the city's first Art Nouveau building, was opened to visitors as an art and design center in 2023.

@casabotter

"Spick and span Grand Dukes who had fled to Turkey from the Bolshevik regime saving only their skins served as head waiters (at Rejans)."

***A Taste of Old Istanbul* by Jak Deleon, 1989**

Old appearance of Narmanlı Han
Ahmet Hamdi Tanpınar

Swedish Consulate

Next to Casa Botter is the **Swedish Consulate**, designed by the Austrian architect, **Domenico Pulgher** in 1869 and set in a large garden. Facing it is the clumpy pillared façade of the **Narmanlı Han** which was the original home of the Russian Embassy. In the 1940s this was another popular meeting place with lots of bookshops and antique shops, the haunt of novelist and parliamentarian **Ahmet Hamdi Tanpınar** (1901-62), amongst others. The restoration project was approved by the conservation board in 2015. Despite the various struggles of non-governmental institutions for a conservation which respected the original building, it ended up as a completely concrete structure which has lost its connection with the greenery. Narmanlı Han also hosts the **Illusion Museum** waiting to give visitors of all ages an experience beyond their senses.

@museumofillusions.istanbul, www.museumofillusions.com.tr
Tel: (0212) 244 06 64

Narmanlı Han after restoration

Crimean Memorial Church (Christ Church)

This unexpectedly British church in Serdari Ekrem Sokak, a short walk east of İstiklal Caddesi, was built to commemorate the Crimean War. A competition to come up with a suitable design was originally won by **William Burges**, the architect behind Cardiff Castle, but the commission then fell to G.E. Street, best known as the architect behind the Royal Courts of Justice in London, England, who came up with the first **neo-gothic** structure in Istanbul (although he never actually came to see it). The church was built between 1858 and 1868 out of Maltese stone on land given to the British by **Sultan Abdülmecid** and its foundation stone was laid by **Lord Stratford de Redcliffe**, known as the Great Elchi (Ambassador) because he played such an important role in contemporary Ottoman politics. Closed in the 1970s, the church was restored by Sri Lankan refugees and reopened for services in 1991. It contains a colorful rood screen painted by the Scottish artist **Mungo McCosh** that depicts notable Istanbul individuals against a backdrop of Sarayburnu; the Christ Child even clutches a simit, a nice touch.

G. E. Street

Facing the church are the **Appartements Papadopoulos,** a set of wonderful Art Nouveau apartments with painted ceilings dating back to 1907.

ADA
TURKCELL
TURKCELL
TURKCELL

TURKCELL

Top of the Funicular

Tünel and Around

048

The Tünel area is a rapidly evolving and hugely fashionable area at the opposite end of İstiklal Caddesi from Taksim Square that is crammed full of trendy bars and restaurants and accessible via one of Europe's oldest funicular railways.

Originally it was the northern end of İstiklal Caddesi that attracted most of the party crowd. However, recently the emphasis has shifted and now the area just off the southern end of the street is one of the most happening parts of Istanbul with new bars and restaurants opening (and closing, of course) on an almost daily basis. In between them a few excellent book and antique shops struggle to compete for the attention of passers-by.

Chimney of the Tünel

The Tünel

To get here you can either walk or hop the tram along İstiklal Caddesi, but the best way is to take the one-stop funicular that runs up from near the Karaköy tram stop to Tünel Square. Modernized in 2008, the Tünel was originally constructed between 1871 and 1874 by the Frenchman **Eugene Henri Gavand** and opened for business in 1875 as the **third oldest underground railway service** in the world after **London** and **New York**. Locals used it mainly to get between their homes up in Pera and their workplaces down in Galata. You can read more about the history of the Tünel at the Karaköy terminal where showcases also display books, newspaper cuttings and cartoons.

When you emerge at the top of the Tünel look across the tram lines and slightly to the left and you will spot a tall **chimney**, a reminder of the period from 1874 to 1970 when the funicular was operated using steam power generated in the basement of the attached building.

The Tünel in numbers

- Built: 1871-1874
- Stops: 1
- Length: 573m
- Duration of journey: 90 seconds
- Number of passengers per journey: 170
- Hours of operation: 7.30am –11pm daily

Galata Mevlevihanesi

Just round the corner from the Tünel station at the top of Galipdede Caddesi stands one of Istanbul's few functioning **dervish lodges** (tekkes) where it is still possible for visitors to watch performances of the **whirling dervishes** several times a month. Dating back to 1492, the lodge is now housed inside an 18th-century complex complete with a graveyard full of finely carved Ottoman headstones including one commemorating **Galip Dede**, a 17th-century Sufi poet.

Dervish performances take place in a wooden-floored octagonal **semahane** (ritual hall), with seating arranged around it and a gallery up above. Unusually, **female dervishes** rotate alongside their male counterparts, dressed in brightly-colored robes that are in sharp contrast to their male colleagues' white ones. Around the arena glasscases show off the collection of the **Museum of Court Literature**, including many fine old manuscripts and musical instruments. If you want to watch the whirling dervishes, please remember that this is a religious ceremony that requires silence and you are not supposed to applaud at the end.

Garden of the Galata Mevlevihanesi

Tel: 0 212 245 41 41
closed Mondays

"The center of the floor is so highly polished by the perpetual friction that it resembles a mirror..."

The Dancing Dervishes **by Julia Pardoe, 1902.**

The Whirling Dervishes

The most famous of all the dervish orders, the Whirling Dervishes were the brainchild of **Celaleddin Rumi** (1207-73) of Konya, better known as **Mevlâna**. Following his philosophy, celebrants circle slowly in imitation of the spheres and in so doing believe that they become closer to Allah. Everything about the ceremony is symbolic: the white robes worn by the dancers are intended to call to mind the **shrouds** they will wear when they die, while their black cloaks symbolize their **tombs** and their tall felt hats their **gravestones**. The dancers whirl with one arm raised high and the other pointing to the ground to transmit the blessings of heaven to earth.

Galipdede Caddesi

Galipdede Caddesi wends its way downhill to the Galata Tower bypassing many of Istanbul's music shops. Perhaps the most interesting building to look out for is **Teutonia**, at No. 65, which was built to house the German Club in 1847 and went on to serve as a Nazi propaganda center in the years leading up to the Second World War. The Goethe Institute still uses it as a venue for German-speaking events. Galipdede segues into **Yüksek Kaldırım** on its way down to Karaköy whereupon it turns into one of Istanbul's most notorious red-light districts.

Teutonia

Sofyalı and Asmalımescit

Where Sofyalı ends Asmalımescit (the Chapel under the Vine) begins and these days both are wall-to-wall eateries. Dotted about amid the cafes and bars are several small art galleries, bookshops, publishing houses and live music venues and Asmalımescit? Originally it was the name of a **chapel** built for **Sultan Bayezid II** (1481-1512) which, unfortunately, did not survive the wrecking balls of the 20th century.

Tünel Geçidi

As you come out of the upper Tünel station you will be facing a small passageway that leads through to the parts of Tepebaşı called **Sofyalı** and **Asmalımescit** where most of the restaurants are. The passageway itself is absolutely delightful, Café filling one side and a couple of antique shops and a Restaurant the other. The fairy lights strung through the trees make this a particularly magical place to come at night-time.

TÜNEL 139 YAŞINDA

The First Intercontinental Flight

Galata Tower and Around

049

Topped with a distinctive witch's-hat roof, the prominent Galata Tower dates back to the days when Genoese traders were settled in this part of town. Today, the restored streets of Galata house many small restaurants and bars. Here, too, you'll find Beyoğlu Hospital, once the British Hospital and housed in a fine early 20th-century building and what was once the British prison, now converted into a restaurant.

Bereketzade Hacı Ali Ağa Fountain

The name Galata is thought to be derived from the **Greek word "gala"** meaning milk and commemorates a milk market that once stood on the site. The area immediately around Galata Tower is called **Kuledibi**, meaning literally "the bottom of the tower".

Galata Tower (Galata Kulesi)

It was the Byzantine **Emperor Justinian** who first erected a tower on this site in 528, but it was the **Genoese** who started work on the hefty tower that currently stands here in 1348-49. At that time what was called the **Tower of Christ** formed part of the walls of what was effectively a separate town facing Constantinople across the Bosphorus.

During the reign of Sultan Süleyman the Magnificent (1494-1566) the tower served as a **prison**. Later it accommodated members of the **Mehter**, the Ottoman military band, while in the second half of the 20th century it was used as a **lighthouse**. Today the 61-meter-tall tower houses a restaurant, as well as providing a vantage point from which visitors can obtain a 360° view of Istanbul.

According to the Ottoman travel writer **Evliya Çelebi**, in 1638 **Hezarfen Ahmet Çelebi** strapped on home-made wings and managed to fly from the top of the Galata Tower in Europe to Doğancılar Meydanı in Üsküdar in Asia, thus completing the first intercontinental flight. In return for his efforts Sultan Murad IV sent him into exile in Algeria. The story featured in the 1996 Turkish film "**Istanbul Under My Wings**".

Recently the small square at the base of the tower has been restored and is now a popular meeting place. Focal point is the fine **Bereketzade Fountain** originally donated to a mosque by Bereketzade Hacı Ali Ağa just after the conquest of Istanbul in 1453 when he became the first Turkish governor of Galata, but rebuilt in 1732 and moved here in the 1950s. It's set into a small surviving piece of the **barbican** that used to back the tower.

Istanbul Under My Wings

Other Genoese survivals

Few other traces of the **Genoese fortifications** survive today since what remained of the walls was demolished in 1864-5. However, the remains of a **medieval gate** adorned with the cross of St George, a symbol of Genoa and two coats of arms can be seen on the Harap (Ruined) Gate in Yanık Kapı (Burnt Gate) Sokak in Azapkapı (see p. 073). A couple of Genoese civil buildings dating back to 1314 survive in Kart Çınar Sokağı. The most important is also the most dejected: what was once the **Podestat** where the Genoese governor held court. Designed by Montano de Marinis, it was a copy of the San Giorgio Palace in Genoa. Its front faces onto Bankalar Caddesi (see p. 074) and looks as if it belongs to the 19th century; only from the rear can you credit that it is an early 14th-century building. The street name "**Büyük Hendek Sokak** (**Big Moat Street**)" also commemorates the lost Genoese fortifications.

The Galata Tower's bell is displayed in the Istanbul Archeological Museum.

"Say Istanbul and towers come to mind:/If I paint one, the others are jealous./ Kızkulesi ought to know better:/She should marry the Galata Tower and breed little towerlets."

***The Saga of Istanbul* by Bedri Rahmi Eyüboğlu, 1974**

The Genoese in Istanbul

During the 11th and 12th centuries the weak Byzantine emperors granted trading concessions first to **Venice** and then to other Italian cities, including **Pisa, Amalfi** and **Genoa**. Most of the Italian traders settled along the shores of the Golden Horn, but, after offering assistance to the Byzantine **Emperor Michael Paleologos** against the Crusaders in 1204, the Genoese were able to move up to what is now **Galata** and settle there behind sturdy walls; in 1261 Paleologos signed a treaty permitting them to govern Galata as a **semi-independent colony** under a podesta (governor) as a reward for their help. In 1453 when **Sultan Mehmed II** arrived to capture Istanbul, the Genoese attempted to safeguard their position by staying neutral in the conflict. Such was Mehmed's success, however, that he was able to insist they disarm and tear their walls down, even though he allowed them to maintain their religious and commercial privileges. Today there is a **Galata Museum** in the port of **Genoa, Italy**.

Golden Horn and part of historic peninsula from Galata Tower

Beyoğlu (British) Hospital

Galata Tower gets all the attention but another unusual tower also juts up on the skyline of Galata and that is the tower that looks like a large eggcup with a diminutive egg inside it that forms part of Beyoğlu Hospital in Camekan Sokak. Designed in 1904 by **Percy Adams** (who was also responsible for Senate House, London University, UK), it originally housed a **British Seamen's Hospital** and the tower was constructed to offer a clear view out to sea so that ships nearing land could signal if they had people on board in need of medical treatment. In 1924 the British donated the building to the Red Crescent since when it has continued in service as a hospital.

Old drawing of the British Hospital

British Prison

Just a short walk down Galata Kulesi Sokak you will come, on the left, to what was, between 1904 and 1919, a British prison in the days when the Ottoman sultans allowed individual nations to punish their own civil wrong-doers; it's still possible to see **graffiti** scribbled by the prisoners on the upstairs walls. Later it served as a British military police station and then as private lodgings. In the 1970s it was used as a workshop by jewelers and metal workers before being bought in 1991 by an architect and planner who oversaw its conversion into a **restaurant** (see p. 330).

St Peter's Han

On Kart Çınar Sokağı this huge soot-blackened building was originally an apartment block built by the French ambassador in 1771 whose coat of arms can be seen on the façade (as can that of the Bourbon kings). A sad little plaque commemorates the French poet **Andre Chenier** who was born in a house on the same site in 1762, only to lose his head to the guillotine in 1794.

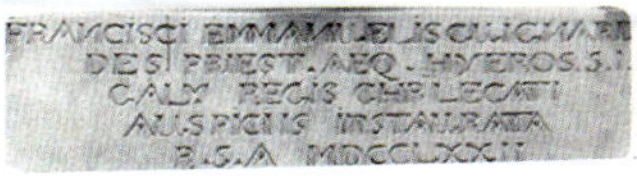

Dome of Sts Peter and Paul Church

Church of Sts Peter and Paul

Also on Galata Kulesi Sokak is the Dominican-built Church of Sts Peter and Paul which was designed by the Swiss architect **Gaspare Fossati** between 1841 and 1843. The **Dominicans** had originally built themselves a church in Karaköy in 1228, but after this was converted into the **Arab Mosque** (see p. 272), they moved into the existing Church of St Peter further uphill. This wooden church was destroyed by fires in 1660 and 1731, before being pulled down in 1841 and replaced with the present stone building in its extensive grounds.

Entrance to Sts Peter and Paul Church

During a storm in 1875 the Galata Tower's conical roof flew off. It was replaced during the 1965-67 restoration.

Neve Shalom Synagogue

This most famous of Istanbul's **Sephardic Jewish** synagogues started life as the reception hall of a Jewish boys school in Büyük Hendek Sokak that was converted into a synagogue in 1938. When the congregation outgrew the building a new purpose-designed but architecturally undistinguished synagogue was erected on the site in 1949. After a **bomb attack** by the Palestinian faction led by Abu Nidal killed 23 worshippers in 1986 security was tightened although this was still not enough to prevent an even more dramatic attack in 2003 when three people were killed by a group of men whose motivation appears to have been a witch's brew of local Kurdish grievances spiced with Al Qaeda-influenced ideas.

Chief Rabbi İshak Haleva

Neve Shalom Synagogue

9th Israeli President Shimon Peres visits Neve Shalom Synagogue

Museum of Turkish Jews

This was moved to its new location in 2015 when the Zülfaris Synagogue (p. 271) was closed down. The museum depicts the past of Jewish people with sections on dowry, marriage and circumcision and other aspects of the social life of the community. It was opened for service with current exhibition technologies, objects and panels for the new generations.

@jewishmuseumofturkey
www.muze500.com
Tel: 0212 292 63 33
closed Saturdays

The Schneider Synagogue is now used as an art gallery.

Italian Synagogue

Serdar-ı Ekrem Caddesi

Until recently virtually derelict, newly recobbled and cleaned-up Serdar-ı Ekrem Caddesi that runs from near the Tower to near the Crimean Memorial Church is shaping up to be Istanbul's Soho, a streetful of designer shops and cafes with the elegant restored Kamondo Han (1861-8), built for the wealthy Kamondo family (see p. 061).

Doğan Apartments

Also in Serdar-ı Ekrem Caddesi is this massive block originally built for the Belgian Helbig family and dating back to 1895. It was named after Doğan, the son of Kazım Taşkent, another owner, who had died in an avalanche in Switzerland, aged just eleven. After changing hands several times in the 20th century, it was turned into a set of apartments that are now very desirable in an area that is rapidly gentrifying.

Tulip Fountain

In the back streets below Galata Tower at the junction of Laleli Çeşme Sokağı and Şair Ziya Paşa Caddesi there lurks an **Art Nouveau** fountain, the Laleli Çeşme (Tulip Fountain), designed by the Italian architect **Raimondo d'Aronco** in 1904. Despite its currently neglected state, it's a beautiful and unique piece of Istanbul street furniture and well worth seeking out.

"(Galata)... the Shanghai of the Levant: a semi-independent colony taking control of regional commerce from the dying Byzantine Empire."

***Constantinople-City of the World's Desire 1453-1924* by Philip Mansel, 1995**

Pearls of Pera

Şişhane, Tepebaşı and Pera Museum

050

In fashionable Tepebaşı, the Pera Museum, one of Istanbul's finest temporary exhibition spaces, also houses one of the city's most impressive small museums, with Osman Hamdi Bey's popular painting The Tortoise Trainer as its best-known exhibit. Just a stone's throw away is the famous Pera Palace Hotel whose guests have included Mustafa Kemal Atatürk and Agatha Christie. Meşrutiyet Caddesi is lined with impressive 19th-century buildings, some of them providing homes to 21st-century consulates. Şişhane is shaped up to be the city's newest trendy hotspot.

Tepebaşı

In the 1870s foreigners and Levantines started to colonize Tepebaşı which now shelters the Pera Museum as well as a growing number of fashionable cafes, restaurants and hotels.

Tepebaşı in old postcard

Deniz Palas

The lovely Deniz Palas in Sadi Konuralp Caddesi overlooking the Golden Horn in Şişhane was designed by Yorgo Kulutros in the 1920s and features some Art Nouveau flourishes. It now houses the Istanbul Culture and Art Foundation, which is responsible for many of the city's festivals. The hall is lit by a lamp in the shade of the old treasury of Hagia Sophia and the second floor houses a small museum in memory of the Istanbul-born opera singer Leyla Gencer (1928-2008), known as the Turkish Diva. There is a restaurant, located on the top floor of the building. It offers a truly spectacural Istanbul view.

@iksv_istanbul, www.iksv.org, Tel. 0212 334 07 00

Şişhane Square and the Frej Apartment Block

Come out of Tünel station, turn left and left again and follow the road as it winds round until you arrive in **Şişhane Square**, a busy traffic intersection over which looms the elaborately carved Sarkuysan Building. This started life in 1906 as the Frej Apartment block which was built for the Frej Family by the Greek architect **Konstantinos Kyriakidis** (1881-1942) in a manner that tops off the Art Nouveau facade with a French-style mansard roof. The statues of nude females that adorned the exterior did not meet with universal approval and had to be covered up during the reign of Sultan Abdülhamid II (1842-1918).

The facade of the Frej Apartments was decorated with statues of naked women.

Frej Apartment Block

The Pera Museum

The Pera Museum is housed in a splendid 19th-century mansion on Meşrutiyet Caddesi, just doors away from the **Grand Hotel de Londres** (Büyük Londra Oteli). The gift to the city of the **Suna** and **İnan Kıraç Foundation**, it houses some of the private collections of its namesakes, as well as providing three floors of temporary exhibition space for both local and international exhibitions. It's one of the centerpieces of rapidly gentrifying Tepebaşı ("Hilltop"), a district within easy reach of popular İstiklal Caddesi and offering great views of the Golden Horn.

The best idea is to take the lift up and work down from the **fourth floor** that is devoted to an exhibition entitled **Istanbul: The City of Dreams**. This shows images of Istanbul and daily life in the Ottoman Empire from the 17th to the 20th century. It's here that you will find **Osman Hamdi Bey**'s popular and unexpectedly large painting "**The Tortoise Trainer**". Many of the paintings were done by foreign artists including the Italian **Fausto Zonaro**, who was court artist to the Ottoman sultans from 1896 to 1909 and the Maltese **Amadeo Preziosi**, who lived in Istanbul from 1842 to 1882. The earliest pictures tend to be simple depictions of Istanbul scenery, often showing buildings that no longer exist, but as time passed so images of daily life became more popular. Particularly interesting are a series of pictures of interiors painted by the French artist **Jean-Baptiste Vanmour** in the early 18th century, but also of note is **Mıgırdıç Civanyan**'s portrayal of the Said Paşa Yalı (waterside mansion) at Sadabad, one of Istanbul's lost architectural gems (see p. 256).

@peramuzesi
www.peramuzesi.org.tr
Tel: 0 212 334 99 00
closed Mondays

Maria Callas

Café Pera

The **ground floor** of the Pera Museum houses a gift shop selling books and reproductions of exhibits, as well as an elegant café with an Art Deco feel that readily evokes early 20th-century Vienna. Centerpiece is a grand piano which was given to the opera singer **Maria Callas** by her father. She in turn gave it to her music teacher who brought it with her to Ankara and then passed it on to the writer **Mordo Dinar**, a teacher at Galatasaray High School. There it caught the eye of **Yiğit Okur** who was inspired by it to write his novel, **"The Piano"**, a copy of which stands on top of the instrument.

Maria Callas' piano in the Pera Museum's café

Pera

Pera was the name given to the cosmopolitan area around **İstiklal Caddesi** where many of the foreign diplomats and merchants, known as Levantines, lived. It is thought that the name came from the Greek **"peran en skai"**, meaning **"the fig gardens on the other side"**. In the 19th century most of the wooden buildings here were reconstructed using stone which put an end to the devastating **fires** that had previously been a regular feature of life here. Pera was renamed Beyoğlu during the early years of the Turkish Republic.

The Tortoise Trainer by Osman Hamdi Bey, 1906

Göksu Outing by Fausto Zonaro

Osman Hamdi Bey and "The Tortoise Trainer"

The extraordinary Osman Hamdi Bey (1842-1910) (see p.598) was not only an archeologist and museum-maker but also the only Turkish artist to have been called an **"Orientalist"**. His many delightful paintings depict aspects of daily life in 19th-century Turkey, with the artist and members of his family often appearing amongst the characters. In *The Tortoise Trainer* he is dressed up as an elderly dervish preparing to train a group of tortoises that would have carried candles on their back to illuminate the parties held at the **Topkapı Palace** during the early 18th-century **Tulip Age**. In 2004 it was sold at auction for $3.5 million, at that time the highest amount that had ever been paid for a Turkish painting. Since then it has cropped up in reproduction on everything from tiles to T-shirts.

Two Female Musicians by Osman Hamdi Bey

The **third floor** of the museum showcases a collection of **Kütahya tiles** and **ceramics**. Sometimes overshadowed by the popularity of İznik tiles and ceramics, the products of the Kütahya kilns are nevertheless some of Turkey's finest works of ceramic art and this collection focuses in particular on pieces that were made between the 18th and 20th centuries, including some fine jugs decorated with images of human figures and strange egg-like objects designed to hang inside churches.

The museum's **second floor** displays a variety of **Anatolian weights and measures.** Admittedly of rather specialist interest, the collection contains items dating back to pre-history that are displayed in chronological order and includes examples of the often ingenious gadgets used to measure everything from land to pharmaceutical products.

The Casa d'Italia is now the Italian Cultural Center.

Meşrutiyet Caddesi

Meşrutiyet Caddesi (Constitutional Monarchy Road) is the street that runs parallel to more famous İstiklal Caddesi, linking the Tünel area at the southern end with the British Consulate to the north. Once nicknamed **Le Petits Champs** because of the sprawling local cemeteries, it's lined with imposing 19th-century buildings that used to house wealthy Europeans. In the 20th century most of them acquired new uses: the Casa d'Italia, for example, became the İtalya Evi and now houses the **Italian Cultural Center**, while the home of Monsieur Glavany became the **Belle Vue** (now the **Büyük Londra**) **Hotel**. Nearby Kallavi Sokak was named after him.

British Consulate

If you walk to the Pera Palace Hotel from Şişhane along the road on the left-hand side you will see an elaborate 19th-century mansion that was built for a family of Genoese bankers, the Corpis, hence its original name, the Palazzo Corpi. For much of the 20th century it served as the **American Consulate**, moved, since 9/11, to a fortress-like building in İstinye. (see p. 449)

Palazzo Corpi

The **Palazzo Corpi** was designed by Italian architect Giacomo Leoni for Ignazzio Corpi. Its neoclassical exterior conceals a hallway with fine frescoes over the stairwell. The ceiling of the Great Hall is decorated with paintings of Diana, Neptune, the Three Beauties and other mythological scenes.

Pera Palace Hotel

Pera Palace Hotel

The Pera Palace Hotel stands on a site overlooking the **Golden Horn.** In 1895 the Belgian **Georges Nackelmackers,** who had founded the **Compagnie Internationale des Wagons-Lits,** had it built by the French Levantine architect **Alexandre Vallaury** to accommodate passengers arriving in Istanbul from Europe on his brand-new **Orient Express** train (see p. 206). At the time the hotel advertised itself as having "a thoroughly healthy situation, being high up and isolated on all sides". Amongst its many famous guests were **Mustafa Kemal Atatürk,** the first president of the Turkish Republic, who stayed in room 101, "Murder on the Orient Express" author **Agatha Christie,** who stayed in room 411, Hollywood screen goddess **Greta Garbo,** spy **Mata Hari, President Tito** of Yugoslavia and **King Edward VIII** of Britain.

A show in old Pera

Beside Pera Palace Hotel, there is a wide open space which offers a fine view out over the Golden Horn; the 19th-century Theatre de Petit Champs once stood here. Right beside it is a glass-and-steel monstrosity of a building that has been described as "a tragedy for Istanbul" – the headquarters of the **TRT** television network. Plans to replace it with a Frank Gehry-designed extension of the Pera Museum have run aground on what would become of TRT afterwards. Across the road is the **Büyük Londra Oteli,** designed by the Italian architect **Guglielmo Semprini,** which, when it opened in 1892, boasted all the latest technology including an elevator and bathtubs. **Ernest Hemingway** was one of its most famous guests.

Originally built in 1801, the **British Consulate** (Pera House) was rebuilt in 1844 after a fire by **William James Smith** and **Charles Barry,** best known as architect of the House of Commons building in London, UK; its design imitated the **Reform Club** in Pall Mall. In 2003 the gatehouse was destroyed by a **bomb** that also killed the then consul, since when security has become very tight. Those fortunate enough to be able to go inside will find a wonderfully British garden with a large lawn where parties are held every June. **St Helena's chapel,** in the consulate grounds, has been restored since the bomb blast.

Şişhane Municipality Building

Martial Music, Magnificent Tents

Harbiye and the Military Museum

051

Easily overlooked because it's a little apart from the main tourist attractions, the Military Museum in Harbiye is well worth visiting not just for its permanent collections but because it's the one place where you can watch the Ottoman Janissary band (Mehter) go through its paces on a regular basis. Harbiye is also home to several important classical and pop music concert venues.

A piece of the chain that closed off the Golden Horn

An architecturally undistinguished area with a busy main road slicing through the middle of it, Harbiye was named after the Military Academy, the **Mekteb-i Harbiye**, built here in 1841 and then rebuilt after a fire in 1853. Much of the land to the south used to be a vast **Armenian cemetery** until the 1930s; since 1945 Turkish Radio and Television (TRT) has had its head office on the nationalized land.

The museum

When the Military Academy was moved to Ankara in 1936, the building that had housed it became the headquarters of several regiments. It finally metamorphosed into the Military Museum in 1993, acquiring collections that had originally been housed in Hagia Eirene and the Tiled Pavilion (Çinili Köşk) in the grounds of Topkapı Palace.

Those who are interested in how war has been waged over the centuries will enjoy the copious collections of arms and armor which include **swords** wielded by Sultans Süleyman the Magnificent and Selim the Grim, **kettledrums** beaten by the Janissaries at the Battle of Mohacs in 1526 and the **chainmail jacket** worn by Uzun (Tall) Hasan, the Akkoyunlu leader defeated by Sultan Mehmed II in 1473. Here, too, you can see the **bloodstained shirt** that the "Young Turk" Talad Paşa was wearing when he was assassinated in Berlin in 1921 and the **remains of the car** in which the Grand Vizier Mahmud Şevked Paşa was killed in 1913.

Even if you're not much interested in matters military, it's still worth coming here to see a piece of the **chain** that used to stretch between Sarayburnu and Karaköy, thus closing off the Golden Horn to approaching ships and the magnificent **embroidered pavilions** used by the Ottoman sultans when in battle – they give a whole new meaning to the word tent!

Students at Military Academy

Turkish and Ottoman medals and badges: Independence Medal; Nişan-i Osmani; Nişan-i Osmani Şemsi (Sun); Meclis-i Mebusan (Parliament) Medal

Military Academy turned museum, from the air

The Military Academy's most revered student was **Atatürk** who studied here from 1899 to 1905. His classroom is preserved intact although all too often behind locked doors. This is a particularly good place to bring children since every afternoon at 3pm the colorful Ottoman **Mehter band** (see opposite) goes through its paces, pounding out the music that is believed to have inspired **Beethoven** and **Mozart** even as it terrified the inhabitants of conquered territories. In summer they do this outdoors so you can listen without buying a ticket; in winter they move sensibly indoors.

Atatürk's seal

Fourteenth-century helmet of Sultan Orhan

The mehter band

In Ottoman times the Janissaries were famous for their Mehter bands, marching bands that date back to the days of the first sultans. The bands would march into newly captured territories ahead of the new governor to impress the authority of the Ottomans upon the subject people, but they fell into disfavor after the Janissaries were overthrown in 1826 and only started to come back into fashion for use on ceremonial occasions in the 1950s. Members of the band wear colorful green and red uniforms and most of them play the kös (a large bass drum), the nekare (small kettle-drum), the davul (drum), the zil (cymbals), the boru (related to a trumpet) or the kaba zurna (a form of flute). The most unusual instrument is a çevgen which looks like a stick but is actually a collection of bells.

Çevgen

First siege of Vienna by Hasan Rıza

Hasan Rıza

Hasan Rıza

The Military Museum contains a large collection of paintings of battle scenes, including depictions of the **Battle of Mohacs** in 1526 and the first Ottoman **assault on Vienna** in 1529 by Hasan Riza (1857-1912), an artist born in Üsküdar who studied at the Naval College on Heybeliada (see p. 587) before taking part in the Russo-Turkish War of 1877-78. There he met and was coached by an Italian war artist, going on to study art more formally in Italy and Egypt. Later he returned to Turkey and earned his living painting portraits and pictures of historic battles while living in Karaağaç, near Edirne. On the outbreak of the **First Balkan War** in 1912 he was sent to work in Edirne Hospital. When the Bulgarians entered the city, he tried to return home to save his pictures but was tragically killed before he could get there. Some of his surviving works hang in **Vienna Museum**.

St Espirit Church

Notre Dame de Sion

In the 1850s a French school for girls was built in Harbiye. Contained inside the compound is the exuberant **Church of St Espirit** designed by the Italian-born Swiss architect Guiseppe Fossati in 1846 and extensively repaired in 1865 after an earthquake. There's also a small **art gallery**.

City secrets

The **chapel** of Notre Dame de Sion was turned into a **concert hall** in 2006 to celebrate the 150th anniversary of the founding of the complex. Concerts are free and popular with the city's resident foreigners. The acoustics are magnificent. We love it.

www.nds.k12.tr
Tel. 0212 219 16 97

Hilton Istanbul Bosphorus

Located at the heart of the city and within walking distance to Taksim and Nişantaşı, Hilton Istanbul Bosphorus is one of the symbolic structures of the city that left a mark in old Istanbul photographs and in everyone's memory. Hilton Istanbul was designed by Skidmore, Owings & Merrill (SOM), one of the world-famous architecture offices of the period and the award-winning Turkish architect Sedad Hakkı Eldem. Opened by Conrad Hilton in 1955, it is the first five-star hotel of Turkey. Another feature of the property structure is that it was the highest building ever built in Istanbul at that time. While featuring the traditional offerings such as 5 o'clock tea and "welcome coffee", the hotel continues to support handcrafts of our country with its interior design and projects. John Kennedy, Bill Clinton, Pavarotti, Enrico Macias, Henry Ford, David Rockefeller, Brigitte Bardot, Marlon Brando, Frank Sinatra, Tina Turner, Sophia Loren, Michael Douglas, Silvio Berlusconi, Prince Charles, George Bush, Sean Connery, Anthony Quinn, Danny Kaye, Mohammed Ali and King Hussein of Jordan were some of the guests of this historical hotel.

Shopper's Paradise

Nişantaşı, Teşvikiye and Maçka

052

If you want to see how the upper echelons of Istanbul society shop, you could do worse than head for Nişantaşı, the upscale suburb that sprawls out east of Democracy Park. Hard as it is to believe it now, this was once forest where the sultans came to get in some target practice. In the 19th century, their successors decided that an area so close to Pera was ripe for redevelopment and slowly but surely their plans swallowed up neighboring Teşvikiye and Maçka too. Visitors come here mainly to browse the many shops, but there are some minor historical monuments waiting to be discovered too.

Valikonaği in the past with Vedat Tek Mansion on the left

Nişantaşı is bisected by **Valikonağı Caddesi**, with the main shopping streets – **Rumeli Caddesi, Teşvikiye Caddesi and Abdi İpekçi Caddesi** – running off on either side. There's some fine 19th-century architecture here including a number of grand apartment blocks although it's sometimes hard to appreciate them through the crush of eager shoppers blocking the pavements.
Nişantaşı means "target stone", a reminder of the **obelisks** that were erected in the woodlands here to mark the furthest points reached by the sultans' arrows. Several of these stones still survive: there is one at the junction where Valikonağı Caddesi meets Teşvikiye Caddesi and a couple more in the grounds of the Teşvikiye Mosque. Yet another stands in front of the **Harbiye police station** just up the road.

Teşvikiye took its name from the word "teşvik (encouragement)" after Sultan **Mahmud II** initiated a policy of encouraging people to move here, while Maçka may have come from the Greek "matsouka" which means "a thick rod".

Abdi İpekçi Caddesi

Abdi İpekçi (1929-79) was a journalist and human rights activist who, while editor of the **Milliyet Newspaper**, was murdered near his home by Mehmet Ali Ağca who went on to try and kill the Pope. The street was renamed in İpekçi's honor and a statue marks the spot where he died.

Vedat Tek Konağı

In Valikonağı Caddesi stands the elaborate house created by the Turkish architect Vedat Tek (1873-1942) as a family home in 1913-14. Tek worked in what became known as the First Nationalist style, which incorporated ornamental tiles, thick lancet windows and overhanging roofs into its designs. Amongst his other works in Istanbul are the main **post office building** in Sirkeci (see p. 207) and the **ferry landing stage** at Haydarpaşa (see p. 493). Today the building houses a restaurant but if the side door is open it's worth popping in to admire the marble staircases, the tiles and the elaborate first-floor ceilings that so distinguished the interior when it was a home.

Vedat Tek

"Many (target) stones are in existence which date from times gone by and are considerably beyond those set up at the present day."

Turkish Letters **by Ghislain Ogier de Busbecq, 1560**

Target stones

Nişantaşı was not the only place where archery used to take place. Dotted about what is now the built-up suburb of **Okmeydanı** (Archery Square) above Hasköy there was once a training ground for archers with 55 more commemorative obelisks.

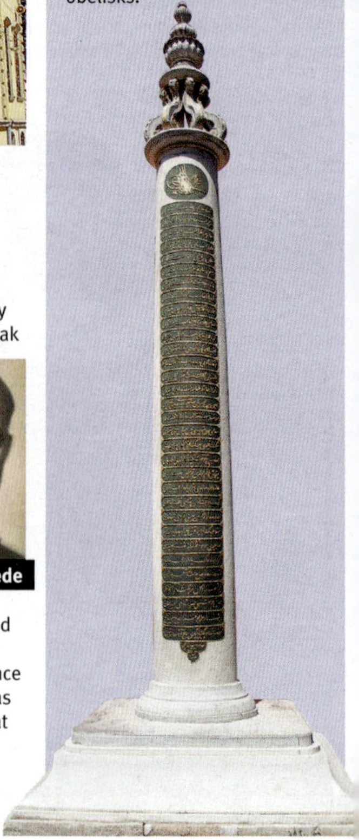

Teşvikiye Mosque

At the south-easterly end of Teşvikiye Caddesi, the Teşvikiye Mosque was built in 1853 to replace an earlier mosque that had fallen into ruins. It has a small dome, a single minaret and a graceful central portico. In the courtyard you'll see two original **target stones**, both with elaborate Ottoman inscriptions. One dates back to the reign of **Sultan Selim III** (1789-1807), the other to **Sultan Mahmud II** (1808-39).

The mosque is associated with a bizarre episode in history when a Jew from Smyrna (modern İzmir) named **Sabbetai Tsvi** (1629-76) proclaimed himself Messiah. Shortly afterwards he was persuaded by the authorities to recant and convert to Islam, but was in any case expelled to Thessaloniki. Those of his followers who followed his lead were called **"Dönme (Converts)"**. During the 1923 population exchange between Greece and Turkey, the Dönme came to Turkey and many settled in Teşvikiye where they were known as **Selanikliler** (people from Thessaloniki). In the way of things, the Sabbatians later underwent their own schism and near the mosque stand two schools, originally founded in 19th-century Thessaloniki, one for each of the two communities.

Lost Messiah

The story of Sabbatia Tsvi and the Dönme is described in detail in John Freely's "The Lost Messiah".

The mosque is a popular venue for high society funerals. It was here that the memorial service for **Ahmet Ertegün** (1923-2006), the founder of Atlantic Records, was held.

Immediately across the road is the imposing, seven-storey **Teşvikiye Palas apartment**. At the junction with Cami Sokak a branch of a restaurant is housed inside what was once a **sebil**. Nearby stands a memorial to **R. Hüsrev Gerede** (1886-1962), an MP, diplomat and national hero described by Atatürk as "a friend for hard times". Gerede was with Atatürk when he landed in Samsun to launch the Turkish War of Independence and also attended the Sivas and Erzurum congresses at which their strategy was thrashed out.

Hüsrev Gerede

Old Maçka Palas

Nişantaşı's Nobel Prize winner

Nişantaşı was the childhood home of the Nobel Prize-winning novelist **Orhan Pamuk** (1952-) whose life with his extended family in the Pamuk Apartments was described in his 2005 memoir **"Istanbul: Memories of a City"**. In it he vividly describes **"hüzün"**, a sort of melancholy that transcends the personal and is inspired by a communal sense of loss tied up with the collapse of the Ottoman Empire and symbolized by the ruined buildings, the rubbish, the gloomy lighting and other evidence of decline he witnessed in the streets of his youth.

Orhan Pamuk

Maçka Palas

On Maçka Caddesi the rather austere Maçka Palas building now houses a deluxe hotel. It was built in 1922 by the Italian architect **Guilio Mongeri** (architect of St Anthony's Cathedral on İstiklal Caddesi, see p. 311) and was home, at various times, to the former president **Celal Bayar** (1883-1986, until 2005 the longest-lived politician in the world); the novelist **Kerime Nadir** (1917-84); and the Galatasaray goalkeeper **Turgay Şeren** (1932-2016). A plaque on the wall commemorates the stay of the poet **Abdülhak Hamid Tarhan** (1852-1937) in 1937.

Facing it is the huge **Anatolian Technical High School (Anadolu Teknik Lisesi)**, also built by **Guilio Mongeri** at the start of the 20th century and originally intended to house the Italian Consulate. When the First World War broke out the building was still incomplete and when it ended the Italians preferred to base themselves in the old **Venetian Palace** in Taksim (see p. 311), so Mongeri's building was demoted into a **depot** for storing tobacco. Work on it was not finally completed until 1970 when it became an extraordinarily beautiful schoolhouse.

Just down the road from the Maçka Palas is the lovely **Izmir Palas apartment block**, with its overgrown rose garden. It was built for the Izmir businessman **Şerifzade Ahmed Süreyya Bey** in 1925 by the architect **J. d'Armi** and was one of the last pure examples of the First National style of architecture.

Turgay Şeren

Kerime Nadir

Abdülhak Hamid Tarhan

Celal Bayar

Anatolian Technical High School

Maçka Barracks (Maçka Kışlası)

Designed by **Simon** and **Sarkis Balyan**, Turkish-Armenian architects from the same family that designed the Dolmabahçe (see p. 386) and Çırağan (see p. 406) palaces, the enormous Maçka Barracks now houses part of **Istanbul Technical University**. Originally it served as a police station and arsenal.

Maçka Barracks

Valide Fountain

Around the corner in Spor Caddesi is the magnificent **Valide Fountain (Valide Çeşmesi)**, built in 1839 for **Bezmialem Valide Sultan**, the mother of **Sultan Abdülmecid** and decorated with inscriptions in goldleaf and the carvings of wreaths and swags typical of the westernized imperial style in favor at the time. Opposite the fountain is a **namazgah**, a corner of a garden set aside for ritual prayer.

Fountain designed by Raimondo d'Aronco

Democracy and Maçka Parks

The back-to-back Democracy and Maçka Parks fill the ravine between Maçka and Elmadağ, divided only by Kadırgalar Caddesi; a **cable car** carries passengers effortlessly from one side to the other. On the Democracy Park side in Maçka there are several cafes along the rim of the valley where you can soak up the view over the Vodafone Park Stadium (see p. 285) to the busy Bosphorus. At the corner where the park meets Abdi İpekçi Caddesi stands a large fountain built in 1901 for **Sultan Abdülhamid II** by the Italian architect **Raimondo d'Aronco**. It used to stand in front of the **Nusretiye Mosque** in Tophane (see p. 382) but was moved here in 1957 when the coast road was widened. It exhibits a mixture of Ottoman baroque features with Art Nouveau twists. At the northern end of Democracy Park there's a bust of historian **Dimitri Cantemir** (see p. 234).

Cable car running between Maçka and Taşkışla

Congress Valley

There are many performance and exhibition venues in Harbiye that have an important place in Istanbul and its art life as well as the people whose names they carry. The events organized throughout the year at Cemal Reşit Rey Concert Hall, Cemil Topuzlu Open-Air Theatre, Lütfi Kırdar Convention and Exhibition centre and Istanbul Congress Centre are important both for the culture, art and the business world. One of the most popular of these events, Contemporary Istanbul, which is organized every year at Lütfi Kırdar Convention and Exhibition Centre, is always a meeting eagerly awaited by art lovers.

@crrkonsersalonu
@istanbullutfikirdar.icec
@iccistanbul
@contemporaryistanbul

"Photographs belong to the Büke Uras Collection"

A couple from Istanbul sitting on the stones which gave their name to Taşlık in the early 1930s.

Western traveller couple posing on the cornerstones of the Aziziye Mosque, which gave its name to Taşlık, in 1918.

Aziziye Mosque

Sultan Abdulaziz (1861-1876), the 32nd Sultan of the Ottoman Empire, ordered a monumental mosque to be built, which could be seen from all coastal villages and palaces, in Maçka Vişnezade Quarter, just above Dolmabahçe Palace, in a high position dominating the Bosphorus. The proposed architect for the project was Sarkis Balyan who almost monopolized the design of the architectural structures of the Ottoman dynasty during the entire 19th century. Abdulaziz named this giant structure "Aziziye Mosque", reminiscent of his sultanate. There are several houses in the area and a small timber mosque belonging to Süleyman the Magnificient era. These structures were expropriated after compensation. Sarkis Balyan was also commissioned to build a row of houses to raise funds for the foundation established for construction costs. This row, named after its initial purpose of Akaretler (see p. 398), constitute the most important example of this type of residence during the Ottoman state. Akaretler also functioned as a timber set that would protect Dolmabahçe Palace from any possible fire that might have started in Beşiktaş neighbourhood, where there were many timber buildings.

The construction of the groundwork of Aziziye Mosque, comprising of large cut stones, was started around the end of 1874 and beginning of 1875. However, Abdulaziz was dethroned by a coup in May 30, 1876. He then died in Feriye Palace (see p. 407), where he was being held in custody, on June 4, 1876 on suspicion of suicide. Sultan Murad V and then Sultan Abdülhamid II succeeded to the throne following the coup. The Aziziye Mosque project was cancelled despite the prolonged construction, most probably to prevent people from remembering the name Abdülaziz.

The story of the mosque from this point on is interesting. The large stone blocks, which constitute the groundwork of the construction, covered the vacant plot completely for more than a half century. The area was publicly named "Taşlık" (Stony Ground) in reference to these abandoned corner stones. It turned into a viewing terrace often frequented by citizens of Istanbul and Western travellers for its proximity to the Dolmabahçe and Yıldız palaces and its view of the magnificent Sarayburnu and the Bosphorus. Taşlık became an important sightseeing area of Beyoğlu and Şişli residential areas, the most densely populated areas of Istanbul, for its visual relationship with the Bosphorus. Since none of these regions had a public viewing terrace of such a size, people came to enjoy this public space which was formed in an organic way.

Hürriyet

20 Aralık 1973 Pazar

Talû göreve devam edecek

•Korutürk'le görüşen Başbakan kabine için temaslara başlayacak

Taksim'e dikilecekti

Her yönüyle İNÖNÜ

13 Ocak 1974 Pazar günü

Hürriyet'te

İnönü'nün heykelini parçalanmış ve başsız olarak bulduk

"İki elim bomboş kaldı" diyen Bayan İnönü televizyonu seyrettikçe ağladı

İsmet İnönü visited Rudolf Belling while the statue was being sculpted.

Homeless Statue: Atlı İnönü Monument

Although the stone blocks of the foundation of Aziziye Mosque fell apart over time, they dominated the area until the end of the 1930s. The area is actually the private garden of Dolmabahçe Palace. In his master plan for Istanbul, Henri Prost, the French expert on urbanisation, suggested transforming the Kadırgalar Valley, which extends from Dolmabahçe to Maçka, into a large park. In 1940, Lütfi Kırdar, the governor and Mayor of Istanbul of the time, demolished the Taksim Barracks in line with the Prost Plan for building Taksim Gezi. He built a continuous park in an area of 30 acres between Taksim Square and Taşlık, named "İnönü Gezisi". As the park, named "Park Number 2" in the Prost plan, was being built, the corner stones of the Aziziye Mosque were also cleared. In 1940, Maçka Taşlık Gazinosu (Club) was built on part of the Taşlık area. This famous club was later run by Fahrettin Aslan.

It is argued that these stones were later used in the construction of Şişli Mosque, which was built between 1945 and 1949. This discretionary use also reminds us that tombstones from the expropriated Armenian cemetery in Elmadağ were used for the construction of the stairs of Gezi Park around the same time.

In 1944 a 7.5-meter high pedestal was placed on the southern part of Taksim Gezisi, which overlooks Taksim Square, by Architect Mehmet Ali Handan. The pedestal was intended for the bronze horse statue commissioned by President İsmet İnönü to be completed by Rudolf Belling, the Austrian sculptor and Head of the Department of Sculpture at the Fine Arts Faculty. It took four years to complete the monument, but in the end it was never placed on the pedestal. As a result of criticism directed at the expenditures of the sculpture, which was being made during the World War with many war-related problems still prevalent, the project was suspended for a while.

Then, in 1950, the Democratic Party came to power and it was impossible for the İnönü Statue to be placed on the pedestal. The monument-statue was kept in storerooms for years (first in the garden of Mecidiyeköy Tekel Factory and then in municipal workshops in Edirnekapı.) After the demise of İnönü in 1973, Hürriyet Newspaper looked for the monument and found it in pieces in a storeroom belonging to the Directorate of Public Works in Bakırköy Osmaniye. In 1982, with it once again on the agenda, the board decided to place the monument in Taşlık Parkı in front of İnönü's house. The pedestal, which had been vacant for years, was dismantled, the statue was repaired and the pedestal and the statue met after 38 years. The monument was unveiled with a ceremony on the 59th anniversary of the Lausanne Agreement. Unfortunately, like İnönü, Rudolf Belling's life did not extend long enough to see the opening of the largest monumental statue he had worked on for more than three years.

The photo of the Taşlık Kahvesi (Stone Coffeehouse) by Sedad Hakkı Eldem, published in the issue 11-22 of the Arkitekt magazine in 1950. The sustaining wall of Aziziye Mosque that the coffeehouse is placed on can be seen clearly.

Maçka Valide Fountain

Istanbul Technical University Maçka Campus

Maçka Poets Park

The Lost Carnival

Kurtuluş, Şişli and Mecidiyeköy

053

A mainly nondescript and heavily built-up area squeezed in between Nişantaşı and Kasımpaşa, Kurtuluş was the old Tatavla, a hilltop district. This was an area which once had a large Greek and Armenian community and even today the cemeteries for the burial of minority groups are a conspicuous feature. Mecidiyeköy is known primarily for its shopping malls.

An old Greek house from the 1890s in Pangaltı

In the side streets a few old buildings still survive.

Kurtuluş

Established in the 16th century, **Tatavla** (also known as **Aya Dimitri**), was originally a completely separate hilltop village overlooking a wooded gorge with a stream running along the bottom which separated it from Tarlabaşı. Its population was made up of men who had been abducted from the Greek islands to work either in the navy or in the **Ottoman shipyards** at Kasımpaşa (see p. 264). They had retreated to the hilltop after their church in Kasımpaşa was turned into a mosque and chose a piece of land that had once been used for pasture, hence the Greek-Turkish hybrid name they chose for it: **Tatavla** which means "**The Stables**". Heart of the new village was the **church of Hagios Demetrios** (Aya Dimitri), which they established in 1535. In 1793 the Sultan decreed that only Greeks could live here, a distinction it shared with what is now **Ayvalık** on the Aegean coast.

The settlement grew rapidly, with a particular surge in residents after Fener was looted in 1821 (see p. 230). It became famous for a raucous **Lent carnival** and for a generally licentious atmosphere with many wine-houses, brothels and even **transvestite dancers**, the ancestors perhaps of those who inhabit Tarlabaşı (see p. 088) today.

Hard though it is to believe it when strolling along today's heavily built-up streets, but reports from the 19th century describe Tatavla as having had an insular community living in privately-owned two-storey houses set around the two churches of **Hagios Georgios** and **Hagios Eleftherios**. It was a little slice of Greece in Turkey, which suffered several severe blows in the early 20th century, culminating in a huge fire that destroyed much of the housing. After that Tatavla was renamed **Kurtuluş** which means "**Salvation**". Modern Kurtuluş is still a neighborhood with a mixed population including some Greeks and Armenians; the Armenian newspaper **Agos** has its offices here. Most of the area is without architectural distinction although there are a few fine late 19th-century mansions around **Pangaltı** and in **Kurtuluş Caddesi**. Kurtuluş forms part of the borough of **Şişli,** which means "with a skewer" in Turkish, a name it may have acquired from the mansion home of a family of skewer-makers.

Baklahorani Carnival

In Greek tradition the Monday before the start of Lent is called "**Clean Monday**" and this was the day when the old Tatavla carnival, called the Baklahorani, got into its stride. A fairground-like atmosphere prevailed in front of the churches and the Haghios Eleftherios cemetery, with people drinking alcohol and tucking into plates of beans, which were regarded as an especially appropriate food on which to feast before a fast. Perhaps the strangest feature of the celebrations was the so-called "**procession of the Amazons**", during which prostitutes from all over Istanbul paraded by on horseback dressed in velvet. Not surprisingly the carnival had an unsavory reputation and by the time it was staged for the last time in 1943 it was down to its last 20 customers. Although only 76 people gathered in the first year of the carnival, which began to be reorganized in 2009 under the personal initiative of author Hüseyin Irmak, this number had increased by 2014. These days, when we are in need of a sense of unity, you can't help but wish that we were not in need of such an effort to keep the colors of our culture alive.

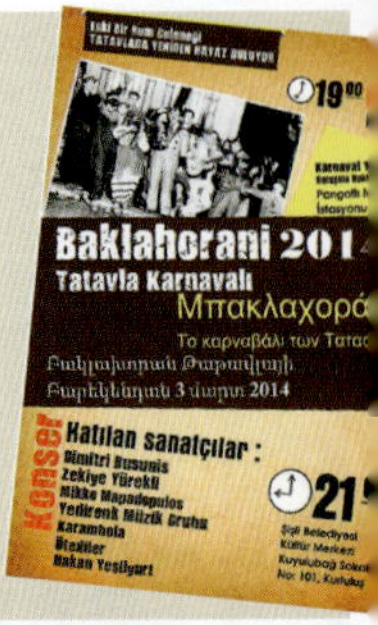

Hagios Demetrios Church

Church of the Dodeka Apostoli

Churches

The current version of the **Church of Hagios Demetrios,** in a pretty walled garden in Safa Meydan (Square), overlooks what is now the local bus station and dates back only to 1726. The derelict but still imposing **Church of Hagios Eleftherios,** built in 1855, was the first church to acquire a dome after the laws prohibiting them were abolished. It's in a dip beside Omuzdaş Sokak, a short downhill walk from the Greek Orthodox cemetery in Bayır Sokak.

The large **Church of the Dodeka Apostoli (Twelve Apostles)** in Avukat Caddesi in Feriköy (Feri's Village) was completed in 1868 and stands on land given to Madame Feri in recognition of her French husband's services as a doctor.

"Pull, driver, pull, let's head to Tatavla!"

Old Constantinopolitan song.

Hagios Eleftherios Church

Protestant Cemetery

The Feriköy cemeteries

The **Protestant Cemetery** in Abide-i Hürriyet Caddesi feels like a little piece of England even though sections of it are reserved for departed members of the German, French, Hungarian, Swedish, Norwegian and American communities. The gravestones here date back to the 19th century and form a record of mixed marriages, refugee status and missionary activity and of deaths from cholera and drowning that seem a world away from modern Istanbul. This is the burial place of the American anthropologist **Josephine Powell** (1919-2007), the last in a long line of doughty female explorers who fell in love with the Middle East. She rests here amid daisies and birdsong not far away from **Hilary Sumner-Boyd**, co-author with John Freely of one of the seminal texts on the city, **"Strolling Through Istanbul"**.

Josephine Powell

Across the road is the bombastic **Catholic Cemetery** with family tombs the size of small houses.

Gallery Baraz

Owned by the famous Turkish art dealer Yahşi Baraz, this gallery at Kurtuluş Caddesi No. 141 showcases the work of the artists he represents including **Burhan Doğançay** (see p. 303).

@galeribaraz
www.galeribaraz.com

Bulgarian Exarchate

Close to the point where Halaskargazi Caddesi meets Abide-i Hürriyet Caddesi a fine **late 19th-century mansion** stands in a large garden. In 1870 the sultan granted the Bulgarian Church independence from the Greek Orthodox Church and this building was intended as the home of its newly independent patriarch, **Joseph I**. Unfortunately by then the congregation had virtually faded away.

Near the D-100 there was also a **Bulgarian hospital** which has since become the Türkiye Hospital, its past commemorated by a cross on the building's façade.

Çankaya Apartments

Houses crammed in together

Halaskargazi Caddesi

Halaskargazi Caddesi stretches from Harbiye to the **Şişli Mosque** (1945-9) where it turns into Büyükdere Caddesi. Its name, which means **"Veteran Savior Street"**, is a reference to **Atatürk**. Although most of it is architecturally undistinguished there are a few fine 19th-century buildings to enliven a walk along it; in particular a lovely house belonging to the **Bulgarian Exarch** stands in a rambling garden just before you reach Sişli Mosque. It was on this street that the Turkish-Armenian journalist **Hrant Dink** was murdered in 2007 in front of the **Agos** offices.

Hrant Dink

Bozlu Art Project

Exhibiting the modern and contemporary artworks collected by **Dr. Şükrü Bozluolçay** in years, Bozlu Art Project is one of the spots that bring history and art together. The **Mongeri Building**, which is one of the important examples of the First National Architectural Movement, was turned into an art center in 2016 after around two years of renovation. Despite the chaos surrounding it, the building designed in 1925 by the famous Italian architect **Giulio Mongeri**, who signed his name on many buildings in Istanbul, reflects the spirit of last century with overtones of classical Ottoman architecture as well as the colorful domed tile boards and pointed arcs. While you can observe the works of important names of contemporary Turkish art, the "Artist Workshops" section of the gallery is also remarkable. Alongside the extensive library and the books published by **Bozlu Art Publications**, the center aims at contributing to the formation of a memory of art history through the artist lectures, documentaries, catalogues and archives parallel to the exhibitions.

@bozluartproject
www.bozluartproject.com
Tel: 0212 233 72 33

Şişli Etfal Hastanesi (Children's Hospital)

If you turn off Halaskargazi Caddesi along Küçükbahçe Sokak you will come to Şişli Children's Hospital whose 20-meter-tall clock tower was built as a **memorial** to Sultan Abdülhamid II's daughter Hatice Sultan who died aged only eight months. Unusually it doubles as a minaret and mescit (chapel) according to a design prepared by **Raimondo d'Aronco.**

Hisart Live History and Diorama Museum

The museum reflects **Nejat Çuhadaroğlu**'s effort and patience, as well as his 30 years of experience in model making, 25 years of experience in diorama making and his identity as a collector for 18 years. Learning that all of the military equipment exhibited such as swords, machetes, guns, rifles and most of the textiles on the mannequins such as uniforms and kaftans are original arouses astonishment, respect and admiration. Since there are not much remaining of the outfits of the **Ottoman** era up to the 19th century, those outfits were prepared true to the original based on the engravings and paintings. When you learn that the preparations of the outfits on the mannequins could take one month, one year or ten years depending on the person or the period it represents, I am sure you will take off your hat to the effort once more.

@hisartmuseum
www.hisartmuseum.com
Tel: 0212 296 98 04
closed Mondays

Atatürk Museum

This museum on Halaskargazi Caddesi is housed in a baby-pink three-storey building where the founder of the Turkish Republic **Mustafa Kemal Atatürk** lived with his mother and sister from December 1918 to May 1919. It contains some of his **personal effects** along with a few portraits and many **photographs**, but the labeling is in Turkish.

closed Tuesday and Mondays

Mecidiyeköy

North of the Feriköy cemeteries the district of Mecidiyeköy was originally developed by Sultan Abdülmecid I in the 19th century, hence its name, "Mecid's Village". It's mainly of interest to shoppers keen to scour the shopping malls for bargains and people in search of computer equipment.

Monument to Liberty (Abide-i Hürriyet)

31 March Incident

In 1909 Şişli was the scene of an attempted fight-back against the Young Turks and in favor of Sultan Abdülhamid II. The uprising was quickly quashed and a new grand vizier, Ahmed Tevfik Paşa, installed. He was the last holder of such office in Turkey. The sultan himself was overthrown only weeks after the uprising. The **Abide-i Hürriyet** (Monument to Liberty) on Şişli's highest hill in **Çağlayan** commemorates the 74 soldiers who died.

Darülaceze

This building, whose door is the only visible part from Okmeydanı, harbors mostly sad but also hope-inspiring stories. It was opened in 1895 on the order of **Sultan Abdülhamid** as a shelter for orphaned children who were living on the streets following the migrations triggered by the **1877 Ottoman-Russian War** and for disabled elderly. Covering an area of 30 acres, the institution kept its doors open to 72,000 people, 29,000 of them children, regardless of their religion, language, race, class and sex. Don't you think that the unity of a mosque, a church and a synagogue all in its garden is proof of that?

Church

Synagogue

Mosque

The entrence of the church and the synagogue.

Bomontiada

Bomonti Brewery was opened in 1890 in Feriköy. The brewery, which was the first mass production facility of its time, also gave its name to the district where it was located. After continuing to manufacture for a long time, the brewery was closed in 1991. It was reopened in 2015 as Bomontiada, when it was organized as a centre of culture, art and entertainment, inspired by global examples. Bomontiada, as was the case with the initial foundation of the historical Bomonti Brewery, has once again changed the fate of the district which had been left to nearby manufacturing workshops. With its galleries, restaurants, cafes and outdoor spaces, it hosts various events throughout the year. Its spacious courtyard, which is particularly refreshing during the summer months, has already turned into a point of attraction for people of all ages.

@bomontiada
www.bomontiada.com.

Just next to it you should definitely visit the Feriköy Organic Bazaar open every Saturday at Gökkuşağı Street and the Feriköy Antique Bazaar which is open every Sunday.

@ferikoyantikpazari
www.ferikoyantikapazari.com.

Gourmet Delights

Etiler and Ulus

054

Forget sightseeing for a moment. Etiler and Ulus are both upscale residential areas in which the main activities are shopping and eating in an array of restaurants where fine dining (and views) are the order of the day.

Etiler is home to some of Istanbul's wealthier residents and the prices in the shops and restaurants inevitably reflect their purchasing power. The historically-minded will struggle to find much to interest them, although Etiler's name is said to refer to the **Hittites**, one of the many ancient peoples who left their mark on central Anatolia. Immediately after the founding of the Turkish Republic in 1923 there was a fad for giving names like this to Istanbul suburbs; so adjourning **Akatlar** is said to be named after the Akkadians, another people from the dim and distant past.

In the hills above Arnavutköy and Kuruçeşme, **Ulus** once had a large **Jewish population** and still has more Jews than other parts of the city. Its name means "the nation" or "the people", a reference to the Turkish Republic. **Ulus Park** is a large open space that houses several revered restaurants and offers spectacular Bosphorus views.

Ahmet Adnan Saygun

Busy Ahmet Adnan Saygun Caddesi links Ulus with Etiler and Zincirlikuyu. Here you'll find two **Jewish cemeteries** catering for the Sephardic and Ashkenazi communities. The victims of the 1986 Neve Shalom massacre were buried in the Ashkenazi Cemetery. Right beside the Ashkenazi Cemetery is the **Oditorium,** a large Jewish High School that stills offers an education to around 500 pupils. Nearby is a statue of **Ahmet Adnan Saygun** (1907-91), a Turkish composer whose works blended Western-style classical music and Turkish folk music. At Atatürk's behest, Saygun penned Turkey's **first two operas**, "Özsoy (Lineage)" and "Taşbebek (Porcelain Doll)", in 1934.

Little New York

Levent and Maslak

055

Not much visited by tourists, Levent and Maslak are Istanbul's booming business districts, areas of high-rise office blocks interspersed with equally high-rise apartment complexes. There are some fine restaurants here to suit the palates and pockets of the business community, as well as upscale shopping malls. The Maslak Pavilions serve as a rare and pleasant reminder of the past, while the Elgiz Museum of Contemporary Art is a must for art lovers.

Levent is apparently named after the **sailors** ("levend") of the Ottoman navy. They acquired that nickname from the Italian word used to describe people from the Eastern Mediterranean. Alternatively its name may commemorate a farm worked here by **Cezayirli Hasan Paşa** in the 18th century. **Maslak** is named after one of the old reservoirs bringing water from the nearby Belgrade Forest. Despite its efforts to create a glitzy "**Mashattan**" image for itself, it's actually an alarmingly inhuman landscape where people come a very poor second to the traffic on busy **Büyükdere Caddesi**. You must walk considerable distances just to cross over it – don't come here if you have mobility problems as the pedestrian overpasses are a nightmare. But, this being Turkey, in amongst the soaring skyscrapers you'll still come across the roughest of **gecekondus** (houses that are thrown up overnight), not to mention a family looking after more than one hundred street dogs. The suburb is also home to the **Istanbul Technical University** campus.

Maslak skyscrapers on Victory Day (30 August)

Maslak Pavilions

The buildings in Maslak Park are thought to have been built on land first developed as a country retreat by Sultan Mahmud II. Later **Sultan Abdülaziz** gave them to his nephew, **Abdülhamid II**, in an attempt to discourage him from sailing at Tarabya, at that time widely thought of as dangerous. The **Imperial Lodge** (Kasr-ı Hümayun), which housed Abdülhamid's office and sleeping quarters, is now a museum set in a large wooded park; the sultan himself carved the banisters of the main staircase as well as the frames for the mirrors over the beds. The **Royal Apartments** (Mabeyn-i Hümayun) are surrounded by rare plants. A café is housed inside the octagonal T**ent Pavilion** (Çadır Kasrı), while the **greenhouse** (Limonluk) shelters camellias imported from France by Abdülhamid. The **Pasha's Quarters** are used for administration. The grounds are offering a pleasant and surprisingly peaceful oasis after busy Maslak central.

Tel: 0212 259 32 92, closed Sundays.

Imperial Lodge (Kasr-ı Hümayun)

Elgiz Museum of Contemporary Art

Opened in 2001, this wonderful modern art gallery in Maslak's Meydan Sokak houses the impressive collection of **Sevda and Can Elgiz**. While hosting temporary exhibitions, the museum also displays Elgiz Collection in the permanent exhibition area, offering free admission. The museum also holds various workshops for groups of young people and children with an aim to pass it on to the next generations. Launched its 2000 m^2 terrace space for open-air sculpture exhibitions, Elgiz Museum has brought the city together with sculpture art with various themes each year since 2010. In an aim to showcase contemporary art projects from all around Turkey on international platforms, Elgiz Museum, in 2015, became the founding member of **Global Private Museum Network** (GPMN) and the member of **International Council of Museums** (ICOM). To reach it from the İTÜ Ayazağa Metro station you have to cross the road and cut through to the second row of office blocks in search of the **Beybi Giz Plaza**.

@elgizmuseum, www.elgizmuseum.org
Tel: 0212 290 25 25
closed Sundays, Mondays and Tuesdays

Atatürk City Forest

This area in Hacıosman which has been secluded for many years is being put in the service of the citizens of Istanbul following the extensive of Istanbul Metropolitan Municipality. Similar to the **Validebağ Woods** in Üsküdar (see p.504), this area arranged paying regard to the natural environment includes a 12 km walking parkour and a natural pond. The city forest that became a new spot of breathing since its opening in 19 May 2020 can be reached by the subway.

Cendere Art Museum

Cendere Pump Station, built by a French company in 1902 during the reign of Abdulhamid, was built to transport Kağıthane spring waters to the city. The facility, which met the water needs of Istanbulites to a great extent in the past, began to lose its function with the development of technology and the preference for modern solutions in water distribution. The station, one of the few industrial heritage buildings in Istanbul that has survived to the present day, opened its doors as an art gallery after the functional and restoration works carried out by Istanbul Metropolitan Municipality.

@cenderesanatmuzesi
Closed on Mondays.

Galatasaray in numbers

- Founded 1905 - Turkey's first football team
- Winner UEFA Cup 2000 – first and only Turkish team to win a major European cup
- 10 times winner of Presidents Cup
- 15 times competitor in Champions League
- 22 times winner of Turkish Cup

Ali Sami Yen Sports Complex

This stadium, which was founded in 2007 in Seyrantepe, changed the name of the neighbourhood to Aslantepe. The facility completed in 2011 has since been hosting Galatasaray Sports Club.

THE BOSPHORUS
(EUROPEAN SHORE)

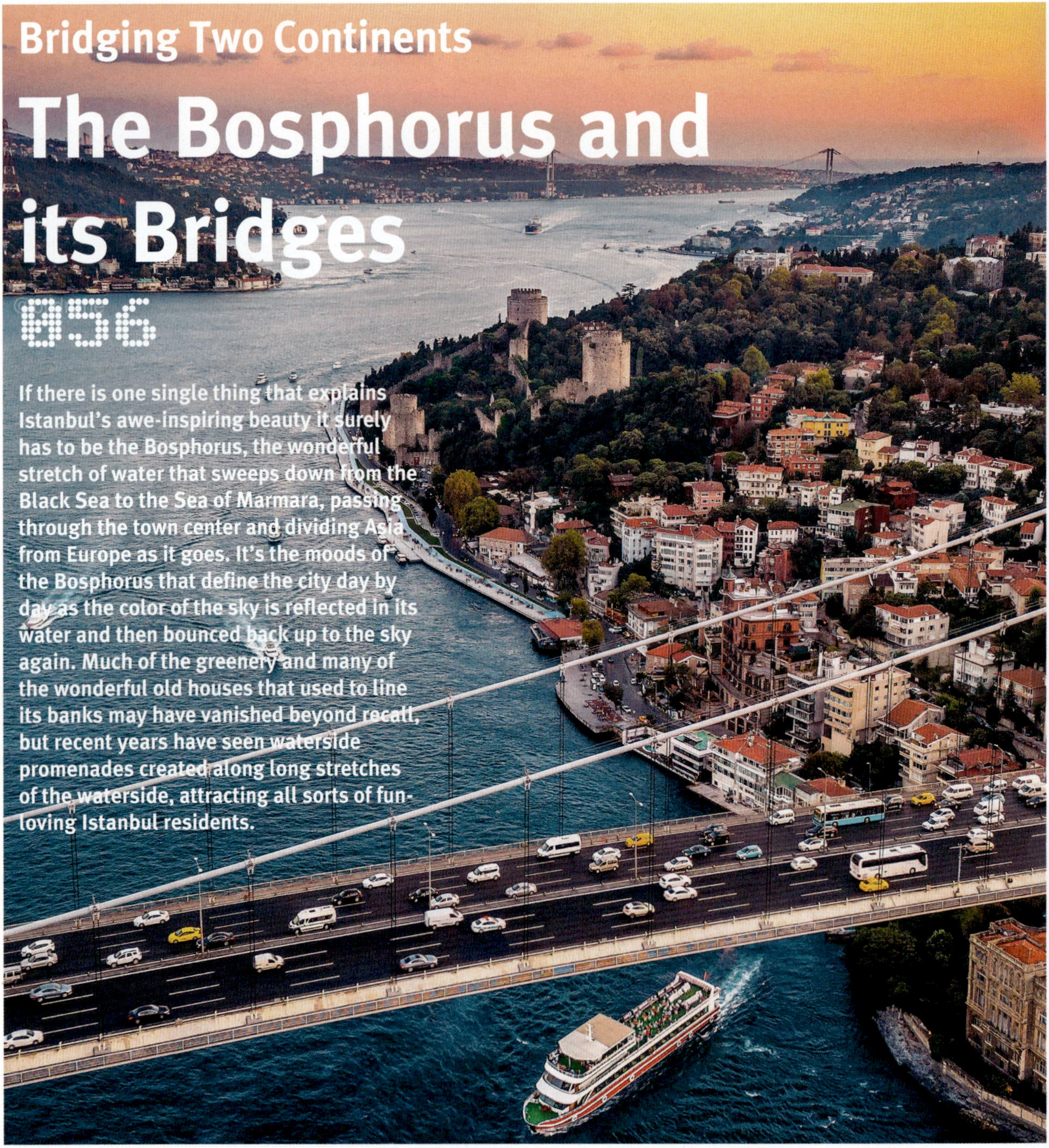

Bridging Two Continents

The Bosphorus and its Bridges

056

If there is one single thing that explains Istanbul's awe-inspiring beauty it surely has to be the Bosphorus, the wonderful stretch of water that sweeps down from the Black Sea to the Sea of Marmara, passing through the town center and dividing Asia from Europe as it goes. It's the moods of the Bosphorus that define the city day by day as the color of the sky is reflected in its water and then bounced back up to the sky again. Much of the greenery and many of the wonderful old houses that used to line its banks may have vanished beyond recall, but recent years have seen waterside promenades created along long stretches of the waterside, attracting all sorts of fun-loving Istanbul residents.

Streching almost 30 kilometers from **Sarayburnu** in the heart of Old Istanbul right up to **Anadolu Feneri** at the mouth of the Black Sea, the Bosphorus is the magnificent stretch of water that separates the European and Asian shores of the city. Even now, when many of the wonderful **wooden yalıs** (seaside mansions) that used to line the shores have been lost, the beauty of the Bosphorus is still absolutely magnetic and few things can be more enjoyable than taking a **cruise** along it, looking out for historic palaces and ancient castles, watching for **birds** and the occasional pod of dolphins and floating beneath the modern bridges without which Istanbul's traffic would grind to a complete halt. At the far end of the strait at Anadolu Kavağı (see p. 558) you can stop for a fish lunch and climb up to the remains of a castle offering a view down to the **Black Sea**. Then it will be time to hop back on to the ferry for the return journey via **Kanlıca**, well-known to Istanbul residents for its thick and tasty yoghurt (see p. 549).

How the Bosphorus got its name

According to Ancient Greek mythology, the name Bosphorus, meaning **"cow's passage"**, is derived from that of the priestess **Io**, the favorite of **Zeus**, the king of the gods. Fearing the wrath of his jealous wife, Zeus had Io turned into a cow, but **Hera** was wise to him and sent a gadfly to hound poor Io who was driven to roam the earth in an attempt to rid herself of it. Eventually she arrived at the Bosphorus, which has commemorated her passing ever since. The story had a happy ending, for when she finally arrived in Egypt Zeus had the decency to return her to human form. In Turkish the Bosphorus is called much less imaginatively **"Boğaz"**, or **"throat"**.

Zeus, Hera and Io the cow

Strategic importance

The Bosphorus has always held great strategic significance as the link between the Mediterranean and Black Seas via the Sea of Marmara, which is one reason why **Constantine the Great** chose to locate the new capital of the Roman Empire (Byzantium) beside it. The result has caused several conflicts, especially the **Crimean War** of 1853-56 and the **Russo-Turkish War** of 1877-78 and the struggle over **Gallipoli** in 1915 during the First World War. Under the terms of the 1936 **Montreux Convention** the Bosphorus has been declared an international shipping lane, although Turkey retains the right to bar access to warships and ships of non-Black Sea nations. The strait is one of the world's busiest shipping routes. Every year approximately **40,000 ships** pass along it. Ten thousand of them are tankers carrying oil and other explosive materials.

In 2003 growing fears over the danger of collisions, especially between oil tankers, on this super-busy waterway led to the erection of a series of white **radar towers** along both sides of the Bosphorus, sometimes sited right beside important historic monuments.

The Bosphorus then and now

At the start of the 21st century the shores of the Bosphorus are built-up for much of their length. To understand what they looked like one hundred years ago you have to imagine the coast roads stripped away and, in their place, a succession of discrete villages, mansions and palaces separated by woodland that would have been accessible only by boat. Today the villages may have been subsumed by urban sprawl but some of them are still extremely beautiful.

"Each villa on the Bosphorus looks a screen/New painted, or a pretty opera scene."

Don Juan **by Lord Byron, 1821**

Bridging the Bosphorus

In 512 BC the Persians under the leadership of **King Darius** built a bridge of 325 boats from Anadolu Hisarı to Rumeli Hisarı, enabling an **army of 700,000 men** to cross from Asia to Europe; Darius is said to have watched them doing so from a spot above Rumeli Hisarı which was called **"Darius' Throne"**. More than a thousand years later the Byzantine **Emperor Heraclius I** created a similar bridge of boats and rode a horse across it.

The first modern bridge was the Bosphorus Bridge (**July 15 Martyrs' Bridge**) built in 1973. The Second Bosphorus Bridge (**Fatih Sultan Mehmet Bridge**) was built 5km to the north of the first bridge in 1988. But since the traffic problem was still not resolved, the Third Bridge (**Yavuz Sultan Selim Bridge**) was opened for traffic in 2016 with its two piers in Garipçe and Poyrazköy.

King Darius

Said Halim Paşa Yalı

Yalıs old and new

In Turkish, the word "yalı" refers to a waterside house. The Bosphorus yalıs are graceful wooden mansions that sit right beside the water with landing-stages for boats to tie up at them. The first yalıs were built in the early 18th-century, during the so-called **Tulip Era**, but most date back to the 19th and early 20th centuries. Unfortunately, as population pressure raised the value of land along the Bosphorus, many were either demolished or caught fire in sometimes suspicious circumstances. Those that still remain are aptly described by the locals as **"the pearls of the Bosphorus"**.

Cruising the Bosphorus: Eminönü to Bebek

Long Bosphorus ferry cruises depart from Eminönü. Soon after starting off you will get a magnificent view of **Sarayburnu** (Palace Point), with the **Topkapı Palace** (see p. 002), **Hagia Sophia** (see p. 026) and **Sultanahmet Mosque** (see p. 038) throwing up a wonderful silhouette on the skyline. Then, on the left, you will see Karaköy and the Complex of Galataport (under construction, see p. 378) on the European shore. A little further along you will spot **Kız Kulesi** (Maiden's Tower, see p. 496), just off Üsküdar on the Asian shore. The elaborate 19th-century **Dolmabahçe Palace** (see p. 086) then looms up on the European side, followed shortly afterwards by the pretty early 20th-century **Beşiktaş landing stage** (see p. 397). A little further along you will see the **Four Seasons at the Bosphorus Hotel** and the luxurious **Çırağan Palace Hotel** (see p. 406), with its wonderful swimming pool right on the water's edge. On the opposite shore is the late 18th-century **Pink Yalı**, more correctly called the Fethi Ahmed Paşa Yalı (see p. 512).

As you approach the 1st **Bosphorus Bridge** look out for **Ortaköy** (see p. 410) on the European shore, which is one of Istanbul's liveliest nightlife hotspots. Facing it and almost immediately beneath the bridge, is **Beylerbeyi Palace** (see p. 517), which resembles a cut-down version of the Dolmabahçe. Then, still on the Asian side, you will spot the twin towers of the **Kuleli Miltary School** (see p. 523).

Back on the European side of the strait the boat sails past lovely **Arnavutköy** (see p. 422), which retains many of its wonderful wooden houses. A little further along you pass the beautiful Art Nouveau building in **Bebek** that houses the **Egyptian Consulate** (see p. 427).

Cruising the Bosphorus: Kandilli to Anadolu Kavağı

Over on the Asian shore you should keep your eyes peeled for the long white **Kıbrıslı Mustafa Emin Paşa Yalı** (see p. 535), **Küçüksu Palace** (see p. 537) and the late 17th-century **Köprülü Amcazade Hüseyin Paşa Yalı** (see p. 544), the oldest surviving wooden mansion on the Bosphorus. Then shortly before the **2nd Bridge** the unmissable castle of **Rumeli Hisarı** (see p. 434) looms up on the European shore. Facing it are the less dramatic remains of **Anadolu Hisarı** (see p. 539), its older and smaller brother.

The ferry continues past **Kanlıca** (see p. 546) and then, on the Asian shore, you'll see, high on a hill, the **Hıdiv Kasrı** (see p. 550), a wonderful Art Nouveau summerhouse built for the last khedive (Ottoman governor) of Egypt in c.1900. On the European side the boat skirts **Emirgan** (see p. 440) and the pretty harbor at **İstinye** (see p. 448) before coming to **Yeniköy** (see p. 550), a particularly upscale suburb where you'll see the 19th-century **Sait Halim Paşa Yalı** and many others.

Further still, you pass **Tarabya** (see p. 458) and **Sarıyer** (see p. 466) before arriving at **Rumeli Kavağı** (see p. 469), which offers a fine selection of fish restaurants. Otherwise you can continue to **Anadolu Kavağı** on the Asian side (see p. 558) and end your run with monumental 3rd Bridge.

The red building on the top of the hill at Kandilli once housed Casanova.

2nd Bosphorus Bridge

3rd Bosphorus Bridge

The Bosphorus in numbers

- Length: 32 km
- Maximum width: 3600 m (Black Sea entrance)
- Minimum width: 698 m (Anadolu Hisarı-Rumeli Hisarı)
- Maximum depth: 110 m (Bebek-Kandilli)
- Minimum depth: 30 m

1st Bridge in numbers

- Built: 1973
- Length (between its towers): 1074 m
- Height to road: 65 m
- Height to top of support struts: 165 m
- Traffic lanes: 6

2nd Bridge in numbers

- Built: 1988
- Length (between its towers): 1090 m
- Height to road: 64 m
- Height to top of support struts: 169 m
- Traffic lanes: 8

3rd Bridge in numbers

- Built: 2016
- Length (between its towers): 1875 m
- Elevation from Sea Level: 72 m
- Length of Towers: 322 m
- Traffic Lanes: 8

Jason and the Argonauts

In Greek mythology Jason was the son of the king of Thessaly who had been overthrown by his brother. Jason’s uncle had told his nephew that he could only become king himself after bringing back the **Golden Fleece** from Colchis (probably modern Georgia). To do this Jason gathered together a group of heroes, including **Hercules and Theseus** and set off in a ship called the **Argo,** after which his followers became known as the Argonauts. Together they traveled up the Bosphorus and through the **Symplegades** (see p. 559) to reach **Colchis** and retrieve the fleece with all sorts of hair-raising adventures along the way.

n holding the Golden Fleece

1st Bosphorus Bridge

A curious and sometimes dangerous feature of the Bosphorus is that the surface current flows down from the Black Sea towards the Sea of Marmara, while the undercurrent flows in the opposite direction.

Cormorant

The birds of the Bosphorus

No sooner does any ferry set sail than a stream of **black-headed gulls** will gather around it, screeching a hopeful plea for a piece of one of the simits (sesame-seed rolls) many locals buy just to toss to them. They are the most conspicuous of the Bosphorus' multitudinous birds, but you will also see many **cormorants** swimming in the water or sunning themselves with their wings spread open on the buoys and flocks of tiny **Mediterranean shearwaters** skimming low across the water. These are the resident birds, but the Bosphorus also lies on an important migratory route and one of the great sights of the city is that of the **storks** arriving back from their winter sojourn in Africa in March and then leaving again in even greater numbers in the third week of August.

Dolphin delight

Dubbed the "street children of the Bosphorus" in a newspaper article, the pods of dolphins that can sometimes be seen swimming in the strait are an encouraging sign that it is becoming less polluted. **Bottlenose dolphins**, **common dolphins** and **harbor porpoises** have all returned to the water recently, delighting fishermen and ferry passengers alike with their antics.

How the Judas tree got its name

If you visit Istanbul in the spring you will hardly be able to miss the beautiful pink-flowering Judas trees (*Cercis siliquastrum)*. Legend holds that **Judas Iscariot**, the disciple who betrayed Jesus Christ, hanged himself from one of these trees, hence its popular name. In reality it is probably a corruption of the French **"Arbre de Judée"**, meaning **Tree of Judea** in recognition of one of the places that it grows.

"Say Istanbul and a seagu comes to mind/Half silve and half foam, half fish and half bird."

The Saga of Istanbul by Bedri Rahmi Eyüboğl 1974

For more information about my "Bophorus by Night" and "Judas Trees" tours please visit www.saffetemretonguc.com/turlar or call +90 541 123 34 34

Deck of the Savarona

The Savarona

The *Savarona* was the largest and most luxurious private yacht in the world. It was built in 1931 for **Emily Roebling**, granddaughter of the man responsible for New York's Brooklyn Bridge, but in 1938 it was bought by the **Turkish Government** and used for several cabinet meetings. It was while on-board the *Savarona* in 1938 that **Atatürk** succumbed to critical illness; he was taken from the yacht to the Dolmabahçe Palace where he died. In 1979 the yacht was badly damaged by fire.

Completely restored, the *Savarona* can be hired for special occasions and past guests have included **Prince Rainier of Monaco, Prince Charles and Princess Diana** of **Britain** and **King Juan Carlos** of **Spain**, as well as **Tom Cruise** and **Nicole Kidman** and **Sharon Stone**. The ship was expropriated in 2014 under the initiative of the Ministry of Culture and Tourism. Today Savarona is used as presidential yatch.

The Fireworks on 29 October (Republic Day/Cumhuriyet Bayramı) over the 1st Bridge.

Moonlight flits

On summer evenings few things could be more pleasant than taking a **late-night cruise** along the Bosphorus and plenty of companies compete to offer ready-made or do-it-yourself boat trips. But just think how much more romantic it must have been in the past when wealthy yalı owners would organize caique trips with musical entertainment of the more classically sedate kind that kept going right through until dawn. On moonlit summer nights boats would be rowed in silence from bay to bay, pausing in front of favored yalıs so that the musicians could serenade the owners. **Sultan Abdülaziz** seems to have been the greatest fan of these excursions, but by the end of the 19th century they had faded into history.

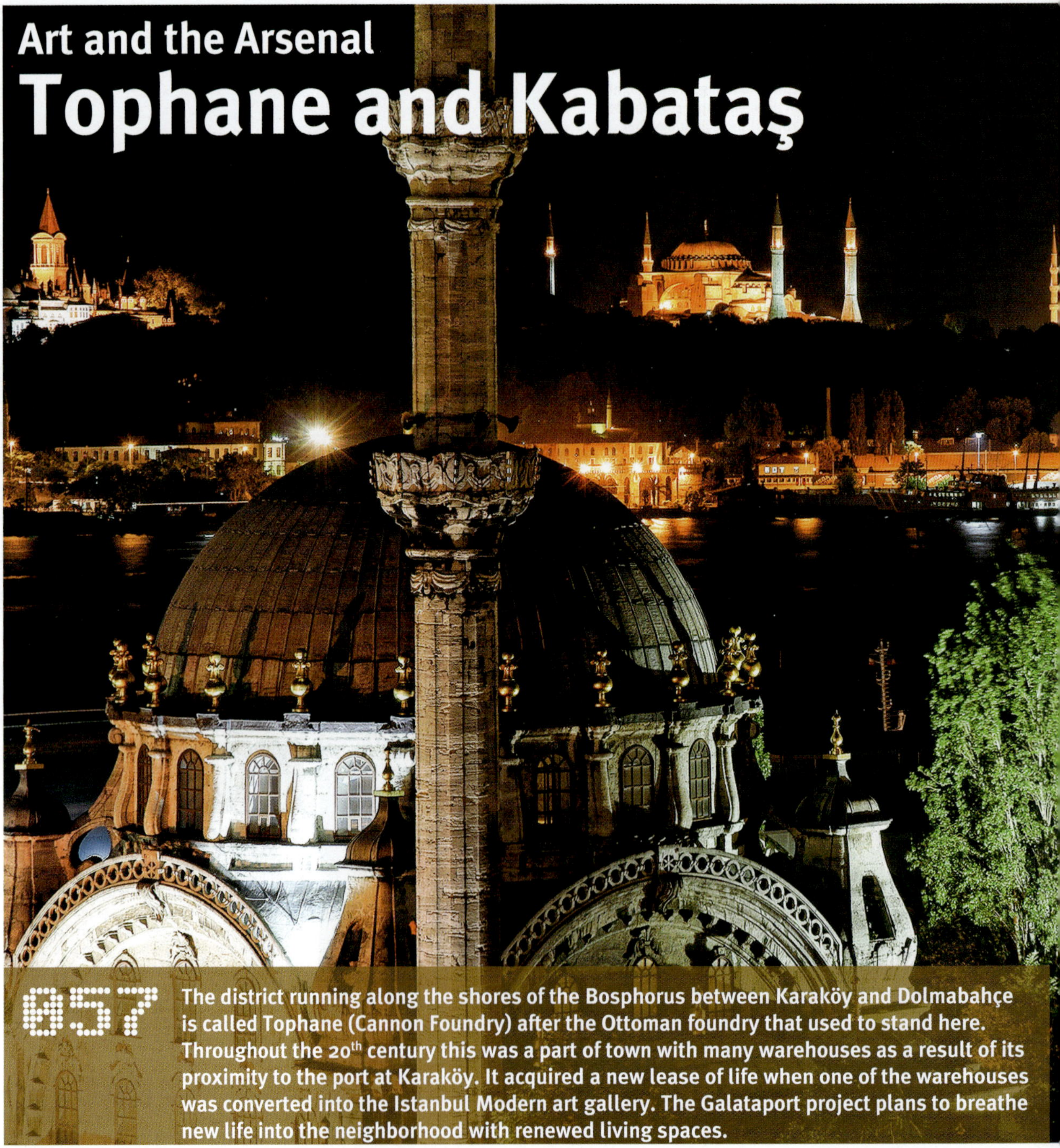

Art and the Arsenal

Tophane and Kabataş

057 The district running along the shores of the Bosphorus between Karaköy and Dolmabahçe is called Tophane (Cannon Foundry) after the Ottoman foundry that used to stand here. Throughout the 20th century this was a part of town with many warehouses as a result of its proximity to the port at Karaköy. It acquired a new lease of life when one of the warehouses was converted into the Istanbul Modern art gallery. The Galataport project plans to breathe new life into the neighborhood with renewed living spaces.

Istanbul Modern

In 2005 the Istanbul Modern housed in an old warehouse, opened as the first permanent showcase for Turkish art of the 19th and 20th centuries. In addition to its rich collection, Istanbul Modern is also occasionally home to exhibitions of art and photography.
The museum, related to all fields of art with its rich library and movie theatre, also has a restaurant and a gift shop. The museum is also attractive for families with children. There are art workshops in another department where children can spend time with art.
Modern Turkish art is not perhaps as well known as it deserves to be and the Istanbul Modern has gone a long way to rectify the problem. It shows both paintings belonging to its own permanent collection and other pieces that are on loan, which means that you can visit again and again and still find something to surprise and delight you. Particular treats to home in on include "Village Women" by **Nuri İyem** (1915-2005), "Woman Knitting" by **Nurullah Berk** (1906-92) and "Child Fishing" by **Orhan Peker** (1927-78). It's also worth looking out for works by **Burhan Doğançay** (1929 -2013) and **Fahrelnissa Zeid** (1901-1991), the wife of a Jordanian prince whose paintings hang in some of the world's most important galleries.
Other names to conjure with include those of **Fausto Zonaro** (1854-1929) who was court painter to the sultans from 1891 to 1910, **Abdülmecid Efendi** (1868-1944), the son of Sultan Abdülaziz, who ended his life in exile in Paris (see p. 011). **Şeker Ahmet Paşa** (1841-1907), **Osman Hamdi Bey** (1842-1910) and **Süleyman Seyyid** (1842-1913) were three men who studied abroad and went on to become professional artists, while **İbrahim Çallı** (1882-1960) and **Hamit Görele** (1894-1980) were leading lights in more modern times whose work tends to reflect trends in art on the international stage.

The museum continued its activities in its first home, warehouse number 4, in Tophane for 14 years. It moved to its building, which was renovated within the scope of the **Galataport Project** and designed by **Renzo Piano**, in 2023.

Free guided tours, held only in Turkish, are organized every Thursday and Sunday at 5.00 p.m. Private tours, customized for individuals or group tours can be organized every day except on Mondays, for a fee per person. Tours are 45 minutes in duration and are available in Turkish and English. Guided tours must be reserved in advance. Audio guides, geared towards adults, are available in English and Turkish, with a duration of approximately 45 minutes.

@istanbulmodern
www.istanbulmodern.org
Tel: 0212 334 73 00
closed Mondays

Village Woman, by Nuri İyem

Contemporary artists

Those keen to know where Turkish art has been going over the last 30 years should look out for works by Kutluğ Ataman, Gülsün Karamustafa, Hale Tenger, Sarkis, Taner Ceylan, Hussein Çalayan, Leyla Gediz, Hüsamettin Koçan, Mithat Şen and İpek Duben.

Galataport, the New Meeting Point of the City

Seeing Galataport only as a shopping mall would be unfair. This project that allows the Karaköy Coast to be used as a port while being open to pedestrian traffic, also includes culture and art centers, shops, restaurants and hotels. Extending along the 1.2-kilometer coastline from Karaköy to Tophane, Galataport also contains many historical and important places for Istanbul. Designed like a neighborhood, the project aims to bring the cosmopolitan structure of the region back to life in a modern form. Do not forget to enjoy one of the most beautiful views of the world, including Sarayburnu, the Anatolian side and the entrance of the Bosphorus from the seaside.

Museum Square, the heart of Galataport, is the first museum square in Istanbul, covering an area of 14 thousand square meters. In the square that was organized in unison with the habitat shaped around it, many artifacts that had been lost among the buildings and traffic for years were revealed again. **The Clock Tower**, located in the center of the square, was behind the **Nusretiye Mosque**, inside the warehouse area used as **Istanbul Modern**. While it was being restored with very special techniques, a floor that was never noticed before since it was covered with earth over time was uncovered. The tower associated with the **Tophane Pavilion**, which was built by **Sultan Abdülmecid** in the same place with his monogram on the sea side of the building, was designed by Balyans in 1848-49 as a flag tower and was probably converted into a clock tower during the reign of **Abdülhamid II**. The clock tower, the first of its kind in the city, was left in the middle when the barracks around it were demolished during road widening works in the 1950s. Once again welcoming visitors from the sea with the Museum Square project, the clock tower is witnessing the new experiences of Istanbulites and visitors.

Istanbul Biennal

Since 1987 Istanbul has been hosting a lively modern art jamboree every two years. The Biennal spreads itself out through venues all over town, some of them indoor, some of them out and it has acquired a reputation for spotlighting unexpected locations.

@iksv_istanbul
www.iksv.org/bienal

If you liked this you'll also like: Doğançay Museum (see p.303)
Elgiz Museum of Contemporary Art (see p.363)
Osman Hamdi Bey Museum (see p.599)
SantralIstanbul (see p.257)

Kılıç Ali Paşa Mosque

Immediately opposite the Tophane tram stop is the Kılıç Ali Paşa Mosque which was built by the great Ottoman architect **Sinan** in 1580 for **Vice Admiral Kılıç (The Sword) Ali Paşa.** Ali seems to have been an Italian who was seized by pirates and then joined his captors in their Mediterranean marauding. Later he worked in the Istanbul shipyard, before going on to serve in the navy under **Turgut Reis**, after whom Turgutreis on the Bodrum Peninsula is named. Kılıç Ali then became governor general in Tripoli in Libya and later took part in the disastrous naval engagement at **Lepanto** in 1571 when the Ottoman fleet was defeated off the coast of Greece, an event that marked a turning point in the Empire's fortunes. Kılıç Ali was the only commander who managed to retreat without his ships being wiped out, whereupon he was promoted to the post of Vice Admiral. He then returned to an earlier occupation and developed the **Royal Shipyard** so that it would be able to turn out larger vessels.

The Kılıç Ali Paşa Mosque was supposedly built on **reclaimed land** after bureaucrats had objected to giving Ali land to build on, saying that "All the seas are yours. What business do you have on the land?" Sinan was in his nineties when he designed it and he seems to have taken **Ayasofya** as his model. Today the entire külliye (complex) still survives, complete with a **tomb, hamam** and **madrasah**. Restoration of the entire mosque complex finished in 2010.

---

www.kilicalipasahamami.com
Tel: 0212 393 80 10

Kılıç Ali Paşa

Interior of Kılıç Ali Paşa Mosque

Tophane Fountain opposite Kılıç Ali Paşa Mosque

Tophane Fountain

Facing Kılıç Ali Paşa Mosque across Tophane İskele Caddesi is a magnificent free-standing baroque fountain with overhanging roof that was built for **Sultan Mahmud I** in 1732. It is decorated all over with naturalistic images of fruit and flowers and has **mukarnas** (stalactites) carved in the corners, a characteristic of early 18th-century fountains. The fountain was badly damaged by fire in the mid-18th century and restored in 1957. Recently it was restored and regilded, making it once again a distinctive feature of the area. Hard though it is to believe it now, the surrounding area once accommodated the city's thriving **fruit** and **vegetable market**. Before that it was a **military parade ground**.

Tophane Fountain in old engraving

The Arsenal (Tophane)

The original arsenal at Tophane was apparently built in the 15th century for **Sultan Mehmed II** and expanded by **Bayezid II**. It was then replaced with a new arsenal by **Süleyman the Magnificent** who needed to stockpile ammunition for his wars against the Holy Roman Emperor. In turn that building was replaced in 1803 by **Selim III** and it is this multi-domed structure that you see today standing on the inland side of the road across from the Tophane tram stop and forming part of the modern **Mimar Sinan University**; look up towards the top corners of the building to see two tiny **carved cannons** that serve as a reminder of its history.

The small adjoining building is sometimes used for **temporary art exhibitions**. Beyond it, a string of ruins heading up towards Cihangir were part of a **barracks** attached to the foundry.

Tomtom Gardens' courtyard

Tomtom Neighborhood

These days a momentous transformation is taking place in Tomtom Neighborhood. Once the richest and most splendid neighborhood, it is now reviving its past glory. The buildings are being restored and brand new designer boutiques, stores, art galleries and cafes are being opened... The Tomtom Neighborhood holds a very special place in Beyoğlu's history. Adjacent to **Çukurcuma** between Karaköy and Galatasaray, it is a unique oasis surrounded by consulates, schools, palaces and large gardens. It rapidly evolved into a design neighborhood similar to Soho in England, Meatpacking in New York and Marais in Paris. Once the **Galataport project** (see p. 378) is finalized, the pedestrian and tourist traffic in Boğazkesen, the connecting axis street between Karaköy and the Istiklal Street, is likely to increase.

The legal cases of French citizens under the protection of the French embassy were held in the yellow-colored French or **Capitulation Court** located at the end of **Tomtom Kaptan Street**. Next to the court is the **Venetian Palace**. The French Palace, with a deep-rooted history, is located just across the court. The architect of the **French Palace**, which assumed its present condition after the great fire of Pera, is the Parisian architect **Pierre Lauracisque.** The palace building with its plain façade is currently used as the residence of the consul general. It has an air of a separate city in the heart of Beyoğlu with its church, school and institute. The residence of the old Franciscan nuns, dating back to the 1850s and the adjacent buildings were harmonized with the European palaces on the same street after a series of restoration works started in the 2000s.

There are numerous addresses like galleries, craft workshops, design stores and restaurants awaiting discovery along **Boğazkesen Street** in the Tomtom Neighborhood. The street is an essential destination for local and foreign tourists who are in love with photography. **The Zanaat Atelye**, located in the historical **French Orphanage** dating back to 1850, is a papier-mâché museum and a cafe. You can admire the original plaster models of many historical spaces and enjoy your time in its garden.

Named after its green gardens, there is an ongoing project at the heart of the Tomtom Neighborhood: **Tomtom Gardens**. Last year it was awarded the "Best Residence" as part of the Sign of the City Awards. It is a spectacular restoration project with seventeen buildings around three different courtyards. The first courtyard of Tomtom Gardens is located on the Tomtom Kaptan Street. The project was carried out with an Italian landscape architect and has achieved an extraordinary result. Art and design spaces are also in operation here. The second phase of Tomtom Gardens, located on Boğazkesen Street, neighbors the French Orphanage and also sports a splendid courtyard. The third phase is located just across the **Tomtom Kaptan Mosque** on Boğazkesen. Architect Han Tümertekin will design a very beautiful building and a modern courtyard on an indoor parking space. Some historical buildings such as the **Yugoslavian School, Austria-Hungary School, the Baltazzi Apartment** and **Hotel Italia Dakar** will be restored. In addition to commercial units, more than a hundred penthouses and flats will be built around the different courtyards.

Tomtom Gardens is located right across from Italian High School

Çukurcuma

Just across the Tomtom Kaptan Street, Çukurcuma is the place where you can find the best antique shops in Istanbul. The best way to discover this place is to get lost among its narrow streets... It's possible to be surprised by the distant and serene atmosphere of this location despite it being just adjacent to the hubbub of İstiklal Street.

Tomtom Kaptan Mosque with tower of St. Anthony's Cathedral behind it.

Tomtom Kaptan Mosque

You may overlook this small mosque, located on Bogazkesen Avenue, between renovated buildings and new shops. It was built by a sailor named Tomtom Mehmet Kaptan in 1592.

Tophane Pavilion (Tophane Kasrı)

The cute little green pavilion standing a little way along the road from the fountain was built as a base from which **Sultan Abdülmecid** (1861-76) could inspect his troops. It was designed by **William James Smith** who was also responsible for the British Embassy (now the consulate) in 1852. The sultans received many foreign statesmen here and the pavilion was also the setting for several international conferences and meetings. After the 1923 Treaty of Lausanne ended the Turkish War of Independence, the **Bosphorus Commission** met here to agree arrangements for using the strait.

Nusretiye Mosque and Arsenal in old picture

Nusretiye (Victory) Mosque

Sultan Mahmud II commissioned the Turkish-Armenian architect **Krikor Balyan** (1764-1831) to build this fine mosque in a style midway between the baroque and imperial styles. It was given its name to celebrate his **victory** over the troublesome **Janissaries** in 1826. Building work took place between 1822 and 1826 and almost immediately the overly thin minarets fell down and had to be rebuilt. For the Nusretiye mosque Balyan abandoned the traditional courtyard and instead built what looks almost like an apartment over the entrance, a feature which was reproduced in the **Dolmabahçe Mosque**, just down the road. Inside the hünkar mahfili (**sultan's pew**) is shielded by a screen so fine that it looks almost like lace.

Hünkar mahfil (Sultan's lodge)

The grand if grubby **sebil** beside the mosque originally stood across the road but had to be moved when the road was widened. It bears a fine calligraphic inscription by **Yesarizade İzzet Efendi**.

Old Clock Tower

Behind Nusretiye Mosque make sure to look out for the little clock tower standing at the back of the grounds. Dating back to 1848-49 and probably a work of Bali Balyan, it was the city's first such clock tower and used to stand beside Tophane Pavilion until it was moved during road-widening in the 1950s.

Molla Çelebi Mosque (Fındıklı Mosque) and around

Continuing north along the coast road towards Dolmabahçe Palace, you will pass the **Meclis-i Mebusan Building**, a pair of Balyan-designed buildings, once called the twin palaces, that were built in 1856 for **Münire Sultan** and **Cemile Sultan**, the daughters of Sultan Abdülmecid. After the declaration of the Republic they hosted sessions of the **Grand National Assembly**. Today they house the **Mimar Sinan University**. Next you will come to the **Molla Çelebi Mosque**, another work of **Sinan** which dates back to 1561-62 and was built for poet and **Chief Justice Mehmed Efendi**.

Molla Çelebi Mosque

One of the statues of Fındıklı Park

Koca Yusuf Paşa sebil serving as a café

Hekimoğlu Ali Paşa Fountain

Detail from an old door

Hekimoğlu Ali Paşa Fountain

Right beside the Molla Çelebi Mosque is the free-standing **Hekimoğlu Ali Paşa fountain** which dates back to 1732 and is a plainer version of the one at Tophane. It was restored in 2008. Across the road is a pretty little **sebil** which was paid for in 1787 by **Koca Yusuf Paşa**, Grand Vizier to Sultan Abdülhamid I. Continuing towards Dolmabahçe Palace there's a second **sebil** at the junction of Meclis-i Mebusan Caddesi, the coast road, with Dolmabahçe Gazhanesi Sokak, which climbs uphill towards Taksim. This sebil was paid for in 1741 by **Hacı Mehmed Emin Ağa**, whose tomb is inside it. Members of his family are buried in the small adjoining graveyard.

In Ottoman times sebils were **staffed fountains** where water and sherbet drinks would be dispensed to passers-by in contrast with **çeşmes** which were self-service fountains. Look out for snack shops and drink stands around town with names such as Café Sebil or Sebil Büfe and you'll be looking at a slice of water distribution history.

Hadika Stone

Kabataş Pier

Despite objections, the old Kabataş pier was demolished as part of arrangements made for the Kabataş Square and the transfer center project. It will integrate the pier with the four existing large piers and the Kabataş-Funicular line, Bağcılar-Kabataş Tram line and new Mahmutbey-Kabataş metro line. By building the land-road underground, the plan is to integrate different means of transportation within the square.

Sultan Abdülmecid ordered a harbor to be built here since the pier suffered from the southwestern storms. That is why this monument facing the sea on one side and the harbor on the other has the benefits of the harbor written on one side and prayers for the sultan on the other.

Did Cervantes work in Istanbul?

Could Cervantes, the world-famous author of **Don Quixote** have had a hand in the building of the Kılıç Ali Paşa Mosque? Cervantes had been wounded during the battle of **Lepanto** in 1571 and recent research in the mosque archives suggests that he was taken captive by the Ottomans and that his handiwork can be detected in the building. More mainstream opinion, however, has Cervantes returning to military life after a lengthy sojourn in hospital.

Picasso sketch of Don Quixote and Sancho Pancho

Baroque Beauty of the Bosphorus

Dolmabahçe Palace

058

By the mid-19th century the Ottoman sultans were obsessed with all things Western and determined to move out of Topkapı Palace and into the Dolmabahçe Palace on the southern shore of the Bosphorus. The palace consists of one large main building divided into two separate wings along with a couple of smaller pavilions and extensive gardens. It's a riot of lavish baroque ornamentation, which will come as a shock to those who like their décor minimalist.

Straight ahead from the garden is the entrance to the Administrative Section.

Unlike Topkapı Palace, which was, like the Byzantine Great Palace, a collection of relatively small buildings, the Dolmabahçe Palace conforms more closely to Western ideas of a palace as a single large structure although Islamic tradition still decreed that there must be two separate sections, one to show off the public face of the state, the other for the private life of the sultan. The fact that **Sultan Abdülmecid** chose to have it built on the far side of the Bosphorus also indicated a mental break with the past; Topkapı harked back to Byzantine times not just in its layout but also in its location; Dolmabahçe in contrast was built on the side of the Bosphorus more usually associated with Westerners.

In Turkish Dolmabahçe means "**filled-in garden**", a reference to the fact that the land on which the palace was built had been reclaimed from the Bosphorus (the area now covers 110,000 square meters). Until 1614 there had been a port here, but under first **Sultan Ahmed I** and then **Sultan Osman II** it was slowly filled in to provide space for a park and cirit ground as well as for the wooden Beşiktaş Palace, a complex of buildings like Topkapı Palace that increasingly came to serve as the sultans' summer residence.

The present Dolmabahçe Palace was designed by **Garabed** and **Nigoğos Balyan** who came from a celebrated family of Ottoman Armenian architects. Work started in 1843. When it was finally completed in 1856 the main building contained **285 rooms, 43 halls and 6 bathrooms**. The palace was even equipped with its own 600-meter-long quay since most visitors would have arrived by water. The entire complex stretches all the way from Kabataş in the south to Beşiktaş in the north although not all of it is open to the public.

The **last six sultans** lived for varying amounts of time in the Dolmabahçe although Sultan Abdülhamid quickly retreated to the greater security of the Yıldız Palace (see p. 402). The last of the imperial family to live here was **Abdülmecid Efendi**, the caliph-artist who was forced into exile in 1924.

The palace's **interior decoration** was the work of a Frenchman called Charles Séchan who also designed the Paris Opera. It's all very over-the-top, with Baccarat and Bohemian crystal, Sevres and Yıldız porcelain and Hereke carpets the order of the day. Some of it could certainly do with a good dust and the rushed guided tours make it hard to take in the excess of detail.

@dolmabahcesarayi
www.dolmabahce.gov.tr
Tel: 0212 236 90 00/1359
closed Mondays and Thursdays
guided tours in English and Turkish

Time management

Allow an hour for the tour of the Selamlık and 25 minutes for the Harem. Unfortunately, you may have to wait in line to buy a ticket before going into the grounds and there may be further waits for guided tours in the appropriate languages. If your time is limited stick with visiting the Selamlık.

"...the Corinthian ice-cream opulence of the Dolmabahçe Palace."

A Traveller's Companion to Istanbul **by Laurence Kelly, 1987**

Fatih's ships

It was from the site where the Dolmabahçe Palace now stands that the warships used by Mehmed the Conqueror for the 1453 conquest of the city were dragged up to Pera and then down again to Kasımpaşa, thus circumventing the chain that blocked the entrance to the Golden Horn.

Dolmabahçe Mosque

Restored in 2009, the mosque near the entrance to the palace was built in baroque style by **Garabed Balyan** for Sultan Abdülmecid's mother **Bezmialem Valide Sultan** and completed after her death in 1855. It's adorned with two minarets, but its most conspicuous features are the **huge arches** studded with windows that provide supports for the dome on four sides. Those same large windows allow light to flood into the interior from the Bosphorus, making it especially delightful. The original courtyard and sebil were sadly sacrificed to road-widening. From 1956-60 the mosque was used to house the Naval Museum, returning to religious duty in 1967 when the museum moved down the road to Beşiktaş (see p. 396).

The palace exterior

Baroque architecture is not to everybody's taste, but the white sandstone exterior of the Dolmabahçe is certainly impressive, especially when viewed from the water. The monumental scale of the building combined with the lavish decoration of the exterior marks it out from the Topkapı Palace; the harem of the Topkapı, for example, is richly decorated on the inside but extremely plain on the outside.

Administrative Section

The clock tower

The path to the palace runs past a 27-meter-high, four-storey clock tower erected by Sarkis Balyan for Sultan Abdülhamid II in the 1890s. Its four faces are still inscribed with **Arabic numerals** and the ground floor is adorned with two thermometers and two barometers.

Clock Tower

The gates

Modern visitors enter the complex via the **Administrative Gate** that was used by politicians and civil servants. In the past the most important visitors would have arrived at the **Shore Gate**, stepping onto the quay from their caiques. Traffic on busy Dolmabahçe Caddesi whisks past the imposing **Ceremonial Gate** that was used by the sultan and grand vizier when they processed to the nearby mosque for Friday prayers.

Ceremonial Gate

Saltanat (Ceremonial) Gate in an old postcard

The Selamlık (Administrative Section)

Visitors enter the palace up stairs from the garden into the huge **Reception Hall** where guests would wait to be received. The 60-branch chandelier, the fine Hereke carpet and the fireplaces with shimmering glass panels above them were all designed to create a grand first impression. On the seaward side of the hall are the rooms that were occupied by the most important officials; members of parliament had offices on the inland side; the grand vizier had a room just beside the entrance on the seaward side. The Reception Hall was the scene of meetings convened by **Atatürk** in 1928 to devise a **new Latin alphabet** to replace the Arabic one that had been used to write Ottoman Turkish.

As is the case throughout the palace the Reception Hall is completely symmetrical

The Surre Procession by Stefano Ussi, 1873

On the landward side of the entrance was a room to store the gifts that the sultan as caliph sent to Mecca every year at the time of **the Haj (Pilgrimage)**. The sultans were never able to perform the Haj themselves because of the length of time it would have taken, but every year a camel train weighed down with gold would set out to make the journey in their stead; **"The Surre Procession"**, a huge painting by the Italian artist **Stefano Ussi** (1822-1901) hanging in one of the clerk's rooms beyond the reception hall, vividly portrays it pressing on from Cairo. The painting is the largest canvas in the palace's extensive art collection.

The tour moves past rooms occupied by the secretariat into the **Entrance Hall** that was used by the sultan when on short excursions; doors opened into the back garden so that he could leave by carriage and into the front garden so that he could leave by boat.

Crystal Staircase

Ambassadors Hall (Süfera Salonu)

Ambassadors Hall

Privy Chamber (Zülvecheyn Salonu)

Crystal Staircase

One of the most spectacular features of the Selamlık is the **Crystal Staircase,** a double flight of stairs lined with crystal banisters that winds up to the second floor, passing beneath an enormous Baccarat chandelier. It leads to the vast and elaborately decorated **Süfera (Ambassadors) Hall,** which was used to host formal receptions and where gifts to the sultans, including a pair of bearskins given by **Tsar Nicolas II**, are displayed. Small rooms opening off from the front of it were used as waiting rooms and are decorated with paintings of sea scenes by the Crimean artist **Ivan Konstantinovic Ayvazovski** (1817-1900), who visited Istanbul eight times and was a particular favorite of **Sultan Abdülaziz**. In one of them you can also see a table inlaid with images of Napoleon and 12 famous European women including his wife, the Empress Josephine, Queen Marie Antoinette and the murderer Charlotte Corday.

Fausto Zonaro

Privy Chamber

A corridor from the Süfera passes a guest room on one wall of which can be seen Fausto Zonaro's wonderful **painting** of Kaiser Wilhelm II arriving at the palace in 1898. It then opens into a glorious **Reception Room,** better known as the Red Room because of its dramatic red and gold decoration. Here ambassadors would wait again before finally being admitted to the sultan's presence. The corridor then dodges past a pair of rooms set aside for the crown princes before re-crossing the Süfera to reach the huge **Privy Chamber,** with its elaborate parquet floor. This was used for **religious ceremonies** especially during Ramadan and for **wedding parties and banquets,** with an orchestra providing music from the stairwell; its alternative Arabic name "Zülvecheyn", meaning "double-fronted", refers to its location midway between the selamlık and harem quarters. A door leads into **Caliph Abdülmecid's Library,** which overlooks the Bosphorus; as well as many leather-bound books, it contains a self-portrait of the caliph who was an artist of considerable ability (see p. 511). Also opening off it is a **Music Room,** equipped with a grand piano and a pair of cellos.

Sultan's Hamam

Sultan's Reception Room

The tour skips through a small sitting room containing another Fausto Zonaro painting, "Women Getting into a Rowing Boat", before reaching the exquisite **Hamam,** the sultan's private Turkish bath which came complete with marble floors and walls of translucent, honey-colored Egyptian alabaster. The last room in the Selamlık is the **Memorial Room,** which contains paintings and photographs of four sultans. A corridor then winds round the Muayede Hall (see below) to the Harem. It's lined with **paintings** by, among others, **Şeker Ahmed Paşa, Osman Hamdi Bey** and **Fausto Zonaro**, including the latter's colorful and much reproduced set of four images portraying **Sultan Mehmed II** and the conquest of Istanbul in 1453; it's also pierced with windows that allowed the women of the harem to observe the goings-on down below without being seen themselves. The corridor ends at the **Sultan's Reception Room** in the Harem, a lovely room also called the Crimson or Domed Room after the most conspicuous features of its décor, which was where the sultan would receive his wives and children.

Osman Hamdi Bey

Caliph Abdülmecid's Library

Atatürk's office

Ceiling above Caliph's Staircase

Blue Hall

Another short corridor furnished with an organ concealed in a wooden case and a portrait of his wife by **Abdülmecid Efendi** leads to the grand **Blue Hall** with its trompe d'oeil columns where the palace women would assemble to celebrate religious holidays. It was also used by the queen mother or the principal wife to entertain **visiting head of states** and as the years passed, some important male guests were also greeted here. In 1937 an elevator was inserted into the room so that it could be used more comfortably by **Atatürk** whose study, just off it, is almost equally elaborate.

Atatürk's deathbed

The tour then passes through one of the most important rooms in the palace, which is the one in which **Atatürk** died in 1938. His bed is draped with the Turkish flag in perpetuity, just as all the clocks in the palace are permanently stopped at the time of his death. Across the corridor is Atatürk's bathroom fitted out with a private pharmacy of medicaments.

Next you will enter the **Pink Hall**, once the living room of the queen mother where she received special guests and celebrated important occasions. A telescope is poised to take in a view of the Bosphorus which would have been so much less built-up in those days. The tour then passes a couple of pretty guestrooms and another hamam before returning through the Blue Room to glance at Sultan Abdülaziz's bedroom. The beautiful **Caliph's Staircase,** illuminated by another wonderful chandelier, then leads back down to the ground floor and the entrance hall to the harem that was guarded by the head maid in her room right beside it. The importance of her position is suggested by the fact that her room is not much less elaborately furnished than the guestrooms.

The tour then makes a circuit of what was once a dining room for some of the sultan's servants but now houses selected items of **glass, porcelain** and **silver** from the palace's collection. Perhaps the single most amusing item on display is a set of decanters that could be concealed inside what looked like a set of leather-bound books.

Atatürk's deathbed

Palace paintings

The Dolmabahçe Palace contains a collection of around 500 paintings including masterpieces by the court artist Fausto Zonaro, the maritime specialist Ivan Konstantinovic Ayvazovski, the orientalist-archeologist Osman Hamdi Bey and the caliph-artist Abdülmecid Efendi. It's a shame that the rushed guided tours make it hard to appreciate any of them.

10 November 1938

At 9.05 am on 10 November 1938 **Atatürk** died in the Dolmabahçe Palace. His body lay in state in the Ceremonial Hall for three days and all the palace clocks have shown the time of his death ever since.

Ceremonial Hall

Ceremonial Hall (Muayede Salonu) with sultan's throne at the back

Finally the tour winds up in the most astonishing room of the entire palace, the breath-taking **Ceremonial (Muayede) Hall,** which stands right in the center dividing the selamlık from the harem. Thirty-six meters high, it's topped with a **dome** that is invisible from the exterior and is supported by 56 columns; it is apparently the largest throne room in the world. The room is so large that it required a silk Hereke carpet covering 124 square meters and a Bohemian crystal chandelier weighing 4.5 tons and requiring 664 lightbulbs; a gift from **Queen Victoria** of Great Britain. It took three months just to install it. A form of central heating could be piped up the columns but required a full three days to take effect.

The hall was used for all the most important imperial ceremonies including those associated with the holiday following Ramadan. At that time the sultan's glittering **250-kilogram throne** would be brought from the treasury at Topkapı and set up against the west wall. The ambassadors would line up in the gallery facing him, with other guests to the left and the orchestra to the right; the space above the sultan would be left empty since no one but Allah could be positioned above him.

Several important events took place in this room. In 1876 the coronation of **Sultan Murad V** was staged here instead of at Topkapı. It was also here that the **first meeting of the Ottoman parliament** was held in 1877, an event that contained within it the seeds of the end of the Empire. Later, it was here that **Atatürk** gave his first speech as president of the Republic of Turkey; a copy is on display in the room.

The Harem

The Ceremonial Hall marks the dividing point between the public part of the palace and the private part where the sultan's family lived. Today you must enter the harem from a separate entrance to the rear.

No matter how Westernized the palace looked on the outside the way of life on the inside continued much as it had at Topkapı, with the **Valide Sultan (Queen Mother)** at the apex of a hierarchy of women who were still closely guarded by **black and white eunuchs.**

The tour of the harem starts in the **Entrance Hall** whose ceiling cornices are painted with images of Istanbul scenery. From here you ascend to the first floor and bypass several rooms before arriving at the **Hall of the Royal Women** that was used to celebrate religious occasions and also the more private achievements of the sultan's children; the decoration of the room, while still elaborate, is toned down a little in comparison with the Selamlık. The same is true of the **Hamam of the Royal Women** which in no way compares with the beauty of the sultan's alabaster bath in the Selamlık.

Young Woman Combing Hair by Osman Hamdi Be

The tour continues through a rather more sparsely furnished **Hall of the Royal Women** and continues to the **Japanese Salon** that was used by the queen mother and features fabrics decorated with sunflowers alongside more overtly Japanese motifs. Next to it is the **Bedroom of the Sultan's Mother** that was furnished for Sultan Abdülaziz's mother **Pernevniyal Valide Sultan** with a French-style cream lacquer bedroom suite. There follow a series of guestrooms fitted out in a variety of styles, some with throne-like beds, others with iron bedframes. The tour then passes back through the Hall of the Royal Women to visit a suite of rooms typical of those that were assigned to the senior women of the harem; it comes with a little lobby equipped with a piano and a sitting area off which open a small bedroom, sitting room and bathroom. Here can be seen **Osman Hamdi Bey**'s lovely painting **"A Young Lady Having her Hair Combed".** You then bypass a room decorated as it might have been if the head maid had been occupying it, before arriving at a second similar suite of rooms.

The tour then returns through the main Hall of the Royal Women, which gives you a chance to peek into the **Circumcision Room** where the royal princes would have rested and received well-wishers after their sünnet (circumcision). You will also get a chance to peek in on a child's **playroom** with a photo of Sultan Abdülmecid's grandson İbrahim Tevfik Efendi on the wall before returning to the Entrance Hall to leave.

Main room of Glass Pavilion

Glass Pavilion (Camlı Köşk)

Attached to the outside wall of the palace and so visible from Dolmabahçe Caddesi is the Glass Pavilion, which many may think the most delightful room in the whole palace. Luxuriantly decorated in red, gold and blue, it's furnished with a piano with crystal legs and features a ceiling cornice painted with images of particularly mild-looking wild animals; four gilded eagles fill in the corners. A conservatory-like room focused on a crystal fountain is attached to it at an L-shaped angle and lets light flood in from one side. The suite served as a private rest room for the sultan apart from the hustle of the main palace building.

Conservatory of Glass Pavilion

Dolmabahçe Clock Museum

This collection housed in a garden museum mainly consists of 19th-century French and British clocks that were used in the palace. While Western clockmaking was the preserve of philosophers and mathematicians, Ottoman timepieces were crafted by mosque officials, most of them senior members of the Mevlevi sect, whose chief duty was to determine the time for the call to prayer. The museum includes examples of clocks crafted by such masters as Eflaki Dede, Mehmet Şükrü and Mehmet Muhsin.

The gardens

The palace gardens provided the gardeners with a wonderful opportunity to show off and they're exceptionally beautiful in the summer when a fountain adorned with stone swans plays as a centerpiece amid lawns on which stone lionesses frolic with their cubs. All sorts of exotic plants can be seen here. The grounds also contain an **aviary** that has recently been brought back to life, with peacocks, chickens, guinea fowl and ornamental pheasants ambling around amid the shady cypress and plane trees.

Imperial gardens

Palace of the Crown Princes (Istanbul Painting Museum)

Glance through the gates at the Beşiktaş end of the palace gardens to see the façade of this completely separate building that now houses the **Museum of Painting.** It was designed by the Balyans in a mixture of Empire, Baroque and Rococo styles in 1856. In 1937 Atatürk had the **Istanbul Fine Arts Academy** (now the Mimar Sinan University) founded here. It was the first such establishment in Turkey. It contains a notable collection of 19th-century Turkish paintings, including three by Osman Hamdi Bey (1842-1910) and was a favored haunt of the young Orhan Pamuk, as described in his "Istanbul: Memories of a City".

www.millisaraylar.gov.tr
Tel: 0212 261 42 98
closed Mondays

Masked Ball by Ali Avni Çelebi (1904-93)

Barbarossa's Backyard

Beşiktaş

059

Frequently overlooked by visitors, Beşiktaş is a frantically busy part of town, with major interchanges for buses and ferries and a new Metro line on its way. The most obvious attraction is the Naval Museum right on the waterfront beside Barbaros Square, but it's also worth venturing into the back streets to find the pretty little Ihlamur Pavilion and the lovely Art Nouveau Şeyh Zafir complex. The W Hotel in Akaretler is housed inside what were once the living quarters for staff at the Dolmabahçe Palace.

In Turkish Beşiktaş means "**cradle stone**", a name which commem-orates a claim that a piece of Jesus' cradle was brought here from Bethlehem by early Christians and stored in a local church. It's possible that it was then taken to Hagia Sophia, only to be stolen by the Fourth Crusaders in 1204.

Like Kadıköy, Beşiktaş is a busy shopping area, its streets crammed with ordinary people shopping on ordinary budgets in contrast with more upscale Nişantaşı, just a short distance away. At the heart of a tight-knit network of shopping streets to the west of busy Barbaros Bulvarı an undercover **fish market** is ringed with neighborhood fish restaurants. Two **eagle monuments** nearby commemorate the 100th anniversary of the much-loved local football team Beşiktaş ("the Black Eagles") whose stadium is in nearby Dolmabahçe.

The Black Eagles in numbers

- Founded in 1910, Beşiktaş was Turkey's first sports club. In the 1936 Olympics in Berlin it was also the first club to showcase a female athlete.
- 15 times League champion
- 9 times winner of the Turkey Cup
- Beşiktaş was also the first team to score 10 goals in an official game, against Adana Demirspor in the 1989-90 season.

Cihanüma Virgin Mary Greek Orthodox Church

Köyiçi Greek Orthodox Church of the Virgin Mary

Tulumbacıs (early fire-fighters)

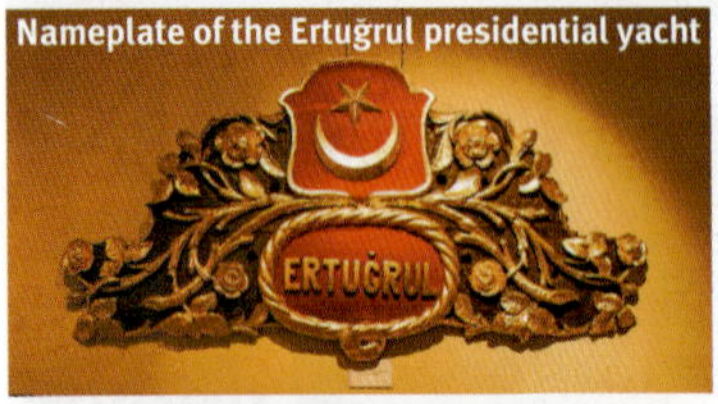

Nameplate of the Ertuğrul presidential yacht

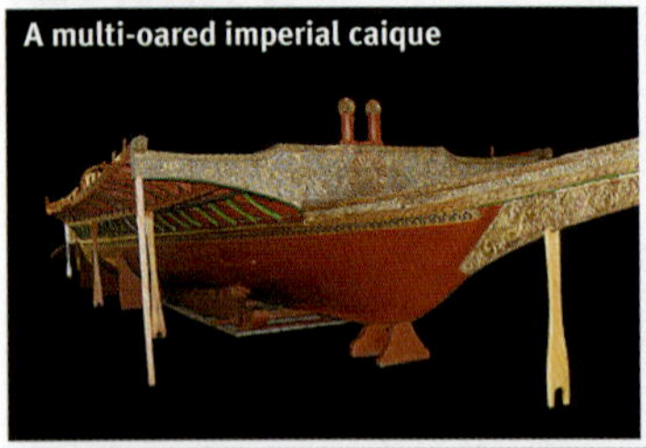

A multi-oared imperial caique

Naval Museum

An important port of call for crusty sea-dogs everywhere, the **Naval Museum** *(closed Mondays)* honors the important role the navy played during the heyday of the Ottoman Empire. Many of the exhibits are of fairly specialist interest, although most people will love the room full of **caiques**, the graceful, gondola-like boats that were used to move people and their belongings around the Bosphorus. Most came equipped with 13 pairs of oars, although the number of oars increased or decreased with the importance of the passengers. The finest caiques were the ones reserved for the imperial family and used to convey the sultan to Friday prayers. These imperial caiques have small enclosed kiosks at the stern; those intended for the sultan bear his coat of arms and decorative weaponry, while those intended for the women of the harem are decorated with fruit and flowers. Many also have an eagle carved like a ship's figurehead at the bow end. The oldest and biggest imperial caique in the collection dates back to the 17th century; it required 24 pairs of oars to convey **Sultan Mehmed IV** about town. Most of the other caiques date from the 19th century.

The **Atatürk Room** preserves the first Turkish president's cabin from the state yacht Ertuğrul, while across the hall a room shows off a collection of souvenir handkerchiefs. You can also so see is a length of the **chain** used in Byzantine times to close off the Golden Horn from the Bosphorus, along with paintings of the many different types of boat that used to ply the strait. One room shows off the different uniforms worn by the Turkish navy over the centuries, while on the landing a glass-case contains the green ensign removed from the tomb of Barbaros Hayreddin in the square outside.

@denizmuzesi_istanbul
www.denizmuzesi.dzkk.tsk.tr
Tel: 0212 327 43 45, closed Mondays

Barbaros Square

Beside the Naval Museum is Barbaros Square, a rather bleak expanse of concrete much loved by skateboarders that is home to a **statue** of Barbaros Hayreddin (c.1478- 1546), a famous pirate turned admiral known as **Barbarossa (Redbeard)** to the Europeans. It was Barbarossa who established the Ottoman control of the Mediterranean that lasted until the **Battle of Lepanto** in 1571. During the reign of Süleyman the Magnificent, he was not just in charge of the Ottoman navy but also governed Algeria and parts of Greece. He left a book of memoirs which detail his many campaigns and formed the basis for **M. Ertuğrul Düzdağ**'s novel **"The Mediterranean Was Ours"**.

Across the square from the statue stands the two-storey octagonal **tomb** designed by Mimar **Sinan** for Barbarossa in 1541. Before setting off on naval engagements sailors still salute the great admiral by firing shots outside the mausoleum.

Tomb of Barbarossa

Barbaros Hayreddin Paşa

The statue of Barbarossa is inscribed with rousing words by the poet **Yahya Kemal Beyatlı** (1884-1958):

"Whence on the sea's horizon comes that roar? Can it be Barbarossa now returning From Tunisia or Algiers or from the Isles? Two hundred vessels ride upon the waves, Coming from lands the rising Crescent lights: O blessed ships, from what seas are ye come?"

Sinanpaşa Mosque

Across the road from the square stands the brick-and-stone striped **Sinanpaşa Mosque,** another work of Mimar Sinan dating back to 1555-56 and built for the Admiral Sinan Paşa (1506-96), a brother of Grand Vizier Rüstem Paşa (see p. 222).

Beşiktaş ferry terminal

Beşiktaş ferry terminal

The **shore** in front of the square hosted Istanbul's busiest quay in the mid-19th century and it was here that the first stone jetty was built for the Bosphorus ferry company, **Şirket-i Hayriye**, which started business in 1854. When catching the ferry to Üsküdar be sure to take a look at the cute little ticket office designed by architect **Ali Talat Bey** (1869-1922) in 1911 in First National Architectural style. It was one of the first buildings in Istanbul to use reinforced concrete although you are more likely to admire the dinky little tiles on the façade.

Beşiktaş ferry terminal in an old photograph

Akaretler means “rentable property”

Fausto Zonaro

Akaretler

Old appearance of Akaretler

Just inland from the main coast road at Beşiktaş is the district called Akaretler. You can find it by walking along Süleyman Seba Caddesi, pausing to inspect the small **Milli Emlak Dükkanları (National Estate Agency Shops),** an attractive minor work by architect Vedat Tek on the corner. Akaretler is where the Armenian architect **Sarkis Balyan** designed a set of row-houses to accommodate the workers from the Dolmabahçe Palace in the 1870s. They have now been restored to form the **W Hotel** whose presidential suite once served as the studio for the Ottoman court artist **Fausto Zonaro** (1854-1929), some of whose work can be seen in the **Pera Museum** (see p. 334) and **Dolmabahçe Palace** (see p. 390). From 1914-18 Atatürk's mother Zübeyde and sister Makbule lived in a house that now forms part of the hotel complex.

Atatürk House Museum

Şeyh Zafir complex

In Yıldız Caddesi, just off busy Barbaros Bulvarı, the unusual and newly restored Şeyh Zafir complex (also known as Ertuğrul Lodge) includes a tomb, fountain and library. It was designed by **Raimondo d'Aronco** in 1903-04 for the leader of a dervish order who had also been a spiritual advisor to **Sultan Abdülhamid II**. It's a wholly unique and beautiful building – you'll find nothing else like it in Istanbul.

Şeyh Zafir's tomb

Palace Collections Museum

This was opened as a store museum in 2006 in the Matbah-ı Amire (Palace Kitchens) buildings to exhibit the works kept in the Dolmabahçe Palace warehouses. The museum exhibits daily objects used mainly in Dolmabahçe Palace and at the Ottoman palaces during the 19th century.

www.millisaraylar.gov.tr
Tel: 0212 236 90 00, closed Mondays

Abbasağa Park

To the west of Barbaros Bulvarı the hillside Abbasağa Park features a group of statues of men and women who have died in the struggle to bring greater democracy to Turkey: Uğur Mumcu, Ümit Yaşar Doğançay, Abdi İpekçi, Ahmet Taner Kışlalı, Asım Bezirci, Bahriye Üçok, Bedrettin Cömert, Çetin Emeç, Doğan Öz, Muammer Aksoy, Onat Kutlar and Orhan Cavit Tütengil.

Continuing downhill from the park you will come to the small **Abbasağa Mosque,** dating back to the mid-17th century but restored in 1834-35 at which time it acquired an unexpectedly delightful wooden ceiling and galleries. It is completely outstripped in the size stakes by the vast Armenian **Church of Surp Asdvadzadzin (St Mary)** nearby with a redundant school facing it across the road. Designed by **Garabed Balyan** in 1838, it has a **false dome** that is invisible from the outside to comply with the law which at the time forbade the minority populations to indulge in such ostentation.

Abbasağa Mosque

Surp Asdvadzadzin (Virgin Mary) Armenian Church

Ali Paşa Fountain

Pavilion of the Linden Trees (Ihlamur Kasrı)

By the 19th century the shores of the Golden Horn were falling from favor as a place for recreation and Ihlamur, a wooded valley close to the new palaces on the Bosphorus, quickly attracted the attention of **Sultan Abdülmecid.** After the Dolmabahçe Palace was completed in 1856 he commissioned **Nigoğos Balyan**, a member of the family responsible for its design, to build him a lodge where he could stay overnight when traveling between Beşiktaş and the shipyards of the Golden Horn, or between the various Bosphorus palaces.

Today the two pavilions at the northern end of Ihlamurdere Caddesi still stand in a pleasant small garden, now hemmed in by traffic but once part of a much larger park; the landscaping, complete with ornamental pool, reflects the western style favored at the time.

The larger **Ceremonial Pavilion** (Mabeyn Köşkü), with its elaborately carved ceilings, porcelain fireplaces imported from Britain and indigo-colored glass door panels, would have been used by the sultan and his guests. Once reserved for the harem and the rest of their entourage, the **Entourage Pavilion** (Maiyet Köşkü) now serves as a simple café. The elaborately carved façades of both buildings mark a move away from traditional Ottoman design that focused all its decorative efforts on the interiors of buildings. With Beşiktaş' registry office just across the road, the steps of the Ceremonial Pavilion now form a popular backdrop for **wedding photos** especially at weekends.

Across the road from Ihlamur Kasrı the small **World Peace Park (Dünya Barış Parkı)** features a small collection of marble sculptures. Keep walking up through the park to reach the **Süslü Karakol (Decorated Police Station),** erected for Sultan **Abdülaziz** in 1866 to replace an older wooden model.

---

www.millisaraylar.gov.tr
Tel: 0212 258 89 03, closed Mondays

Ceremonial Pavilion (Mabeyn Köşkü)

Ihlamur Pavilion in old postcard

"Ihlamur Köşkü is a miniature version of Dolmabahçe, Göksu and Beylerbeyi Palaces."

***Saray ve Ötesi (The Palace and Beyond)* by Halid Ziya Uşaklıgil. 1942**

Kaymakçı Pando (the Clotted Cream Seller)

A description of Beşiktaş would be incomplete without mentioning Pando the Cream Seller, who was one of the symbols of Beşiktaş Çarşısı (Bazaar) and who passed away soon after he was removed from his shop. I fondly commemorate Pando with his delicious breakfasts with honey and clotted cream as Istanbul loses all her past colours from the old days.

Kaymakçı Pando

Fire Brigade Museum

The museum which was first opened by the Metropolitan Municipality of Istanbul in the fire brigade building in Fatih (see p. 118) in 1932, has been open for visitors in Beşiktaş Kılıç Ali Paşa Cistern since 2013. The museum exhibits fire extinguishers as old as 200 years, water pumps and the costumes of fire brigades.

Tel: 0212 259 91 24
closed Saturdays and Sundays

The Sultan's Last Retreat

Yıldız Park, Chalet and Palace

060

First there was the Eski Saray (Old Palace) on the Third Hill, near Beyazıt Square. Then came Topkapı Sarayı at Sarayburnu (Seraglio Point). Then there was Dolmabahçe Palace on the Bosphorus waterfront. Finally the Ottoman sultans withdrew to the Yıldız (Star) Palace as their empire gradually slipped away from them. Today Yıldız Park acts as one of the lungs of the city, a vast open space adorned with mature trees and shrubs and dotted with historic buildings in an otherwise very built-up area.

The wooded slopes of **Beşiktaş Hill** were left untouched well into Ottoman times when **Sultan Ahmed I** finally had a hasbahçe (royal park) laid out around a small hunting lodge here. Covering 500,000 square meters of hillside, what is now Yıldız Park was originally laid out in the early 19th century for **Mihrişah Sultan**, the mother of **Sultan Selim III**, on land that had originally formed the gardens of the Çırağan Palace (see p. 407). Over the course of the 19th and 20th centuries the park was slowly developed until it consisted of a complex of buildings and gardens of varying dates and styles more reminiscent of the layout of the Topkapı Palace than the Dolmabahçe. Several of the buildings are now open to the public, who can, in any case, come here just to explore the many paths and driveways and to walk around a lake where wild animals were once kept on the islands. Seen from above, the lake turns out to be shaped like **Abdülhamid II**'s **"tuğra (monogram)"**. In the 1980s the park was rescued and restored by the tireless Turkish Touring and Automobile Association although it has now passed back into municipality hands.

The last Ottoman sultan to wield absolute power, **Abdülhamid II** was nonetheless terrified of everyone and retreated to Yıldız Palace from the waterside palaces fearing an attack from the Bosphorus. Even then he was unable to relax. The men who carried out the building work on the palace were not allowed to discuss the plans with each other and the sultan had some of the corridors blocked with stones to slow the progress of intruders. Finally he was deposed in 1909 and **exiled to Salonica** whereupon the palace was plundered of many of its valuables. When Salonica fell to Greece in 1912, the ex-sultan was brought back as a prisoner to **Beylerbeyi Palace** (see p. 517) where he died in 1918. The last days of this unhappy man who was reduced to spying on his subjects through a telescope are vividly evoked in **Brian Unsworth**'s marvelous novel **"The Rage of the Vulture"**.

"The wilderness of ugly kiosks, pavilions, chalets and belvederes which go under the general name of Yıldız has no master thought, no dominant inspiration unless it be – Fear."

The Fall of Abd-ul-Hamid **by Francis McCullagh, 1910**

Sultan Abdülhamid II in front of Yıldız Palace during the Friday Salute

The first visit of Kaiser Wilhelm II to Sultan Abdülhamid II was immortalized in a painting by the Italian-born court artist Fausto Zonaro. It's on display in the Dolmabahçe Palace.

Yıldız Chalet (Yıldız Şale)

Despite its cohesive look, the graceful two-storey Yıldız Chalet was actually built in three stages. The oldest part dates back to the 1870s when it was designed as an **official guesthouse** completely separated from the imperial complex by a high wall. In 1889 it was expanded by **Sarkis Balyan** for the state visit of **Kaiser Wilhelm II**, the first such visit ever hosted by the sultans. The Kaiser visited again in 1898 when a third section, designed by **Raimondo d'Aronco**, was added for his benefit. Amongst the many other visiting dignitaries to be accommodated here were the British prime minister **Sir Winston Churchill**, the French president **Charles de Gaulle** and the Romanian dictator **Nicolae Ceaucescu**.

The most impressive room in the 60-room Chalet is the huge **Ceremonial Hall**, which measures 30 by 15 meters and is home to the **largest Hereke carpet** ever woven; 60 weavers worked on this single piece of floor covering that spreads out over 400 square meters of ground. During the early years of the Republic the hall was turned into a luxurious **casino**. After the Marmara earthquakes of 1999 then US president **Bill Clinton** was guest of honor at a cocktail party held here.

More decoratively interesting is the **Banqueting Hall**, also called the **Mother-of-Pearl Room** (Sedefli Salon), a grand dining room with Moorish ceilings and doors inlaid with mother-of-pearl that were transferred here from **Çırağan Palace.** It's set up today as if anticipating diners at any moment.

Ultimately Abdülhamid ended up living in the Chalet guesthouse rather than in the State Apartments, as did the very last of the Ottoman rulers, **Mehmed VI**, who finally fled to Malta in secret with his family in 1922. He died and was buried in Syria.
The first visit of Kaiser Wilhelm II to Sultan Abdülhamid II was immortalized in a painting by the Italian-born court artist Fausto Zonaro. It's on display in the Dolmabahçe Palace.

---

www.millisaraylar.gov.tr
Tel: 0212 259 32 92
closed Mondays

Malta Pavilion

Park and pavilions

Yıldız Park is a wonderful place to while away a few hours. Many of the trees and shrubs are labeled to help you identify them and you'll see squirrels foraging for nuts and hear green parakeets screeching overhead.

The park contains two beautiful pavilions, both designed by the ubiquitous **Balyan brothers**. The finer of the two, the lovely **Malta Pavilion (Malta Köşkü),** was built during the reign of Sultan Abdülaziz and became a **prison** for Sultan Murad V and his mother after Murad was deposed in 1876. It now houses a restaurant with stunning painted ceilings and great views out over the Bosphorus. Centerpiece of the ground floor is what would once have been a magnificent **indoor pool**, its central fountain adorned with marble fish and swans; two more fountains against the wall have matching swan motifs. Even the ladies' restroom is impressive as it retains the original marble washbasin; you can also examine, although not use, the original marble toilet.

Çadır Pavilion

Despite its demure exterior, the **Çadır Mansion (Çadır Köşkü),** right beside the lake, has rather a grim history since it was here that Abdülhamid had the Grand Vizier Midhat Paşa and his associates tortured in an attempt to prove that they had murdered Sultan Abdülaziz. It now houses a café and restaurant too.

Midhat Paşa

Described as the father of the 1876 constitution, Midhat Paşa (1822-84) was a would-be reformer and two-times grand vizier who found himself battling against the obduracy and/or incompetence of the later Ottoman sultans. Accused of complicity in the possible murder of **Sultan Abdülaziz** in 1876, he was tortured in the **Çadır Köşk**; only foreign intervention saved his life. There's a bust of Midhat Paşa in front of the old TC Ziraat Bankası building in **Cağaloğlu** (see p. 060).

Yıldız Palace buildings

State Apart (Büyük Mab

The heart of the last imperial complex, the **State Apartments (Büyük Mabeyn)** were completely rebuilt in 1866 by **Sarkis** and **Agop Balyan** but are not currently open to the public.
It was allocated to the Presidency in recent years. The German Prime Minister **Angela Merkel** was one of its most famous visitors.
Just to the east of the state apartments are two small museums. The **City Museum** (**Şehir Müzesi**) houses a collection of **Yıldız porcelain** as made at the factory in the Park (see opposite), as well as examples of the sort of **wooden toys** once sold at Eyüp (see p. 252) and some fine paintings by **Şevket Dağ**, **İbrahim Çallı**, **Hamit Görele** and **Bedri Rahmi Eyüboğlu** among others. The adjoining **Yıldız Palace Museum** displays miscellaneous items from the palace in the old Carpentry Workshop (Marangozhane) where Abdülhamid himself used to work. There are also some magnificent examples of Art Nouveau furniture here too.

City Museum

**Warning!
It is not possible to pass directly from Yıldız Park and the Şale to the Yıldız Palace buildings.**

Facing the museums across the courtyard the **Armory (Silahhane)** is not currently open to the public. Another work of Raimondo d'Aronco, the **Assistants' Apartments (Yaveran Dairesi),** used to house the sultan's aide-de-camp.

In a separate courtyard behind the State Apartments is the gorgeous d'Aronco-designed **Yıldız Palace Theatre,** a private entertainment center where Sultan Abdülhamid would come to watch plays sitting all alone in a box over the entrance – the stalls below him could not be used since no subjects could sit with their backs to the sultan. Amongst the performers he would have seen in action was the French actress **Sarah Bernhardt**, a habitué of the Markiz Pastanesi on İstiklal Caddesi (see p. 313). The theater is decorated in blue and gold and the dome is adorned with **stars** ("yıldız" is Turkish for star), but is not currently open to the public.

The museum at the **Gedikli Cariyeler** (Regular Concubines) building adjacent to it exhibits costumes of the Palace Theatre, archival documents of traditional and westernized Turkish theatre and some personal belongings of famous artists.

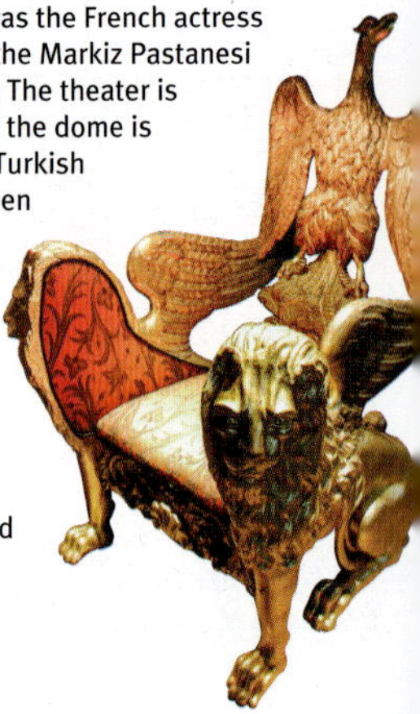

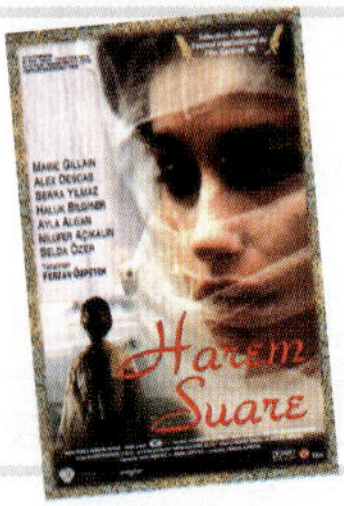

A Tragical End

By the time Abdülhamid II was forced into exile in Salonica there were some 230 women aged between 15 and 50 in his harem, almost all of them Caucasian. Telegrams were dispatched to their families and some fathers and brothers arrived to reclaim their daughters who were then officially freed from slavery. For others there was to be no such happy ending as no trace could be found of their families. This story forms the backdrop for **Ferzan Özpetek**'s lavishly beautiful 1999 film **"Harem Suare (The Last Harem)"**.

Imperial Porcelain Factory

At the top end of the park stands a factory, designed by the Italian architect **Raimondo d'Aronco** to resemble a medieval castle from Europe. This began turning out **Sevres-style porcelain** in 1896, possibly as a cost-cutting measure to reduce the expense of importing popular European dinner services for the palace. Production stopped between 1909 and 1911 and had only just recommenced when the factory was taken over to produce insulation materials for use in the **Turkish War of Independence.** From 1920 to 1957 it once again ceased production. Since 1995 it has been operating as a **museum-factory** churning out decorative china for export and sale in its gift shop.

The mosques

Abdülhamid was far too paranoid to travel far for Friday prayers, so in 1886 he had the **Hamidiye Mosque** built close to the palace on Barbaros Bulvarı (and even worked on carving the minbar himself). The calligraphy above the main entrance is especially fine. The three-storey **clock tower** beside the gate was completed in 1890. He would have had rather further to walk to the delightful, Balyan-designed **Küçük (Little) Mecidiye Mosque,** near the park's lower entrance opposite Çırağan Palace, which dates back to 1848 and the reign of **Sultan Abdülmecid.** Its complex incorporated a school, madrasah and caravanserai. Soil brought from Mecca was used in creating the walls which are decorated with pretty swags of flowers rendered in white plaster.

Yıldız Hamidiye Mosque built by Sultan Abdülhamid II

Küçük Mecidiye Mosque

Phoenix of a Palace

Çırağan Palace

061 Today one of Istanbul's most beautiful and exclusive hotels with an infinity swimming pool stretching right to the edge of the Bosphorus, the original Çırağan Palace was erected in 1856 on the site of a series of older palaces and is intimately linked to events in later Ottoman history. Like so many Istanbul landmarks it was destroyed by fire in 1910 and the site stood abandoned until the 1980s when the palace was restored and turned into a hotel. Across the road are the shrine of Yahya Efendi and Yıldız Park.

"(Ferahabad Palace)...the guardian assured me there is 800 rooms in it...wainscotted with mother-of-pearl fastened with emeralds like nails."

***The Turkish Embassy Letters* by Lady Mary Wortley Montagu, 1718.**

Çırağan Palace Kempinski Hotel

The site of the Çırağan Palace has a long history dating back to the reign of **Sultan Ahmed I** (1603-17) when it was part of the royal Kazancıoğlu Gardens. Later Ahmed III's Grand Vizier **Damat İbrahim Paşa** had the Ferahabad Palace built here for his wife, Fatma Sultan. It became the setting for many of the lavish **Tulip Era parties** for which he was famed (see p. 265) and this included the **candle-lit soirees** after which the district is believed to have taken its name (in Persian "cereğan" means "full of light").

When **Ahmed III** was overthrown in 1730 (see p. 265), the palace fell into disuse until **Sultan Mahmud I** started to use it to entertain foreign ambassadors. Towards the end of the 18th century it was replaced with a new summer palace intended for Sultan Selim III's sister, **Beyhan Sultan**. During the reign of Sultan Mahmud II the Turkish-Armenian architect **Garabed Balyan** expanded the palace and made it habitable in winter; what was called the **"Beyaz Saray" (White Palace)** then started to play a big part in imperial life, as home to **Sultan Abdülmecid**; **Sultans Murad V**, **Abdülhamid II** and **Mehmed V Reşad** were all born here. However, once the larger Dolmabahçe Palace was completed, Abdülmecid moved there and in 1856 the White Palace was torn down to make way for a new building.

If you like this you'll also like:
Eyüp Mosque (see p. 245)
Shrine of Sümbül Efendi in Kocamustafapaşa (see p. 097)
Shrine of Telli Baba in Sarıyer (see p. 467)
Shrine of Yuşa Baba in Beykoz (see p. 556)

Yahya Efendi Tomb

Shrine of Yahya Efendi

Just a short uphill walk across the road from the hotel is a delightfully secluded and much revered shrine which houses the remains of Yahya Efendi (1495-1570), one of Sultan Süleyman the Magnificent's brothers-in-law. It was built by **Sinan** in around 1570 and became a popular place with sailors who would visit it to give thanks for their safe return from a voyage. Several minor members of the imperial family are buried here, including one of Sultan Süleyman's daughters.

The Feriye palaces

At one time the part of the coast extending from **Beşiktaş** to **Defterdarburnu**, the headland at Ortaköy just beyond the Bosphorus Bridge, was reserved for the summer palaces of the nobility and on either side of the Çırağan Palace stand lovely old waterside mansions whose workaday modern uses disguise their previous importance. The one that was closest to Beşiktaş is now the **Four Seasons at the Bosphorus Hotel**, the one that was furthest from Beşiktaş is what was the **Hatice Sultan Palace** in Ortaköy (see p. 414). In the middle of Palace Row was what now houses the **Kabataş Boys' High School** in which Sultan Abdülaziz died in 1874. Many of the buildings belong to **Galatasaray University** whose language department is housed in one of the finest. Unfortunately, the wooden building built in 1871 was burnt down, together with all the documents and archives in it, during a fire in 2013. The restoration of the building started in 2016 after three-and-a-half years in its derelict state.

Security for all these palaces was provided by the grand 19th-century **Feriye (Tabya) police station** that now houses the Feriye Lokantası. Across the road stand the **Zaptiye Barracks,** which have been restored recently.

Sultan Abdülhamid II at the Friday Salute

Sultan Abdülaziz employed the **Balyans** to complete the work on the new palace, asking them to incorporate Moorish details into what was otherwise a typically "Western" design; architects were sent to inspect the **Alhambra** and other Moorish buildings in Spain but still the sultan is said to have interfered so frequently with the plans that they had to be redrawn 20 times. Work on the palace was finally completed in 1874 and the sultan moved in, only to move straight out again, complaining that it was damp (although others think that he had been scared away by rumors that ill luck would come to those responsible for moving a dervish lodge that had stood on the site). The sultan died less than two years later in suspicious circumstances; some believe he killed himself, others that he was murdered. He was succeeded by his nephew **Murad V** who proved too mentally unstable to govern and was deposed after 93 days in favor of his brother, **Abdülhamid II.**

Sultan Abdülaziz

Murad was then imprisoned in the Çırağan Palace where, in 1878, there occurred an event known as **"the Çırağan Incident"** during which **Ali Suavi**, a teacher at the Şehzade Mosque, led a band of insurgents in an unsuccessful assault on the palace from the Bosphorus, hoping to rescue Murad and reinstate him on the throne. Soon afterwards the ex-sultan was moved to the **Malta Pavilion** in Yıldız Park which was thought to be more secure (the park is connected to the Çırağan Palace via a marble bridge). Ultimately Murad stayed a prisoner for 28 years until his death.

When he died in 1905, the building was abandoned, only to spring to life again briefly as a home for the new **Turkish Parliament** that was elected in 1908.

Sultan Murad V

Then in 1910 disaster struck and the palace burnt down in a mere five hours, taking with it many priceless antiques and historic documents. The site then languished for decades, playing a walk-on part in **footballing history** as a temporary pitch for Beşiktaş before the construction of their stadium at Dolmabahçe (see p. 393). It wasn't until the 1980s that it was rebuilt to form the centerpiece of a new **Kempinski Hotel** (see opposite) which opened in 1990. The hotel was restored again in 2007 and has played hosts to many famous guests including **John F. Kennedy Jr**, **Pavarotti**, **Sting**, **Bill Clinton**, **Kofi Annan** and **Oprah Winfrey**.

Old Çırağan Palace in an engraving of 1839

The Feriye Palaces. On the left the building used as Galatasaray University, on the right the one used as Kabataş Boys High School

GAZEBO

Most Beautiful Scene

Ortaköy

062

From the Bosphorus, Ortaköy is one of the least missable suburbs, partly because it sits right beside the 1st Bridge on the European side and partly because its mosque stands on a promontory jutting out into the water. This is one of Istanbul's more happening suburbs, with a cluster of restaurants hugging a small waterside square and a lively Sunday handicrafts market. Amid all this fun and games a few reminders of the past –churches, synagogues and hamams– often get completely overlooked.

Ortaköy ferry terminal

Ortaköy (Middle Village) has a history dating back to Byzantine times when there were several monasteries here. By the 17th century Evliya Çelebi was able to report a large mixed population of **Jews**, **Greeks** and **Muslims** living side by side; the village had already established a reputation as a place with a lively nightlife as he reports that there were "a great number" of taverns here. Today that reputation is well-earned and on summer evenings the traffic on the coast road around Ortaköy can be murderous.

The focal point of daytime life remains the waterside square which is overlooked by a collection of old houses, most of them now housing cafes and restaurants. Lost amid the weekend melee is a wonderful 18th-century **fountain** erected by **Damat İbrahim Paşa**, son-in-law and Grand Vizier to Sultan Ahmed III (1713-30).

Dome of Ortaköy Mosque

Ortaköy Mosque (Büyük Mecidiye Camii)

Sitting on **Defterdarburnu**, a promontory right beside the Bosphorus Bridge, the light-filled, baroque style Ortaköy Mosque was designed by **Nigoğos Balyan** for **Sultan Abdülmecit** in 1853-55 on the site of an earlier 18th-century mosque (he was also responsible for the Dolmabahçe Mosque (see p. 388) and there are similarities between the two buildings). Attached to the rear a two-storey pew for the sultan was designed so that he could enter it directly from his caique without having to walk round to the main entrance. Inside the dome is decorated with painted clouds floating between columns, a touch of whimsy that fits with the Bosphorus setting.

The interior of Ortaköy Mosque is absolutely breath-taking.

Mimar Sinan

The Kethüda (Steward) Hamam

The bath is one of four monuments in Beşiktaş designed by **Mimar Sinan**. It is located where the traffic is at its densest and is known as the first monument to be built after the Turks settled in Ortaköy. Also known as the Ortaköy Turkish Bath, the building was used a restaurant, a night club and a design office after its restoration. It currently functions as a cultural center of the **Beşiktaş Municipality**. It is thought to have been built for Hüsrev Kethüda, a steward to the Grand Vizier **Sokullu Mehmet Paşa** (see p. 178) in the 1570s. The internal layout is unusual, with four doomed rooms replacing the usual single chamber of the hot room. I hope the building will be used as a Turkish bath.

The road linking Beşiktaş to Ortaköy

The "18 Houses" whose occupants are thought to have been Jews

Etz Ahayim Synagogue

Hagios Fokas Greek Orthodox Church

On the right is Hagios Fokas belltower

Churches and synagogues

Almost invisible behind the shops stands the huge Greek Orthodox **Church of Hagios Fokas.** It only dates back to 1856 although a Byzantine church with the same dedication originally gave its name to the surrounding area. Look out for the small belfry perched above the gate that leads into the courtyard from the main road.

Not far away is the **Etz Ahayim (Tree of Life) synagogue,** which dates back to the 14th century although the current building mainly dates from 1813 and 1941. Behind it lies a long story of fires and more fires, the congregation having been considerably expanded in the early 17th century after a conflagration drove them out of the Grand Bazaar.

Along Dereboyu Caddesi you'll see the Armenian **Church of Surp Lusavoriç,** built in 1839.

Esma Sultan Yalı

Hatice Sultan Yalı

Fehime Sultan Yalı

Waterside mansions

Just past the Ortaköy Mosque it's impossible to miss the stone-built remains of the **Esma Sultan Yalı,** built for the fun-loving sister (1778-1848) of Sultan Mahmud II who had been widowed at the age of 25 and went on to make the most of her wealth and connections. As time passed the mansion became first a school, then a tobacco warehouse and finally a coal depot before a terrible fire in 1975 reduced it to a ruin. In the 1990s the shell was bought by the Marmara hotel group. It's now used for **social events,** including high-society weddings.

Hatice Sultan and her daughter Selma Sultan

At Defterdarburnu beneath the Bosphorus Bridge stand the charred remains of the **Fehime Sultan Yalı.** This was originally given by Sultan Abdülhamid II to **Gazi Osman Paşa,** the hero of the battle of **Plevne,** in 1883. After his son Kemaleddin Paşa married the sultan's daughter Naime Sultan they lived in the yalı, so that it is sometimes confusingly called the **Naime Sultan** or even **Gazi Osman Pasa Yalı.** In 1910 it was given as a present to Fehime Sultan, one of the daughters of Sultan Murad V and went on to house a secondary **school**. It burnt down in 2003.

Almost next door to it, the **Hatice Sultan Yalı** had been given to Fehime's elder sister Hatice Sultan. After serving time as an orphanage and primary school, it then housed a sports center. To add to the confusion there had also been an earlier palace here that was designed for another Hatice Sultan, the sister of Sultan Selim III, by the Dutch architect **Antoine-Ignace Melling** (1763-1831) who left a beautiful drawing of it. Work to convert both mansions into a **hotel** began in 2009.

Forbidden love

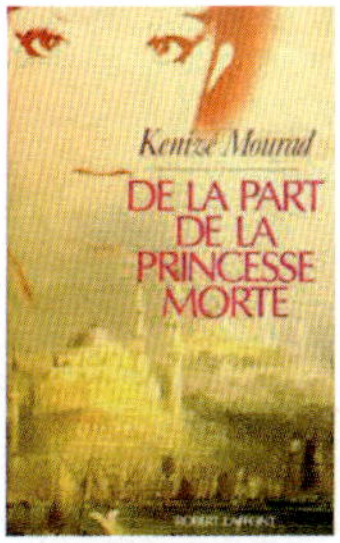

Hatice Sultan (1870-1928) was one of history's many female victims. The daughter of **Sultan Murad V** who was deposed, she was still unwed at the age of 31 and pleaded with her uncle, the new sultan **Abdülhamid II**, to let her marry. The husband he found for her was an ugly old man, so, perhaps to get her own back, Hatice embarked on an affair with her cousin Naime Sultan's husband **Kemaleddin Paşa**. Inevitably, Kemaleddin was forced to divorce his wife and was sent into exile. When Abdülhamid was, in turn, deposed, Kemaleddin returned and proposed to Hatice who refused him in favor of an ordinary but handsome man called **Rauf Hayri Bey**. Hatice's granddaughter Kenize Murad told the story in his book "Saraydan sürgüne (From the Palace to Exile)".

Bruno Taut

Taut lived in Istanbul from 1932 to 1938.

Who was Bruno Taut?

A German Jew born in Königsberg in 1880, Taut had already made a name for himself as an architect especially with some Modernist housing estates in **Berlin** which are now listed as a world heritage site when he was forced to leave the country in 1932. After spending time abroad, he was made a professor of architecture at what is now the **Mimar Sinan University of Fine Arts** in 1936. He lived in Turkey until his death in 1938 and was responsible for several buildings in Ankara and Trabzon. As his final commission he designed the **catafalque** used for Atatürk's state funeral in Ankara in November 1938.

Taut House (Taut Evi)

As you drive across the Bosphorus Bridge towards Ortaköy you may glimpse a house on the right-hand side of the hillside that looks rather like a burgundy-colored pagoda. This was the home of the German architect **Bruno Taut** who said that he had designed it to "express the Orient's spiritual values...in a modern house".

The Taut House on the Ortaköy hillside

Balyan Family

Many visitors of Istanbul have heard about Sinan, the great Ottoman architect of 16th century. However, only a few know about the Armenian Balyan family, even though they have left many monuments around the city in the 19th century. Balyans adapted the Western style on their works, completely reversing the old Ottoman style which looks rather modest from the outside but intensifies the ornaments on the inside and used all the subtleties of the art of ornamentation generously on the exterior.

Coming from Middle Anatolia, **Bali Kalfa** had succeeded in finding a place for himself and his son in the palace. **Magar** taught architecture to his sons, **Krikor** and **Senekerim.** Krikor Amira Balyan built the **Nusretiye (Victory) Mosque** in Tophane (see p.382) for Sultan Mahmud II and the **Feshane** (see p.251) on the coast of Haliç and the **Valide and Topuzlu Aqueducts** (see p.564) in the Belgrad Forests are among his works. Krikor's younger brother Senekerim built the **Tower of Beyazıt** (see p.083). On the other hand, it was Magar's youngest son **Garabed Amira Balyan** who decorated and furnished the palace as if it was his own. With his son **Nigoğos,** they built the **Dolmabahçe Palace** (see p.386) for Sultan Abdülmecid. **Gümüşsuyu Military Hospital** (see p.285), **Abud Efendi Mansion** (see p.533) and the **Adile Sultan Palace** in Kandilli (see p.530) are also their works.

Waterside Art Nouveau

Kuruçeşme and Arnavutköy

063

Arguably the most beautiful of the Bosphorus suburbs, Arnavutköy is distinguished by its magnificent wooden houses, a reminder of what many of the villages must have looked like in the past. Famed at one time for its vineyards, Arnavutköy came to be better known for the strawberries introduced here in the early 19th century. On the hillside above the lovely houses stands the modern incarnation of the famous and influential Robert College. There are also a growing number of excellent restaurants in this part of town.

Tezkireci Osman Efendi Mosque

Kuruçeşme

Kuruçeşme (Dry Fountain) was probably named after the 17th-century **Köprülü Hemşire Fountain** attached to the **Tezkireci Osman Efendi Mosque**, although the area may originally have been called Koruçeşme, meaning "the Fountain of the Woods" because at that time it was lush and green and the fountain well supplied with water. Then it dried up and the name had to be changed. Given how fashionable the area is now it's surprising to learn that until recently it was an industrial zone where coal and sand were stored. Almost the only reminder of that these days is the bus stop named "Kömür Tevzii (Coal Distribution Point)".

Kuruçeşme is a pretty place to take a waterside stroll, with a newly laid promenade along the Bosphorus from which you can admire the tethered yachts of the wealthy and gaze across at the fairy-tale building that houses **Kuleli Military High School** (see p. 523).

Surp Haç Armenian Church

Ali Vafi Mansion

Hagios Demetrios Church

Churches

There are a number of churches in Kuruçeşme, including the **Surp Haç (Holy Cross)** Armenian church, a rectangular brick-and-stone building designed by **Garabed Balyan** in 1881, standing on the site of a much earlier structure. It's on the left as you head inland along Kırbaç Sokak. At the top of some steps at the end of the same road is the **Church of Hagios Demetrios** (St Demetrius), which was built in 1798. The latter is especially interesting as it was here that the contentious theological school now on **Heybeliada** (see p. 586) started out in 1804. Those signing up to train for the priesthood used to stand on the symbol of a double-headed eagle inset in the ground just inside the entrance and vow to observe the teachings of the Church. At the back of the church a **tunnel** runs uphill to the **Hagios Sotiros Ayazma (sacred spring)** whose source is a cave some 40 meters away. The continual dripping of water over the last hundred years or so has caused the walls to calcify so that they now look like the inside of a cave. It's a minor but rather remarkable sight. Finally, the small **Church of Ioannes Prodromos (John the Baptist)**, with its round wooden turret, is half-hidden behind high walls at the point on the Kuruçeşme-Arnavutköy Yolu where Kuruçeşme meets Arnavutköy.

Hagios Sotiros sacred spring

Ioannes Prodromos Church

Galatasaray Island

Just offshore at Kuruçeşme is a **small island** that was given to the Armenian architect **Sarkis Balyan** by **Sultan Abdülhamid II** in 1880 as a reward for his work on the nearby **Esma Sultan Yalı** (see p. 414) and **Çırağan Palace** (see p. 406). Of the two-storey yalı he built on the island and in which he carried out physics experiments there remains no trace. Later the island became a walled garden and then a water sports center. It was belonging to **Galatasaray Sports Club.** All the buildings on the island, which had long been home to a complex of restaurants and night clubs, were demolished in 2017 on the grounds that they were not consistent with the zoning plan. I don't know what the fate of the deserted island will be.

The Red Yalı

On the waterside heading north towards Arnavutköy the **Halet Çambel Yalı** is a rusty-brown ("Ottoman rose") mansion built for an Armenian who was a gardener for Sultan Mahmud II in the 1830s. Educated in the girls school beside the house, Halet Çambel was the archeologist who excavated the Hittite site at Karatepe-Aslantaş near Osmaniye. She was married to the award-winning, self-taught architect **Nail Çakırhan**. She donated it to Bosphorus University.

Robert College

In 1871 an American College for Girls affiliated to the boys' college at Bebek was founded on the hilltop above Arnavutköy. In 1971 the two colleges amalgamated and the new co-ed establishment retained the famous Robert College name.

"Freedom and independence are the foundations of my character."

Mustafa Kemal Atatürk quoted on the Arnavutköy waterfront memorial.

Wooden houses at Arnavutköy

Who was Halide Edip Adıvar?

Born in 1884, Halide Edip Adıvar was a Turkish novelist and feminist who became a lecturer in literature and then went on to fight in the **Turkish War of Independence** (1919-22). Later she traveled in France and Britain before returning to become a professor of English literature at **Istanbul University** and, briefly, a **member of parliament.** She died in 1964 and there's a **bust** in her memory behind the Milion in Sultanahmet (see p. 063). Her 1926 autobiography, "The Memoir of Halide Edip", describes her years in Arnavutköy. Her childhood also formed the basis for **Frances Kazan's novel "Halide's Gift".**

Old Arnavutköy ferry terminal

Hagios Elias Chapel

Arnavutköy

A short walk north of Kuruçeşme, Arnavutköy ("Albanian Village") is named after the **Albanian builders** who were brought here by Sultan Abdülmecid in the 19th century to lay sidewalks for Istanbul. At one time it had a large population of Greeks and Jews. Today a few Greeks remain but the Jews are all gone.

Cruising along the Bosphorus it's impossible to miss Arnavutköy where a dense cluster of wooden houses still adorn the waterside. That's all that most visitors get to see. However, if you disembark at the landing stage and wander inland you will discover even more fine houses climbing up the hillside, some of them designed with an **Art Nouveau** flair. Most of these houses probably date back to the early 20th century and although to modern eyes they appear both beautiful and individual, experts believe that the Art Nouveau twists were often just additions to preexisting buildings, the patterns being mass produced rather than individually designed. An exception is the house at **4 Dulkadiroğulları Sokak** which was almost certainly designed by an architect rather than being put together by a builder from standard patterns.

Greek Primary School

Mansions lined up behind a road on reclaimed land.

Arnavutköy's back streets are full of wooden houses.

Taksiarkhes Church

Tevfikiye Mosque

Heading inland from the Tevfikiye Mosque near the water you will come to the huge late 19th-century **Taksiarkhes Church**, built beside a sacred spring. Its central dome looks exactly like those of the larger mosques, although it has a bell tower over the entrance too. Inscribed on the bell tower are Jesus' words "Come to me".

At the westerly end of the waterfront the **Arnavutköy Mosque** dates back to 1832 and the reign of Sultan Mahmud II. Beside it stands a fine 19th-century **Karakol (Police Station)**.

If driving between Etiler and Arnavutköy along Sekbanlar Sokak, you might want to divert briefly along Körkadı Sokak to see the pretty little 19th-century **chapel** built over an ayazma sacred to Elijah. Its dome is especially attractive. The chapel is kept locked after several thefts but the caretaker may be willing to open it for you (he lives in a house in the cemetery across the road).

Akıntıburnu

At the eastern end of Arnavutköy the coastline juts out into the Bosphorus and the current becomes so powerful that it is not always possible for small boats to pass. In the past porters on the shore would have had to tow some of the more fragile boats around Akıntıburnu, the **Cape of the Current**. According to the 16th-century French writer Pierre Gilles, the paving stones here had been worn down by the passage of crabs that came ashore and walked around the cape rather than risk the current.

Bayraktar Holding has its headquarters in the İzzeabad Mansion between Arnavutköy and Bebek.

The stylite lifestyle

Back in the days when Kuruçeşme was still the Byzantine settlement of **Anaplous** it was home to two of those extraordinary **Christian hermits** called stylites, or men who sat on top of pillars. From 433-60 **Simeon the Stylite** perched atop a perch overlooking the Bosphorus and from 460-93 **St Daniel the Stylite** did likewise. So impressed by this was **Emperor Leo I** that he supplied Daniel with a second column linked to the first by a beam so that he could stretch his legs. Later he even added a shelter against the wind and rain which Daniel reluctantly agreed to use. Not surprisingly, the crowds flocked in to stare at them.

ALARKO

Türkan Saylan

A doctor of medicine, an academician, a writer and an educator... Of course all these titles are not sufficient to describe Türkan Saylan, one of the old residents of this neighborhood. Her name is more often associated with the Association for Supporting Modern Life (ÇYDD) as one of the association's founders and president. The association contributed significantly to the education of girls and their participation in modern life. The World Health Organization issued a report about the "significant reduction of leprosy" in Turkey thanks to the country-wide work of this idealist woman, who came to be the first woman awarded with the Gandhi Award in India. I very much hope that her house on the Beyazgül Street will one day be reopened as a museum to inspire women across Turkey and in the world.

Beautiful "Baby" Bebek

064

Midway along the western shore of the Bosphorus, Bebek (Baby) is an unabashedly upscale suburb set round a pretty harbor and dominated by the academic might of the Bosphorus University. It's centered on an attractive waterside park and filled with alluring shops and restaurants where the well-heeled can be seen going about their business. Both Rumeli Hisarı and Arnavutköy are within enjoyable walking distance along the waterside promenade.

Bebek (Hümayun-u Abad) Mosque

Across the park from the Egyptian Consulate building, this small and not especially distinguished mosque right next to the site of the old **Hümayunabad Palace** was built by architect **Kemaleddin Bey** in 1912. Although he was one of the leading lights in the First National Architecture movement, the mosque is fairly classical in its design. However, some of the interior woodwork is very impressive.

Bebek Mosque by İbrahim Çallı

Where Bebek gets its peculiar name from is unclear. Some people think it was taken from the Turkish expression **"beautiful as a baby"**, while others think it was named after the Turkish official **Mustafa Çelebi** who was **nicknamed "Bebek"** because of his good looks and who was put in control of this part of the Bosphorus after the Ottoman conquest of 1453. The area first acquired importance in the early 18th century when **Sultan Ahmed III** had the **Hümayünabad Palace** built here, spurring many other members of the nobility to build luxurious homes nearby. The palace was destroyed in the reign of **Abdülmecid** (1839-61) who is said to have been incensed when it was suggested that it would outlive many sultans.

Today Bebek is arguably the trendiest of the Bosphorus suburbs, a place where female fashionistas can feel comfortable strolling around in shorts and where some of the cafes cater unashamedly to the see-and-be-seen crowd. It's also a notorious traffic bottleneck especially at weekends.

Egyptian Consulate

The single most impressive building in Bebek is a huge Art Nouveau mansion with a mansard roof right on the waterfront that was designed for **Emine Hanım**, the mother of the last Egyptian Khedive, **Abbas Hilmi Paşa** (see p. 551), in 1902. For that reason it is also called **Hıdiva Sarayı** (Palace of the Female Khedive). Although it is often listed as a work of Raimondo d'Aronco, it was probably designed by one of two Austrian architects, Fabricius or Antonio Lasciac. The Khedive used the mansion as a summer house until he was deposed in 1914 whereupon it was bequeathed to the Egyptian government on condition that it was used as an embassy (a consulate after the embassy was moved to Ankara in 1923). In 2010 it was completely renovated, which returned some of the original coloring to the stonework.

Don't forget to pass the Pink Mansion in March when the magnolia is in bloom.

Buildings being restored as part of Bebekoy project

Churches and mansions

The Lazarist Church of Sacre Coeur in Mektep Sokağı dates back to 1908 when it formed a vast complex with a school which is now closed; the **Old French Orphanage (Eski Fransız Yetimhanesi)** adjoining it was built in 1856 and now serves as a summer school for **St Benoit High School** in Karaköy (see p. 275). A **second orphanage**, also on the hillside, was taken over by the state and given to a company which is now turning it into Bebekoy, a luxury housing development. The **Minorities Foundation** apparently plans to challenge their right to do this in the European Court of Human Rights.

Nearby in İnşirah Sokak, the hill road that leads to Etiler, stands the Greek Orthodox **Church of Hagios Haralambos**, dating back to 1830. The bell tower was added in 1962. Immediately opposite it is a fine white mansion with a magnificent magnolia tree in its garden. When the tree is in flower in March it's almost worth coming to Bebek just to see it.

If you continue along the same road you will come to the Armenian **Kavafyan Mansion**. Built in 1751, it is one of Istanbul's oldest (and largest) surviving **wooden houses**, originally built for Christian shipowners in classic konak style with the rooms opening off a central hall (sofa). Unfortunately it has been locked up for years so we were unable to discover whether it retains its original painted ceilings. It is slowly fading away before our very eyes, at perpetual risk of fire from a carelessly discarded match.

Hand-drawn mural detail

Kavafyan Mansion

The Lazarists

The Lazarists (also known as the Congregation of the Mission) are a Roman Catholic order of secular clergymen dating back to the 17th century who are **followers of St Vincent de Paul**. Their curious name was acquired from one of the first properties they owned, the Priory of St Lazare in Paris. In 1783 Lazarist missionaries arrived in Turkey. Grateful for having found exceptionally fertile ground in Poland, it was the Turkish Lazarist community that provided the land for Polish settlers in what is now **Polonezköy** (see p. 570).

Lazarist Sacre Coeur Church

Hagios Haralambos Greek Orthodox Church

French Orphanage

Science Faculty Building

A place worthy of its name – Manzara (View)

Robert College and Bosphorus University

Robert College, the first American college to be opened outside the United States, was founded in 1863 by the American missionary **Cyrus Hamlin** who had worked in Florence Nightingale's hospital at Selimiye (see p. 495). It took its name from that of his financial backer, Christopher R. Robert.

Cyrus Hamlin

In 1971 the college land was given to the Turkish Ministry of Education who founded **Bosphorus University** (Boğaziçi Üniversitesi) on the site. The college itself reopened on the site of the Robert College for Girls in Arnavutköy. Past alumni include two ex-prime ministers of Turkey: **Bülent Ecevit** (1925-2006) and **Tansu Çiller** (1946 -), Turkey's first –and so far only– female prime minister.

Bülent Ecevit

Tansu Çiller

Old photo shows Kennedy Lodge housing a canteen for teaching staff

Albert Long Hall

Türkan Sabancı Park in Bebek

Join the locals for a stroll in **Türkan Sabancı Parkı** which is equipped with a large children's playground, exercise machines, fountains and a dog-running compound. Many of the plane trees here have preservation orders on them and you may see (or hear) green parakeets roosting in their branches. Right in the middle stands a statue of the poet **Fuzuli**

Snake Mansion

As you head out of Bebek towards Rumeli Hisarı you will pass turnings to the **Ayşe Sultan** and then **Arifi Paşa Woods** before coming to the **Kayalar Mescidi**, a rare surviving 17th-century wooden chapel. Beside it is a fine wooden mansion which is a reproduction of the **Yılanlı Yalı** (Snake Mansion) built here in the 18th century. Its curious name came about after **Sultan Mahmud II** showed too much interest in the house; a quick-witted official distracted him by claiming that it was so full of snakes that it was virtually uninhabitable. Unfortunately the original building burnt down in 1964. In 1989 one half of it was faithfully reconstructed by its new owner. The other half is an ugly concrete apartment block which has had the cheek to misappropriate the original name!

Kayalar Mescid

Manually operated roundabout

Who was Fuzuli?

Fuzuli was the pen name of the much-admired Iraqi poet **Mohammed bin Süleyman** (1480-1556), who wrote in Azerbaijani Turkish, Persian and Arabic. After the Ottomans captured his home town in 1534 he became a court poet to Sultan Süleyman the Magnificent. Despite his posthumous fame, he always struggled to make a living and eventually died of cholera or the plague. The mystery is why he should be commemorated here.

City Secrets

The Bebek Cistern, which belongs to the waterside mansion in the principality garden of Mabeyinci İbrahim Paşa, dates from the 19th century. Unfortunately, the waterside mansion and the nearby police station building have not survived to the present day. The building, which was used for different purposes for many years, was restored by Istanbul Metropolitan Municipality and opened as an art gallery.

"Bebek catches the heart with
its fragile, fadeless beauty..."
Portrait of a Turkish Family by İrfan Orga, 1948

The Conqueror's Castle

Rumeli Hisarı and Aşiyan

065

As you sail along the Bosphorus you can hardly miss the enormous fortifications that make up Rumeli Hisarı (European Castle) lurking just beside the 2nd Bridge. Rumeli Hisarı may not be the largest but it is certainly the most impressive castle along the Bosphorus. The suburb that grew up around it is well-known for its many pleasant waterside cafes and restaurants.

Having determined to conquer Constantinople, in 1452 **Sultan Mehmed II** built a vast castle on the European shore at the point where the Bosphorus is at its narrowest and where it would be facing the considerably **smaller castle** (Anadolu Hisarı, see p. 541) built by his grandfather, Beyazid I, on the Asian shore. Even though the building of the castle has been described as "tantamount to a declaration of war", the Byzantine **Emperor Constantine XI Dragases** was forced to give him the land on which to build, apparently on the same spot that **Darius the Great**, the king of the Persians, had watched while his army of 700,000 men crossed the Bosphorus using a bridge of boats on their way to attack the Scythians in 512 BC. In a stupendous feat of speed-building, Mehmed employed 1,000 craftsmen and 2,000 laborers to complete work on the fortress, which he had designed himself, in a mere four months. His three grand viziers, **Halil Paşa**, **Zağanos Paşa** and **Saruca Paşa**, were put in charge of work on the three main towers that now bear their names. Once the castle was built, Mehmed was able to prevent supplies of grain being shipped from the Black Sea to Constantinople, weakening the city and making its defeat more likely. Only one **Venetian ship** attempted to breach the blockade; it was sunk and its crew impaled for their pains.

Constantine XI Dragases

Once Constantinople had fallen, Rumeli Hisarı had served its purpose and became a **customs collection point**. In time even this function was lost to Rumeli Kavağı further north (see p. 466) and parts of the castle were used as a **gaol** for foreign prisoners of war.

The castle was badly damaged by an **earthquake** in 1509 and the floors of two of the towers were lost to fire in 1746. Sultan Selim III had the castle restored but by the 19th century it had been completely abandoned and some locals even set up home inside the grounds. Drawings made at that time show the tall main towers capped with witch's hat roofs rather like the Galata Tower. In 1953 to celebrate the **500th anniversary** of the conquest of Istanbul the castle was completely restored but with flat roofs to replace the pitched ones.

Wooden houses inside Rumeli Hisarı in the 19th century

Bird's eye view of Rumeli Hisarı

The Castle

Built on a slope, the castle had one large tower near the shore (the Halil Paşa) and two others on the hillside above. In between the sturdy walls were broken up with 13 smaller towers; in all the walls enclosed an area of more than 31,000 square meters. Sultan Mehmed had a **mosque** built inside the walls over a cistern, although it has since vanished, with only the stump of the minaret to mark its passing. The castle was one of the first in Europe to be built with the use of cannons in mind. As so often in Turkey, close inspection of the walls reveals that they were constructed reusing material from much older structures. You can walk along some stretches of the walls which offer great views, although parents should be warned that there are no safety railings.

Tel: 0212 263 53 05
closed Mondays

Cannon

The castle's names

Rumeli Hisarı has gone under many guises over the years, including Kulle-i Cedide (New Castle), Yenice Hisarı (Quite New Castle) and Boğazkesen Kalesi (Bosphorus-dividing Castle).

Dragging the boats

In 1453 when **Sultan Mehmed II** determined to seize Constantinople he faced a serious problem because the Byzantine Emperors had always been able to prevent access to the Golden Horn by stringing a heavy metal chain across it. To solve this problem Mehmed had 80 special flat-bottomed boats built. These were than dragged from **Tophane**, over the **Galata heights** and down into the Golden Horn at **Kasımpaşa**, thereby circumventing the chain and making it possible to attack the great sea walls of Fener and Balat (see p. 243). It was an event memorably immortalized by the Italian court artist **Fausto Zonaro** whose painting **"The Siege"** hangs in the Selamlık of the Dolmabahçe Palace (see p. 390).

Fatih Sultan Mehmed Gives Orders to the Fleet by Fausto Zonaro

The size of a cowhide

The 17th-century travel writer Evliya Çelebi reported that after Fatih Mehmed decided to build a castle here he approached the Byzantine Emperor for a piece of land big enough to create a hunting lodge. The emperor agreed, specifying that the building should not exceed the size of a cowhide. The sultan then had a cowhide cut into fine strips which were stitched together and spread out to create the huge space now covered by the fort. Since this is the same story as is told about Queen Dido and the founding of Carthage in what is now Tunisia, it's probably fair to assume that it's apocryphal.

"I was sitting in Rumeli Hisarı
with a folk song running through my head
about Istanbul's marble stones
And the seagulls are landing on my head."

***Istanbul Folk Song* by Orhan Veli**

Sis (Mist) by Abdülmecid Efendi

Tevfik Fikret

Statue of Orhan Veli

Aşiyan (Nest) Museum

Was there ever a bedroom with a more beautiful view than this? On the hillside as you leave Bebek heading for Rumeli Hisarı stands the small house built by the poet, idealist and critic of the government **Tevfik Fikret** (1867-1915) who had been a professor of Turkish literature at Robert College and who was reinterred here in 1961. In 1945 his house was turned into a museum which displays many of his possessions as well as a superb painting entitled simply **"Sis (Mist)"** by **Abdülmecid Efendi**; beside it hangs the Fikret poem of the same name that had provided his inspiration. Also here are reminders of **Abdülhalk Hamid** and **Nigar Hanım**, two other members of the Edebiyat-ı Cedide (New Literature) movement associated with Fikret. From the benches outside you can gaze out on the **Küçüksu Palace** and the twin streams that used to form the **Sweet Waters of Asia** (see p. 541).

Between the house and the road stretches the peaceful **Aşiyan Cemetery** where local notables including the poets **Orhan Veli** and **Yahya Kemal Beyatlı** and the playwright **Ahmed Vefik Paşa** are buried. Nearby there's a **statue** of Orhan Veli being eyed up by the seagull who features in one of his best-known poems.

@asiyanmuze
Tel: 0212 263 69 86
closed Sundays and Mondays

Surp Santuht Church

Mosques and churches

Hacı Kemaleddin Mosque

The conspicuous and pretty **Hacı Kemaleddin Mosque** may date back to the reign of Sultan Mehmed II. However, it was completely rebuilt in 1746 by **Sultan Mahmud I**, which is when the fountain in front of it was added.

The much less conspicuous **Ali Pertek Mosque**, opposite the Rumeli Hisarı İskele Restaurant, dates back to the mid-17th century although it was largely rebuilt in the 1960s and restored in 2009.

There seems to have been an Armenian community in Rumeli Hisarı since the days of Mehmed the Conqueror, but no trace remains of their original wooden church. The present hillside Church of **Surp Santuht** was built in 1856 and is still in use today.

The Paşa's Library

Today it's private property and concealed from view behind a steel gate, but the Paşa's Library with the to-die-for view that plays a leading role in **Maureen Freely**'s revisiting of the tense political scene of the 1970s in her 2007 novel **"Enlightenment"**, really does exist. It was built for **Ahmed Vefik Paşa** (1823-91), a politician, playwright and compiler of the **first Turkish dictionary** who eventually sought a retreat from the world here. He originally owned the land now occupied by Bosphorus University but lost it on account of his debts. In 1902 his "birdcage" was given a makeover by Levantine architect **Alexandre Vallaury**.

Ahmed Vefik Paşa

Arpacı Çeşme Street beneath the snow

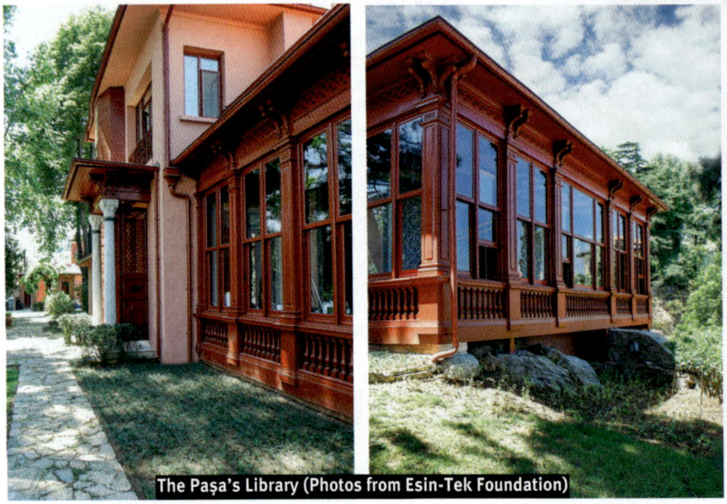
The Paşa's Library (Photos from Esin-Tek Foundation)

The Fairy Mansion

If you stand in front of the Rumeli Hisarı landing stage and look up to the right you will see a stepped and turreted red-brick building in front of the bridge. Left unfinished by the death of its original owner, **Mısırlı (Egyptian) Yusuf Ziya Paşa**, aide-de-camp to **Khedive Abbas Hilmi Paşa**, it was completed with results that don't seem to please everybody. It's better known locally as the Perili Köşk (the Fairy Mansion). After the restoration, the mansion was rented by **Borusan Holding**. The mansion is used by the offices and administration of the holding during weekdays and welcomes art-lovers as a museum on weekends. This makes it the first "office museum" in Turkey. Apart from the permanent collection, which focuses on works of contemporary art that are shaped by technology, it also hosts temporary exhibitions all year round. The museum also has a nice café that is ideal for a break by the Bosphorus.

@borusancontemporary, www.borusancontemporary.com
Tel: 0212 393 52 00

Field Marshall Zeki Paşa Yalı

A rare example of a stone yalı, this fine stone mansion standing right beside the bridge was designed by **Alexandre Vallaury** for the wealthy field marshal **Zeki Paşa** some time in the early 20th century. Zeki Pasa was intensely loyal to Sultan Abdülhamid and for 17 years he was in charge of the Arsenal at Tophane. Later the yalı passed into the ownership of **Sabiha Sultan**, the daughter of **Mehmed VI**, the last Ottoman sultan and her husband **Ömer Faruk Efendi**, a son of the last caliph **Abdülmecid Efendi**. Their eldest daughter Neslişah Sultan was born in the house and the family continued to live here until the whole family was sent into exile. The building, which has more than 20 rooms, now belongs to the Baştımar family (see p. 513).

Baltalimanı

Just past the Fatih Sultan Mehmed Bridge lies the suburb of Baltalimanı which is named after **Admiral Baltaoğlu Süleyman Bey**, the man responsible for building the boats that Fatih Mehmed used for the assault on Constantinople. "Balta" means axe in Turkish; the admiral acquired this nickname because of the vast quantity of trees he had cut down to build the ships.

Mustafa Reşid Paşa

The most impressive building here is what started life as the pink-painted waterside **Palace of Mediha Sultan** and is now an orthopedic hospital. It was designed in the mid-19th century by **Sarkis Balyan** for **Mustafa Reşid Paşa** who held the office of grand vizier under Sultan Abdülmecid no less than six times and who kickstarted the **Tanzimat** reform movement (see p. 202). Later it was occupied by his son Galip Paşa who had married Abdülmecid's daughter Fatma Sultan. Later still it became the property of Damat Ferit Paşa who renamed it for his wife. It was here that a **trade treaty** between the Ottomans and the British was signed in 1838. It eased the restrictions on foreign traders and encouraged a mini economic boom.

Mediha Sultan Palace

Japanese Garden

In an easily accessible spot of Istanbul, in Baltalimanı, this park quietly welcomes visitors. Those who are interested come to see the Japanese cherry blossoms in March and April. When 2003 was declared the Turkish Year in Japan, one of the first steps taken was declaring Shimonoseki and Istanbul twin cities. A Turkish garden was created in Shimonoseki while a Japanese garden was created in Istanbul. When you visit the park, you can see details of Japanese landscaping with bridges, ponds and plant arrangements. The importance of tea in Japanese culture and the tea ceremonies also find place in the garden with a tea house. The entrances to the 6137-square-meter garden are free. Since the opening hours change in winter and summer, make sure to check before you go.

Tulip Fever

Emirgan and Boyacıköy

866 One of the most delightful of the Bosphorus suburbs, Emirgan is centered on a very pretty main square where inviting tea gardens nestle beneath ancient plane trees. Just inland are the Emirgan Woods, once the playground of the Egyptian Khedive İsmail Paşa, now a public park with a lake and three inviting cafes housed in 19th-century mansions. In spring the park is full of tulips, making it one of the most beautiful spots in the whole city.

Emirgan was originally called Emirgune after **Emir Güne Han**, an Iranian nobleman who had surrendered the castle of **Yerevan** (now in Armenia) to Sultan Murad IV without a fight in 1635. In return for this, the Sultan brought him to Istanbul, renamed him Yusuf Paşa and gave him what were then the Feridun Bey Gardens and are now the 500,000-square-meter **Emirgan Woods**. For a long time, the sultan and noble remained friends and passed many a drunken night together in the gardens which are described in lyrical terms by the contemporary Ottoman traveller **Evliya Çelebi**. After Murad's death, his successor **İbrahim I** had Yusuf executed.

In the 19th century **Sultan Abdülaziz** gave the woods to the Egyptian **Khedive İsmail Paşa** (1830-95) who built himself a seaside palace and then adorned the garden with the Yellow (Sarı), White (Beyaz) and Pink (Pembe) pavilions. Forced to abdicate under pressure from the French and British in 1879, İsmail, known as the Magnificent despite running up huge debts for Egypt, lived out the remainder of his days at Emirgan as a **virtual state prisoner**.

In 1943 the Istanbul authorities bought the Emirgan Woods and turned them into a public park.

Small lake in front of Yellow Pavilion

Egyptian Khedive İsmail Paşa

Yellow Pavilion beneath the snow

White Pavilion

The pavilions (köşks)

Designed to look like a Swiss hunting lodge by **Sarkis Balyan** in the 1870s, the **Yellow Mansion (Sarı Köşk)** now houses a restaurant and café, while the Neoclassical **White Mansion (Beyaz Köşk)** has a cafe. The **Pink Mansion (Pembe Köşk)** was modeled on a townhouse. The oldest of the three, it was restored in 1982 and now hosts –you've guessed it– a café! All three mansions were restored in the 1980s by the Turkish Touring and Automobile Club.

"Victory is a shattering beauty with a rose face and tulip kisses."

Yahya Kemal

It was Khedive İsmail who commissioned Guiseppe Verdi's opera "Aida" to celebrate the opening of the Suez Canal in 1871.

Hamid-i Evvel Mosque

Beautifully restored in 2009, the present mosque was built in 1838 during the reign of **Mahmud II**, but stands on the site of a much older mosque from which only a fountain survives. Jutting out from the side is the room that served as the sultan's private pew, a more prosaic version of the elaborate hünkar mahfilis in buildings like the New Mosque (see p. 213). Facing it across the square is what was once the timekeeper's lodge built in 1844 by **Ağa Hüseyin Paşa** (1776-1849), who also paid for the **Serasker fire tower** in Beyazıt (see p. 083).

Emirgan Square

Few squares along the Bosphorus are as immediately inviting as Emirgan's where **ancient plane trees** provide shade for a cluster of pretty little **cafe** right beside a picturesque mosque and a gracefully restored octagonal **fountain** dating back to 1783 and paid for by the wife of Sultan Abdülhamid I. There are few better places to while away a few hours in the middle of a hot summer day before heading on to visit the Sakıp Sabancı Museum, just up the road (see p. 444).

Surp Yerits Mangants Armenian Church

Hüseyin, Sherif of Mecca

Lawrence of Arabia

Şerifler Yalı

South of the main square, the graceful 18th-century Şerifler Yalı stands on the probable site of Emir Güne Han's 17th-century palace. Badly damaged and cut off from the water when the coast road was built in 1940, it is still the **oldest surviving yalı** (mansion) on the European shore of the Bosphorus and belonged at one time to a Sherif of Mecca called **Hüseyin** (1854-1931), who served in the Ottoman parliament before throwing in his lot with **Lawrence of Arabia** in the Arab revolt that led eventually to the creation of Jordan. One son, **Abdullah**, became the Emir of Jordan, while another, **Faisal**, became King of Iraq. In 1924 Şerif Hüseyin proclaimed himself caliph and fled to Cyprus and then Jordan where he eventually died. **Ağa Hüseyin Paşa**, who built the Hamid Evvel timekeeper's lodge, also owned the house for a while. It contains fabulous frescoes.

Boyacıköy

Between Emirgan and Baltalimanı lies the beautiful and barely noticed suburb of Boyacıköy (Dyers' Village), so named because this was where, in the 18th century, a large family of dyers from **Kırklareli** in Thrace were resettled by **Sultan Selim III** to enable them to prepare all the **fezes** (see p. 251) needed in the capital. Its pretty back streets conceal the small Armenian **Church of Surp Yerits Mangants (The Three Holy Infants)**, built over an ayazma (sacred spring), which dates back to 1836. It was wholly reconstructed in 1885 and restored again as recently as 2004 even though the congregation is down to the last 10 families.

Stained-glass image of Three Holy Children

Greek Orthodox Primary School

Panagia Evangelistria Greek Orthodox Church

In Fırın Sokağı stands the Greek Orthodox **Church of Panagia Evangelistria (St Mary)** which dates back to 1834. Round the corner in **Tebdil Eskisi Sokağı** is the attractive double-fronted **schoolhouse** dating back to 1905. With its original cobbles, shady trees and old wooden houses this street looks like a slice of Safranbolu somehow strayed into the metropolis.

Tulip Festival

A **tulip festival** has been taking place in Emirgan Woods for decades, but in 2006 the Istanbul authorities expanded the idea to take in the rest of the city and remind visitors that tulips originally reached Europe from Turkey and not the other way around. Every winter millions of bulbs are planted and then in mid-April concerts, exhibitions and other events are organized to coincide with their flowering. The park looks absolutely magnificent at this time, with beds of primulas planted so densely together that they resemble Persian carpets and the sweet scent of thousands of hyacinths filling the air.

If you liked this, why not also enjoy the tulips in:
Gülhane Park (see p. 200)
Khedive's Villa gardens (see p. 550)
Sultanahmet Square (see p. 033)

Behind the Horse

Sakıp Sabancı Museum

067

In a superb location high up in a sloping garden on the shores of the Bosphorus close to Emirgan Woods, the Sakıp Sabancı Museum is one of Turkey's finest privately owned museums, with a small permanent collection and a regular program of high-profile touring shows.

Opened in 2002, the Sakıp Sabancı Museum is housed inside an imposing white mansion also known as the Atlı Köşk (Horse Mansion) because of the prominent **statue of a horse** that stands near the gate. It occupies land which **Sultan Abdülmecid** gave to the **Khedive Mehmed Ali Paşa** in the 19th century and which was later bought by another Egyptian prince who rebuilt the crumbling mansion that stood on it. This came to be known as the Prince Mehmed Ali Hasan Mansion after its new owner and it was this mansion, complete with its furnishings, that businessperson **Hacı Ömer Sabancı** bought in 1951. On his death in 1966 his son Sakıp moved into the house which remained the family home of one of Turkey's most important families of industrialists until 1998. Apart from the permanent collections, the Sakıp Sabancı Museum hosts regular blockbuster exhibitions, for example of works of Picasso and Dali.

@sakipsabancimuzesi
www.muze.sabanciuniv.edu
Tel: 0212 277 22 00, closed Mondays

Miniature Koran

One of the museum's prize exhibits is a tiny leather-bound Koran written in 1635 and measuring only 3.5 by 2.2 centimeters, making it too small to be read by the naked eye.

One of the sitting rooms

The rooms

Inside the house three ground-floor rooms retain the grandiose 18th and 19th-century **furnishings** in use when this was a Sabancı family home as well as paintings by well-known artists. One sitting room contains a 19th-century Hereke carpet, a Bohemian crystal chandelier and portraits of Ömer Sabancı and his wife by Bedri Koraman. The hall and stairwell are decorated with seascapes by **Fausto Zonaro** (1854-1929), while a second sitting room contains two paintings of young girls by the last caliph **Abdülmecid Efendi** (1868-1944) and pictures by the Russian artist **Ivan Konstantinovic Ayvazovski** (1817-1900). The corridor features a series of prints of the sultans commissioned by **Sultan Selim III** who had been impressed by the propaganda value of European royal portraiture. They were made in London in 1814 by **John Young** after originals by **Konstantin Kapıdağlı** whose works are also on display in Topkapı Palace (see p. 7).

Rodin statue

Mae West's lips at Salvador Dali exhibition

Young Girl Carrying a Pumpkin by Fausto Zonaro, 1889

The paintings

The museum also contains a fine collection of 19th and 20th-century paintings, including works by the Turkish orientalist artist Osman Hamdi Bey (see p. 335). Other artists represented include Şevket Dağ (1875-1944), İzzet Ziya (1880-1934), David Çıracıyan (1839-1907), Süleyman Seyyid (1842-1913), Bedri Rahmi Eyüboğlu (1911-75) and Fikret Mualla (1903-67). Unfortunately, they are usually on view only when there is a temporary exhibition in the same part of the building.

The "Byzantine" horse

The statue of a horse that stands in front of the museum is a copy of one of those from a **quadriga** (chariot group) that used to stand in the **Hippodrome** (see p. 7) before it was stolen by the Fourth Crusaders in 1204 and removed to Venice. After admiring it while on a business trip, Sakıp Sabancı had it copied to adorn his garden. The original bronze horses had been brought to Constantinople from Chios in Greece in the 5th century.

Calligraphy collection

A bust in the Rodin exhibition

The calligraphy

The museum also contains a fine collection of Turkish **calligraphy** spanning a 500-year period, including several lovely old **Korans** and many imperial **tuğras** (monograms) and fermans (decrees), some of them dating back to the 15th century. Look out in particular for the work of **Şeyh Hamdullah of Amasya** (1433?-1520), who was a teacher of Sultan Bayezid II and of **Ahmed Karahisari** (1468-1556), who worked at the court of Sultan Süleyman the Magnificent. Striking, too, are the **hilyes**, curious calligraphic pictures used to describe the physical attributes of the Prophet Mohammed according to a pattern designed by Hafız Osman in the 17th century.

The garden

The garden contains fine old fountains and other marble pieces dating back to Roman and Byzantine times. A second bronze **horse** also stands just in front of the museum building; French-made, it was brought here from its original home in Moda (see p. 484).

From the garden terrace it is possible to gaze across the Bosphorus to **Çubuklu** and the conspicuous flat-topped tower of the **Khedive's Villa** (see p. 551).

A second statue of a horse stands in front of the mansion.

Bosphorus view from the garden

Supplementary gallery

Best of the Yalıs

İstinye and Yeniköy

068

Continuing along the shore of the Bosphorus you come to the largest and certainly one of the prettiest bays at İstinye and then, beyond that, to the upscale suburb of Yeniköy which is renowned for its fine yalıs, or waterside mansions. Neither suburb has any specific tourist attractions, although they make perfect places to while away a few peaceful hours on a sunny afternoon. The newly-built "castle" that has housed the American Consulate since 2003 is hardly an improvement to the scenery.

İstinye Bay

Istanbul Stock Exchange (Borsaistanbul)

İstinye

İstinye is said to take its name from a footnote in the tale of **Jason and the Argonauts** (see p. 373), it being a possible corruption of the Greek name Sosthenion (Thanksgiving). According to the story, the Argonauts paused here to erect a statue in gratitude for the help given to the hero **Polydeuces** in defeating **Amycus**, the son of Poseidon and king of the Bebryces, who was in the habit of challenging all comers to box with him. Since he used nail-studded gloves he normally succeeded in killing them, but on this occasion he had met his match. A big and attractive bay, it was for many years used as a **dry dock** (hence the bus stop labeled Tersane (Shipyard), but is now happily full of pleasure boats again.

Taksiarchis Greek Orthodox Church

İstinye Hamam

Opposite the Neslişah Hanım Sultan Mosque, this hamam is one of the few along the Bosphorus and is thought to date back to immediately before or after the conquest of Constantinople in 1453. It has long since lost its women's section but still opens daily for men.

Deli ("Crazy") Fuad Paşa Yalı

In İstinye the **Deli ("Crazy") Fuad Paşa Yalı** was home to Fuad Paşa (1835-1931), a fearless fighter in the Russo-Turkish War and a notoriously plain speaker, hence his nickname. Later he plotted against Sultan Abdülhamid II and was sent into **exile** in Damascus. It now houses the offices of Turkey's delegation to BSEC, the Black Sea Economic Cooperation Organization.

Mihrişah Valide Sultan Fountain

Yeniköy

Immediately to the east of İstinye is **Yeniköy**, the Greek Neohorion which eventually became Nihori and was later Turkified into Yeniköy (New Town). This is a part of town. This is a part of town where many rich and famous people, including Tansu Çiller, who was Turkey's first female prime minister, live in magnificent mansions with security systems that wouldn't look amiss in downtown Lagos.

Don't miss the tall and graceful **Mihrişah Valide Sultan Fountain** in the park. It dates back to 1805 and was completely renovated in 2008.

Cavafy's ancestors

The famous Greek poet Constantine Cavafy's mother Hariklia was born in Yeniköy/Nihori and married there at age 14.

The mansion on the hill at the far left belongs to Şehzade Burhaneddin Efendi Yalı.

"Oh, stranger, should you ever catch a glimpse of
a village where nature smiles at you
and a beautiful girl, fine as a rose
hides behind each plane tree
Stop: You've arrived at Nihori."

Constantine Cavafy (1863-1933)

The ferryboat lines, which have run between İstinye and Çubuklu to ease traffic problems since 2017, offer an escape from the rush of the city and you can enjoy the view.

Churches, a synagogue and a mosque

On the hillside above Yeniköy's Villa Park, at the northern end of town, stands the wood-faced, Gothic-style Armenian **Church of Surp Hovhannes Mıgırdıç**. Behind it are the 19th-century Greek **Orthodox Churches of Hagios Georgios** and **Nikolaos**, with a rotting schoolhouse close by. The **Church of Panagia**, dating back to 1837 and with a detached belltower, stands on a slope in the center of Yeniköy just north of Simitçi Salih Sokağı which is lined with picturesque wooden houses.

Yeniköy Synagogue

Yeniköy's small and inconspicuous **synagogue** right in the center of the suburb was built in 1870 by **Abraham Kamondo** (see p. 261) who had a summer home here.

The first **Osman Reis Mosque** was built here in 1635-36 but nothing now remains of it. In 1904 a small new version in the First National architectural style was built. It stands on the main road in front of the **Ahmed Afif Paşa Yalı** (see p. 452).

Of the city's many Greek schools, today only three high schools (Zapyon, Zoğrafyon and Fener) and one primary school still accepts pupils.

Osman Reis Mosque

Surp Hovhannes Mıgırdıç Church

Greek Primary School

Hagios Georgios Church

Panagia Church

Yeniköy Yalıs

Vaniköy, Kandilli, Kanlıca and Arnavutköy aside, Yeniköy retains the largest number of original yalıs, the oldest of them the **Dadyan Yalısı**, built in the late 18th century for the Armenian family in charge of the gunpowder works in Ataköy (see p. 190). Most are hidden from casual sightseers behind lofty walls. The best way to catch a glimpse of them is from a boat on the Bosphorus.

Recaizade Mahmud Ekrem Bey Yalı

The very first building after the İstinye ferry terminal is the **Recaizade Ekrem Bey Yalı.** Recaizade Ekrem Bey (1847-1914) was an important author and a member of the literary group called Edebiyat-ı Cedide (New Literature) around Tevfik Fikret (see p. 435) who published a magazine called "Servet-i Fünun (The Wealth of Knowledge)". The same family also had a yalı in Vaniköy (see p. 552).

Faik Bey Yalı

Next to the Recaizade Ekrem Bey Yalı, the **Faik Bey Yalı**, also called "Pakize Hanımefendi Yalı", was built in the 19th century for a governor of Gümüşhane in north-eastern Turkey.

Ahmed Afif Paşa Yalı

The **Ahmed Afif Paşa Yalı**, built at the end of the 19th century in a style that combines elements of eastern and western architecture by **Alexandre Vallaury**, architect of the Ottoman Bank and Pera Palas Hotel, was later bought by Misbah Muhayyeş, who had owned the Pera Palas. When **Agatha Christie** visited Istanbul to write her famous novel "Murder on the Orient Express", she stayed here as a guest. It's now owned by a member of the Sabancı family. The tiny **Osman Reis Mosque** in front of it is another work of Vallaury dating back to 1903-4.

The building on the left is the Selahattin Adil Bey Yalı.

Şehzade Burhanettin Efendi Yalı

One of the biggest yalıs on the Bosphorus with 64 rooms, the **Şehzade Burhanettin Efendi Yalı** is named after a son of Sultan Abdülhamid II who bought it in 1911. There's a large pavilion in the back garden. It's valued at $150 million, making it one of the ten most valuable homes in the world. After the Kıbrıslı Yalı in Kandilli, it boasts the longest pier on the Bosphorus.

Rasim Ferid Talay Yalı

The white **Rasim Ferid Talay Yalı** is home to ex-prime minister Tansu Çiller and her husband Özer Uçuran Çiller. It's distinguished by its blue-tinted glass windows.

Kara Todori Yalı

On the far right the **Kara Todori Yalı** was constructed by **Sarkis Balyan** in 1871, using materials left over from the building of the Çırağan Palace (see p. 406). It belonged to Alexandros Todori, the son of the Stefenos Todori, director of Turkey's first medical school. The yalı in the middle is the Beyazcıyan, the one on the left the Muzafer Gazıoğlu.

Şehzade Burhaneddin Efendi Yalı

Sait Halim Paşa Yalı

In 1863 the Aristarhis family paid for a large yalı on the site of an older building. This was later bought by Mehmed Abdülhalim Paşa who commissioned **Petraki Adamantini**, a Çanakkale architect, to rebuild it on a grander scale. When he died one of his sons, **Sait Halim**, bought out the shares of his eight siblings to take over the property. Sait Halim was a grand vizier from 1913 to 1917. Despite his efforts to keep the Empire neutral during World War I, it was in his yalı that the Young Turks signed an **agreement with Germany** in 1914 that resulted in Turkey joining the First World War on their side. Later Sait Halim was **exiled** to Malta; he was **assassinated** in Rome in 1921. Sometimes called the Pembe Aslan Yalı (Mansion of the Pink Lions) because of the statues in front of it, the Sait Halim Paşa Yalı burnt down in 1995 and has since been rebuilt to serve as a popular venue for society wedding parties.

@saithalimpasayalisi
www.saithalimpasa.com

The Sandoz, Dadyan and Hamapulos yalıs standing side by side in Yeniköy Harbor.

Mısırlı (Egyptian) Fuad Bey Yalı used to belong to the owner of the Son Havadis (Latest News) newspaper, Mustafa Özkan.

Faik and Bekir Bey Yalı

The **Faik and Bekir Bey Yalı**, to the right of the Yeniköy ferry terminal, was designed in 1906 by the Italian architect, **Raimondo d'Aronco** who was responsible for the summer residence of the Italian Consulate in Tarabya. As it was built for the twin daughters of Sara Sultan, it was also called the "Twins' Mansion". It was later sold in two separate parts, called the Faik Bey Yalı and Bekir Bey Yalı respectively.

Armenian Catholic Church behind Kalkavan Yalı

Some of the yalıs have been turned into apartments.

Franz Joseph I

The Austrian Consulate

On the northern outskirts of Yeniköy as it merges into Kalender, the vast Austrian consulate was originally housed in a building called the **Cezayirliyan Yalı** which was given by Sultan Abdülhamid II to the Austro-Hungarian Emperor **Franz-Joseph** I in 1883 at a time when gifts of desirable real estate were seen as a good way to consolidate political alliances. At the end of the First World War most of its contents were sold to provide funds for citizens of the defeated empire to return home. It was briefly owned by the **British,** before being returned to the Austrians and then given to the Germans during the Second World War. Today the wheel has come full circle and it once again houses the Austrian Consulate and Cultural Center.

An old postbox

Austrian Consulate

A mansion in a wood on the Kalender road

BEYDEN 2 BL. İST.

ISKELE
BALIK

A Place Called Therapy

Kalender, Tarabya and Kireçburnu

869

The further along the Bosphorus you travel, the leafier it becomes. At Kalender you can pause to admire the enormous Huber Yalı, then round the bend you arrive in Tarabya, a huge and beautiful bay whose loveliness is diminished only by presence of the ugly Grand Tarabya Hotel. This was where many of the European embassies supported summer establishments so that their staff could escape the suffocating heat of the inner city. The pleasant restaurants suggest that many people are still seeking escape here today.

Tiny **Kalender** is sometimes said to have been named after a dervish lodge that used to stand here. However, it is more likely that it took its name from the **summer palace** built in the 17th century by Kalender Çavuş, caretaker of the Sultanahmet Mosque. This was replaced in the 18th century by the **Kalender Garden Palace**, another work of Sultan Ahmed III's busy Grand Vizier **Damat İbrahim Paşa**. Although this was restored in the 19th century, nothing now remains of it bar the garden walls.

"The long road that led across the hills from Therapeia to the city was dotted with ox-wagons carting furniture back from the villas to the town."

Sweet Waters **by Harold Nicholson, 1921**

Auguste Huber's wife

Huber Mansion (Huber Köşkü)

The huge Art Nouveauish Huber Mansion in Kalender, with its wonderful garden, takes its name from its former owner **Auguste Huber** who was the representative of Mauser and Krupp, the company that sold **rifles** to the Ottoman Empire at the end of the 19th century. For some years it was used as a French Catholic girls **school**. Since President Kenan Evren had it renovated in 1985, the mansion has served as a delightful **summer residence** for the presidency. A story claims that the mansion was given as a bribe to the lady-in-waiting of **Empress Eugenie**, the wife of Napoleon III, who was rumored to have had an affair with **Sultan Abdülaziz**. Despite its grandeur, not a great deal is known about the building which may or may not have been a work of **Raimondo d'Aronco**.

The old Huber Mansion is now used as a summer residence for the president.

Tarabya

Is a much bigger and more impressive place. Its name is said to be a corruption of the Byzantine name Therapeia (Therapy), which some claim had been given to the area because of the **hot springs** with healing properties that could be found here but were apparently destroyed by an earthquake in the 14th century. Others say that Patriarch Attikos gave it the name in the 5th century because of the area's generally **healthy atmosphere**. To confuse matters further, others insist that **Sultan Selim II** bestowed the name on the area after enjoying a fish supper here so much that he had **Grand Vizier Sokullu Mehmed Paşa** build him a palace in the place he dubbed simply **"Tarabiye (Pleasure)"**.

Tarabya's two Greek Orthodox **churches**, one of them, at the entrance to the Sümer Woods, dedicated to Hagia Paraskeve and the other to Hagios Konstantinos, stand as reminders of the large Greek population who used to live here.

Tarabya bay is dominated by the high-rise Grand Tarabya Hotel. It stands on the site of the summer retreat associated with the historic **Tokatlıyan Hotel** in Pera (see p. 304) that burnt down in 1954.

The old Tokatlıyan Hotel

German Summer Consulate

Summer residences

Kaiser Wilhelm II

In the 18th century several of the **embassies** opened new out-of-town bases in huge houses with gardens in **Büyükdere** (see p. 463). Here their staff could hope to escape the oppressive summer heat. Later Tarabya became a more popular base for the embassies, probably because it was not quite so far away. Many of the **Greeks** from crowded Fener also kept summer homes here, just as some people keep summer houses on the Princes' Islands today. The summer home of the British Embassy burnt down in 1911.

Abdülhamid II passed his adolescence in what later became the summer residence of the **German Consulate** to the south of Tarabya. Later he gave it to **Kaiser Wilhelm II** in return for his re-establishing the Ottoman navy. The mansion was designed by the Belgian architect Cingria who had won a prize in a competition to come up with the best plans. It was restored in 1990 but has lost most of its original internal features. The mansion sits in 45 acres of gardens and a path through them leads to a small **cemetery** containing 265 graves and an obelisk-shaped war memorial that records the stay of **Sultan Mahmud II** in a military camp here in 1829 and the part played in helping him reform the Ottoman army by **Marshall Helmuth von Moltke the Elder** (1822-88).

As you head out of Tarabya towards Kireçburnu you'll pass a duo of summer residences. The **Italian Consulate** was housed in a spectacular mansion designed by **Raimondo d'Aronco** and completed in 1908 in a style that mixed and matched Ottoman and Palladian styles of architecture. It was given as a wedding present to **Princess Elena of Montenegro** by Sultan Abdülhamid II and is currently undergoing particularly slow restoration.

Italian Summer Consulate

The oldest of the embassies here, the French Embassy had a rather convoluted history. It was housed in a building that had originally belonged to the Phanariot Greek governor of Wallachia, Prince Alexander Ipsilanti, who had been executed for treason in 1806. Since the French had helped dissuade the British from attacking Istanbul, Sultan Selim III was persuaded to give the building to the Emperor Napoleon Bonaparte. Unfortunately it caught fire in 1913 and only rather mundane portions of the original structure survive.

The poisoner

In antiquity Tarabya appears to have been called Pharmakeus which means "the poisoner" because it was here that **Medea**, abandoned by her lover **Jason** (see p. 373), threw away the poison with which she had been intending to kill him. An alternative story claims that a witch poisoned the drinking water as the Argo was sailing past in an attempt to kill its occupants. Her fiendish plot failed because the goddesses Hera and Athene stepped in to clean up the water.

There are fine wooden houses along the shore at Kireçburnu.

Kireçburnu

The promontory just north of Tarabya bay is called Kireçburnu (Lime Point), perhaps because of the past existence of **lime quarries** in the area. But the most important thing about Kireçburnu is that it is here for the first time that you start to be able to see the **Black Sea** straight ahead of you, an enthralling sight were it not for the pylons, electricity wires and 3rd Bridge that disfigure it.

Dikranyan Yalı

Ural Ataman
Classic Car Museum

A stunning collection of 63 vehicles from the days before American car manufacturing hit the bumpers, this small privately-owned museum is only open on Saturdays but is a great place to bring boys who are tired of historic sightseeing and their dads. It's inland from the coast, across the road from the Metin Oktay sports center.

@uralatamanmuseum, www.atamanmuseum.com
Tel: 0212 299 45 39

Escaping the Heat

Büyükdere and Sadberk Hanım Museum

078

In 1980 Turkey's first privately-owned museum opened in Büyükdere, which comes just before Sarıyer on the European shore of the Bosphorus. Resembling a cut-down version of Ankara's Anatolian Civilisations Museum crossed with the Ethnography Museum, it houses the collections of Sadberk Hanım who was the wife of the businessperson Vehbi Koç. Come here to see everything from Ancient Greek pottery to the finest Anatolian embroidery. The museum is housed in two magnificent old yalıs. Several others stand close by.

There are many old yalıs and mansions in Büyükdere.

Piyasa Caddesi

Büyükdere in an old photograph

Büyükdere takes its name from the "büyük dere (big stream)" at the head of the bay where the battalions of the **First Crusade** paused to catch their breath before crossing the Bosphorus into Asia Minor on their way to Palestine in 1096. **Evliya Çelebi** left a breathless description of it as a beautiful wooded place inhabited mainly by Greeks and Armenians in the 17th century. Today, of course, it is very built up and of the Greeks and Armenians only their churches remain. However, this is still a very charming part of the Bosphorus, where the coast road has been built on reclaimed land a little way in front of the yalıs and where there are still many lovely **wooden houses** surviving in the back streets.

Büyükdere houses

Summer retreats

Heading back from the museum towards the center of Büyükdere you come to the magnificent neoclassical summer residence of the **Spanish Consulate** that was built by Franciscan friars and given to the Spaniards in 1783 following a cholera epidemic. It has lost its original gardens to the coast road but acquired in their place some parkland to the rear. The Franciscans also built the **Church of the Immaculate Conception** here in 1866; it's further west, just before the main road running inland rejoins the coast road heading for Tarabya.

East of the Sadberk Hanım Museum, what eventually became the **Russian Consulate** was originally built in 1840 for **General Nikolai Ignatiev**, the "shrewd paşa", also known as "the vice-Sultan", who was extremely keen to secure the Bosphorus for the Russians. Since he never succeeded in achieving that his ghost is said to haunt the old consulate building, in any case a sad sight today with its black and white pebble-mosaic path leading through an overgrown garden to an abandoned building.

Russian Consulate

Spanish Consulate

Greek Primary School

Hagia Paraskeve Greek Orthodox Church

Surp Boğos Church

Church of the Immaculate Conception

Churches

Originally built as an Armenian Catholic chapel in 1847, the **Church of Surp Boğos,** near the Spanish Consulate, was expanded into a gothic-style church in 1893; it wouldn't look out of place in Britain or France. A little further inland, the Greek Orthodox **Church of Hagia Paraskeve** stands on the site of a church dating back to the early 17th century. The current model may be far more modern but it stands in a particularly pretty **cobbled courtyard** shaded with huge trees. The old **schoolhouse** with which it was once associated stands derelict at the top of the stairs behind it.

Keçecizade Fuad Paşa

Fuat Paşa Yalı

Housed inside a late 18th-century yalı, the 60-room hotel takes its name from a later owner, **Keçecizade Fuat Paşa,** who was a Grand Vizier to Sultan Abdülaziz in the late 19th century. Not as glitzy as some of its more recently refurbished competitors, the Fuatpaşa still has history and Bosphorus views.

Kocataş ve Sait Paşa Yalıs

Kocataş Mansion, built in the 19th century, was bought by **Necmettin Molla Kocataş,** who served as the Minister of Justice and Deputy Vizier in the Ottoman Government. The neighbouring Sait Paşa Mansion was commissioned by **Mehmet Sait Paşa,** who was the Grand Vizier of Abdulhamid II in the second constitutional era. Both mansions are revived today with the modern touches of Six Senses, while paying regard to their original architecture.

Sadberk Hanım Museum

If this marvelous small museum were in Sultanahmet, it would be heaving with visitors. As it is you may well find you have it to yourself.

The museum is housed inside what was originally the wooden **Azaryan Yalı** built at the start of the 20th century by Manuk Azaryan Efendi who was a member of parliament towards the end of the Ottoman era. It was sometimes called the **Vidalı (Criss-crossed) Yalı** because of the wooden latticework on its façade. In the 1950s the Koç family bought the mansion and turned it into a family home. In 1980 it opened to the public as Turkey's first privately museum, expanding to incorporate the next door yalı in 1988.

The original building contains collections related to **Turkish and Islamic art** and **Ottoman Turkish life,** while the second building houses the **archeological collections** arranged in chronological order. In the first section the rooms set up to show off the rituals associated with circumcision and engagement as well as what the bedroom of a new mother would have looked like are particularly interesting. Also wonderful are the exquisite samples of embroidery, the colorful Ottoman clothing and some delicate examples of 18th-century **oya** (the embroidery stitched around the edge of women's headscarves) amongst which those shaped like pansies are especially lovely.
The museum also houses one of the finest collections of 16th-century **İznik pottery** in the country. Be sure, too, to take a look at the **Beykoz glass** originally produced at the glass-making works on the opposite side of the Bosphorus (see p. 554).

Normally the museum also showcases artworks typical of the Selçuk, Mameluk, Safavid and other Islamic styles. However, these are sometimes sidelined in favor of temporary exhibitions. Check *Time Out Istanbul* for details.

The archeological section in the Sevgi Gönül wing contains exhibits dating from **Neolithic through to Byzantine times** and includes some wonderful cuneiform tablets, Phrygian bowls, glass perfume bottles, coins and gold jewellery as well as a fine collection of Roman lamps, some of them carved with scenes that are very naughty indeed. Most of the exhibits were collected by the late Hüseyin Kocabaş, although Sevgi Gönül, the daughter of Sadberk Koç, was also responsible for recovering many items that had been removed from the country illegally.

This is a state-of-the-art museum in which every-thing is beautifully presented, with English labeling and explanations to supplement the Turkish. There's an excellent giftshop on the ground floor along with a **tea garden** in the secluded back garden.

@sadberkhanimmuzesi
www.sadberkhanimmuzesi.org.tr
Tel:0212 242 38 13
closed Wednesdays

Sadberk Hanım

Sadberk Hanım (1908-73) was the wife of the hugely successful Turkish businessperson, Vehbi Koç and an enthusiastic collector, especially of historic fabrics and embroidery. Sadly, she died before she could see the museum that was her dream open its doors.

Ceramics collection in museum

Floatplanes

Did you know that there were flights from Turkey to Italy as early as 1924? And with floatplanes that took off from the **Harbor of Büyükdere!** The flights that were scheduled on two main courses (Istanbul-Athens-Brindisi and Istanbul-Athens-Rhodes) between 1924-1936 were carried out with the **Italian Aero Espresso Airlines**. The Dornier Wal planes with a passenger capacity of 10 were flown by Turkish and Italian pilots.

Shrine of the Silver Saint

Sarıyer, Rumeli Kavağı, Garipçe and Rumeli Feneri

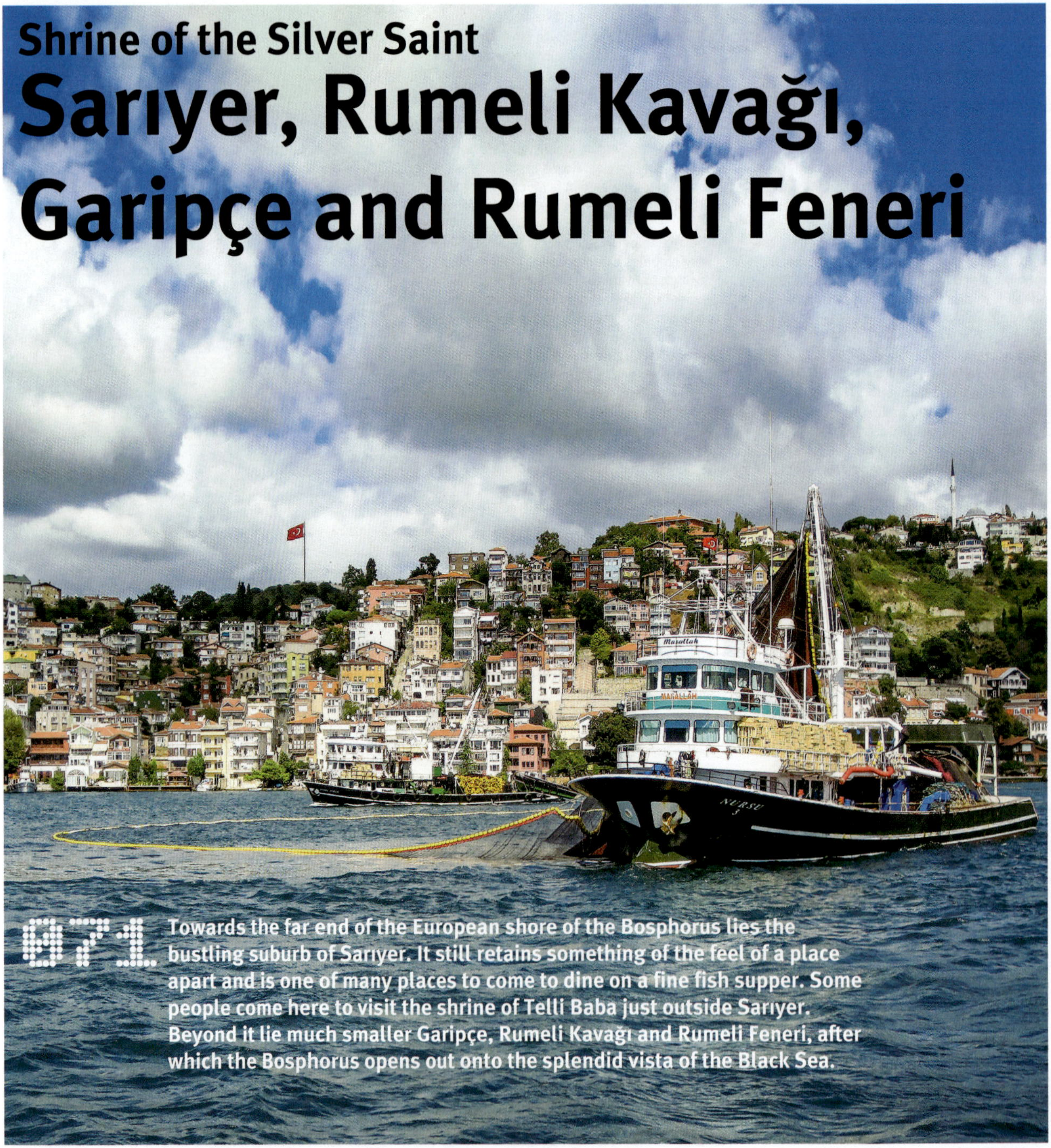

071 Towards the far end of the European shore of the Bosphorus lies the bustling suburb of Sarıyer. It still retains something of the feel of a place apart and is one of many places to come to dine on a fine fish supper. Some people come here to visit the shrine of Telli Baba just outside Sarıyer. Beyond it lie much smaller Garipçe, Rumeli Kavağı and Rumeli Feneri, after which the Bosphorus opens out onto the splendid vista of the Black Sea.

Sarıyer

Sarıyer Ordu Evi (Army House)

There is some debate as to how Sarıyer got its name which means simply "**yellow place**" in Turkish. Some say that it took it from a yellow-hued local soil, others that Sarıyer is a corruption of Sarıyar meaning "blonde beloved", a name it had acquired in memory of one of the sultans' favorites. Yet others suggest that it was named after a local holy man, Sarı Baba, about whom nothing is known. Then there is a suggestion that it was named after two blond soldiers ("sarı erler") associated with Sultan Mehmed II and buried near a town center mosque. In desperation some people have even suggested that it acquired the name because it was a place where people spent many yellow (gold) coins.

St John the Baptist Church

A surprisingly conservative backwater which has acquired a sizeable population of expatriate Iranians and Arabs in recent years, Sarıyer still retains a **fishing fleet** with the accompanying fish market and restaurants serving an array of fresh fish dishes. Right beside the quay a turreted building dating back to 1911 houses the **Naval Officers' Club**; other fine if forgotten buildings lurk in the back streets, including one now owned by Kızılay that must be amongst the finest wooden mansions in all Istanbul.

Amid the lovely old wooden buildings hidden in the back streets of **Yeni Mahalle** there is a 19th-century church dedicated to **Hagios Ioannis Prodromos (St John the Baptist)**, although it no longer offers regular services. Above Yeni Mahalle there are great Bosphorus views from **Havantepe.**

Shrine of Telli Baba

Heading up the Bosphorus towards Rumeli Kavağı you pass the tomb of **İmam Abdullah Efendi,** better known as Telli Baba, an **evliya** or holy man who is thought to be able to help the single find husbands or wives. When pilgrims leave the shrine they take away a piece of **silver wire** which they return to attach to it once they are securely married. The shrine is so popular that whole wedding parties often visit it as part of their celebrations. In the past local fisherman also sought Telli Baba's intercession to protect them on their voyages.

Not much seems to be known about Telli Baba and the two stories most commonly told about him belong to two completely different periods in time. According to the first he fought alongside **Sultan Mehmed II** at the conquest of Istanbul in 1453, while according to the second he was fighting alongside **Sultan Mahmud II** when Cossacks attacked Rumeli Kavağı in the 19th century. He is thought to have been a dervish who established a lodge on the site where his shrine now stands. He may have been a member of the Qadiri sect who adorned their turbans with the same sort of silver threads as were used to decorate bridal veils, hence his nickname Telli Baba (Silver-Threaded Father).

Bird watcher's paradise

The far end of the Bosphorus is one of the best places in the world for spotting **raptors** as they pass over on their way to and from their winter homes in Africa. To cite just one example, around 40,000 **lesser spotted eagles** pass this way every year, although **common and honey buzzards, marsh harriers** and **steppe eagles** are also familiar sights. The best times and places to observe the birds are at **Rumeli Feneri** in spring and at **Toygar Hill in Beykoz**, (see p. 552) Otağtepe Fatih Woods in **Kavacık** (see p. 545) and **Çamlıca Hill** (see p. 506) in autumn.

Many lovely wooden houses survive in Sarıyer and Yeni Mahalle

The castle

Rumeli Feneri with 3rd Bosphorus Bridge behind it

Rumeli Kavağı

This last stopping place for the public ferries on the European side of the Bosphorus is little more than a cluster of houses and fish restaurants attached to a fishing harbor, a great place to stop for lunch. Rumeli Kavağı might have been named after the **poplar trees** (kavak) that used to grow here, although it is much more likely that it acquired its name from the secondary meaning of "kavak", which is "control point". Certainly there has been a castle, **İmroz Kalesi**, on the hillside here since the 12th century when Manuel I Comnenos built it to enable him to levy **tolls** on passing ships. This was later occupied first by the Genoese and then by the Ottomans, before **Sultan Murad IV** turned the whole area into a military base to guard the mouth of the Bosphorus.

Garipçe

In ancient times Garipce was **Gyropolis (City of Vultures)**, a place closely associated with the gods of the winds. It may have acquired its modern name as a corruption of "Karibce", meaning "quite near" in Turkish, because of its proximity to the lighthouse at Rumeli Feneri. Today it is little more than a pretty, secluded fishing harbor with a couple of rickety wooden houses interspersed with fish restaurants and the remains of a castle dating back to 1778. Unfortunately, once the abutment of the 3rd Bridge was built here, the place lost its unspoiled beauty.
Out on the headland are the remains of a twin-towered castle dating back to 1769 and offering fine views of the Black Sea and the Symplegades from its arched exterior wall.

Rumeli Feneri

There has been a lighthouse at Rumeli Feneri (European Lighthouse) since at least the 16th century. Just off-shore are a pair of rocks – Kocataş ("Great Stone") and Körtaş (Blind Stone) – which the Ottomans called the **Kanlı Kayalar (Bloody Rocks)** because of the hazard they presented to shipping. To the Ancient Greeks these were the Symplegades between which Jason and the Argonauts managed to sail en route to finding the Golden Fleece
(see p. 373).

The current 30-meter-tall **lighthouse** here was built in 1769 and modernized by the British during the Crimean War in 1856. It forms a pair with the one across the Bosphorus at **Anadolu Feneri**.

Rumeli Feneri on the Bosphorus by Jean Laurens, 1853

THE BOSPHORUS
(ASIAN SHORE)

Football Fanatics and Moonlight Fanciers

Fenerbahçe and Kalamış

072 Fenerbahçe will always be associated primarily with the mega-league football team whose stadium can be found here. For non-football fans, however, it's also the location of a delightful park that opened to the public back in the 19th century. Neighboring Kalamış is home to a large marina. This is a well-heeled residential area with some suitably upscale restaurants to go with it.

The "dragon mansion"

"Ver Leftere
yaz deftere.
(Give Lefter a
look, he'll put it
in the book)"

Fenerbahçe football chant.

Statue of Lefter

Fenerbahçe in numbers

- Founded 1907
- 8 times winner of Presidents Cup
- 19 times Turkish League champions
- 6 times winner of Turkish Cup

Fenerbahçe takes its name, which means "lighthouse garden" in Turkish, from a **lighthouse** that stands on the coast here. It's a district of well-maintained low-rise apartment blocks in leafy streets, with the occasional fine old mansion surviving as a reminder of the past. One of the best stands near Fenerbahçe Park; its wooden facade is decorated with a protruding classical-style bust while two lively green dragons serve as brackets supporting the top floor cumba (bay window).

Şükrü Saraçoğlu Stadium

The **"Yellow Canaries"** have their home base in the Şükrü Saraçoğlu Stadium in Fenerbahçe, which was built in 1908 but expanded as recently as 2006 to hold a crowd of almost 54,000 supporters. Visitors can buy souvenir kits at the Fenerium shop attached to the stadium, where there's also a small **museum**.

Across the road stands a **statue of Lefter Küçükandonyadis** (1925-2012), Fenerbahçe's all-time hero, who scored 423 goals in the 615 games he played for the team in addition to the 20 goals he scored while playing in 50 matches for the Turkish national team. He retired to Büyükada (see p. 588) where a street is named after him.

An old tree in Fenerbahçe Park

Fenerbahçe Park

Just south of the Kalamış Marina, the Byzantine emperors and Ottoman sultans built themselves **summer palaces** on a peninsula that juts out into the Bosphorus, a location that is perfect for watching the moon reflected on the water. In the 19th century the area was turned into a public park, which became an extremely popular recreation center. However, by the middle of the 20th century it had fallen into a dereliction from which it was only rescued in 1990 by the efforts of the indefatigable **Çelik Gülersoy** and his Turkish Touring and Automobile Association. The views out towards **Sarayburnu** (see p. 202) and the **Princes' Islands** (see p. 578) are superb and this is a very popular park for strolling especially at weekends. Although this is a great place to come to see tulips in spring, parts of the park are also set aside for the cultivation of **wild flowers**.

Fenerbahçe remembered by poet Yahya Kemal

Kalamış and the Marina

The small 19th-century **Church of Hagios Ioannis Khrysostomos (John Chrysostom)** stands opposite the entrance to the Kalamış Marina. Externally it's not much to look at although the icon-filled interior is atmospheric. In the narthex look out for a fine old 19th-century stone printing block depicting a much older Istanbul.

One of Istanbul's two marinas, Kalamış is larger than Ataköy (see p. 193), with berths for more than 1000 yachts. Like all Turkey's marinas, it is operated by Setur.

www.seturmarinas.com

Hagios Ioannis Khrysostomos Church

Ancient Chalcedon

Kadıköy and Moda

073

Hard though it is to imagine it today, Kadıköy was once a completely separate settlement gazing at Byzantium across the water. This was the Chalcedon of the Megarians which was founded in c. 635 BC, but fell to the Turks long before Byzantium. Of all the suburbs on the Asian side of the city, today's Kadıköy has to be one of the liveliest, with a large student population and plenty of nightlife opportunities especially along its famous "Bar Street". Adjoining Moda is one of Asian Istanbul's glitziest residential suburbs.

Kadıköy shoreline

Arriving by ferry in Kadıköy (the Village of the Judge), its attractions are not immediately obvious – you will find yourself stranded in a shapeless concrete plaza facing onto what looks like an unbroken line of high-rise shop and apartment blocks. The sole building of distinction is the low-rise (**Old Market Building) Eski Hal Binası** on the shore which was built to house a wholesale market in the 1920s but is now home to the **Istanbul Conservatory** and Haldun Taner Theater. Still, appearances can be deceptive and you only have to delve down the side streets behind the high-rises to find narrow pedestrianized streets lined with interesting shops, enticing restaurants and lively bars that cater to a large local student population; it's a bit like Beşiktaş but with heavy metal T-shirts and attitude. Here, too, are a number of small, discreet churches dating back to the 19th century. Kadıköy is within handy walking or ferry distance of **Haydarpaşa station**, the imposing, German-designed terminal for train services to Anatolia. 1

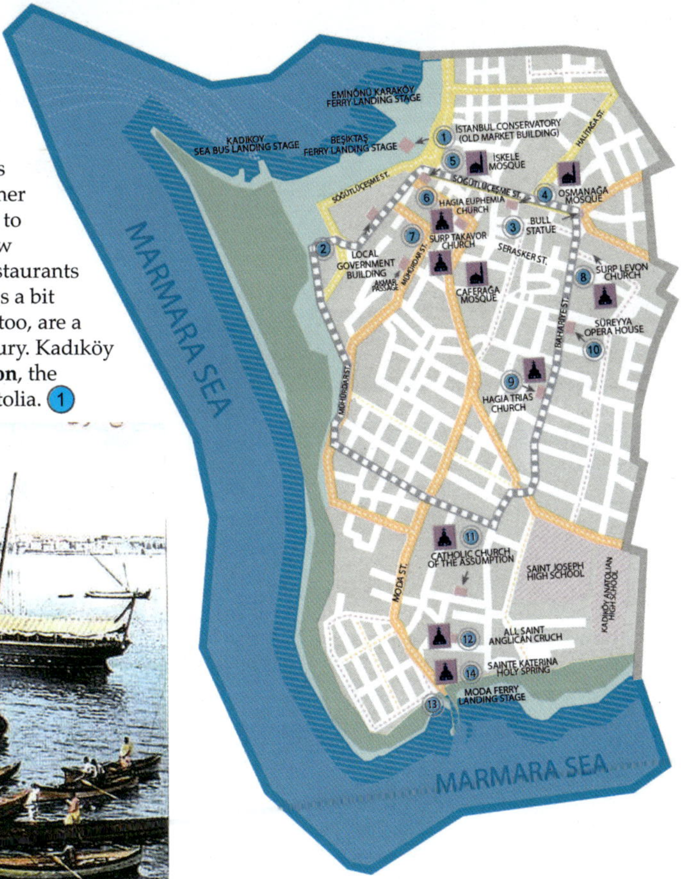

Kadıköy harbor
in old photo

Next to the Eski Hal Binası, an unusual **statue of Atatürk** commemorates the changeover from writing Turkish in the Arabic script to writing it using the Roman alphabet in 1928. A huge step forward in enabling ordinary people to learn to read and write, the change had the unintended consequence of cutting Republican Turks off from Ottoman history which was sealed in the archives in suddenly mysterious Ottoman Turkish. Behind the statue stands the **Kadıköy Kaymakamlığı** (local government building), a fine example of First National Architecture dating back to around 1913 and designed by the Greek architect **Constantinos P. Kyriakides**.

Amid the maze of busy shopping streets there are a couple of landmark monuments to look out for. Just as Wall Street in New York has its monumental bull, so too does Kadıköy. Watch out, too, for the monumental slab with a tiny crocodile perched on the corner and use it to get your bearings inside the market. Now it serves as Kadıköy History, Literature and Art Library since 2014. It also functioned as Kadıköy Mayor's Office and underwent a thorough restoration in 1995. 2 3

Kadıköy History, Literature and Art Library

On the right the Old Market building as it was in the past; on the left how it is now

The Land of the Blind

Fable has it that Byzas, the founder of Byzantium, was advised by the famous oracle of Apollo at Delphi in Greece to build his new town opposite "the Land of the Blind". Arriving at the point where the Golden Horn and Bosphorus met the Sea of Marmara, Byzas gazed across at Chalcedon and decided that its inhabitants must have been blind not to have recognized the advantages of this location as opposed to their preferred spot in Asia. So in 667 BC he went ahead and founded Byzantium on the site that went on to become Constantinople and Istanbul. More than 2,000 years later that inveterate Ottoman travel writer Evliya Çelebi retorted that the truly blind had to have been those who settled across the water and didn't recognize the beauty of Kadıköy!

The Kadıköy crocodile

Deep in the bazaar you may come across a slab of inscribed stone with a tiny bronze statue of a crocodile in the corner. Believe it or not, the 1st-century geographer **Strabo** recorded that people would feed the crocodiles at a spring a little inland from Chalcedon!

Fish market

The streets of Kadıköy host giant works of world-famous mural artists.

Hagia Euphemia Greek Orthodox Church

Surp Levon Armenian Catholic Church

Hagia Trias Greek Orthodox Church

Surp Takavor Armenian Church

Churches 6 7 8 9

Facing the small square adorned with the sculpture of a crocodile is the best known of Kadıköy's Christian places of worship, the Greek Orthodox **Church of Hagia Euphemia** that started life in 1694, although the current building only dates back to 1830. As the story goes, Hagia (Saint) Euphemia was a local Christian who rejected the governor's instructions to pray to a pagan god. For her obstinacy she was tortured, before being thrown to a bear in c. 305. Later, it was believed that her spirit intervened at the **Fourth Ecumenical Council**, held in Chalcedon in 451, when two groups of Christians were unable to agree on whether Jesus was possessed of one or two natures. Following her intervention, the Council ruled that Jesus was both wholly man and wholly god (i.e. that he had two natures), a distinction that may seem unimportant today but was, in the 5th century, as contentious as arguments over gay priests today. Hagia Euphemia's remains were removed to Constantinople during the **Persian invasion of Chalcedon** in the 7th century. Today a casket purportedly containing her remains can be seen in the church of the Greek Patriarchate in **Fener** (see p. 232). A late 19th-century painting of the Council of Chalcedon can be seen in the narthex.

Nearby is the Armenian **Church of Surp Takavor (Christ the King)**, originally built in the 17th century but only dating back to the late 19th century in its present form. It has a pleasant central dome inset with oval windows.

The basilica-shaped **Church of Surp Levon (St Leo)**, at the start of Bahariye Caddesi, is unusual in that it is an Armenian Catholic church, the sole example in Anatolian Istanbul. The current building dates back only to 1911 although there is believed to have been an older wooden church on the site.

Finally, not far from "Bar Street" in Hacı Şükrü Sokak is the huge **Church of Hagia Trias (the Holy Trinity)**, which dates back to 1902 and boasts an especially colorful dome.

Mosques 4 5

Unlike nearby Üsküdar, which is dominated by Islamic religious buildings, Kadıköy's mosques keep a relatively low profile. The oldest of them, the low-slung **Osman Ağa Mosque** on Söğütlüçeşme Caddesi, was built during the reign of Sultan Ahmed I (1603-17) for Mısırlı (Egyptian) Osman Ağa who also paid for the decorative fountain nearby. More obvious as you head into the market from behind the ferry terminal is the **Harbor (İskele) Mosque** that dates back to 1760 but was completely rebuilt in 1858.

Synagogue

Kadıköy's only synagogue, the **Hemdat Israel (The Loveliness of Israel)**, stands between İzettin and Uzun Hafız Sokaks, a little inland and uphill from the harbor. It dates back to 1899 when many Jews moved into Kadıköy after a fire devastated nearby Kuzguncuk (see p. 508).

The entrance of Hemdat Israel Synagogue

Sürreya Opera House

Süreyya İlmen

Bahariye Caddesi 10

Pedestrianized Bahariye Caddesi (officially General Asım Gündüz Caddesi but no one calls it that) is the İstiklal Caddesi of the Asian side of Istanbul with a similar old-fashioned **tram** trundling along it en route to Moda. The most striking monument on the street is the grand **Sürreya Opera House** donated to the city by Süreyya and Adalet İlmen in 1924. This was later converted into a **cinema** but was restored to its original function in 2007. The facade is decorated with carvings of the Muses and masks of tragedy and comedy and many people will find the elaborate interior more than worth the price of a concert ticket. Beside it stands a modern marble sculpture by **Neslihan Pala** called Vodvil (Vaudeville). To find Bahariye Caddesi walk up Söğütlüçeşme Caddesi from the harbor until you reach the statue of the bull and then turn right.

www.sureyyaoperasi.org

Özgen Berkol Doğan Library of Science Fiction

The first and only science fiction library in Turkey was established in commemoration of the young scientist Özgen Berkol Doğan, who passed away in 2007. The library that provides service since 2012 includes around 12 thousand books and periodicals about science fiction and fantastic literature, as well as Turkish and World Literature, social sciences, physical sciences, technology, art, sports, cinema, philosophy and psychology. You can find every science fiction, fantastic and horror literature book published in Turkish and also works in several languages. In their monthly program, they include speeches, film screenings and mini concerts. Don't miss if you happen to pass by.

@bilimkurgukutuphanesi
www.ozgenberkoldogan.com
Tel: 0216 349 31 31

Yeldeğirmeni

Once populated mostly by **Greeks** and **Jews**, Yeldeğirmeni is a neighborhood around the streets which trail down to Kadıköy Rıhtım Street. Its churches and its location as home to the only synagogue in Kadıköy is living proof of this. The **Germans** and **Italians** who came to build the **Haydarpaşa Station** (see p.492) often chose to live in this neighborhood and they built nice buildings to remind us of their history. Throughout the years, particularly during the events of 6-7 September and following the Cyprus Operation, Yeldeğirmeni lost its Greek population. For many years it stayed as an unsafe and uninhabited group of streets just next to Kadıköy. But, particularly because the young population are choosing to live in this neighbourhood in ever increasing numbers, new venues have been opened and it has now reassumed its past glory. As a result of this change, the **Kadıköy Municipality** opened the **Notre Dame du Rosaire Church**, built in 1895 as a monastery, school and church, as **Yeldeğirmeni Art** in 2014. The church had been used as a gym during the 1980s but was evacuated after the 1999 earthquake.

Gazhane Museum

The Gashouse in Hasanpaşa began working in 1892 and served for Istanbul until 1993. Later, with the use of natural gas, it became obsolete. This important industrial legacy was left to its fate for a long time, and in 2015 the preparation for its revival began. The restoration is finally over and in July 2021 the Gazhane Museum opened its doors. The 31,500-meter square space includes the climate and cartoon museums, exhibition halls, theaters, libraries, playgrounds, showgrounds, and cafés and restaurants. Being a central spot on the Anatolian side, the place is likely become the address of many meetings and cultural activities.

Baylan

Baylan stands out among the modern stores with its different style as you walk up from the main post office building. This is a very old but quite popular patisserie serving its customers since 1961. Its owner was originally a Greek but it changed hands in 2010. It offers a great opportunity to relax in the hubbub of the bazaar and to taste the nostalgic flavors which have been preserved for years.

Nightlife

For a fun night out head straight for Kadife Sokak (AKA Bar Street), a street full of old wooden houses which have been turned into bars each with their own distinctive character. The Nâzım Hikmet Cultural Center offers a program of music, films and art exhibitions.

www.nazimhikmetkulturmerkezi.org
Tel: 0216 414 22 39

A tea garden in Moda

Moda ferry terminal

Moda 11 12 13

Facing out towards the Sea of Marmara and the Princes' Islands, Moda is an unexpectedly swish residential neighborhood with some trendy restaurants and bars. Although there may have been settlement here since Phoenician times, Moda only really became fashionable (which is what its name means in Turkish) in the dying days of the Ottoman Empire when many Greeks and Armenians made it their home. Buried in the back streets are several churches that serve as a reminder of these lost Christian populations. One of the most imposing is the 19th-century Catholic **Church of the Assumption**, which was built by the French. Considerably smaller is the Anglican **Church of All Saints**, built in 1878 to a design by **G. E. Street** who was also responsible for the Crimean Church (see p. 315). Just across the road from Barış Manço's house, it holds services every Sunday morning.

Moda streets

Many of Istanbul's ferry landing stages are an architectural cut above their mundane function and Moda's, built in 1917 by architect **Vedat Tek** as the first stop for ferries en route for the Princes' Islands, is certainly one of the finest. Destroyed by a high wind in 1937, it was restored in 2000 with a little help from pop star **Barış Manço**. The pier, which was used for different functions for a while and then abandoned to its fate, became a living place with its café and library of 9 thousand books after the restoration carried out by Istanbul Metropolitan Municipality.

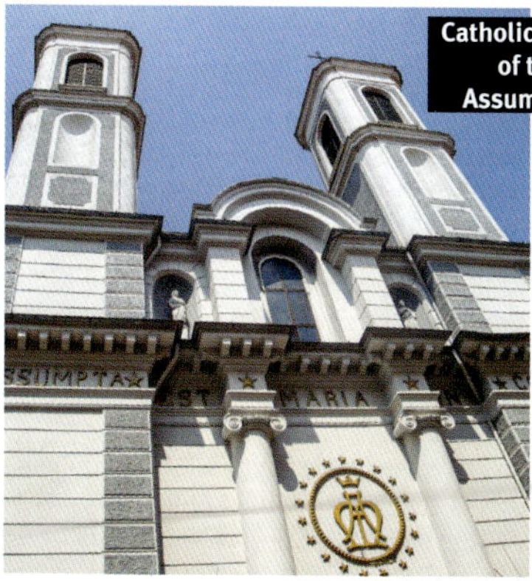

Catholic Church of the Assumption

All Saints Anglican Church

Remembering Barış Manço

The much-loved Turkish pop singer Barış Manço (1943-99), whose music spanned the spectrum from supermarket favorite "Domates, Biber, Patlıcan (Tomatoes, Pepper, Aubergine)" to the sublime "Gülpembe (Pink Rose)", had a house on Yusuf Kamil Paşa Sokak in Moda and regularly signed off his TV show with an airy "Barış Manço, Moda, 81300", the postcode to which fans could write in the days before email. When he died the outpouring of grief was compared to that bestowed on Princess Diana of England. Now his personalized car number plates hang off one gate while another shows the Messiah-like singer greeting his youthful followers.

www.barismanco.kadikoy.bel.tr
Tel: 0216 337 94 13
closed Mondays

Barış Manço House Museum

St. Catherine Ayazma (14)

An important feature of the Meyhane Koço, serving since 1928 and located on the slope going down to Moda Pier, is its underground ayazma (holy spring). An entrance was later built next to the restaurant for the ayazma, which is dedicated to Saint Katerina, an important religious figure for the Greeks.

Mahmut Muhtar Paşa Mansion

Mahmut Muhtar Paşa Mansion

Settlement in Moda dates back to the 1850s. The few mansions which survive from that period will pop up as if to remind you of the old aristocratic days of Moda as you stroll along its streets. These mansions, some in good condition and trying to survive among modern buildings and others about to fall down, are the last witnesses of Moda's bygone days.

The building, which is also called the Marble Mansion because of its marble covering, was built for an Englishman named **James Baker** in 1886. The mansion is located within the walls of the school close to the pier as you walk along Moda Street. It was later bought by Princess Nimetullah Hanım and her husband **Mahmut Muhtar Paşa**. **Princess Nimetullah Hanım**, daughter of the **Egyptian Khedive İsmail Paşa**, lived there until her death. After their demise, the mansion was inherited by their children. However they sold the mansion to the Ministry of National Education owing to disagreements between them. The valuable pieces of furniture and objects in the mansion were put to sale at an auction. Among these were two statues in the garden. The horse statue was bought by the **Sabancı Family** after heated competition at the auction and is currently located in front of the restaurant building of **Sakıp Sabancı Museum** (see p. 447). The gazelle statue, which can be seen in front of the Divan Hotel in Elmadağ, was bought by the **Koç Family**. The building has been used as Kadıköy High School for Girls since 1957, which was later named **Kadıköy High School**. The high school is still open, but the mansion stands in a derelict condition in its garden.

Dr. Arif Sarıca Paşa Mansion

The mansion is on the left side once you leave the Mahmut Muhtar Paşa Mansion behind. It used to belong to **Dr. Arif Sarıca**, the physician of **Sultan Abdülhamid II**. Arif Sarıca Paşa's brother was one of the eminent bureaucrats of the period and he also had a mansion on the Caddebostan coast. The mansion was built by the Greek **Pape Kalfa** in 1903 as a five-storey building made of cut stone. The building, which still belongs to the Sarıca Family, is inhabited by the pianist **Ayşegül Sarıca** who was honoured as a State Artist in 1971.

Antipa Mansion

This grey building, which will strike you immediately as you stroll on the Cape of Moda, was built for a Greek physician named **Dr. Andreas Antipa**. The last owner of the mansion was **Ferit Tek** who was the Tokyo Ambassador. The street was later named after him.

The Road to Baghdad

Bağdat Caddesi and Sahil Yolu

074

The premier shopping street on the Asian side of the city, Bağdat Caddesi (Baghdad Avenue) runs for six kilometers from Kadıköy to Bostancı, passing through or skirting round Kızıltoprak, Feneryolu, Selamiçeşme, Çiftehavuzlar, Göztepe, Caddebostan, Erenköy, Şaşkınbakkal, Suadiye and Çatalçeşme. Somewhat fancifully dubbed the Rodeo Drive or Bond St of Istanbul, it's more like a more modern version of İstiklal Caddesi without the tram and historic buildings. Come here to shop for big-name brands, to eat at classy restaurants and to watch the Turks watching each other. For much of its length the parallel Sahil Yolu provides an alternative walking route with several pleasant seaward-facing parks.

From as long ago as Byzantine times there was a road that ran out from **Üsküdar** to **Anatolia**, although this seems to have followed a different route from the modern Bağdat Caddesi as far as Kızıltoprak. In 1638 **Sultan Murad IV** captured Baghdad and renamed the road east to celebrate the event (which was also commemorated by the **Baghdad Pavilion** inside Topkapı Palace – see p. 8). He and his successors lined it with **fountains** to serve thirsty travelers; a few still survive while others are remembered in place names such as **Çatalçeşme** (Fork Fountain), **Selamiçeşme** (Selami's Fountain) and **Söğütlüçeşme** (Willow Fountain). Several of these fountains were originally part of **namazgahs**, or open-air prayer areas; the Çatalçeşme was designed with three spouts to facilitate the watering of passing **camel trains**.

In the 19th century some of the suburbs around Bağdat Caddesi became fashionable residential areas, hence some of the magnificent buildings that survive especially in **Caddebostan**. Before the opening of the Bosphorus Bridge in 1973, many people also built small **summer houses** along the waterside and there are still a handful of pleasing wooden houses lost amid the concrete. Otherwise, there's little left to show for the area's past history bar the small **Zühtü Paşa Mosque** at Kızıltoprak, which dates back to 1885 and the **Galip Paşa Mosque** at Caddebostan, which was built in 1899.

Today Bağdat Caddesi, especially between Caddebostan and Suadiye, is a place to promenade or to drive slowly up and down adding to the traffic congestion. It's at its most exuberant whenever the Fenerbahçe football team has a win. At such times non-football fans might like to steer well clear. There are several pleasant local parks including the waterside **Dalyan Park** in Caddebostan and the huge **Özgürlük (Freedom) Park** in Selamiçeşme. **Göztepe Park** also has a pleasant rose garden running alongside it. The modern **synagogue** in Taş Mektep Sokak is a reminder of Göztepe's relatively large Jewish population.

Zühtü Paşa Mosque

Galip Paşa Mosque

Özgürlük Park, Selamiçeşme

Cemil Topuzlu Mansion, also known as İpar Mansion

Cemil Topuzlu

Çiftehavuzlar

Designed by **Alexandre Vallaury** in 1900 in a style that mixed classical Turkish design with Art Nouveau, the **Cemil Topuzlu Mansion (Köşkü)** on Operatör Cemil Topuzlu Caddesi is one of the most magnificent of the forgotten mansions in this part of Asian Istanbul and was designed for a then mayor of Istanbul. Before road widening in the 1980s it stood right on the shore.

Nearby is the imposing building that houses the **Büyük Külüp (Big Club)**, successor to the famous Cercle d'Orient founded in 1882 by the British ambassador Sir Alfred Harrison on İstiklal Caddesi and frequented by all the foreign movers and shakers. It's a members only venue, sadly.

Nasreddin Hoca and Keloğlan

Nasreddin Hoca is familiar throughout the Middle East as a funny man who sits astride his donkey facing backwards and wearing a giant turban. His stories have something of the flavor of Aesop's Fables usually with a pointed punchline. **Keloğlan** (Bald Boy) is more uniquely Turkish, a poor youth who overcame adversity to marry a sultan's daughter in a story filmed as recently as 2005. Models of both characters stand in the grounds of the **Toy Museum.**

Göztepe Toy Museum

The leafy residential area of Göztepe is home to Istanbul's wonderful **Toy Museum** which houses more than 5,000 toys collected over the years by its writer-owner **Sunay Akın**; the oldest is a French-made violin dating back to 1817. A reconstructed toyshop shows off examples of the types of non-figurative **wooden toys** that used to be made in Eyüp (see p. 252). Children swoon over the room that resembles a railway compartment and over toilets housed in a replica submarine; their parents will be almost as enthralled by the unexpectedly stylish **café** on the ground floor. Outside in the courtyard are larger than life models of two Turkish folk heroes, Nasreddin Hoca and Keloğlan. The museum is in Dr Zeki Zeren Sokak, off Ömerpaşa Caddesi and is well signposted from Göztepe bus stop.

@istanbuloyuncakmuzesi, www.istanbuloyuncakmuzesi.com
Tel: 0216 359 45 50, closed Mondays

Giraffe-shaped street lamps

Where else in the world could you bump into streetlights shaped like life-sized giraffes? The three that stand in front of Göztepe's Toy Museum are copies of a much-loved original that used to stand in the garden of the home of the Minister for Education **Mehmed Münif Tahir Paşa** (1830-1910) in Erenköy. Not surprisingly, the house used to be called **Zürafalı Köşk (Giraffe Mansion).**

Tevhide Hanım Mansion

Caddebostan

The small beach and larger park beside the water at Caddebostan are overlooked by a pair of superb 19th-century mansions. The most impressive is the **Ragıp Paşa (Mansion) Köşkü**, built in 1906 by **August Jasmund** (who also designed Sirkeci Railway Station, see p. 206) at a time when it would have stood right on the waterfront. **Ragıp Paşa** (1857-1920) was aide-de-camp to **Sultan Abdülhamid II** and was sent into exile on Rhodes in 1908, which meant that he never got to live in his beautiful home. A single-storey stone building on the main road opposite the a restaurant used to serve as the selamlık (men's area). The adjacent building belonged to his daughter, **Tevhide Hanım**. Ragıp Paşa was also responsible for three hans on and off İstiklal Caddesi (see p. 302)

Ragıp Paşa Mansion

Mansion where Atatürk stayed and Çatalçeşme

Suadiye

The part of Bağdat Caddesi that stretches between Caddebostan and Suadiye is the trendiest bit, with the upscale department store Vakko anchoring an area of globalized **brand-name heaven** from its lovely white-wooden premises. Pluck a name from the air and it's bound to be represented here along with an unfeasibly large number of banks and a complete line-up of cafes to keep weary shoppers lubricated. Come here to shop if you find İstiklal Caddesi too crowded or touristy. The pavements are level, the street hawkers few and far between and mature palms and fig, plane and chestnut trees do their best to conceal the relentlessly prosaic architecture.

At the Bostancı end of Suadiye stand the sad relics of a **wooden house** that hosted **Atatürk** on five occasions. It is restored in 2018.

Bostancı

One of the main boarding points for ferries to the Princes' Islands, Bostancı still boasts one of those pretty little terminals that were built in the early years of the boat services, although there's also a more utilitarian modern terminal for inner-city services just down the road.

Amusement Park in Bostancı

Coast Road (Sahil Yolu)

It's possible to walk almost all the way from **Kadıköy to Bostancı** along a sea-facing esplanade laid out with walking and cycle tracks and dotted with exercise machines, beaches, small marinas and even areas set aside for rollerbladers. In early evening this part of town springs to life with enthusiastic joggers, dog walkers and cyclists. It has something of the atmosphere of the Kordon in İzmir and is a great place to watch the sun set over the Princes' Islands.

Caddebostan Cultural Center

CKM, one of the largest and most established cultural centres on the Asian Side, was opened in 2005. The centre, covering an area of 19,000-square-meter, continues to play a pioneering role in artistic events.

www.ckm.kadikoy.bel.tr
Tel: 0216 467 36 00

Ataşehir Mimar Sinan Mosque

The mosque that you can see on the edge of the road among the chaos of the ongoing construction for the Financial Centre in Ataşehir, was built on the basis of plans for the Selimiye Mosque by Architect Sinan The mosque, designed to host 10,000 people in an area of 36,758-square-meter, is also significant in combining traditional details with the characteristics of modern architecture. The adjacent Mimar Sinan Park offers a calm space both for children and for those who would like to take a breath among the buildings.

Nezahat Gökyiğit Botanical Garden

One of the places where you can get lots of fresh air on the Asian side pops up at an unexpected location. The garden, situated on eight parcels between the main road and ring road at the junction where the roads from Atatürk and 2nd Bosphorus bridges and the Anadolu highway meet, was built in 1995 by **Ali Nihat Gökyiğit** in memory of his wife **Nezahat Gökyiğit**. After landscape work, its function was changed and it was opened as a botanical garden in 2002. Other than the different plant species from different geographies, the garden also functions as a research, education and training centre. You can trace the building process of the garden through the photographs which depict the tunnels for passage along the parcels. You can also find detailed information about the endemic plants there. As well as the ponds and the animals living inside, the exploratory garden and the maze attract children's attention, too. There are no facilities inside, but there are tables and benches where you can enjoy your drinks and snacks on condition that you obey the rules.

@ngbb_official, www.ngbb.org.tr

Gateway to Anatolia

Haydarpaşa and Selimiye

075

Sirkeci Station may have been robbed of much of its setting, but Haydarpaşa, the waterside station from which trains depart for Anatolia, Syria and Iran, more than makes up for it, especially if you approach by ferry. German-designed, it is huge and imposing.

The piece of land immediately to the north of Kadıköy was named after one of two Ottoman grand viziers: either **Hadım Haydar Paşa**, who served **Sultan Süleyman the Magnificent** (1520-66) and owned a local vineyard, or the **Haydar Paşa** who served **Sultan Selim III** (1789-1807) and had barracks built here. It seems to have remained mainly agricultural land right through until the 19th century when it became the assembly point for armies heading east. The original station was built in 1833 and the port beside it in 1899, after which time the entire area took on an industrial hue. The fate of this splendid building, which has become a symbol of the migration from Anatolia to Istanbul, stayed obscure for a long time after the closing of the suburban line. The building is one of the most beautiful examples of the German style. After the fire and the consequent closure of the suburban line in 2010, it remained unclear for a long time. When the news about it being turned into a hotel caused controversy this project was laid aside, but the fate of the building is still not certain. The suburban train now works on the Halkalı-Gebze line, going through Ayrılıkçeşme. There were occasional small-scale events during the time it stayed vacant. The book days organized on the platforms in 2017 piqued the interest of both book-lovers and fans of trains. Exciting information is obtained from the archaeological excavations, which started in the region in 2019, on the remains found during the arrangement works. The history of **Chalcedon** is being reshaped before our eyes, starting from the 5th century BC.

Haydarpaşa ferry terminal is decorated with Kütahya tiles

The birds of Haydarpaşa

For keen ornithologists one of the pleasures of the boat ride to Haydarpaşa will be the long sea wall that juts out from the shore and provides a preening post for hundreds of cormorants and gray herons.

The station

In 1898 **Kaiser Wilhelm II** visited Istanbul, a visit most famously commemorated by the fountain that still stands in the Hippodrome (see p. 047). This state visit was instrumental in improving relations between the Ottoman and German courts as a result of which the business of building a railway network for Turkey was transferred from the British to the Germans. In 1906 when a new station was required for Istanbul the work was funded by the German government as part of their plans for a **Berlin to Baghdad railway.** Responsibility for its design was given to two German architects, **Otto Ritter** and **Helmut Cuno**, who created the present monumental building. Ironically it is Sirkeci on the European side of town which favors the oriental look; in contrast, Haydarpaşa on the Asian side of town looks as if it has somehow strayed from its natural home on the Rhine. Despite damage caused by accidents in 1917 and 1979, the station still appears much as it did when it first opened to the public in 1908. If you arrive at the station by ferry you will disembark at the pretty little landing stage provided for it by architect Vedat Tek in 1917. It is decorated with fine Kütahya tiles by Hacı Hafız Mehmed Emin Efendi. What looks like a chimney jutting out of the roof turns out to be a bird house.

Haydar Baba Shrine

The number of shrines in Istanbul is quite high. Although their real stories are not well known, all of them hold a special meaning for people. Here's a shrine, with an obscure story and an interesting location. Although it is located among the railways in the platform, called Haydar Baba, the inscription of the tomb belongs to Lahuti Abdullah. All the machinists used to visit the shrine before embarking on their journey and they used to salute as they passed in front of it to ensure a safe trip. Throughout the years, this person who rests here has become a protector of railways, as with the saints who were believed to protect sailors.

Clock towers beside the entrance

Haydarpaşa Campus

Haydarpaşa Campus

Created in 1894 to house the **Imperial School of Military Medicine**, this imposing building, which is visible from the ferry as you approach Haydarpaşa and from Topkapı Palace, was designed by **Alexandre Vallaury** and **Raimondo d'Aronco** in a style known as Neo-Ottoman. The striking clock towers on either side of its entrance are actually the minarets of a mosque. The building went on to serve as a **high school** for boys before becoming the medical faculty of Marmara University in 1983. It was later acquired from Marmara University and allocated to another foundation university.

Behind the building lies the **Crimean War Cemetery** where many British and Commonwealth soldiers who succumbed to their wounds in the Selimiye Barracks or at Gallipoli were buried. Alongside them lie prominent members of the 19th-century expat community. Also here is the tomb of **Edward Barton** which was relocated here from **Heybeliada** (see p. 587).

Crimean War Memorial

Selimiye Barracks

Centuries in the planning, the Selimiye Barracks were first built to the north of Haydarpaşa in 1799 and took their name from **Sultan Selim III** who intended them to act as a base for the new army with which he was hoping to replace the troublesome Janissaries. In 1808 the barracks were burnt down, only to be rebuilt in much stronger materials in 1825 by **Sultan Mahmud II**, just two years after he finally saw off the Janissaries. Mahmud II's barracks only had one wing; the other three were added by architect **Krikor Balyan** during the reign of **Sultan Abdülmecid** to create an enclosed parade ground. During the early years of the Republic, the barracks were turned into a **school**, only to revert to their original function in 1963. Today the vast four-towered structure still houses the headquarters of the **Turkish First Army**, the largest division in the country.

Even for those not generally gripped by military history the Selimiye Barracks are interesting as the site of the **British military hospital** where **Florence Nightingale** worked during the Crimean War (1853-56). The famous "Lady with the Lamp" is credited with having reduced mortality from war wounds enormously by introducing simple rules of hygiene. One tower of the barracks was housing the small **Florence Nightingale Museum**, with mementoes of the nurse preserved rather soullessly in her living room and surgery, but it's permanently closed.

The famous "Lady with the Lamp" was named after her birthplace of Florence.

Büyük (Big) Selimiye Mosque

Across the road from the barracks is the baroque-style mosque that **Sultan Selim III** had built for the soldiers in 1803-4. Its twin minarets proved too weak to support themselves and had to be completely rebuilt. Selimiye itself was the city's first officially planned neighbourhood.

Who were the Janissaries?

The Janissaries were one of the world's first uniformed standing armies and provided the household guard of the Ottoman sultans right through from the 14th century, when the corps was probably established by **Sultan Murad I**, to 1826 when **Sultan Mahmud II** abolished them. The original Janissaries were **Christians** seized as **slaves**, converted to Islam and turned into soldiers loyal to the sultan. However, by the early 18th century they had become so powerful that they could often dictate policy to the sultans; even as their once formidable power as a fighting force declined, they were still able to remove any sultan foolhardy enough to try and improve matters. Eventually, Sultan Mahmud II inspired them to rebel by threatening to set up a modern army. During the ensuing riot, a fire broke out in the barracks and thousands of Janissaries were killed. This so called **"Auspicious Incident"** marked the end of their power. To find out more about the Janissaries visit the **Military Museum** in Harbiye (see pp.341-2).

Low-ranking Janissary officer flanked by orderlies

"(Selimiye Barracks)... a cross between the Escorial and Sandhurst."

***Constantinople: City of the World's Desire 1453-1924*, by Philip Mansel, 1995**

The Snake in the Basket

The Maiden's Tower

076

Just off the Bosphorus coast at Üsküdar, the cute little Maiden's Tower (Kız Kulesi in Turkish) crops up in many old pictures of Istanbul and has attracted many romantic stories over the years.

Maiden Tower before restoration

The Athenian General Alcibiades

Although the tower currently standing on the rock off Üsküdar dates back only to the 19th century the earliest building there seems to have been a small fort built by the Athenian general **Alcibiades** in 408 BC to keep the Persians at bay. Later the Byzantine Emperor **Manuel I Comnenos** (1143-80) had a miniature castle created to discourage invaders. **Sultan Mehmed the Conqueror** replaced this mini-castle with one of his own which was restored by **Sultan Selim I**. Like Istanbul's larger islands, this islet also served time as a **prison**, with Sultan Mahmud I locking up the **Chief White Eunuch Beşir Ağa** here before beheading him and then Sultan Osman III locking up his **Grand Vizier Hekimoğlu Ali Paşa** here before exiling him to Cyprus.

Like so many Istanbul buildings, the Maiden's Tower has also fallen foul of a fire, this time one started by torches at a party that got out of control in 1719. It was replaced almost immediately by Sultan Ahmed III's Grand Vizier **Damat İbrahim Paşa**, at which point it appears to have been turned into a **lighthouse**. The final version was created by **Sultan Mahmud II** in the early 19th century.

Since then the rock has served a predictable collection of functions as a **semaphore station**, a **quarantine outpost** during a cholera outbreak and a **tollbooth**.

Fabulous stories

There's something about off-shore islands which brings out the fantasist in everyone, so it's hardly surprising that a story rather like that of Rapunzel crossed with Cleopatra quickly developed around the Maiden's Tower. According to the tale, a king had a beautiful daughter whom he loved greatly although a prophecy had predicted that she would be killed by a snake bite. Anxious to circumvent cruel fate, the king had his daughter confined on the rock until eventually someone delivered a basket of fruit to her that turned out to contain the predicted snake. The rest, as they say, is history.

That story is fanciful enough, but a second version stirs the Turkish hero **Battal Gazi** into the mix. Battal Gazi was an 8th-century Umayyad soldier who used to farm land immediately across from the tower and fell in love with the Byzantine emperor's daughter. While he was away fighting in Damascus, the emperor imprisoned his daughter on the rock. On his return Battal Gazi was able to free her, but only with the help of a highly unlikely-sounding 700 soldiers. A third version of the story has a fairy-tale ending with the princess rescued from the tower by a **Persian prince** but only after she had been poisoned by a snake hidden in a basket of flowers that he sent to her.

Finally the story of the Maiden's Tower, sometimes called Leander's Tower, became hopelessly entangled with that of **Hero and Leander**, lovers who lived on opposite sides of the Dardanelles near Çanakkale. Every evening Leander would swim across to meet Hero, guided by a light that she hung in a tower. One night the wind blew the lamp out and Leander was swept away by the tide and drowned. Cast into despair, Hero committed suicide by jumping from the tower. How the two disparate venues became so mixed up is, however, unclear.

James Bond in town

In 1999 the Maiden's Tower featured as a hideway for the fiendish Elektra, played by Sophie Marceau, in the James Bond movie "The World is Not Enough". It also featured in the smash-hit Turkish television series "Kurtlar Vadisi (The Valley of the Wolves)".

Multitude of Mosques

Üsküdar, Bağlarbaşı and Çamlıca

077

Just up the coast from Kadıköy, Üsküdar was first settled almost as long ago but could hardly be more different. It's historically interesting, with many fine mosques and a waterside promenade that provides delightful views of the pretty little Maiden's Tower. Afterwards you can climb up the hill to Çamlıca to soak up the panoramic views, or stroll amid the silent tombstones in the enormous Karacaahmet Cemetery.

Üsküdar harbor as it was in the past...

...and as it is today.

The area that is now Üsküdar appears to have been settled at about the same time as Kadıköy. It was originally called **Chrysopolis** (the City of Gold), although whether because the Persian invaders stored their plunder from Anatolia here, or because of the way the setting sun lit up the Bosphorus in front of it is unclear. Although Chalcedon (Kadıköy) was originally the more important of the two settlements, Chrysopolis grew very quickly and soon became the main departure point for military expeditions into Anatolia. Over time its name changed to **Scutari**, which could have been derived from the Greek word "skitos", which described the leather used to coat the shields of the imperial guards stationed here; or from Scutarion, the name of a long-lost Byzantine palace situated on land immediately across from the Maiden's Tower. This in turn evolved into the modern Üsküdar. Legend has it that the neighbourhood was named after in reference to its geographical characteristics. Since it has a wide coastline which gets narrower towards the slope, it was defined as "narrow at the top".

Although Chrysopolis pre-dated Byzantium it lacked the other city's naturally defensible site and was occupied several times before the Turks finally seized it in the 14th century. Today visitors who arrive by ferry find themselves in a fairly chaotic transport interchange which stands where the great caravan trains bearing pilgrims to Mecca for **the Haj** used to start out. Once upon a time many of Istanbul's rich and powerful came here to make their homes in what Italian writer Edmondo de Amicis could still describe in the second half of the 19th century as "like a rural city." Today only the great mosques they endowed survive.

Recent excavations associated with the **Marmaray project** (see p. 185) have uncovered traces of a medieval bazaar, tannery, monastery and wooden pier near the ferry terminal.

Harbor (İskele) Mosque

Facing the ferry landing stage across the busy main road is the magnificent mosque built by **Mimar Sinan** for **Mihrimah Sultan**, daughter of **Sultan Süleyman the Magnificent** and wife of his grand vizier **Rüstem Paşa**, in 1548. It was the first building in which he made use of the semi-domes that were to become one of his trademarks. When it was first built the mosque stood right on the **waterfront** and the sultan was able to disembark straight from his caique onto its steps; the view from the şadırvan (fountain) was regarded as one of the best in Istanbul. The medrese to the side that was once part of the complex now houses a local **clinic**, while the school on the other side now houses a **children's library**. Note the fine **sundial** attached to the wall as you exit at the back towards the library.

Sundial

Sultan Ahmed III Fountain

In front of the mosque amid the swirling traffic is the free-standing baroque **fountain of Sultan Ahmed III** dating back to 1728. All four sides are decorated with **poetry**, including a couplet composed by Ahmed III himself. It's a less elaborate version of the one in front of Topkapı Palace (see p. 004).

Shrine of Aziz Mahmud Hüdayi Efendi

In Aziz Mahmud Efendi Sokak, this shrine (1541-1628) commemorates a holy man born in Koçhisar, near the Salt Lake, who lived through the reigns of eight different sultans and founded the **Celveti sect**. Asked a question by Sultan Ahmed I in a letter, he sent back his reply without even needing to open it. An inscription inside the **Bulgurlu Hamam** records that he was the imam who read the first sermon in the **Blue Mosque** in 1616.

Yeni Valide Mosque

Very close to the ferry terminal is the imposing Yeni Valide (Queen Mother) Mosque built by **Sultan Ahmed III** for his mother **Valide Rabia Gülnüş Ümmetullah** in 1710. Despite its huge size it has a pleasingly rustic appearance brought about by the combination of the queen mother's tomb, which has been described as resembling a giant aviary, the house-like wooden façade of the sultan's pew and an especially beautiful fountain. Of relatively late date, it was still designed with a large courtyard surrounded on three sides by domed porticoes and with an elaborately carved şadırvan (ablutions fountain) as its centerpiece. Not much else of the complex survives apart from a small **school** building and much larger **imaret** (soup kitchen).

Across the road an **old hamam** has been converted into a small shopping center. Its attribution to Sinan is unlikely to be true although it may well date back to the 16th century.

On the left the Valide Sultan's tomb

In front of the Yeni Valide Mosque stands the İskele Mosque. Across the Bosphorus Galatasaray University and the Kabataş Boys High School occupy the old Feriye Palaces.

Marmaray

The project, which was launched in 2013 as a solution to traffic issues in Istanbul and in particular to ease the Bosphorus transits, started to operate with five stations between **Ayrılıkçeşme** and **Kazlıçeşme** (Ayrılıkçeşme-Üsküdar- Sirkeci- Yenikapı- Kazlıçeşme). The project consists of an immersed tunnel, approximately 1.4 km in length and bored tunnels on both sides, each almost 11 km in length. The project, integrated with the suburban line between Gebze and Halkalı, significantly eases public transportation in Istanbul. The first project to build a tunnel under the Bosphorus from Üsküdar to Sarayburnu was designed in the 1860s. The project, which had been planned for years, only came to realization for the first time with the Marmaray. During the construction work on Yenikapı station, the **Byzantine Port** was unearthed (see p. 185). During the excavations, which ignited great excitement all around the world, the world's largest port from the Antiquity and thirty-seven shipwrecks dating back to periods between the 5th and 11th centuries were discovered along with bones of humans and animals and more than 35,000 artefacts dating back as far as the **Neolithic Period**. Even the loads of the ships survived. The findings of the shipwrecks, which survived to this day in the mud carried over by the **Lykos Stream** (see p. 147) and the photographs of the excavation work have been exhibited at **Istanbul Archeology Museum** in recent years. According to **Istanbul University Research Center for Yenikapı Wrecks**, the findings from Yenikapı might again highlight the role of Byzantine shipbuilding and maritime commerce in Constantinople and the Late Roman period. The conservation and reconstruction work of the wrecks is ongoing as part of the project. 'Yenikapı 12', whose reconstruction was completed, had her first sailing course in the Sea of Marmara and an exhibition was put on at Istanbul Archeology Museum. The project to exhibit the artefacts kept in the stores of the Archeology Museum is still waiting.

---

www.yenikapibatiklari.com

Şemsi Paşa Mosque

As you follow the road round towards the Maiden's Tower you will pass the twin-domed **Cedit Valide Soup Kitchen** (İmaret) and the wooden **Balaban Lodge (dervish tekke)** which is being completely rebuilt. Finally you will reach the small Şemsi Paşa mosque complex that was designed by Mimar Sinan in 1580 for the Vizier **Şemsi Paşa** whose tomb opens, unusually, straight into the mosque. Another name given to the mosque is "Kuşkonmaz" (birds don't land). Since the mosque is located at the intersection of the air streams from the Marmara and the Black Sea, the reverse effect of the wind and the boom penetrating into the minarets prevents birds from perching in the mosque. The legend has it that the reason for choosing such a location was because Şemsi Ahmet Paşa wanted a mosque which could not be soiled by birds. The mosque, enjoying the nice view of this location, was restored in 2012.

As you walk along the coast road towards Salacak and the ferry to the Maiden's Tower you will pass two **sculptures** -1453 and 1923- by Faruk Akın (the artist also responsible for the giant alarm clock facing the ferry terminal).

Şemsi Paşa Mosque

Rum Mehmed Paşa Mosque

A short walk away from the Şemsi Paşa Mosque is this small mosque built in 1471 for one of Fatih Sultan Mehmed's grand viziers. Mehmed Paşa was a "Rum", the Turkish word for a Greek, which is sometimes offered as an explanation for why this building, with its taller than average central dome, is so Byzantine in appearance.

Ayazma Mosque

Close to the Rum Mehmed Paşa Mosque is the huge baroque **Ayazma Mosque** complex built by Sultan Mustafa III for his mother Mihrişah Emine Sultan in 1760 and designed by Mehmet Tahir Ağa. Note the small birdhouses on the façade and on the gateway. Look out, too, for what are probably the last remaining Janissary tombstones in the city, identifiable from the flamboyant headgear carved onto the top of them. This is the mosque that dominates the eastern skyline of Üsküdar as you approach by ferry.

Interior of Ayazma Mosque

Also on the coast road you will see an imposin building originally erect in 1842 to house a **polic station** but since given life as the Air Force Club

Salacak in an old engraving

Salacak

Muharrem Nuri Birgi Yalı

The Üsküdar waterfront facing the Maiden's Tower (see p. 496) has been laid out as a promenade. On the hillside up above it the **Muharrem Nuri Birgi Yalı** is a fabulous 18th-century Ottoman rose-colored wooden mansion restored by architect **Turgut Cansever** in 1971, with wonderful interior décor for those who get to see it. The famous violinist **Yehudi Menuhin** (1916-99) was once a guest here.

Ahmediye Mosque

Inland on Gündoğumu Caddesi the Ahmediye Mosque complex was built in 1722 by **Eminzade Hacı Ahmed Paşa** who was in charge of the arsenal during the reign of **Sultan Ahmed III**. It still retains many of its subsidiary buildings including a **sebil** (water dispensary), **medrese** (seminary) and **kütüphane** (library) grouped round a small courtyard.

Nevmekan-Sahil (shoreline), which was transformed from the former Üsküdar Registry Office into a library, offers a different experience with its architecture and unique sea view.

"(The mosque) of the (Atik) Valide is... the most beautiful structure I ever saw."

***Turkish Embassy Letters*, by Lady Mary Wortley Montagu, 1718**

Nurbanu Sultan

Atik Valide Mosque

Cannonball dating back to 1453

High up on a hill and with particularly tall minarets, Üsküdar's most important mosque is another work of **Sinan**, this time designed in 1583 for **Nurbanu Sultan**, the wife of **Sultan Selim II**. To find it you need to walk up Eski Toptaşı Caddesi (Old Cannonball Street), readily identifiable by a small monument in the middle of the road incorporating a cannonball said to have been used during the siege of Istanbul in 1453.

Described by **John Freely** as one of the half-dozen most impressive Ottoman monuments in the country, the Atik Valide Mosque has a delightful **courtyard** filled with plane trees and rosebushes, a place where old men while away the day over glasses of tea and their newspapers. A narthex of twelve arches filled with fine metalwork opens onto an interior that seems unexpectedly small after the grand exterior. The mihrab is surrounded with İznik tiles but of a late period when the colors tended to run.

Ablutions Fountain

Unfortunately, the surrounding complex is not being well maintained. Not only are the walls of the mosque and medrese plastered with graffiti, but the lovely old **caravanserai** with its fine wooden portal leading into a domed antechamber is falling into rack and ruin despite being the property of Marmara University's School of Fine Arts. **The mekteb** (school) at the back is also in ruins, as is the **imaret** (soup kitchen) with its graceful brick chimneys. Külliye (social complex) underwent a bad restoration, which looks good from the outside, in 2014.

The Çinili Mosque is remote from the center.

Tiled (Çinili) Mosque

Kösem Sultan

It's even further uphill to this mosque but you won't regret it once you can inspect the fine **İznik tiles** on its walls.
The mosque dates back to 1640 when it was built by **Mahpeyker Kösem Sultan**, the mother of **Murad IV** and **İbrahim I**. Facing it across a square is the **Çinili Hamam** which, despite its name, is not tiled at all.

Karacaahmet Cemetery

Heading south towards Kadıköy the hillside is covered with a vast cemetery, the largest in Turkey and second only to Eyüp for the quality of its Ottoman tombstones. Named after a warrior companion of Orhan I whose tomb is still greatly revered, the cemetery was seen as being on the side of the city closest to the holy cities of Mecca and Medina, hence its great popularity as a burial place. The artist **Fikret Mualla** was buried here in 1967 as was the rock musician **Cem Karaca** in 2004.

Mehmed Naci Aköz Kite Museum

The small, special museum which you will see in Üsküdar will surprise you. This is Turkey's first and only and one of the world's eighteen, kite museums. Exhibiting about 750 colourful kites collected from all over the world, the museum has a collection of more than 2,500 pieces collected from six different continents and thirty-three countries (kites, publications, materials and various objects). It is located just across the Municipality of Üsküdar, at the end of Uncular Main Street on Bakıcı Street. Open on weekdays, the museum can be visited by appointment on Saturdays. There are kite-making courses as well.

@ucurtmamuzesi, www.ucurtmamuzesi.net
Tel: 0216 553 23 37

Zeynep and Kamil

By tradition girls born at the Zeynep Kamil Hospital are given the name Zeynep in addition to their normal name, while boys have Kamil tagged onto theirs.

A few old wooden houses survive in Üsküdar.

Abdülaziz Hunting Lodge (Abdülaziz Av Köşkü)

The Abdülaziz Hunting Lodge stands in the **Validebağ Wood** off Tophanelioğlu Caddesi in **Altunizade**. Built in 1856 in neo-Turkish style, it features a delightful wooden portico. There was a scout museum which I thought was never open whenever I visited. There is a "Writing Workshop" signboard placed on the lodge, which was later restored for a second time. Its present use is still not in harmony with its texture and history. The Validebağ Wood, a first degree protected area, offers you some fresh air in the middle of the city.

Adile Sultan Pavilion

Altunizade İsmail Zühtü Paşa, who is the namesake of the neighborhood of Altunizade has an amazing mansion built. After a while, he gifts it to Sultan Abdülaziz, who admires the mansion. **Sultan Abdülaziz** has the mansion demolished and has this pavilion built for his little sister, **Adile Sultan**. Next to the hunting seat of Abdülaziz, Adile Sultan Pavilion is used as the Validebağ Teacherage today. And its architect is **Nigoğos Amira Balyan**.

Şakirin Mosque

Zeynep Fadıllıoğlu

On the north-eastern side of the cemetery, facing the Zeynep Kamil Hospital, is the brand-new **Şakirin (Gratitude) Mosque**, a futuristic building commissioned by the **Şakir Family**, which mixes minarets of reinforced concrete with a sweeping dome that looks like an off-cut from the Guggenheim in Bilbao and a courtyard centered on a giant silver ball symbolizing the world that reflects the mosque back to itself. It was decorated by **Zeynep Fadıllıoğlu**, already well known for her work on the **Ulus 29** restaurant (see p. 361), who thereby became the first woman in modern times to adorn a mosque in Turkey. With its utterly original **arched mihrab** of turquoise and gold, a **minbar** decorated with stylized leaves and a **chandelier** of dripping plastic adorned with the 99 names of Allah and the Nur (Light) verse of the Koran, the mosque is a first in every way and a godsend to those whose hearts sink whenever they see yet another debased version of Sinan's great masterpieces. Conservatives have criticized the Şakirin as resembling a casino. I prefer to congratulate the architects for their originality.

Marmara Faculty of Theology Mosque

The mosque was rebuilt with a modern architectural design in 2012 after it had been demolished for not meeting earthquake regulation. The mosque was opened for service again in 2015. As part of the Marmara University Faculty of Theology, it has a capacity of 4,500 people and covers an area of 30,000 square meters with its square and cultural center. Its helix-shaped dome with glass tunnels and minarets with different styles are striking.

Çamlıca' Girls High School

Above Üsküdar is Çamlıca (Pine Wood), which is best known for its large public parks. Here, too, is **Acıbadem** where **Vice-Admiral Ahmed Ratip Paşa** commissioned a fine mansion from **Kemaleddin Bey** (see p. 009); unfortunately for him, he was exiled for taking bribes over the building of the Hejaz railway before he got to live in it. The work was completed in 1908 and in 1938 the 54-room mansion was turned into **Çamlıca Girls' High School**, albeit a high school decorated with **Murano glass** stair rails and Villeroy and Boch bathroom tiles. Now that a new modern school has been built right next door for the girls, this masterpiece is standing sadly empty.

Hamams

Üsküdar retains several historic Turkish baths that receive relatively few foreign visitors and all of which have separate sections for men and women. The oldest of them is the **Şifa (Healthy) Hamam** which appears to have been built in the late 15th century. The **Valide Atik Hamam** is a work of Sinan dating back to 1583. The **Çinili (Tiled) Hamam** dates back to 1648 and was carefully restored in 1964; unusually, the women's section is larger than the men's. The **Bulgurlu Hamam** proudly preserves the basin used by Aziz Mahmud Hüdayi Efendi (see p. 500). Finally there is the **Ağa Hamam** that dates back to 1610.

Büyük Çamlıca Mosque

Büyük (Big) Çamlıca Mosque
The mosque that was recently added to the silhouette of Istanbul has increased interest in the area. The construction of the mosque began in 2013 and was opened for worship in 2019. It's the largest mosque in Turkey with a capacity of 65,000 people. As we are familiar from historical mosques, most typically those in Süleymaniye, there are several symbols contained within its architecture. Four of the minarets are 107.1 meters high, referring to the Victory of Malazgirt, which was the turning point that brought Turks into Anatolia. And the diameter of the dome is 34 meters, the number that represents Istanbul.

Büyük (Big) Çamlıca

The 262-meter-high Büyük Çamlıca on **Mt Bulgurlu** is Istanbul's highest point and used to be a famous beauty spot, much hymned by writers as various as **Procopius, Evliya Çelebi, Lady Mary Wortley Montagu** and **Lord Byron**. Now, however, its beauty is marred by serried ranks of radio and phone masts although the views are still magnificent and there's an inviting Ottoman-style coffee house as well as a restaurant and private picnic kiosks to make up for them. There are also shady walks to be had beneath the pine trees (çam) that gave their name to the site.

Küçük (Little) Çamlıca

Less well known but perhaps even prettier is Küçük Çamlıca, a hillier park covered with trees and adorned with a complex of kiosks loosely based on **Topkapı Palace.** Between them stands a copy of the İftariye Canopy (see p. 8) from which you can gaze out on the city, a **magnificent panorama** stretching from the Princes' Islands on the left, through Fenerbahçe and Haydarpaşa in the middle, to Topkapı Palace on the right.

Çamlıca Tower

A television tower with a height of 388.5 meters is being built to prevent the visual pollution caused by the radio and television towers in Büyük Çamlıca. The tower, which is visible from many parts of İstanbul, also has two restaurants on 39th and 40th floors and viewing platforms on 33rd and 34th floors.

@camlica.kule
www.360kule.com
Tel: 0216 440 40 40

Marmara Faculty of Theology Mosque with European Shore behind it.

Television's Favorite Suburb

Kuzguncuk

078

On the Asian side of the Bosphorus, just north of Üsküdar, Kuzguncuk is a pleasant, leafy suburb with many old wooden houses and a mosque, church and synagogue virtually side by side. Its traditional appearance has made it a favorite with Turkish television companies who have used it in several recent soap operas.

Kuzguncuk pier in the 1890s

Building with date according to three calendars

The Byzantine **Kosinitsa**, Kuzguncuk lacks any major attractions although it is a great place to wander around and admire the frilly wooden houses that dot the main drag or perhaps come for a bite to eat in one of several unexpectedly sophisticated restaurants. Unusually, it has a **church, mosque and synagogue** all grouped together near the waterfront, a reminder of how cosmopolitan a city Istanbul was in the 19th century. It's thought that the first settlers were **Jews** expelled from Spain at the end of the 15th century who were followed here by **Greeks and Armenians**, before Turks finally moved in too. At one time there may have been as many as 10,000 Jews living here and the area was sometimes called "**Little Jerusalem**". Today there are hardly any Jews, Greeks or Armenians left, although their place is slowly being taken by expats from the USA and the UK.

According to **Evliya Çelebi** the area was named after a wise man called Kuzgun Baba who lived here in the 15th century. However, others think it took its name, more prosaically, from the Turkish word for "little raven". In reality, it's probably a corruption of the original Kosinitsa.

Can Yücel

Kuzguncuk was sometime home to the translator and poet Can Yücel (1926-1999), known for his prolific use of slang. It also features as the setting for Buket Uzuner's best-selling novel "Mediterranean Waltz".

"I Anatolia"

One of Kuzguncuk's most famous residents was the playwright **Güngör Dilmen** (1930-2012) whose most famous play, "I Anatolia", relates the history of Anatolia through the mouths of 16 famous women.

Güngör Dilmen

Fine example of a wooden house in Kuzguncuk

Üryanizade Mosque

Synagogues

The **Beth Ya'akov Synagogue**, in Icadiye Caddesi, was built in 1878 and used to provide services in summer; in winter the congregation would move to Yakup Sokak to another synagogue, **Kal de Ariva**, that dated back to 1840; its name meant "lower synagogue" to distinguish it from Bath Ya'akov which was also called **Kal de Abaşo** (Upper Synagogue). The hamam next door to Bath Ya'akov used to function as a **mikvah** (ritual bath) for the Jewish community.

Beth Ya'akov Synagogue

Mosques

Built in 1860, the waterside **Üryanizade Mosque** was built for Sultan Abülhamid's religious leader Üryanizade Ömer Efendi. It boasts a distinctive **wooden minaret** and a design that that recalls the neighboring yalıs.

The much newer **Kuzguncuk Mosque** dates back only to 1952 (hence its nickname, the "Yeni Cami (New Mosque)" and stands right beside the Armenian church of **Surp Krikor Lusavoriç**. The domes of the mosque and the church have the same shape and reach the same height.

Churches

Beside the main road, the huge Armenian church of **Surp Krikor Lusavoriç** was built in 1831 and rebuilt in 1861. On İcadiye Caddesi, the Greek Orthodox **Church of Hagios Panteleimon** was built in 1821 on the site of an earlier church dating back to 550. Its magnificent detached bell tower (1911) doubles as an entrance gate. A third, smaller church, dedicated to Hagios Georgios, stands beside the Beth Ya'akov Synagogue. The church also has a holy spring.

Surp Krikor Lusavoriç Armenian Church

Hagios Panteleimon Greek Orthodox Church

Nakkaştepe

On the lower slopes of **Nakkaştepe** (Embroiderers' Hill), just to the east of Kuzguncuk, there's a walled Jewish Cemetery full of gravestones with inscriptions in Hebrew, Ladino, Ottoman and Turkish. Views from the top of the hill are superb. Tourists are sometimes brought to cafes here in the mistaken impression that it is Çamlıca Hill!

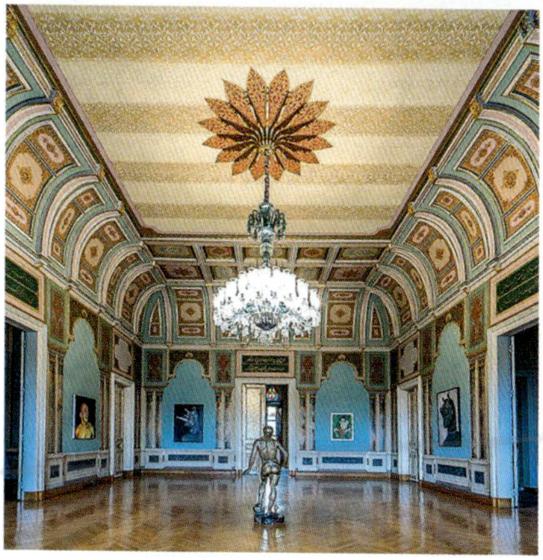

Abdülmecid Efendi the painter born to be sultan

His name may not ring many bells with foreign visitors but Abdülmecid Efendi was an extraordinary man who would, had he been born just a few years earlier, have become sultan. The son of **Sultan Abdülaziz**, he was born in 1868 either in the old Beşiktaş or new Dolmabahçe Palace. In 1922 the sultanate was abolished but he was appointed **caliph**, or head of the Islamic congregation worldwide. Exiled in 1924, he died in **Paris** in 1944 and was later re-buried in **Medina**. In the meantime he had made a name for himself as an **artist** of considerable ability. His paintings are on display in the **Dolmabahçe Palace** (see p. 390), **Aşiyan** (see p. 435) and the **Istanbul Modern** (see p. 377).

This old photo shows Caliph Abdülmecid Efendi with his daughter Dürrüşehvar and grandson of Hyderabad Nizam. The other bride is the writer Kenize Mourad's mother, Selma Sultan, the granddaughter of Sultan Murad V.

Abdülmecid Efendi Mansion (Abdülmecid Efendi Köşkü)

A very beautiful and colourful mansion strikes one's eye just across from the Jewish Cemetery on Gümüşyolu Street. The mansion, located in Bağlarbağı Grove, was built at the end of the 19th century as a hunting lodge by the **Egyptian Khedive İsmail Paşa**. Its original size was bigger but only its Selamlık (the portion of a house reserved for men) part has survived. A Cufic inscription at the entrance writes "God is the only victor".

Its architect is **Alexandre Vallaury** who designed many beautiful buildings including Istanbul Erkek Lisesi (High School for Boys) (see p.060), Istanbul Archeology Museum (see p.020), SALT Galeri and the former Haydarpaşa High School (see p.494). Following the death of İsmail Paşa, **Sultan Abdülhamid II** bought the mansion for the last caliph **Abdülmecid Efendi**, who was the son of his uncle. Abdülmecit Efendi lived in this mansion, located in its land of 200 decares, for 28 years. Sultan Abdülhamid II, his cousin who had granted him the mansion, did not allow him to come to the city. Hence, Abdülmecid Efendi told **Pierre Loti** that he saw the place as his grave.

Known for his love of the arts, Abdülmecid Efendi used the mansion for meetings about art and literature. Abdülmecid Efendi, son of Sultan Abdülaziz, was a well-educated personality of many talents. He is especially known for his paintings, with some of his work even being exhibited in Europe. Moreover, he worked on nudes on a couple of his paintings and produced ground-breaking work for his time.

Abdülmecid Efendi was the honorary president of the Ottoman Artists Association, founded in 1909 and offered financial support for the publication of the newspaper of the Ottoman Artists Association. The 1918 Vienna Exhibition, the first exhibition to be opened by Turkish artists in Europe, included four of his works.

During the time of Kâzım Taşkent, the founder of the first private Turkish bank Yapı ve Kredi Bankası, the mansion was bought for protection. All its originality was preserved during the renovation work and it survives to this day. Its entrance hall, the tiles decorating the walls, the fireplace, the fountain and all its details are reflective of his fine taste. Thanks to the occasional exhibitions held in the mansion, you may have a chance to admire both the works of art and this beautiful structure.

Cemil Molla Mansion

Cemil Molla Mansion

Heading north from Kuzguncuk you are soon forced to divert inland by a waterfront naval base. Just as the road turns you will see on the right a wonderful wooden house with a turret that was built by the Italian architect **Albeti** in 1885 for **Mahmud Cemil Efendi**, a Minister for Justice under Sultan Abdülhamid II. Its decor was so impressive that it was sometimes nicknamed **"the eighth wonder of the world"** and it was regularly used for poetry readings and musical recitals.

At the time that it was built the only building allowed to be illuminated using electricity was the Yıldız Palace. Regardless of this, Cemil Molla had an **electricity generator** installed in the grounds of his house and on the anniversary of the sultan's accession to the throne risked his wrath by turning it on to light the building. His argument that the only way to commemorate such an important occasion properly was with electricity eventually won the day and so he paved the way for the rest of the city to be electrified. The mansion also housed one of the Empire's first telephones, as well as a private **cinema** and **photographic studio**. Today, sadly, all this remarkable history has been forgotten.

Fethi Ahmed Paşa Yalı

Kuzguncuk's finest building is the **Fethi Ahmed Paşa Yalı**, otherwise known as the **Pink Yalı**, which was built in the 18th century. Fethi Ahmed Paşa was married to Sultan Abdülmecid's sister **Atiye Sultan** and was responsible for the yalı's interior decoration. The building was apparently a favorite of the Swiss-French architect **Le Corbusier** who made two visits to Istanbul in 1911 and 1948.

Franz Lizst

Le Corbusier

The composer **Franz Liszt** also stayed here when he visited the city. Only the men's part of the mansion survives; the women's quarters were used as a tobacco depot and burned down in 1927.

In 1846 Fethi Ahmed Paşa became responsible for the creation of Istanbul's first military museum, then housed in Hagia Eirene Church (see p. 041).

Hüseyin Avni Paşa Fountain

Paşalimanı

Just before Kuzguncuk on the way from Üsküdar is Paşalimanı (the Paşa's Harbor) which acquired its name when **Admiral Piyale Paşa** built himself a palace here (since lost). Facing the waterfront a large, newly restored **warehouse** used to store tobacco; it has now been restored to provide administrative offices for the Istanbul opera, ballet and orchestra. Immediately opposite it is what used to be the monumental **Nemlizade Tobacco Warehouse**, built by **Vedat Tek** in 1923.

Şevket Mocan

Fethi Ahmed Paşa's grandson was a playboy who became MP for Tekirdağ during the period when the Democratic Party led by Adnan Menderes was in power. A habitué of the Tokatlıyan Hotel (see p. 459), he fell in love with Gönül Yazar who was nicknamed "Taş Bebek (The Porcelain Doll)". His daughter Ayşe married the nephew of the leader of the Communist Party Zeki Baştımar which so enraged her father that he called for membership of the CP to attract the death penalty. Baştımar's family owned the **Zeki Paşa Yalı** in Rumeli Hisarı (see p. 437). The Fethi Ahmed Paşa Yalı is sometimes called the **Mocan Yalı** after this man.

"...the mansions were built facing Kuzguncuk... 'It would've been rude to have their backs to the Sultan when he went by, so they turned their face to the street and their back to the water, m'boy,' grandpa used to say."

***Mediterranean Waltz*, by Buket Uzuner, 2000**

Old warehouses

Kuzguncuk Vegetable Garden

The story of the "Ilia's Vegetable Garden", as mentioned by the locals, dates back to the 1990s. The locals of the neighbourhood united under the name "Garden Solidarity Volunteers". The garden is a refreshing area both for the locals in Kuzguncuk and visitors coming from other places with its cultivable areas, a small park, openair cinema open during summer months and as a gathering place for the locals on religious holidays.

The Empress' Love-Nest

Beylerbeyi

079

The 1st Bosphorus Bridge separates Kuzguncuk from Beylerbeyi, best known for its palace but also home to a fine baroque mosque, a yalı-hotel and a collection of inviting restaurants grouped together around the ferry terminal. It was used as a setting in the famous 1964 heist movie "Topkapı" starring the late Peter Ustinov.

Beylerbeyi is sneakily two-faced. From the water its charms are immediately obvious as you drift past the palace and its alluring landing stage. From the road, however, it appears at first sight to be just another congested suburb, the only hint of something more interesting being the imposing gateway leading through to the mosque.

The area was originally called "**Stavros (The Cross)**", apparently because of a large cross erected here by **Constantine the Great**. Later it was renamed "Lord of the Lords", possibly in memory of **Mehmed Paşa** who served as Governor of Rumelia (the Balkans) during the reign of **Sultan Murad III** and built himself a fine house here (although the name could be much later in origin). In the dying days of the Ottoman Empire this was a place where religious leaders made their homes. Today it's a suburb that has moved steadily upmarket and there's a very chi-chi corner full of restaurants, art galleries and upscale shops tucked away out of sight of the busy main road near the ferry terminal. Think the **Ortaköy** (p.410) of the Asian shore and you'll get the general picture.

Tunnel

"(Beylerbeyi Palace) the most elegant edifice on the Bosphorus."

***The City of the Sultan and the Domestic Manners of the Turks in 1836* by Julia Pardoe.**

Beylerbeyi Palace

The first Beylerbeyi Palace was built here between 1829 and 1832. But, as so often, fell victim to a fire in 1851. Although enough of the palace survived for him to continue to use it, **Sultan Abdülmecid** never returned there and in 1865 Sultan **Abdülaziz** had it replaced with the present relatively restrained baroque building that was designed by **Sarkis Balyan**. It was here that Sultan **Abdülhamid II** lived after he returned from exile in Salonica in 1912 and here that he died in 1918.

Sultan Abdülaziz

Originally the palace would have been approached from the Bosphorus and it has a delightful **private landing stage** of marble flanked by exquisite **boathouses** that look like tents rendered in stone. Today of course most visitors have to be content with creeping up on it from the rear before joining a guided party in the hall.

Empress Eugenie

Intended for summer use and to house official guests, the palace has a very manageable 26 rooms divided into the public men and private women's quarters. The single most impressive room is focused on a large **marble pool** with a fountain carved with dolphins; the sound of the cascading water must have been marvelously cooling in summer. Also very impressive are two rooms facing each other across a hallway whose walls, ceilings and furniture are all carved with **Moorish-style woodwork**. Like the larger and older Dolmabahçe Palace (see p. 386), Beylerbeyi is decorated throughout with Hereke carpets, Baccarat glass and Yıldız porcelain. However, one of its more conspicuous features is the omnipresence of **maritime scenes** painted by **Stanislas Chlebowski** (1835-84), a Polish artist much admired by Sultan Abdülaziz, on the walls and ceilings. There is also a series of decorative panels inscribed with poetry and with quotations from the Koran.

Famous visitors to the palace included the **Shah of Iran** and those other well-known, the **Duke and Duchess of Windsor**. But the most famous visitor was **Empress Eugenie** of France who dropped by on her way to the **opening of the Suez Canal** in 1869 and was supposedly so impressed by what she saw that she had copies of the windows made for the Tuileries Palace in Paris. She is believed to have embarked on an affair with **Sultan Abdülaziz**, as described in **Pablo Martin Asuero's book "El Palacio de las Columnas Azules (The Palace of the Blue Columns)"**.

A particularly delightful feature of the palace is the **terraced garden** that rises up the hillside behind it. Here can be found the **Stables (Ahır Köşk)**, one of the few imperial stable blocks to survive, as well as the decorative **Yellow Pavilion (Sarı Köşk)** and **Marble Pavilion (Mermer Köşk)**, the latter overlooking a small **lake** on which swans used to swim. A unique **tunnel** was built beneath the terraced part of the garden during the reign of Sultan Mahmud II; this enabled road traffic to pass without it being cut off from the waterside part. Some might wish that a similar solution could have been found so that the 1st Bridge did not soar so noisily above it today.

---

www.millisaraylar.gov.tr
Tel: 0216 321 93 20
closed Mondays and Thursdays

Beylerbeyi Mosque

Right on the waterfront, this large mosque with a small garden was built by **Sultan Abdülhamid I** for his mother **Rabia Sultan** in 1778; the architect was **Mehmed Tahir Ağa** who was also responsible for **Laleli Mosque** (see p. 088). A second minaret was added in the early 19th century by Sultan Mahmud II. Beside it stands an attractive two-storey oval building that used to house a **library** and **time-keeper's lodge**. The mosque boasts a particularly fine minbar and a imam's chair made from wood inlaid with ivory.

Mosque interior

Kürsü (preacher's chair

Beylerbeyi Hamam

Inconspicuously located behind what looks like the façade of a wooden house **Beylerbeyi Hamam** was built in 1789 as part of the Beylerbeyi Mosque complex. It still serves men and women, with women mainly welcomed during the middle part of the day and men in the early morning or evening.

Tel: 0216 321 46 83

Beylerbeyi Yalıs

Mabeyinci Faik Bey Yalı

This elaborately decorated yalı once belonged to **Esra Bereket**, the wife of **Bereket Şah**, the Nizam (Governor) of Hyderabad and the richest man in the world in the 1930s. It was used in the making of the 1964 film **"Topkapı"** starring Peter Ustinov and Melina Mercouri.

The Hasip Paşa Yalı belongs to Demir-Aslıhan Sabancı.

Debreli İsmail Paşa Yalı

Like so many yalıs, the Debreli İsmail Paşa Yalı fell victim to fire. When it was rebuilt along the lines of the Alexandre Vallaury-designed original, it was turned into a 14-room waterside hotel with spacious, light-filled rooms. The decor is sorely dated which will appeal to some guests more than others

The pink-colored Hüseyin Kazım Kadri Yalı is used as a restaurant.

Özdemir Sabancı Yalı

Anchor Village

Çengelköy, Kuleli and Vaniköy

North of Üsküdar, beyond Kuzguncuk and Beylerbeyi, lies the waterside suburb of Çengelköy, known for its pretty main square which is shaded by ancient plane trees. This is not a place to come in search of major sights so much as somewhere where you can while away a few hours beside the water and shop the way the locals do. The most prominent landmark between Çengelköy and Vaniköy is the lemon-walled, twin-towered, oddly asymmetrical Kuleli Military School, clearly visible as you cruise along the Bosphorus.

In Turkish, Çengelköy means "Anchor Village" and two possible explanations have been given for how it acquired this strange name. The usual story is taken from the Ottoman travel writer **Evliya Çelebi** who suggested that a stash of Byzantine hooks and anchors had been found here after the Conquest of Istanbul in 1453. However, it is also possible that the village was named after **Admiral Çengeloğlu Tahir Paşa** who built a waterside mosque here.

As long ago as the 6th century the Emperor Justin II had a palace built for his empress **Sophia** after whom the area that is now Çengelköy was called **Sophianae**. In the 19th century a summer palace, the **Hümayun Kasrı**, stood here, its grounds watered by streams that flowed down from the forests on the hillside above. Today no trace of either structure survives.

Church of St George

At the Kuleli end of Çengelköy, in Tanrıverdi Sokağı, the large 19th-century Greek Orthodox church of Hagios Georgios (St George) stands on sloping land with a bell tower at the top of a flight of steps. From the outside (which is all that you are likely to be able to see) it looks almost like a warehouse. Inside, however, it contains a particularly fine iconostasis.

On 6 January (Epiphany) swimmers retrieve crosses thrown into the sea during an ancient ceremony known as **tossing the cross** at Çengelköy, Kuzguncuk, Fener, Ortaköy, Yeniköy, Arnavutköy and Yeşilköy.

Hagios Georgios Church at Easter

Vahdeddin Köşkü

High on the hillside above Çengelköy stands a huge 19th-century mansion distinguished by a tower topped with an onion dome. Originally built for the **Armenian Köçeoğlu Family**, it became home to Sultan Abdülaziz's nephew **Prince Burhaneddin** and then to **Vahdeddin Mehmed VI**, the last of the sultans who reigned from 1918 to 1922 before being sent into exile. It is used by Presidency of Turkey.

Çengelköy Yalıs

Sadullah Paşa Yalı

Like most of the Bosphorus suburbs, Çengelköy and Vaniköy still retain plenty of lovely old waterside mansions in varying states of repair. One of the oldest in Çengelköy is the burgundy-colored Sadullah Paşa Yalı which was given to **Mehmed Ağa**, a eunuch at Topkapı Palace, by **Sultan Abdülhamid I** in the late 18th century. Its baroque-style upper floor contained a room designed to imitate an Ottoman tent (otağ).

Sadullah Paşa

After the death of **Necibe Hanım** (see The haunted house below) the house passed to Ferit Tek, a distant relative. His daughter married an Egyptian prince and set up a foundation to maintain it. One tenant was **Ayşegül Tecimer** who married **Asil Nadir**, the Polly Peck entrepreneur who fled to Northern Cyprus when his business empire collapsed. She was later accused of selling antiquities illegally and left Turkey to live in **Marrakesh** in Morocco.

Oval Hall

The haunted house

In 1872 the Mehmed Ağa Yalı was bought by **Sadullah Paşa** who fell from favor with the court. Suspected of plotting against the sultan, he was sent as an ambassador to **Berlin** and forbidden to return. Eventually he fell in love in **Vienna** and committed suicide there in 1892. Unable to believe he was never coming back, his wife, **Necibe Hanım**, continued to keep the house spotless and waited for his return clad in a dress he loved. She was still wearing it when she, too, died in 1917. Some people believe that her **ghost** haunts the house to this day.

Bostancıbaşı Abdullah Ağa Yalı

The early 19th-century Bostancıbaşı Abdullah Ağa Yalı was built for a man who rose from poverty to become a grand vizier to **Sultan Mahmud II** for a brief four months and who was nicknamed **"Deli Abdullah (Crazy Abdullah)"**. The mansion was expropriated by the Ministry of Culture and Tourism in 1981. All its original pieces were preserved before its demolishment in line with the relief and restoration projects prepared by the Taç Foundation. It was rebuilt with a concrete-brick interior and a timber-covered façade. It was planned to be turned into a Judgeship Building and was transferred to the Ministry of Justice. The mansion was restored under this function and assumed its present shape. It is currently home to a branch of an old pudding shop, which is now a worldwide chain store.

Server Bey Yalı

Right next to the landing stage is the recently restored and elegant four-storey Server Bey Yalı that has changed hands many times.

The yellow bulding at the back is a church.

Muazzez Hanım Yalı's staircase is inside a graceful tower.

The area in front of the building is perfect for fishing.

Kuleli Military School (Kuleli Askeri Lisesi)

When the Janissaries were disbanded in 1826, **Sultan Mahmud II** founded a regular army to take their place and a wooden barracks was built for them on the shores of the Bosphorus just up from Çengelköy. After it burnt down **Sultan Abdülmecid** commissioned **Garabed Balyan** to build a stone replacement which came to be known as the **Tower Barracks** after its most conspicuous feature. Following another fire **Sultan Abdülaziz** had it rebuilt with a second storey. During the Crimean War of 1855-56, the barracks were turned into a **military hospital** supervized by **Florence Nightingale.** Over the years the building has served as a school, orphanage and military school. One of its most famous students was İrfan Orga, the author of the poignant "A Portrait of a Turkish Family".

The site on which the Military School now stands has been identified as the probable location of a convent called **Metanoia (Repentance)** established by the Emperor Justinian's wife **Theodora** to house forcibly reformed prostitutes, a story gleefully related by the Byzantine historian **Procopius** (c. 500-c. 565) who claimed that Theodora herself had started out as one of them.

After the decision to close down the military schools in the aftermath of the July 15 coup attempt, this building was also evacuated, full of its memories. The front part of the building was planned to be transferred to the Ministry of Culture and Tourism to be turned into a museum. The function of the remaining part will be decided and announced later on.

Kaymak Mustafa Paşa Mosque

This pretty wooden mosque was built in 1720 for Kaymak Mustafa Paşa whose father, Boşnak Kara İbrahim Paşa, had been brother-in-law to the Tulip Age Grand Vizier Damat İbrahim Paşa. Like him, Kaymak Mustafa Paşa was killed during the Patrona Halil uprising of 1730. The mosque was restored by Sultan Mahmud II.

Kuleli in a 19th-century Thomas Allom engraving

Vaniköy Yalıs

Mahmud Nedim Paşa Yalı before restoration

Just after you pass the Kuleli Military High School you'll see two unexceptional yalıs sharing a garden. They belong to the Ülker family, Turkey's most famous chocolate-makers. The brown one is the **Neşet and Şirin Yalçın Yalı**, the yellow one the **Yusuf Paşa Yalı.**

Mahmud Nedim Paşa Yalı

Further north in Vaniköy, the **Mahmud Nedim Paşa Yalı** was built for an Ottoman ambassador to Vienna and grand vizier who was so fond of the Russians that he was nicknamed **"Nedimof"**. It features a distinctive wooden tower. The yalı came into the hands of Kızılay (the Red Crescent) who sold it to Yalçın Sabancı for just $3 million in 2006. It has since been beautifully restored.

Anadolu Kazaskeri Necmettin Efendi Yalı

The **Anadolu Kazaskeri Necmettin Efendi** Yalı has had a troubled history featuring damage caused by fires and boat collisions. It belonged to the **Sapmaz**, a wealthy family of textile manufacturers from Adana. In 1973 Coşkun Sapmaz married the Turkish pop singer and actress **Ajda Pekkan** but his family disapproved so strongly of the match that it lasted only six days. Later the family was hit by a financial crisis and lost everything including this yalı.

The Suna-İnan Kıraç Yalı was designed by Sedad Hakkı Eldem

The yalı on the right is the İffet Hanım

Vaniköy Mosque was built in 1665 by Van (Vanlı) Mehmed Efendi who gave his name to the suburb. The Sultan's Lodge was added in Sultan Mahmud I's reign.

Serasker Rıza Paşa Yalı

Next door to the Anadolu Kazaskeri Necmettin Efendi Yalı, the Serasker Rıza Paşa Yalı, which dates back to the late 19th century, retains more of its original appearance. Rıza Paşa was an ambassador and a favorite of Sultan Abdülhamid I. During the Second Constitutional Period he was forced to flee to France. His son Sürreya İlmen became an MP and established the Sürreya Beach and the Sürreya Opera House in Kadıköy (see p. 481).

Ahmet Nazif Paşa Yalı

Ahmet Nazif Paşa (1842-1905) was three times Minister of Finance under Sultan Abdülhamid II. He had a great reputation for being well-adjusted and honest. The larger building on the left was the haremlik of the yalı while the separate smaller building on the right was the selamlık.

Vaniköy has many lovely yalıs. Some have succumbed to fire while some are in the process of restoration. During the research for this book one of the hardest tasks was establishing the names of some of them. I'd be grateful for any advice.

Melek Hanım Yalı

Mihrengiz Kadın Efendi (Melek Hanım) Yalı

The daughter of **Esvapçıbaşı Sabıt Efendi**, Melek Hanım grew bored with yalı life and rented the property out. Amongst its tenants have been the archeologist **Halet Çambel** (see p. 421) and the writer and translator **Mina Urgan**. The three-storey mansion on the left is the **Kadınefendi Yalı**.

Recaizade Yalı

The **Recaizade Yalı** belonged to Recai Mehmed Efendi was the birthplace of his son, the poet **Mahmud Ekrem Bey** (1847-1914), author of "Araba Sevdası (Carriage Liaisons)", regarded as one of Turkey's first realist novels. Mahmud Ekrem had his own yalı in **Yeniköy** (see p. 452). Accused of secretly signaling to **Khedive Abbas Hilmi Paşa** over in Çubuklu, he was forced to sell it and move to Cihangir. Until the 1980s the Vaniköy yalı was used as a corn-oil factory. It was then seized by the local authorities, but is now back in private ownership. The garden boasts some beautiful bougainvillea plants.

Recaizade Mahmud Ekrem

Postcard of Vaniköy at the end of the 19th century with the Ahmed Nazif Paşa Yalı in the foreground and the tower of the Mahmud Nedim Paşa Yalı to the right.

Vaniköy in 2012. To the left is Ender Mermerci's yalı with the Ahmed Nazif Paşa Yalı beside it. The tower of the Mahmud Nedim Paşa Yalı appears after its restoration.

The Hilltop Observatory

Kandilli and Küçüksu Mansion

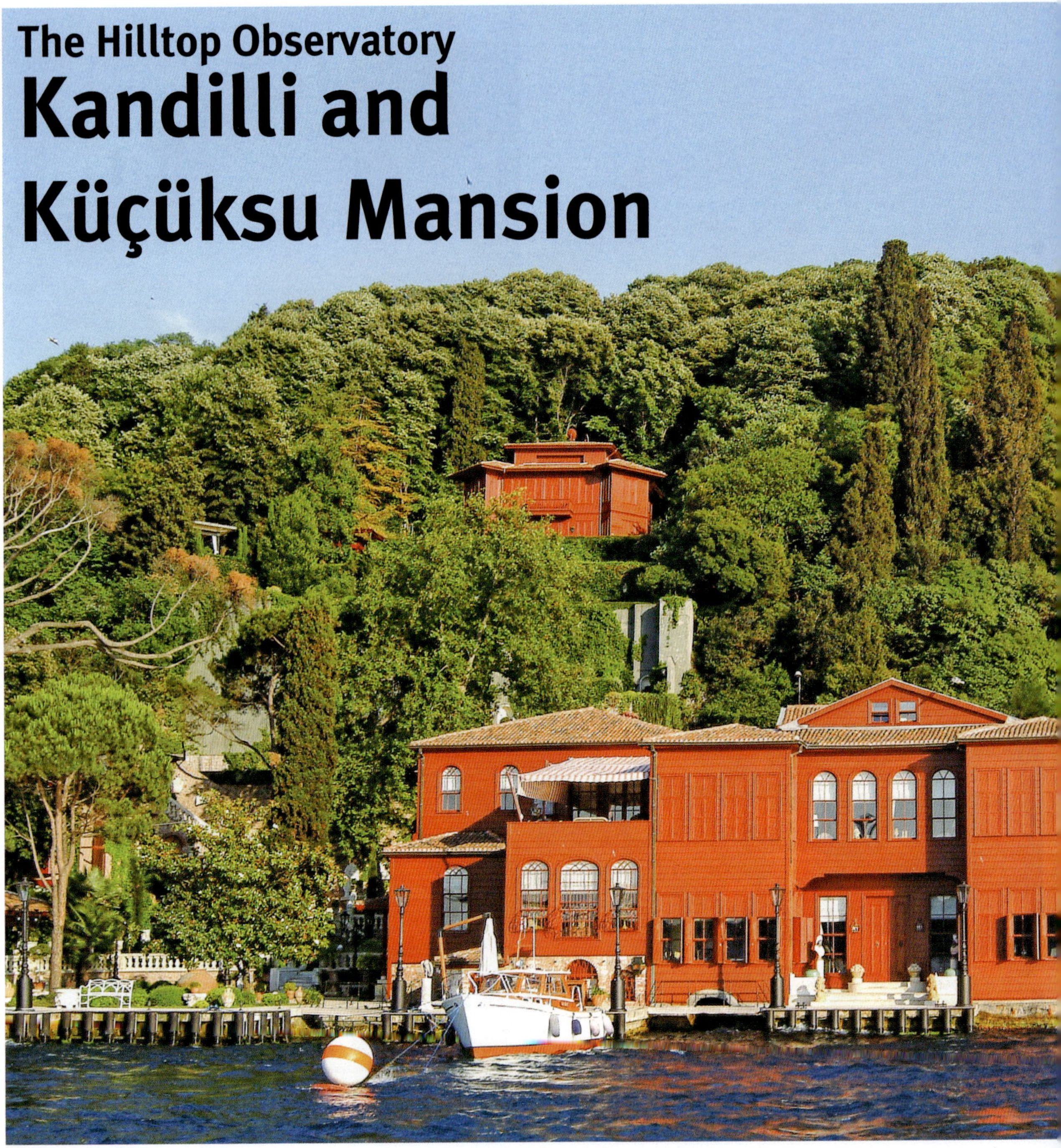

081 For Turks the suburb of Kandilli is best known as the location of a famous observatory that issues bulletins after earthquakes. It is home, too, to the Küçüksu Kasrı (Mansion), perhaps the prettiest of the minor 19th-century imperial lodges. Kandilli also boasts many fine yalıs, including the Kıbrıslı Yalı, the longest such waterside mansion on the Bosphorus and Abud Efendi Yalı, the setting for a popular soap opera.

Demosten Corpi Mansion

The lost mansions

Like so many areas of Istanbul, Kandilli has suffered from relentless and often unthinking "development". In particular, the number of wooden houses declines day by day; some were supposedly being restored although the end results often look nothing like the originals. A more conspicuous victim of brutalist restoration was the **Demosten Corpi Mansion**. This four-storey building in Sıraevler Street opposite the Armenian church, was built by members of the same Italian family responsible for the **old American Consulate** in Tepebaşı (p.336). Its walls and ceilings were once richly decorated, with especially adorable animal paintings. The exceptionally big and beautiful garden embraced a chalet and pool. But then one day the walls were suddenly whitewashed, an act of vandalism almost as crass as whitewashing over the walls of the Sultanahmet Mosque.

When this photo was taken in the 1980s some of the paintings still survived.

Greek Orthodox Church of Christ

Surp Yergodasan Arakelotz (12 Disciples) Armenian Church

The Greek Orthodox Primary School has been closed for decades.

...and lost churches

Although it was one of the smaller villages on the shores of the Bosphorus, Kandilli once had **three churches and a mosque**. The Catholic Church was converted into a house and although the other two churches still exist they are no longer open to the public. The **Istanbul Riots** of 6-7 September 1955 left an indelible mark on Kandilli; the minority religious populations disappeared and the Greek primary school, which had boasted 88 students in 1914, closed in 1972 (I later found one of its old desks, still with the old pupil's names carved into it, on sale in an antique shop). At that time, **the sense of community** was still strong. Everybody knew and greeted each other, so a stranger really stood out. One day I spotted a stranger standing on the quayside. The village headman identified him as his old friend, Marko, who had had to leave along with the other Greeks. Now he had returned to visit his elderly aunt and his old homeland before he died. In the 1990s his aunt, the last Greek in the village, passed away and the Greek cemetery opened and closed its doors for a funeral for the last time. It was the end of an era. Neither Kandilli nor Istanbul was ever the same again. The **mansion of Fatin Gökmen**, founder of the Kandilli observatory, stood beside the old Greek cemetery. A gorgeous structure originally built for a Levantine family, it was converted into a monstrous shape in the process of "restoration". Another stone building in the same street was built for the Galvany family after whom **Kallavi Street** was named. Despite the magnificent murals decorating its walls and ceilings the house was turned into a social facility for a school, leaving only the original outside walls still standing. In their heyday, these two houses boasted **breathtaking views** of a small forest and a valley running down to a beach. Then, despite the fact that construction along the shore of the Bosphorus had been prohibited, it was suddenly surrounded by serried ranks of new villas.

The Glavany family mansion and coat of arms

Casanova's Bosphorus bolthole

The façade of another traditionally maroon-colored yalı known as the Casanova Mansion, conceals an interesting footnote to **erotic history**. When describing his varied experiences on a visit to Istanbul in 1745 in his 12-volume **"Story of My Life"**, the famous Italian playboy Giacomo Casanova (1725-98) mentioned in particular the love and kindness shown to him by Reis-ül Küttap İsmail Efendi. Later an artist named Türkan Hanım lived here. Finally it was bought and restored by the construction company STFA.

Casanova Mansion

Giacomo Casanova

Dabkoviç Mansion

Kandilli Yokuşu (Kandilli Hill)

Kandilli Yokuşu contains the mansion home of the **Trabzon MP Şükrü Bey** whose huge, tree-filled garden contained an ayazma (sacred spring). Eventually this fine building also fell victim to the sort of "restoration" that effectively replaces an old building with a brand-new one. In this case, however, the good news is that building had provided an inspirational childhood home for **Bünyamin Derman** who went on to become an award-winning architect.

ingly, people still lived in this house a few years ago.

Kurt Bağrı Sokak

Poetic inspiration

I lived in Kandilli for 25 years. It is and always will be the most special place in the world for me. This section was the last part of the book to be finished. As I was writing these lines and putting a full stop to the work, I remembered a poem of **Constantine Cavafy** entitled **"The City"** which reads:

"You will not find new places;
other seas
you will not find. This city will
follow you.
You will walk the same familiar
streets,
Get older in the same
neighborhood,
Grow white hair in the same
house.
Always you will return to this
same city.
Don' t expect anything elsewhere;
There is no ship, no road
As you have destroyed your life
here
In this little corner,
So you have ruined it
Everywhere in the world.

Kandilli ferry terminal

The view from the palace is spectacular.

Kandilli

IV. Murad

In Turkish Kandilli means **"with oil lamps"** and there are several suggested reasons as to how the suburb acquired such a romantic name. Two of them relate to **Sultan Murad IV** who is said to have built a palace here and ringed it with oil lamps; alternatively, he is said to have hung a cypress tree with decorative lamps. In another version of the same story a priest in need of a favor is said to have placed candles in the sultan's garden every evening, thus giving rise to the name. More prosaically, lamps are thought to have been placed at **Kandilli Point** as a form of primitive lighthouse. Finally, the name could have come from the proliferation of candle-makers' workshops in the area. Take your pick. Today the Küçüksu River is a polluted trickle of water and it's hard to believe that it was once, with the Göksu River at nearby Anadolu Hisarı (see p. 538), one of the two stretches of water to which revelers flocked in the 18th century and which were known collectively as "the Sweet Waters of Asia". Dredging work currently in progress should eventually improve its appearance and smell, a step in its rehabilitation,

Adile Sultan Palace

In the old days...

Adile Sultan

One of Sultan Mahmud II' s 31 children, Adile (1825-98), a published poet and philanthropist whose life was blighted by the deaths of her husband, children and younger brother ***Sultan Abdülaziz,*** *employed the* ***Balyan*** *Family to build a palace for her in Kandilli. In 1916 it became Turkey' s second girls' school and then a girls' high school. Destroyed in a fire in 1986, it has since been restored with grants from an ex-upil Prof. Dr. Türkan Saylan* *(see p.425)* *and the businessman Sakıp Sabancı and reopened in 2006 as an* ***education and cultural center*** *and* ***restaurant*** *(see below) with a spectacular 180-degree view of the city.*

Oval Hall

On the hilltop stands the Adile Sultan Palace. On the shore to the left is the Edip Efendi Yalı. The twin green-roofed yalıs belong to Yalçın Sabancı and Hasan Aslanoba.

The Observatory (Rasathane)

Istanbul's first observatory was built above **Tophane** in the 16th century, roughly where the Maison de France is now in Tom Tom Kaptan Sokak. It was the brainchild of **Takıyyüddin** (1526-85), a talented astronomer and physicist who had worked at the observatory in **Samarkand** and arrived in Istanbul in the 1550s. However, after the religious authorities ruled that it was a sin to study the heavens, **Sultan Murad III** ordered **Admiral Kılıç Ali Paşa** (see p. 379) to destroy it. A surviving account of the first observatory describes several different instruments that were in use there. It is thought that it may have had an influence on the work of the famous Danish astronomer, **Tycho Brahe**.

Takıyyüddin

Two years later a new observatory, the Rasathane-i Amire, was established in **Beyoğlu**, before being moved again, this time to **Maçka**. Finally in 1911 the Observatory arrived in its present location on İcadiye Hill where once there had stood a mansion called **Hekimgörmez Sarayı (Never Needs a Doctor Palace)**, a name apparently given to it because the strong sunlight on the hilltop was believed to keep its residents healthy. Until this time the religious authorities had been in control of everything to do with **time-keeping** but from then on this responsibility passed to the observatory. Today as part of the **Bosphorus University** (see p. 429) the observatory also serves as an earthquake research institute. One of its managers **Ahmet Mete Işıkara** made a name for himself in the aftermath of the 1999 earthquakes when people hung so desperately on his words that children started to call him **"deprem dede" (grandfather earthquake)**.

Ahmet Mete Işıkara

You can find out more about the Observatory at the Museum of Islamic Science and Technology in Gülhane Park (see p. 201).

Kandilli Yalıs

Edip Efendi Yalı

Visible from a waterside walkway at the Bosphorus' narrowest point and overlooking the city's fastest-flowing current, **Şeytan Akıntısı (Devil's Current),** the Edip Efendi Yalı has borne the name of many Ottoman officials over the years. Unusually, it features the same ground plan for the male and female sections of the building (the female part is usually larger). From 1881 to 1907 the British woman **Dorina Lady Neave** lived in the **Clifton Yalı** at Kandilli that was eventually burnt down by the Germans. In her *Romance of the Bosphorus* she left a lively account of growing up there that includes descriptions of an earthquake, seeing Sultan Abdülhamid II visiting the mosque for Friday prayers and an extraordinary day when many Bosphorus fish literally froze to death.

Behind the yalı one of the Bosphorus radar control towers can be seen.

Passing in front of the yalı, the Devil's Current is one of the fastest flowing waters on the Bosphorus.

The Monheim Yalı which belonged to Selahattin Beyazıt is a rare example of a single-storey Bosphorus building. It was built by Sedad Hakkı Eldem.

Hadi Bey Yalı

Once called the Manford House, this beautiful 19th-century Ottoman-rose-colored yalı was bought by a Greek ship-owner called Licardopulos after the British occupation of Istanbul. The lawyer Hadi Bey later acquired it from a Salonican Turk in settlement of a debt. It now belongs to Hasan Çolakoğlu, the owner of the TEB bank.

Kont Ostorog Yalı

Of the many other yalıs one of the most impressive is the **Kont Ostorog Yalı**, built in the 19th century for the Polish count Leon Ostorog who was an adviser to the Ottoman court and which was visited in the past by Pierre Loti (see p. 252). It's now owned by Rahmi M. Koç (see p. 259).

Abud Efendi Yalı

Between the Kont Ostorog and Kıbrıslı yalıs stands the mid-19th-century Abud Efendi Yalı designed by the famous **Garabed Amira Balyan.**

Living room

Landward Entrance

Sofa Room

Lounge

Kıbrıslı (Cypriot) Yalı

Of all the Bosphorus yalıs, the 21-room Kıbrıslı (Cypriot) Yalı, which was built in the 18th century for the Grand Vizier Mehmed İzzet Paşa, is the longest. Later it passed into the hands of Kıbrıslı Mehmed Emin Paşa whose wife **Melek Hanım** wrote a book called **"Thirty Years in the Harem"** which was published in 1872 and is still in print. Past guests at the yalı included Pierre Loti, the Empress Eugenie and King Faisal II, the last king of Iraq.

Who was Melek Hanım?

An Ottoman woman of Greek, Armenian and French lineage, Melek Hanım met **Kıbrıslı Mehmed Emin Paşa** in Paris and married him in Istanbul. As the wife of a grand vizier she traveled extensively with her husband. However, in his absence she seems to have plotted to replace her sickly son with another child in the event of his death. The child survived, but one of her co-conspirators killed another one and in the ensuing **scandal** her husband divorced her. Sent into exile, she passed her time plotting to get revenge on him and writing an account of the life of upper class women in late Ottoman society, which, despite being called "Thirty Years in the Harem", had little to do with what most people think of as the harem at all.

Kıbrıslı Yalı in the early 20th century.

2nd Bridge and Rumeli Hisarı from Kandilli

The parapet bears the monogram of Sultan Abdülmecid

"I saw you in Küçüksu
I knew you by your eyes.
No matter how much you pain me
my heart longs for thee."

***Song* by Tamburi Mustafa Çavuş.**

The fountain in an old photograph

Küçüksu Mansion

Küçüksu (Mansion) Kasrı makes the perfect escape for those who want to see how the 19th-century sultans lived but find the Dolmabahçe Palace overwhelming. Designed by **Nigoğos Balyan** in 1856-7 as a hunting lodge for **Sultan Abdülmecid** on the site of an older wooden palace, it has only eight perfectly maintained rooms, enough for you to appreciate the lavish baroque decoration without feeling swamped by it.

The mansion stands on the banks of the **Küçüksu River** in a pleasant small garden complete with lily ponds. Of course the sultan would have approached in his **caique** from the Bosphorus where he would have been looking straight at the elaborate ornamentation of the façade. Today's visitors, however, approach from the rear which is a great deal less heavily decorated.

Inside, a delightful double staircase spirals round beneath an internal dome that is painted, like all the ceilings, with goldleaf. The rooms all feature **parquet floors** made from walnut, mahogany and chestnut, on top of which are laid Hereke carpets and one fine Persian carpet that is distinctive for its animal designs. Most of the chandeliers are Bohemian crystal, although one was made in Italy. It's worth taking a peek at the bathroom which features an over-the-top marble sink and then a super-plain shower unit. Because it was just a **hunting lodge** there was no formal bedroom, although Turkey's fourth president **Cemal Gürsel** (1895-1966) sometimes slept here, hence the daybed in one of the upstairs rooms.

www.millisaraylar.gov.tr
Tel: 0216 323 33 03

Mihrişah Sultan Fountain with Küçüksu Mansion in the background

Mihrişah Sultan Fountain

As if it wasn't enough that Küçüksu Mansion is the prettiest of the imperial lodges, it also has, right next door in the shape of the **Mihrişah Sultan Fountain**, which was commissioned by Sultan Selim III for his mother in 1807, the most elegant fountain to be found anywhere along the Bosphorus. Much hymned by writers and artists, it stands on a plinth to protect it against flooding roughly midway between the **"Sweet Waters of Asia"**.

Bohemian crystal chandelier

The Junior Fortress

Anadolu Hisarı

082

It was here at the narrowest point of the Bosphorus that Sultan Bayezid I chose to build his castle and it was here, much later on, that many wealthy individuals chose to build their yalıs, including the magnificent Amcazade Hüseyin Paşa Yalı, the oldest such waterside mansion to survive. This was also the part of Istanbul famed as the "Sweet Waters of Asia".

Anadolu Hisarı in an old engraving

Anadolu Hisarı is the suburb that grew up around the "**Anatolian Castle**" started by **Sultan Bayezid I** and completed by Sultan **Mehmed II**. Today the remaining fortifications are overshadowed by the **2nd Bridge**, although this is still a pretty place with a number of impressive **yalıs** clustered around the castle. The banks of the **Göksu River** may be built up now but they once served as one of Istanbul's premier pleasure gardens and even today there's the occasional whiff of the Thames at Maidenhead in England about it.

The white yalı at the far left by the entrance to Göksu River is named after Riyaziyeci İzzet Bey.

The castle

Long before Sultan Mehmed II rode up to capture Istanbul in 1453 the early Ottoman sultans had yearned to seize the city and in 1394 **Sultan Yıldırım (the Thunderbolt) Bayezid** identified the site of an ancient temple to Jupiter at the narrowest point on the Bosphorus as the best location for a castle. It was from here that he launched the first Ottoman attack on Constantinople which came to an unsuccessful end in 1402 when Tamerlane came thundering across the country and carted the sultan off in chains. Later Sultan Mehmed II decided to expand his great-grandfather's fortress at the same time as he built his own much more magnificent castle on the opposite shore at Rumeli Hisarı; Anadolu Hisarı is sometimes called the **Güzelce Hisarı** (Rather Pretty Castle) to distinguish it from its more impressive rival.

The new Asian Castle consisted of a keep with a surrounding wall enclosing an area of some 7,000- square meters/23,000- square feet together with an outer barbican with three towers. Unfortunately, in the 20th century a road was driven through the walls rendering them considerably less impressive.

From the bridge over the Göksu River a narrow road winds down to the river and in one of the gardens in front of the fortress you can see a rare **namazgah**, an outdoor prayer arena complete with stone mihrab and minbar that was probably built in the early 18th century.

Göksu River

While fairly insignificant today, the stream that runs beside the fortress was once extremely important as one of the two waterways (the other was the Küçüksu River), which together made up the playground called **"The Sweet Waters of Asia"**. Its banks were once lined with parks and green spaces and wooden bridges allowed pedestrians to gaze down on boats bringing yet more visitors to frolic on the banks. The area was especially busy on Wednesdays, Fridays and Sundays when people flocked in to participate in what were called the **Göksu Galas**. As recently as the 1960s the area was still undeveloped. Even in 1972 **John Freely** and **Hilary Sumner-Boyd** could write: "If you continue up the valley on foot, you find at the beginning of spring banks and meadows covered with the earliest snowdrops of the year and with wild cyclamen." Now, of course, they are solidly carpeted with concrete, although pleasure boats still moor in picturesque order alongside the banks.

Anadolu Hisarı Yalıs

Zarif Mustafa Paşa Yalı

The Zarif Mustafa Paşa Yalı at Aandolu Hisarı is one of the most beautiful and valuable of the Bosphorus mansions. Right beside it is the Amcazade Hüseyin Paşa Yalı, the oldest such mansion on the Bosphorus shore. Below in a nutshell is the story of the 300 years of history that lies behind its lovely façade.

One of the biggest and most conspicuous of the mansions is the Zarif Mustafa Paşa Yalı, built on the site of a **Byzantine monastery** with a sacred spring (ayazma) in the ground and purchased in the early 19th-century by **Kani Bey,** official coffee-maker to Sultan Mahmud II. In 1848 it passed into the possession of the **Zarif Mustafa Paşa** after whom it is named. The Paşa's son-in-law Sadık Bey soon tired of all the partying that went on there and bought the selamlık (male quarters) and boathouse for himself before erecting a high wall between the two properties.

The family were related to **Şeyh Talat Efendi** from whom they acquired a piece of the Prophet Mohammed's beard. After Sadık's son **Esat Bey** donated one hair to the **Fatih Mosque** the yalı was sometimes called the Esat Bey Yalı in his honor. The mansion's cihannüma (lantern) was used to display the rest of the beard.

The yalı stayed in the same family until 1992. During the Turkish War of Independence and the British occupation of Istanbul Esat Bey's sons used it to store weapons to be smuggled to the resistance in Anatolia. Because the harem section had been used by English soldiers it was later pulled down. In 1926 the building was painted yellow in celebration of the wedding of Sadiye Hanım, after which it was sometimes called the **Yellow Yalı.**

The **Montreux Convention** of 1936 had designated the Bosphorus an international waterway which meant that all non-military shipping was free to pass through it, a potentially dangerous situation. Sure enough, in 1974 a ship hit the yalı and severely damaged it. Speedily restored, it fall victim to another **shipping accident** in 1990. After a long legal struggle the owners finally sold the remains for $7 million to the then **Saudi energy minister** whose mother had wanted to live somewhere where she would be able to hear the call to prayer. A stroke meant that she never actually lived in the mansion but it was nevertheless restored by her family.

Since 2000 the house has been back in Turkish hands and the current owner acts as an unofficial ambassador for the country, welcoming such eminent visitors as Colin Powell, Oprah Winfrey and the Grand Duchess Maria Vladimirovna Romanova of Russia to her home.

Fruit Room

Living room

It retains many **original features** including a mehtabiye (room for looking at the full moon) and a maltalık (coffee room) whose walls are decorated with painted fruit and flowers; a built-in **sea hamam** filled with water from the Bosphorus that once allowed the women of the house to bathe in privacy now serves as an indoor fish pond. In the past a **track** used by horse carts passed through the garden but the family eventually donated some land behind it to create a proper road.

Bahriyeli Sedat Bey Yalı

Dating back to the late 19th century, one of the finest waterside mansions in Anadolu Hisarı is the neo-baroque **Bahriyeli Sedat Bey Yalı**, also called the Manolyalı Yalı (Magnolia Mansion), which has been divided into two separate properties.

Marki Necip Bey Yalı

The **Marki Necip Bey Yalı**, believed to date back to the early 19th century, took its name from that of a Frenchman who became a Muslim in order to be able to marry the woman he loved. The building with a tower immediately behind it was used as a winter home. The yalı was restored after a fire in 1983.

Komodor Remzi Bey Yalı

Built in 1917, the **Komodor Remzi Bey Yalı**, a grey-painted mansion right on the waterfront, was bought by **Erdal İnönü**, a son of Turkey's second president and a prime minister in his own right, in 1972.

Nuri Paşa Yalı

The **Nuri Paşa Yalı**, built in 1895 for an officer of Sultan Abdülhamid I, was for some time the home of industralist Rahmi M. Koç(see p. 532). After he moved to the Kont Ostorog Yalı in Kandilli. it became the home of his son Ali Koç. According to the gossip Nuri Paşa's son Hami ran away with the daughter of Marki Necep Bey who owned the yalı next door.

"This ceiling (of the Amcazade Hüseyin Paşa Yalı) is the most precious thing of its kind in all Constantinople".

***Constantinople Old and New* by H.G. Dwight, 1907**

Köprülü Amcazade Hüseyin Paşa Yalı

It may not look much now but this yalı is very important not only architecturally but because of events that took place inside it. It was built in 1698 for **Grand Vizier Hüseyin Paşa**, nicknamed "The Wise", a member of the powerful Köprülü family who also bequeathed several buildings to **Divan Yolu** and **Çemberlitaş** (see p. 064 and 068). As the representative of Sultan Mustafa II, Hüseyin Paşa negotiated with the Europeans at Carlowitz in 1698 and the final articles of the **Peace of Carlowitz,** which resolved the Austro-Ottoman War (1683-99), were signed in this house in 1699. Its terms forced the Ottomans to cede many of their European holdings to Poland, Russia, Austria and Venice and marked the beginning of the end of their power.

Today all that survives of the yalı is the central section with its cumba (bay window), both wings having long since collapsed. It's painted the popular rust-red color that was called **"Ottoman rose"**. 19th-century drawings show an interior of unmatched sumptuousness and **Pierre Loti** (see p. 252)was one of those who campaigned to save the building for posterity. In 2009 restoration work on the yalı finally began.

Hekimbaşı Salih Efendi Yalı

In much better shape although minus its left wing is the yalı built in the mid 19th century for **Salih Efendi** who was the court physician in attendance when **Sultan Abdülmecid** died of tuberculosis in 1861. He didn't challenge the verdict that **Sultan Abdülaziz** had committed suicide in 1876 even though he may well have been murdered. However, he drew the line at agreeing when, in the same year, **Abdülhamid II** deposed his brother **Murad V** on the grounds of "emotional instability" and took his place on the throne. Despite the new sultan's efforts to exile him, Salih Efendi was able to retire to the yalı he had bought in the 1840s where he planted a **physic garden** and remarried at the age of 63 to a beautiful 16-year-old Circassian girl called Payidar. Some of his medical instruments are still preserved in the house. In the mid-20th century British travel writer **Freya Stark** was a guest here. Beautifully restored, the yalı is still in the hands of Salih Efendi's descendants and was restored in 2010.

Living room facing the Bosphorus before the accident.

In 2005 the yalı appeared in Conde Nast Traveler magazine's "Fabulous 50" list of places that are not always open to the public but which give an added insight to a culture. I think it has an air of the "1001 Nights" about it and love its original Turkish bath. Unfortunately the sea mansion had its share from the traffic in the Bosphorus and a ship struck the mansion in April 2017, severely damaging its façade.

Otağtepe Fatih Woods

On **Otağtepe (Tent Hill)** in Kavacık above Anadolu Hisarı, this small and rather overgrown park offers fine views along the Bosphorus in both directions.

Yoghurt and Yalıs

Kanlıca

083

Dominated today by the 2nd Bridge, Kanlıca's great claim to fame is its yoghurt which has been held in high regard since the 17th century when the Ottoman travel writer Evliya Çelebi spoke of it in mouth-watering terms. Modern passengers on the longer Bosphorus cruises will have a chance to sample it without leaving the boat since yoghurt-sellers always board at Kanlıca to sell their wares. Otherwise, the main reason to visit the suburb is to inspect some of the finest surviving Bosphorus yalıs, none of them open to the public.

"Lying down on a stone in Kanlıca
My tearful eyes turn towards the castle
There is nothing to do, he wanted to go and he went
I both understand and feel bitter that it ended so one-sidedly"

***From "Since Istanbul became Istanbul"* by singer Sezen Aksu**

Originally Kanlıca seems to have been called **Glaros (Seagull)**, but there is uncertainty over the origin of its modern name, which means "**quite bloody**" in Turkish. Some suggest that it is a corruption of "**kağnis (ox-cart)**" since such carts were once made in this area. Others suggest that local cows used to graze on a **red grass** that turned their milk pink; this grass was supposedly called "kanglı" which might have evolved over time into Kanlıca.

The Kanlıca landing stage opens onto a pretty little main square with a handful of fishing boats still moored alongside an inlet running up to the mosque. It has something of the feel of the old Istanbul, the one jarring feature being the white radar tower, which competes for height supremacy with the minaret. It would have had poor Mimar Sinan turning in his grave.

Gazi İskender Paşa Mosque

This small, much modernized mosque facing the ferry landing stage was originally built by **Mimar Sinan** in 1559-60 for İskender Paşa (1492-1571), a governor of Van, Erzurum, Diyarbakır and Baghdad during the reign of Sultan Süleyman the Magnificent, who is buried in a tomb attached to the time-keeper's lodge beside his son Ahmed Paşa. Today there's nothing left of Sinan's handiwork.

Keeping time

Accurate time-keeping is important in most societies, but in Muslim tradition it's especially critical because of the need to summon the faithful to prayer at the correct times in the day which change according to the phases of the moon. Pinpoint accuracy becomes even more important during Ramadan when the start and end of each day of the month-long fasting period is announced from the mosques. In the past the start of each day of fasting was taken to be the point at which it was light enough for someone to be able to distinguish between a black and white thread. Today telling the time is a mechanized business, but once it was the responsibility of special time-keepers (muvakkit) and many mosques had special lodgings (muvakkithane) where their time-keepers could sleep. You can see many devices to do with time-keeping in the Museum of the History of Islamic Science and Technology in Gülhane Park (see p. 201).

Quadrant

Astrolabe

Timekeepers in a miniature

"Yesterday I came here and gazed on holy Istanbul from the hill..."

Poet Yahya Kemal Beyatlı remembers Mihrabat Woods

Mihrabat Woods

On the hillside above Kanlıca a 200-acre wooded park with marked walking trails offers a pleasant place to drink tea, smoke a nargile and gaze out over the Bosphorus and two of its bridges. There has been woodland here since the reign of **Sultan Mahmud I** (1696-1754) and the Grand Vizier **Damat İbrahim Paşa** built a mansion here as a gift for **Sultan Ahmed III** (1703-30). The mansion may be long gone, but many writers and poets, including **Yahya Kemal Beyatlı** (1884-1958) and **Özdemir Asaf** (1923-81), used to come here to draw inspiration from the view.

Kanlıca Yalıs

Princess Rukiye Yalı

This late 19th-century yalı, once one of the largest of all the waterside mansions, was a gift from her husband's family to Princess Rukiye, the daughter of **Khedive Abbas Hilmi Paşa** (see p. 551). The yalı in the Mihrabat Woods behind was bought in 1957 by Özdemir Atman, a stalwart of the Turkish Jockey Club (TJK).

Ethem Pertev Yalı

Most distinctive of all the Kanlıca yalıs is the graceful Ethem Pertev Yalı which was built for Saraylı Fatma Hanım in the 1860s but is named after an Ottoman pharmacist who created a famous **skin cream** (Pertev kremi) that is still on sale today. Unfortunately one of his sons was killed when a wave hit their boathouse and in 1932 his other children sold the building to a sea captain. The influence of **Art Nouveau** is apparent in the frilly balcony on the ground floor, hence its nickname the **"Süslü (Decorated) Yalı"**. The sea mansion was severely damaged when a cargo ship's steer was locked in 2015.

Yağlıkçı Hacı Reşit Bey Yalı

Built in the 1850s, this yalı was restored in the 1980s by Barlas Turan. The bay here was a popular venue for **moonlit musical soirees** in late Ottoman times.

Saffet Paşa Yalı

Built in 1907, this yalı has one of the longest mooring places on the Bosphorus. It was completely rebuilt in 2008 after a fire destroyed the original. It takes its name from the grandfather of Sedat Simavi who set up the **Hürriyet** newspaper in 1948.

Hacı Ahmet Bey Yalı

Atatürk is known to have attended a circumcision celebration in this late 19th-century yalı that belonged to the Ramazanoğlu Family.

Sadrazam Kadri Paşa Yalı

Built in the mid-19th-century, this yalı belonged to **Kadri Paşa**, a grand vizier and **governor of Edirne** who married the daughter of İsmail Paşa, Sultan Abdülmecid's personal physician. This is one of those unlucky waterside mansions that was hit by a ship as recently as 1991. It has since been restored and members of the same family still live in it. When you look at it from the water, the yalı to the left belongs to pop superstar **Sezen Akzu** while the tiny one to the right belongs to **Cem Boyner,** owner of the Boyner chain of clothes shops.

Yağcı Şefik Bey Yalı

This yalı was built in 1905 on the site of the lost Cemile Sultan Palace and beautifully restored in 1989. A successful businessperson, **Şefik Bey** built the larger structure as the haremlik, or family quarters and the smaller one as the selamlık for the men. The current owner is the daughter of multi-millionaire tycoon Faruk Yalçın who founded the **zoo in Gebze** (see p. 601).

Yedi-Sekiz (7-8) Hasan Paşa Yalı

Some of the oldest yalıs on the Bosphorus can be seen in Kanlıca.

Yedi-Sekiz Hasan Paşa Yalı

The late 19th-century **Asaf Paşa Yalı** is also known as Yedi-Sekiz Hasan Paşa Yalı because the illiterate paşa used to sign his name as 7/8 – "yedi-sekiz" in Arabic numbers.

Necmettin Erbakan Yalı

Kanlıca Yoghurt

The original Kanlıca yoghurt was made with a mixture of cow, buffalo and ewe's milk and, like Maraş ice-cream, was thick enough to slice with a knife. Much of the ready-packaged stuff sold today comes automatically sweetened although the waterside retailers will ladle in as much or as little icing sugar as you want. In and around the main square shops compete to sell the famous local yoghurt.

Ahmed Rasim Paşa Yalı houses a boutique hotel

The Egyptian Summer-House

Çubuklu and the Khedive's Villa

084

One of Istanbul's more easily overlooked delights is the Khedive's Villa (Hıdiv Kasrı) at Çubuklu near Kanlıca on the Asian side of the Bosphorus, which is clearly visible from the ferries and from the grounds of the Sakıp Sabancı Museum but which vanishes from sight once you get closer to it.

In Turkish the word "çubuk" has several meanings, so inevitably there are several stories about how the suburb of Çubuklu got its name. In the more prosaic version the "çubuk" refers to the stems of the clay pipes that were manufactured here in the 19th century; in the more romantic version the "çubuk" was a cornelian cherry tree planted by the later **Sultan Selim I** who visited here when he was just a crown prince. The sapling matured and produced fruit overnight, a phenomenon miraculous enough to justify its name being bestowed on the surrounding area.

A short walk to the right of Çubuklu landing stage is the late 19th-century neoclassical **Halil Edhem Yalı** that was built for Edhem İbrahim Paşa, a grand vizier to Sultan Abdülhamid II and the father of Osman Hamdi Bey (see p. 335). Unlike many other yalıs it still retains its architectural integrity. It was restored in 1988.

The Villa

The Khedive's Villa (Hıdiv Kasrı) was intended as a summer home for the **Egyptian Khedive Abbas Hilmi Paşa** whose mother commissioned the fabulous building used as the Egyptian Consulate across the water in Bebek. Abbas Hilmi already owned a palace on two waterside plots of land in Çubuklu, but in 1907 he bought the slope behind them and began work on a property that was called the **Çubuklu Summer Palace.** Hard though it is to believe that the architect of such a superb and prominent building could be unknown, there is no certainty about who created it; some list it as a work of **Raimondo d'Aronco,** others as the handiwork of the Italian architect **Delfo Seminati** or the Austrian architect **Antonio Lasciac** .

The Khedive used the villa in summer right through until the 1930s during which time **Pierre Loti** (see p. 252) visited it and expressed a preference for the original waterside palace. Eventually the Egyptian sold his retreat to the Istanbul authorities and departed for Switzerland where he died in Geneva in 1944. In the way of things, the beautiful building was then left to molder until 1984 when the Turkish Touring and Automobile Association under the far-sighted leadership of **Çelik Gülersoy** (see p. 034) took it over and restored it. It now offers a **restaurant** and **garden café**.

The villa was designed in a style, which has been dubbed **neo-Renaissance** and its most striking feature is the lofty flat-roofed tower, which offers panoramic views across the Bosphorus. In the elaborate metalwork over the main entrance the Khedive's coat of arms can be seen, while inside **Art Nouveau** glass doors open onto a circular lobby ringed with paired marble columns with a fountain playing in the center. In its heyday a steam-powered elevator with padded velvet seats would whisk the favored to the top. A circular restaurant is wrapped around this lobby, but don't miss the **door-frame** that leads into the main dining room which is decorated with gilded bears, leaves thrown over their shoulders like cloaks, happily plucking berries from the trees. Even the rest rooms merit a quick look as they still retain their original Art Nouveau tiles.

Behind the villa is a formal **rose garden** laid out in 1909 and a park shaded with pine trees and full of hydrangeas. It's at its fragrant finest in spring when the lawns are planted with tulips and the sweet scent of hyacinths fills the air.

The Khedive's Villa

"The Khedive built himself a new palace on the hill, but I adore greenery and preferred the old palace. I never like change."

***Journeys* by Pierre Loti, 1910**

Halil Edhem Yalı

Who was the Khedive?

Abbas Hilmi Paşa

"Khedive" was a term used to describe the virtually autonomous governors of late Ottoman Egypt. From 1892 to 1914 **Abbas Hilmi Paşa** was the last khedive of Egypt and Sudan while they were a British protectorate. In 1914 he was deposed by the British who feared that he would side with the Ottomans in the First World War. Stripped of his property and forbidden to return to Egypt, he finally accepted defeat and abdicated in 1931.

From Nightingale to Kitchen Glass

Paşabahçe and Beykoz

085

Towards the northern end of the Asian shore of the Bosphorus are the twin suburbs of Paşabahçe and Beykoz, the former well known for the glassware that used to be produced here. Both are very built-up today, although large stretches of woodland still survive behind Beykoz. Some of the best views of this end of the Bosphorus can be had from the Hill of Joshua.

Paşabahçe

Once known as **İncirliköy** (Fig Village), **Paşabahçe**, "the Pasha's Garden", took its modern name from the gardens of **Hezarpare Ahmed Paşa** that existed here in the 17th century. Today it's best known for the large glass factory that was founded in 1934. Although the factory has been relocated, the Paşabahçe name lives on and modern Paşabahçe glassware is sold all over the world.

Paşabahçe products

There's a small **ayazma** (sacred spring) in the main square, while the Greek Orthodox **Church of Hagioi Constantinos and Helene** dating back to 1894 can be found in the back streets just a little way inland. Both are likely to be locked. The large and undistinguished modern **mosque** in the main square was built in 1971 and replaces a wooden one dating back to the reign of Sultan Mustafa III.

Hagioi Constantinos and Helene Greek Orthodox Church

Paşabahçe Bay

It was in Paşabahçe Bay that the British and French fleets assembled in 1854 before setting sail through the Black Sea to take part in the Crimean War.

Paşabahçe Yalıs

Twin Andonaki Yalıs

Originally the twin Andronaki yalıs were symmetrical, in the photo they didn't match! In 2011 the yalı on the left was finally completed.

A few wooden yalıs still survive in Paşabahçe.

Beykoz

Beykoz has a somewhat enigmatic name which means **"the Sultan's Walnut"** in Turkish. This seems to have been bestowed upon it by **Osman Gazi**, the first of the Ottoman leaders, in memory of one of his commanders, **Akçakoca Bey**, although conceivably it was derived from the Persian word "koz", meaning village. Before that it had been called Amycus after **King Amycus**, the ruler of a people called the Bebryces, who used to challenge all comers to boxing bouts which he would invariably win until he met his match in Polydeuces, one of the heroes traveling in the Argo with Jason in search of the Golden Fleece.

Beykoz Museum of Glass and Crystal

Chamberlain to the Egypt Khedive İsmail Pasha, Abraham Pasha was an incredibly rich state official who received the title of admiralship and raised to viziership by Sultan Abdulaziz. This Armenian admiral who was also a hunter and gambler owned the famous Cercle d'Orient in Pera (p. 302). He also had a more secluded place made for himself in Beykoz, inside today's Beykoz Grove including mansions, aviaries, pools, theater building and barns. The barn buildings in Abraham Pasha's farm were turned into the Museum of Glass and Crystal in 2021, after three years of restoration. The museum that gets its name from the Ottoman Beykoz Imperial Factory of Glass and Crystal displays 1500 pieces from the Seljuks to the late Ottoman era. Within the museum a library with 600 books, a periodical exhibition area, an educational workshop for children, a café with exquisite delicacies and a giftshop are also in service. The garden of the farm is also nicely tended. The garden that has 117 different tree species will make you feel like in a botanical museum.

www.millisaraylar.gov.tr
Tel: 0216 424 16 32

İshak Ağa Fountain

Beykoz's attractive main square is dominated by the İshak Ağa Fountain, a magnificent fountain with 10 water spouts (hence its alternative name, the On Çeşme (Ten Fountains) and a large water tank which is accessed via steps down into a dip. The original fountain dated back to the reign of **Sultan Süleyman the Magnificent**, but it was completely restored in 1746 by **İshak Ağa** who was customs superintendent during the reign of **Sultan Mahmud I**. Restored again in 2008, it now boasts glittering new paintwork but no taps on the spouts. In spite of this snag there's nothing else quite like it in Istanbul.

Near the fountain the 18th-century **Beykoz Mosque** is architecturally undistinguished but still retains a little time-keeper's lodge (see p. 547).

On (10) Fountain in Beykoz by Hoca Ali Rıza (1858-1930)

Field Marshal Fevzi Çakmak

Beykoz high street is named after Field Marshal Fevzi Çakmak (1876-1950) who was born locally and fought alongside Atatürk at the **Battle of Dumlupınar** in 1922.

Beykoz Wood

Originally called Abraham (Avram) Paşa Wood, this extensive stretch of forest on the hillside between Paşabahçe and Beykoz was laid out in the 19th century during the reign of **Sultan Abdülhamid II**. Today it's a popular recreation area with cafes and children's play areas. **Abraham Paşa** (1830-1918) was a fabulously wealthy Armenian civil servant, hunter and gambler, the owner of the famous **Cercle d'Orient** in Pera (see p. 302) and vast tracts of the northern Bosphorus. He built himself a house in the woods in which to hold lavish parties. Later debt forced him to sell it and retreat to his yalı in Büyükdere. In 1937 his house burnt down, but in 2007 it was reconstructed and opened to the public as a reasonably priced restaurant.

Kavalalı Mehmed Ali Paşa

Beykoz Mecidiye Kasrı (Mansion)

On a hilltop a little way west of Beykoz stands an imposing marble mansion designed by **Sarkis and Nigoğos Balyan** for **Kavalalı Mehmed Ali Paşa** who, as Governor of Egypt, led an uprising against the Ottomans. This was only suppressed with Russian assistance and the **Treaty of Hünkar İskelesi**, signed in Beykoz in 1833, resulted in the

Ottomans having to cede to the Russians the right to move their warships through the Bosphorus and Dardanelles. To try and make up for this Mehmed Ali began work on the mansion in 1855 during the reign of Sultan Abdülmecidl; his grandson **Said Halim Paşa** (see p. 454) saw it through to completion in 1866, by which time Sultan Abdülaziz was in charge of things. **Empress Eugenie** of France was one of its more illustrious guests.

After serving as an orphanage and hospital, the mansion was taken over by the Ministry of Culture in 1999. The large grounds contain a European-style **grotto** studded with seashells. It was taken over by the Turkish National Palaces in 1997. After restoration work was completed in 2016, the pavilion was reopened for visitors as a museum.

www.millisaraylar.gov.tr
closed Mondays

French Empress Eugenie

Dalyan fishing

Off the coast at Beykoz in spring and early summer you will be able to see an unusual method of fishing that has been in operation at least since the 17th century when it was described in his usual colorful style by Evliya Çelebi. Poles are set up in the water with nets attached beneath it. The fish are frightened into swimming towards the nets which are then pulled in around them. Although Çelebi says it was a method used to catch swordfish, today lüfer (bluefish) and other common fish are caught in the same way. Dalyan fishing is also carried on near Anadolu Kavağı and Poyrazköy (see p. 558).

Nightingale glass

Historically the area around Beykoz was strongly associated with glass-making and in particular with a technique called **"çeşm-i bülbül (the eye of the nightingale)"**, in which stripes of blue, white, green and red glass were created. The technique was apparently introduced from Venice in the 18th century by a dervish and craftsman called **Mehmed Dede**. It took its name from the fact that the first factory set up to produce it in 1843 was right beside the **Çeşm-i Bülbül** fountain, now lost.

Beykoz Yalıs

The Hamamcı Hafız and Niyazi Kaptan are among beautiful yalıs of Beykoz.

Some historic yalıs have stood the test of time.

Hill of Joshua

For a truly spectacular view of the northern end of the Bosphorus you should make your way up the Hill of Joshua (Yuşa Tepe), at 198m the second highest hill along the Bosphorus, after Çamlıca Hill (see p. 506). On the summit a small 18th-century mosque stands over what are thought to be the remains of the Church of St Panteleimon, dating back to the reign of the **Emperor Justinian.** There's also a beautiful 19th-century fountain. From here you can also gaze down on the **Selviburnu** and **Macarburnu headlands.**

Fountain on Hill of Joshua

In ancient times a mysterious 17-metre-long trench here was called the **Bed of Hercules,** although it is probably better known as the **Giant's Grave** mentioned in Lord Byron's **"Don Juan"**. Muslims believe it was the grave of **Yuşa,** a local holy man, sometimes thought to be synonymous with the **Prophet Joshua.**

Ahmed Mithad Efendi Yalı

The Istanbul-born writer and publisher Ahmed Mithad (1844-1912) spent some of the reign of Sultan Abdülaziz in exile on Rhodes because of his writing. When Sultan Abdülhamid II ascended to the throne he wrote in praise of him and was permitted to return. His yalı was built in 1887.

"While the sun was setting on the Hill of Joshua I looked at/ the 17-meter-long prophet and the weary plane trees, my friend"

The Hill of Joshua
by Haluk Levent, 2006

Gateway to the Black Sea

Anadolu Kavağı

086

As its very last stop the Bosphorus excursion boat from Eminönü calls in at Anadolu Kavağı on the Asian shore where the remains of a huge Byzantine-Genoese castle sit astride the hill offering views out towards the Black Sea. Anadolu Kavağı is still a real village separated from Beykoz by dense woodland. However, its main square is full of fish restaurants catering to the boat trippers.

Just as Rumeli Hisarı and Anadolu Hisarı gaze at each other across the Bosphorus, so do Rumeli Kavağı and Anadolu Kavağı, believed to have been the ancient Serapion and Hieron of the Greeks. According to legend, **Jason of the Argonauts** erected altars in both locations to give thanks when he returned from Colchis at the far end of the Black Sea with the fabled Golden Fleece (see p. 373). Later, **temples** were erected at both sites, the one on the Asian site being a shrine to the twelve Olympian gods and goddesses of Ancient Greece. Passing mariners would pause here to offer **sacrifices** to Zeus Ourious (of the Favorable Wind) before sailing into the Black Sea.

It's possible that the name Anadolu Kavağı refers to the poplar trees that once grew here, but, as with Rumeli Kavağı, it's more likely that the name commemorates its role as a "border" point where the Black Sea merged with the Bosphorus. Certainly both locations were fortified by the Byzantines who levied **customs dues** on passing mariners.

Anadolu Kavağı's life is firmly focused on the area immediately behind the ferry landing stage which is chock-a-block with fish restaurants ringing the elaborately-carved 18th-century **Cevriye Hatun Çeşmesi** (fountain), sadly reset into a far less impressive modern cistern.

"The wind swept down the Euxine and the wave broke foaming o'er the blue Symplegades."

Don Juan **by Lord Byron, 1863**

The Clashing Rocks

So important is the passage from the Bosphorus to the Black Sea that it was bound to attract a colorful mythology. In ancient times it was believed that the strait was guarded by two huge rocks, **the Symplegades** or Clashing Rocks, which would move towards each other and clash, making a noise like thunder, thereby preventing ships from passing. On his way to seek the Golden Fleece the famous mariner **Jason** stopped off to help the blind local king **Phineus** who was plagued by monsters who constantly attacked him and ate all his food. Jason and his fellow heroes (see p. 373) saw off these monsters and in return Phineus advised Jason how to trick his way through the Symplegades by sending a pigeon ahead of the ship; if it managed to pass through safely, so would the ship. Jason followed his instructions and the rocks only clipped the pigeon's tail. When the ship followed behind, urged on by the playing of Orpheus' famous lyre, it suffered only minor damage to its stern.

Midillili Ali Reis Mosque

Anadolu Kavağı's small mosque dates back to 1593, but it was thoroughly rebuilt in the 20th century and is of no great architectural significance. There are a few old tombstones in the grounds.

Yoros Castle

It's not clear exactly when the castle on the Asian side of the Bosphorus was built although it's assumed to date from the period when the Palaelogos Family ruled Constantinople; it's still possible to make out their motto on an inside wall above the entrance - a cross surrounded by four "b"s (for "basileus") which stand for "King of kings who kings it over kings". In 1352 the **Genoese** seized the castle and started to collect the customs dues for themselves. In 1452 **Mehmed the Conqueror** took over the castle, but he doesn't seem to have made use of it and it was allowed to tall into ruin.

The castle is usually referred to as Yoros Castle, a name thought to derive either from the Greek for "oros (mountain)" or "ourios (fair winds)". Today Rumeli Hisarı may look far more impressive but in its heyday Yoros Castle covered twice as much ground, making it the largest castle on the Bosphorus. In 2010 archeological excavations began at the castle.

Anadolu Feneri and Poyrazköy

The road north of Anadolu Kavağı leads to Anadolu Feneri (Anatolian Lighthouse) where the eponymous lighthouse sits inside the remains of the **Gözetleme (Watch) Castle** beside a small mosque; it dates back to 1769 but was modernized in 1856. Before Anadolu Feneri the small beach resort of Poyrazköy, in the shad of the 3rd Bridge, is named after the freezing "poyraz" wind which blows down the Bosphorus from the north-east. This is a place to come to sunbathe in high summer although there's also another 18th-century fortress, **Poyraz Castle**, to explore.

Marko Paşa Mansion (Marko Paşa Köşkü)

Inside the grounds of the naval base at Anadolu Kavağı stands the magnificent **Marko Paşa Köşkü (Mansion)**, once home to a famously wise Greek doctor **Marco Apostolidis** (1814-1888) who became the chief physician to Sultan **Abdülaziz** and then to the army and was also the founder of the **Red Crescent** in Turkey. If you catch the ferry to Sarıyer you will get a superb view of it, a white mansion topped lantern a gazebo, as you pull away from the harbor. Marko Paşa died on **Burgaz Island** where he liked to spend his summers. He is buried in **Kuzguncuk** (see p. 508) where his winter house has become a primary school. The Turkish expression **"Anlat derdini Marko Paşa**'ya (Tell your problem to Marko Paşa)" parodies the fact that he never actually listened to anyone's problems.

ISTANBUL ESCAPES

The Enchanted Forest

Belgrade Forest

087

The Belgrade Forest, which runs down from the slopes of the Istranca Mountains in Thrace almost to the coast, is to Istanbul what Epping Forest is to London or Central Park to New York – a large expanse of wooded open space within easy reach of the city center. Contained within the forest are several aqueducts and dams, survivors from a water distribution system that dates back to Roman times. The forest is especially impressive in the fall when the trees take on their autumnal hues.

The Forest takes its name from the **village of Belgrade** that used to stand in its center. This in turn was named after Belgrade (now the capital of Serbia), which was captured by **Sultan Süleyman the Magnificent** in 1521, after which he brought some of its inhabitants to live here and care for the water system that supplied the city. In the 18th century some of the **foreign embassies** constructed summer residences around the village and it was here that **Lady Mary Wortley Montagu** spent a few days with her diplomat husband in 1717, a visit immortalized in her book **"The Turkish Embassy Letters"**.

In the 19th century the summer residences were moved to the waterside at Tarabya and Büyükdere and slowly Belgrade village contracted. The last straw was a **fire** of 1826 deliberately planned by **Sultan Mahmud II** who had ordered his new model army to set the forest ablaze to rid it of renegade Janissaries; they had taken refuge there after he had had most of them killed and only managed to survive by preying on passers-by. In 1898 Belgrade's few remaining inhabitants were moved elsewhere; nothing remains to mark the village's existence bar the **foundations** of some of the buildings and the church.

Today the forest is full of beeches, oaks, poplars, pines, plane trees and chestnut trees. It's a popular place for picnics, especially over summer weekends, with the main formal picnicking facilities at **Neşetsuyu (Water)**, near Bahçeköy. However, it's also home to the historic aqueducts and dams that served the **Taksim** and **Kırkçeşme (Forty Fountains)** water distribution systems. Still in use today and so in an excellent state of repair, some of these structures date back to Roman times while others are works of the incomparable **Mimar Sinan** (see p. xxvi). I was at first confused as to how the systems actually worked. Then I stumbled upon the offices of the city water supplier, İSKİ and soon everything had become clear.

Neşet Water is named after the teacher Neşet Bey.

"...this place, which perfectly answers the description of the Elysian fields".

The Turkish Embassy Letters
by Lady Mary Wortley Montagu, 1717

Kırkçeşme water distribution system

He may be best known for his mosques but **Mimar Sinan** was also responsible for several forest aqueducts that were commissioned by **Sultan Süleyman the Magnificent** between 1554 and 1563. These served the more westerly side of the city, bringing water down to just outside **Eğrikapı** on the land walls (see p. 149) via a series of four dams and 33 aqueducts. The Kırkçeşme system is itself divided into two branches, one coming from the **Ayvad Dam (Ayvad Bend)** and the other from the **Big Dam (Büyük Bend)**. They join at the **Main Pool (Başhavuz)**, a circular stone reservoir said to be as deep as the Galata Tower is high.

The British artist W.H. Bartlett drew the Mağlova Aqueduct before it was partially drowned by a dam on the Alibey River. The photo shows it as it is today.

"Every rill, however trifling, is arrested in its progress when it descends from a height into the lower lands; by which means the valleys become inundated."

Julia Pardoe describes the water distribution system in The Beauties of the Bosphorus, 1839

The very finest surviving structure on the Kırkçeşme system is also unfortunately the least accessible today. The stunning two-storey **Mağlova Kemer (Aqueduct)** straddles the **Alibeysuyu (stream)** in the depths of the forest with no road leading to it. Its four central arches are believed to be the widest such arches on any aqueduct in the world; it is thought that the different size of the openings helped the structure stand up to floods and earthquakes over the centuries. Sometimes erroneously called **Justinian's Aqueduct**, the Mağlova would have been enough to cement **Sinan**'s reputation as a genius, even without the Süleymaniye Mosque. Also on the Alibeysuyu is the 165-meter long two-tier **Güzelce Kemer (Quite Charming Aqueduct)**, constructed by Sinan in 1563-64.

Quite Charming Aqueduct

If you drive directly from Bahçeköy to Kemerburgaz you will pass under the 102-meter-long **Pasha's Aqueduct (Paşa Kemer)**, commissioned in the 12th century by Emperor Andronicus I Comnenos but later repaired by Sinan. At the end of the road a turn to the right leads through the awe-inspiring, 711-meter-long, two-tier **Long Aqueduct (Uzunkemer)**, restored in 2009. If instead you turn left you will come to the 342-meter-long **Crooked Aqueduct (Eğrikemer)**, which seems to have started life in late **Roman** times but was rebuilt by **Sinan** in 1564; it takes its name from the fact that it has two branches, one three stories high and 216 meters long, the other running off at an angle and merely one storey high and 126 meters long.

Crooked Aqueduct

Also part of the Kırkçeşme system are four large dams – the **Dark Dam (Karanlık Bend, 1620), the Great Dam (Büyük Bend, 1724), the Cherry Dam (Kirazlı Bend, 1818)** and the **Ayvad Dam (Ayvad Bend, 1765)**, all of them lovely stone structures with Ottoman dedication tablets that remind us that carefully designed engineering projects can also be works of art in their own right; indeed, 18th-century drawings show people gathered on the tops of the dams to picnic, listen to music and smoke nargiles in these beauty spots.

Pasha's Aqueduct

Long Aqueduct

Taksim water distribution system

The second branch of the water system within the forest brought water down to the eastern side of the city and ended in the "taksim" at **Taksim Square** (see p. 283). It was constructed between 1731 and 1839 to serve the growing population of the European part of town.

Near the entrance to the forest at Bahçeköy, the most prominent surviving aqueduct from this system is the 490-meter-long **Mahmud I Aqueduct** commissioned by Sultan Mahmud I in 1732 and originally attached to a vast dam made of Proconnesian marble from Marmara Island; from its top it's theoretically possible to gaze out towards the opening of the Bosphorus into the Black Sea although you won't be allowed to climb up there today. Also surviving are a series of dams built across branches of the **Kağıthane stream**: the 88-meter-long **Topknot Dam (Topuzlu Bend, 1750), the Valide Dam (Valide Bend)**, commissioned by Sultan Selim III's mother Mihrişah Sultan in 1796 and the arc-shaped **Mahmud II Dam** (also known as the New Dam, 1839).

Atatürk Arboretum

This 296-hectare site on the road from Bahçeköy to Kemerburgaz is primarily a research establishment but is open to the public on weekdays. Some **2,000 species of plant** including 100 species of oak tree can be seen here and most are clearly labeled. It's a beautiful, peaceful place with well-maintained gardens and the lakes in the middle that deserves to be better known. Leaflets at the gate suggest routes round the arboretum and highlight plants to look out for.

Beach Club Bonanza

Kilyos

888

Beyond Sarıyer the road continues for 15 kilometers to Kilyos on the European side of the Black Sea which boasts several long stretches of sandy beach. In summer it's a popular escape from the city, with a number of exclusive beach clubs, but inevitably, the urban sprawl is creeping up – don't come here expecting a rural idyll especially over a summer weekend.

"A small reservoir is on the summit of each; and tubes...pour the water into this tank on one side and discharge it on the other. Each pillar is six inches lower...; and thus a gradual descent is produced along the tops of these (water pressure towers)... from the mountains to Stamboul."

Julia Pardoe describing how the water pressure towers work in *The Beauties of the Bosphorus*, 1839

Modern Kilyos is one of Istanbul's premier summer retreats, playing on its biggest assets, which are its sandy beaches; its official name is **Kumköy (Sandy Village)**. That it has a history that predates its popularity as a beach resort is clear from the remains of a 14th-century **Genoese castle** perched on the hilltop; it's not possible to go inside it although it apparently contains the remains of an ancient cistern. The remnants of three stone **water towers (su terazi)** are also reminders of the role it once played in the process of bringing water into the city from the Belgrade Forest (see p. 562). Also visible high up in the hills on the outskirts of town is a restored ancient Greek watchtower called **Ovid's Tower**, giving it a probably spurious connection with the great Roman poet who passed along the Bosphorus in AD 8 on his way to exile in Tomis (now Constanta) on the Black Sea. To see it close up you will need to drive through the modern settlement of Zekeriyaköy.

vid

Not much of Kilyos' past glory is apparent today when the coast has become so built-up. The hotels overlook a long strip of sand which qualifies for Blue Flag status. The Turban Tatil Köyü, currently out of action except for its beach, opened in 1955 as Turkey's **first holiday village**.

In high summer Kilyos is a popular escape from the city heat, especially with younger people who pour in for **beach raves**. Since this is the Black Sea the waters can be chilly even in August. There's also a dangerous **undertow**, so it's unwise to swim out of sight of lifeguards.

Ovid's Tower

Beach clubs

As you move away from the centre, you see better beach clubs, especially in Demirciköy near Kilyos. You pay more at the weekends than you pay on weekdays in these paid-clubs. The clubs offer many activities such as football, basketball and windsurfing. They are closed during offseason, but the restaurants in Demirciköy continue serving. The venues also host concerts and festivals.

Sea Daffodil Festival

The best way to raise awareness in society is through art, because art has no age or limits. The 9th Sea Daffodil Festival took place in 2018 as part of the environment and art events organized in September by Sarıyer Municipality to raise awareness of the endemic sea daffodils in Kilyos. The second of the Sarıyer Sculpture Composition also took place as part of the program. Since this is Turkey, the continuity of everything is doubtful. If you happen to come to Kilyos, you can find information about the festival from the website www.sariyer.bel.tr and join the event.

Turkey's Largest Lighthouse
Şile

889

A growing beach resort north of Istanbul on the Asian side, Şile boasts long sandy beaches, some offshore rock formations, a crumbling castle and Turkey's largest lighthouse. It's a popular escape from the city - come here mid-week to escape the crowds.

Şile's few tile-roofed wooden houses are in urgent need of protection if they are not to vanish altogether in favor of the usual concrete.

There seems to have been a settlement at Şile since c.700 BC. However, it didn't really come into its own until Ottoman times when a lighthouse was first built here. It remained a fairly sleepy small beach resort until the 1990s when it was discovered by the Turkish middle classes. Since then many people have bought second homes here. After the 1999 earthquake destroyed some of the competitor resorts around the Sea of Marmara, Şile grew even more rapidly. Today lovely old wooden houses crumble away forgotten in the back streets alongside the ever-growing number of concrete newcomers.

Şile has a string of **sandy beaches**, the best of them, especially the long and wild one at **Kumbaba**, not yet too built-up. Although it's possible to swim here, strong undercurrents can be dangerous; enter the sea only when lifeguards are on-duty. The **Ağlayankaya (Weeping Rock)** sometimes pointed out to visitors is a fairly unspectacular rock formation.

Sultan Abdülmecid

Şile Bezi

Şile is famous for a crinkled, sweat-absorbent, see-through fabric called Şile bezi (Şile cloth) that is popular for making shirts. Originally hand-woven, it is now usually machine-made but is popular with labels like Denizli's stylish Buldan. You can buy it in Istanbul shops, but it's more fun to browse the rails here, especially during the annual **Şile Festival** which takes place every year in the last week of July.

Şile Castle

The remains of a picturesque small castle dating back to Byzantine times but rebuilt under the Ottomans bestride a rock overlooking a colorful fishing harbor. This was originally the harbor of the ancient settlement of **Calpe** through which Xenophon's 10,000 Greek mercenaries passed on their way home from sorting out problems in Persia in 400 BC, as recounted in the **"Anabasis"**.

"(Şile) has a sleepy, indolent air that both pleases and frustrates..."

Life with a View by Toni Sepeda, 2007

The lighthouse

The largest lighthouse in Turkey and the second largest lighthouse still in operation in the world, Şile's stripy black and white "fener" dates back to 1859 when it was built at the command of Sultan Abdülmecid. The lighthouse was built 60 meters above sea level and stands at 19 meters high. Apart from looking nice, it was painted with black and white stripes in order for it to be seen easily during the day. In the past it worked with gas lamps but since the late 1960s it's been illuminated with electricity, sending its light as far as 35 miles. The interior of the lighthouse is open to visitors as a museum.

The Polish Village

Polonezköy and Riva

098

Istanbul keeps many surprises up its sleeve and one of them is certainly Polonezköy, the "Polish Village" tucked away in the countryside east of Beykoz on the Asian side of the city. A historical anomaly, Polonezköy was founded in the 19th century at a time when "Poland" had been partitioned between Russia, Prussia and Austria to provide a safe haven for ethnic Poles. Today it's a popular weekend retreat with a string of hotels, pensions and restaurants in leafy gardens. Nearby Riva offers lots of sand and fish restaurants by a river.

The Church of the Virgin Mary

Technically still in Istanbul although at the point where it fades out into the countryside, Polonezköy was established in 1842 on land leased from Istanbul's Lazarist community (see p. 428) as a place where Polish soldiers fleeing compulsory military service in the Russian army could start a new life. It was originally called **Adampol** ("the Town of Adam" in Polish) in honor of Prince **Adam Czartoryski**, the man who negotiated the right for his fellow citizens to establish an agricultural colony here. At first there were only 12 colonists who built wood-and-stone houses here whose design reflected that of their homes in the Carpathians, but following a failed uprising in Hungary in 1848 and then another in Poland in 1863 many more settlers started to arrive. In 1853 Poles from the village fought for the Ottoman Empire during the **Crimean War** after which **Sultan Abdülmecid** granted them the land in perpetuity.

In 1918 Poland regained its independence and some villagers considered returning there. Few actually did so, however and when **Atatürk** visited in 1934 he found a flourishing settlement, still earning most of its living from farming as well as from the sale of firewood and articles made from the skin of wild boars. The house where he stayed is still pointed out to visitors today.

Even in the 19th century **Franz Liszt**, **Gustave Flaubert** and **Pierre Loti** had included Polonezköy in their itineraries but a century later Polonezköy's otherness meant that it was starting to attract more tourists for whom the villagers started to build purpose-designed guesthouses.

Today tourism is the lifeblood of the village which has attracted visits from such eminent modern Poles as **Lech Walesa** in 1994 and President **Aleksander Kwesniewski** in 1996 and 2000.

For more information on the village go to www.polonezkoy.com

Polonezköy Today

It goes without saying that all the original settlers spoke Polish and learnt Turkish only as a second language. Nowadays, however, most locals speak Turkish and only a few can speak fluent Polish. At first no local could sell their property to an outsider. Now they can sell to whomsoever they please which inevitably means that the Polish nature of the settlement has been diluted by incomers. Unfortunately many of the newer hotels and pensions are also concrete buildings that completely ignore the village's unique architectural heritage.

The church

There are few specific sights in Polonezköy, although the **Church of St Mary** is worth a quick look. Built in 1912, it was requisitioned as a military headquarters during the First World War, before being restored and returned to use as a church in 1918. The garden contains a memorial to the poet **Adam Mickiewicz** who died and was buried here in 1869. There's a museum in his memory in **Tarlabaşı** (see p. 292).

Zofia Rizi's House (Zofia Rizi Anı Evi)

An unmodernized late 19th-century house set in a wild garden and decorated with displays of old photographs and other mementoes of a lost lifestyle, Zofia Rizi's house stands as symbol of Turkish-Polish friendship and is normally open to the public on Sundays and public holidays.

Hiking

Polonezköy is an attractive centre for nature enthusiasts. The almost 5 km-long hiking trail in the forest offers its visitors a distinct pleasure every season. There are also challenging trails hidden in the forest for those who want to ride a bike.

Wood Carving Sculpture Exhibition

These wooden sculptures, located right in front of the Polonezköy House of Culture, will catch your eye as soon as you enter the village. Sit on benches in the greenery and listen to the stories of these monuments, which have now become the symbols of the village.

Riva

Just 20 minutes' drive from the 2nd Bridge on a good day, Riva seems to have it all: the remains of a Genoese castle, a big swathe of sandy beach and a river lined with fish restaurants. It makes a surprisingly pleasant escape from the city without having to travel too far.

The village signs on the way promises to present you hidden paradises. While Ali Bahadır Köyü (Village) attract attention with its natural products, the glass furnace in Öyümce Köyü provides a delightful environment for visitors of all ages with its amazing nature and the activities carried out in the biggest and best-equipped glass arts center in Turkey.

@theglassfurnace
www.camocagi.org
Tel: 0216 433 36 93

Tour boats for hire on the niver.

Riva Castle

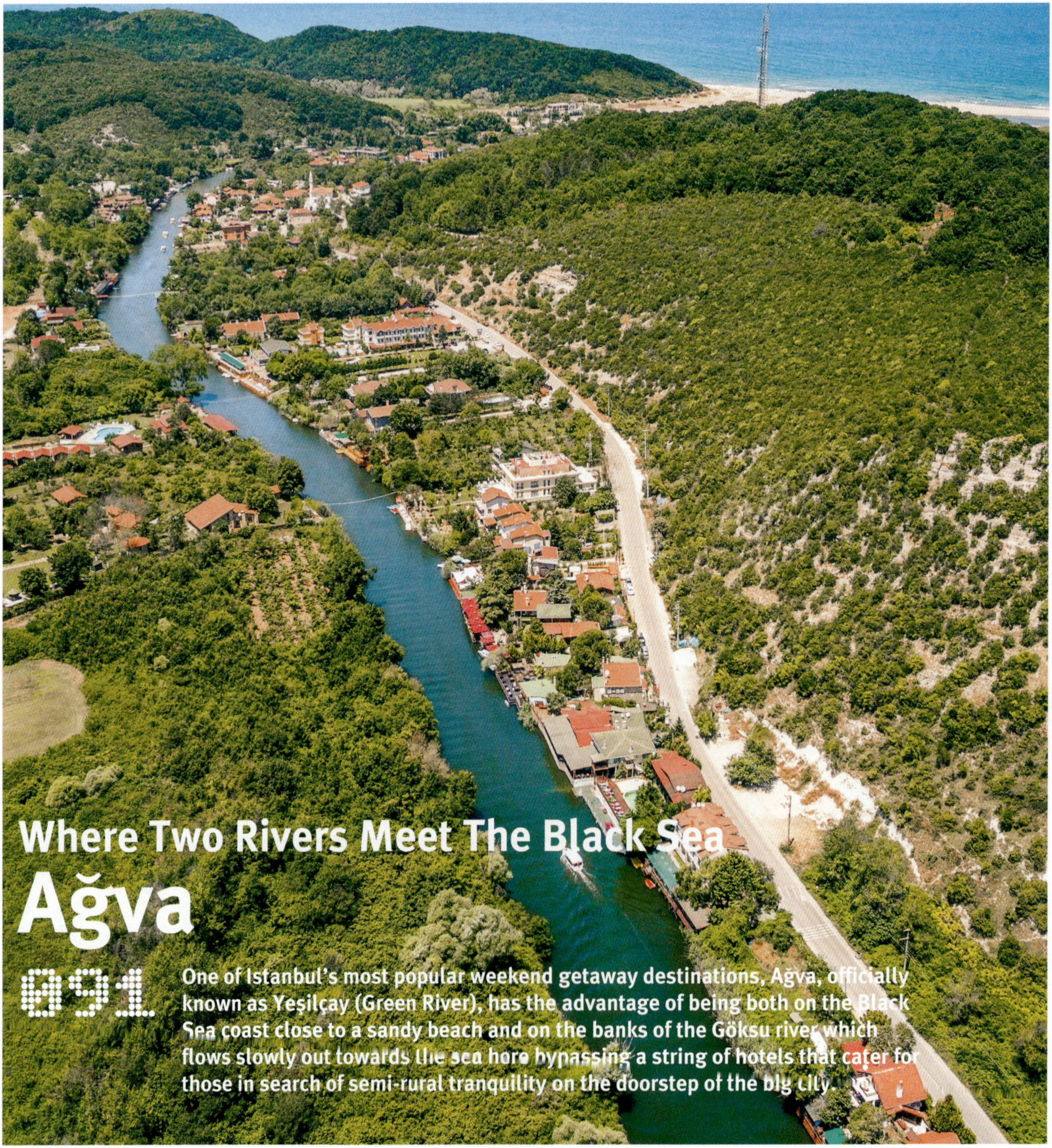

Where Two Rivers Meet The Black Sea

Ağva

091

One of Istanbul's most popular weekend getaway destinations, Ağva, officially known as Yeşilçay (Green River), has the advantage of being both on the Black Sea coast close to a sandy beach and on the banks of the Göksu river which flows slowly out towards the sea here bypassing a string of hotels that cater for those in search of semi-rural tranquility on the doorstep of the big city.

What is there to do in Ağva? Well, not a lot actually which is precisely why people come here in their hundreds to relax and unwind in the growing number of hotels which line the river banks, the best of them offering spacious gardens and comfortable lounges, if rather small bed and bathrooms. The **Göksu** makes the perfect backdrop for all this inactivity; to reach some of the hotels you actually have to cross it on primitive **cable cars** or pulley-assisted **rafts** which all adds to the sense of adventure.

Most hotels offer canoes and pedaloes for guests to explore the river, as well as organized **boat trips** up and down stream. Ağva has a small **beach** with the Yeşilçay and Göksu rivers running down to it but it's nothing much to write home about. More energetic guests can hike to assorted local waterfalls and caves in which Christians once took refuge from the Romans. The whole area is surrounded by lovely deciduous **woodland** and is especially beautiful in autumn.

Accommodation is usually offered on a bed, breakfast and dinner basis and there are few stand-alone restaurants here. Most hotels also offer long weekend packages from Thursday through to Sunday night.

Aqua

The name **"Ağva"** is said to be a corruption of the Latin **"Aqua"**, meaning simply **water**. It was renamed **Yeşilçay** as part of a general policy of Turkifying place names in the mid-20th century.

Akçakese

Just three kilometers off the road from Şile to Ağva is Akçakese, a cluster of Olympos-style treehouses right on the waterfront with a few luxury Jacuzzi-equipped models thrown in. Development near the site is offputting, but once you're there it vanishes thankfully from view.

Kilimli Koyu

With a car you might like to drive the five kilometers from Ağva to Kilimli Koyu where there are some unexpectedly wonderful off-shore rock formations reminiscent of Dorset or Cornwall in the UK. Best of all is the circular cove where locals point out the Gelinkaya, a rock said to be a woman whose parents refused her permission to marry the man of her dreams and who reacted by praying to be turned to stone for all eternity.

Tip: Avoid visiting Ağva over summer weekends when the best places fill up quickly and prices rise accordingly.

Island of Exile

Kınalıada

092

Originally called Proti ("First" in Greek), tiny, arid Kınalıada is the first island visited by the ferries from Istanbul. Its Turkish name means "hennaed island", a reference to the orangey-red sandstone cliffs on its eastern side. Although the radio masts on top of Teşrifiye Hill have robbed the island of much of its natural beauty it's still worth a brief stop, especially in high summer when the Armenian community descends en masse.

The basilican Church of Genissa Panagia Theotokou (the Birth of the All Holy Mother of God), founded in 1886, contains several silver-framed icons.

The only Armenian church in the islands, the whitewashed Church of Krikor Lusavoriç (St Gregory the Illuminator) was completely rebuilt in 1988. There's an overgrown Armenian cemetery behind it.

With an area of less than 1.5 square kilometers / 0.93 miles, Kınalıada could hardly be more compact and its proximity to the mainland means that it is the most built-up of the Princes' Islands. It is dominated by three hills: **Plane Tree Hill** (Çınar Tepesi, 115m / 377ft), **Visiting Hill** (Teşrifiye Tepesi, 110m / 360ft) and **Monastery Hill** (Manastır Tepesi, 93m / 305ft). There are no phaetons (or cars) on the island so you must explore it on foot or by bike.

The island is a taster for the main course of the larger islands, with many of the same attractions. As soon as you step ashore you will appreciate the peace and quiet brought about by the absence of cars and if you visit out of season you may find the population of cats far outstripping that of human beings. Down on the promenade that backs the thin strip of shingle beach seagulls and hooded crows crack open the shells of purple mussels by dropping them on the pavement. Houses and apartments line up on the hillside terraces; the Taş Köşkü in Fazıl Ahmet Aykaç Sokak is one of the finest restored wooden mansions.

Monastery of Christ

At one time there were three monasteries on the island, but the only one to survive today is the Monastery of Christ (Hristos) where the **Emperor Leo V** was buried after he was killed in a clash between the iconoclasts and iconodules (see p. 583) in the Church of Hagia Eirene on the mainland in 820. It's also where poor **Romanos Diogenes IV** ended his life. Since then the monastery buildings have been put to many uses, housing an **orphanage** at the start of the 20th century, the **military** during the First World War and **White Russian refugees** after the Bolshevik Revolution of 1917.

Imperial Exiles

Over the centuries, the island's proximity to the mainland made it the perfect dumping ground for those with whom the Byzantine emperors had fallen out. Of the many people exiled here the most famous was probably **Romanos Diogones IV**, who had been defeated by the Selçuk leader Alparslan at the battle of **Malazgirt** (Manzikert) in eastern Turkey in 1071 and who had his eyes put out to worsen his punishment, a gruesome practice that already had a long pedigree.

In the 9th century **Nicephoros I** exiled the rebellious Armenian general Bardanes to Proti. Shortly afterwards Leo V sent the deposed emperor **Michael I Rhangabe** there together with his wife and children. The wife and daughters became nuns, the ex-emperor and his sons monks, although not before the boys had been castrated to ensure they could not father a rival dynasty. Of the two boys, Niketas changed his name to Ignatius and eventually returned to Istanbul to serve as patriarch and achieve canonization. Having murdered Leo V, **Michael II** promptly despatched his widow and her four children to Proti too.

In the 10th century **Romanos I Lecapenus** was deposed by his two sons, Stephen and Constantine, who exiled their father to Proti, only to find themselves overthrown in their turn and sent to follow him. Later in the 10th century Proti became the place of banishment for **Theophano**, the wife of **Nicephoros II Phocas**. Theophano is believed to have conspired with her lover **John Tzimisces** to have him murdered, only to have Tzimisces round on her in turn and despatch her to Proti.

Kınalıada Mosque

At a time when so many newly built mosques lack any architectural originality, the small waterside mosque on Kınalıada, designed by **Turhan Uyaroğlu** and **Başar Acarlı** in 1964, was designed to evoke the shape of a **yacht** and is strikingly original in its use of materials, although much in need of a good scrub.

Watchtower Island

Burgazada

093

Previously called Antigoni and Panormos ("Safe Harbor" in Greek), Burgazada is the third largest of the Princes' Islands and the second stop on the ferry ride. Its original population of Greek fishermen was replaced in the 1950s with one of well-heeled Jews. They, in turn, have been replaced with Turkish second-home owners. The island's beauty has been somewhat diminished since 2003 when a fire wiped out most of its pine forest covering, but it's still a pleasant place to while away a few sunny afternoon hours.

Yassıada and Sivriada from Burgazada

"When my soul felt stifled, I used to set out with my pocket knife in my pocket to whittle away at small sticks while strolling the island's uncrowded streets. I sharpened my new pencil. Then I kissed what I had made. If I couldn't write I would have gone crazy."

Sait Faik Abasıyanık

With an area of only 1.5 square kilometers/5 square miles, Burgaz is small enough to manage without transport; the phaetons that serve as taxis are only really necessary if you want to get to the more remote restaurants. Its modern name is a corruption of the Greek word **"pyrgos"** meaning a tower and recalls the **watchtower** that used to stand on top of the solitary hill, **Bayraktepe** (Flag Hill, 170m/558ft), which was described by the 17th-century travel writer **Evliya Çelebi** and sketched in 1794 by the Italian traveller **Cosimo Comidas**. Just to confuse matters, the hill is also known as Hristos Tepesi (Hill of Christ).

Burgaz's loveliest houses are along **Gezinti**, **Gönüllü** and **Mehtap streets**. As you walk around keep an eye out for a hollowed-out **600-year-old plane tree** in the back streets. The small island visible immediately off-shore is **Kaşıkadası** (Spoon Island, see p. 595).

Coast of Burgazada

Sait Faik Museum

The lovely wooden **Spanudis Mansion** was home to the writer **Sait Faik Abasıyanık** *(1906-54)*, sometimes nicknamed "Adalı (the Island Dweller)", for 20 years. Faik was famous for his short stories, many of them set on the island and usually focusing on ordinary people such as fishermen. Museum is restored in 2013 and it is free as Sait Faik willed to. A tiny **bust** of Sait Faik can be seen near the ferry terminal.

Tel: 0216 381 20 60
closed Sundays, Mondays and Tuesdays

Sait Faik Museum

Ioannes Prodromos Church

Churches

Dominating the skyline as you approach Burgazada is the imposing but not particularly beautiful **Church of Ioannes Prodromos (John the Baptist)**, which dates back in its present incarnation only to 1899. It stands on the site of a much older church built by **St Methodius the Confessor** who had been banished by the Emperor Michael II ("the Stammerer") in 822 as punishment for his opposition to Iconoclasm (see below). Poor Methodius was really made to suffer. Whipped 700 times, he was then dropped into a pit with two murderers, one of whom soon died, his body being left in the pit to worsen the misery of the other prisoners. Fortunately when the emperor died in 829, his son **Theophilos** allowed Methodius to return to the mainland where he became patriarch and convened a church council that agreed to restore the icons. Later Theophilos' empress Theodora built a church over the site of his imprisonment which still exists as a cellar beneath the narthex of the modern building. As for Methodius, when he died in 846 he was buried in the Church of the Holy Apostles which used to stand where the Fatih Mosque does today (see p. 115). Damaged in the 1999 earthquake, the church has since been completely restored and every year on 29 August Greeks assemble here to celebrate the feast day of St John.

In 1938 the denizens of the Austrian School in Galata founded the Roman Catholic **Church of St George** so that they would still be able to go to church during their summer holidays.

Remains of church from Byzantine times

There's a Greek cemetery on top of the hill.

Monasteries

Burgaz has two monasteries where 19th-century buildings mask much longer histories. The Greek Orthodox **Monastery of Hagios Georgios Garipi** probably dates back to Byzantine times even though the first reference to it is in the late 17th century. It was associated with the monastery of **Megalo Spelaoi at Kalavryta** in Greece and it was a monk from there who was responsible for the current dormitory which was added in 1859. It's unclear why it is called **"Garipi"**. Some commentators suggest that this is derived from an Arabic word meaning **"poor"**, others that it refers to the **well** in the grounds. The monastery was used as a place of refuge for **White Russians** in the aftermath of the Bolshevik Revolution in 1917. Although mimicking a Byzantine building, the church only dates back to 1897. Just inside the entrance there are frescoes of St George and the Annunciation, while the body of the church contains a glitteringly beautiful **iconostasis**. The building was badly damaged in the 1999 earthquake but was restored in 2005.

The **Monastery of the Transfiguration** was probably founded somewhere between the 9th and 11th centuries on the site of an ancient **Greek temple** atop the Hill of Christ. Today a 19th-century church on the site is surrounded by pieces of Byzantine masonry, including many finely carved capitals, that testify to its origins. People still visit the church to celebrate the **Feast of the Transfiguration** on 6 August.

Iconoclasts Versus Iconodules

In the 8th and 9th centuries the Byzantine Empire was wracked by controversy over whether it was or wasn't acceptable to display icons (religious images of saints) in churches. The first period of Iconoclasm (image-smashing) lasted from 730 to 787 and was brought to an end when the Second General Council of Nicaea ruled in favor of the icons. The dispute broke out again in 814 and raged until 842 when the death of an Iconoclast emperor, Theophilos and his replacement by an Iconodule (icon-loving) regent, Theodora, finally brought it to an end.

İnönü's Island Retreat

Heybeliada

094

Called Halki in the past, Heybeliada (Saddlebag Island) is the second largest of the Princes' Islands with a resident population of about 5,500 that swells enormously in summer. It shares many of the attractions of Büyükada; pine-covered hillsides, lovely old wooden houses and streets blissfully devoid of cars. Here, too, you can avail yourself of a phaeton ride around the island although since it is less than 2.5 kilometers in area, walking and cycling make good alternatives. Come here to visit the monasteries and to soak up the peace and quiet.

"The size and pace of Heybeliada are just right for strolling. This is not a place for hurry or stress. Only an arriving ferry or sea bus causes islanders to quicken their pace."

***An Island in Istanbul: At Home on Heybeliada* by M A Whitten, 2006**

The Ancient Greek philosopher **Aristotle** records that **copper** used to be mined on Halki, hence the name which means copper in Greek. The copper mines have long since closed down, despite a brief attempt to revive them in the 19th century and instead the island is now rather fancifully named after the Turkish word "**heybe**", meaning **saddlebag**, supposedly because the dip between the pine-covered hills resembles such a bag. None of these hills is as high as those on Büyükada although there are more of them: **Hope Hill** (Ümit Tepesi, 85m/278ft), **Windmill Hill** (Değirmen Tepesi, 136m/446ft), **Village Hill** (Köy Tepesi, 128m/420ft) and **Son of the Woodcutter Hill** (Baltacıoğlu Tepesi, 98m/322ft).

In the 16th century, the island provided shelter for rich Christians who wanted to escape an outbreak of plague in Istanbul. Later, it suffered considerably from a fire and a series of earthquakes in the early 20th century. In 1924, a **sanatorium** at Yeşil Burnu helped revive the island's fortunes. **İsmet İnönü**, the first prime minister and later second president of the Turkish Republic, spent some time there and always maintained his ties with the island, which helped increase its popularity. The sanatorium closed in 2006.

İsmet İnönü

The island was long famous for a seminary which trained Greek Orthodox priests. This was closed in 1971 and the struggle to have it reopened is a running sore between Greece and Turkey.

Ahmet Rasim

Hüseyin Rahmi Gürpınar

The shoreline near the landing stage is dominated by a naval base which is off-limits to visitors but there is also a broad **promenade** lined with seats commemorating Turkey's many writers. Both **Hüseyin Rahmi Gürpınar** (1864-1944), a celebrated writer and politician and **Ahmed Rasim** (1865-1932), a journalist, writer and historian, lived on the island.

İsmet İnönü Museum

One of Heybeli's most regular summer visitors was İsmet İnönü (1884-1973), the second president of the Republic. His family stayed in the **Mavromatakis Köşkü** in Refah Şehitler Caddesi which is sporadically open to the public as a museum.

www.ismetinonu.org.tr, Tel: 0216 351 84 49
closed Mondays

İsmet İnönü Museum

The son of darkness

Cyril Lucaris

What on earth would cause a pope to brand someone "the son of darkness and the athlete of hell"? Cyril Lucaris (1572-1638) was an extraordinary man who became patriarch of Constantinople six times and patriarch of Alexandria in Egypt once. Regardless of this he was a troubled soul who dabbled with the Protestantism practised at the Dutch Chapel in Pera until eventually he came up with a Declaration of Faith that was effectively Calvinist. Furious Greek Orthodox believers denounced him to the sultan as a spy and he was executed and his body thrown into the Bosphorus, only to be dredged up again and buried on Halki.

Places of worship

Hagios Nikolaos Church

In the main village the brightly colored **Church of Hagios Nikolaos (St Nicholas)** was built in 1857 on the site of a much older Byzantine church. Damaged by an earthquake in 1894, it has since been completely restored and its tower contains a bell brought from Tsarist Russia. In the grounds there's a **sacred spring** dedicated to Hagia Paraskeve. In summer Armenians and Syrian Orthodox Christians also use this church. A mosque and synagogue can be found nearby, reflecting the mixed population that used to inhabit the island.

The **Monastery of Hagios Georgios tou Kremnou (St George on the Cliff)** was probably founded in 1583-84 and became a refuge for Istanbul Greeks during times of plague. It has a link with Jerusalem, whose patriarch **Nikodemos I** was buried here in 1910.

The **Monastery of Hagios Spyridon** at Pine Harbor (Çam Limanı) dates back to 1868, when it started life as a tiny chapel. Rebuilt after an earthquake in 1894, it has gone through several more refits but is now in ruins.

Monastery of Hagia Triada (Halki Seminary)

Patriarch Photius I

Halki's early monastic history is some-what obscure, but it seems likely that the Monastery of Hagia Triada (the Holy Trinity) was originally built on Ümit Tepesi some time before the 9th century when **Theodore,** the abbot of the monastery of St John of Studius on the mainland, was banished there by **Emperor Leo V** because of his opposition to iconoclasm (see p. 583). However, in 820 when the emperor was assassinated and his wife and daughters were also exiled to Halki, Theodore was moved to another monastery which suggests there were at least two separate monasteries already in existence.

Holy Trinity was restored by the **Patriarch Photius I** who had himself been exiled there twice and when he died in 890 he was buried there. Later he was canonized, becoming the patron saint of the school that grew up on the site.

Entrance to Halki Seminary

In 1453 the monastery was destroyed. It was not rebuilt until 1550 when

Metrophanes III, who went on to become patriarch, not only oversaw the work but endowed the **library** with more than 300 books, some of them since moved to the Patriarchal Library in Fener or lost to overseas libraries.

After a period in the financial doldrums, Holy Trinity received a much-needed endowment from Tsar Peter the Great of Russia (1672-1725), who saw his country as the successor to Byzantium as **"the Third Rome"**. It was rebuilt in 1773, but badly damaged in 1821 at the start of the Greek War of Independence. In 1844 the Halki Seminary was founded here, only to be destroyed by an earthquake in 1894. The complex was rebuilt by the architect **Pericles Photiades** in 1896 and functioned as a school and a seminary preparing young men for the priesthood. It was renowned for its extensive library and attracted students from all around the Orthodox world. In 1971 the seminary was forcibly closed. Talks between Turkey and Greece aimed at reopening it are ongoing.

Naval High School (Deniz Lisesi)

This school originally started life on the island in 1773 but soon moved to **Kasımpaşa,** returning to Heybeli in the mid 19th century. With the birth of the Turkish Republic it was renamed the Naval War Academy but this was moved to Tuzla in 1985 since when the property has served as a naval high school. It's one of those places that everyone who is anyone has visited: **Riza Pahlavi,** the last but one shah of Iran, **Marshall Tito** of Yugoslavia and Prime Minister **Zülfikar Ali Bhutto** of Pakistan amongst others.

One of the gems of Heybeli is unfortunately virtually impossible for casual visitors to see since it lies on land that now belongs to the naval base. **The Church of the Panagia Kamariotissa (Our Lady of the Arches)** used to be part of a monastery of the same name that is now lost but contained the last Byzantine church to be built before the Ottoman conquest of Constantinople in 1453. It housed some religious items which were removed to the Halki Seminary. The church became the last resting place for six of Istanbul's patriarchs including **Cyril Lucaris** who held the post on six separate occasions until he was executed by **Sultan Murad IV** in 1638. In 1828 many Russian prisoners-of-war were housed here during the Russo-Turkish War; around 300 of them died and there's a **memorial** to them on Aşıklar Yolu (Lovers Lane). During the Greco-Turkish population exchange of 1923 many displaced Greek children from Anatolia wound up in an **orphanage** housed in what had been a school attached to the monastery. Also in the grounds of the base is a large **cemetery** that contains the remains of **Edward Barton,** the second ambassador of **Queen Elizabeth I** of England to the Ottoman court, who died in 1597 (the gravestone has been removed to the English Cemetery near the Selimiye Barracks (see p. 494). The Naval Base is closed since July 15, 2016.

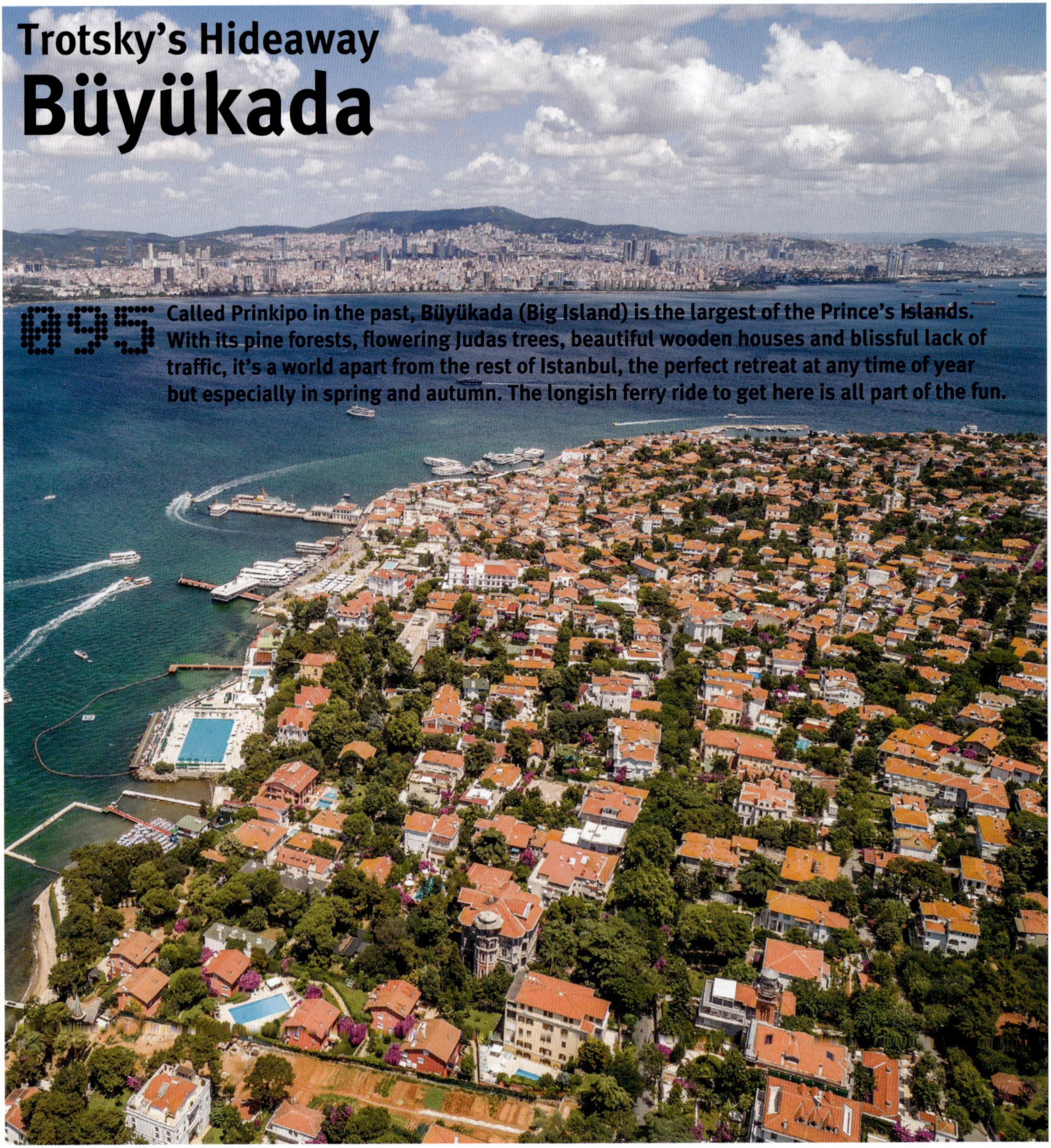

Trotsky's Hideaway
Büyükada

095 Called Prinkipo in the past, Büyükada (Big Island) is the largest of the Prince's Islands. With its pine forests, flowering Judas trees, beautiful wooden houses and blissful lack of traffic, it's a world apart from the rest of Istanbul, the perfect retreat at any time of year but especially in spring and autumn. The longish ferry ride to get here is all part of the fun.

Beautiful Büyükada may be the furthest of the Princes' Islands from the mainland but it's also the jewel in their crown. It consists of two hills – the **Hill of Christ** (İsa Tepesi; 164m / 538ft) and the **Great Hill** (Yücetepe; 202m / 663ft) – with a valley in between them and thin stretches of beach around the perimeter. The entire island is only 4.3 kilometers / 2.6 miles long by 1.3 kilometers / 0.80 miles wide which means that getting around it on foot or by bicycle is an easy matter.

Büyükada has a history stretching right back to the 6th century when the **Emperor Justin II** (r. 565-78) had a **convent** built here, probably in the area that is now called Maden (Mine). This convent was expanded in the late 8th century by the **Empress Eirene** (c. 752-803), a colorful character who took responsibility for the blinding of her own son (see opposite) and very soon there began a tradition of banishing those who proved awkward or inconvenient to this and other monasteries on the islands. The last self-imposed imperial exile was another **Eirene**, the wife of **Emperor Alexios I Komnenos** who retired to Prinkipo on his death in 1118.

The island is thought to have been one of the last places to surrender to the Ottomans in the 15th century. It wasn't until 1846 that a ferry service brought Büyükada within easy reach of the rest of Istanbul after which it slowly acquired a population of pleasure-lovers who found it the perfect place to escape from the oppressive heat of high summer. In 1909 the "**Young Turks**" toppled **Sultan Abdülhamid II** in a coup and many of his associates were exiled to the island. In 1929 they were joined here by the Russian revolutionary **Leon Trotsky** (see opposite). Since then the only exiles have been of the voluntary kind – city-dwellers in search of a less stressful life.

With its palms, pines and plane trees, Büyükada is exquisitely beautiful, but for all that it's not immune to the familiar problems of litter and shoddy building work. Even today one half-built structure still mars the scenery on the waterfront, visible to everyone as the ferry pulls in.

The Evil Empress

Empress Eirene

Born in Athens to a noble family, the **Empress Eirene** became the wife of **Leo IV** (r. 775-80). On his death their son **Constantine VI** ascended to the throne despite the fact that he was only 10 years old. As his regent, Eirene was responsible for restoring the icons to the churches after the Iconoclastic period had seen them removed (see p. 583). When he was twenty Constantine seized power from his mother and confined her to her palace, only to set her up again as co-ruler a mere two years later. In 797 Eirene had Constantine blinded and banished to the convent on Büyükada where he died two days later. She then became the first woman to rule Byzantium on her own and managed to hold onto power for five years. In 802 she was deposed and exiled first to **Büyükada** and then to the Greek island of **Lesbos** where she died. Eventually her remains were returned to Büyükada and buried alongside those of her son.

Revolutionary in exile - Trotsky and Büyükada

In 1929 Leon Trotsky was exiled from Russia and arrived on Büyükada where he worked on his **"History of the Russian Revolution"** while living in the **İliasko (İzzet Paşa) Köşkü** on Çankaya Caddesi, ironically built originally for a Greek banker, Konstantinos İliasko and then lived in by the chief of Sultan Abdülhamid's secret police. Trotsky stayed on the island until 1933, constantly on the alert for potential assassins. He was eventually stabbed to death with an ice-pick in Mexico City.

The house where Trotsky lived from 1929 to 1933

"An island of peace and forgetfulness."

Farewell to Prinkipo **by Leon Trotsky, 1933.**

Harbor (İskele) Building

Ferries to Büyükada arrive at a two-storey landing stage that was designed in First National Architecture style in 1899 by the architect **Mihran Azaryan** although it was not actually built until 1915. It's decorated with tiles by the great master of the Kütahya art, **Hacı Hafız Mehmed Emin Efendi** who was also responsible for the tiles on the landing stage at **Haydarpaşa Station** (see p. 493). Internally it has a fine octagonal booking hall. Over the years it has served a variety of functions including housing the island's **first cinema.** The top floor now functions as a **café** with a pleasant outdoor terrace.

Other places of worship

At one time Büyükada had a large Greek population and there are still two Greek Orthodox churches in the main settlement. The **Church of the Panagia (Virgin Mary)** started life in 1735 in another part of the island and moved to its current location in 1793; it was completely renovated in the late 19th century. Today its most impressive possession is a fine pulpit. The second church, designed by the Greek architect **Fistikos Kalfa** in 1856-60, is dedicated to **Hagios Demetrios** who is the island's patron saint and serves as the seat of the bishopric for all the islands. A third building, the Franciscan **Church of San Pacifico,** dates back to 1866 and contains a painting by the Italian artist **Giovanni Battista** which shows San Pacifico, Ignatius and Sophia flying over the Princes' Islands. Of similar date is the austere Armenian Catholic **Church of Surp Astvadzadzin Verapolium.**

Büyükada's finest mosque is the **Hamidiye,** built during the reign of **Sultan Abdülhamid II** in 1892-3. The island also has a **synagogue** dating back to 1903.

Muslims visiting Hagios Georgios Church

Armenian Catholic Church of Surp Astvadzadzin Verapolium

The monasteries

Although much of the pleasure of a trip to Büyükada lies in simply taking it easy, there are a few specific attractions that are worth seeking out, including the monasteries that sit atop the two hills. On Yücetepe stands the **Monastery of Hagios Georgios Koudonas (St George of the Bells),** which was probably founded in 963 during the reign of the Emperor **Nicephoros II Phokas** (r. 963-9), although the first mention of it is in the mid-12th century. A pretty story dating back to 1625 tells how a shepherd boy heard **the sound of bells** coming from underground and dug down to uncover an ancient **icon of St George** apparently buried there by priests in 1204 when they saw the Crusaders approaching, hence the name of the monastery (their actions were probably just as well since the monastery was completely destroyed). The original icon is preserved at the Patriarchate in Fener (see p. 232) but a copy is on display here too.

The present monastery consists of half a dozen **churches and chapels** ranging in date from 1752 to 1909 and spread over three levels, with one still containing the metal **chains** to which mentally disturbed individuals used to be tied in the hope of a miraculous cure. Several miracles were, in fact, attributed to the icon of St George and there is an annual **pilgrimage** to the church on **St George's Day (23 April).** Primarily a Greek Christian event, it is nonetheless observed by non-Christians too. Pilgrims, some of them barefoot, walk up the steep stone path, pausing to tie pieces of paper and plastic to the trees beside it and unwind reels of cotton in defiance of notices instructing them not to do so.

On İsa Tepesi the **Monastery of Sotiros Christou (Christ the Savior)** dates back to the Byzantine era although the earliest confirmed reference to it only crops up in 1158. The Greek Patriarchate had it restored at the end of the 16th century but it was only kept going through the Ottoman era with the help of funding from Greek merchants and a Phanariote nobleman. During the 19th century several patriarchs lived in the monastery which was restored again in 1869. Today all that remains of the original buildings is the **katholikon** (the church with the iconostasis), a two-storey south wing and some of the outbuildings.

A third monastery dedicated to **Hagios Nikolaos (St Nicholas)** stands on the east side of the island near the coast. The earliest reference to it only dates back to the 17th century and in any case that building was completely burnt down in 1852. The current structure dates from 1860, the narthex from 1873.

Greek Orphanage

On the slopes of **İsa Tepesi** stand the six-floor ruins of what is believed to be Europe's largest - and the world's second largest wooden building (after the Todaiji Temple in Nara, Japan) - covering 23,255 square meters. It was originally erected in 1898 by a French company who intended it to serve as a **hotel-cum-casino** and was designed by **Alexandre Vallaury.** When Sultan Abdülhamid II refused permission for this, it was bought in 1902 by the widow of a wealthy Greek banker who gave it to the Patriarchate on condition that it was turned into an **orphanage.** Perhaps pleased to be rid of an embarrassment, the Sultan not only made a donation towards the orphanage but also gave it tax-exempt status. The orphanage opened in 1903 and continued to function until 1964, with a break during the First World War when the Kuleli Military School (see p. 523) was relocated here. It was returned to the Patriarchate in 2008 since when it has continued to languish.

Mizzi Mansion

Houses and Mansions

Büyükada is renowned for its fine wooden houses. One of the most magnificent mansions on Çankaya Caddesi is the newly restored **Con Paşa Köşkü**, built by Achilleus Politis in 1880 for **Trasivolos Yannaros** (Con Paşa, pronounced John Pasha) who was responsible for introducing the ferry service to the islands. This mansion is in the incredibly elaborate style popular on the mainland at the time. However, some of the other mansions exhibit features clearly copied from Europe. For example, the **Yelkencizade Köşkü** at No. 3 Kadıyoran Caddesi appears to be a direct copy of a design initially created for a Viennese property by the architect **Josef Maria Olbrich.** Often decorative features added to door and window frames give otherwise quite ordinary houses an Art Nouveau twist.

Another wonderful mansion to look out for is the **Fabiato Köşkü** at No. 21 Çankaya Caddesi, which was built in 1878 and restored in 1998 by **Çelik Gülersoy** (see p. 034) who eventually died here. It has been turned into a **cultural center** with an inviting garden where **concerts** are held in summer. Nearby at No. 31 is the **Mizzi Köşkü**, an extraordinary red-brick construction complete with observation tower which was built by **Raimondo d'Aronco** for the lawyer **Giovanni Mizzi** in 1894-5. While the building's heavy, squared-off proportions barely nod towards Art Nouveau, the details of the balconies and lamp-holders are pure Jugendstil – and the drawings for them still survive today. A little further along the road at No. 44 the **Adalar Kaymakamlığı** (local government headquarters) is housed inside what was once the **Hotel Imperial**; despite the peeling paintwork of the façade it still retains its fine **frescoed ceilings.**

Çankaya Palas

Vural Suiçmez Mansion

Who was who on Büyükada?

Other famous residents or visitors to the island have included Angelo Guiseppe Roncali, later **Pope John XXII**, who lived in the **Vatican Embassy Mansion** on Şehbal Sokağı while papal nuncio to Istanbul from 1933-34; and **Princess Fahrelnissa**, the artist wife of the Jordanian Emir Zeid, whose paintings are on display at the Istanbul Modern (see p. 377) and her brother **Cevat Şakir Kabaağaçlı**, "the Fisherman of Halicarnassus" who popularized blue cruises out of Bodrum, both of whom lived in the **Rosolato Köşkü**, on Şehbal Sokağı.

Cevat Şakir Kabaağaçlı

Büyükada Anatolian Club

In 23 Nisan Caddesi, this attractive building was originally created for the Prinkipo Yacht Club by the British in 1906 and has hosted everybody from President İsmet İnönü through to the last shah of Iran and Nikolae Ceaucescu, the Romanian dictator. Of course Atatürk stayed here too and his room has been preserved as it was in his day. It's open to members and their guests only.

Turkey's most beautiful street

Çankaya Caddesi is a millionaire's row of exquisite houses in all the styles of the 19th and 20th centuries, most of them set in lush, well-kept gardens. If there's a prettier street in Turkey it's hard to think where it could be.

According to the unanimous decision of the Istanbul Metropolitan Municipality (IBB) Council, the era of carriages in the Prince's Islands is over as of 2020. It was decided for the horses to be bought by IBB and the transportation to be provided by electrical vehicles. The senior horses will be released in the natural habitats of the Ministry of Agriculture and Forestry under supervision of veterinaries.

The Marmara's Forgotten Gems

The Other Princes' Islands

096

In all, nine islands, plus Vordonisi Island, make up the Princes' Islands. Only four of them are permanently inhabited, but although Sivriada, Yassıada, Kaşık Island, Sedef Island and Tavşan Island lack residents that doesn't mean they don't have interesting histories to fall back on; only Kaşıkadası is without the ruins of a medieval monastery. Sedef adası has found new life for itself with an upscale summer beach club. Otherwise you'll need to hire private boats to explore these forgotten gems.

Yassıada

The sixth largest of the islands, Yassıada, to the west of Burgazada, used to be called Plati by the Greeks, both names referring to its flat shape, although more unkind people also called it Hayırsızada, meaning "the useless island". From the 4th century onwards Yassıada was used as a convenient dumping ground for political prisoners. It boasted the habitual 9th-century **monastery**, as well as a small chapel, although no traces of either building remain.

More unexpected are the remains of the "medieval" **castle** built here by the British ambassador **Sir Henry Bulwer** (1801-72), brother of the novelist Edward Bulwer-Lytton, who bought the island in 1857 and turned it into a love-nest to share with his Greek mistress, the **Princess Eurydice**. Eurydice was eventually deported from Turkey as a Russian spy in 1872, whereupon the **Khedive İsmail Paşa of Egypt** paid handsomely to buy the island and then let the folly fall into ruins. In 1960-61 the castle played an ignominious role in modern Turkish history when it was turned into a courthouse where the deposed **Prime Minister Adnan Menderes**, the **Foreign**

Yassıada hearings, 1960

Affairs Minister Fatih Rüştü Zorlu and the **Finance Minister Hasan Polatkan** were tried and sentenced to death for violating the constitution (all three have since been posthumously pardoned). The islands of Yassıada and Sivriada were consigned by the Ministry of Culture and Tourism Directorate for Cultural Heritage and Museums in 2011 to be used as museums. Yassıada's name was later changed to "Democracy and Freedom Island" and a series of hotel and facility constructions were begun in 2015. The Bulwer Building was demolished during the construction and the church and the dungeon were also damaged. The project will be completed in 2019 with a hotel of 125 rooms, about 30 concrete bungalows, a conference room for 600 people, a mosque, a museum and exhibition areas.

Kaşık Island

The smallest of the islands is officially tiny spoon-shaped Kaşıkadası (Spoon Island) which was called Pita (Bread) by the Greeks. It is the only one of the islands not to have had a monastery built on it and is now privately owned with a couple of summer houses on it.

Vordonisi Island

When is an island not an island? Perhaps when it's as tiny as Vordonosadası (Vordonos Island), a pinprick of a place which is only occasionally included in a list of the Princes' Islands even though it too managed its 9th-century **monastery**.

Tavşan Island

Called Neandros by the Greeks, Tavşanadası (Rabbit Island) is the second smallest of the Princes' Islands. It lies just south of Büyükada and boasts the by now predictable ruins of a **monastery** dating back to the 8th century which served as a place of exile for several imperial cast-offs, including **Theodora**, the wife of the **Emperor Theophilos**, who was banished here by her son **Michael III** in 856. Like Sivriada, Tavşanadası proved a convenient place to abandon **street dogs** with the result that it was sometimes nicknamed **Köpekleradası (Island of Dogs)**. It's a great place for bird-watchers since a cliff to the south of the island provides nesting perches for thousands of **cormorants** and **seagulls**. Here, too, is a **cave** which can be entered by boat.

Sedef Island

Once called Terebinthos (Turpentine Tree) by the Greeks, Sedefadası, just east of Büyükada, is the fifth largest island in the group and takes its Turkish name either from "sedef", meaning mother of pearl, or from "sedefotu" meaning the rue plant. There are slight remains of a 9th-century **monastery** to the north-west of

the island and a cluster of luxury villas, inhabited only in summer. Otherwise the main feature of Sedef-adası is Port Sedef, an upscale summer beach club-cum-restaurant which opened amid the cypresses and umbrella pines in 2008. Guests are ferried to and from the other islands. It's a great place to come for a really special occasion.

Sivriada

The third smallest of the Princes' Islands, Sivriada, to the west of Burgazada, used to be called Oxia in Greek; both names refer to its pointed hill shape. The port side of the island was quarried out to provide the building materials for Kadıköy harbor, but nearby stand the ruins of a **monastery** which was built some time before the 12th century.

The islands were not just popular as places to abandon unwanted human beings. Sivriada had a wretched reputation as a place to which packs of **street dogs** were periodically dispatched to starve to death or eat each

Sivriada

other. Modern visitors are often surprised to see how many dogs live wild on the streets of Istanbul, but their numbers are tiny in comparison with those reported by visitors in the 19th century when between 40,000 and 50,000 dogs may have been roaming free. **Sultan Mahmud II** was probably the first to try and solve the problem by sending the dogs to Sivriada. However, the boat in which they were traveling was quickly blown ashore again. This was seen as a sign that Allah didn't approve of their banishment, which soon put the brakes on the scheme. Later **Sultan Abdülaziz** had another try. This time several fires broke out after the boat carrying the dogs set sail and this, too, was interpreted as a sign of Allah's displeasure, resulting in another reprieve for the hounds. In 1911 yet another attempt to banish the dogs was followed by an earthquake and yet another reprieve.

Beach Breakaways

The Marmara Islands

097

Often confused with the Princes' Islands which are also in the Sea of Marmara, the Marmara Islands are much further away from the center of Istanbul on the south side of the sea. In summer there are regular ferries from Yenikapı but at other times of year access is easiest from the small town of Erdek, also on the southern shore. The Marmara Islands are in many ways the antithesis of the upscale Princes' Islands, their visitors mainly drawn from Istanbul's middle and working classes who flock here in their thousands especially during the long school holidays.

"...no smog, no revving engines, no car alarms going off in the middle of the night."

Irene-Marie Spencer on Ekinlik in *Travelers' Tales: Turkey*, 2002

Peace dominates the islands.

The Marmara Islands are a group of seven islands, only four of them inhabited. While not quite as car-free as the Princes' Islands, these little beach hideaways still have relatively little vehicular traffic meaning that they are pleasantly quiet in comparison with the mainland. Until the First World War all the islands had sizeable Greek populations but these are long gone, leaving less to show for their passing than on the Princes' Islands.

Marmara Island

The largest of the islands, originally called **Procennesus** by the Greek descendants of Miletian colonists who lived here, modern Marmara is named after its **marble quarries** that once supplied the grey-white marble for some of the columns of **Hagia Sophia** (see p. 026). The quarries are on the north side of the island while most of the residential development, including Marmara Town, is to the south. The interior is largely occupied by **Mt İlyas** (İlyas Dağı, 700m).

Marmara Town has a certain vaguely rural charm, with a pleasant waterside promenade lined with shops and restaurants, but there are no historical monuments, bar the fine **Marmara High School** (Lisesi) and **Government** (Hükümet Konağı) buildings, a backstreet cartouche that recalls a lost church, a couple of old marble **fountains** and a fine collection of Ottoman tombstones. There's a better beach at **Çınarlı,** which is named after the 1000-year-old **plane trees** at the entrance to the village. Houses here have pretty gardens and there's another beachside promenade. Narrow your eyes and you could just about imagine yourself on one of the Greek islands.

Avşa Island

The second largest of the islands, Avşa has been hideously over-developed with a mish-mash of summer homes, beach restaurants and tacky souvenir shops. The beaches are not especially wide but they are sandy and during the school holidays they are wall-to-wall bodies, with some matrons taking to the water in Islamic bathing costumes that billow around them like barrage balloons. The ruins of the **Church of Hagia Triada** are the sole reminder of the days when the Greek residents called the island Ophioussa.

Paşalimanı Island

The third largest of the islands is "the Pasha's Harbor", a 10-kilometer-long strip of rock dotted with plane trees and with a few private rooms available for rent in its main "town", **Balıklı**.

Ekinlik Island

Also known as Kaşık (Spoon) Island because of its shape, Ekinlik, the smallest of the inhabited islands, lacks beaches but does have a reasonably pretty village with a ruined church and a pleasant tea garden.

İmralı Island

Way out to the east, İmralı merits a mention not because you can visit it (you can't!) but because it houses the high-security prison holding the PKK terrorist leader **Abdullah Öcalan**. In 1961 it was also the place where **Prime Minister Adnan Menderes** and his associates were hanged (see p. 146). Until 1923 and the Greco-Turkish population exchange there were three Greek villages on the island whose inhabitants made a living from fishing, viticulture and silk production. After their departure, the prison was opened in 1935.

An Artist's Waterside Studio

Eskihisar

098

Hidden in the generally grim outskirts of eastern Istanbul the small port settlement of Eskihisar boasts an "eski hisar (old castle)" as well as the summer home of Osman Hamdi Bey, the late 19th-century archeologist and artist who founded the Istanbul Archeology Museum. Here, too, is his grave in a pretty, forgotten cemetery.

In the Coffee-house (1879)

Women on a Pleasure Trip (1887).
They are shown on the northern side of Sultanahmet Mosque.

Woman with Mimosa (1906)

In the 19th century Istanbul's wealthier residents generally maintained two homes, one in town for the winter and a second on the islands or somewhere close to the water such as Eskihisar where they could take advantage of the cool sea breezes in summer. Osman Hamdi Bey (1842-1910), Turkey's only orientalist artist and the man behind the Istanbul Archeology Museum and the Istanbul Academy of Fine Arts (now the Mimar Sinan University of Fine Arts), was no exception, keeping a winter house at Kuruçeşme, (see p. 419) and then moving with his family to Eskihisar in the summer. Such was his love of what was then a completely separate small town that on his death he was buried here in a graveyard where most of the tombstones resemble those of the medieval Menteşe emirs who ruled south-western Turkey from their capital at Beçin, near Milas.

The castle

The hilltop castle at Eskihisar dates back to Byzantine times but has been given a makeover that has completely stripped it of the patina of age. To make up for this, in summer an open-air cinema with a wonderful sea-view backdrop screens movies inside the battlements.

Where to see Osman Hamdi Bey's paintings

- *The Tortoise Trainer* (1906) and *Two Musician Girls* (1880) are both in the **Pera Museum** (see p. 335),
- *The Shore and A Young Lady Having her Hair Combed* are in **Dolmabahçe Palace** (see p. 386),
- *Woman with Mimosas* (1906), *Portrait of a Young Girl* (1891) and *Man with a Yellow Robe* (1905) are in the **Museum of Painting** (see p. 393),
- *Street Scribe* is in the **Sakıp Sabancı Museum** (see p. 444).

Osman Hamdi Bey Museum

The house in which Osman Hamdi Bey lived has been beautifully restored and is a fine example of the wooden yalıs (waterside mansions) that used to grace many parts of the city. Painted white, it has a verandah and balcony overlooking a **harbor** where small fishing boats still bob up and down. There's a pleasant **tea garden** in the grounds, although the once lovely garden that appears in his paintings is now very overgrown.

Inside the house are **copies** of many of Osman's paintings, although unfortunately none of the originals is on display, nor is there any information about where they can be seen. Visitors are given a **guided tour** (in Turkish only) and can view the room in which the artist completed his paperwork which still retains much of its original furniture as well as some pretty door panels that he hand-painted himself. Upstairs, his light-filled **studio** has been equipped with a mannequin modeling the lovely portrait he painted of his second wife clad in yellow and filling a basket with flowers.

Tel: 0262 655 63 48, closed Mondays

Osman Hamdi Bey and his family

Hannibal's Last Resting Place

Gebze

099

A seemingly uninviting suburb that is nevertheless home to the magnificent Çoban Mustafa Paşa Mosque which retains the complex of other buildings that used to be associated with it. Gebze also deserves a footnote in Tunisian history since it was here that the famous Carthaginian general Hannibal (he of the elephants and the Alps) died and was buried.

Çoban Mustafa Paşa Mosque

Right in the center of Gebze stands this magnificent mosque complex, one of the finest outside the heart of Istanbul and built on such a grand scale because Gebze was one of the first places through which **caravan trains to Anatolia** would have to pass. It was constructed in 1523 for **Çoban (Shepherd) Mustafa Paşa**, a shepherd who had abandoned his flocks to fight in Sultan Selim I's campaign which led to the **conquest of Egypt.** For his pains he became the Governor of Egypt in 1522 and so decided to employ **Egyptian craftsmen** to work on his mosque, both inside and out. The complex is listed in the **Tezkeret-ül Ebniye**, the standard list of all Mimar Sinan's works created by his friend Mustafa Sai and it's thought that he may have worked on it as an assistant to another court architect. Alternatively, he may have enlarged it in 1538.

There are many things that make this such an especially wonderful place. The elaborate **Mamluk-style carvings** created by the Egyptian workmen on the interior and exterior walls are impressive enough, but high walls also square off the complex from the outside world and enclose a series of other amenities that make this one of the most complete külliyes (mosque complexes) to survive: guestrooms, a caravanserai and stables, a medrese, a dervish lodge, a soup kitchen and a hospice as well as the tomb of Çoban Mustafa Paşa himself. To add to all this the buildings also look onto a beautiful **peaceful courtyard** where old men snooze beneath the plane trees. It's a delightful spot and completely unexpected amid its concrete-jungle surroundings.

Interior of Çoban Mustafa Paşa Mosque

"...at the caravanserai, every evening every room is provided with a fireplace, a dish of soup, a loaf of bread, a candle and a bag of forage for every horse, ass, mule or camel."

***Seyahatname* by Evliya Çelebi, 1640**

Memorial stone

Hannibal's grave

The great Carthaginian general Hannibal (248-183 BC) is remembered for his part in the **Second Punic War** against the Romans during the course of which he drove an army of war elephants right round the Mediterranean from what is now Tunisia to confront the Romans in their Italian homeland in 218 BC. Eventually Hannibal retired to Libyssa (Diliskelesi) in Bithynia (the area immediately east of what is now Istanbul) which was governed by his friend, **King Prusias I**. Unfortunately the Romans were not prepared to let their great enemy die in peace and pressed Prusias to extradite him to Rome. Rather than submit to this Hannibal poisoned himself and was buried in what are now the grounds of TÜBİTAK (the Scientific and Technological Research Council).

In the 20th century **Atatürk** decided that his grave should be marked with a memorial.

GOSB Mosque

Among the newest mosques with modern architectural features in Istanbul, the GOSB Mosque that was opened to service in 2015 is one of the firsts to come to mind. The building symbolizing infinity with its wide dome mounted on a square base with single yard has a minaret rising from the stone pool that was designed in the shape of a factory chimney as a tribute to the industrial zone.

Faruk Yalçın Zoo

At **Bayramoğlu** in Darıca near Gebze, this zoo set in 200,000 square meters of grounds suffers from the same problems as most small zoos, its elderly cages filled with bored-looking animals and birds. The gardens are pleasant enough, but most children seem more interested in the **large playground** than in the animals.

@farukyalcin.zoo
www.farukyalcinzoo.com.

Birthplace of Palace Carpets

Hereke

100

In the world of oriental carpets few names are more resonant than that of Hereke where many of the finest silk carpets ever made were woven. The building that housed the factory still survives on the outskirts of Istanbul just a stone's throw away from a picturesque fishing harbor. Nearby is a pretty guesthouse built for the visit of Kaiser Wilhelm II.

"The art of the workshop carpet is the art of the designer."

***Carpets From the Tents, Cottages and Workshops of Asia* by Jon Thompson, 1983**

Hereke stands on the site of the ancient **Ankyron** on the shores of the Bay of İzmit where Constantine the Great died in 337. Nothing now remains of Ankyron although there are slight traces of a medieval **castle** on a nearby hilltop which **historian Geoffrey de Villehardouin** attributed to the period of the Crusader occupation of Constantinople from 1204 to 1261.

In 1843 **Sultan Abdülmecid** created a factory at Hereke to produce the many hand-knotted silk carpets needed for the royal palaces. At the same time a workshop staffed by Hereke weavers was also established in the grounds of the **Dolmabahçe Palace**. Between them they produced 140 large carpets and 115 prayer rugs, including some of the finest examples of the carpet craft ever produced. The factory burnt down in 1878 but reopened in 1882. With the loss of its imperial sponsors Hereke carpet-weaving went into a decline between 1923 and 1945, but in the 1950s the craft started to pick up again, with some of the weaving contracted out to workers in their own homes.

The best Hereke carpets have more than a million knots per square meter.

While woven in Turkey and utilizing the **Turkish double-knot**, Hereke rugs took much of their inspiration from Persia (Iran), India and Egypt. They also incorporated motifs from popular carpet patterns, such as 16th-century Uşak medallions, which means that they are sometimes mistaken for much older pieces. Many were given as **gifts** to visiting heads of state.

Modern-day Hereke is a sleepy backwater bypassed by the main Istanbul to Kocaeli highway. With a cluster of fish restaurants around the harbor and a small park, it offers enough entertainment to fill a comfortable half-day excursion.

Kaiser II. Wilhelm

Kaiser Wilhelm's Guesthouse

A lovely whitewashed guesthouse was built right on the waterside near the factory for the visit of **Kaiser Wilhelm II** (1859-1941) and his wife **Victoria** in 1898. It was constructed from panels that had been prefabricated using boat-building techniques and no nails in the carpentry workshops of the **Yıldız Palace** (see p. 403). The Kaiser brought with him a set of **color-fast chemical dyes** and a microscope and slides to enable the factory workers to study the parasites that could damage their carpets and so improve production techniques. The guesthouse was restored in 2009.

Hereke Silk Fabric and Carpet Museum

Old weaving loom

Close to the landing stage for the İzmit ferries, the old Hereke factory now houses a small museum showing off a selection of **silk carpets and brocade**, including examples of patterns that can still be seen in the **Dolmabahçe and Beylerbeyi Palaces**. Also preserved here is some of the old machinery used in the silk production, together with photographs of the factory in its heyday. It's open free of charge.

www.millisaraylar.gov.tr
open weekdays

And the West Side of Istanbul...

101

As you make your way towards the west side of the city, you will be welcomed by antique remains, important monuments and natural beauties scattered among the modern urban buildings. Especially the amazing bridge in Büyükçekmece is one of the masterpieces of architect Sinan...

The construction of the bridge which is another monument reflecting Sinan's genius began with the order of Suleiman the Magnificent before the Szigetvar Expedition. Hundreds of stonemasons and sculptors worked in its construction, the water of the lake was drawn with huge water pumps. 2 or 3 men-high pilings were connected with the lead cast between them. The bridge consists four sections and 28 arches (636 meters).

Küçükçekmece

The connection of **Region** located in today's county center to the main city of Bizantion was made through **Via Egnatia** (see p.191), which was built by command of **Emperor Constantinus** in late 4th century. In the Ottoman era, the town named Çekme-i Küçük (Small Drawer) served as an entrance to Istanbul for those who traveled from the west with its bathhouses, fountains, mosques, madrasas and taverns. The westerners chose to name here as **Ponte Piccolo**, which means "small bridge" in Italian

The building of Halkalı Land College that was opened in 1884 and contributed to the evolvement of husbandry in Turkey now hosts the rectorate of a foundation university.

Near Lake Küçükçekmece, the **Yarımburgaz Cave** is a treasure with findings from all the periods of a duration of 400 thousand years, from Paleolithic ages to Byzantium. The archeological digs reveal that the settlers here were occupied in fishing, hunting and farming. During the Byzantian era, it is known that the place was used as a monastery complex. The findings from several archeological digs are exhibited in **Istanbul Archeological Museum** (see p.020). Today the cave carries traces of the damage caused by neglect and especially the improper use of the film industry.

Küçükçekmece Bridge

Expanding in an area of 16 km², Lake Küçükçekmece was formed about 18 thousand years ago, as a result of the rise of sea levels with the melting of glaciers in the last geological era. Don't miss the **Küçükçekmece Bridge** located along this lake. In the place of this bridge, there was probably a wooden bridge in the Roman era. The bridge that was repaired by command of **Mehmed the Conqueror** is known to have been repaired in different periods because of its strategic importance. In Seyahatname (Book of Travel), **Evliya Çelebi** states that the construction of the bridge began by **Süleyman the Magnificent**, but it was finished as late as the period of Selim II.

Avcılar

Located near Marmara Sea and west of Lake Küçükçekmece, Avcılar attracts attention with its beautiful coastline and recent archeological digs, even though it's mostly referred with the campus of Istanbul University.

During the digs in the **Bathonea Antique City** near Lake Küçükçekmece in 2009, two ancient harbors dated to **Hellenistic** and **Roman** eras and the second antique lighthouse in our country buried in the lake were discovered. Besides these a huge open cistern built in the time of **Emperor Constantinus**, remains of a fortress, a palace complex with a mosaic base, underground water canals and antique roads were revealed. The digs also found traces of the earthquake that happened in 7 May 558, which caused the collapse of the dome of Hagia Sophia.

---

www.bathonea.org

Beylikdüzü

Located between Büyükçekmece and Küçükçekmece Lakes, the research made in Beylikdüzü, especially around Haramidere reveals some traces and tools used by the people of **Paleolithic Age**. Resources mention that these were also from settlements around the **Via Egnatia**. The fact that the district has remains of what is thought to belong to an antique harbor and the archeological findings that were discovered in a construction pit by chance are the recent evidence that the area has been a residential place since antiquity.

West Istanbul Marina

Providing service in Beylikdüzü since 2012, West İstanbul Marina serves marine lovers with its anchorage, recreational facility and high-quality technical service. With its cafés, restaurants, spa centers, beach club and sailing school, the place provides its guests a living space beyond a marina. I recommend you discover the most beautiful place by the seashore in Beylikdüzü.

@westistanbul_marina
www.westistanbulmarina.com
Tel: 0212 850 22 00

Bridges

Even though the research about which period **Yakuplu Bridge** was built in continues, the evidence at hand shows that it was one of the bridges of Via Egnatia.

Haramidere (Kapıağası) Bridge was built by architect Sinan, on the Istanbul-Rumelia caravan route. The bridge built with uniform face stones and a neat workmanship is under protection, but it can only be seen passing by in a car since it's located between belt highways.

Büyükçekmece

It was **Hellenes** who established Beylikdüzü, where the first settlements began in 7th century B.C. The settlements in the area were not dense since it was a town of resort and agriculture called **Athyra** during Byzantian times and also a stopover for armies during Byzantian and Ottoman eras. Many Turkish refugees settled in the area especially after the **Ottoman-Russian War** in 1829.

Don't leave Büyükçekmece before visiting the small and simple **Sokullu Mescidi** (Masjid), the caravansary and the Sultan Suleiman Fountain with three sections that were ordered by Süleyman the Magnificent before the Szigetvar Expedition and supervised by Sinan. The caravanserai is also known as "The Lead Inn" since its roof was fully covered with lead when it was first built.

Sokollu Mescidi

Sancaklar Underground Mosque

Those who will visit this mosque should not expect a classical mosque form or glamour. Instead you will experience how impressive the feeling of simplicity can be. The mosque is located towards the slope of the hill with a panoramic view of Büyükçekmece Lake while passing through luxurious sites in the area. The first eye-catching structure is the minaret designed as a rectangular column. No other characteristic of the mosque can be discerned from outside. But the real glory will welcome you when you go down the stairs and enter the mosque, as if you were entering a cave. Everything is simple, but the details are well thought out. The mosque, designed by Architect Emre Arolat, has won numerous awards and has an international reputation.

Did you know that the only festival in UNESCO's International Council of Organizations of Folklore and Folk Arts' (CIOFF) Category A is **International Büyükçekmece Festival of Culture of Arts?** In the **Museum of World Costumes**, outfits and objects of 173 countries; vests, cloaks, shirts, kilts, shoes, kerchiefs, handkerchiefs, scarves, tarbooshes, hats, jodhpurs, pants, 145 suits and 555 pieces of jewelry and accessories are exhibited

Tel: 0212 883 07 22

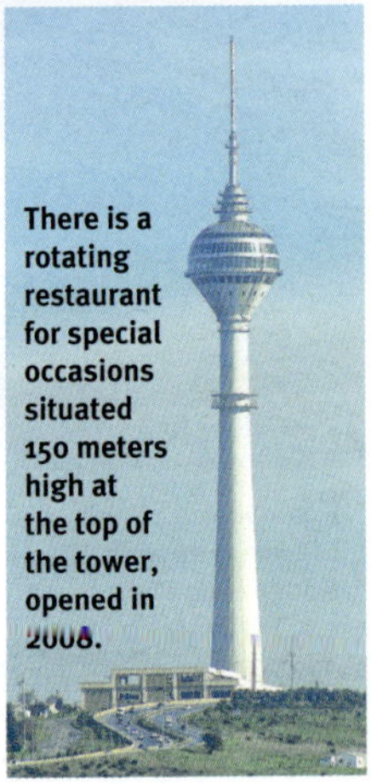

There is a rotating restaurant for special occasions situated 150 meters high at the top of the tower, opened in 2008.

Çatalca

With a history of around 2500 years, Çatalca is the biggest district of Istanbul on European grounds. The first known settlement in Çatalca area was established in **Roman** era around 450 B.C. in where is now known as **İnceğiz Köyü** (Village). When Çatalca was first established in the antique era by Thracians, it was called **Ergiske,** dedicated to Poseidon's son Ergiscus. After the Ottoman domination it was first called Çatalburgaz and in time the name evolved to Çatalca. The hardest times in the history of Çatalca were during the Balkan Wars. When the enemy advanced to Çatalca, many soldiers from several cities of Anatolia were dispatched to the fronts. The **Alaiye Martyrdom** was built in commemoration of those who fell martyr in these battles. After the Treaty of Bucharest was concluded one year later, Bulgarians returned the area they conquered.

Çatalca Aqueducts

Museum of Population Exchange

Before the 1923 Population Exhange, Çatalca was a residential area that **Orthodox Greeks** and **Muslim Turks** lived together. After the decision of the exchange was finalized, refugees were inhabited in the houses of the Greeks who left the residential area within the Çatalca Province. This museum was founded with the aim of preserving, recording and handing the cultural heritage of refugees to the next generations. Since 2010, the first migration themed museum in Turkey has been bringing past stories to the present.

www.lozanmubadilleri.org.tr/catalca-mubadele-muzesi/ closed Mondays

Silivri

Established by **Megarans** in 677 B.C., Silivri was first named **Selymbria**. In the Byzantian era it was an important place of viticulture and winemaking. After Byzantian **Emperor Arkadius** (377-408) married Eudoxia, he had the **Selymbria Castle** rebuilt and changed the name of the city to Eudoxiapolis. Towards the end of the fifth century, the Byzantian built a wall to prevent the Bulgarians from entering the city. The 56 kilometers long **Anastasia Wall** extends from the west of Silivri to Evcik at the coast of Black Sea. The castle and the walls were repaired after big earthquakes but only a few monuments inside the **Kale Park** remained to this day. There are few specific sights in Silivri, although **Piri Mehmed Camii** and **Silivri Bridge** built by architect **Sinan** are worth a quick look. The **Village Market** that brings the natural goods produced by farmers of Silivri to consumers in a decent environment is next to the historical **Kısa Köprü** (Short Bridge) on the seaside and open every day.

The three-storey Byzantine Monastery Caves and Rock Churches built by human hands near İnceğiz Village in the northwest of Çatalca, were discovered by the scientific world in the 1950s. A crucifix relief in one of the rooms blinks at us from the time it was made.

Piri Mehmed Mosque

The Yoğurthane Buildings (Yoghurt Production Facilities), known to have been built by the Greeks in the 19th century and the location where the famous Silivri Yoghurt used to be produced, is being repurposed under the initiative of Silivri Municipality.

The bridge with 32 arches (340 meters) is closed to vehicular traffic.

Kale Park

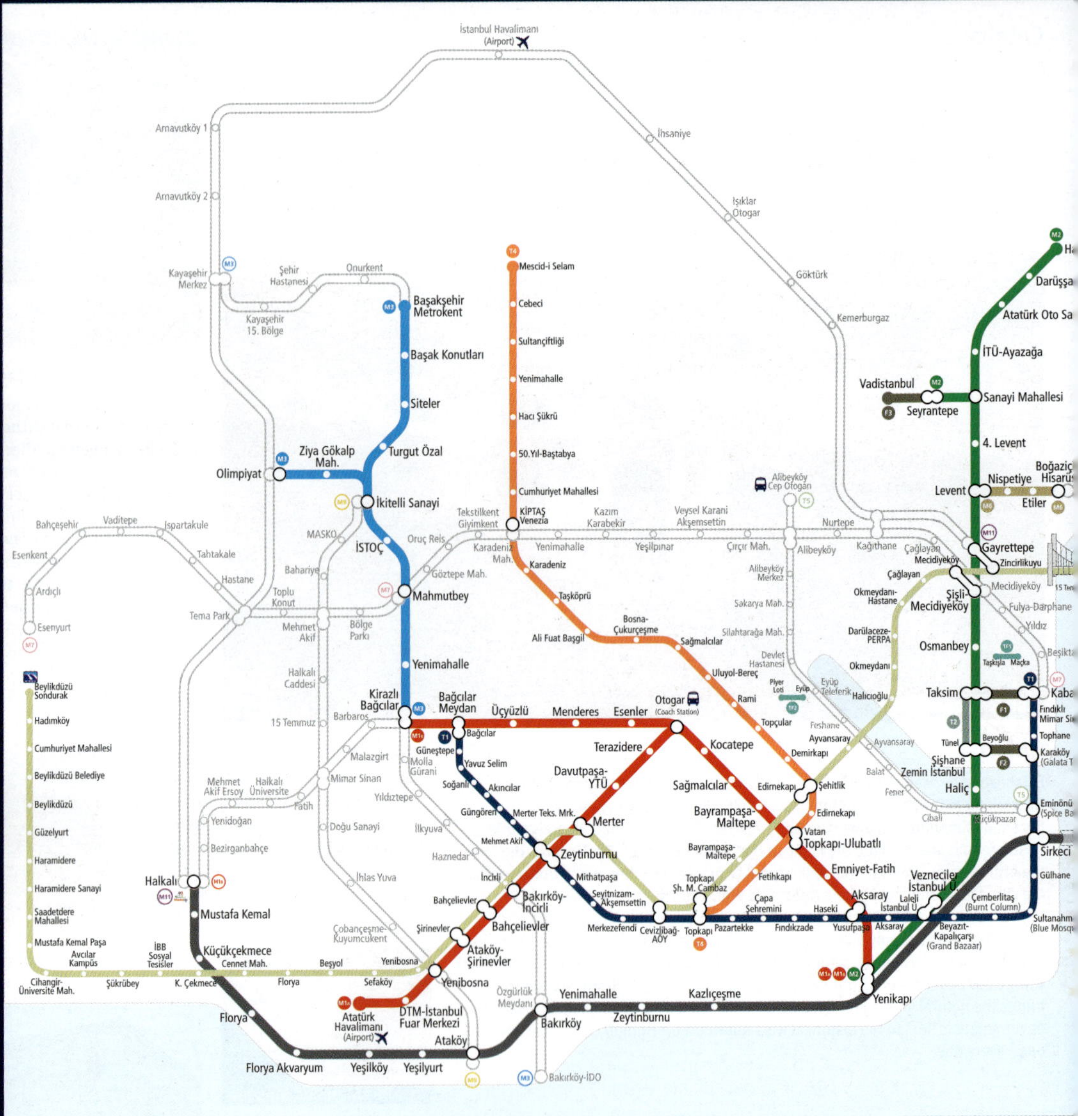

Yapımı Devam Eden Hatlar / Lines under construction

- **M1B** Kirazlı Bağcılar-Halkalı Uzatması
  Metro Line Extension
- **M3** Bakırköy İDO ve Kayaşehir Uzatmaları
  Metro Line Extensions
- **M4** Tavşantepe-SGH ve Tuzla Uzatmaları
  Metro Line Extensions
- **M5** Çekmeköy-Sultanbeyli Uzatması
  Metro Line Extension
- **M7** Kabataş-Mahmutbey-Esenyurt Metro Hattı
  Metro Line
- **M8** Bostancı-Dudullu Metro Hattı
  Metro Line
- **M9** İkitelli Sanayi-Ataköy Metro Hattı
  Metro line
- **M10** Pendik-SGH Metro Hattı
  Metro Line
- **M11** Gayrettepe-İstanbul Hvl.-Halkalı Metro Hattı
  Metro Line
- **M12** Göztepe-Ümraniye Metro Hattı
  Metro Line
- **M13** Yenidoğan-Hastane Metro Hattı
  Metro Line
- **F4** Hisarüstü-Aşiyan Füniküler Hattı
  Funicular Line
- **T5** Eminönü-Alibeyköy Tramvay Hattı
  Tram Line

İşaretler / Signs

- İstasyon-Durak / Statio
- Hat Başı-Sonu / Termin
- Aktarma İşaretleri / Transfe
- Boğaz Köpr
  Bosphorus Bri

METRO İSTANBUL

İSTANBUL BÜYÜKŞEHİR BELEDİYESİ

İstanbul Raylı Sistemler Ağ Haritası / *Istanbul Railway Network Map*

LEJANT / Legend

Mevcut Hatlar / Lines In Operation

- M1A Yenikapı-Atatürk Havalimanı Metro Hattı – Metro Line
- M1B Yenikapı-Kirazlı Metro Hattı – Metro Line
- M2 Yenikapı-Hacıosman Metro Hattı – Metro Line
- M3 Kirazlı-Olimpiyat-Başakşehir Metro Hattı – Metro Line
- M4 Kadıköy-Tavşantepe Metro Hattı – Metro Line
- M5 Üsküdar-Çekmeköy Metro Hattı – Metro Line
- M6 Levent-Boğaziçi Ü./Hisaüstü Metro Hattı – Metro Line
- TF1 Maçka-Taşkışla Teleferik Hattı – Cable Car
- TF2 Eyüp-Piyer Loti Teleferik Hattı – Cable Car
- T1 Kabataş-Bağcılar Tramvay Hattı – Tram Line
- T2 Taksim-Tünel Nostaljik Tramvay (İETT) – Heritage Tram
- T3 Kadıköy-Moda Tramvay Hattı – Tram Line
- T4 Topkapı-Mescid-i Selam Tramvay Hattı – Tram Line
- F1 Taksim-Kabataş Füniküler Hattı – Funicular
- F2 Karaköy-Beyoğlu Tarihi Tünel (İETT) – Tunnel
- F3 Seyrantepe-Vadistanbul Füniküler Hattı – Funicular Line
- Halkalı-Gebze Marmaray (TCDD) – Suburban Line
- Metrobüs (İETT) – Metrobus / BRT Line

Haritayı QR kod ile mobil cihazlarınıza indirebilirsiniz.

You can download the network map in your mobile devices via the QR code.

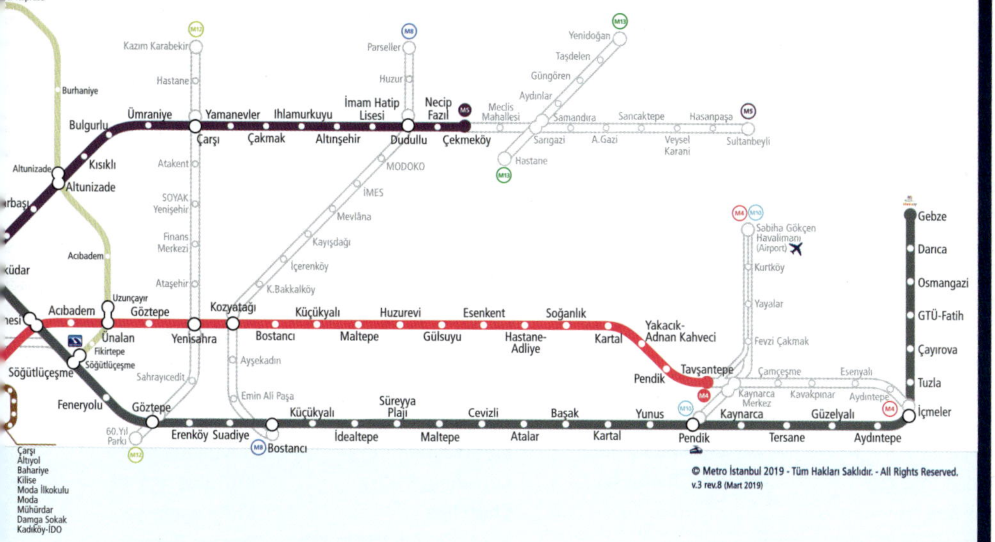

v.3 rev.8 (Mart 2019)

Havalimanı / Airport

Otogar / Coach Station

YHT-Hızlı Tren Garı
High Speed Rail Transfer Station

Marmaray Boğaz Tüneli
Marmaray Undersea Tunnel

İletişim / Contact

Sayın Yolcularımız, raylı sistemler cep haritasını istasyon görevlilerinden temin edebilirsiniz.

Dear Passengers, you can obtain the network map from the station staff.

Sefer saatlerini Cep Haritalarından ya da istasyon bilgilendirme panolarından öğrenebilirsiniz.

You can get information about timetables through the pocket maps or the information boards located in the stations.

ALO 153

SMS 1530

/metroistanbul_

/metroistanbulas

/metroistanbul_

0552 153 00 34

/metroistanbul

www.metro.istanbul

Index

Photo Credits by page number

Saffet Emre Tonguç
4, 7, 10, 13, 14, 15, 17, 19, 21, 22, 23, 24, 25, 30, 31, 34, 35, 36, 40, 43, 48, 51, 52, 55, 56, 57, 61, 63, 69, 70, 71, 72, 73, 76, 77, 81, 82, 83, 84, 93, 94, 95, 96, 100, 101, 110, 111, 119, 127, 132, 134, 135, 136, 137, 138, 139, 140, 141, 142, 146, 149, 158, 159, 160, 161, 162, 169, 170, 174, 177, 178, 179, 186, 187, 188, 189, 201, 202, 208, 209, 215, 219, 221, 222, 223, 227, 229, 231, 232, 234, 236, 237, 238, 241, 242, 243, 245, 256, 260, 270, 271, 274, 275, 276, 282, 284, 297, 301, 305, 307, 310, 311, 312, 313, 316, 317, 321, 323, 326, 327, 328, 329, 333, 334, 335, 340, 355, 363, 364, 374, 378, 381, 382, 383, 387, 388, 389, 390, 391, 393, 395, 397, 398, 399, 400, 401, 404, 405, 408, 413, 414, 415, 416, 420, 421, 423, 424, 425, 428, 429, 430, 431, 436, 438, 439, 440, 442, 443, 444, 445, 446, 447, 449, 450, 451, 452, 453, 454, 455, 456, 459, 460, 462, 463, 464, 466, 467, 468, 474, 478, 480, 481, 489, 491, 499, 503, 506, 508, 510, 511, 512, 517, 518, 519, 522, 523, 526, 527, 530, 531, 532, 533, 534, 535, 536, 537, 539, 543, 544, 545, 548, 549, 551, 552, 553, 556, 558, 559, 563, 564, 565, 567, 569, 571, 572, 575, 576, 577, 587, 590, 591, 601, 602, 603

Aydın Sertbaş(@aydinsert)
XXXI, 4, 5, 8, 12, 13, 18, 19, 21, 22, 23, 24, 25, 27, 28, 30, 31, 33, 34, 36, 39, 40, 42, 44, 45, 49, 53, 56, 60, 61, 63, 65, 66, 68, 69, 75, 76, 82, 88, 89, 90, 92, 94, 95, 96, 97, 98, 101, 102, 103, 104, 106, 107, 108, 109, 110, 111, 116, 118, 119, 120, 122, 123, 124, 126, 127, 131, 134, 143, 148, 150, 152, 158, 159, 163, 167, 170, 172, 173, 175, 176, 177, 178, 195, 196, 201, 203, 207, 209, 210, 212, 213, 214, 219, 221, 225, 226, 228, 229, 233, 235, 244, 247, 261, 273, 274, 277, 280, 283, 288, 289, 293, 294, 296, 298, 301, 306, 309, 314, 316, 320, 322, 330, 333, 337, 338, 348, 354, 356, 357, 358, 362, 363, 365, 369, 372, 373, 378, 384, 386, 394, 396, 397, 398, 400, 405, 406, 407, 411, 414, 417, 422, 424, 427, 435, 437, 438, 441, 443, 456-457, 461, 469, 475, 476, 478, 480, 482, 483, 485, 489, 491, 494, 495,496, 498, 499, 500, 502, 503, 504, 505, 506, 507, 511, 512, 514, 517, 519, 521, 527, 541, 546, 549, 550, 551, 554, 556, 558, 567, 568, 569, 573, 588, 590, 604, 610, 614

Pat Yale
15, 18, 21, 22, 24, 25, 34, 45, 47, 53, 55, 59, 60, 63, 73, 78, 79, 81, 82, 83, 87, 88, 89, 94, 95, 96, 97, 99, 102, 104, 110, 111, 112, 113, 117, 118, 119, 122, 123, 125, 130, 135, 140, 143, 146, 147, 148, 149, 153, 157, 160, 161, 162, 163, 167, 168, 169, 170, 174, 177, 178, 181, 182, 186, 187, 188, 189, 191, 192, 193, 196, 197, 201, 202, 203, 205, 208, 209, 210, 221, 222, 223, 227, 228, 229, 232, 234, 243, 245, 247, 248, 249, 250, 251, 252, 253, 255, 256, 257, 259, 260, 270, 273, 276, 277, 285, 290, 292, 298, [illegible], [illegible], [illegible], 311, 312, 314, 319, 322, 325, 327, 328, 329, 333, 336, 341, 342, 345, 346, 349, 352, 353, 354, 355, 357, 380, 381, 382, 383, 388, 390, 393, 396, 398, 399, 400, 401, 404, 419, 420, 422, 425, 428, 441, 442, 445, 446, 451, 455, 460, 461, 463, 464, 465, 467, 468, 469, 472, 473, 474, 478, 479, 480, 481, 487, 488, 490, 494, 502, 503, 504, 505, 506, 508, 512, 513, 527, 545, 548, 549, 553, 554, 559, 563, 565, 567, 571, 572, 573, 575, 576, 577, 578, 579, 586, 591, 600, 601, 603

Halit Bilen (@Bildrone)
III, VII, IX, XII, XIV, XVI, XVII, XIX, XXV, XXVII, XXVIII, XXXI, XXXIV, 20, 46, 60, 70, 84, 86, 111, 114, 145, 149, 198, 216, 230, 239, 278, 280, 283, 285, 300, 366, 387, 410, 411, 431, 432, 449, 476, 502, 506, 508, 509, 516, 517, 520, 526, 527, 538, 540-41, 547, 552, 557, 558, 562, 565, 566, 578, 584, 622

Uğur Soyata (@Emrkrm)
XIX, XXI, 54, 493, 497

Hasan Tolga Sıtkı (@tolgy75)
26, 57, 240, 374, 545

Barış Hasan Bedir (@barishasanbedir)
434, 562, 565, 570, 574, 583, 592

Sinan Doğan (@_sinandogan_)
42, 63, 70, 85, 90, 94, 95, 98, 99, 102, 116, 125, 130, 147, 150, 178, 207, 220, 242, 250, 256, 272, 297, 311, 327, 346, 371, 375, 376, 379, 380, 382, 388, 396, 397, 411, 412, 423, 500, 501, 502, 507, 516, 523, 564, 568, 605

Rebecca Erol
53, 70, 99, 100, 217, 219, 224, 230, 258, 266, 274, 275, 282, 305, 308, 312, 313, 314, 315, 318, 321, 377, 492, 505

Alexandros Massavetas
24, 78, 86, 90, 145, 149, 157, 176, 182, 184, 186, 231, 235, 238, 261, 270, 276, 277, 292, 301, 302, 329, 353, 383, 413, 455, 502, 521, 582, 590, 591, 592, 593

Şebnem Köken
9, 66, 69, 120, 190, 200, 203, 205, 206, 213, 226, 236, 237, 241, 244, 245, 246, 247, 251, 264, 278, 304, 306, 348, 396, 434, 477, 479, 493, 521, 523, 564, 589

Gülgün Asutay
5, 8, 15, 23, 25, 50, 51, 52, 72, 88, 112, 203, 214, 222, 228, 232, 253, 281, 302, 304, 311, 312, 389, 390, 403, 410, 443, 450, 454, 476, 520, 535, 585

Erman Tezgör
38, 117, 122, 178, 219, 246, 269, 343, 604, 605

Serhan Güngör
67, 102, 151, 232, 257, 260, 284, 375, 394, 401, 434, 499, 508, 547, 605

Aydın Kudu
28, 280, 370, 413, 432, 513

Mehmet Özcan
156, 157, 158

Kate Russell
8, 35, 39, 76, 167, 170, 215

Ufuk Sarışen
296, 419, 442, 557, 596, 597

Servet Dilber
21, 22, 215, 253, 364, 508, 510, 514, 528, 537

Bünyad Dinç
11, 12, 92, 142, 392, 504

Fatih Pınar
5, 133, 138, 144, 147, 164, 241, 256, 267, 273, 288, 290, 291, 320, 344, 348, 350, 368, 411, 413, 422, 423, 424, 448, 449, 451, 457, 474, 475, 515, 560

Ozan Kutsal 2, 7, 267, 591, 594 **Michael Constantini** 79, 217, 414, 415, 426, 579, 580, 581, 595 **Kemal Adıbelli** 40, 70, 72, 81, 213, 369, 496, 526 **Aynur Koç** 52, 69, 598, 599 **Altan Tuzluoğlu** 430, 534, 549 **Nil Yüzbaşıoğlu** 297, 586 **Mısra Öncel Erkaya** 238 **Duygun Soysal** 261, 480 **Didem Alp** 421 **Serhat Şahin** 428 **Arzu Brumendi** 534, 581, 583, **Billur Tufan** 453, 551 **Sinem İpek** 429, 454 **Aslı Özlen** 531, 532 **Pınar Okyaltırık Özdikicioğlu** 518, 522 **Alişan Özkan** 140, 548 **Uğur Akbulut** 58, 59 **Refika Birgül** 225 **Aydın Sert** 511 **Teoman Cimit** 198 **David Thomas Scarff** 412 **David Grenier** 53 **Mehmet Çubuk** 214 **John Armstrong** 18, **Mustafa Kirazlı** 363, **Alp Boneval** 169 **Gül İnan** XXXVII **Bahar Gökten** 485 **Sevtap Tonguç** 525 **Ece Azoz** 18 **Nadide Göksun** 42 **Harry Tzimitras** 18 **Sunset Arşivi** 360 **Sabancı Müzesi Arşivi** 445 **Istanbul Modern Arşivi** 378 **Khaftan Arşivi IV,** 20, 69 **Büke Uras Koleksiyonu** 349

Acknowledgements

Most of the information contained in this book was collected during the course of our combined decades of guiding and guidebook writing, or by pounding the streets and squeezing our friends for tips. We would also like to acknowledge the following as important written sources:

Altun, Selçuk *Songs My Mother Never Taught Me*, Telegram, 2008
Ascherson, Neal *Black Sea: The Birthplace of Civilisation and Barbarism*, Virago,1996
Barillari, Diana & Godoli, Ezio *Istanbul 1900*, Rizzoli, 1996
Belge, Murat *Boğaziçi' nde Yalılar, İnsanlar*, İletişim, 1997
Boppe, A *The Painters of the Bosphorus*, 1911
Busbecq, Ghislain Ogier de *Turkish Letters*, Eland, 2001
Byron, Lord *Don Juan*, 1863
Çelebi, Evliya *Seyahatname*
Deleon, Jak *A Taste of Old Istanbul*, 1989
Deleon, Jak *The Bosphorus: A Historical Guide*, 1999
Deleon, Jak *The Pera Palas: A Historical Hotel Overlooking the Golden Horn*, Gözlem, 1991
Devrim, Şirin *A Turkish Tapestry: The Shakirs of Istanbul*, Quartet, 1996
De Amicis, Edmondo *Constantinople*, Hesperus Classics, 2005
Diehl, Charles *Byzantine Empress*, 1904
Dorina, Lady Neave, *Romance of the Bosphorus*, 1949
Dünden Bugüne Istanbul Ansiklopedisi, Tarih Vakfı, 1993
Dwight, H.G. *Constantinople: Old and New*, 1907
Dwight, H.G. *Constantinople: Settings and Traits*, 1927
Eyüboğlu, Bedri Rahmi *Istanbul Destanı*, 1974
Eyüp Gezi Rehberi, Atölye Yayıncılık, 2005
Freely, John *Istanbul: The Imperial City*, Viking, 1996
Freely, John *Stamboul Sketches*, Redhouse, 1974
Freely, John *The Lost Messiah*, Penguin, 2002
Freely, John *The Princes' Islands*, Adalı Islander Editions, 2007
Freely, Maureen *Enlightenment*, Marion Boyars, 2007
Goodwin, Jason *The Janissary Tree*, Faber & Faber, 2006
Günay, Reha *A Guide to the Works of Sinan the Architect in Istanbul*, 2006, YEM Yayın
Hinkle, Richard & Vander Sluis Rhonda *From the Bosphorus*, Çitlembik, 2005
Hürel, Haldun *Anlat Istanbul*, Kapı, 2009
Istanbul 1900-50, Boyut, 2003
Istanbul 1950-2003, Boyut, 2003
Istanbul Türküsü, Orhan Veli
Karaca, Zafer *Istanbul' da Tanzimat Öncesi Rum Ortodoks Kiliseleri*, YKY, 2008
Karaz, Claire *Topkapı Palace: Inside and Out*, Çitlembik, 2004
Karmi, İlan *Jewish Sites of Istanbul*, Isis Press, 1992
Kayra, Cahit & Üyepazarçı, Erol *Mekanlar ve Zamanlar Kandilli, Vaniköy, Cengelköy*, İBB, 1993
Kelly, Laurence ed. *A Traveller' s Companion to Istanbul*, Interlink Books, 2005
Kelsey, Tim *Dervish: Travels in Modern Turkey*, Penguin, 1996
Kılıçkaya, Ali *Churches of Istanbul*, Uranus, 2008
Loti, Pierre *Ayizade*, Amphora, 2008
Loti, Pierre *Constantinople: The Way it Was*, 2006
Loti, Pierre *Voyages*, 1910
Mak, Geert *The Bridge*, Harvill Secker, 2008
Mansel, Philip *Constantinople: City of the World' s Desire 1453-1924*, John Murray, 1995
Massavetas, Alexandros *Going Back to Constantinople: Istanbul - A City of Absences*, Athens News Publications, 2007
McCullagh, Francis *The Fall of Abdülhamid*, Kessinger Publishing, 2009
Mershon, Anne Marie & Weissenbacher, Edda Renker *Istanbul' s Bazaar Quarter*, Çitlembik, 2009
Montagu, Lady Mary Wortley *The Turkish Embassy Letters*, Virago 1994
Nadel, Barbara *Pretty Dead Things*, Headline, 2008
Nicolson, Harold *Sweet Waters: An Istanbul Thriller*, Sickle Moon Books, 1999
Norwich, John Julius *Byzantium: The Decline and Fall*, Penguin, 1996
Orga, İrfan *Portrait of a Turkish Family*, Eland, 1993
Pamuk, Orhan *Istanbul: Memories of a City*, Faber & Faber, 2005
Pardoe, Julia *The Beauties of the Bosphorus*, 1840
Pardoe, Julia *The City of the Sultan and the Domestic Manners of the Turks*, 1836
Pardoe, Julia *The Dancing Dervishes*, 1902
Petersen, Paulann *Blood Silk*, Quiet Lion Press, 2003
Procopius, *The Secret History*, Penguin Classics, 2007
Seal, Jeremy *A Fez of the Heart*, Picador, 1995
Sepeda, Toni *Life with a View: A Turkish Quest*, Çitlembik, 2007
Shanahan, Brendan *In Turkey I Am Beautiful*, Harper Collins, 2008
Step by Step Istanbul, Intermedia, 1992
Stratton, Arthur *Sinan*, 1972
Sumner-Boyd, Hilary & **Freely**, John *Strolling Through Istanbul: A Guide to the City*, Redhouse, 2000
Taksim Water System/Kırkçeşme Water System, İSKİ
Thompson, Jon *Carpets from the Tents, Cottages and Workshops of Asia*, 1983
Trotsky, Leon *Farewell to Prinkipo*, 1933
Tuğay, Emine Foat *Three Centuries: Family Chronicles of Turkey and Egypt*, 1963
Twain, Mark *Innocents Abroad*, Penguin, 2003
Uşaklıgil, Halit Ziya *Saray ve Ötesi*, 1942
Van den Graven Robert *Byzantine Istanbul: A Self-Guided Tour*, Çitlembik, 2001
Van Millingen, Alexander *Byzantine Churches in Constantinople*, 1912
Venola, Trici *Drawing on Istanbul*, Mira Publishing, 2006
Villers, James Jr ed, *Turkey*, Travelers' Tales, 2002
Walking Through Byzantium: Great Palace Region, 2007
Weissenbacher, Edda Renker *A Self-Guide to İznik Tiles in Istanbul*, 2004
White, Charles *Three Years in Constantinople*, 1846
White, Jenny *The Abyssinian Proof*, Phoenix, 2008
Whitten, M.A. *An Island in Istanbul: At Home on Heybeliada*, Adalı Islander Editions, 2006
Yılmazkaya, Orhan *Turkish Baths: A Guide to the Historic Turkish Baths of Istanbul*, Çitlembik, 2006

TEN